Regulation

Gregory Carnes, Ph.D., CPA
Gaylord A. Jentz, MBA, JD
Robert A. Prentice, J.D.

PO Box 4223 Sedona, AZ 86340-4223
888.884.5669 N.America 928.204.1066 International

www.cpaexcel.com

Edward Foley, President & CEO
Gun Granath, Editor

ISBN 978-0-9746541-1-9

Printed in the United States of America

ABOUT THE CPAexcel™ CPA EXAM REVIEW COURSES

The Surest Way to Pass the CPA Exam

Since 1998, a growing number of CPA exam candidates have used CPAexcel to pass the CPA exam. The performance of our students on the exam, as well as their feedback to us, confirms that CPAexcel is the easiest way to pass the CPA exam.

Key reasons why our students chose CPAexcel:

- They consistently pass the exam at a rate almost twice that of all other candidates
- They learn from leading professors who are CPA exam experts at top accounting schools
- They master more knowledge in less time than other students, by using CPAexcel's unique bite-sized lessons℠ and software-driven, highly-interactive Efficient Learning System™
- They benefit from using the most powerful learning tools of any CPA exam review course
- They select from among CPAexcel's basic learning modules to create customized courses that fit their individual learning needs, lifestyle, schedule, and budget.
- They have unlimited use of Simulated CPA Exams with exam-identical formats, functions and time limits – plus representative scores and identification of weak spots.
- They receive free electronic updates and their CPAexcel course has no expiration date
- They pay about half the price of other leading review courses

CPAexcel's Basic Learning Modules Are:

- ***Core Study Materials***. All CPAexcel courses include: Bite-sized lessons, Efficient Learning System, Diagnostic Exams, Study Text, Proficiency Questions, Past Exam Questions, Simulations, Electronic Flashcards, Performance Metrics, Exam Tutor, Simulated CPA Exams, Final Review, and Student Discussion Groups.
- ***Guided Seminars.*** Provide a structured distance-learning environment with assignments, grades, and prompt answers to each student's questions from subject-expert professors.
- ***Video Lectures with Printable Slides.*** Leading professors from top accounting schools present information essential to passing the exam. These lectures are integrated into bite-sized lesson and typically run between five and fifteen minutes.
- ***Textbooks.*** Include copies of CPAexcel's Study Text typically organized into 3 to 10 page lessons that follow the same sequence as our courseware.
- ***Printed Flashcards.*** 1000 printed flashcards help you learn and test yourself on the go.

How CPAexcel's Basic Learning Modules Fulfill the Needs of Different Types of Learners:

Learners' Needs	Appropriate CPAexcel Course
You learn best in a classroom-type setting watching and listening to an instructor and then using textbooks to study the details.	**Video Gold Medal Course.** (Core Study Materials, Guided Seminars instructor and then using textbooks to study Video Lectures, Textbooks)
You learn best in a structured learning program, with assignments and grades. You learn well by simply reading.	**Gold Medal Course** (Core Study Materials, Guided Seminars program, with assignments and grades. Textbooks)
You learn best studying at your own pace in your own way using recorded lectures, with reading materials and self-scoring tests.	**Video Self-Study Course Plus** (Core Study Materials, Video Lectures, your own way using recorded lectures, with Textbooks)
You learn best studying at your own pace in your own way using reading materials and self-scoring tests.	**Classic Self-Study Course** (Core Study Materials, Textbooks)

ABOUT THE CPAexcel™ CPA EXAM REVIEW COURSES

OUR AUTHORS & MENTORS

CPAexcel™ content is authored by a team of accounting professors and CPA exam experts from top accounting colleges such as the University of Texas at Austin (frequently ranked the #1 accounting school in the country), California State University at Sacramento, Northern Illinois University, and University of North Alabama. Via the Internet, students using CPAexcel's Guided Seminars receive unlimited mentoring and personalized answers to their questions from subject-expert professors. Team members are:

Professor Craig Bain
CPAexcel Guided Seminar Professor
Ph.D., CPA
Northern Arizona University - Flagstaff

Professor Allen H. Bizzell
CPAexcel Author, Guided Seminar Professor and Video Lecturer
Ph.D., CPA
Former Associate Dean and Accounting Faculty, University of Texas (Retired)
Associate Professor, Department of Accounting, Texas State University (Retired)

Professor Gregory Carnes
CPAexcel Author and Video Lecturer
Ph.D., CPA
Raburn Eminent Scholar of Accounting, University of North Alabama
Former Dean, College of Business, Lipscomb University
Former Chair, Department of Accountancy, Northern Illinois University

Professor B. Douglas Clinton
CPAexcel Video Lecturer
Ph.D., CPA, CMA
Alta Via Consulting Professor of Management Accountancy, Department of Accountancy, Northern Illinois University

Professor Charles J. Davis
CPAexcel Author, Guided Seminar Professor and Video Lecturer
Ph.D., CPA
Professor of Accounting, Department of Accounting, College of Business Administration, California State University - Sacramento

Professor Donald R. Deis Jr.
CPAexcel Video Lecturer
Ph.D., CPA, MBA
Ennis & Virginia Joslin Endowed Chair in Accounting, College of Business, Texas A&M University - Corpus Christi
Former Director of the School of Accountancy, University of Missouri - Columbia
Former Professor and Director of the Accounting Ph.D. Program, Louisiana State University - Baton Rouge

Professor Janet D. Gillespie
CPAexcel Author and Guided Seminar Professor
Ph.D.
Lecturer, Department of Accounting, McCombs School of Business, University of Texas - Austin

Professor Marianne M. Jennings
CPAexcel Video Lecturer
J.D.
Professor of Legal and Ethical Studies, W.P. Carey School of Business, Arizona State University

Professor Gaylord A. Jentz
CPAexcel Author
J.D., MBA
Herbert D. Kelleher Centennial Professor Emeritus in Business Law, Department of Management Science and Information Systems, McCombs School of Business, University of Texas - Austin

Professor John E. Karayan
CPAexcel Guided Seminar Professor
J.D., Ph.D
Chair, Department of Accounting and IT, Woodbury University - Burbank, California

Professor Claire Latham
CPAexcel Guided Seminar Professor
Ph.D, CPA
Washington State University

Professor Christopher Meakin
CPAexcel Guided Seminar Professor
MA, J.D., BBA
University of Texas - Austin

Professor Pam Smith
CPAexcel Video Lecturer
Ph.D., MBA, CPA
KPMG Professor of Accountancy, Department of Accountancy, Northern Illinois University

Professor Dan Stone
CPAexcel Video Lecturer
Ph.D., MPA
Gatton Endowed Chair, Von Allmen School of Accountancy and the Department of Management, University of Kentucky

Professor Donald Tidrick
CPAexcel Author and Video Lecturer
Ph.D., CPA, CMA, CIA
Deloitte Professor of Accountancy, Northern Illinois University
Former Associate Chairman of the Department of Accounting, Director of the Professional Program in Accounting and Director of the CPA Review Course, University of Texas at Austin, 1991 - 2000

Professor Jeanne Yamamura
CPAexcel Guided Seminar Professor
Ph.D., CPA, MIM
University of Nevada - Reno (Retired)

ABOUT THE CPAexcel™ CPA EXAM REVIEW COURSES

CPAexcel's BITE-SIZED LESSONS℠ AND EFFICIENT LEARNING SYSTEM™

A key reason why CPAexcel students pass the CPA exam at rates almost twice that for all other students is that they study using CPAexcel's bite-sized lessons℠ and Efficient Learning System.

Bite-Sized Lessons:

CPAexcel's course materials are broken down into many lessons each one of which covers a single topic that can often be learned in about 30 minutes. The course materials available in each bite-sized lesson are shown below in an image of a typical "Lesson Overview" panel displayed alongside a part of the Table of Contents for that section of the course materials. Each of the learning resources listed in the Lesson Overview are linked to that particular learning resource for that lesson.

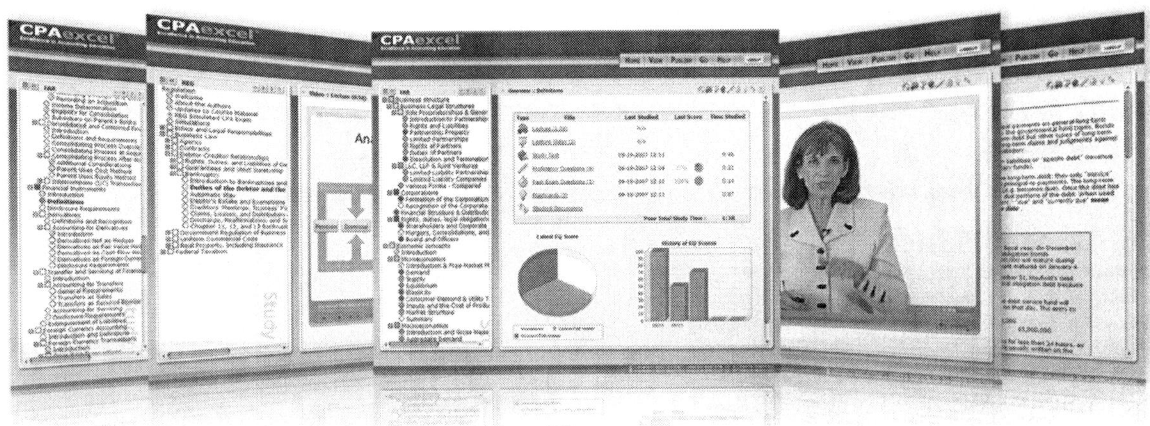

Students may use each lesson's learning resources in any desired sequence. Typically, a student will first watch and listen to the Video Lecture and then either review the Study Text or go directly to the Proficiency Questions to test and reinforce his or her knowledge of the lesson content. Then he or she might test his or her knowledge on Past Exam Questions. Note that each of the learning resources are just one click away from each other, enabling the student to easily access all the resources needed to quickly master that bite-sized topic before moving to the next topic.

Compared to other review courses, CPAexcel's bite-sized lessons are a much more efficient way to master the large body of knowledge required to pass the CPA exam. They are a key contributor to the exam success of CPAexcel's students.

Efficient Learning System:

CPAexcel's software-driven Efficient Learning System tightly-integrates the use of all CPAexcel's learning functions including bite-sized lessons. Key benefits to students are:

- Significant increases in knowledge gained and retained per hour of study
- Increased student focus and motivation
- Automatic progress measurement, tracking, and reporting
- Two-click access to fellow students and professors worldwide
- Exact replication of the formats and software functions used in the CPA exam itself
- 24/7/365 courseware access from any computer anywhere, with synchronization of scores
- Online and offline personalized updates with automatic alerts

Free Demonstration:

Free demonstrations of CPAexcel are available at http://www.cpaexcel.com/tutorial/

Table of Contents

Welcome

From the Author:
The scope of material in the Regulation-Business Law Section that is "fair game" under the AICPA content guidelines is still vast. The student's best approach is to cover all the material as thoroughly as possible in each subject area, to try to see the big picture (without ignoring the minutiae). The problem is that the emphasis of the material for the exam has been reduced to 20-25% from approximately 60%, but the subject areas remain 90% unchanged. There is a lot of detail in these subject areas, and the exam questions can come from any and all of these areas. Going over the material just once is inadequate to fully master it. For many of you, some of these subject areas will be a completely new learning experience.

In addition, I recommend the following:

1. Review the Overview for each General Subject area. The Overview gives you my opinion where to emphasis your study.
2. Review Previous CPA and Sample Questions (with answer rationales).
3. Read the examples in the text material to be sure you understand each of the various laws in each subject area.

~ *Dr. Gaylord Jentz.*

The challenge in the tax area is that there are so many topics that can be tested. However, once a topic is chosen for the test, the question asked is usually somewhat basic. So make sure you know the foundational concepts very well and do not be as concerned about the complex areas.

When you take the exam, you will be working problems, so that is what you must practice. Do not just read the problems and the solutions. That will not prepare you. Work as many problems as you possibly can.

~ *Prof. Gregory A. Carnes*

The ethical and legal environment in which accountants operate is highly regulated. On the one hand, this is a good thing because few professionals enjoy more specific guidance as to what they are to do - and are not to do - than accountants. On the other hand, there is a lot to learn, both about specific ethical standards and about the legal consequences of violating ethical and other professional standards. The good news is that this material, which constitutes 15-20% of the Regulation section of the CPA exam, is intensely valuable information for your post-exam professional life. You are not wasting your time in any sense when you learn this material. You are preparing for the CPA exam and improving your chances of succeeding as a professional. In the post-Enron, post-Sarbanes-Oxley world in which accountants now operate, nothing could be more important than having a good grasp of both professional and legal responsibilities.

There are few short cuts to learning this material. Regarding professional responsibilities, always remember that appearances count. Your cause may be just and your heart may be pure, but if an activity does not pass the "smell test," it probably does not comport with the AICPA's Code of Professional Conduct either. Learn the rules as best you can, but in a close call where you don't know the answer specifically, use your common sense because most of the rules are consistent with commonsense notions of good conduct.

The most frequently-tested aspect of legal responsibilities has traditionally been the third-party liability of auditors and other accountants. When can an accountant be held liable for careless errors to those other than her client (such as the client's creditors, lenders, and investors)? Pay particular attention to that area.

~ *Prof. Robert A. Prentice*

About the Authors

Meet Our Authors

Professor Robert Prentice

Professor Robert A. Prentice is the Ed and Molly Smith Centennial Professor of Business Law at the University of Texas at Austin and has taught both UT's and other CPA courses for fifteen years. He created a new course in accounting ethics and regulation that he has taught for the last decade. Professor Prentice has written several textbooks, many major law review articles on securities regulation and accountants' liability, and has won more than thirty teaching awards.

Professor Gaylord Jentz

Dr. Jentz is the Herbert D. Kelleher Emeritus Centennial Professor in Business Law at the University of Texas at Austin McCombs School of Business. He received his B.A., M.B.A., and J.D. degrees from the University of Wisconsin at Madison.. Dr. Jentz has been past President of the Academy of Legal Studies in Business, the Southwestern Federation of Administrative Disciplines, the Southern Business Law Association, Phi Kappa Phi (UT Chapter), and the Texas Association of College Teachers. He is the author or co-author of six monographs and forty-four books and editions, including West's Business Law: Text and Cases, ninth edition (2004) and West's Business Law Alternate ninth edition (2005), Fundamentals of Business Law, sixth edition (2005), and four versions of Business Law Today, sixth edition (2003-2004). He has also published in learned journals and is past editor-in-chief of the American Business Law Journal. Dr. Jentz has given advanced purchasing seminars throughout the United States and taught at four regional and graduate banking schools.

Dr. Jentz is the recipient of eleven teaching, academic, and service excellence awards, including the CBA Foundation Award for Excellence in Education, the CBA Foundation Advisory Council Distinguished Scholastic Contributions Award, the Academy of Legal Studies in Business Faculty Excellence Award, the Western States School of Banking's Banking Leadership Award, the James C. Scarboro Memorial Award for Outstanding Leadership in Banking Education, and The University of Texas "Civitatis" Award.

Prof. Greg Carnes

Gregory Carnes is the Raburn Eminent Scholar of Accounting, University of North Alabama. Former Dean of the College of Business at Lipscomb University in Nashville Tennessee. Former Department Chair and Crowe Chizek Professor of Accountancy at Northern Illinois University. He taught *Partnership Taxation* and *Taxation of Compensation and Benefits* in NIU's Masters of Science in Taxation Program. Greg has published approximately 20 articles in journals such as *The Journal of Economic Psychology, Journal of the American Taxation Association, Advances in Taxation, The Journal of International Accounting, Auditing, and Taxation, The Tax Adviser, Taxation for Accountants, Taxation for Lawyers*, and *The CPA Journal*,. He is a contributing author on Federal Taxation (ARC Publishing), a popular textbook used in undergraduate and graduate taxation courses. He currently serves on the board of the *Federation of Schools of Accountancy* and is vice-president of communication for the *Accounting Program Leadership Group.* He is a member of the AICPA, the Illinois Society of CPAs, the American Accounting Association, and the American Taxation Association.

Greg received his Ph.D. from Georgia State University, his M.S. (Tax Specialization) from University of Memphis, and his B.S. (Accountancy) from Lipscomb University. He previously taught at Louisiana State University, and worked for Ernst & Young in Nashville, Tennessee. He currently resides in Rockford, Illinois.

Ethics and Legal Responsibilities

Code of Professional Conduct

The AICPA Code of Professional Conduct consists of (1) Principles (which provide a broad framework) and (2) Rules of Conduct (which govern the specifics of members' performance of professional services). Bylaws require adherence to the Rules and to technical standards promulgated under them.

By the time one studies the Principles, the Rules, Interpretations of the Rules of Conduct, and specific Ethics Rulings, one is immersed in a considerable amount of detail. There is probably more information in this course than you need to pass the test. The question is, of course, what to leave out and what to concentrate upon. Your attention should center upon the areas that the outline emphasizes (especially the tables which summarize key rulings) and upon the past test questions.

I. Code of Professional Conduct

A. Introduction

1. Applies to all AICPA members.
   a. By accepting membership, CPAs assume an obligation of self-discipline above the simple requirements of the law.
2. Even nonmembers are expected to follow.
3. Reason for adoption: a distinguishing mark of a profession is an acceptance of responsibility to the public.

B. Code Provisions: Where applicable (i.e., some do not apply to CPAs not in public practice), Code provisions establish minimum levels of acceptable professional conduct.

C. Principles are Organized into 6 Articles:

1. Responsibilities.
2. The Public Interest.
3. Integrity.
4. Objectivity and Independence.
5. Due Care.
6. Scope and Nature of Services.

D. Supplementation: The Principles are supplemented by Rules of Conduct, Interpretations, and Rulings.

II. Article I: Responsibilities -- "In carrying out their responsibilities as professionals, members should exercise sensitive professional and moral judgments in all their activities."

III. Article II: The Public Interest -- "Members should accept the obligation to act in a way that will serve the public interest, honor the public trust, and demonstrate commitment to professionalism."

A. Accountants are expected to act with integrity, objectivity, due professional care, and a desire to serve the public.

IV. Article III: Integrity -- "To maintain and broaden public confidence, members should perform all professional responsibilities with the highest sense of integrity."

A. Requires observance of principles of:

1. objectivity,
2. independence,
3. due care.

B. Provides that service and the public trust should not be subordinated to personal gain and advantage.

V. **Article IV: Objectivity and Independence --** "A member should maintain objectivity and be free of conflicts of interest in discharging professional responsibilities. A member in public practice should be independent in fact and appearance when providing auditing and other attestation services."

A. Objectivity is a state of mind, featuring:

1. impartiality,
2. intellectual honesty,
3. freedom from conflicts of interest.

B. Independence precludes relationships that even appear to impair objectivity in performing attest functions.

Requirements:

	Audit	**Compilation**	**Tax**	**Consulting**
Integrity	Yes	Yes	Yes	Yes
Objectivity	Yes	Yes	Yes	Yes
Independence in Fact	Yes	No	No	No
Independence in Appearance	Yes	No	No	No

VI. **Article V: Due Care --** "A member should observe the profession's technical and ethical standards, strive continually to improve competence and the quality of services, and discharge professional responsibility to the best of the member's ability."

A. Competence and diligence are key components of due care.

B. Competence is a synthesis of education and experience.

C. Competence may require consultation or referral when a professional engagement exceeds the member's personal competence.

D. Due care requires adequate planning and supervision for any professional activity undertaken.

VII. **Article VI: Scope and Nature of Services --** "A member <u>in public practice</u> should observe the Principles of the Code of Professional Conduct in determining the scope and nature of services to be provided."

A. In addition to serving the public interest and evidencing integrity, objectivity, and due care, professionals should consider whether their attest activities may render inappropriate the offering of other services to an attest client.

B. Additionally, members should:

1. Have in place appropriate internal quality control procedures,

2. Avoid conflicts of interest, as potentially between the role as auditor and a role providing other services, and
   a. Sarbanes-Oxley (2002) dramatically limits the forms of consulting services that audit firms may offer to audit clients that are public companies.
   b. For private company audit clients, AICPA guidelines still apply. They allow quite a bit of consulting by auditors.
3. Assess whether an activity is consistent with their role as professionals.

Proficiency, Independence, and Due Care

Independence (Rule 101)

For those involved in the attest function, nothing can be more important than being conversant with the rules regarding independence.

I. Introduction

A. Especially with the SEC and PCAOB looking over auditors' shoulders, independence problems can lead to all sorts of liability. Two simple but critical points to take away from this section are:

- those involved in tax and consulting need not be independent, and
- for those involved in the attest function, independence in appearance is as important as independence in fact.

> "A member in public practice shall be independent in the performance of professional services as required by standards promulgated by bodies designated by the Council."

3. **Areas of Concern:** Those who perform the attest function must act independently. Whereas consultants and tax professionals may be advocates for their clients, auditors owe their highest duty of loyalty not to the attest client but to the consumers of the financial statements.
4. There are four major areas of concern regarding independence:
   - **a.** **Financial ties** to clients; e.g., an auditor should not own stock in a client.
   - **b.** **Employment ties** to a client; e.g., an auditor should not be on a client's board of directors.
   - **c.** **Non-Audit services** provided clients; e.g., an auditor should not audit financial statements that he himself has produced on the client's behalf.
   - **d.** Auditors' **family ties** to clients; e.g., an auditor's spouse should not be CEO or a large stockholder of an audit client.

B. **Rule 101:** The AICPA Code of Ethics addresses independence in Rule 101 but, to the extent that the Code conflicts with federal guidelines promulgated by the Securities Exchange Commission (SEC) and the Public Company Accounting Oversight Board (PCAOB), its provisions must give way.

II. Who is Covered -- Only "covered members" must follow the independence rules. Who is a "covered member?" Until recently, that question was answered with a "firm-oriented" approach. For example, all partners of the firm had to be independent, meaning that a tax partner in the Seattle office of a Big Five firm could not own stock in an audit client of the Miami office. The SEC has recently changed its focus to an "engagement team-oriented" approach. The AICPA agrees in ET sec. 92 (definitions).

III. Who Must Be Independent

A. Those who participate on the attest engagement team, including those who perform concurring and second partner reviews, all employees and contractors retained by the firm who participate in the attest engagement, irrespective of their functional classification (tax, consulting, etc), but not individuals who perform only routine clerical functions, such as word processing and photocopying;

B. Those who are in a position to Influence the Attest Engagement:

- Evaluate the performance or recommend compensation of the attest engagement partner
- Directly supervise the attest engagement partner and all successively senior levels through the firm's chief executive
- Consult with the attest engagement team during the engagement regarding technical or industry-specific issues, transactions, or events
- Provide quality control or other oversight of the attest engagement, including internal monitoring.

C. Other Partners or Professionals of the Firm:

1. Partners and Managers who provide 10 or more hours of non-attest services to the client
2. Other partners in the office in which the lead attest engagement partner primarily practices in connection with the attest engagement.

D. The Firm.

E. Entities Controlled by Any of the Above.

IV. Who is "a covered member"

	Covered	**Not Covered**
The Firm	x	
Partners who work on the engagement	x	
Managers who work on the engagement	x	
Staff members who work on the engagement	x	
Receptionists and copy staff who work on the engagement		x
Partners in the office of the lead attest partner who don't work on the engagement	x	
Managers in the office of the lead attest partner who don't work on the engagement (unless they perform 10 hours of non-attest service)		x*
Partners in other offices		x*
Those who do concurring and second partner reviews	x	
Those in a position (by reason of review, setting compensation, etc.) to influence members of the engagement team	x	

* Although these persons are generally not "covered members," even they and all other professional employees in the firm, may not own more than 5% of an audit client's stock nor serve as director, officer, other manager, promoter, underwriter, voting trustee, or trustee of a pension or profit-sharing plan of an audit client.

V. The Conceptual Framework.

A. Before we examine the four major areas of independence problems (financial relationships, employment relationships, consulting services, and family relationships), it is worth noting that although there are many, many rules to learn, even this multitude cannot cover every possible situation. To give guidance for situations that are not specifically provided for in the rules, the AICPA in 2006 promulgated a "conceptual framework" for handling such situations.

B. The idea is that by adopting a "risk-based" approach, CPAs may be able to determine how to handle unique, problematic situations. This risk-based approach involves three steps:

1. Identifying and evaluating threats to independence.
2. Determining whether safeguards already eliminate or sufficiently mitigate identified threats and whether threats that have not yet been mitigated can be eliminated or sufficiently mitigated by safeguards.
3. If no safeguards are available to eliminate an unacceptable threat or reduce it to an acceptable level, independence would be considered impaired.

C. There are three types of safeguards that might prevent impairment of independence:

1. Safeguards created by the profession, legislation, or regulation, such as: education and training requirements, external reviews of a firm's quality control system, and professional monitoring and disciplinary procedures.
2. Safeguards created by the client, such as: hiring skilled and experienced personnel, a tone at the top emphasizing fair financial reporting, and effective corporate governance structures.
3. Safeguards implemented by the accounting firm, such as: policies and procedures designed to implement and monitor quality control, documented independence policies, and policies and procedures designed to monitor the firm or partner's reliance on revenue from a single client.

VI. Financial Relationships -- The first major way an auditor may impair his or her independence is to develop inappropriate financial relationships with a client. Interpretation 101-1 spells out the key rules which seek to prevent an auditor or audit firm from having any important financial interest in a client, whether that interest is held directly or indirectly.

A. Interpretation 101-1 -- Independence is impaired if during period of professional engagement or at time of expression of opinion:

	Impaired	**Not Impaired**
Member (or firm) had material direct financial interest in client	x	
Member had immaterial direct financial interest in client	x	
Member had material indirect financial interest in client	x	
Member had immaterial indirect financial interest in client		x
Member committed to obtain material indirect financial interest in client	x	
Member had any material joint investment with client	x	
Member had any loan to or from client, officer, or stockholder (except as permitted by 101-5)	x	
Member accepted more than a token gift from a client	x	

Member leases to or from client via a capital lease	x	
Member leases to or from client via an operating lease		x
Member has not been paid for more than a year.	x	
Member has put investment in client in a blind trust	x	
Partner or professional employee and/or his or her immediate family owned 5% or more of client's equity stock*	x	

*Under new AICPA revision, being a trustee or executor creates a problem only if (i) the covered member had authority to make investment decisions for the estate or trust, or (ii) the trust or estate owned or was committed to acquiring more than 10% of the client ownership interests, or (iii) the value of the trust or estate's holdings in the client exceeded 10% of the total assets of the trust or estate.

B. Direct vs. Indirect Financial Interests -- To help clarify the distinction between direct and indirect financial interests (because interests that are both indirect and immaterial do not impair independence), the AICPA issued new guidelines in 2006 that look like this:

1. A **financial interest** is an ownership interest in an equity or a debt security issued by an entity, including rights and obligations to acquire such an interest and derivatives directly related to such an interest.
2. A **direct financial interest** is a financial interest:
    - a. Owned directly by an individual or entity (including those managed on a discretionary basis by others); or
    - b. Under the control of an individual or entity (including those managed on a discretionary basis by others); or
    - c. Beneficially owned through an investment vehicle, estate, trust, or other intermediary when the beneficiary:
        - i. Controls the intermediary; or
        - ii. Has the authority to supervise or participate in the intermediary's investment decisions.
3. An **indirect financial interest** is a financial interest beneficially owned through an investment vehicle, estate, trust, or other intermediary when the beneficiary neither controls the intermediary nor has the authority to supervise or participate in the intermediary's investment decisions.
4. A financial interest is **beneficially owned** when an individual or entity is not the recorded owner of the interest but has a right to some or all of the underlying benefits of ownership. These benefits include the authority to direct the voting or the disposition of the interest or to receive the economic benefits of the ownership of the interest.

C. Interpretation 101-5 -- Loans From Financial Institution Clients. Generally, shouldn't loan to or borrow from financial institution client or its subsidiary. However, if obtained pursuant to normal lending procedures, terms, and requirements, two types of loans are permitted:

	Permitted	Not Permitted
Grandfathered Loans		
1) Loans from Financial Institution (FI) before it became a client	x	
2) Loan from FI which then sold loan to attest client	x	
3) Loan to CPA before s/he joined firm which had FI as client	x	
4) Falling behind on repayment of #1-3		x
5) Renegotiating #1-3		x
6) Collateral on loans #1-3 (if secured) worth less than loan balance		x
Other Permitted Loans		
7) Auto loan from current client if collateralized by the auto	x*	
8) Loan of surrender value of insurance policy	x	
9) Passbook loans collateralized by cash deposits ("passbook loans")	x	
10) Credit cards and cash advanced on checking accounts < $10,000	x	

*The AICPA recently established similar rules for the leasing of an automobile.

D. **Interpretation 101-6 --** Effect of Threatened Litigation Upon Independence.

	Impaired	Not Impaired
Suit by present management alleging deficient audit	x	
Suit by member against present management for fraud or deceit	x	
Strong possibility present management will sue for deficient audit	x	
Suit over billing dispute or other matter not related to audit (such as consulting or tax matters) if it is for nonmaterial amount		x
Suit against auditor by client's shareholders (assuming no cross claim by member against management claiming fraud)		x
Suit against auditor by client's creditors (assuming no cross claim by member against management claiming fraud)		x

E. **Interpretation 101-8 --** CPA's financial interests in nonclients may impair independence when those nonclients have financial interests in the CPA's clients.

Example: CPA Firm owns 60% of XYZ Co. stock.

XYZ Co. owns 51% of ABC Co.

CPA Firm audits ABC Co.

F. **Additional Financial Threats to Independence. --** In this section, we note some new rules that address some intractable problems with independence that arise from financial ties.

1. **Unsolicited Financial Interests:** For example, what if an audit engagement team member's aunt just out of the blue gives her a block of stock as a gift, and the stock happens to have been issued by an audit client? The rule on unsolicited financial interests provides:

   a. If a "covered member" receives a gift or inheritance of stock in an audit client, no independence problem exists so long as the covered member disposes of the stock as soon as practicable, but definitely within 30 days.

   b. If a "covered member" becomes aware that she will receive a gift or inheritance of stock in a client but does not yet have the right to dispose of it, independence would be considered to be impaired unless (a) the covered member does not participate on the attest engagement team, and (b) the covered member disposes of the stock as soon as practicable after acquiring the power to do so, but definitely within 30 days.

G. **Mutual Funds.** Obviously, if Sam audits XYZ Mutual Fund, he cannot own a direct interest in the mutual fund. But can he own an interest in ABC Corp. if XYZ holds ABC shares in its portfolio? The rule looks like this:

1. An interest in a mutual fund is a direct financial interest, but the mutual fund investor's interest in the underlying securities held by the fund would be indirect.
2. If the mutual fund is diversified, a covered member's ownership of 5% or less of the shares of the fund would not be considered a material indirect interest in the underlying investments.
3. If a covered member owns more than 5% of the shares of a diversified fund, or if the fund is not diversified, then the member should evaluate the underlying investments to determine if their indirect interest is material.

H. **Retirement, Savings, Compensation, or Similar Plans.** These types of employee benefit plans can cause complications because they may own shares of audit clients. The general rule is this:

1. A covered member who participates in one of these benefit plans has a direct interest in the plan but only an indirect interest in the underlying financial interests, *unless* the member has the ability to supervise or participate in the plan's investment decisions.

I. **Gifts and Entertainment.** What happens if a covered member accepts gifts or entertainment from an attest client? Or from one of its key employees or an owner of 10% of its stock? The answer for gifts is slightly different than the answer for entertainment.

1. Answer for Gifts: Independence would be considered to be impaired if the firm, a member of the attest engagement team, or one in a position to influence the engagement accepted a gift from an attest client unless the value is *clearly insignificant to the recipient*.
2. Answer for Entertainment: Independence is not considered impaired if a covered member accepts entertainment, provided the entertainment is "*reasonable in the circumstances.*"

VII. **Employment Relationships --** The second way that an auditor can impair independence is to develop an employment relationship with an audit client. Clearly, a member of the audit team should not go to work for the client, yet remain on the audit team.

	Impaired	Not Impaired
Member was trustee of any trust or executor of any estate with direct or material indirect interest in client*	x	
Member was trustee of any pension or profit sharing plan of client	x	
Member is on client's board of directors	x	
Member is promoter of client's stock	x	
Member is officer of client	x	
Member is a voting trustee of a client	x	
Also, partner or professional employee (who are not otherwise "covered members") and/or his or her immediate family cannot be employed by client or serve as director, promoter, underwriter, voting trustee, or trustee of any pension or profit-sharing trust of the client	x	

*Under new AICPA revision, being a trustee or executor creates a problem only if (i) the covered member had authority to make investment decisions for the estate or trust, or (ii) the trust or estate owned or was committed to acquiring more than 10% of the client ownership interests, or (iii) the value of the trust or estate's holdings in the client exceeded 10% of the total assets of the trust or estate.

A. Interpretation 101-4: A CPA who is a director of a nonprofit organization where the board is large and representative of community leadership is not lacking in independence if:

1. Position is purely honorary,
2. Is identified as honorary on external materials,
3. CPA does no more than contribute use of name,
4. CPA does not vote or participate in management affairs.

B. Former Client Employees Now Working for Audit Firm -- What happens when the auditor jumps to the client after resigning at the audit firm? **Rule 101-2** provides that an accounting firm's independence will be considered impaired when a partner or professional employee goes to work for an audit client unless all of the following six conditions are met:

1. Amounts due the former employee for previous interest in the firm and for unfunded, vested retirement interests are not material to the firm, and the underlying formula used to calculate payments remains fixed during the payout period.
2. The former employee is not in a position to influence the accounting firm's operations or financial policies.
3. The former employee does not participate or appear to participate in, and is not associated with, the firm whether or not compensated for such participation. The Code states that an "appearance of participation" results from such actions as:
   - The individual provides consultation to the firm.

- The firm provides the individual with an office and related amenities (for example, secretarial and telephone services).
- The individual's name is included in the firm's office directory.
- The individual's name is included as a member of the firm in other membership lists of business, professional, or civic organizations, unless the individual is clearly designated as retired.

4. The ongoing attest engagement team considers the appropriateness or necessity of modifying the engagement procedures to adjust for the risk that, by virtue of the former partner employee's prior knowledge of the audit plan, audit effectiveness could be reduced.

5. The firm assesses whether existing attest engagement team members have appropriate experience and stature to effectively deal with the former employee when that person will have significant interaction with the attest engagement team.

6. The subsequent attest engagement is reviewed to determine whether the engagement team members maintained the appropriate level of skepticism when evaluating the representations and work of the former employee, when the person joins the client in a key position within one year of dissociating from the firm and has significant interaction with the attest engagement team.

7. Cooling-off Period

a. Sarbanes-Oxley imposes a one-year *"cooling-off period"* that requires the lead partner, the concurring partner, or any other member of the audit engagement team who provides more than 10 hours of audit, review, or attest services to observe a one-year cooling-off period before going to work for a client: (a) as CEO, CFO, controller, CAO, or any equivalent officers, (b) in any financial oversight role, and (c) preparing financial statements. Because the focus is the year preceding commencement of the audit of the current year's financial statements, the time period could effectively last as long as 23 months.

b. When a member of the attest engagement team (or a person in a position to influence that team) intends to seek or discuss potential employment or association with an attest client or is in receipt of a specific offer of employment from an attest client, independence will be impaired with respect to that client unless:

i. The person promptly reports such consideration or offer to an appropriate person in the firm

ii. Removes himself or herself from the engagement until the offer is rejected or the position is no longer sought. When a "covered member" learns that another person on the attest engagement team (or a person in a position to influence) is considering employment with a client, that member should alert the firm. Then the firm must consider what additional procedures may be necessary to provide "reasonable assurance" that the person performed his/her work for the client with objectivity and integrity.

c. What About Covered Members Formerly Employed by or Associated with a Client? For example, what if a member of the engagement team used to work for the audit client?

i. An individual who was formerly (i) employed by a client or (ii) associated with a client as an officer, director, promoter, underwriter, voting trustee, or trustee for a pension or profit-sharing trust of the client would impair independence if the individual

1. Participated on the attest engagement team or was an individual in a position to influence the attest engagement for the client when the attest engagement covers any period that includes his or her former employment or association with that client; or

2. Was otherwise a covered member with respect to the client unless the individual first disassociates from the client by (a) terminating any relationships with the client, (b) disposing of any direct or material indirect financial interest in the client, (c) ceases to participate in all employee benefit plans sponsored by the client, and (d) liquidates and transfers all vested benefits in the client's benefit plans (but need not liquidate or transfer if there is a significant penalty attached).

VIII. Nonaudit Services to Audit Clients

A. A third concern in the independence realm is the provision of nonaudit services to audit clients. The worry is that auditors will subordinate their objective judgment in order to keep the client happy and purchasing consulting services.

B. The following are now the rules only for audits of private companies. Sarbanes-Oxley overrides for audits of public companies and does not allow most of these activities.

1. **Interpretation 101-3**: When a CPA performs nonattest services for an attest client, that member must be careful not to perform management functions, not to make management decisions, and not to appear to do these things. Also, do not take custody of client assets.

2. Client must agree to perform the following functions:

   a. Make all management decisions and perform all management functions;

   b. Designate an individual who possesses suitable skill, knowledge, and/or experience, preferably within senior management, to oversee the services;

   c. Evaluate the adequacy and results of the services performed;

   d. Accept responsibility for the results of the services; and

   e. Establish and maintain internal controls, including monitoring ongoing activities.

3. The member should be satisfied that the client will be able to meet these criteria and make informed judgments on the results of the member's nonattest services.

4. Before performing nonattest services, the member should establish and document in writing his or her understanding with the BOD or audit committee regarding:

   a. Objectives of the engagement,

   b. Services to be performed,

   c. Client's acceptance of responsibility,

   d. Member's responsibilities,

   e. Any limitations to the engagement.

5. The following are activities that would impair a member's independence:

   a. Authorizing, executing, or consummating a transaction, or otherwise exercising authority on behalf of a client or having the authority to do so

   b. Preparing source documents, in electronic or other form, evidencing the occurrence of a transaction

   c. Having custody of client assets

   d. Supervising client employees in the performance of their normal recurring activities

e. Reporting to the board of directors on behalf of management

f. Serving as a client's stock transfer or escrow agent, registrar, general counsel, or its equivalent

g. Establishing or maintaining internal controls, including performing ongoing monitoring activities for a client

6. The following guidelines give specifics regarding various areas of practice:

Bookkeeping	Impaired	Not Impaired
Record transactions in client's general ledger		x
Prepare F/S based on trial balance information		x
Propose standard, adjusting, or correcting journal entries, provided that client reviews and member is satisfied that client understands nature and impact		x
Make changes in records w/o client approval	x	
Approve or authorize client transactions	x	
Prepare source documents or originate data	x	
Make changes to source documents w/o client approval	x	

Nontax Disbursement	Impaired	Not Impaired
Use payroll time record provided by client to generate unsigned checks or process client's payroll		x
Transmit client approved payroll or other disbursement information to a financial institution chosen by client		x
Accept responsibility to authorize payment of client funds	x	
Accept responsibility to sign or cosign checks	x	
Maintain client's bank account, take custody of client funds, or make credit or banking decisions for client	x	
Approve vendor invoices for payments	x	

Benefit Plan Administration	Impaired	Not Impaired
Communicate summary plan data to plan trustee		x
Advise client management regarding impact of plan provisions		x
Process transactions initiated by plan participants		x
Prepare account valuations		x
Prepare and transmit participant statement to plan participants		x
Make policy decisions on client's behalf	x	
Interpret plan for participants w/o management's concurrence	x	

Make disbursements on plan's behalf	x	
Take custody of plan assets	x	
Serve as a plan fiduciary	x	

Investment - Advisory or Management	Impaired	Not Impaired
Recommend allocation of funds that a client should invest in various asset classes		x
Perform bookkeeping and reporting of client's portfolio balance		x
Review management of client's portfolio by others to determine if managers are meeting client's investment objectives		x
Transmit client's investment selection to broker		x
Make investment decisions on client's behalf	x	
Execute transactions to buy or sell for client	x	
Take custody of client assets, such as a security purchased	x	

Corporate Finance - Consulting/Advisory	Impaired	Not Impaired
Assist in developing corporate strategies		x
Assist in identifying or introducing client to sources of capital		x
Assist in analyzing effects of proposed transactions		x
Assist in drafting offering documents		x
Advise client in transaction negotiations		x
Commit the client to a transaction or consummate on client's behalf	x	
Act as a promoter, underwriter, broker-dealer, or guarantor of client's securities	x	
Act as a distributor of client's private placement memoranda	x	
Maintain custody of client securities	x	

Executive or Employee Search	Impaired	Not Impaired
Recommend position description or candidate specifications		x
Solicit, screen, and recommend candidates on client-approved criteria		x
Advise employer on employee hiring or benefits		x
Hire or terminate client employees	x	
Commit client to employee compensation or benefits	x	

Business Risk Consulting	Impaired	Not Impaired
Provide assistance in assessing client's business risks and control processes		x
Recommend a plan for improving control processes and assisting in implementation		x
Make or approve business risk decisions	x	
Present business risk consideration to board on management's behalf	x	

Information Systems	Impaired	Not Impaired
Install or integrate a client's financial information system (FIS), that was not designed or developed by member		x
Assist in setting up the client's chart of accounts and financial Statement format with respect to the client's FIS		x
Provide training and instruction to client's employees		x
Design or develop a client's FIS	x	
Design, develop, install, or integrated a client's FIS that is unrelated to the client's F/S or accounting records		x
Make other than insignificant modifications to source code underlying a client's existing FIS.	x	
Supervise client personnel in the daily operation of its FIS	x	
Operate client's local area network (LAN)	x	

Appraisal, Valuation or Actuarial	Impaired	Not Impaired
Results would be material to the F/S and services involve a high degree of subjectivity*	x	
Services not requiring a high degree of subjectivity**		x
Services performed for nonfinancial statement purposes***		x
*Ex: valuing ESOP, business combination, or appraisals of assets and liabilities		
**Ex: valuing a client's pension or postemployment benefit liabilities		
***Ex: appraising or actuarial services for tax planning, estate and gift taxation, and divorce proceedings		

7. **Internal Audit Outsourcing**

   a. Finally, regarding internal audit outsourcing, an auditor should not perform internal auditing for an audit client unless it ensures that the client understands its responsibility for establishing, maintaining, and directing the internal audit function (IAF).

b. The member should ensure that client management: (a) designates a competent manager to be responsible for the IAF; (b) determines the scope, risk, and frequency of internal audit activities; (c) evaluates the findings and results arising from those activities; and (d) evaluates the adequacy of the audit procedures performed and the resultant findings.

c. Additionally, member should be satisfied that the client's board of directors or audit committee is informed about the member's and the client's respective roles. That said, certain internal audit activities would, in any event, impair independence. These include, as examples:

Internal Audit Consulting	Impaired	Not Impaired
Performing ongoing monitoring activities or control activities (e.g., reviewing customer credit info as part of sales process) that affects execution of transactions	x	
Determining which, if any, recommendations for improving internal control system should be implemented	x	
Reporting to the board or audit committee on behalf of management regarding internal audit affairs	x	
Approving or being responsible for the overall internal audit work, including determining internal audit risk and scope, project priorities, and frequency of performance of audit procedures	x	
Being connected with the client as an employee or in any management position	x	

Forensic Accounting Services	Impaired	Not Impaired
Expert witness for a client	x	
Expert witness for a large group where attest clients (a) <20% of members, voting interest, and claims of the group, (b) aren't "lead" plaintiffs, and (c) don't have sole decision-making power to select expert witness		x
Litigation consulting: providing advice to attest client (w/o serving as expert witness)		x
Litigation consulting: serving as trier of fact, special master, court-appointed expert, or arbitrator	x	
Litigation consulting: mediator		x

Tax Compliance Services	Impaired	Not Impaired
Assuming that the CPA does not have custody or control over the client's funds and a client employee reviews and approves the tax return prior to transmission to taxing authority, and, if required for filing, signs the tax return, then:		
- Preparing tax return		x

- Transmitting tax return to taxing authority		x
- Transmitting payment		x
Signing and filing a tax return *on behalf of client management*	x*	
Representing client in administrative proceedings before a taxing authority		x
Representing client in court or a public hearing to resolve a tax dispute	x	

*Signing and filing a tax return on behalf of client management impairs independence, unless several restrictive conditions are met: (a) the member has legal authority to do so; (b) the taxing authority has prescribed procedures in place for a client to permit a member to file a tax return on behalf of the client (e.g., Forms 8879 or 8453), and such procedures meet, at a minimum, standards for electronic return originators outlined in Form 8879; and (c) an individual in client management provides the member with a signed statement that clearly identifies the return being filed and represents that (i) such individual is authorized to sign and file the return; (ii) such individual has reviewed the tax return, including its accompanying schedules and statements, and it is true, correct, and complete to the best of her knowledge and belief; and (iii) such individual authorized the member to sign and file on behalf of the client

d. Although the SEC and PCAOB considered banning provision of tax services, they ultimately decided not to. PCAOB rules now provide, however, that a public company's auditor's independence is impaired regarding a tax client if:

- the firm enters into a contingent fee arrangement with an audit client;
- the firm provides marketing, planning, or opinion services in favor of the tax treatment of a "confidential transaction," or if the transaction is based on an "aggressive" interpretation of tax law; and/or
- the firm provides tax services to members of management who serve in financial-reporting oversight role for a client (or to their immediate family).
- Also, when a firm seeks the permission of an audit client's audit committee to provide tax services, it must describe the proposed services in writing to the committee, discuss with the committee the potential effects on independence, and document that discussion.

IX. Family Members

A. A fourth independence concern relates to family members. Obviously, an auditor would have difficulty being objective and independent if a close relative were CEO of the audit company. The rules establish two sets of relatives - an inner circle known as "immediate family members" and a broader circle known as "close relatives."

B. **Interpretation 101-1**: Meaning of certain independence terminology and the effect of family relationships on independence.

C. **Immediate Family Members**: spouse, spousal equivalent, and dependents (whether or nor related). Independence is not impaired solely as a result of an immediate family member:

1. Working for the client in other than a "**key position**."

Definition:
Key Position: A position in which an individual (a) has primary responsibility for significant accounting functions that support material components of the financial statements; (b) has primary responsibility for the preparation of the financial statement; or (c) has the ability to exercise influence over the contents of the financial statements, including when the individual is a member of the board of directors or similar governing body, chief executive officer, president, CFO, COO, general counsel, chief accounting officer, controller, director of internal audit, director of financial reporting, or any equivalent position.

2. In connection with his or her employment, an immediate family member participating in a retirement, savings, compensation, or similar plan that is sponsored by a client or that invests in a client, provided such plan is normally offered to all employees in similar positions: (a) a partner or manager who provides 10 or more hours of non-attest services to the client; or (b) any partner in the office in which the lead attest engagement partner primarily practices in connection with the attest engagement.

D. **Close Relatives**: Parent, sibling, or nondependent child. Independence is considered impaired if:

1. An individual participating on the attest engagement team has a close relative who had:
   a. A key position with the client, or
   b. A financial interest in the client that
      i. was material to the close relative and of which the individual has knowledge; **or**
      ii. enabled the close relative to exercise significant influence over the client.
2. An individual in a position to influence the attest engagement or any partner in the office in which the lead attest engagement partner primarily practices in connection with the attest engagement, has a close relative who had:
   a. A key position with the client; or
   b. A financial interest in the client that
      i. Was material to the close relative and of which the individual or partner has knowledge; **and**
      ii. Enabled the close relative to exercise significant influence over the client (5% threshold).

E. **Immediate Family Members**

	IFM of Audit Team	**IFM of PTI***	**IFM 10 hours Non-Audit**	**IFM of OPIO****
Key Position With Client	No	No	No	No
Non-Key Position	Yes	Yes	Yes	Yes
Participate in Client Benefit Plan	No	No	Yes	Yes

*PTI is shorthand for a "person in a Position To Influence." Example: supervisors, those who decide compensation, etc. of the audit team.

*OPIO means "Other Partners in the Office" of the auditor in charge of an account. Example: The Austin office of PwC audits Dell. All partners in that office, including tax partners, would be OPIOs.

NOTE: "No" indicates impairment.

F. Close Relatives

	CR of Audit Team	CR of PTI	CR Partner of OPIO
Key Position with Client	No	No	No
Fin. Interest in Client That's not Material or Enables Significant Influence	No	Yes	Yes
Fin. Interest in Client That's Material and Enables Significant Influence	No	No	No

X. The Sarbanes-Oxley Act of 2002 -- contained many provisions, some of which related directly to independence. To the extent that they conflict with the AICPA Code (e.g., regarding consulting services), they override the Code when the audit client is a public company.

A. An independent auditor cannot perform the following services for a public company audit client:

1. Bookkeeping or other services related to the accounting records of financial statements
2. Financial information systems design and implementations
3. Appraisal or valuation services, fairness opinions, or contributions-in-kind reports
4. Actuarial services
5. Internal audit outsourcing services
6. Management functions or human resources
7. Broker or dealer, investment adviser, or investment banking services
8. Legal services and expert services unrelated to the audit
9. Any other service that the PCAOB determines is impermissible

B. Firms may provide these services to non-audit clients and to private companies, even if they are audit clients.

C. Other non-audit services may be performed by public audit clients if preapproved by the audit committee and disclosed in client's periodic reports.

D. Tax Services. Although the SEC and PCAOB have determined not to bar provision of tax services to audit clients generally, the PCAOB has issued Rules 3522 and 3523, which bar provision of two types of tax services: (a) those involving confidential or aggressive tax transactions (tax shelters), and (b) personal tax services provided to a person in a Financial Reporting Oversight Role (FROR) at the audit client, such as a CFO.

E. Audit Partner Rotation

1. There are no requirements for issuers to rotate audit firms.

2. But audit firms must rotate both the lead audit partner and the reviewing audit partner at least every 5 years. They must then serve a 5-year "time out" and can thereafter return.

3. Other partners playing a significant role in the audit are subject to a 7-year rotation requirement with a 2-year time out period.

F. **Auditor Compensation --** An accountant is not independent if any audit partner earns or receives compensation based on that partner selling non-attest services to an audit client.

G. **Auditor Report to Audit Committee**

1. Audit firms are now selected and compensated by the audit committee rather than management.

2. Each firm must timely report to the client's audit committee:

   - all critical accounting policies and practices to be used;
   - all alternative treatments of financial information within GAAP that have been discussed with management officials, ramifications of the use of such alternative disclosures, and the treatment preferred by the accounting firm; and
   - other material written communications between the accounting firm and the issuer's management, such as any management letter or schedule of unadjusted differences.

H. **Cooling-Off Periods --** As noted earlier, SOX provides:

1. An audit firm may not perform an audit for a client if its CEO, controller, CFO, CAO, or any person serving in an equivalent capacity was employed by the firm and participated in the audit during a one-year period preceding the date of the initiation of the audit.

2. If the individual worked for the audit firm but did not participate in the client's audit: no problem.

Integrity and Objectivity (Rule 102)

Every CPA, whether involved in auditing, tax work, or consulting must comply with standards of integrity and objectivity. Unlike independence principles, these are not confined mainly to the audit function. In a close case, use your common sense, for the AICPA Code of Conduct specifies that integrity is, at the bottom, judged in terms of what is "right and just."

I. "In the performance of any professional service, a member:

A. shall maintain objectivity and integrity,

B. shall be free of conflict of interest, and

C. shall not knowingly misrepresent facts or subordinate his or her judgment to others."

II. **Interpretation 102-1: --** Not only may a member not knowingly make a false representation, but that member may not permit or direct another to make a false entry in an entity's financial statement, according to Interpretation 102-1.

III. **Interpretation 102-2: --** A conflict of interest may occur if a CPA performing a professional service has a significant relationship with another person, entity, product, or service that could be viewed as impairing the CPA's objectivity, according to Interpretation 102-2.

A. **Exception: No problem if:**

1. Full disclosure to client, and
2. Client consents.

B. **Examples of potential conflicts of interest:**

1. A member is asked to perform litigation services for a plaintiff in a lawsuit against one of the firm's audit clients.
2. A member has provided tax planning advice to a married couple that is now divorcing and is asked by both parties to provide services during the divorce proceedings.
3. In giving financial advice, a member suggests that the client invest in a business in which the member has a financial interest.
4. A member provides tax or financial planning services for several members of a family who may have opposing interests.
5. A member has a significant financial interest in a company that is a major competitor of a client for which the member performs management consulting services.
6. A member serves on a city's board of tax appeals, which considers matters involving several of the member's tax clients.
7. A member has been approached to provide services to the potential buyer of real estate owned by a client of the member's firm.
8. A member refers a tax or financial planning client to an insurance broker which refers clients to the member under an exclusive arrangement to do so.
9. A member recommends or refers a client to a service bureau in which the member or partners in the member's firm hold material financial interests.

IV. Interpretation 102-3 -- provides that a member must respond accurately to his or her employer's external accountant's inquiries. SOX, of course, makes it a crime to lie to outside auditors.

V. Interpretation 102-4: -- Consider the situation where an auditor disagrees with his or her supervisor regarding the proper recording of transactions or preparation of financial statements. In order to ensure that a member's professional judgment is never improperly subordinated, Interpretation 102-4 provides that a member who has such a disagreement with his or her supervisor should take the following steps:

A. The member should consider whether

1. the entry or the failure to record a transaction in the records, or

2. the financial statement presentation or the nature or omission of disclosure in the financial statements as proposed by the supervisor, represents an acceptable alternative and does not materially misrepresent the facts.

B. If appropriate research and consultation indicate that the supervisor's position has authoritative support and does not result in a material misrepresentation, the member may accept the supervisor's position and need do nothing further.

C. If the member concludes that the supervisor's position would lead to material misstatement of records or financial statements, the member should make her concerns known to the appropriate levels of management, such as the supervisor's immediate superior, the audit committee, the board of directors, etc. The concerns should be documented.

D. If, after discussing the matter with the appropriate persons in the organization, the member concludes that appropriate action will not be taken, the member should consider whether or not s/he should continue the employment relationship and whether s/he has a responsibility to contact a regulatory authority or the organization's external accountant. An attorney should be consulted.

VI. Interpretation 102-5 -- reminds members who teach or engage in research and scholarship that their activities are professional services and should be rendered with objectivity and integrity, that they shall be free of conflicts of interest, and that they shall not knowingly misrepresent facts or subordinate their judgment.

VII. Interpretation 102-6: -- Client advocacy can raise interesting dilemmas. Interpretation 102-6 recognizes that a member may be requested by a client to perform tax or consulting services that involve acting as an advocate for the client, and that auditors may be asked to be advocates in support of their clients' positions on accounting or financial reporting issues. Again, these are professional services and should be rendered with objectivity and integrity, free of conflicts of interest, and without subordination of judgment.

A. Inappropriate Services: Additionally, if the requested services involving client advocacy appear to stretch the bounds of performance standards or to compromise credibility, the member should consider whether it is appropriate to perform such services.

VIII. Examples of Integrity and Objectivity Issues Embodied in Past Ethics Rulings.

Question: During the performance of an engagement, an individual participating in the engagement may be offered employment by the client or may seek employment with the client. What are the implications of these actions?

Answer:
An individual participating in an engagement who is offered employment by, or seeks employment with, that client during the conduct of the engagement must consider whether or not his or her ability to act with integrity and objectivity has been impaired. When the engagement is one requiring independence, the individual must remove himself or herself from the engagement until the employment offer is rejected or employment is no longer being sought, in order to avoid any appearance that integrity or objectivity has been impaired.

Question: A member serves as a director or officer of a local United Way or similar organization that operates as a federated fund-raising organization from which local charities that are clients of the member receive funds. Does the member have a conflict of interest?

Answer:
Interpretation 102-2 provides that a conflict of interest may occur if a member performs a professional service for a client and the member or his or her firm has a relationship with another entity that could, in the member's professional judgment, be viewed by the client or other appropriate parties as impairing the member's objectivity. If the member believes that the professional service can be performed with objectivity and the relationship is disclosed to, and consent is obtained from, the appropriate parties, performance of the service shall not be prohibited.

Question: A member has been approached by a private company, for which s/he may or may not perform other professional services, to provide personal financial planning or tax services for its executives. The executives are aware of the company's relationship with the member, if any, and have also consented to the arrangement. The performance of the services could result in the member recommending to the executives actions that may be adverse to the company. What rules of conduct should the member consider before accepting and during the performance of the engagement?

Answer:
Before accepting and during the performance, the member should consider the applicability of Rule 102. If a member believes that he or she can perform the personal financial planning or tax services with objectivity, the member would not be prohibited from accepting the engagement. The member should also consider informing the company and the executives of possible results of the engagement. During the performance of the services, the member should consider his or her professional responsibility to the clients under Rule 301. However, if the client is a public company, SOX would prohibit its auditor from providing tax planning services to the client's top executives.

General Standards and Accounting Principles

No matter what type of professional service a CPA is providing -- audit, tax, consulting, etc. -- that CPA must act with professional competence.

Remember (because these are often possible selections on multiple choice questions) that professional competence entails, among other things, undertaking only tasks that you are competent to perform, exercising due professional care in the completion of those tasks, adequately planning those tasks and supervising those who perform them for you, and obtaining sufficient relevant data to serve as a basis for any conclusions you reach or recommendations you make.

I. **General Standards --** A member must comply with the following standards for all professional engagements:

   A. **Professional Competence:** Undertake only those professional services that the member or member's firm can reasonably expect to be completed with professional competence.

   B. **Due Professional Care:** Exercise due professional care in the performance of professional services.

   C. **Planning and Supervision:** Adequately plan and supervise the performance of professional services.

   D. **Sufficient Relevant Data:** Obtain sufficient relevant data to afford a reasonable basis for conclusions or recommendations in relation to any professional services performed.

II. **Interpretations**

   A. An agreement to perform professional services implies that the member has the necessary competence to perform those services according to professional standards, applying his or her knowledge and skill with reasonable care and diligence, but the member does not assume a responsibility for infallibility of knowledge or judgment.

   B. Competence to complete an engagement includes:

      1. Technical qualifications of CPA and staff.

      2. Ability to supervise and evaluate work.

      3. Knowledge of technical subject matter.

      4. Capability to exercise judgment in its application.

      5. Ability to research subject matter and consult with others where necessary.

Compliance with Standards

A member who performs auditing, review, compilation, consulting, tax, or other services shall comply with standards promulgated by bodies designated by the Council.

I. **Public Company Accounting Oversight Board** (PCAOB): will establish auditing, fraud detection, and other standards for audits of public companies under the supervision of the Securities Exchange Commission (SEC)

II. **Financial Accounting Standards Board** (FASB): at least for the moment, is being relied upon by the PCAOB to establish generally accepted accounting principles (GAAP) for nongovernmental entities.

III. **Governmental Accounting Standards Board** (GASB): establishes governmental accounting standards.

IV. **Auditing Standards Board** (ASB): establishes generally accepted auditing standards (GAAS).

V. **Accounting and Review Services Committee** (ARSC): sets standards for unaudited statements of nonpublic entities.

VI. **Management Advisory Services Executive Committee** (MASEC): sets professional standards for consulting services

Accounting Principles and Interpretations (Rule 203)

As a practical matter, if financial statements do not comply with GAAP, a jury will likely find at least negligence by the accountant.

As a practical matter, if financial statements do not comply with GAAP, a jury will likely find at least negligence by the accountant. However, if the financial statements do comply it is still possible (although, fortunately, somewhat unlikely) that a jury might find the accountant negligent on grounds that, in this particular case, more than compliance with GAAP and GAAS was necessary for a careful job.

I. **Principles --** Members cannot provide positive or negative assurance that financial statements are in conformity with GAAP if the statements contain departures from GAAP that have a material effect on statements taken as a whole, except when unusual circumstances would render financial statements following GAAP misleading. When such unusual circumstances exist, CPA must disclose:

   A. the departure,

   B. the approximate effects of departure, and

   C. the reasons why compliance with GAAP would mislead.

II. **Interpretations**

   A. **Interpretation 203-1:** CPAs are allowed departure from SFAS (Statements of Financial Accounting Standards issued by FASB to establish GAAP) only when results of SFAS will be misleading, as where, for example:

      1. New legislation has been passed, or

      2. New forms of business transaction have evolved.

   B. **Interpretation 203-2:** FASB and GASB Interpretations are covered by Rule 203.

   C. **Interpretation 203-3:** A member shall not state affirmatively that financial statements or other financial data of an entity are presented in conformity with GAAP if such statements or data contain any departure from an accounting principle promulgated by a body designed by the AICPA to establish such principles that has a material effect on the statements or data taken as a whole.

Responsibilities To Clients

CPAs owe a number of responsibilities to their clients, many arising out of simple agency law. Two that often receive attention on the CPA exam relate to matters of confidentiality and contingency fees. Always remember that if a client consents to disclosure of confidential information, the CPA cannot be held liable for disclosure.

I. **Rule 301 --** "A member in public practice shall not disclose any confidential client information without the specific consent of the client."

   Exceptions: This prohibition does not

   A. Relieve a member of his or her professional obligations;

   B. Affect the member's obligation to comply with validly issued subpoenas and summonses, and with applicable laws and government regulations;

   C. Prohibit review of a member's professional practice under AICPA or state CPA society rules; or

   D. Preclude a member from initiating or responding to a complaint filed by the professional ethics division or trial board of the AICPA or a duly constituted state disciplinary body.

II. **Interpretation 301-3 --** A review of a member's professional practice (which is a confidentiality exception) is authorized to include a review in conjunction with a prospective purchase, sale, or merger of all or part of a member's practice so long as the member takes appropriate precautions (such as through written confidentiality agreements) so that the prospective purchaser does not disclose any information obtained in the course of the review, since such information is deemed to be confidential client information.

   A. **Confidential Information:** Members reviewing a practice in connection with a prospective purchase or merger shall not use it to their advantage nor disclose any member's confidential client information that comes to their attention.

   B. **Examples of Confidentiality Issues Embodied in Past Ethics Rulings.**

Question:
May a member in public practice disclose the name of a client for whom the member or the member's firm performed professional services?

Answer:
Rule 301 allows a member to disclose the name of a client, whether publicly or privately owned, without the client's specific consent unless the disclosure of the client's name constitutes the release of confidential information. For example, if the member's practice is solely in the bankruptcy area, release of a client's name might also disclose that the client is having financial difficulties, which could be confidential information.

C. Chart illustrating some of the key rules: When may client confidences be disclosed?

	May Disclose	May Not Disclose
Unless recognized exceptions apply		x
In order to comply with Rule 202 obligations to comply with professional standards	x	
In order to comply with Rule 203 obligations to follow GAAP	x	
In order to comply with an enforceable subpoena or summons	x	
Pursuant to AICPA review of professional practice	x	
Initiating complaint or responding to inquiry made by a recognized investigative or disciplinary body	x	
To potential purchaser of practice who has signed a confidentiality agreement	x	
Of working papers to CPA after that CPA has purchased practice		x
Any time client consents	x	

D. Accountant-Client Privilege

1. Traditionally, there has been no federal accountant-client privilege comparable to the attorney-client privilege.
2. Some states have adopted such a privilege statutorily, however, and it applies only in the courts of those states.
3. However, in the Internal Revenue Service Restructuring and Reform Act of 1998, Congress created a confidentiality privilege between clients and the CPAs who represent them before the IRS. The privilege essentially covers all tax advisers, including accountants. However, it applies only to noncriminal matters before federal courts in which a federal tax authority is involved. It does not apply:
   a. in criminal cases;
   b. in matters not before the IRS or federal courts in cases brought by or against the United States;
   c. to tax advice on state or local matters; or
   d. written tax shelter advice.
   e.

III. Contingent Fees - Rule 302

A. General Rule: A member in public practice shall not:

1. Perform for a contingent fee any professional services for, or receive such a fee from, a client for whom the member or the member's firm performs:
   a. an audit or review of a financial statement; or
   b. a compilation of a financial statement when the member expects, or might reasonably expect, that a third party will use the financial statement and the report does not disclose a lack of independence; or
   c. an examination of prospective financial information.

2. Prepare an original or amended tax return or claim for a tax refund for a contingent fee for any client.

B. **Public Authority Exception:** A fee is not regarded as contingent if fixed by the courts or other public authorities.

C. **Variable Fees:** A member's fees may vary depending on various factors, including the complexity of services rendered.

D. **Permissible Situations:** Interpretation 302-1 provides the following examples of situations in the tax area where a contingent fee would be permitted:

1. Representing a client in an examination by a revenue agent of the client's federal or state income tax return.
2. Filing an amended federal or state income tax return claiming a tax refund based on a tax issue that is either the subject of a test case (involving a different taxpayer) or with respect to which the taxing authority is developing a position.
3. Filing an amended federal or state income tax return (or refund claim) claiming a tax refund in an amount greater than the threshold for review by the Joint Committee on Internal Revenue Taxation ($1 million) or state taxing authority.
4. Requesting a refund of either overpayments of interest or penalties charged to a client's account or deposits of taxes improperly accounted for by the federal or state taxing authority in circumstances where the taxing authority has established procedures for the substantive review of such refund requests.
5. Requesting, by means of "protest" or similar document, consideration by the state or local taxing authority of a reduction in the "assessed value" of property under an established taxing authority review process for hearing all taxpayer arguments relating to assessed value.
6. Representing a client in connection with obtaining a private letter ruling or influencing the drafting of a regulation or statute.

E. **Non-permissible Situation:** Interpretation 302-1 gives the following example of a circumstance where a contingent fee would not be permitted:

F. Preparing an amended federal or state income tax return for a client claiming a refund of taxes because a deduction was inadvertently omitted from the return originally filed. There is no question of the propriety of the deduction; rather the claim is filed to correct an omission.

G. **Examples of Contingent Fee Issues Embodied in Past Ethics Rulings.**

Question:
Rules 302 and 503 prohibit, among other acts, the receipt of contingent fees for the performance of certain services and the receipt of a commission for the referral of products or services under certain circumstances. When is a contingent fee or commission deemed to be received?

Answer:
A contingent fee or a commission is deemed to be received when the performance of the related services is complete and the fee or the commission is determined. For example, if in one year a member sells a life insurance policy to a client and the member's commission payments are determined to be a fixed percentage of the future years' renewal premiums, the commission is deemed to be received in the year the policy is sold.

H. Summary Chart: Summarizing some of the basic rules regarding contingency fees:

	Permitted	Not Permitted
1) Performing audit or review		x
2) Perform compilation knowing third party may use it		x
3) Examine prospective financial information		x
4) Perform any service for client while also performing #1-3.		x
5) Prepare original or amended tax return or claim for refund		x
6) Represent client in an examination by revenue agent	x	
7) File amended tax return based on tax issue that is subject of a test case involving a different taxpayer	x	
8) Prepare an amended tax return for a client claiming a refund that is clearly due the client due to an inadvertent omission		x

IV. Ethics Rulings for Rules 301 and 302

A. A member may utilize outside computer services to process tax returns as long as there is no release of confidential information.

B. Members may reveal the names of clients without client consent unless such disclosure releases confidential information.

C. In divorce proceedings, a member who has prepared joint tax returns for the couple should consider both individuals to be clients for purposes of requests for confidential information relating to prior tax returns. Under such circumstances, the CPA should consider reviewing the legal implications of disclosure with an attorney.

D. A member's spouse may provide services to a member's attest client for a contingent fee and may refer products or services for a commission.

V. Contingent Fees -- The PCAOB has provided that a public company auditor cannot perform any tax services for the client on a contingent fee basis. It has also ruled that independence is impaired if:

A. the firm provides marketing, planning, or opinion services in favor of the tax treatment of a "confidential transaction," or if the transaction is based on an "aggressive" interpretation of tax law; and/or

B. the firm provides tax services to members of management who serve in financial-reporting oversight roles for a client (or to their immediate family).

Rule 501. Acts Discreditable

"A member shall not commit an act discreditable to the profession."

I. **Interpretation 501-1** -- The AICPA has recently delineated new categories of records and provided new rules regarding when they may be retained in the face of a client request for their return.

   A. *Client-provided records* (such as accounting or other records given by the client to the member) should be returned to the client.

   B. *Client records prepared by the member* (such as tax returns or general ledgers) should usually be returned to the client, but may be withheld if the client has not paid the fee for preparation of the documents.

   C. *Supporting records* (information not reflected in the client's books and records that are otherwise unavailable to the client, such as adjusting, closing, or consolidating journal entries produced by the member) should also be returned, unless fees for preparing them are due.

   D. Members' *working papers* (such as audit programs, analytical review schedules, and statistical sampling results) belong to the member and need not be provided to the client, unless state law, federal law, or contractual obligations so require.

   E. **Additional rules:** Client requests should normally be honored within 45 days. Reasonable fees may be charged for the work. Members may keep copies of all records. If applicable state or federal laws require more than AICPA provisions, they, naturally, must be followed.

II. **Interpretation 501-2 -- Discrimination and Harassment in Employment Practices**: Discrimination (on basis of race, color, religion, sex, age, or national origin) and harassment (sexual and other forms) are discreditable acts.

III. **Interpretation 501-3 -- Failure to Follow Standards and/or Procedures or Other Requirements in Governmental Audits**: It is a discreditable act to fail to follow appropriate procedures for governmental audits, unless the member discloses in the report that required procedures were not followed and the reasons therefore.

IV. **Interpretation 501-4 -- Negligence in the Preparation of Financial Statements or Records**: Negligently making (or permitting, or directing another to make) false or misleading journal entries is a discreditable act.

V. **Interpretation 501-5 -- Failure to Follow Requirements of Governmental Bodies, Commissions, or Other Regulatory Agencies in Performing Attest or Similar Functions**: Failing to extend procedures beyond GAAS when governmental bodies, commissions, or other regulatory agencies such as the SEC, the FCC, and state insurance commissions so require is a discreditable act.

VI. **Interpretation 501-6 -- Solicitation or Disclosure of CPA Examination Questions**: Soliciting or knowingly disclosing the May 1996 or later Uniform CPA Examination questions and/or answers without the written authorization of the AICPA is a discreditable act.

VII. **Interpretation 501-7 -- Failure to File Tax Return or Pay Tax Liability**: CPAs who fail to pay their own or their firm's tax liabilities act discreditably.

VIII. Interpretation 501-8 -- Failure to Follow Requirements of Governmental Bodies, Commissions, or other Regulatory Agencies on Indemnification and Limitation of Liability Provisions in Connection with Audit and Other Attest Services: Government agencies, such as the SEC, often oppose indemnification provisions and other limitations of liability provisions in auditors' contracts. They wish auditors to be held liable for their errors. Therefore, if an engagement letter for an audit of a public company contained an indemnification provision wherein the audit client agreed to completely reimburse the auditor for any liability it might incur arising out of the audit, the SEC would not be pleased and the auditor would have committed a discreditable act. On the other hand, the SEC does not oppose contribution (where the client would partially reimburse the auditor if the auditor paid not only its share of damages to third-parties, but the client's share as well), so a contribution provision would be allowed.

Rule 502. Advertising

"A member in public practice shall not seek to obtain clients by advertising or other forms of solicitation in a manner that is false, misleading, or deceptive. Solicitation by the use of coercion, over-reaching, or harassing conduct is prohibited."

I. **Interpretation 502-2 --** CPAs may normally engage in accurate advertising ("commercial speech"). Examples of prohibited false, misleading, or deceptive advertisements include:

   A. Creating false or unjustified expectations of favorable results;

   B. Implying the ability to influence any court, tribunal, regulatory agency, or similar body or official;

   C. Representing that specific professional services in current or future periods will be performed for a stated fee, estimated fee, or fee range when it was likely at the time of the representation that such fees would be substantially increased and the prospective client was not advised of that likelihood; and

   D. Making any other representation that would be likely to cause a reasonable person to misunderstand or be deceived.

II. **Interpretation 502-5 --** Members who obtain engagements through the efforts of third parties have the responsibility to ascertain that all promotional efforts used by the third parties comply with the rules of conduct; otherwise, the member would be doing through others what the member is prohibited from doing personally.

Example:
In a 1993 case, the Supreme Court held that an accountant could not be prohibited from making "in-person" solicitations. Lawyers may be so prohibited by their bar associations, but accountants' clients are viewed as more sophisticated and less vulnerable to high-pressure tactics.

Rule 503. Commissions and Referral Fees

Requirements regarding commissions and referral fees.

I. A member in public practice may not accept a commission for recommending a product or service to a client when that member or his firm also perform:

A. audits or reviews of financial statements;

B. compilations to be used by third parties; and/or

C. examinations of prospective financial information.

II. When a member does accept a permitted commission or referral fee, such must be disclosed to the client.

III. Making a profit by purchasing a product from a third party and reselling it to a client does not constitute receipt of a commission and is permissible, even if the profit is not disclosed.

Rule 505. Name

Requirements for the form of and naming of an organization.

I. Requirements for the form of and naming of an organization

A. Member Restrictions: A member may practice public accounting only in a form of organization (proprietorship, partnership, professional corporation, limited liability company, limited liability partnership, etc.) permitted by state law whose characteristics conform to AICPA resolutions.

B. Misleading Firm Name: A member shall not practice public accounting under a misleading firm name.

1. Names may include past owners.
2. Members may practice in name of former partnership for 2 years when all others have died or withdrawn.
3. If not misleading, a name may:
    - **a.** include a fictitious name, or
    - **b.** indicate a specialization.
4. Firms may not designate themselves as members of AICPA unless all partners or shareholders are members.

II. Interpretation 505-2

A. A member in public practice may own an interest in a separate business that performs nonaudit services for clients.

B. If the member, individually or collectively with his firm or members of the firm, controls the separate business, then that entity and all its owners and employees must comply with the Code of Professional Conduct.

1. Ex: Would have to follow rules on commissions and referral fees.

C. If member and colleagues do not control the separate business, the Code would apply to the member and colleagues, but not to the separate business or its other owners and employees.

1. In this case, the entity could enter into a contingent fee arrangement with an attest client.

III. Interpretation 505-3

A. A majority of the financial interests in an attest firm must be owned by CPAs.

B. When alternative practice structures (APS) are involved, the bottom line is that the public interest will be considered protected if CPAs who own the attest firm remain financially responsible under applicable law or regulation.

Examples: Past Ethics Rulings

Examples of Responsibilities and Practices Requirements Embodied in Past Ethics Rulings.

Examples:
The proficiency questions attached to this lesson are Examples of Responsibilities and Practices Requirements Embodied in Past Ethics Rulings.

Responsibilities in Consulting Services

At least up until the exam was closed, questions regarding consulting services tended to be fairly rudimentary. The AICPA essentially wanted CPAs to know (a) that there are separate standards (SSCS) that govern the consulting function, (b) what types of activities are considered "consulting" and therefore subject to the standards, and (c) that consulting, like other areas of service, requires professional competence, which in turn, requires that CPAs not attempt tasks for which they are not competent, that they adequately plan and supervise, and that they gather sufficient relevant data.

SSCS

Consulting services that CPAs provide to their clients are governed by Statements on Standards for Consulting Services (SSCS).

I. **Consulting Services under SSCS --** Consulting services governed by these standards can include one or more of the following types of consulting services:

A. **Consultations**

> **Definition:**
> *Consultations*: To provide counsel in a short time frame based mostly, if not entirely, on existing personal knowledge about client.

1. **Examples:** Reviewing and commenting on client business plan, suggesting software for further client investigation.

B. **Advisory Services**

> **Definition:**
> *Advisory Services*: To develop findings, conclusions, and recommendations for client consideration and decision-making.

1. **Examples:** Operational review and improvement study, analysis of accounting system, strategic planning assistance, information system advice.

C. **Implementation Services**

> **Definition:**
> *Implementation Services*: To place an action plan into effect.

1. **Examples:** Installing and supporting computer system, executing steps to improve productivity, assisting with mergers.

D. **Transaction Services**

> **Definition:**
> *Transaction Services*: To provide services related to a specific client transaction, generally with a third party.

1. **Examples:** Insolvency services, valuation services, information related to financing, analysis of a possible merger or acquisition, litigation services.

E. Staff and Other Support Services

> **Definition:**
> *Staff and Other Support Services*: To provide appropriate staff and possibly other support to perform tasks specified by the client.

1. **Examples:** Data processing, facilities management, computer programming, bankruptcy trusteeship, and controllership activities.

F. Product Services

> **Definition:**
> *Product Services*: To provide the client with a product and associated professional services in support of the installation, use, or maintenance of the product.

1. **Examples:** Sale, delivery, installation, and implementation of training programs, computer software, and systems development methodologies.

II. Standards for Consulting Services

A. General Standards of Rule 201 of Code of Professional Conduct Apply to Consulting

1. Professional Competence
2. Due Professional Care
3. Planning and Supervision
4. Sufficient Relevant Data.

B. Duties to Client

1. A member performing consulting services:
   - **a.** Must serve client interest while maintaining:
     - **i.** Integrity, and
     - **ii.** Objectivity,
     - **iii.** But not: independence.
   - **b.** Must establish understanding with client (orally or in writing) about the nature, scope, and limitations of services to be performed.
   - **c.** Must communicate with client regarding:
     - **i.** conflicts of interest,
     - **ii.** significant reservations about engagement, and
     - **iii.** significant engagement findings, etc.
   - **d.** Must use professional judgment in applying SSCS.

III. Independence

A. Performing consulting services for an attest client does not necessarily create a conflict of interest, but all members performing both types of services should comply with all applicable rules regarding independence.

B. Consulting Spin Off

1. After the Enron scandal and passage of Sarbanes-Oxley, three of the Big Four firms spun off their consulting units.

Ethics and Responsibilities in Tax Practice

SSTS No. 1 - Tax Return Positions

With Respect to Tax Return Positions

I. **Strength of Position --** A CPA should not recommend to a client that a position be taken with respect to the tax treatment of any item on a return unless the CPA has a good faith belief that the position has a realistic possibility of being sustained administratively or judicially on its merits, if challenged.

   A. **Realistic Possibility --** A "realistic possibility" generally means at least a one-in-three chance.

      1. In determining whether a realistic possibility exists, a CPA should:

         a. Establish relevant background facts,

         b. Distill the appropriate questions from those facts,

         c. Search for authoritative answers to those questions,

         d. Resolve the questions by weighing the authorities uncovered by that search, and

         e. Arrive at a conclusion supported by the authorities.

   B. **Good Faith Belief:** A "good faith" belief may arise from a CPA's study of well-reasoned articles, treatises, IRS General Counsel Memoranda, a General Explanation of a Revenue Act prepared by the staff of the Joint Committee on Taxation, and IRS written determinations (e.g., private letter rulings).

   C. **Signing a Return:** A CPA should not prepare or sign a return as an income tax return preparer if the CPA knows that the return takes a position that the CPA could not recommend as having a realistic possibility of being sustained.

   D. **Non-frivolous Position Recommendations:** A CPA may recommend a position that the CPA concludes is not frivolous so long as the position is adequately disclosed on the return or claim for refund. (Note: "Frivolous" means patently improper.)

   E. **Potential Penalty Consequences:** In recommending certain tax return positions and in signing a return on which a tax return position is taken, a CPA should, where relevant, advise the client as to the potential penalty consequences of the recommended tax return position and the opportunity, if any, to avoid such penalties through disclosure.

Note:
"realistic possibility" generally means at least a *one-in-three* chance
" **frivolous**" generally means "*patently improper*"

Chart summarizing tax return position responsibilities

	OK w/o Disclosure	OK w/ Disclosure	Never OK
Recommend position with "realistic possibility" of being sustained	x		
Prepare or sign return taking a position with "realistic possibility" of being sustained	x		
Recommend position that is "not frivolous" but may not have a "realistic possibility" of being sustained		x	
Recommend frivolous position			x

1. The "realistic possibility" standard of SSTS No. 1 has been coordinated with the federal statutory standards in U.S.C. 6694. In May of 2007, Congress surprised most accountants by abruptly raising the standard in 6694 from "realistic possibility" to "more likely than not." Henceforth, if a tax professional is to avoid penalty under 6694, he or she must recommend only positions that are more likely than not to be sustained (rather than having merely "realistic possibility" of being sustained). The standard was basically changed from 33% to 51%. That change means that the AICPA will probably very soon change the language of SSTS No. 1 from "realistic possibility" to "more likely than not," although, at this writing (Nov. 2007), the AICPA has asked the IRS for a delay in implementation of the provision.

F. **CPA Recommendations:** A CPA should not recommend a position that:

1. Exploits the IRS audit selection process; or

2. Serves as a mere "arguing position" advanced solely to obtain leverage in the bargaining process of settlement negotiation with the IRS.

G. **CPA as Advocate:** A CPA has both the right and responsibility to be an advocate for the client with respect to any positions satisfying the proper standards.

II. **Specific Illustrations for SSTS No. 1 provided by the AICPA's Tax Practice Interpretations.**

A. The CPA's client has engaged in a transaction that is adversely affected by a new statutory provision. Prior law supports a position favorable to the client. The client believes, and the CPA concurs, that the new statute is inequitable as applied to the client's situation. The statute is clearly drafted and unambiguous. The committee reports discussing the new statute contain general comments that do not specifically address the client's situation.

1. The CPA should recommend the return position supported by the new statute. A position contrary to a clear, unambiguous statute would ordinarily be considered a frivolous position.

B. The CPA's client has engaged in a transaction that is adversely affected by a new statutory provision. Prior law supports a position favorable to the client. The client believes, and the CPA concurs, that the new statute is inequitable as applied to the client's situation. The statute is clearly drafted and unambiguous. However, the committee reports discussing the new statute specifically address the client's situation and take a position favorable to the client.

1. In a case where the statute is clearly and unambiguously against the taxpayer's position but a contrary position exists based on committee reports specifically addressing the client's situation, a return position based on either the statutory language or the legislative history satisfies the realistic possibility standard.

C. The CPA's client has engaged in a transaction that is adversely affected by a new statutory provision. Prior law supports a position favorable to the client. The client believes, and the CPA concurs, that the new statute is inequitable as applied to the client's situation. The statute is clearly drafted and unambiguous. The committee reports can be interpreted to provide some evidence or authority in support of the taxpayer's position; however, the legislative history does not specifically address the situation.

1. In a case where the statute is clear and unambiguous, a contrary position based on an interpretation of committee reports that do not explicitly address the client's situation does not meet the realistic possibility standard. However, since the committee reports provide some support or evidence for the taxpayer's position, such a return position is not frivolous. The CPA may recommend the position to the client if it is adequately disclosed on the tax return.

D. A client is faced with an issue involving the interpretation of a new statute. Following its passage, the statute was widely recognized to contain a drafting error and a technical correction proposal has been introduced. The IRS issues an announcement indicating how it will administer the provision. The IRS pronouncement interprets the statute in accordance with the proposed technical correction.

1. Return positions based on either the existing statutory language or the IRS pronouncement satisfy the realistic possibility standard.

E. A client is faced with an issue involving the interpretation of a new statute. Following its passage, the statute was widely recognized to contain a drafting error, and a technical correction proposal has been introduced. The IRS has not issued a clarifying announcement.

1. In the absence of an IRS pronouncement interpreting the statute in accordance with the technical correction, only a return position based on the existing statutory language will meet the realistic possibility standard. A return position based on the proposed technical correction may be recommended if it is adequately disclosed, since it is not frivolous.

F. A client is seeking advice from a CPA regarding a recently amended Internal Revenue Code section. The CPA has reviewed the Code section, committee reports that specifically address the issue, and a recently published IRS Notice. The CPA has concluded in good faith that, based on the Code section and the committee reports, the IRS's position as stated in the Notice does not reflect congressional intent.

1. The CPA may recommend the position supported by the Internal Revenue Code section and the committee reports, since it meets the realistic possibility standard.

G. A client is seeking advice from a CPA regarding a recently amended Internal Revenue Code section. The CPA has reviewed the Code section, committee reports that specifically address the issue, and a recently published IRS temporary position. The CPA has concluded in good faith that, based on the Code section and the committee reports, the IRS's temporary position does not reflect congressional intent.

1. To determine whether the IRS's temporary position meets the realistic possibility standard, the CPA should determine the weight to be given the regulation by analyzing factors such as whether the regulation is legislative, interpretative, or inconsistent with the statute. If the CPA concludes the position does not meet the realistic possibility standard, the position may nevertheless be recommended if it is adequately disclosed, since it is not frivolous.

H. A tax form published by the IRS is incorrect but completion of the form as published provides a benefit to the client. The CPA knows that the IRS has published an announcement acknowledging the error.

1. In these circumstances, a return position in accordance with the published form is a frivolous position.

I. The client wants to take a position that the CPA has concluded is frivolous. The client maintains that even if the return is examined by the IRS, the issue will not be raised.

1. The CPA should not consider the likelihood of audit or detection when determining whether the realistic possibility standard has been met. The CPA should not prepare or sign a return that contains a frivolous position even if it is disclosed.

J. Congress passes a statute requiring the capitalization of certain expenditures. The client believes, and the CPA concurs, that in order to comply fully, the client will need to acquire new computer hardware and software and implement a number of new accounting procedures. The client and the CPA agree that the costs of full compliance will be significantly greater than the resulting increase in tax due under the new provision. Because of these cost considerations, the client makes no effort to comply. The client wants the CPA to prepare and sign a return on which the new requirement is simply ignored.

1. The return position desired by the client is frivolous and the CPA should neither prepare nor sign the return.

K. Congress passes a statute requiring the capitalization of certain expenditures. The client believes, and the CPA concurs, that in order to comply fully, the client will need to acquire new computer hardware and software and implement a number of new accounting procedures. The client and the CPA agree that the costs of full compliance will be significantly greater than the resulting increase in tax due under the new provision. The client has made a good faith effort to comply with the law by calculating an estimate of expenditures to be capitalized under the new provision.

1. In this situation, the realistic possibility standard has been met.

L. On a given issue, the CPA has located and weighed two authorities. The IRS has published its clearly enunciated position as a Revenue Ruling. A court opinion is favorable to the client. The CPA has considered the source of both authorities and has concluded that both are persuasive and relevant.

1. The realistic possibility standard is met by either position.

M. A tax statute is silent on the treatment of an item under the statute. However, the committee reports explaining the statute direct the IRS to issue regulations that will require specified treatment of this item. No regulations have been issued at the time the CPA must recommend a position on the tax treatment of the item.

1. The CPA may recommend the position supported by the committee reports, since it meets the realistic possibility standard.

N. The client wants to take a position that the CPA concludes to meet the realistic possibility standard based on an assumption regarding an underlying nontax legal issue. The CPA recommends that the client seek advice from its legal counsel and the client's attorney gives an opinion on the nontax legal issue.

1. A legal opinion on a nontax legal issue may, in general, be relied upon by a CPA. The CPA must, however, use professional judgment when relying on a legal opinion. If, on its face, the opinion of the client's attorney appears to be unreasonable, unsubstantiated, or unwarranted, the CPA should consult his/her own attorney before relying on the opinion.

O. The client has obtained from its attorney an opinion on the tax treatment of an item and requests that the CPA rely on the opinion.

1. The authorities on which a CPA may rely include well-reasoned sources of tax analysis. If the CPA is satisfied as to the source, relevance, and persuasiveness of the legal opinion, the CPA may rely on that opinion when determining whether the realistic possibility standard has been met.

Note:
Note that in May 2007, Congress surprised tax professionals by raising the standard for tax return preparers. Rather than the "realistic possibility" standard, tax return preparers are now judged by the "unreasonable position" standards, which may impose penalties if the tax preparer did not have a "reasonable belief" that the position would "more likely than not" be sustained on its merits. Rather than alter SSTS No. 1 to conform to the new federal standard, the AICPA has, as of this writing (Oct. 2008), been attempting to induce Congress to return to the earlier "realistic possibility" standard.

SSTS No. 2 - Answers to Questions on Return

Answers to Questions on Return

I. A CPA should make reasonable effort to obtain and provide for client appropriate answers to all questions on a tax return. Rationale:

- **A.** A question may be of importance in determining taxable income or loss, or the tax liability shown on the return, in which circumstance the omission tends to detract from the quality of the return; and
- **B.** The CPA must sign the preparer's declaration stating that the return is true, correct, and complete.

II. Nonetheless, there may be reasonable grounds for omitting an answer, including:

- **A.** The information not readily available <u>and</u> the answer is not significant in terms of the tax liability;
- **B.** Genuine uncertainty exists as to meaning of the question in relation to the particular return; and
- **C.** The answer is voluminous and the return states that data will be supplied upon examination.

III. It is not appropriate to omit an answer because the answer might prove disadvantageous to the client.

IV. A CPA is not required to provide an explanation of the reason for the omission, although reasonable grounds must exist.

SSTS No. 3 - Procedural Aspects

Certain Procedural Aspects of Preparing Returns

I. A CPA may in good faith rely without verification upon information furnished by client or third parties, but:

   A. should not ignore "red flags,"

Example:
A client provides a list of dividends and interest received during the tax year. From the organization of the list, it clearly appears that it is incomplete and that some dividends and interest have been omitted from the list. The CPA who normally may accept the client's numbers is not allowed to accept without question obviously incomplete data.

   B. should make reasonable inquiries if the information furnished appears to be incorrect, incomplete, or inconsistent either on its face or on the basis of other facts known to the CPA; and

   C. when feasible, should refer to client's past returns.

Example:
A CPA is hired by a new client to prepare the client's income tax returns. One of the CPA's first steps should be to ask the client for copies of the client's past returns.

II. **Where the IRS imposes a condition --** for deductibility or other tax treatment, a CPA should make appropriate inquiries to determine whether the condition is met.

III. **A CPA who signs a tax return --** should consider information known from the tax return of another client when preparing a tax return if that information is relevant to this return.

Example:
A CPA prepares the tax return for both a limited partnership and some of its limited partners. Distributions that the partnership's return indicate were made to limited partners do not appear on the limited partners' individual returns. The CPA cannot ignore this inconsistency.

SSTS No. 4 - Use of Estimates

Use of Estimates

I. A CPA may use the client's estimates to prepare tax returns, if:

A. it is impracticable to obtain exact data,

1. numerous transactions involved very small amounts, or

2. records are missing or precise information is not available

B. the estimated amounts are reasonable given known facts, and

C. the estimates do not imply greater accuracy than truly exists.

II. It is usually not required that the use of estimates be disclosed, but such disclosure is required in certain unusual circumstances to avoid misleading the IRS regarding the reliability of the figures, including where:

A. the taxpayer has died or is ill at the time the return must be filed;

B. the taxpayer has not received a K-1 for a flow-through entity at the time the tax return is to be filed;

C. there is litigation pending (e.g., a bankruptcy proceeding) which bears on the return; or

D. fire or computer failure destroyed the relevant records.

SSTS No. 5 - Departure From a Position

Departure From a Position Previously Concluded in an Administrative Proceeding or Court Decision.

I. Unless the taxpayer is bound to a specified treatment in a later year, such as by a formal closing agreement, the treatment of an item as part of concluding an administrative proceeding or as part of a court decision does not restrict the CPA from recommending a different tax treatment in a later year's return.

II. While a CPA will usually recommend the same position that was previously consented to by the taxpayer, s/he is not required to do so and may decide not to based on the following considerations:

- **A.** The IRS tends to act consistently with the manner in which an item was disposed of in a prior administrative proceeding, but is not bound to do so. Similarly, a taxpayer is not bound to follow a previous position.
- **B.** An unfavorable court decision does not prevent a taxpayer from taking a position contrary to the earlier court decision in a subsequent year.
- **C.** The consent in an earlier administrative proceeding and the existence of an unfavorable court decision are factors that the CPA should consider in evaluating whether the "realistic possibility" and "not frivolous" standards are met.
- **D.** The taxpayer's consent to the treatment in the administrative proceeding or the court's decision may have been caused by a lack of documentation, whereas supporting data for the later year is adequate.
- **E.** The taxpayer may have yielded in the administrative proceeding for settlement purposes or not appealed the court decision even though the position met the "realistic possibility" or "not frivolous" standards.
- **F.** Court decisions, rulings, or other authorities that are more favorable to the taxpayer's current position, may have developed since the prior administrative proceeding was concluded or the prior court decision was rendered.

SSTS No. 6+7 - Knowledge of Error

Knowledge of Error: Return Preparation

I. **Informing Client of Material Error:** -- A CPA should inform the client promptly upon becoming aware of a material error in a previously filed return or upon becoming aware of a client's failure to file a required return (whether or not the CPA prepared or signed the erroneous return).

   A. **Informing the IRS:** The CPA need not inform the IRS, and may not do so without client's permission, except where required by law.

II. **Preparing a Return When Previous Return in Error:** -- If CPA is requested to prepare current year's return, and the client has not taken appropriate action to correct an error in prior year's return, the CPA should consider whether to continue a professional relationship with the client or to withdraw. If the CPA does prepare such current year's return, the CPA should take reasonable steps to ensure that the error is not repeated.

   A. **Signing a return:** When a CPA learns the client is using an erroneous method of accounting and it is past the due date to request IRS permission to change to a proper method, the CPA may sign a return for the current year, providing the return includes appropriate disclosure of the use of the erroneous method.

III. **Representing a Client Before the IRS:** -- When a CPA is representing a client before the IRS in an administrative proceeding with respect to a return containing an error of which the CPA is aware, the CPA should follow the same basic procedures as under Rule 162 -- notify the client of the error and advise that the client disclose the error to the IRS.

SSTS No. 8 - Form and Content of Advice to Client

Form and Content of Advice to Client

I. No standard format is required.

II. Although a CPA may choose to communicate with client about subsequent developments that affect previous advice, such communication is not required unless:

- **A.** the CPA has agreed to do so, or
- **B.** the CPA is assisting in implementing procedures or plans associated with the advice provided.

III. Written communications are preferable for complicated or important matters.

Summary of Tax Accountant Duties

This section contains a chart that summarizes the responsibilities of accountants under the SSTSs.

	YES	NO
Be independent of client		x
Verify all data provided by client or third party		x
Be an advocate for client's realistically sustainable position	x	
Be an advocate for client's frivolous position		x
Be an advocate for client's not frivolous position if it is disclosed	x	
Advise client of potential penalty consequences of any recommended tax position	x	
Explain why answers are omitted where there is legitimate reason for omission		x
Make appropriate inquiries to determine whether IRS conditions for tax treatment are present	x	
Consider information known from one tax return in preparing another	x	
Use reasonable estimates where exact data cannot be practicably obtained	x	
Inform client when material error in previously filed tax return comes to light	x	
Inform IRS when material error in previously filed tax return comes to light		x
Take frivolous position on behalf of client when chances of IRS audit are nil		x
Notify client of legislative changes in the tax law affecting previous advice offered (absent contractual undertaking to so update)		x
Comply with accountant/client privilege in noncriminal cases	x	

Disciplinary Systems

In recent years, the AICPA has made the profession's disciplinary proceedings a subject for the law portion of the exam. At least before the exam was closed, this area had not received significant attention on the exam. Fortunately, the material is fairly straightforward and easily grasped.

I. Professional Ethics Division

- **A.** Investigates violations and sanctions minor cases.

II. Joint Trial Board

- **A.** Hears more serious cases.
- **B.** Has power to
  - **1.** acquit,
  - **2.** admonish,
  - **3.** suspend, or
  - **4.** expel.
- **C.** Initial decisions are by a panel whose actions are reviewable by the full trial board whose decisions are conclusive.

III. Automatic expulsion

- **A.** Automatic expulsion without a hearing results when a member has been convicted or received an adverse judgment for:
  - **1.** Committing a felony.
  - **2.** Willfully failing to file a tax return.
  - **3.** Filing a fraudulent tax return on own or client's behalf.
  - **4.** Aiding in preparing a fraudulent tax return for a client.
    - **a.** If a member has already been convicted or received an adverse judgment, then there has already been an opportunity for the member to have a full-blown criminal or civil trial. Consequently, it would be a waste of resources to have a second hearing and summary punishment is justified.

IV. Revocation of Certificate

- **A.** Automatic expulsion also follows revocation of a CPA certificate by any governmental agency, such as a state board of accountancy.
  - **1.** However, expulsion from AICPA does not bar an individual from the practice of accounting.
  - **2.** Loss of state license does.

V. Joint Ethics Enforcement Program (JEEP)

- **A.** The AICPA and most state societies have agreements to split ethics complaints.
- **B.** Typically, AICPA handles:
  - **1.** matters of national concern,
  - **2.** matters involving more than one state, and

3. matters in litigation.

C. The state societies handle the rest.

VI. **SEC Disciplinary Mechanisms --** SEC Rule of Practice 102(e) authorizes SEC to conduct quasi-judicial proceedings pursuant to which it may suspend or permanently revoke the right to practice before the SEC, including the right to sign any document filed by an SEC registrant on grounds of:

A. lack of qualifications;

B. lack of character or integrity;

C. unethical or professional misconduct; or

D. willful violation of the federal securities laws or rules.

E. Carelessness that consists of:

1. A single instance of highly unreasonable conduct that results in a violation of applicable professional standards in circumstances in which an accountant knows, or should know, that heightened scrutiny is warranted.

2. Repeated instances of unreasonable conduct, each resulting in a violation of applicable professional standards, that indicate a lack of competence to practice before the SEC.

Example:
C was auditing a small company. A million dollars seemed to be missing. The company's officers told C that it was in a safe but that they couldn't open the safe because it had a 3-key lock and the holder of one of the three keys was out of town. C later inquired again about looking at the cash but was told that although the one holder of a key had come back into town, another was unavailable. C certified the financial statements on the assumption that the million dollars was in the safe, which of course it was not. The SEC suspended C from practice before the SEC under Rule 2(e).

VII. **IRS Disciplinary Mechanisms --** The IRS can prohibit an accountant from practicing before the IRS if the person:

A. is incompetent,

B. is unethical, or

C. does not comply with tax rules and regulations.

Example:
A CPA failed to file his own individual tax returns for three consecutive years. The Treasury Department found this to be disreputable conduct and barred the CPA from practicing before the IRS.

VIII. **State Boards & State CPA Societies --** State Boards of Accountancy and State CPA Societies also have codes of ethics and/or rules of conduct.

A. States license CPAs and can prohibit non-CPAs from performing the attest functions.

B. It is only state licensing boards that can "disbar" CPAs.

Common Law Liability to Clients and Third Parties

Breach of Contract

Whereas other theories of liability often involve the courts making public policy in setting up the rules, breach of contract law focuses on the parties' agreement. Remember that punitive damages may not be recovered by a plaintiff in a simple breach of contract suit.

Definition:
Breach of Contract: An accountant breaches the contract when s/he fails to perform substantially as agreed under contract.

I. **Accountants' Duties --** Accountants' duties arise from:

  A. **Express Agreement** of the Parties.

    1. Hopefully, in a written engagement letter.
    2. Oral agreement may also be enforceable.

  B. **Implied agreement** (read in as a matter of law) to perform in a nonnegligent manner consistent with the standards of the profession.

Example:
An accountant carelessly performs a tax (or audit or consulting) engagement. When the client sues for breach of contract, the accountant points out that nowhere in the contract did he promise to perform nonnegligently. The accountant is nonetheless in breach of contract because the law implies such a promise on the accountant's behalf.

II. **An accountant is not a guarantor or insurer.**

  A. "Normal" audit is not intended to uncover fraud, shortages, defalcations, or irregularities in general (although it may do so), but is meant to provide auditor evidence needed to express opinion on fairness of financial statements. (Note: Juries often have difficulty grasping this concept.)

  B. An accountant is generally not liable for failure to detect fraud or irregularities, unless:

    1. a normal audit by a careful accountant would have detected them, or
    2. in the engagement letter, accountant undertakes greater responsibility to detect fraud, etc., or
    3. the wording of the audit report indicates that the auditor does have such a duty.

  C. An accountant should follow up on "red flags" and that investigation should not accept explanations at face value.

III. **Client Breaches the Contract --** The client breaches the contract when it interferes with or prevents the accountant from performing.

IV. Consequences of Breach by Accountant

	Yes	No
Accountant entitled to fee		
-- if breach is major		x
-- if breach is minor	x	
Client entitled to:		
-- compensatory damages	x	
-- punitive damages		x

V. Disclaimers -- Attempts by accountants to avoid liability by disclaimers in the contract are generally ineffective.

Note:
Misconception: Two forms of disclaimers are often confused. If an accountant clearly provides in an engagement letter that s/he is not performing an audit, but merely an unaudited compilation, that provision will generally be honored. The accountant cannot be liable for not having performed a full-fledged audit. However, if the accountant in either an audit engagement or a compilation engagement (or any other) provides in an engagement letter that s/he will not be liable for any negligence s/he may commit, that attempted disclaimer will typically not be honored.

Negligence: Liability to Clients

When one hears of an accountant "malpractice" action, that suit is usually brought by a client against its accountant on a negligence theory. This section spells out the basic things that a client must prove to recover from an accountant in such a case.

The basic elements apply whether the auditor has erred in audit, tax, or consulting work. The more complex issue of when accountants should be liable to third parties (nonclients) is addressed later.

I. **Negligence vs. Breach --** In many jurisdictions, the proper cause of action is breach of contract if an accountant simply failed to perform a contract, but negligence if the accountant performed the contract but did so carelessly.

  A. On the other hand, in some jurisdictions a negligence claim cannot be brought for mere economic injuries; such a theory is reserved for personal injury claims and all claims of economic loss must be brought as breach of contract or warranty.

II. **Elements of recovery to be proved by plaintiff in a negligence case**

  A. Duty,

  B. Breach,

  C. Damages, and

  D. Proximate Cause.

III. **Duty**

  A. **Standard:** That degree of judgment and skill possessed by a reasonable accountant under all the circumstances.

  B. **Sources of standard:**

    1. State and federal statutes.

    2. Court decisions.

    3. Contract with client.

    4. GAAP and GAAS (persuasive, not conclusive)

      a. Evidence of violation of GAAP or GAAS almost automatically establishes negligence.

      b. Evidence of compliance with GAAP and GAAS does not necessarily establish reasonable care.

Example:
In one famous case, an accountant had six experts testify that GAAP and GAAS had been followed in his audit. Yet, a jury found him criminally guilty because there was evidence that the accountant knew that the particular financial statements were misleading, notwithstanding the compliance with GAAP and GAAS.

5. Customs of the profession (persuasive, not conclusive).

C. The standard can be raised above that of the reasonable accountant by:

1. An accountant being a specialist;
2. An accountant holds self out as having special expertise; or
3. A contractual provision in which the accountant undertakes higher duty.

IV. **Breach of Duty by Accountant --** An error of judgment or other mistake is not actionable unless it is negligent. (Accountants, like others in our society, are not expected to be perfect.)

V. **Damages**

A. Of course, a plaintiff cannot recover from a careless accountant unless the plaintiff has suffered some injury.

B. **Key Point:** Punitive damages are not allowed in a mere negligence action.

Damages Recoverable by Client in a Negligence Action	Yes	No
Compensatory damages for reasonably foreseeable injuries	x	
Compensatory damages for unforeseeable injuries		x
Compensatory damages for injuries caused by client's contributory negligence		x
Punitive damages		x

VI. **Proximate Cause --** A plaintiff must prove that the accountant's negligence directly (proximately) caused his injuries.

A. **Elements:**

1. "But for" Causation (that is, a court can say that "but for" the accountant's negligence, the loss would not have occurred), and
2. Reasonable Foreseeability - i.e., no "independent intervening causes" unforeseeable to, and beyond the control of, the accountant broke up the chain of causation between the accountant's careless act and the plaintiff's loss.

Example:
A CPA negligently fails to discover during an audit that diamond rings are missing from the client's inventory. In fact, an employee stole rings both before and after the audit. The CPA would not be liable for the rings stolen before the audit because it cannot be said that "but for" the accountant's carelessness the rings would not have been stolen. The CPA would likely be liable for the rings stolen after the audit, however, because successful defalcations by employees are one of the reasonably foreseeable consequences of a defective audit.

VII. **Loss with Multiple Causes --** If loss had multiple causes, accountant is liable if his negligence was a "substantial factor" (but perhaps not the sole proximate cause) in bringing about the loss.

VIII. Defenses to a Negligence Claim - Contributory Negligence of Client -- There are **two types** of client carelessness.

A. All jurisdictions recognize that accountants can raise as a defense the client's carelessness when that carelessness interferes with the accountant's performance of his task.

Example:
An auditor's request for all of the client's records of a certain type is frustrated when the client carelessly overlooks several of the records. The auditor performs the audit not knowing of the existence of these records and not taking into account the extra expenses reflected therein. Perhaps the auditor was careless in not realizing that the records were missing, but it seems clear that the client's carelessness impeded the auditor's attempt to do the audit. The auditor could raise this carelessness as a defense to defeat, or at least minimize, the client's recovery in a malpractice suit.

B. Most jurisdictions, but not all, recognize that accountants can raise as a defense the client's carelessness that contributes to a loss even when that carelessness does not interfere with the accountant's performance of his task.

Example:
An auditor carelessly audits a company and does not discover that one of its employees is embezzling large sums from the company. On the other hand, the company did not investigate the employee's background before it hired him (it would have discovered an extensive criminal record), does not monitor the employee after giving him access to large amounts of cash, and asks no questions when the employee (who makes $20,000 a year) buys an expensive new home and sports car. Most jurisdictions would allow the auditor to raise the company's own careless monitoring of the employee as a defense. However, a few jurisdictions would place the entire loss upon the auditor on the theory that the company discharged its obligation of due care when it hired the auditor.

IX. Chart

Status of Contributory Negligence Defense	All Jurisdictions	Most Jurisdictions
Client's carelessness interferes with accountant's performance of audit	x	
Client's carelessness helps create the situation which the audit fails to detect		x

Fraud Liability

No accountant wants to be accused of fraud, but each year many are. The most important things to derive from this section are these: (a) an ability to compare and contrast the elements of fraud and simple negligence, (b) an appreciation of the difference between actual fraud and constructive fraud, and (c) the knowledge that a fraud claim can lead to imposition of punitive damages, whereas punitive damages are not available in cases involving breach of contract, simple negligence, or federal securities law claims.

I. Elements

A. Accountant made a false representation of fact (or omitted to state a fact in the face of a duty to do so).

1. A false statement of expert opinion is deemed tantamount to a representation of fact.

Example: If A sells B his car, telling B that the car gets 50 miles per gallon when, in fact, it gets only 25, this is a false statement of fact and B can sue A for fraud. If A sells B his car, telling B -- "I really love this car" when, in fact, A hates the car, B cannot sue for fraud because A merely stated an opinion (even though it was a false one). However, when an accountant issues a professional opinion, for example, by certifying financial statements as accurate, the statement carries more weight by virtue of the accountant's expertise. It is treated as tantamount to a statement of fact and actionable if fraudulent.

B. The misrepresented (or omitted) fact was material.

Example: An auditor determines that a client company made a profit of $999,950 but certifies as accurate the client's financial statements, which show a profit of $1,000,000, because that is a nice, round number. This is a false statement of fact but the inaccuracy is so small that it is probably not material.

C. The accountant knew or recklessly disregarded the falsity.

1. Knowledge (scienter) = **actual fraud.**

Example: A famous rock singer gave his money to D, accountant, to invest. The accountant issued to the singer monthly reports indicating that the money was being wisely invested and that the rock singer's fortune was growing. In fact, D had invested the money in several ventures that he operated and most of it had been lost. The monthly reports were mere fictions. This is a clear case of actual fraud on the part of the accountant.

2. Reckless disregard or gross negligence = **constructive fraud**.

Example:
D, accountant, is hired to issue an audit report on a client company. When D shows up for the job, the client's own accountant hands him a finished audit report to sign. D signs the audit report, hoping that it is accurate. It turns out that it is not accurate and lenders who lent money to the client company based on the inaccurate financial statements sue D in fraud. The accountant is liable for fraud of the constructive type. He had no reasonable grounds to believe that the report he signed was accurate. He is guilty of reckless disregard of the truth.

D. The accountant intended to and did induce plaintiff's reasonable reliance on the misstatement or omission.

Example:
D, accountant, certified a client company's financial statements as accurate knowing that they were not and knowing that lenders and investors would rely upon those financial statements in making lending and investment decisions. In such a case, the accountant's intent to induce reliance by the lenders and investors would be clear. The auditor's best defense would be if he could show that some of the lenders and investors knew facts about the client that should have put them on alert that the client was in financial trouble and, thus, that their reliance on the accountant's report was not "reasonable." Unfortunately for accountants, this defense seldom works.

E. The client suffered damages.

Example:
Client calls D, accountant, and asks D to audit and certify 80 copies of financial statements. Client tells D that it intends to seek lenders and/or investors. D certifies the financial statements, which vastly overstate client's worth. ABC Bank makes a loan to the client based on the financial statement and later loses lots of money when the client files bankruptcy. ABC sues D for fraud, showing that D knew or was reckless in not knowing that the financial statements were inaccurate. ABC can recover from D even though D did not know before the audit that ABC specifically would be a recipient of one of the 80 copies of the false financial statements. D did know that its report would be widely circulated and relied upon by lenders or investors.

1. Fraud is an intentional tort, whereas the essence of negligence is mere carelessness.
2. A defrauder's liability runs to all foreseeable victims of the fraud, whereas a negligent accountant's liability is much more limited in scope.
3. A defrauder may be liable for punitive damages as well as compensatory damages; a defendant who was merely negligent is not liable for punitive damages.

II. Summary Chart

Differences Between Fraud and Negligence Causes of Action	Fraud	Negligence
Plaintiff must prove bad intent or recklessness	Yes	No
Plaintiff must prove carelessness	No	Yes
Plaintiff must prove proximate cause	Yes	Yes
Plaintiff must prove compensatory damages	Yes	Yes
Plaintiff can recover punitive damages	Yes	No
Contributory negligence is a defense	No	Yes
All reasonably foreseeable persons may recover	Yes	No

Negligence Liability: Third Parties

The most important and controversial issue in the area of accountants' liability under the common law relates to auditors' exposure to liability in negligence suits brought by third parties (usually investors and/or creditors). The area is controversial and has spawned at least three points of view.

If you can understand the table presented in this section, you should be able to answer any question that can be thrown at you on the exam. Remember that the Restatement view is the majority view around the country, but that several states have adopted the privity point of view either judicially or via statute. If a question is silent as to which approach is to be used, assume that the Restatement view applies. It is the majority rule.

I. Three Primary Approaches

A. The Privity Approach of Ultramares v. Touche -- Accountant is liable only to those with whom s/he is in privity of contract, i.e., the client, or third-party beneficiaries of the contract.

1. **Rationale --** Whereas plaintiffs suing for fraud, recklessness, or gross negligence may recover simply by being reasonably foreseeable victims of the fraud, courts adopting the privity approach are worried about accountant liability for simple carelessness extending to an indeterminate class for an indeterminate time and for an indeterminate amount. Therefore, they limit liability to the client and third parties expressly mentioned in the engagement letter.
2. **Fact --** A substantial number of jurisdictions have adopted the privity approach either through judicial decision or by legislation.

Note:
The Restatement Approach is the majority approach; more states follow it than any other view.

B. The Restatement "Limited Class" Approach -- An accountant is liable to a limited class of nonclients where the accountant knows:

1. the information being supplied to the client will be given to, or is for the benefit and guidance of, a limited group of third persons.
2. the information will influence those third persons in a specific transaction or type of transaction.

II. The Reasonable Foreseeability Approach -- An accountant is liable to whomever s/he can reasonably foresee may use the financial statements s/he certifies or prepares.

A. This view imposes the same scope of liability for negligent accountants as applies in any other type of negligence suit. It also applies the same basic scope of liability as exists in fraud cases against accountants.

B. Very few jurisdictions still use the reasonable foreseeability approach.

Examples:

	Will Plaintiffs Recover Under:		
Scenarios:	**Ultramares**	**Restatement**	**Foreseeability**
1) D, accountant, contracts to do audit for client. D botches the job and employees steal large sums. Client sues D in negligence.	Yes	Yes	Yes

2) D contracts to do audit for client. Letter of engagement specifies that the audit is for the benefit of ABC bank, which will use the certified financial statements to determine whether to double client's current line of credit at the bank. D botches the job certifying financial statements that vastly overstate client's worth. ABC doubles the line of credit but loses tons of money when client goes under. ABC sues D in negligence.	Yes	Yes	Yes
3) Client calls D and asks D to audit and certify a copy of its financial statements so that it may borrow money. During audit, D learns that client will probably borrow from ABC Bank and calls ABC Bank to ask if it has any particular concerns about client's status that D should pay special attention to during the audit. D certifies the financial statements, which vastly overstate client's worth. Client sends financial statements to ABC, which makes loan based thereon. ABC sues D in negligence.	No	Yes	Yes
4) Client calls D and asks D to audit and certify 5 copies of financial statements which, it tells D, it intends to provide to five unidentified banks in the area in hopes of receiving a loan. D certifies the financial statements, which vastly overstate client's worth. Longhorn National Bank, which loans money to client based on the financial statements, later sues D in negligence.	No	Yes	Yes
5) Client calls D and asks D to audit and certify 80 copies of financial statements. Client tells D that it intends to seek lenders and/or investors. D certifies the financial statements, which vastly overstate client's worth. ABC Bank makes loan based on the financial statement and later sues D in negligence.	No	No	Yes
6) Client calls D and asks D to audit and certify one copy of financial statements. Client tells D that it intends to show the statements to its long-time banker in hopes of receiving an extension of current line of credit. Instead, client shows copies of the financial statements to several out-of-state banks that loan money to client and later sue D when they discover the financial statements were error-filled.	No	No	No

Federal Statutory Liability

Foreign Corrupt Practices Act (FCPA)

Scandals involving U.S. companies paying bribes to the officials of foreign governments to obtain and retain business led to passage of the FCPA. These scandals led to the overthrow of some foreign governments. The SEC was scandalized that these companies could pay millions of dollars in bribes, sometimes tens of millions, without ever having an entry on their financial statements reading: "Bribes paid to foreign officials: $4.2 million." The SEC was also upset that the upper level officials in these companies could get away with saying: "Golly, we didn't know this was happening." Therefore, the FCPA contains not only antibribery provisions, but also accounting provisions to ensure that such bribes do not go unnoticed.

I. Introduction -- The FCPA was a post-Watergate response to illegal foreign bribes paid by U.S. companies. It contains two major provisions.

- **A.** It contains anti-bribery provisions aimed at preventing U.S. companies from gaining or retaining foreign business by bribing foreign government officials. A 1998 amendment banned foreign bribery as a means of obtaining a competitive advantage.
- **B.** More relevant to accountants, it contains accounting provisions aimed specifically at preventing companies from hiding huge bribes on their financial statements.

II. Accounting Provisions

- **A.** All companies registered with the SEC must keep "reasonably detailed" records which "accurately and fairly" reflect the company's financial activities. The accounting portion of the FCPA does not require that the company do any business abroad.
- **B.** These companies must devise internal accounting controls (IACs) sufficient to provide "reasonable assurance" that:
  - **1.** transactions are executed in accordance with management's general or specific authorization;
  - **2.** transactions are recorded as necessary to:
    - **a.** permit preparation of proper financial statements, and
    - **b.** maintain accountability for assets
  - **3.** access to assets is authorized; and
  - **4.** recorded assets are compared with existing assets at reasonable intervals.

III. Penalties:

- **A.** Criminal:
  - **1.** Individual: maximum of $100,000 fine and/or 5 years in jail.
  - **2.** Corporation: maximum of $1,000,000 fine.
  - **3.** There will be no criminal prosecutions for inadvertent or insignificant errors.
- **B.** Civil: maximum civil fine of $10,000.

IV. Examples

Example:
D bought 51% of an NYSE-listed company engaged in the wholesale and retail trade in rare coins, precious metals, and the like. D was warned about the company's internal accounting controls but did nothing to remedy the problem. Inventory controls were lax. Rare coins were left unguarded, employees were allowed to take large quantities of assets off the premises, appraisals were inadequate, and the company could not even determine how much had been paid for coins in the inventory. There was no separation of duties. One employee could, without supervision, appraise a particular coin, buy it from a customer, draw a check for the coin, count the coin into inventory, value the coin for inventory purposes, and sell the coin to another. No employees were bonded. Poor control of checks caused the company to bounce over 100 checks. $1.7 million in checks were written to D without supporting documents. Ultimately, the company went from 40 employees to just three and from $2 million in assets to less than $500,000 in just a couple of years. The SEC successfully brought FCPA charges proving violations of the accounting rules.

Example:
A company paid a large sum in a bribe to an infamous African dictator. The bribe payment showed up nowhere on the company's books. The company was held to have violated the FCPA's accounting provisions.

Example:
M, a company's CEO and 47% owner, received $100,000 for non-business related expenses in a period of a few years. The company had no procedure for independent review of M's expenses. Occasionally, M would sit down with the company's accountants and mark vouchers with a "C" (company) or a "P" (personal). This was held to be a violation of the FCPA accounting provisions.

Internal Revenue Code

The Internal Revenue Code carries provisions for both civil and criminal penalties for accountants who violate the Code. There is substantial overlap between civil and criminal punishment.

I. The Code contains several civil liability provisions

A. Understatement of Tax Liability (Sec. 6694(a)).

Example:
Interest expense deductions were being taken by a professional corporation. However, the corporation's sole shareholder was not reporting those payments on his/her individual tax return. The court held that the CPA preparing the corporation's tax returns should have inquired further as to who was receiving those payments.

B. Willful Understatement of Tax Liability (Sec. 6694(b)).

Example:
A CPA preparing a company's taxes was given a tip that company employees and officers charged personal expenses to the company. S/He ignored the tip. The court held that s/he had willfully refused to investigate.

C. Failure to Comply With Disclosure Provisions (Sec. 6695).

1. A tax preparer may be punished for:
    - **a.** failure to furnish a copy of the return to the taxpayer;
    - **b.** failure to sign the return and show own identity;
    - **c.** failure to furnish the preparer's identifying number; or
    - **d.** failure to keep a copy of the return.

D. Aiding and Abetting the Understatement of Tax Liability (Sec. 6701).

1. Even if accountants are not the preparers of a tax return, they may be liable for aiding and abetting an understatement of liability if they:
    - **a.** aid, assist, procure, or advise in preparation or presentation of any portion of any return or other document;
    - **b.** know, or have reason to know, that it will be used in matters arising under tax law; and
    - **c.** know that if the return or document is so used, an understatement of the tax liability of another person will result.

Example:
An accountant provided tax and financial advice to investors in a bogus tax shelter scheme. S/He prepared tax returns only for the enterprise, but sent transmittal letters to the investors with a schedule of the tax shelter attached. This was held sufficient to constitute aiding and abetting understatement of tax liability by the investors.

E. **Disclosure or Use of Information by Preparers of Returns** (Sec. 6713).

1. This provision penalizes:

    a. disclosure or any information furnished to the preparer in connection with preparation of a return, or

    b. use of any such information for any purpose other than to prepare the return.

II. **The Code contains several criminal provisions**

A. **Fraud and false statements** (Sec. 7206).

1. Criminalizes:

    a. willfully making and subscribing to any document made under penalty of perjury, which the accountant does not believe to be true as to every material matter;

    b. willfully aiding the preparation of any tax related matter, which is fraudulent as to any material matter; or

    c. concealing client's property with intent to defeat taxes.

Example: A CPA advised a client to backdate a document to obtain a deduction to which the client was not otherwise entitled. This was held to violate Sec. 7206.

B. **Attempts to evade or defeat tax** (Sec. 7201).

1. Criminalizes evasion of taxes where there exists:

    a. an affirmative act;

    b. willfulness; and

    c. existence of a tax deficiency.

Example:
A client won $2.7 million in a state lottery and began receiving $135,000 in annual payouts. S/He offset much of that income by claiming gambling losses of $65,000 and filed for a $26,000 refund. The IRS audited the client whose accountant arrived at the audit with 200,000 losing lottery tickets as proof of the losses. The accountant had obtained the lottery tickets from a man who collected them, promising to return them to the man after the audit. This looks like a violation of Attempts to Evade or Defeat Tax (Sec. 7201).

C. **Willful failure to file return, supply information, or pay tax** (Sec. 7203);

D. **Willful failure to collect or pay over a tax** (Sec. 7202);

E. **Fraudulent returns, statements, or other documents** (Sec. 7202);

F. **Attempts to interfere with administration of the Internal Revenue laws** (Sec. 7212); and

G. **Unauthorized disclosure of information** (Sec. 7312).

Racketeer Influenced Corrupt Organizations Act (RICO)

Although RICO is still fair game for the CPA exam, its importance for accountants has been dramatically reduced by a recent Supreme Court decision and a recent statute enacted by Congress. If you're going to skip a section, this one is a good choice. The bottom line is that RICO, once fearsome, can no longer be the basis for a civil damage action against accountants in a situation where the essence of the claim is securities fraud, unless the accountant has already been criminally convicted of the offense. This will almost never have happened.

Purpose: prevent organized crime's infiltration into legitimate business.

I. **RICO has two sides**

   A. Criminal: charges can be brought by Department of Justice (DOJ).

   B. Civil: injured individuals can sue for treble damages and attorneys' fees.

II. **RICO prohibits**

   A. receiving money or property through a pattern of racketeering activity and subsequently investing that money into an enterprise (Sec. 1962(a));

   B. acquiring and controlling an enterprise through a pattern of racketeering activity (Sec. 1962(b));

   C. conducting or participating, directly or indirectly, in the conduct of an enterprise's affairs (Sec. 1962(c)); and

   D. conspiring to violate #1, #2, or #3 (Sec. 1962(d)).

III. **Sec. 1962(c)** -- Most RICO cases are brought under Sec. 1962(c), which has four elements. (1) Defendant conducted or participated in the conduct (2) of an enterprise (3) through a pattern of (4) racketeering activity.

   A. **Conduct or Participation - Defendant conducted or participated in the conduct**

      1. The Supreme Court has held that the "conduct or participation" test is met only by those who actually manage a business. If an accountant sticks to accounting and does not become involved in "calling the shots," the accountant will not meet this test. Since this case was decided, RICO has become much less fearsome to accountants.

Example:
An accounting firm provided audit, accounting, and consulting services for an insurance company that became insolvent. Investors sued the firm under RICO proving that it had issued inaccurate audit reports, provided other accounting services, and attended board meetings of the insurer. Despite this activity, the court held that there was no evidence that the accounting firm had made managerial decisions for the insurance company. Therefore, the "conduct or participation" element was not met and the firm could not be liable under RICO.

B. Of an enterprise

1. The enterprise requirement means that the "person" being charged under RICO must be separate and distinct from the "enterprise."
   a. **Example:** the auditor could be the "person," the client could be the "enterprise."

C. Through a pattern

1. A "pattern" is defined in the statute as two acts of racketeering occurring within a 10-year period, but the Supreme Court has held that the pattern requirement is not met unless the acts:
   a. are related, and
   b. threaten a continuity of racketeering activity.

D. Of racketeering activity

1. Racketeering activity is defined in the statute by example and includes:
   a. Mail fraud: any lie told through the mail.
   b. Wire fraud: any lie told over the phone. ("The check is in the mail.")
   c. And about 30 other listed acts.
   d. Plaintiff usually must prove that these racketeering acts occurred but not that Defendant has been convicted of them already.
      i. **Exception --** Any civil plaintiff bringing a RICO claim for damages in a case involving acts that could constitute securities fraud (any lie told involving the sale or purchase of securities) must prove that D had already been criminally convicted of securities fraud.
      ii. **Fact --** This greatly reduces accountants' exposure to liability under RICO because most RICO claims brought against accountants have involved securities fraud and accountants are seldom criminally convicted of securities fraud.

Mail and Wire Fraud

Any time someone tells a lie over the phone ("The check is in the mail.") he has likely committed the criminal offense of wire fraud. Any time someone tells a lie in a letter, he has likely committed mail fraud. These are broad criminal provisions and it pays to know their basics.

Note:
Misconception: It seems logical to assume that if the defendant communicates a fraudulent statement through the mail or over the phone he or she could be liable for mail or wire fraud. However, the rule is that the use of mail or wires must be an essential part of the fraudulent scheme for liability to attach.

I. Any fraud committed with use of the mail or telephones (telegraphs, internet, etc.) is a federal crime.

Example:
An accountant mails fraudulent financial statements to a potential investor in the audited company. This would be mail fraud.

II. Mail and wire fraud are two of the most important federal provisions under which accountants can be held criminally liable. However, one cannot overlook the securities law, tax law, FCPA, and RICO criminal provisions.

Sarbanes-Oxley Act of 2002

In response to the Enron/Arthur Andersen scandal, Congress passed Sarbanes-Oxley, which not only impacted regulation of the accounting profession, but also amended and supplemented the federal securities laws and added new provisions to prevent destruction of evidence.

When Congress passed Sarbanes-Oxley (SOX) in 2002 in response to the Enron/Arthur Andersen scandal, it enacted a wide-ranging law.

I. **Regulation of Accounting Profession --** We have already discussed its impact directly on regulation of the accounting profession -- creation of the Public Company Accounting Oversight Board (PCAOB), restrictions on provision of nonaudit services to audit clients, requirements for rotation of senior audit partners and review partners, etc.

II. **Federal Securities Laws --** We have also noted certain changes it made in the federal securities laws, including stronger criminal penalties for 1934 Act violations, a longer statute of limitations (was within one year of discovery and within 3 years of the wrong; now within two years of discovery of the wrong and within 5 years of its occurrence).

   A. Additionally, Sarbanes-Oxley contained a new federal securities crime provision:

      1. "Whoever knowingly executes, or attempts to execute, a scheme or artifice--(1) to defraud any person in connection with any security [of a public company]; or (2) to obtain, by means of false or fraudulent pretenses, representations, or promises, any money or property in connection with the purchase or sale of any security of an issuer [of a public company]...shall be fined under this title, or imprisoned not more than 25 years, or both."

III. **Destruction of Evidence --** It also added new provisions to prevent destruction of evidence:

   A. **Destruction of Records --** SOX creates a new federal crime relating to destruction of records involved in *any* federal governmental matter or bankruptcy, making it a crime punishable by fine, imprisonment up to 20 years, or both to "knowingly alter, destroy, mutilate, conceal, cover up, falsify, or make a false entry in any record, document, or tangible object with intent to impede, obstruct, or influence the investigation or proper administration of any matter within the jurisdiction of any department or agency of the United States or any case filed under [the Bankruptcy Code]."

      1. This statute is meant to eliminate the technical requirement that a subpoena already be issued or a preceding be imminent.

   B. **Willful Failure to Retain Audit and Review Workpapers --** SOX also creates a new federal crime relating to the willful failure to retain audit and review workpapers. It provides that any accountant who audits an issuer of securities must maintain all audit or review workpapers for a period of five years from the end of the fiscal period in which the audit or review was conducted.

      1. The SEC is to issue rules relating to retention of relevant workpapers, memoranda, correspondence, and other records created in connection with an audit or review.

      2. A "knowing and willful" violation subjects one to fine and imprisonment up to 10 years, or both.

      3. **Note**, that yet another SOX provision mandates that the PCAOB establish rules requiring auditors to prepare and maintain audit work papers for not less than 7 years.

C. **Corrupt Tampering with Documents to Be Used in an Official Proceeding --** SOX also creates a new federal crime for tampering with documents to be used in an official proceeding, providing that any person who "corruptly" (1) alters, destroys, mutilates, or conceals a record, document, or other object, or attempts to do so, with the intent to impair the object's integrity or availability for use in an official proceeding, or (2) otherwise obstructs, influences, or impedes any official proceeding, or attempts to do so, shall be fined, or imprisoned up to 20 years, or both.

Business Law

Agency

Introduction and Definitions

As with many areas of the law, grasping the essential terminology pays dividends in terms of mastering the substantive material. This section defines agency and describes key aspects of it.

Definition:
An agency relationship: is a fiduciary relationship in which one person undertakes to consummate transactions or undertake business through the actions of another.

I. There are two parties to an agency relationship: Principal and Agent

Definitions:
Principal: one who wishes to accomplish something by acting through another.

Agent: one who acts on a principal's behalf to achieve the principal's purposes.

II. Examples of agents

A. Employees.

B. Partners.

C. Spouses.

1. Spouses are automatically agents only if they are buying necessities for the family.

III. Typical form of agency relationship -- Customer (third party -- T) buys from a salesperson (agent -- A) goods owned by store owner (principal -- P).

IV. Types of agents

A. Special Agent: one authorized to conduct a single transaction or series of transactions on the principal's behalf.

Example:
A real estate agent authorized only to sell principal's house.

B. General Agent: one authorized to conduct all necessary transactions in connection with a business.

Example:
A manager is hired to run a restaurant owned by the principal who lives in another city.

C. Universal Agent: one authorized to do all acts that can be legally delegated to an agent.

Example:
A soldier who is to be stationed abroad for three years appoints his sister to handle all his business affairs during his absence.

D. Power of Attorney

Definition:
Power of Attorney: a formal written authorization of agency.

1. A power of attorney is not generally required for a valid agency relationship, except when:
   a. the contract the agent is to enter into must be in writing under the statute of frauds, such as a real estate contract, or
   b. the agency relationship cannot reasonably be completed within one year.
2. A power of attorney must be signed by the principal (but not by the agent).
3. A power of attorney is generally construed narrowly.

Formation and Termination

The key to formation of an agency relationship is usually not formalities; it is the consent of the principal and the agent.

I. Formation of the Agency Relationship

A. The basis for an agency relationship is the consent of the parties -- the consent of the principal (P) to have the agent act on his/her behalf and the consent of the agent (A) to act on behalf of the principal.

B. The following elements are <u>not</u> necessary to the formation of an agency relationship:

1. Capacity.

Example:
A minor agent can bind an adult principal, and vice versa (although, of course, the minor agent can quit at any time and the minor principal can disaffirm any contract negotiated by the adult agent).

2. Consideration.

Example:
If A agrees to be P's agent as a favor to P, contracts A negotiates on behalf of P are binding on P (of course, A can quit at any time).

II. Termination of the Agency Relationship

A. The way in which an agency relationship is terminated has important ramifications for post-termination liabilities. The two most important things in this section are (a) the two ways agency relationships are terminated (by act of the parties and by operation of law) and (b) the concept of an agency coupled with an interest.

B. Agency relationships are terminated in two major ways:

1. Termination by Act of the Parties.

a. Fulfillment:

Example:
A was hired to sell P's house and has done so.

b. **Lapse of Time:**

Example:
A was hired for a two-year period and that period has expired.

c. **Specified Event:**

Example:
A is hired to manage P's properties until P returns from Europe and P has returned.

d. **Mutual Agreement:**

Example:
A has been managing P's restaurant and A and P mutually agree to terminate their relationship.

e. **Act of One Party:**

Example:
A has promised to work for P for two years. P has promised to pay A $500/month for that period. Either party has the power (though not the right) to terminate the relationship at any time but may have to pay damages for breach of contract to the other party.

i. **Exception:** A principal cannot (that is, has neither the right nor the power to) terminate an *agency coupled with an interest.*

ii. An **agency coupled with an interest** is a power conferred by a writing, which vests in the agent an interest in the property that is the subject of the agency.

Example:
P borrows $5,000 from A. To secure the loan, P grants A a security interest (a property interest for the sole purpose of securing a debt) in P's antique store inventory. To protect his status as a lender, A inserts in the agreement a provision whereby P makes A his agent for the sale of the inventory in the event that P defaults on the loan. Because A has an interest in the subject matter of the agency (the inventory), the arrangement is an agency coupled with an interest and P cannot terminate A's authority to sell without A's consent. Of course, if P repays the loan then A no longer has an interest in the subject matter and the agency terminates.

2. **Termination by Operation of Law**

   a. **Death of Insanity:**

Example:
P hires A to sell P's house. P dies. The agency terminates.

   b. **Bankruptcy:**

      i. **Limitation:** Bankruptcy terminates an agency relationship only if the agent's bankruptcy would impair A's ability to act as an agent or if the principal's bankruptcy would cause the agent to realize that P would no longer wish A to enter into transactions on P's behalf.

   c. **Change of Law:**

Example:
A is hired to buy a race track for P and racing is declared to be illegal.

   d. **Loss or Destruction:**

Example:
A is hired to sell P's warehouse, which is destroyed by a tornado.

Duties of Agent and Principal

This section describes both the duties of a principal to an agent and the duties of an agent to a principal.

The duties that a principal owes to an agent are few and fairly straightforward.

I. To comply with agency agreement

Example:
The principal should provide all compensation and benefits promised in the parties' agreement.

II. To reimburse reasonable expenses

A. Absent contrary agreement, the principal is responsible for expenses the agent incurs in reasonably performing his or her activities on the principal's behalf.

Example:
A, a truck driver delivering furniture for P Furniture Store, fills the truck up with gasoline so he can complete the delivery. Absent agreement to the contrary, P should reimburse A for the expense.

III. Fiduciary Relationship -- The agency relationship is a fiduciary relationship. Most important in this section is the notion that an agent owes a supreme duty of loyalty to his or her principal.

A. Obedience: The agent should follow the principal's instructions unless those instructions call for illegal or immoral acts.

B. Reasonable Care: The agent should discharge all responsibilities carefully and is theoretically liable in negligence to the principal for damage caused by carelessness.

C. Accounting: The agent should always keep any funds of the principal in agent's custody separate from agent's own funds and should always be able to tell the principal exactly where the funds are located.

D. Notification: The agent should immediately inform the principal of any important information that the principal would want to know.

E. Loyalty:

Example:
Agent, a sales representative, learns that a long-established credit customer is on the brink of bankruptcy. Agent should inform principal so that principal can evaluate whether to continue selling to the customer on credit.

1. No competition.

Example:
Agent, an accountant, siphons tax business away from his/her accounting firm, the principal, by telling small clients to come to his/her house on weekends where s/he will do their taxes for much less than the firm charges.

2. No conflict of interest.

Example:
Agent is a buyer for a major retailer and begins buying goods from a company that agent establishes in a friend's name.

3. No appropriation of business opportunities.

Example:
Two partners are in the oil and gas business and one learns of a fabulous oil and gas opportunity in Mexico. S/He invests in that opportunity for himself/herself only.

4. No disclosure of confidential information.

Example:
Agent learns trade secrets while working for principal. Agent should not sell or give those trade secrets to anyone.

Note:
Misconception: Many believe that trade secrets can be disclosed and used for the agent's benefit unless the agent has signed a covenant-not-to-compete. This is erroneous. The common law of agency imposes a duty of nondisclosure of confidential information that extends beyond the existence of the agency relationship regardless of whether the agent has signed a restrictive covenant.

Liabilities and Authority of Agents and Principals

Contract Liabilities

In general, an agent acts on behalf of a principal when contracting. When everything is said and done, the two parties to the contract are the principal and the third party. The agent is not liable on the contract. This can be altered when the agent acts on behalf of a partially disclosed or undisclosed principal. In terms of past exam questions, the most important rules to understand in the entire agency section are those relating to undisclosed principals.

I. Conditions

A. Contract Liability: Principal will be held liable on a contract to third-party if agent acted within the scope of authority.

B. Express Authority

Example:
Principal hires agent to sell P's house for at least $90,000. Agent finds a ready, willing, and able buyer for $100,000. Principal is bound.

C. Implied Authority

1. Customary

Example:
Principal hires Agent to manage Principal's restaurant. Principal does not spell out Agent's authority. The law implies that Agent has the authority customarily exercised by managers of comparable businesses in the area, which likely includes the authority to hire and fire employees, to open bank accounts, to purchase supplies, to sell to customers, etc.

2. Incidental

Example:
Principal instructs Agent to deliver a truckload of furniture to a customer. The truck has a flat tire as the delivery is being made. Although Principal did not instruct Agent to do so, Agent has the authority to replace the tire if it is incidental (necessary) to completion of the assigned task.

3. **Emergency**

Example:
When Principal is out of town, a flash flood threatens his retail store. Agent, manager of the store, without ever having been expressly authorized to do so by Principal, incurs substantial bills in a good faith effort to protect the store from the flooding. Principal would be liable for payment of these funds because Agent's exercise of emergency authority.

D. **Apparent Authority:** Even if the agent lacks express or implied authority (both being types of "actual authority"), the principal may still be liable upon contracts negotiated by the agent if:

   1. Principal held Agent out as Principal's agent;
   2. Agent acted within scope of apparent authority; and
   3. Third party reasonably relied on the appearance in entering into a contract.

Example:
Principal hires Agent to manage Principal's motel but instructs Agent not to hire or fire employees. Agent takes out an ad in the paper for custodial help and hires X for the job. It is customary in the area for motel managers to hire and fire and X does not know of the limitation on Agent's authority. Because Principal held Agent out as his manager, Agent acted as motel managers generally do and X reasonably believed that Agent had the authority to hire X, the contract is binding on Principal.

Example:
Agent is a traveling sales representative for Principal for ten years. Principal then fires Agent for dishonesty. Agent goes to long-time customer X who has not heard of the firing and negotiates a contract to sell Principal's goods to X and accepts a down payment, which he then steals. X can bind Principal to the contract because it appeared to X that Agent still had authority to work for Principal.

E. **Terminating Agent's Authority:** To effectively terminate Agent's authority in the previous example, Principal should first, give direct notice that Agent no longer works for Principal by phone or mail to all of Agent's regular customers and second, give constructive notice to all potential customers by publishing in a newspaper of general circulation a notice to the same effect.

   1. **Limitation:** Such a procedure is not necessary in situations where agency relationships end by operation of law, as when the principal dies, for such a termination ends all actual and apparent authority. However, the procedure is required in cases of termination by act of the parties.

F. Apparent Agency: Related to the notion of apparent authority is the concept of apparent agency (also known as **ostensible agency** or **agency by estoppel**).

Example:
Apparent Agency: Agent is not an employee of Principal but in the presence of the Principal, Agent tells X that she is such an employee. If Principal does not object, X may justifiably assume that Agent is indeed an employee of Principal and enforce subsequent contracts negotiated by Agent against Principal.

G. Principal's Liability: Even if Agent acted outside the scope of any actual or apparent authority, Principal is still liable if he *ratifies* the contract:

1. expressly (by words),

Example:
Without either actual or express authority, A negotiates the sale of P's car to X. P wasn't planning on selling his car but is so pleased with the purchase price that he telephones X and tells him he embraces the deal and intends to promptly deliver title.

2. or impliedly (by actions).

Example:
Without either actual or express authority, A negotiates the sale of P's car to X. A delivers X's check for the purchase price to P. P cashes the check.

H. Agent's Liability: Agent will <u>not</u> be liable to the third-party for contracts negotiated on the Principal's behalf if the agent:

1. acts within actual authority;
2. discloses P's identity; and,
3. if the contract is written, signs in representative capacity on a written contract.

Example:
Nichols v. Seale (Tex.Civ.App.1974)

"The Fashion Beauty Salon"

Carl V. Nichols

/s/ Carl V. Nichols

Nichols is personally liable, because he did not sign in a representative capacity.

Example:
Lerner v. Amalgamated Clothing Textile Union (2d Cir. `91)

Dated: 11-27-87 T.F.M. Ind. Firm

By: Frank Lerner, its President

/s/Frank Lerner

Lerner is not personally liable.

I. Nonexistent, Partially Disclosed, and Undisclosed Principals

1. **Nonexistent Principals:** if an agent purports to act for a principal who does not exist at the time, the agent is usually liable on the contract to the third party.

Example:
Principal is dead, or has been declared insane, or is an organization without the capacity to contract.

2. **Partially Disclosed Principals:** if A tells the third party that s/he is acting on behalf of a P but does not disclose P's identity, P is liable on the contract (if its identify is disclosed) and so is A, unless the third party agrees to the contrary.

Example:
Agent negotiates to buy a house on behalf of a principal but does not tell the seller who the principal is.

3. **Undisclosed Principals:** If A hides from the third party the fact that she is acting on behalf of P, and the third party believes A is acting on her own behalf, A is personally liable on the contract and P will be also, if P later makes himself known.

Example:

1. Agent negotiates to buy a house on behalf of a principal but tells the seller that she is buying for herself.

2. In the undisclosed principal situation, the agent is functionally a party to the contract and may enforce it against the third party.

3. The principal, once revealed, can also enforce it, except that in three situations the third party can refuse to perform for the undisclosed principal and continue to treat the agent as the sole party to whom she is obliged:

- if the third party has already performed for A before P is revealed, the third party need not perform again for P;

- if, prior to the transaction, third party indicated that s/he would not do business with P and P acted through A to disguise his/her identity, the third party need not perform when s/he learns of the deception, and

- if the contract is the type that cannot typically be assigned (e.g., it calls for personal service by A or A's personal credit standing, judgment, or skill played an important part in the third party's decision to deal with A), the third party can refuse to perform.

Tort Liabilities

Agents who commit torts are liable for those torts. The most important thing to learn in this section is when the principal will be liable for those torts also. The general answer is that the principal will be liable any time the agent was acting within the "scope of employment" when he or she committed the tort, but the specifics of this rule can be somewhat detailed.

I. **Agent's Liability --** Agents are liable for the torts they commit.

II. **Principal's Liability**

Note:
Misconception: Many people believe that agents are not liable for the torts they commit if they were ordered to commit the torts by their boss. However, this is no excuse and the agents are liable notwithstanding their obedience to their boss's instructions.

A. **Direct Liability:** A principal is liable for the agent's torts if the principal is at fault:

1. Directs the tort

Example:
Principal tells Agent that X owes Principal money and Agent should beat on X until he pays. If the Agent does so, the Principal is liable for assault and battery because he directed the commission of the tort.

2. Negligent entrustment

Example:
Principal owns a construction company and entrusts Agent, a high school student without a driver's license, with a large dump truck, which Agent drives carelessly causing injury to X. X can recover from Principal because Principal negligently entrusted the truck to an agent incapable of handling it.

3. Failure to properly supervise

Example:
Principal hires Agent who has a known history of violence as a door-to-door sales representative. While along on a sales call, Agent assaults a customer in the customer's home. Principal is likely liable for not supervising the Agent.

4. Negligent hiring and/or retention

Example:
Principal hires Agent as a truck driver, not checking Agent's driving record, which would have disclosed multiple arrests for DUI. Agent causes an accident while driving under the influence. Principal is probably liable for negligent hiring.

Example:
Principal hires Agent as a truck driver. Agent has a good driving record but later develops a drinking problem that principal is aware of. Agent causes an accident while driving under the influence. Principal is probably liable for negligent retention.

B. Vicarious Liability -- Even if the principal has not done anything wrong personally, he may be vicariously liable under the doctrine of *respondeat superior*.

1. **Elements of vicarious liability:**
   a. Existence of a master-servant relationship; and
   b. the agent acts within his scope of employment.
2. **Principal-Agent Information**
   a. The principal-agent relationship has two forms:
      i. **Master-servant relationship**: The principal is usually liable for the agent's torts.

Example:
A works as a carpenter for the P Construction Co. He carelessly drops his hammer on passerby X's head. P is probably liable to X.

ii. **Employer-independent contractor**: The principal is usually not liable for the agent's torts.

Example:
A hail storm damages P's roof. P looks in the yellow pages and finds the name **Al's Roofing.** P hires Al to fix her roof. Al carelessly drops a hammer on passerby X. P is probably not liable to X.

Note:
Misconception: Many people believe that a defendant cannot be liable unless he or she has done something morally blameworthy. But a completely innocent principal with the best motives in the world who has been totally careful may still be liable for her agents' torts within the scope of authority. The rationale is based in part on the notion that the principal profits when the agent does things right and therefore should incur the costs when the agent errs. The rationale is also based in part upon a natural desire to compensate the innocent victims of the agent's torts.

b. **Other Details**
   i. **Exception**: Even the principal of an independent contractor will be liable for that agent's torts in two general circumstances:
      1. where "extrahazardous activity" is involved (e.g., use of explosives, radioactive material, etc.).

Example:
Principal wishes to "implode" a downtown office building to make way for new construction and hires independent contractor A Construction Co. If A botches the job, Principal is liable.

ii. where a statute imposes a "nondelegable duty" (e.g., the duty of a railroad to maintain railroad crossings, the duty to repossess cars without breach of the peace).

3. **Agent is a Servant:** The **key to determining** whether the agent is a servant for whose torts the principal is liable, or an independent contractor for whose torts the principal usually is not liable, is this question: Does P have the right to control the method and manner of A's work?

   a. If the answer is Yes: master-servant relationship.

   b. If the answer is No: independent contractor relationship.

4. **Additional factors** in determining whether an agent is a servant or an independent contractor:

   a. Does A work regular hours for P (e.g., 9-5)?

   b. Does P provide A's tools?

   c. Is A paid by the hour or week rather than by the job?

   d. Is P A's major source of income, rather than being simply one of A's many customers?

      i. If the answer is Yes: indicates a master-servant relationship.

      ii. If the answer is No: indicates an independent contractor. Relationship.

III. Scope of Employment

A. **Within Authority:** An agent will be held to have acted within the scope of employment when committing the tort if these three questions are answered affirmatively:

1. Was this the type of work agent was hired to do?

2. Did it occur substantially within normal time and space limitations?

3. Was it done to serve the principal in some way?

   a. While delivering furniture for his employer, P Furniture Co., Agent carelessly drives the truck through a stop sign injuring X. P is liable to X.

   b. While on vacation from his job at P Furniture Co., Agent carelessly drives his family car through a stop sign injuring X. P is not liable to X.

B. **Deviations from the scope** of employment will not alter the principal's liability if:

1. they are minor, or

Example:
While delivering furniture for his employer, P Furniture Co., Agent leaves the highway in order to get a soda at a fast food restaurant he has spotted just off the highway. Agent carelessly drives his car in the fast food restaurant's parking lot injuring X. P is liable to X.

2. after deviation, A is returning and "reasonably close" to the point of departure.

Example:
While delivering furniture for his employer, P Furniture Co., Agent leaves the highway to visit an old friend several miles away. After the visit, Agent is returning to the highway in order to complete the delivery and carelessly causes an accident on the on-ramp injuring X. P is liable to X.

C. **Special Considerations:** The principal is less likely to be held liable for an agent's intentional torts than for an agent's mere negligence because it is more likely that the agent is not acting within the scope of employment when committing intentional torts. However, if the agent is motivated in any important way by a desire to serve the principal, then the principal is probably liable.

Example:
Agent is a bouncer at Principal's bar. X, a customer, walks in and Agent exclaims: "That's the guy who stole my girlfriend!" Agent beats up X. Principal is not liable because Agent acted for purely personal motives.

Example:
Agent is a bouncer at Principal's bar. X, a customer, becomes unruly. Agent uses excessive force in ejecting X, even though Principal has warned Agent to be careful. X is seriously injured and sues Principal. Principal is probably liable.

Contracts

Introduction and Classification

An overview of the Contract area of Business Law including discussion of types of contracts and UCC vs. Common Law.

Definition:
A Contract: is an agreement supported by consideration between two or more persons with competent capacity for a legal purpose.

I. **Basic Requirements**

  A. **Offer and Acceptance.**

  B. **Consideration.**

  C. **Capacity of Parties.**

  D. **Legality.**

II. **Governing Law**

  A. Real Estate - Statutory and Common Law.

  B. Sale of Goods - Uniform Commercial Code.

  C. Services - Common Law.

III. **Classifications of Contracts**

  A. **Formation Classification**

    1. **Express Contract --** A contract formed wholly by oral and/or written words.

Example:
Over the phone, I offer to sell you my personal computer for $400. Later in the day, you send me a fax accepting my offer. The combination of the oral offer (phone) and written acceptance (fax) creates an express contract.

    2. **Implied-in-fact Contract:** A contract formed, at least in part, based on the conduct of the parties.

Example:
You call a tax accountant and inquire how much the accountant charges to prepare a tax return. The fee charged is given by the receptionist who answered your call. The next day, you drop off at the office canceled checks, W-2 forms, and other information. The accountant prepares your return. Your conduct in dropping off the tax materials and the conduct of the accountant in preparing the tax return creates an implied-in-fact contract.

    3. **Quasi-contract** (also called an implied-in-law contract): A contract imposed by law, despite the fact no actual intent to make a contract exists, to prevent unjust enrichment.

Example:
A doctor comes upon an unconscious motorist and renders valuable medical aid saving the motorist's life. Even though no aid was solicited by the motorist, to prevent an unjust enrichment, the motorist could be required to pay the reasonable value of the medical aid.

4. **Bilateral Contract:** A promise in exchange for a promise.

Example:
I offer to sell you my watch for $200 (promise). You respond. I accept (promise to pay) your offer.

5. **Unilateral Contract:** A promise in exchange for an act (which act is the offeree's total performance).

Example:
Upon completion of mowing my yard, (offeree's act and total performance) I will pay you $50 (promise). You mow the yard.

B. **Performance Classification**

1. **Executed Contract:** A fully performed contract by both parties.

Example:
I offer to sell you my watch for $200. You accept and we exchange the watch for $200 cash. Since the contractual obligations of both parties have been completed, it is now an executed contract.

2. **Executory Contract:** A contract not fully performed by the parties.

Example:
I offer to sell you my watch for $100 with payment and transfer of the watch to take place ten days later. You accept. Since no performance has taken place, it is called an executory contract.

C. **Enforceability Classification**

1. **Valid Contract:** A contract which meets the four basic requirements (offer and acceptance, consideration, parties with legal capacity, legal purpose).
2. **Void Contract:** An agreement missing an essential basic requirement for a valid contract.

Example:
You and I agree that for $10,000 I will pay you, you will burn down the classroom building. Since the performance is not for a legal purpose, the contract is void.

3. **Voidable Contract:** A valid contract but one party has the option to avoid liability from it.

Example:
I offer to sell you a Picasso painting, which I know is a fake, for $100,000. You accept. Due to my fraud, you can avoid any liability under this contract.

4. **Unenforceable Contract:** A valid contract but it cannot be enforced because of a legal defense.

Example:
I orally offer to sell you my real property for $125,000. You accept. This contract is unenforceable, although valid, because it is not in writing as required by the Statute of Frauds.

Formation

Offer and Acceptance

You cannot have a contract unless an offer is made by the offeror and the offer is accepted by the offeree. Pay particular attention to the methods and the time an offer can be and is terminated, as compared to when an acceptance becomes effective, creating the contract. This is an important subsection.

I. Parties

Definitions:
Offeror: Party making the offer

Offeree: Party accepting the offer

II. Requirements of an Offer

A. Intent -- Offer must be made with serious intent (objective theory) - Same for acceptance.

1. Objective intent is measured by a reasonable person's interpretation from the acts and words of the parties and the circumstances surrounding the transaction.
2. Offers made in an apparent moment of anger, jest, or undue stress do not meet the objective theory test.

Example:
Three workers get in an owner's 2002 car to go to work and the car will not start. Owner says "I'll sell this car to anyone for $500." One of the passengers drops $500 into the owner's lap. Offer was obviously made in an apparent moment of anger; thus, no contract.

3. Advertisements usually are not offers but an invitation to the reader to make an offer. An advertisement, however, which only invites acceptance is an offer.

Example:
Ad in newspaper from a clothier: "Dresses 50% off marked price." This is not an offer but is inviting the reader to come to the store and offer to buy a dress less 50% of the marked price.

Example:
Ad by a dog owner: "I offer a $100 reward to the person who returns to me my lost dog, Lasso (description)." The ad only invites an acceptance and is an offer.

4. Preliminary negotiations and other invitations to make offers are not offers.

    a. **Price Lists --** Invites a buyer to offer to purchase at the seller's listed prices (usually notation: "price subject to change"). Thus, prices stated in the price list are not offers but invitations to the buyer to offer to buy at that price.

    b. **Solicitation of Bids --** A solicitation invites bids (offers) to perform certain duties. The bid is the offer.

    c. **Auctions --** The seller, through an auctioneer, invites bids (offers) from prospective buyers. The buyer, not the seller, is the offeror.

    d. **Negotiations --** Words which elicit offers but are <u>not</u> offers.

Example:
Will you sell your car for $2,000? I will not sell my car for less than $2,500. I plan on selling my car next month for $2,500.

B. **Definite Terms --** Terms of the offer must be definite (same for acceptance) to enable a court to determine rights and obligations of the parties and to determine whether there is a breach.

    1. For contract terms to be definite, generally, the parties must be identified, the subject matter of the contract stated, price stated, and time for performance stated or inferred.

    2. **Definiteness --** is important for creation of all service and real estate contracts.

    3. **Uniform Commercial Code (UCC) --** In sale of goods, the Uniform Commercial Code relaxes requirements of definiteness as long as the parties intend to make a contract. Thus, a contract to sell you my watch would be binding without a statement of price, place of delivery, or time of performance. The UCC would supply these terms (see Sales of Goods under Uniform Commercial Code).

C. **Communication of Offer --** Offer must be communicated by the offeror or authorized agent and received by the offeree or authorized agent.

Example:
Your assistant accountant offers to sell me your watch for $100. Unless your assistant is authorized to make this offer, there is no offer to bind you to a contract by my attempted acceptance.

Example:
In the newspaper, I offer $100 reward for the return of my lost dog. You do not read the newspaper nor know of the reward offer upon finding my dog and returning it to me. Since you did not know of the offer upon returning my dog, there was no offer in existence for you to accept.

III. Termination of an Offer

A. An offer can be terminated by an act of the parties:

- **Revocation:** Withdrawal of an offer by offeror.
- **Rejection:** Clear indication by offeree that the offer in its present form will not be accepted.
- **Counteroffer:** A rejection by the offeree and at the same time the making of a new offer.

B. Revocation - General Rule -- An offer can be revoked at any time before acceptance without liability, unless the offer is irrevocable.

1. Irrevocable offers are:

a. Options - a separate contract whereby the offeree gives consideration in exchange for the offeror's promise to keep the offer open (not to withdraw) for a specified period of time.

Example:
A seller of land has offered to sell a school district a parcel of land. The school district is not sure it wants to buy this tract but does not want the seller to be able to withdraw the offer. The school district offers the seller $5,000 if the seller will keep the offer open for three months. If the seller agrees, the school district has an option (but no obligation to accept) and the seller must keep the offer open (not sell to someone else) for three months.

b. Sale of goods - Firm offers: In the sale of goods, if the following three criteria are met the offer is irrevocable without consideration for the time period stated in the assurance (or if none is stated, for a reasonable period of time), but without consideration only for a period not to exceed three months. (UCC2-205):

i. offeror (seller or buyer) is a merchant, and

ii. offeror, using a signed writing,

iii. gives assurance offer will remain open.

Example:
Sue owns a retail TV store. Sue, by a signed letter, offers to purchase from Adam, a TV manufacturer, fifty (50) TVs at Adam's catalog price. Her letter states that her offer would remain open and not be withdrawn for sixty (60) days. Sue's offer is irrevocable without having to pay consideration for the stated sixty (60) days. If Sue had stated a six (6) months period (rather than sixty (60) days), her offer would be only irrevocable for three months and after this period she could revoke her offer at any time during the last three months.

c. Irrevocable by estoppel - conduct of a party, which prevents (by law) the offeror from withdrawing the offer.

Example:
Bud, in Chicago, makes the following unilateral offer to Sally in Detroit: "Upon delivery of your car to my Chicago home, I'll pay you $18,000." Sally immediately, with all title papers, leaves Detroit and drives to Chicago. One mile from Bud's house, Bud calls Sally on her cellular phone and withdraws his offer. The modern view in equity is that Sally's substantial performance to accept Bud's offer makes his offer (estops him from withdrawing his offer) now irrevocable.

2. Revocation of a revocable offer is not effective until it is received or known by the offeree. Public offers can be withdrawn without the knowledge of the offeree if the revocation is made in the same medium the public offer was made.

Example:
Jane offers to sell Jim her textbook for $50. That evening, Jane changes her mind and mails Jim a letter of revocation. The next morning, Jim accepts Jane's offer. That afternoon, Jane's letter of revocation is received. Jane's revocation was not effective until received in the afternoon. Jim's acceptance in the morning binds Jane to the contract.

C. **Rejection and Counteroffer - General Rule --** An offer can be rejected or a counteroffer made at anytime before acceptance by the offeree terminating the original offer.

1. A counteroffer is a rejection of the original offer by the offeree, and at the same time, the making of a new offer.

Example:
David offers to sell to Doris his textbook for $60. Doris responds "I would not buy your textbook for $60 but I will offer to pay you $50 for it." This is a counteroffer and David's offer for $60 is terminated, and Doris has made to David an offer to buy his book for $50.

2. An inquiry by the offeree is not a rejection, and thus does not terminate the offer.

Example:
David offers to sell his textbook to Doris for $60. Doris responds, "I'm a little short on cash today. Could you lower your price?" This is merely an inquiry and not a rejection. Thus, later in the day, Doris could still accept and bind David to a contract. Even if Doris had said, "I'm a little short on cash today, but I do have $50, and if you wish to sell it today, I'll buy it for $50," this is not a counteroffer, even though a new offer was made. It is an inquiry and a new offer. Two offers are in existence (David's for $60 and Doris's for $50).

D. **Termination by Operation of Law**

1. An offer can be terminated by operation of the law automatically upon the happening of an event:

   a. **Lapse of time**.

   b. **Death or insanity of the offeror or offeree**.

   c. **Destruction of the specific subject matter of the offer**.

   d. **Intervening illegality**.

2. **Lapse of Time: General Rule --** An offer automatically terminates at the end of a stated period for its existence, or if no period is stated, it terminates after a reasonable period has lapsed.

3. **Death or Insanity of the Offeror or Offeree: General Rule --** Death or insanity of either party before acceptance terminates the offer unless the offer is irrevocable (such as an option).

   a. **Reason for General Rule --** Offerees are incapable of accepting and offerors cannot withdraw their offers after death. Irrevocable offers are an exception because offerors cannot withdraw anyway.

4. **Destruction of the Specific Subject Matter of the Offer: General Rule --** If the specific object of the offer is destroyed prior to acceptance, the offer terminates automatically (perishes) with the destruction. If the items that are destroyed are fungible goods or commodities, the general rule does not apply because the offeror can easily obtain the same product to deliver to the offeree.

   a. **Reason for General Rule --** The specific object is the offer and with its destruction there is nothing to accept.

Example:
Mary offers to sell her horse, Showboot, to Jim for $10,000. That evening, Showboot is killed by lightning. The next morning, Jim sends a letter of acceptance. There is no contract. If Mary had offered to sell Jim any one of her horses (she has four) for $10,000, and that evening one of her horses is killed by lightning, Jim's acceptance would bind Mary to a contract because no specific subject matter (a particular horse) was stated in the offer and destroyed.

5. **Intervening Illegality: General Rule --** If the object of the offer becomes illegal before acceptance, the offer is automatically terminated.

IV. **Acceptance of an Offer**

A. **Unilateral Offer: General Rule --** Acceptance takes place upon completion (total performance) of the act required by the offer. Generally, no notice to the offeror is required unless such is required by law [see UCC 2-206(2)] or offeror would have no means to know act has been completed.

B. **Bilateral Offer: General Rule --** Acceptance (promise) must be unequivocal and communicated to the offeror.

1. If sent by an **authorized medium**, the acceptance is effective binding the parties to a contract the moment the offeree delivers the acceptance to the authorized medium -- even if never received by the offeror.

   a. Express authorization - the medium stated by the offeror in the offer.

b. Implied authorization -

i. same medium used as offer was made,

ii. mail,

iii. in sale of goods - any reasonable medium.

2. If sent by **unauthorized means**, acceptance is effective only when received by offeror.

Example:
On May 1, Mary sends John a letter offering to sell her accounting textbook. John receives the offer on May 2. On May 3, Mary sends John a letter withdrawing her offer. On May 4, John sends a properly addressed letter with correct postage to Mary accepting her offer. On May 5, John receives Mary's letter of revocation. Mary does not receive John's letter of acceptance because of destruction of a mail sack with the letter in it. Mary and John have a contract formed on May 4 when John used mail (impliedly authorization under all three of the above) as the medium for acceptance. Her letter of revocation was not effective until received, which was after John had accepted.

C. **Mirror Image Rule --** In common law, any deviation in the terms of acceptance from those in the offer constitutes a counteroffer, not an acceptance. This is true today for service and real estate contracts, but under UCC 2-207(1) in a sale of goods, a definite expression of acceptance creates a contract even if the terms of the acceptance modify those of the offer.

D. **Silence: General Rule --** Silence is not an acceptance unless the offeree's actions indicate an attempt to accept or the offeree (such as soliciting the offer) has a duty to reject.

Consideration

Consideration is a dying concept requirement for contract formation, but past exams have stressed knowledge on preexisting duty, releases, and accord and satisfaction.

I. Consideration/Legal Detriment

Definition:
Consideration: is the value promised by the offeror (promisor) and the legal detriment promised or performed by the offeree (promisee). In a bilateral contract, both the offeror and offeree are promisors (those making a promise) and promises (those receiving the promise).

A. Legal detriment: The promise must be

1. **for legal value**,
2. **legally sufficient**,
3. **bargained-for**.

Example:
Mary's offer to purchase Jim's accounting text for $50 and his acceptance constitute consideration. The text and $50 are legal value, legally sufficient to show this is not a gift, and a bargained-for action to take place now or in the near future.

B. Legal detriment can consist of doing, or promising to do, an act not required by law or a contract, or by refraining from, or promising to refrain from, doing something one has a legal right to do.

Example:
Sam negligently runs over Jim causing injury. Sam promises in writing that if Jim will not sue Sam in tort (negligence), Sam will pay Jim for all medical costs plus $10,000. Jim's agreement (forbearance to file a tort suit) is consideration to contractually obligate Sam to pay all of Jim's medical costs plus $10,000.

C. **Moral obligations** are not with consideration (agreement to take a friend to lunch).

D. **Adequacy of consideration** is immaterial, thus differences in the value of the promises is not the key - what is controlling is whether the value promised is legally sufficient (serious to be paid) so as not to constitute a gift or moral obligation.

II. Preexisting Duty

Definition:
Preexisting Duty: a promise (agreement) to do whatever one is already legally obligated to do without consideration.

Example:
Able contracts to build you a home for $150,000 according to a set of specific plans and specifications. Later, Able tells you that he will lose money building your house and that he will complete the house only if you agree to pay him an additional $5,000. You agree. This agreement to pay $5,000 is without consideration and it is unenforceable. Able gave up nothing of legal value for the $5,000 - already legally obligated to build the same house for $150,000.

A. **Exceptions**

1. **Rescission and new contract --** the tearing up the old contract (rescission) and making a new one ($155,000 to build the house above).
2. **Unforeseen hardship --** only for risks not assumed in ordinary business. (Inflation cost is not an unforeseen hardship, but running into an unknown buried cement slab in digging a basement is.)
3. **Sale of goods --** UCC 2-209(1) can have a binding modification of an existing contract without consideration.

Example:
Sue and Mary have a requirements contract to sell all the gasoline Sue needs to operate her three delivery trucks for one year at $1.39 per gallon. Due to a shortage of gasoline, the wholesale price to Mary of gasoline climbs from $1.15 to $1.35 per gallon. Sue agrees in writing to modify the contract for the remaining term paying $1.50 per gallon. This modification is binding.

III. **Contracts with Uncertainty of Total Performance**

A. **Requirements Contract --** The contract is with consideration if the requirements contract is based on the needs of the buyer and the contract requires the buyer's needs to be purchased from seller.

B. **Output Contract --** The contract is with consideration if the contract is based on an established production or ability to produce by the seller and the seller must sell the seller's production to the buyer.

C. **Option to Cancel Clauses In Term (time) Contracts --** The terms of the time contract are enforceable if the party with the option to cancel would be required to give consideration to exercise the option.

Example:
Jim hires Mary as his accountant for a one-year (term) contract for $8,000 per month. Jim reserves in the contract the right to cancel the contract at any time upon notice. This contract is unenforceable because Jim is not required to give Mary consideration if he were to exercise the option. Jim and Mary simply have a contract at will with no specific salary terms. If Jim had to give Mary 30 day's written notice, this would be consideration to exercise the option because even if notice were given to her the first day on the job, she would be entitled to $8,000 for the month.

IV. Contracts for Settlement

A. Release -- To be an enforceable and a bar to further recovery, releases require consideration be given.

Example:
Sam negligently runs his car into the rear of John's car. Sam, in a signed writing, promises to pay John $1,000 if John will release Sam from any further property liability due to the accident. This accepted release by John is binding and bars John from any further recovery.

B. Covenant Not to Sue -- A substitution of a contract for a different cause of action.

Example:
Joe, in his most recent will, leaves all of his assets to his son, Able, and nothing to his two married daughters who both were unaware of Joe's heart condition. It is learned that Able had not informed his sisters of their dad's condition and Joe has told friends that Able had said that his daughters did not care about him. The daughters have indicated they would contest the will. Able and his sisters agree that if the sisters do not contest the will, he will give each $15,000 from monies he will receive under the will. This (giving up the legal right to contest the will for $15,000) is a covenant not to sue (contract) and enforceable.

C. Accord and Satisfaction -- A payment by a debtor of a lesser sum than the creditor purports is owed as full payment of the debt. You cannot have satisfaction (termination of the debt) unless there is accord. Accord is the acceptance by the creditor of the lesser sum knowing this is all the debtor intends to pay ("Payment in full"). Creditor can avoid the legal issue by returning the payment (no accord) to the debtor. Whether accord is a satisfaction of the purported debt depends upon whether the debt is liquidated (one reasonable persons would not differ over the amount owed) or unliquidated (a debt reasonable persons would differ over). The majority rule is accord is not satisfaction if the debt is liquidated (creditor can sue for the balance), and accord is satisfaction (debt canceled) if the debt is unliquidated.

Example:
Jim borrows $100 from Joan payable back without interest. Jim sends to Joan a check clearly marked as "payment in full" for $90. If Joan cashes the check, accord has taken place, but since reasonable persons would all claim that Jim owes Joan $100, the debt is liquidated and Joan can still legally pursue recovery of $10 from Jim.

Example:
Jim contracts to purchase from Joan a new file cabinet for $250. Upon delivery, Jim discovers that the cabinet is scratched. Jim tenders to Joan a check clearly marked "payment in full" for $200. Joan has no idea as to the cost of damage due to the scratches. She can avoid the issue and return the check (no accord) but if she cashes it (since reasonable persons could disagree as to the cost of damage), the purported debt is canceled because this is an unliquidated debt.

D. **Past Consideration --** A promise to pay for an act already completed is without (not bargained-for) consideration.

Example:
Employer states "In consideration of the twenty years of loyal service you have given the company, I promise to pay you $10,000") - promise is unenforceable because it is for an event which has already taken place.

V. Promises Enforceable Without Consideration

A. **Promissory Estoppel --** A promise, which induces another party in reliance therein to materially change their position, is estopped in justice from claiming no consideration.

Example:
Jim pledges (promises) $50,000 to the church to add a childcare room to the church. In reliance (induces church to change its position) thereon, the church contracts for the addition (changes substantially their position). In the interest of justice, the church can hold Jim to his pledge denying his claim that his pledge lacked consideration.

B. **Promises Barred By The Statute of Limitations --** A promise to pay a debt barred from recovery by law - the statute of limitations - atolls the debt anew and is enforceable.

Capacity and Legal Purpose

Very few persons do not have capacity to enter into contracts; rather, the law deals mainly with the liability of those with limited capacity who do so. The exam stresses the limited liability of a minor, his or her right of disaffirmance, and the two major exceptions to disaffirmance law -- a minor's ratification and a minor's contract for necessities. A brief listing of the types of contracts that are subject to an illegal purpose should be known. Be sure to know the legality of exculpatory clauses, covenants not to compete clauses, and the effect of illegal contracts.

General Rule: Almost all persons have the legal capacity to enter into a valid contract, but because of some incapacity they can avoid their performance or liability under it (called a voidable contract).

I. Most Common Types of Persons with Limited Capacity

A. Minors.

B. Mentally Incompetent.

C. Intoxicated.

II. Minors

A. General Rules of Disaffirmance -- In most states and for most contracts, a minor is any person under the age of 18. A minor can make almost any contract an adult can, except, for example, contracts for liquor or cigarettes. If a minor can make a contract, a minor can avoid liability under it at any time before reaching majority and for a reasonable time thereafter. If a minor does wish to avoid liability (disaffirm), the minor must show intent to do so and must return any consideration derived from the contract that the minor still possesses or controls. If the minor does not possess or control, or has returned the consideration, the minor is entitled back any consideration he or she has paid and cannot be held further on the contract.

B. Exceptions

1. **Necessities --** To be a contract of necessity, the following criteria must be met:
   - **a.** It must be an item of necessity (e.g., food, clothing, shelter, etc.).
   - **b.** It must be in value what the minor is accustomed to (standard of living).
   - **c.** Minor must not be under the care of a parent or guardian.
2. If all three criteria are met, the minor may disaffirm the contract but the minor is liable for the reasonable value of the goods used.
3. **Ratification --** Any minor's contract that is affirmed by the minor after reaching the age of majority (now an adult), is fully liable on the contract.

Example:

Able, a minor age 17 fully supporting his way through college (parents deceased), leases an apartment from Sue for one year with rental payments of $400 per month. Able makes five payments, turns 18, and makes one more payment before Able and Sue have a dispute with Able turning the apartment back to Sue upon moving. What are the possible claims and results of liability for Able?

Possible Results:

If Able can disaffirm (within a reasonable time after becoming 18), Able (by majority rule) is entitled to return of all six payments made to Sue and has no further liability (remaining six months' rent).

If Able's payment after reaching age of majority (18), is considered by the court to be a ratification of the lease contract made when Able was a minor, Sue gets to keep the six payments made and Able can be held liable for the remaining six months' rent.

If a court determines this is a contract for a necessity, Sue can keep the six payments made (reasonable value based on use) but cannot collect for the remaining six months' rent.

4. **Other Exceptions**

   a. Marriage removes the right to disaffirm most contracts.

   b. The marriage contract, an enlistment contract in the armed services, certain types insurance by statute, etc., cannot be disaffirmed.

C. **Minor's Torts: General Rule --** A minor is liable for his or her torts except, if in imposing tort liability, it would enforce a contract against a minor (would in effect remove right of disaffirmance). Parents can be held liable for a minor child's torts by statute (such as vandalism by children who are living at home) or where parents failed to exercise proper parental control.

III. **Mentally Incompetent Persons --** Contracts made by a person mentally incompetent, but before a court has adjudged that person incompetent, are voidable by the person or legal guardian (the same as a minor) during period of incompetency and for a reasonable time after regaining his or her competency. To avoid liability, however, the mentally incompetent party must be able to return the consideration received under the contract. If the contract is made after the person has been adjudged incompetent by the court, the contract is void (can only be made by legal guardian), not voidable. Laws on necessity and ratification on voidable contracts after regaining competency are the same as a minor.

IV. **Intoxicated Persons --** Any person who becomes voluntarily intoxicated can avoid any contract made while intoxicated at any time while he or she is still intoxicated or for a reasonable time after becoming sober. Apply basically same rules as if person was mentally incompetent (not yet court adjudged) at time contract was made.

V. **Legal Purpose: Two Types**

A. **Contracts Contrary to Statute --** (to commit a crime or tort):

1. **Usury --** Charging a higher interest rate than permitted by law (maximum rate). Do not confuse with:

   a. **Legal Rate --** When parties intend a rate of interest but do not fix the amount in the contract.

b. **Judgment Rate --** Rate of interest to be applied to a monetary judgment until judgment is paid.

c. **Prejudgment Rate --** Rate of interest to be applied if plaintiff wins a judgment from date of filing suit to date judgment is entered by court. In absence of contract, this rate (where allowed) is usually either the same as the legal or judgment rate of interest.

2. **Gambling Contracts --** Contract itself is illegal and void but payment of the gambling debt may be only voidable.

3. **Sunday (Sabbath or Blue Laws) --** Some states prohibit certain contracts being made on Sunday.

4. **Licensing Statutes --** If purpose of the licensing law is mainly revenue generation, the contract with the unlicensed person may be enforceable. If purpose is to regulate for welfare of public (such as a doctor or lawyer), the contract with the unlicensed person is null and void.

5. **Contracts Contrary to Statute --** Contracts to commit any crime or tort contrary to statute are illegal and void.

B. **Contracts Contrary to Public Policy**

1. **Contract in Prohibition of Marriage**

2. **Contracts in Furtherance of Immorality**

3. **Unconscionable Contracts or Clauses Against Public Policy**

a. **Exculpatory Clauses --** A clause in a contract, which disclaims any liability regardless of type or degree of fault. These clauses are usually illegal if the bargaining power is one-sided and are so grossly unfair to be deemed unconscionable. Clauses disclaiming liability are legal if conspicuous and reasonable. (Thus, a clause disclaiming one's intentional acts would be illegal but a conspicuous clause disclaiming liability to acts such as theft, fire, etc., is legal.)

4. **Conflict of Interest --** Any contract, which is in conflict of interest by public officials or those with fiduciary duties is illegal.

5. **Contracts Obstructing the Legal Process --** One which virtually constitutes bribery -- paying a legislator to vote a certain way.

6. **Discriminatory Contracts --** Any contract, even if not in violation of a statute, which discriminates as to race, color, sex, national origin, or religion.

7. **Contracts in Restraint of Trade**

a. **Exception --** A covenant not to compete is legal if it is:

i. ancillary - a part of a larger contract, and

ii. reasonable in restraint in time and area.

Example:
Charles owns a successful Italian restaurant. Cameron wants to start an Italian restaurant across the street. Charles contracts for $5,000 with Cameron not to start the restaurant. This is an illegal (contract in restraint of trade) contract.

Example:
Charles contracts to sell his Italian restaurant to Susan. In the contract is a clause that prohibits Charles from starting an Italian restaurant in the city for six months. This is probably a legal covenant not to compete because it is ancillary -- part of the sale of business contract and the restraint is reasonable in time and area.

VI. **Effect of Illegal Contracts --** If both parties are at fault (pari delicto), the courts will leave the parties as they find them.

A. **For illegal covenants not to compete, the courts can**

1. Declare the covenant void and, because it is ancillary and divisible, the court can enforce the main purpose of the contract.

Example:
Contract is for sale of a business and the covenant not to compete clause provides that the seller of the business shall never start a restaurant anywhere in the world. This clause is divisible and could be held void, yet the other terms of the sale of the business enforced.

2. - or - the court could reform the covenant to be reasonable and enforce it.

B. **Innocent Party --** When a party is totally innocent, or a party entered into the illegal contract because of fraud or duress imposed by the other party, the innocent party may be able to enforce the contract, but not the guilty party.

Statute of Frauds and Interpretation

A favorite question under the contracts section concerns those contracts which, although valid, require a signed writing or a legally recognized exception for the enforceability of the contract. There are four such types of business contracts: guaranty of debt contracts, sales of goods priced at $500 or more, contracts impossible to perform within one year of contract formation, and contracts involving any interest in real property -- all of which are fair exam game. Besides some general rules, such as "any ambiguity in a written contract is construed most strongly against the drafter," the parol evidence rule that a fully integrated, clearly worded written contract cannot be contradicted or varied with certain exceptions is stressed.

A valid contract, but to be enforceable in a court of law the contract must be in writing, or have written evidence of the oral contract (called a memorandum), or meet a legal exception to the writing requirement. Has virtually nothing to do with fraud but requires proof of an oral contract's existence for its enforceability.

I. Types of Contracts Which Come under the Statute of Frauds

- **A.** Guaranty of Debt Contracts
- **B.** Contracts Involving an Interest in Realty.
- **C.** Contracts Impossible to Perform within One Year of Formation.
- **D.** Contracts for the Sale of Goods Priced at $500 or More.
- **E.** Premarital or Antenuptial Contracts -- not mutual exchange of promises.
- **F.** Promises of Executors for Personal Liability for Debts of the Deceased.

II. Contracts to Guaranty the Debt of Another.

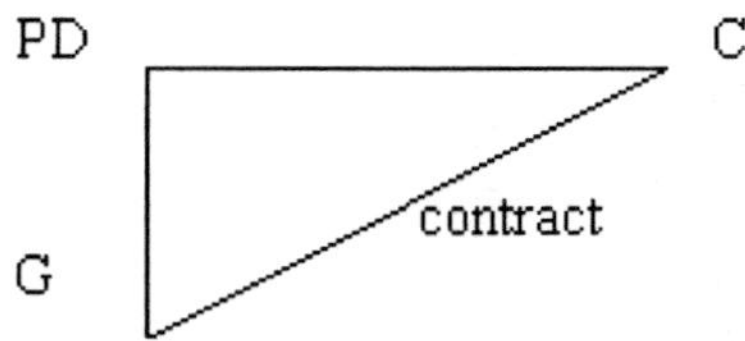

- **A.** If these three criteria are met, the contract comes under the Statute of Frauds:
  1. Applies only to contracts that bind G (guarantor) and C (creditor).
  2. The terms of the contract make PD's (principal debtor) obligation primary and G's obligation secondary. (For example, "If PD does not pay and is in default, then I (G) will pay.") Note: If G's debt obligation is primary, G is a co-debtor and the contract is outside the Statute of Frauds.
  3. The contract is an express contract.

B. **Exception --** If the guarantor is to benefit economically or pecuniary from the making of the guaranty, the contract no longer requires a writing for enforceability. This is referred to as the "main purpose" or "leading object" doctrine.

Example:
Able is a commission agent selling Peter's products. Peter has a rule that his agents only sell to customers for cash. Able knows she can sell more, and thus make more commissions, if she can also sell to customers on credit. Able orally contracts with Peter allowing Able to sell to customers on credit, and if any customer does not pay when due, she agrees she will pay Peter. Some customers who were sold Peter's products on credit fail to pay Peter. Peter demands Able pay.

Question: Does the Able-Peter contract allowing Able to sell on credit come under the Statute of Frauds?

Answer: Yes - It is an express contract (formed by words) between a guarantor (Able) and a creditor (Peter) creating a secondary debt obligation. (Able is liable only if customer, the principal debtor, fails to pay.)

Question: Does the "main purpose" exception apply?

Answer: Yes - Able is making the guaranty for personal financial gain -- more commissions -- and thus the oral guaranty contract (if proved) is enforceable.

III. Contracts Involving An Interest In Realty

A. **General Rule --** Any contract involving an interest in realty, to be enforceable, must be in writing, or have written evidence thereof, or an applicable exception.

1. Real Estate Purchase Contracts.
2. Leases of Realty; Exception in most states for leases of a year or less than one year.
3. Mortgages of Realty.
4. Easements.
5. Creation of Life Estates.
6. Real Estate Broker Contracts.

B. **Exception in Equity (Partial Performance) --** If the performance is such that the parties cannot be returned to the status quo, the exception is applicable. Partial performance includes:

1. payment - full or partial,
2. possession,
3. valuable improvements.

Example:
Mary orally contracts to purchase Jim's house and lot. Mary sends Jim a check for 5% of the purchase price, which Jim cashes. The closing (passage of deed and payment) will not take place for two months. Mary's lease has expired and it is agreed that Mary can move onto the premises paying Jim a rental payment. Mary moves into the house, plants a number of trees, and adds a deck to the back porch. Just before closing, Jim is offered $20,000 more than Mary's purchase price. Jim tenders return of Mary's down payment and claims the oral contract is unenforceable.

Question: Does this contract come under the Statute of Frauds?

Answer: Yes - A purchase of realty contract is an interest in realty.

Question: Can Jim successfully claim that the oral contract is unenforceable under the Statute of Frauds?

Answer: No - The partial performance in equity rule applies (in all states) because there was a payment, possession, and valuable improvements, which will not allow the parties Jim and Mary to be returned to the status quo.

Question: What if only the payment had been made (no possession or valuable improvement)?

Answer: In many states, since the return payment returns the parties to the status quo, the exception would not apply and the oral contract would be unenforceable.

IV. Contracts Impossible to Perform Within One Year of Formation -- Any contract objectively impossible to perform within one year from the date of contract formation (date of acceptance) without breaching the terms must be in writing or have written evidence of it to be enforceable. Year begins the next day after acceptance.

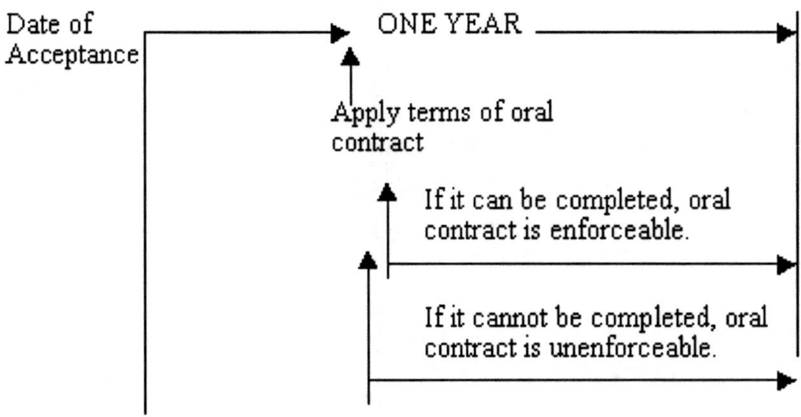

V. Contract for the Sale of Goods -- Any contract for the sale of goods priced at $500 or more must be in writing or have written evidence of it (memorandum), or an applicable exception [UCC 2-201(1)(2)(3)].

A. **Applicable Exceptions --** [UC-201(2)(3)]

1. **Between merchants (only) --** if one sends the other a written confirmation, and the other, after receipt, does not object in writing within ten days, the oral contract is enforceable by either party.
2. **Special Ordered Goods --** Goods that a seller cannot resell in his/her ordinary course of business are special ordered goods. An oral contract for special ordered goods is enforceable if the seller has substantially begun performance or has made an irrevocable commitment to do so before the buyer cancels the order claiming the Statute of Frauds.
3. **Admission Under Oath --** Any admission under oath (disposition, interrogatory, signing of answer, or on the stand during trial) that an oral contract was made removes the Statute of Frauds as a defense.
4. **Performance by Buyer --** If the buyer takes possession or makes a payment accepted by the seller, the Statute of Frauds is removed (oral contract enforced) at least to the quantity possessed or paid for.

VI. **Memorandums --** A memorandum is written evidence of the existence of an oral contract and, if it is a valid memorandum, it removes the requirement of a writing under the Statute of Frauds.

A. **Criteria for a Valid Memorandum**

1. **Generally**

a. Need identity of the parties stated,

b. Object of the contract stated

i. Realty - need legal description and, in some states, price

ii. Sale of Goods - quantity

c. Signed by the party to be held liable on the oral contract.

2. <u>Some States Also Require</u>

a. essential terms and conditions.

VII. **Interpretation**

A. **Meanings of Terms --** Terms are assumed to have their ordinary meaning; if technical, their technical meaning.

B. **Ambiguities --** any ambiguity will be construed against the party who drafted the contract.

C. **No Contradictions --** In sale of goods (UCC 2-202) a written contract can be explained, but not contradicted, by usage of trade, course of performance, or course of dealing.

VIII. **Parol Evidence Rule --** A fully integrated contract (complete embodiment of terms) clearly written cannot be contradicted, varied, or altered by evidence of the parties' prior negotiations, prior agreements, or contemporaneous oral agreements.

A. **Exceptions**

1. **Subsequent Modification --** either oral or written evidence that parties, after written formation, agreed to modify the terms is admissible. This evidence may have to be in writing as required in the contract or because of the Statute of Frauds.

2. **Voidable or Void Contract --** oral evidence can be introduced to show the contract is voidable by a party or void. (For example, contract was induced by fraud or mistake or object of contract is illegal.)
3. **Ambiguous Terms --** oral or written evidence can be introduced only to clean up the ambiguity.
4. **Obvious Clerical or Typographical Error --** in reducing oral contract into a writing, parol evidence can be introduced to show true agreement.
5. **Incomplete Contracts --** Parol evidence can be admitted to "fill in" the gaps.
6. **Agreed-upon Conditions --** Parol evidence can be admitted if entire contract is subject to an agreed-upon oral condition (this contract is expressly conditioned upon my attorney's assent). This does not alter the written contract but goes to whether the contract is enforceable.

Genuineness of Assent

Even with an offer and acceptance, true meetings of the mind may be lacking due to mistake, fraud, duress, or undue influence. Usually stressed are the laws on bilateral and unilateral mistake, and the elements for a fraud or misrepresentation action.

I. Assent (true meeting of the minds) may be lacking because of

- **A.** Mistake
- **B.** Fraud or Misrepresentation
- **C.** Duress
- **D.** Undue Influence

II. Types of Mistakes

- **A.** Unilateral Mistake - **General Rule:** If only one of the parties makes a mistake, the mistake is binding on the mistaken party, unless:
  - **1.** the other party knows or should know of the mistake; or
  - **2.** the error was due to a mathematical calculation (addition, subtraction, division, or multiplication) and such was done inadvertently and without gross negligence.

Example:
Jim tells everyone that he is going to offer to sell Mary his laptop computer for $550. That evening when Jim is typing up his offer, he inadvertently types the price at $500 rather than $550. Mary, upon receiving Jim's letter writes back a simple "I accept" message.

Question: Do Jim and Mary have a contract?

Answer: Yes.

Question: What is the price in the contract?

Answer: Even though Jim intended to sell Mary the laptop computer for $550, he made a unilateral mistake, which Mary did not know had been made. Thus, the mistake falls on Jim and the contract is for $500.

Question: Would your answer be different if Jim had typed $5.50?

Answer: Yes, because here Mary would know Jim had made a mistake and such cannot be held against Jim.

- **B.** Bilateral (mutual) Mistake - **General Rule:** If both parties are mistaken and the mistake goes to the value or quality of the subject matter of the contract, the contract is fully binding on the parties. If, however, the mistake goes to the identity, existence, or quantity of the subject matter, the contract cannot be enforced by either party.

Example:
John is invited to Mary's house for dinner. John admires a painting Mary had purchased two years ago. John inquires as to the value of the painting. Mary responds truthfully she does not know but paid $500 for it and believes it is worth more today since the artist is deceased. John offers to buy the painting for $800 and Mary agrees to sell. Later, John learns from an art expert that the value of the painting is only $500.

Question: Have John and Mary made a bilateral mistake?

Answer: Yes.

Question: Can Mary enforce the contract against John?

Answer: Yes, because although a bilateral mistake was made, the mistake goes to the value of the painting.

Question: Suppose both John and Mary believed the painting was painted by Picasso and after the contract for sale learned it was a forgery. Could Mary enforce the contract against John?

Answer: No, because the mistake went to the identity of the subject matter and this rendered the contract unenforceable.

III. Fraud or Misrepresentation

A. Elements

1. Intentional Deceit (includes negligent misrepresentation),
2. Deceit of a Material Fact,
3. Reliance on the party deceived.
   - a. If all three elements are present, the deceived party is entitled to damages (including punitive damages) or can rescind (cancel) the contract.
   - b. The basic difference between fraud and innocent misrepresentation is intent and for innocent misrepresentation the remedy is usually limited to rescission.

B. Forms of Deceit

1. **Untrue Statements**
2. **Concealment:** Only where there is an intent to hide in order to deceive. (Having car repaired and repainted after an accident is not in and of itself deceit, but stuffing steel wool in a muffler with a hole in it is.)
3. **Half-truths:** To the question how far is the nearest railroad, a truthful answer of 15 miles could still be deceit if the railroad could not be reached by truck due to an impassible gorge.
4. **Duty to Disclose:** Generally, when dealing at "arm's length" there is no duty to disclose, except:
   - a. When the parties are in a fiduciary relationship (one of trust such as doctor-patient, lawyer-client, trustee-beneficiary, partner-partner, etc.).

b. Knowledge of a serious defect or damages. (I would not have to tell you the car had been in an automobile accident three years ago, but I would have to tell you the brakes do not work.)

C. Material Facts

1. Statements of value, or the opinions of nonexperts, or predictions for the future are not fact, and thus their falsehood is not actionable fraud or misrepresentation.

   a. "This car is in A-1 condition," is merely one's opinion and sellers are allowed to huff and puff their wares without liability.

2. An expert's opinion to a lay person, however, may be a fact.

   a. Thus, misrepresentation of law by a lay person is opinion, but by a lawyer licensed to practice in that state is a fact.

D. Reliance

1. Unless the party is actually deceived (relied on), there is no fraud or misrepresentation.

   a. A sign on a Longhorn steer in Texas that this is a race-horse would not be fraudulent to almost everyone and certainly not a Texan.

IV. Undue Influence -- Arises usually from a special relationship whereby one, because of this relationship, can exercise undue influence overcoming the free will of the other in rendering decisions. These contracts are voidable.

A. A sister, upon whom a brother heavily relies for advice, talks her brother into contracting to sell his only asset, his house, to her at a price of 50% of the market value. This relationship allowed the sister to overcome her brother's free will and the brother can set aside this contract or sale.

V. Duress -- A forcing of a party to enter into a contract under the fear or threat of violence to that party or member of his or her family, or use of economic pressure to overcome the party's free will.

A. An employer threatens to fire and have an employee "black-listed" in an industry the employer controls unless the employee contracts to sell the employer mineral rights in a piece of land the employee has just purchased. This threat of economic sanctions, loss of job, plus not being able to work and apply his or her industry skills to earn a living, is economic duress.

Third Party Rights

Third party rights in a contract in which the third party was not a party in formation, assignment and delegation of contract rights, and duties to third parties are important topics. You should know when assignments can and cannot legally be made, what the effects are when an assignment is made, and the criteria for donee and creditor beneficiary rights to incur.

I. **General Rule --** Generally, unless a party is privity (a party thereof) to a contract, that party (called a third party) has no enforceable rights to or obligations under the contract.

   A. **Exceptions**

      1. Assignees and Delegatees of a contract
      2. Third Party Beneficiaries

II. **Assignments and Delegations**

   A. **Terminology**

Rights: enforceable actions can be assigned

Duties: are delegated

Assignor: party (usually one of the original contracting parties) who makes the assignment

Assignee: party to whom rights are assigned

Delegator: party who makes the delegation

Delegatee: party to whom the duties are delegated

   B. **General Rule**

      1. Any right can be assigned or delegated unless an exception applies.

   C. **Assignment Exceptions**

      1. Contract Terms Prohibit Assignment (anti-assignment clause). In most states you cannot prohibit an assignment of a money claim.

Example:
In a typical term lease, the tenant cannot (by the lease contract terms) assign the lease without the landlord's consent. Most fire insurance policies prohibit assignment of the policy without the insurer's consent, but the policy holder can assign a money claim for a loss sustained covered by the policy.

2. Statute Prohibits Assignment

Example:
Future social security or workers' compensation benefits, in many states future wages, and some rights which are intended only for a particular person, such as alimony or child support are not assignable by statute.

3. Personal Contracts - contracts unique to the person receiving services.

Example:
You contract to tutor Green's children after observation of them. Green assigns her right to your services to Hope. This assignment is prohibited without your consent. The reason is that Hope's children may be different in needs and temperament.

4. Assignments which materially increase the risks of the obligor (party obligated to perform the contract). For sale of goods see UCC 2-210(2).

Example:
Green owns a restaurant and has a fire insurance policy (contract) with ABC Insure. Green cannot assign the policy to Able to cover a restaurant Able owns on the other side of the city without ABC Insure's consent. The reason is that ABC Insure's policy was made and based on risks assumed on ABC's evaluation of Green's circumstances. Able's circumstances and resulting risks can be quite different and thus could substantially increase ABC's risks.

D. Delegation Exceptions

1. Contract terms prohibit delegation

Example:
Green wants to have her products locally delivered to her customer's front porches. Any local delivery carrier can make these deliveries. Green contracts with ABC Del Inc. to make her deliveries and places in the contract that the contract cannot be delegated to any other carrier. This clause prohibits delegation.

2. Contract is based on the personal skill of the obligor, or a special trust has been placed in the obligor.

Example:
You hire a famous heart specialist (doctor) to perform a heart transplant. This doctor cannot delegate the surgery to any other doctor - even one with equal skills - because your contract was made dependent upon this doctor's skill and the trust you have placed in him or her.

3. Contract performance will materially vary that expected by obligee.

Example:
Green contracts with Smith to clean a surface by use of sandblasting. Green delegates the duty to Able who specializes in cleaning the same type of surface by hot water. Even though the result is the same, Green's expectation of sandblasting is materially different from that of hot water.

E. **General Rules - On Assignment --** (apply equally to delegation)

1. An assignee can acquire no better rights than those possessed by the assignor (can acquire lesser rights).
2. An assignment is not binding on an obligor until the obligor has notice of the assignment:
   a. Between two assignees to the same contract:
      i. U.S. Rule - first in time of assignment, first in right
      ii. English Rule - first to give obligor notice
   b. Until notice, obligor can discharge the contract by performance to the assignor.

Example:
John owes Jane $100. Jane assigns her right to the money to Sam. Until John has notice of the assignment, John can discharge his obligation by payment to Jane. If John has notice, John can only discharge the debt by payment to Sam. If Jane had also assigned, the next day after her assignment to Sam, the payment to Mary, and Mary gave John notice, as between Sam and Mary's priority, it depends upon whether the US rule (Sam gets priority by first in time) or the English rule (Mary gets priority by first to give notice) applies.

3. Any defense the obligor (unless waived - see UCC 9-206) has against the assignor is also a defense against the assignee.
4. Any defense the assignor has against the other contracting party, except the assignor's minority or bankruptcy, is also a defense which is available to the assignee.

Example:
ABC Appliance store contracts to sell Jones a TV, model X, for $1,450. Jones, through fraud, gives ABC false credit information. ABC is to make delivery at the end of the week on Friday. On Wednesday, ABC discovers that it had sold its last model X TV earlier. ABC assigns its contract for delivery and sale to XYZ Appliance who had model X TVs in stock. On Thursday, ABC learns of the fraud and notifies XYZ. ABC's defense of fraud (avoid the contract) is also a defense available to XYZ, who does not have to deliver the TV set to Jones.

5. Unless released, the assignor remains liable to the other contracting party.

Example:
Assume a tenant is allowed to assign the balance of a five-year lease with a landlord to an assignee. Unless the assignor (tenant) is released by the landlord, the assignor is still liable for any default by the assignee.

III. **Beneficiary Contracts --** An intended beneficiary is one for whose benefit the contract is made, and thus the beneficiary has legal rights in a contract to which the beneficiary is not a party.

A. **Types**

1. Donee Beneficiary
2. Creditor Beneficiary
3. Incidental Beneficiary

B. **Donee (Intended) Beneficiary: Criteria**

1. The contract must be made for the direct benefit of the beneficiary, and
2. the donee's rights must have vested (have unconditional legal effect).

Example:
You contract with ABC Life Insurance Company for a $25,000 policy on your life with your spouse as the named beneficiary. You reserve the right to change beneficiaries. Although this contract is made for the direct benefit of the spouse, the spouse's right is not vested; first, because while you are alive you can change beneficiaries, and second, the spouse, even if still the named beneficiary, has no rights in the policy until you are dead.

C. **Creditor (Intended) Beneficiary: Criteria**

1. There must exist a debtor-creditor relationship, and

2. the debtor must make a contract with a third person, which benefits the creditor.

Example:
ABC is the mortgagee (creditor) on a home owned by Green (debtor). Green contracts to sell the home to Able (third person), with Able agreeing to assume the mortgage (become personally liable to make payments to ABC). Although ABC is not a party to the purchase contract, ABC is a creditor beneficiary and can enforce mortgage payments against Able.

D. **Incidental Beneficiary**

1. A third party who receives an unintended benefit has no legal rights in a contract between two parties.

Example:
A contractor has a contract with the city to build a swimming pool in a neighborhood small park. The swimming pool will increase the value of the homes in the neighborhood. The contractor breaches the contract. The city decides not to sue. The homeowners wish to file suits against the contractor as a beneficiary of the contractor-city contract. Since the homeowners are only incidental beneficiaries, they have no legal rights in the contractor-city contract.

Remedies for Breach and Discharge of Contracts

It is important to understand the scope and limitation for four basic remedies for breach of contract: damages, specific performance, rescission and restitution and reformation. Discharge deals mainly with performance and when completion or lack of completion causes a discharge of the contract. This total area should be divided into performance of a condition versus a promise, discharge by performance, discharge by agreement such as a release, novation, and accord and satisfaction, and discharge by operation of the law, such as objective impossibility situations and a bankruptcy decree.

I. Types of Remedies

A. Remedies at Law

1. Damages

B. Remedies in Equity

1. Specific Performance
2. Rescission and Restitution
3. Reformation
4. Quasi-Contract Recovery

II. Damages

A. Nominal -- There is a breach but no financial loss has been suffered. Court awards a nominal amount ($1 or some other small amount).

B. Compensatory -- All costs or loss actually suffered and proved caused by the breach. The term **incidental damages** means all expenses incurred by the nonbreaching party due to the breach [See UCC 2-715(1)]. The term **consequential damages** include any foreseeable loss known by the breaching party [UCC 2-715(2)].

Example:
Able contracts to purchase for $40,000 from Sallar Inc. 100 transmissions to be installed in custom-made recreational vehicles to be driven in the mountains. Delivery is to be on or before May 1. On April 20, Sallar tells Able that Sallar cannot deliver on time. Able immediately, with notice to Sallar, purchases on the open market the transmissions from Green Inc. at a price of $42,000. Able can collect from Sallar all expenses incurred in the making of the new contract and those incurred from Sallor's breach plus the actual increase in price of $2,000.

Example:
Able contracts with Sallor Inc. to deliver on or before May 1 parts for a special oil field value Able is making for Oiltax. Able's contract with Sallor specifically states "time is of the essence" and "any delay in our production and delivery will result in Able paying Oiltax liquidated damages of $1,000 per day." Sallor does not deliver on time and by the time Able can purchase the parts elsewhere, it is late in delivery to Oiltax by five days. Here Able can recover not only from Sallor all expenses and the increased parts price purchase costs, but also the foreseeable liquidated damages ($5,000) caused by Sallor's breach.

C. **Punitive Damages --** Damages awarded to punish a wrongdoer -- rarely given in breach of contract cases.

D. **Liquidated Damages --** A specific sum is agreed to be paid in the formation of the contract in the event that in the future the contract is breached. These provisions are enforceable as long as (a) at the time of formation of the contract it is apparent damages would be difficult to estimate in the event of breach, and (b) the amount stated is a reasonable sum estimate. The provision cannot be constituted as a penalty. [See UCC 2-718]

Example:
Able has agreed to construct a 100-unit apartment complex for Green. Completion date is agreed to be May 1 or earlier. Since Green will be preleasing the apartments with one-year leases to begin on May 1, it is agreed to include a liquidated damage clause to cover breach of lease actions and costs incurred in housing by some tenants if the apartments are not completed on time. The liquidated damage amount is based upon average occupancy for new apartment buildings when first available in the community and the estimate that at least 70% of those would require substitute housing and storage. This was broken down on a daily basis and this was the liquidated damage amount per day for late construction. This clause would probably be enforceable because of the difficulty in estimating damages and the reasonable amount per day (determination).

E. **Mitigation of Damages --** In most situations when a breach takes place, the law imposes on the nonbreaching party the duty to take actions to mitigate (reduce) the amount of damages owed. Some states require such in breach of real estate lease cases.

Example:
Able has a one-year lease with Green for $1,000 per month. After six months, Able breaches the lease and abandons the property. If mitigation is required, Green must use reasonable means to find and lease the property to a suitable tenant. Able is still liable for any difference and, if no tenant can be found, for the balance of the lease.

III. Remedies in Equity

A. **Specific Performance --** If the object of the contract is unique and damages inappropriate as a remedy, the nonbreaching party (usually a buyer) can, by court order, force the breaching party to perform the contract. This is not applicable to personal service contracts.

Example:
Able contracts to sell his lake lot to Green for $10,000. Able now has a better offer and refuses to deed the lot to Green. Because land is unique (no two parcels have same legal description) and damages would hardly satisfy Green who wants the lot, specific performance is an appropriate remedy.

B. **Rescission and Restitution --** The undoing of a contract so as to return the parties to their original position. Generally, both parties must make restitution -- returning anything each has received. As a remedy, this is where one party is in breach and the nonbreaching party with notice rescinds the contracts. (Remember in mutual rescission there is no breach but discharge of the contract.) The breaching party must restore the nonbreaching party to his or her original position, but the nonbreaching party cannot retain benefits he or she has received as unjust enrichment.

C. **Reformation --** Used by the court to correct an imperfectly expressed contract. It is applied most often to correct clerical errors, or errors in reducing a valid oral contract into a written form, or to make a covenant not to compete reasonable in time or area -- all to reflect the true intentions of the parties.

D. **Quasi-contract Recovery --** A remedy to give a reasonable value benefit to one party and avoid an unjust enrichment received by the other party.

Example:
Able has a one-year $50,000 employment contract with Green. The contract contains an option to cancel clause "at any time" which renders the one-year contract unenforceable because of a lack of consideration. Able works for 15 days and is dismissed for no reason. Although there was no one-year contract for $50,000, Able has given Green valuable services. Green must pay Able a sum equal to the reasonable (market) value of those services. To not be required to do so would give Green an unjust benefit.

IV. Election of Remedies -- Under common law, when multiple remedies were available, the nonbreaching party had to elect which remedy to pursue. The object was to prevent double recovery.

Example:
In a land sale contract, the buyer could not have the remedy for damages and specific performance. In service and real estate contracts this common law doctrine is still applied, but has been eliminated in part in the sale of goods (see UCC 2-703 and UCC 2-711), which hold that remedies are not exclusive but cumulative -- including all available remedies for breach of contract. Obviously, remedies that conflict -- specific performance and damages are not permitted -- but a suit based on fraud could include damages plus rescission and restitution.

V. Discharge of Contracts: Methods of Discharge

A. Discharge by Occurrence or Failure of a Condition.

B. Discharge by Performance or Breach of Contract.

C. Discharge by Agreement.

D. Discharge by Operation of the Law.

VI. Discharge by Condition -- A condition requires exact and complete performance and any failure or occurrence discharges a party from any liability. Failure to have exact and complete performance is a material breach. A promise of performance requires substantial performance of the contract to be completed. Only failure to have substantial performance constitutes a material breach. Unless a condition, performance is based on a promise.

A. Types of Conditions

1. **Precedent --** An event is required before a party has an absolute duty to perform.

Example:
Before a life insurance company is liable on a life insurance contract, the policyholder must pay a premium or pay for a binder. Thus, payment is a condition precedent to policy liability.

2. **Subsequent --** An event must take place after an absolute duty is imposed, to hold a party liable on the contract.

Example:
A fire policy has a provision, which requires after a loss that a proof of loss must be filed within sixty days after the fire in order for the policyholder to recover for the loss. The requirement of the filing of a proof of loss after the fire to receive payment for the fire loss covered by the policy is a condition subsequent.

3. **Concurrent --** Each party's absolute duty to perform is dependent upon the other party's absolute duty to perform at the same time.

Example:
A buyer of oranges promises to pay for the oranges only upon seller's delivery. Thus, the seller's duty to deliver is absolute only on buyer's tender or payment, and buyer's duty to tender or pay is absolute only upon seller's tender or delivery of the oranges.

B. **General Rules**

1. Unless specified, most contracts for performance are only construed as promises.

Example:
Specifications for the building of a house call for Kohler plumbing fixtures. The contractor installs American Standard, a comparable value fixture. Unless the contract payment was conditioned upon installation of only Kohler plumbing fixtures, the specification is a promise and the installation of a comparable fixture is substantial performance and not a material breach.

2. Contracts which require personal satisfaction - If a condition precedent, it requires the actual satisfaction or approval for discharge of the contract.

Example:
The President of the United States hires you as an artist to paint his or her official portrait to the personal satisfaction of the President. This is a condition and any real dissatisfaction causes a failure of the condition and no liability for the President.

Example:
Smith is hired to clean the lobby of an office building to the personal satisfaction of the building manager. This is merely a promise for satisfaction and a reasonable person test would be used to see if substantial performance had been achieved. If so, there is no material breach even if the building manager claims dissatisfaction.

VII. **Discharge by Performance -- General Rule**: A contract is automatically discharged when both parties fully perform. If a contract requires only a promise, substantial performance in good faith is a discharge, and the only recovery allowed the nonbreaching party is an allowance (if proven) between the value of full performance and the value of substantial performance. Any lack of total performance under a condition or lack of substantial performance under a promise is a material breach.

Example:
Able contracts to sell Baker his car for $2,000. Able delivers to Baker his car and Baker gives Able $2,000. Contract fully performed discharges both parties.

Example:
Able contracts to build Baker a house specifying (promise) Kohler plumbing fixtures. Able installs American Standard comparable in quality fixtures but totaling $300 less in price. Baker has an absolute duty to pay for the house. Able's promise was substantially performed but not fully performed. Baker may be able to deduct only $300 from the purchase price because Able is not in material breach.

A. **Material Breach** -- Any material breach in performance allows the nonbreaching party the full array of remedies available by law or contract and excuses the performance of the nonbreaching party and discharges the nonbreaching party's contract obligations.

B. **Anticipatory Breach** -- If either party repudiates a contract prior to the time of performance, the nonbreaching party may treat the repudiation as an anticipatory and immediate material breach. This permits a party to pursue remedies prior to the stated date for performance. [see UCC 2-610 and 2-611].

VIII. Discharge by Agreement or Party Action

A. **Release** -- A release is a discharge of a breaching party's obligations under a contract. It usually must be in writing, it must be secured or given voluntarily and in good faith, and it usually requires consideration.

B. **Waiver** -- A waiver by the nonbreaching party is a relinquishment of a right due to a party's breach. This is often binding without consideration [See UCC 1-107].

C. **Mutual Rescission** -- An enforceable mutual agreement to discharge all contract obligations and restore the parties to their pre-contract positions.

Example:
Able contracts with you to sell her accounting book for $70. Later, both of you change your mind about the sale and you both agree to cancel the contract. This is mutual rescission. Had you already paid the $70, upon mutual rescission Able must return to you the $70 paid.

D. **Novation** -- By a valid contract, a new party is substituted for one of the original parties thereby terminating (discharging) the original contract.

Example:
Son Able, on a loan from West Bank, will not be able to pay the debt when due. Able's mother, Sue, Able, and West Bank agree that if West Bank will release son Able, and provide for a thirty-day extension, Sue will pay the loan. This is a novation whereby Able is discharged (released) terminating the old contract, and creating a new contract by substituting Sue as the debtor.

E. **Accord and Satisfaction --** An agreement whereby the original contract can by satisfied by completion of either the original performance or by a different performance.

Example:
Green owes you $5,000 due on May 1. On April 20, Green tells you he is not sure he can pay you the $5,000 but, if not, offers to deed to you a lot Green owns. You agree (which is the accord). On May 1, Green can satisfy the debt by either paying you $5,000 or by transfer of the deed to the lot.

IX. **Discharge by Operation of the Law**

A. **Material Alteration --** The law automatically discharges an innocent party's obligations upon a material alteration by the other party.

B. **Statute of Limitations --** If a suit for breach of contract is not filed in a court of law or equity within a statutory period of time, the nonbreaching party is barred from pursuing a remedy. This effectively discharges the contract. The statutory periods of time vary from state to state and depends upon the type of contract. For the sale of goods, it is a four-year period from date of cause of action but this period can be reduced to one year by agreement . [See UCC 2-725]

C. **Bankruptcy Decree --** Most obligations of a bankrupt debtor can be fully discharged by a decree in bankruptcy.

D. **Objective Impossibility or Impracticability of Performance: Types:**

1. **Death or Insanity** of a person whose performance is essential to completion of a contract.

Example:
For $500, Able contracts with Sue to sing at her party on Friday. On Thursday, Able dies. This contract is objectively impossible to perform, discharging the contract.

2. **Destruction of the Specific Subject Matter** of the Contract is an automatic discharge of the contract.

Example:
Able contracts to sell you her boat "Flying Cloud." Before she can deliver the boat specified, the boat is destroyed through no fault of Able. This contract is automatically discharged at the time of destruction.

3. **Illegality** which now renders the contract illegal, discharges the contract automatically upon the change in the law.

Example:
You have a contract with Able to build an apartment complex on your lot. Before construction, but after the contract has been formed, laws are changed which only permit single residences to be built.

4. Contracts which become **Commercially Impractical** or there is a **Frustration of Purpose** are discharged. Here, the failed performance must meet the objective standard and not be merely more difficult to perform. Extreme difficulty or cost may meet the objective standard test.

Example:
Able rents the roof of a building to watch a circus parade with friends. At the last moment, the parade route is changed so that it does not pass where it can be viewed from the roof. This is a frustration of purpose.

Example:
Able contracts to move hazardous waste ten miles through a city to a hazardous waste site for $50 per load ($5 per mile). The city now prohibits hazardous waste to travel through the city. The only other safe route to the site is around a series of mountains for a distance of 300 miles. The costs to travel far exceed the contracted price per load. This contract would probably now be rendered commercially impractical.

Contracts Review Question

This comprehensive review question test the following areas of contract law: 1. Offer, acceptance, and revocation, 2. Statute of Frauds, 3. Breach, 4. Rescission, 5. Assignment

I. Background

A. On January 15, East Corp. orally offered to hire Bean, CPA, to perform management consulting services for East and its subsidiaries. The offer provided for a 3-year contract at $10,000 per month.

B. On January 20, East sent Bean a signed memorandum stating the terms of the offer. The memorandum also included a payment clause that had not been discussed and the provision that Bean's acceptance of the offer would not be effective unless it was received by East on or before January 25.

C. Bean received the memorandum on January 21, signed it, and mailed it back to East the same day. East received it on January 24. On January 23, East wrote to Bean revoking the offer. Bean received the revocation on January 25. On March 1, East Corp. orally engaged Snow Consultants to install a corporate local area network (LAN) system for East's financial operations. The engagement was to last until the following February 15, and East would pay Snow $5,000 twice per month.

D. On March 15, East offered Snow $1,000 per month to assist in the design of East's Internet home page. Snow accepted East's offer. On April 1, citing excess work, Snow advised East that Snow would not assist with the design of the home page. On April 5, East accepted Snow's withdrawal from the Internet home page design project. On April 15, Snow notified East that Snow had assigned the fees due Snow on the LAN installation engagement to Band Computer Consultants. On April 30, East notified Snow that the LAN installation agreement was canceled.

II. East Corp. and Bean

A. The following 5 questions are based on the transaction between East Corp. and Bean. For each item, select the best answer from List I. An answer may be selected once, more than once, or not at all.

B. List I

1. Acceptance of a counteroffer.
2. Acceptance of an offer governed by the mailbox rule.
3. Attempted acceptance of an offer.
4. Attempted revocation of an offer.
5. Formation of an enforceable contract.
6. Formation of a contract enforceable only against East.
7. Invalid revocation because of prior acceptance of an offer.
8. Offer revoked by sending a revocation letter.
9. Submission of a counteroffer.
10. Submission of a written offer.

C. Questions

1. What was the effect of the event(s) that took place on January 20?

    a. The memorandum that East sent Bean was a submission of a written offer. The oral offer from East Corp. to Bean was not enforceable because an agreement that cannot be performed within 1 year must be in writing to be enforceable according to the statute of frauds.

2. What was the effect of the event(s) that took place on January 21?

    a. Bean attempted an acceptance of the offer on January 21 by signing and mailing the memorandum. This action did not form an enforceable contract because the terms of the offer stated that acceptance would not be effective until received by East on or before January 25.

3. What was the effect of the event(s) that took place on January 23?

    a. East attempted to revoke the offer on January 23. Revocation is effective when it is received by the offeree prior to acceptance. By January 25, a valid acceptance had already occurred.

4. What was the effect of the event(s) that took place on January 24?

    a. An enforceable contract was formed on January 24 according to the stated terms of the offer made by East in the memorandum. The offeror received the valid acceptance 1 day before the offeree received the attempted revocation.

5. What was the effect of the event(s) that took place on January 25?

    a. The revocation received on January 25 was invalid because an enforceable contract had already been formed the day before.

III. East Corp. and Snow Consultants

A. The following 3 questions are based on the transaction between East Corp. and Snow Consultants. For each item, select the best answer from List II. An answer may be selected once, more than once, or not at all.

B. List II

1. Breach of contract.
2. Discharge from performance.
3. Enforceable oral contract modification.
4. Formation of a voidable contract.
5. Formation of an enforceable contract.
6. Formation of a contract unenforceable under the statute of frauds.
7. Invalid assignment.
8. Mutual rescission.
9. Novation.
10. Unilateral offer.
11. Valid assignment of rights.
12. Valid assignment of duties.
13. Valid assignment of rights and duties.

C. Questions

1. What was the effect of the event(s) that took place on March 1?

   a. Oral contracts are usually enforceable unless they are within the Statute of Frauds. A services contract is not within the Statute of Frauds if it can be completed within a year of entering into the contract. The oral contract between East and Snow is enforceable because it was entered into on March 1 and will be completed by February 15 of the following year.

2. What was the effect of the event(s) that took place on March 15?

   a. The contract entered into on March 15 by East and Snow is enforceable because it had all of the following requirements of a contract: offer and acceptance, mutual assent, consideration, legality, and capacity of parties.

3. What was the effect of the event(s) that took place on April 5?

   a. The parties to a contract may, by agreement, end it without performance or alter their performance obligations. Mutual rescission occurs when the parties to an executory bilateral contract agree to cancel it. They are restored to their original positions. The agreement to rescind is itself a contract. The mutual surrender of rights constitutes the consideration necessary for, and the performance of, the contract of rescission.

Debtor-Creditor Relationships

Rights, Duties, and Liabilities of Debtors and Creditors

Secured Parties/Lien Holders and Other Collection Methods

This area is divided into three parts. They are possessory liens (bailee liens, artisan liens, and pledges); nonpossessory liens (secured transactions, real estate mortgages, mechanic's liens -- note that secured transactions are detailed in the section under the Uniform Commercial Code, and real estate mortgages are detailed in the section on Property); and judicial liens (writ of attachment, writ of execution, and garnishment). Of all these, for this section, the most important for the exam are artisan's lien, mechanic's lien, writ of attachment, writ of execution, and garnishment.

I. Possessory Liens - Common Law

Definitions:
Bailee's Lien: a bailee, such as a warehouse company, a common carrier, an innkeeper, etc. has a right to compensation (by contract) or reimbursement (expenses incurred in the keeping of the bailed property). To enforce this right of payment from the bailor, the bailee has a lien on the bailed property and can sell the property to satisfy the lien.

Artisan's Lien: (sometimes referred to as a worker's lien) - a contract bailee who improves or repairs bailed property to increase its value. Failure of bailor to pay as contracted allows the bailee to place a possessory lien on the bailed property and the bailee, with proper notice, can sell the property to satisfy the lien.

A. Important Rules:

1. To **create either lien** the bailee creditor must
   a. **not have agreed to extend credit** (cash only), and
   b. **not voluntarily give possession back to the bailor** (does not cover temporary possession such as allowing an owner to test drive a car after an engine overhaul).

Example:
Mary takes her car to Jim's Auto Shop to have some major repairs. A sign and a notice above her signature authorizing the repairs states clearly "All Repairs Are For Cash Payment." Mary authorizes Jim to repair the car. When she comes to pick up her repaired car, she does not have sufficient cash to pay the $900 repair bill as estimated. Jim refuses to give Mary her car until she tenders $900 cash. Jim has met both criteria above to create an artisan's lien on the car and, following any statutory procedure, may sell the car, deducting from the proceeds the cost of sale, costs suffered due to default, and the $900. Any balance will be turned over to Mary.

   c. In most states, an artisan's lien has priority over a previously perfected statutorily filed lien (such as a filed UCC-1 financing statement under Article 9). There is a conflict, however, as to whether a bailee's lien (such as a storage company lien) has priority.

Example:
Farmer John, to purchase a tractor, signed a security agreement with West Bank putting up the tractor as security for the loan. West Bank has properly perfected its security interest by filing a UCC-1. Later, Farmer John takes the tractor to I.M. Implement and has some engine repairs made. All repairs are for cash. Farmer John, having fallen on hard times, cannot pay cash and is in default to West Bank. In this case, even though West Bank's lien is first in time, it is a filed lien and I.M. Implement's artisan's lien, being a possessory lien, has priority over West Bank's perfected secured interest. I.M. Implement can "foreclose on its lien," and from the proceeds satisfy all of its costs and repair charges before West Bank has any entitlement.

Definition:
Pledge: a bailment of personal property by a pledgor (owner and debtor) as security for the performance of an obligation (a debt to be repaid) to a pledgee (creditor) whereupon, if the pledgor fails to repay the obligation within a specific period of time, the pledgee can either keep or sell the pledged property in full satisfaction of the obligation (treated lightly on CPA exam under Secured Transactions).

B. Important Rules:

1. To create, you need a delivery (actual or symbolic) with intent to create a security interest.
2. Any increase in value or profits derived from the pledged property can be retained by the pledgee as further security, except cash (must be returned to pledgor or pledgee to reduce the debt). Particularly important when stock is pledged. If pledgee registers the stock in its name held in trust for pledgor, then stock dividends and stock splits can be kept by pledgee as additional security but cash dividends must be turned over to the pledgor or used to reduce the debt.

II. Nonpossessory Liens - Filed Liens

A. Secured Transactions -- See material under Secured Transactions

B. Real Estate Mortgages -- See material under Property

C. Mechanic's Lien -- (sometimes referred to as a materialman's lien) is a statutorily filed lien by a creditor who has rendered services, labor, or material to repair or improve real estate and the creditor has not been paid.

1. **Important Rules**
   - **a.** To create a mechanic's lien, the person furnishing the labor or materials must file the lien, usually within 60-120 days of the last date the services or materials were furnished.
   - **b.** The creditor can be
     - **i.** a materials supply store (like a lumber yard, plumbing supply store, etc.),
     - **ii.** a subcontractor,
     - **iii.** a general contractor,
     - **iv.** or any employee of either of the latter two.

c. The lien is upon the entire realty and if the homeowner doesn't pay the lien can be foreclosed (same as a real estate mortgage).

d. In most states, the mechanic's lien and real estate mortgage have equal dignity, thus one does not have priority over the other.

e. Upon foreclosure, only surplus goes to the former owner.

Example:
Sue has owned her home for twenty-five years. She contracts with Joe's Remodeling to completely remodel the guest bathroom in the house. Joe's Remodeling contracts with Ace Plumbing Fixtures for the purchase of a new bathtub, which is installed by John Pool, a sole proprietorship plumber. Upon completion of the remodeling, Sue pays fully Joe's Remodeling. Joe's Remodeling did not pay either Ace Plumbing Fixtures or John Pool. In this situation, either or both (if they have properly filed) have a lien on Sue's house and can foreclose (have the house sold) to satisfy their claims.

III. Judicial Liens - Court-ordered Liens -- Remember, a prior perfected secured party has priority over a judicial lien creditor.

A. Attachment -- an action by a creditor for a court-ordered seizure for the taking into custody the debtor's nonexempt property **prior** to the creditor getting a judgment.

1. Important Rules

a. Usually only available if a creditor has a reasonable belief the debtor will hide, dispose, or remove nonexempt property from the jurisdiction of a court.

b. Must be done in strict compliance with statutory procedures or creditor can be liable for the tort of wrongful attachment (conversion). Procedures include filing of an affidavit as to debtor's default, legal reason for attachment, and posting of a bond.

Example:
Farmer Smith has an installment loan with West Bank and has missed four monthly payments. West Bank has notified Smith in writing that he is in default and, by the terms of the loan, it has accelerated the note and loan so that the total amount owed is due. Smith has refused to discuss the matter despite West Bank's encouragement to see if the default could not be resolved. West Bank now learns from a neighbor that by the weekend Smith intends to move all nonexempt farm machinery etc. into another state. West Bank cannot get a judgment by the weekend. Here, West Bank could proceed by attachment to take into custody by court order Smith's nonexempt property and hold such pending the securing of a judgment.

B. Writ of Execution -- after receiving an unsatisfied judgment, a creditor can seek from the court a writ to levy (possess and sell) on nonexempt property of the debtor. The order usually directs the sheriff or an official of the court to seize and sell the nonexempt property.

Note:
Misconception: The term "judgment proof" is a misnomer. With a proper claim, the plaintiff can almost always get a judgment. The problem is collecting the amount of the judgment. Many believe this is easy if the debtor has assets. The problem is that frequently many of the assets of individuals are exempt from collection of a judgment. Assets such as homesteads, cars, household furniture and appliances, farm animals, cemetery plots, clothing, books, and even tools of one's trade are exempt and not subject to a writ of execution. Thus, instead of being "judgment proof," it might be a better to use the term "execution proof."

Note:
Misconception: Bank accounts of the debtor cannot be garnished because they are not wages. This is incorrect because a bank account is the bank's obligation to pay to the depositor (debtor) the amount of money in the account. This is a debt the bank owes to the debtor, which permits the garnishor creditor to garnish (order the garnishee bank) the account (money the bank owes the creditor).

C. Garnishment -- a court order requiring third parties (garnishee) to deliver a debtor's property held in their possession, or to pay debts they owe to the debtor to the creditor to satisfy a debt or judgment.

1. Important Rules

a. Usually a post-judgment remedy, but can be a prejudgment remedy after a hearing.

b. Property typically garnished include:

i. Bank accounts

ii. Wages - usually limited by Federal or state law to 25% of take-home pay. (Only two states prohibit garnishment of wages, except for child support.) Employer must pay to the court 25% and 75% to the debtor-employee. Some states permit continuous garnishments -- that is, one court order covers all wages owed by a particular employer without the creditor having to file for each period the wage is paid.

c. Cannot garnish such payments as Social Security, and employers cannot fire an employee because of garnishment.

IV. Other Creditor Collection Methods -- There are other things creditors can do to resolve the debt before the debtor seeks relief through bankruptcy. Three of the most important of these involve a composition of creditors' agreement (a contract between the debtor and his or her creditors); an assignment by the debtor of assets to a third party to sell and distribute the proceeds among creditors -- called an assignment for the benefit of creditors; and situations where a creditor can set aside a fraudulent conveyance made by the debtor.

A. Composition of Creditor's Agreements -- A contract between the debtor and his or her creditors whereby the creditors agree to discharge the debtor's debts upon a payment (usually a lesser sum).

1. IMPORTANT RULES

a. Creditors who do not contract are not bound by the composition agreement. (The advantage, however, of composition agreements is an immediate payment and it avoids costs and delay of bankruptcy proceedings; plus, many times the payments made exceed those a creditor would receive through bankruptcy.)

B. Setting Aside Fraudulent Conveyances -- Transfers by a debtor of property to a third party by gift or contract, which are done to defraud creditors, can be set aside. Title reverts back to the debtor subject to remedies of the creditors. There are two types of fraud.

1. Fraud in Fact -- Debtor transfers property with the specific intent to defraud.

Example:
Creditor Smith is about to get a judgment against debtor Jones, whose major nonexempt asset is a boat. Just before the judgment is issued, Jones transfers the boat by gift to his ten-year-old son. This transfer is made strictly with the intent to deny Smith a writ to levy execution on Jones's boat, thus to defraud Smith. Smith can have title of the boat to the son set aside and then secure a writ of execution and levy on the boat.

2. **Fraud in Law --** Due to the circumstances, there is a presumption of fraud, which can be rebutted.

Example:
Creditor Smith is seeking repayment of a loan from debtor Jones. About a month before Smith files an action to get a judgment for the debt owed, Jones sells his boat (nonexempt property) to his neighbor (a nonmerchant) Evans at a price of about 60% of its market value. The neighbor takes title to the boat but allows Jones to keep and use the boat. Smith now gets a judgment and wants to set aside the sale of the boat so that she can get a writ of execution and levy on the boat. To prove fraud in fact would be difficult, but the circumstances of a greatly reduced price and allowing Jones to retain possession and use of the boat allow Smith to claim fraud in law. This creates proof of a presumption of fraud, and shifts the burden of proof (no fraud) to Jones and Evans.

C. **Assignment for the Benefit of Creditors --** Involves generally an insolvent debtor who voluntarily transfers certain of his or her assets to a trustee or assignee who is to liquidate the assets and tender to each creditor on a pro-rata basis a payment in satisfaction of that debt.

1. **Important Rules**

   a. The amount of property turned over to the trustee or assignee, and thus pro-rata share is entirely at the discretion of the debtor.

   b. Creditors can accept or reject amount tendered.

      i. Referred as a "cram-down" or "take-it-or-leave-it" choice of the creditor.

      ii. Acceptance by the creditor is a complete discharge of the debt.

      iii. Rejection eliminates a creditor's right to the property assigned, but creditor can

         1. go after nonexempt property not assigned.

         2. receive surplus, if any, after participating creditors have been paid.

         3. petition debtor into involuntary bankruptcy

Example:
Debtor Smith has come upon difficult financial times and has not found his twenty (20) creditors willing to accept a lesser sum in a creditors' composition agreement. Smith's debts amount to $100,000. Smith turns over to a trustee (Jones) $20,000 worth of property, and instructs Jones (for a fee) to sell the property and pro rate the proceeds among his twenty creditors. Jones sells the property and then on a pro-rata basis offers each creditor a sum. Creditors who accept the lesser sum discharge their debt. If all creditors accepted the sums offered by Smith, the entire $100,000 in debt is discharged. If none of the creditors accepted or only some, Smith could petition himself into bankruptcy.

Note:
Retention of possession by a **merchant debtor** after a sale to a buyer is not evidence of fraud in law.

Guarantees and Strict Suretyship

Definitions, Rights, Duties, and Liabilities of Creditors and Guarantors

A legal relationship in which a person called a surety or a guarantor and another called a principal debtor are obligated to perform on the same obligation to a person called a creditor, and the surety or guarantor can recover from the principal debtor for any performance the surety or guarantor gives to the creditor. A definition can tell you a great deal about the law concerning a subject, such as this one, which covers both a suretyship and a guaranty. The most common type of guaranty is an absolute guaranty. There are others, and once you know the classification type, you will know a great deal about the liability of the guarantor. Only guaranty contracts (see Contracts Section) come under the Statute of Frauds requiring a signed writing or main purpose doctrine exception for the contract to be enforceable. Strict suretyship contracts with a creditor are enforceable even if orally made because these contracts do not come under the Statute of Frauds.

I. **Definition --** Simply - for a loan of money from a creditor in a guaranty or suretyship relationship, the following takes place:

   A. The money from the creditor goes to the principal debtor.

      1. The surety or guarantor is liable to the creditor in a strict suretyship at time debt is due because the surety is primarily liable and, in a guaranty, usually only upon principal debtor's default because the guarantor is secondarily liable.

      2. Any payments the surety or guarantor make to the creditor can be legally recovered (reimbursed) from the principal debtor.

II. **Types of Guarantees**

Definitions:
Absolute Guaranty: There are no conditions for guarantor's liability to a creditor and the guarantor is liable upon the principal debtor's default (most common type).

Conditional Guaranty: A guarantor is liable only upon the principal debtor's default and one or more conditions for liability having been met. A "guaranty of collection" is a conditional guaranty.

Example:
The guaranty contract with the creditor states that the guarantor is only liable upon debtor's default and the creditor securing an unsatisfied judgment against the principal debtor. This condition requires the creditor to ascertain the principal debtor's default, file a suit, and receive a judgment, which cannot be satisfied out of the principal debtor's nonexempt assets before the guarantor can be held liable.

Definition:
Continuing Guaranty: A guaranty which extends to a series of debt transactions.

Example:
Sue, a land developer, wants to be able to make numerous contracts to develop a ninety-acre tract of land. West Bank agrees to guaranty all contract payments Sue will be required to make to a variety of contractors. This is a continuing guaranty.

Definition:
Limited or Unlimited Guaranty: The guarantor's liability can be limited in amount guaranteed and/or duration (time period), or the guarantor's liability can be unlimited as to amount and/or time.

Example:
Sue seeks a five-year $100,000 loan from West Bank. Sue has in her possession approximately $50,000 in nonexempt assets. West Bank will not make the loan unless the loan is guaranteed by Sue's father. Sue's father contracts with West Bank to guaranty the loan for only the first four years of the loan and only for the amount of $70,000. This is a limited guaranty. If Sue's father had agreed to an unlimited guaranty, Sue and West Bank could later contract to extend the loan period and raise the debt level without Sue's father's consent.

Definitions:
General Guaranty: A guaranty in which the guarantor is liable to anyone (the public) who knows of and contracts with the principal debtor in reliance on the guaranty -- such as a letter of credit.

Special Guaranty: A guaranty limited to a particular person or persons who deal(s) with the principal debtor.

III. Statute of Frauds

A. If the guaranty is made by an **express contract with the creditor** making the **guarantor secondarily liable**, the guaranty contract must be **in writing** and **signed by the guarantor** (or a written memo) for it **to be enforceable against the guarantor**. The only **exception** is if the **"main purpose"** or **"leading object"** doctrine can be applied -- that is, that the **guarantor will benefit financially or economically, then an oral guaranty is enforceable**.

Example:
Smith is a commission sales agent. Smith makes her salary from the commissions she receives for each sale. Peters, her boss, will only let Smith and other commission agents sell to buyers for cash. Smith goes to Peters and orally contracts that she be allowed to sell to customers on credit and, should any customer not pay Peters, she would. Note, this is a guaranty contract (express contract) made between Peters (creditor) and Smith (guarantor) whereby Smith has agreed to pay Peters for a customer's debt only if the customer is in default (secondary liability). Ordinarily, this express contract must be in writing to be enforceable, but here the "main purpose" of Smith's guaranty is to benefit Smith financially. Thus, the oral contract is enforceable.

IV. **Rights of the Creditor and Surety or Guarantor --** Generally, upon a principal debtor's default, the creditor has a choice to proceed against the principal debtor, the guarantor, or the collateral of the debtor. There are basically four rights of the Surety or Guarantor: the equitable right of exoneration, the right of the surety or guarantor to be reimbursed or indemnified by the principal debtor, the right of subrogation, and among co-sureties the right of contribution. Be sure to know the right of contribution.

A. **Rights of the Creditor**

1. Proceed against the principal debtor personally and/or the debtor's nonexempt property. If creditor receives a payment and debtor owes more than one debt to the creditor of which only some of these are guaranteed, the law is the creditor must apply the payment to the debt as directed by the debtor, but if no direction is given, creditor has choice.

Example:
Daniel owes two debts to Carl, one for $500, and another for $1,000. The $1,000 debt is guaranteed by Gloria. If Daniel makes a $500 payment to Carl and does not designate to which debt the payment should be applied, Carl has the choice and can extinguish the $500 debt over Gloria's objection.

2. Proceed against the guarantor personally according to the guaranty contract. Can even reduce the claim to judgment and by writ of execution go after the guarantor's nonexempt assets.

3. Proceed against collateral of the debtor held either by the creditor or the guarantor. Creditor can sell the collateral to satisfy the debt and default costs and any balance must be turned over to the principal debtor. Upon payment by the principal debtor, any collateral subject to the debt must be returned to the principal debtor.

Note:
If the collateral is in possession of the guarantor, even before principal debtor's default, creditor can, through an equity action, require the guarantor to preserve the value of the collateral.

B. **Rights of the Surety or Guarantor**

1. **Exoneration --** this is a right rarely granted. It is an equitable right, which permits the guarantor to petition the court to order the creditor by court decree to exhaust recovery against the principal debtor before holding the guarantor liable. If the principal debtor has a defense against the creditor, there is no right of exoneration.

Example:
Phillip is in default on a guaranteed loan made by West Bank. Phillip has numerous nonexempt assets but these are located in another state. Evans, the guarantor, presently has most of her assets tied up (such as long-term CDs) to the extent that if she is required to pay now she will suffer severe financial losses. Under these circumstances, Evans could petition a court of equity for exoneration, which the court may grant.

2. **Reimbursement and Indemnity** -- Applies whenever the guarantor has fully or partially fulfilled the debtor's obligation to the creditor. Upon payment to the creditor, the guarantor has a right to seek reimbursement from the principal debtor.
    a. Right is contractual if guarantor became a guarantor at request of the principal debtor.
    b. Right is based on quasi-contract theory of recovery if guarantor was not requested by the principal debtor.
    c. Right of reimbursement covers all costs guarantor has incurred because of guaranty.
    d. If principal debtor has a defense against paying the creditor, the guarantor's right of reimbursement is correspondingly reduced.

Example:
Principal debtor is a minor on a guaranteed loan made by West Bank. The principal debtor disaffirms the loan contract debt claiming the defense of minority. West Bank then collects from the guarantor because a principal debtor's defense of minority is not a defense available to the guarantor. The guarantor, however, has no right of reimbursement from the principal debtor.

3. **Subrogation** -- Generally, assists the guarantor's right of reimbursement upon the guarantor's payment to the creditor. Upon payment, the guarantor succeeds to any rights the creditor has (stands in the shoes of the creditor). These include:
    a. Creditor's rights against the principal debtor, including right to file a claim in bankruptcy.
    b. Creditor's rights to the principal debtor's collateral held by the creditor or the guarantor.
    c. Creditor's rights against third parties; for example, those who damage the principal debtor's collateral held by the creditor.
    d. Creditor's rights against a co-surety.

Example:
Evans has guaranteed a loan made to Phillips by West Bank. West Bank has in its possession collateral owned by Phillips of which some has been damaged due to the negligence of a third party, Green. Phillips files for bankruptcy and the bankruptcy court, upon West Bank's petition, allows West Bank to collect from Evans.

Question: What are Evans's rights in this situation?

Answer: Evans has the right of subrogation. This allows Evans to file West Bank's creditor's claim against Phillips's bankruptcy estate, to sue Green for damage to the collateral due to Green's negligence, and to take possession of any remaining collateral held by West Bank.

4. **Right of Contribution --** Applies when two or more sureties or guarantors are liable on the same obligation to the same creditor and upon debtor's default one co-surety pays more than his or her proportional share of the obligation. Entitles this co-surety to recover from the other co-surety the amount paid above his or her share owed.
   a. **Generally --** Co-sureties are jointly and severally liable. They can become co-sureties by contract, can be bound as co-sureties for different amounts, and can become co-sureties even without knowledge of each other's existence.
   b. **Release of Co-surety --** If the creditor releases a co-surety without the other co-sureties' consent (or reserving rights in the release in the remaining co-sureties), the remaining co-sureties' liability is released to the extent that the right of contribution cannot be obtained.
   c. **Reimbursement --** If a co-surety is fully reimbursed, there is no right of contribution.
   d. **Collateral --** In absence of agreement, co-sureties are entitled to share in proportion to their liability a debtor's collateral in the hands of the creditor or acquired by a surety after the co-suretyship relationship was created.
   e. **Amount --** If co-sureties become such by contract or consent, their agreement on amount of contribution is binding. In absence of agreement, contribution is determined by a ratio of the proportionate maximum liability of each co-surety.

Formula:

$$\frac{\text{Max Liability of Co-Surety}}{\text{Total Max.Liability of All Co-Surety}} \times \text{Amount Paid by Co-Surety Seeking Contribution} = \text{Amount of Contribution Entitlement}$$

Example:
Able, Baker, and Carl are co-sureties on a $50,000 debt owed by Daniel. Able's maximum liability is $10,000, Baker's $16,000, and Carl's $24,000. Daniel is in default and still owes $40,000. The creditor collects the full amount from Carl and Carl seeks rights of contribution from Able and Baker. Carl has these rights because Carl has paid more than his proportionate share. Using the formula above:

Able: $10,000/$50,000 x $40,000 = $8,000

Baker: $16,000/$50,000 x $40,000 = $12,800

which means Carl's proportionate share owed is:

$24,000/$50,000 x $40,000 = $19,200

Defenses of the Guarantor

The general rule is that any defense available to the principal debtor, except the principal debtor's incapacity, bankruptcy, or statute of limitations, is also available to the guarantor. In addition, the guarantor has his or her own personal defenses. Most important are defenses available to a guarantor due to something the creditor has done. Divide these creditor acts into those that create a complete discharge of guarantor liability and those acts that serve mainly to discharge the guarantor only to the extent the guarantor suffers a loss. This section is important.

I. **General Rules --** Defenses derived from the principal debtor - such as a creditor's fraud, duress, failure of consideration, or breach of loan contract upon the principal debtor, are defenses available to the guarantor against the guarantor having liability to the creditor.

Example:
Creditor, by fraud, induces a principal debtor to incur a large debt guaranteed by Jones for the purchase of land from the creditor, which later proves to be worthless. The principal debtor can avoid the loan due to the creditor's fraud. Jones also can avoid his/her guaranty because of the creditor's fraud on the principal debtor.

A. **Exceptions**

1. the principal debtor's incapacity,
2. the principal debtor's bankruptcy,
3. the Statute of Limitations running out on the principal debtor's debt.

Example:
Daniel is the minor son of Emily and Emily is the guarantor of a loan West Bank made to Daniel. Daniel, being a minor, has legally disaffirmed his liability on the loan. Although West Bank cannot hold Daniel liable, Emily cannot escape her guaranty liability by claiming her son's minority as a defense.

II. **Defenses of the Guarantor**

A. Guarantor's incapacity - note, that in some states a minor does not have capacity to contract as a guarantor.

B. Guarantor's discharge decree in bankruptcy.

C. Statute of Limitation runs out on guarantor's obligation - period begins on date guarantor becomes liable for principal debtor's debt.

III. **Guarantor Defenses Due to Actions by the Creditor**

A. **Release --** Release of the principal debtor without the guarantor's consent is also a release from liability of the guarantor. Collateral of the principal debtor held by either the creditor or the guarantor can still be used by the creditor to satisfy the debt.

> **Note:**
> If the creditor, in the release to the principal debtor, reserved rights against the guarantor, this is no longer a release but a covenant not to sue, which does not discharge the guarantor from liability.

B. **Refusal of Principal Debtor's Tender --** If the principal debtor tenders payment to the creditor under a guaranty contract, and the creditor refuses the proper tender, the guarantor is completely discharged from liability.

Example:
Peter has a loan from West Bank fully guaranteed by Susan. Peter sends to West Bank a check for the full amount of the debt, which includes interest. Peter has on deposit more than sufficient funds to cover the check. The check clearly states that payment is in full accord and satisfaction of the loan. A bank officer, by mistake, believes that the amount of the check is insufficient to cover both the principal and interest owed and sends back the check to Peter. Since this was a proper tender, under these circumstances, Susan is discharged from her guaranty liability and only Peter remains liable to West Bank.

> **Note:**
> The principal debtor is not discharged, but principal debtor is not liable for future interest or other charges.

C. **Material Alteration by Creditor --** Any material alteration of the written loan or guaranty contract by the creditor such as amount of debt, time for payment, etc. is a complete discharge of the guarantor's liability.

> **Note:**
> Alteration is the sole act of the creditor. Modification, discussed later, is an agreement between the principal debtor and the creditor.

D. **Failure to Disclose --** A creditor's failure to disclose material facts, which affect the risks of liability to a prospective guarantor in most states is presumed fraud and permits the guarantor to disaffirm the guaranty contract (complete discharge of liability).

Example:
Peter seeks a loan from West Bank. After a careful credit analysis, West Bank denies the loan because of two factors that West Bank feels would make the loan too risky to make. The next day, Peter comes to West Bank with a prospective guarantor, Gloria, a wealthy customer of West Bank. Gloria tells West Bank that if it will make the loan to Peter, she would sign a guaranty contract. In this case, if West Bank is willing to make the loan with Gloria's guaranty, West Bank must tell Gloria of the material risk factors, which caused it to deny the loan. Failure to do so is presumed fraud and this allows Gloria, at any time, to disaffirm her guaranty liability. Note: to avoid a violation of privacy, West Bank must have Peter's permission for disclosure.

E. **Modification of the Loan Contract --** A material and binding modification of the loan contract made between the principal debtor and the creditor without the consent of the guarantor in most states:

1. If the guarantor is gratuitous, the guarantor's liability is completely discharged.
2. If the guarantor is compensated (receives financial or economic benefit), the guarantor's liability is only discharged to the extent of loss suffered by the guarantor due to the modification.

Example:
Gloria is the mother of Phillip and she has guaranteed a loan West Bank has made to Phillip. Later, Phillip and West Bank, without Gloria's consent, raise the amount of the loan interest rate and extend the loan period. This is a binding (with consideration) and material modification of the loan contract. Since Gloria is a gratuitous (noncompensated) guarantor, this modification completely discharged her guaranty liability.

Example:
Phillips wants a loan to start a restaurant. West Bank will not make the loan to Phillips unless she can secure a satisfactory guarantor. Evans, a financial entrepreneur, agrees with Phillips to be a guarantor if Phillips will turn over to Evans 5% of all gross proceeds for three years. Phillips agrees and the guaranteed loan contract is made with West Bank. Later, Phillips and West Bank make a material, binding modification of the loan without Evans' consent. Upon Phillips default, because Evans is a compensated guarantor, Evans can only escape guaranty liability to the extent of loss Evans can prove he suffered due to the modification.

F. **Surrender or Impairment of Debtor's Collateral --** If the creditor surrenders the debtor's collateral held in the creditor's possession without the consent of the guarantor or commits acts that impair the value of the collateral, the guarantor is discharged to the extent of loss suffered by the guarantor due to the surrender or impairment.

Example:
West Bank made a $100,000 loan to Phillip with Phillip transferring to West Bank 5,000 shares of stock (value $25,000) and having Evans as guarantor. Later, without Evans consent, West Bank releases back to Phillip the 5,000 shares. Upon Philip's default, Evans' guaranty liability on the $100,000 guaranty will be reduced by the value of the shares released to Phillip.

G. **Guaranty of Collections --** Any failure of the creditor to give the guarantor proper notice of the principal debtor's default, or any material delay in attempting to collect first from the principal debtor, discharges the guarantor from liability to the extent of loss suffered by such failure.

Bankruptcy

Introduction to Bankruptcies and Commencement

Bankruptcy is governed by federal law and administered by Bankruptcy Courts. There are five types of bankruptcy. You should know all five, whether a debtor can choose a particular chapter, and whether the debtor can be involuntarily petitioned into bankruptcy under a given chapter. Who can file and under what circumstances a debtor can be petitioned into bankruptcy is very important. Chapter 7 is not available to all debtors.

I. **Author's Advice for Studying Bankruptcy --** The text is detailed and the law on Bankruptcy is complicated. Add to this the fact that the percentage of the value of the subject has been reduced substantially but the content coverage has not been reduced and even expanded with the enactment of the 2005 Bankruptcy Act, and you have a dilemma. That dilemma is how much time should I spend on detail when there will only be a few questions on the exam.

II. **Here are some suggestions --** prefaced by the fact that the text is detailed for those who want or need some in-depth knowledge. Even limiting your study for the test to the basics under the 12 recommendations below is a lot to chew. Good luck.

   A. Do Not memorize numerical amounts in the text. You will never remember them and these will change every three years. If you feel you need to know a few of the numerical amounts, I suggest the following:

      1. The amount of the debt required for the filing of an involuntary Chapter 7 petition,

      2. The monetary limits for the filing of Chapter 12 and Chapter 13 petitions, and

      3. The maximum debt for employee-owed wages and benefits for priority of payment.

   B. Know the five (5) different petition filing Chapters - 7, 9, 11, 12, & 13 and who cannot file under each.

   C. Under the 2005 Bankruptcy Reform Act, be sure to understand what is "means testing," when abuse of Chapter 7 is presumed, the effect if there is abuse, and the requirement of credit counseling.

   D. Generally, what is a debtor required to file beside the petition to commence the bankruptcy proceedings.

   E. What basically constitutes the debtor's estate, including gifts etc., acquired after petition is filed.

   F. Generally, know what the federal exemptions are, and if the debtor elects the state exemptions, what the limitation is on the homestead equity amount.

   G. What constitutes a preference for trustee avoidance of the transfer.

   H. Know a summary of the order of priorities among creditors. Note, on unsecured creditors, that the top priority is domestic support obligations and tax claims are low priority.

   I. What debtors or debts will not be discharged. For example, partnerships and corporations cannot get a Chapter 7 discharge; only one Chapter 7 discharge every eight years; no discharge for domestic support obligations; student loans; and generally due to conduct of the debtor.

Note:
The law on bankruptcy will be constantly changing. There are a number of reasons. First, the 1994 amendments to the Bankruptcy Act created a Bankruptcy Review Commission of nine members to review and make recommendations for possible yearly legislative reform. Recent recommendations have resulted in passage of the Bankruptcy Abuse Prevention and Consumer Protection Act of 2005 (referred to as the Bankruptcy Reform Act of 2005). Second, beginning on April 1, 1998 and every three years thereafter, almost all dollar amounts will be adjusted automatically to reflect the Consumer Price Index rounded off to the nearest $25. The following text has the April 1, 2007 adjustment figures and the Bankruptcy Reform Act of 2005.

Note:
MISCONCEPTION:
Persons with substantial assets cannot file a petition into bankruptcy if their liabilities are less than their assets. This statement is incorrect. There are numerous reasons why debtors file for bankruptcy to discharge debt. For example, corporations who have substantial assets and are making a profit may file a Chapter 11 bankruptcy because of a number of lawsuits filed against it.

J. Requirements of reaffirmations.

K. The essentials for filing and proceeding under a Chapter 11 Bankruptcy.

L. Chapter 12 and Chapter 13 essentials for filing (note the inclusion of a Family Fisherman under Chapter 12) and the filing of a three-five payment plan.

III. IMPORTANT - See Note.

IV. Generally

A. Bankruptcy is governed by **federal law**. It began with the Bankruptcy Act of 1898, with major amendments with the Bankruptcy Reform Act (effective in 1979) and with amendments principally in 1984, 1986, 1994, and 2005.

B. **Administration** of bankruptcy proceedings is by **Bankruptcy Courts**, adjuncts of the U.S. District Courts. A Bankruptcy Court is basically an **administrative court** with judges appointed for fourteen-year terms.

C. A **debtor** does **not** have **to be insolvent** (liabilities exceed assets) in order to petition himself or herself into **any chapter (except Chapter 9)** in bankruptcy.

V. Types of Bankruptcy (Very Important)

A. There are **five** types.

1. **Chapter 7 --** Referred to as **"straight bankruptcy"** or **Liquidation**
   - a. Permits **voluntary and involuntary petitions.**
2. **Chapter 9 --** Allows for **Adjustment of Debts of a Municipality** -- a rehabilitation of municipalities, defined as any political subdivision, public agency, or instrumentality (includes any taxing unit) of a State.
   - a. Permits **voluntary petitions** by the municipality.
3. **Chapter 11 --** Allows for a **Reorganization** of a debtor to pay debts -- a rehabilitation of a debtor.
   - a. Permits **voluntary and involuntary petitions.**
4. **Chapter 12 --** Allows for **Adjustment of Debts of a Family Farmer and Family Fisherman** -- a rehabilitation of a person (including a corporation or a partnership) who meets **the definition of a family farmer or fisherman**.
   - a. Permits only **voluntary petitions** by the family farmer or family fisherman.
5. **Chapter 13 --** Allows for **Adjustment of Debts of an Individual with Regular Income** -- a rehabilitation of only individuals (not partnerships or corporations) with limited total secured and unsecured debt amounts.
   - a. Permits only **voluntary petitions**.

VI. Commencement

A. Who May Petition

1. Any **person** (individual, partnerships, or corporations) may **voluntarily** petition themselves into a Chapter 7 bankruptcy (spouse can jointly file)

a. except

i. Banks

ii. Savings (buildings) and loan associations

iii. Credit unions

iv. Railroads

v. Insurance companies

vi. Governmental units (usually)

vii. Small business investment companies licensed by the Small Business Administration.

b. IMPORTANT: Before debtors can file a petition, they must receive credit counseling from an approved non-profit agency within 180 days prior to the date of filing.

> **Note:**
> **IMPORTANT:** Prior to commencement of a filing, the clerk of the Bankruptcy Court is required to give "consumer" debtors detailed notice of each chapter available under which the debtor may proceed and the clerk must provide informational materials on the types of services available from credit counseling agencies.

2. Any **person** may be **involuntarily petitioned** into a Chapter 7 bankruptcy

a. except

i. All of the above exclusions from a voluntary petition

ii. Nonprofit (not for profit) corporations

iii. **Farmers** (those that receive 80% or more of gross income from a farming operation and family farmers who meet that definition under a Chapter 12 bankruptcy).

B. Creditors' Petitions

1. For creditors to **involuntarily petition an eligible debtor** into bankruptcy:

a. If the debtor has **twelve (12) or more unsecured creditors with non-contingent claims**, the petition must be signed by three or more of these creditors whose **aggregate claims** are **$13,475 or more**.

b. If the debtor has **less than twelve (12) unsecured creditors with non-contingent claims**, the petition requires only one (more can sign) of these creditors **with an aggregate debt of $13,475 or more to sign the involuntary petition**.

2. Debtor's can **challenge involuntary petitions**. If so, creditors must prove either:

a. Debtor has not been paying debts as they become due, or

b. Debtor's property has been placed in receivership, or debtor has made an assignment for the benefit of creditors within 120 days of the filing of the involuntary petition.

> **Note:**
> If court dismisses the creditor's petition on the debtor's successful challenge, the Bankruptcy Court can assess all costs against petitioners (including reasonable attorney fees and any damages). If the petition was filed in bad faith, recovering could include punitive damages.

C. Upon the filing of a **voluntary petition** or the filing or **granting of an involuntary petition**, the court will grant an **order for relief**. This sets in motion proceedings that lead to the discharge of the debtor's debts.

Duties of the Debtor, the Trustee, and Automatic Stay

This section describes requirements imposed on the debtor during bankruptcy proceedings. Failure by the debtor to comply is grounds for denial of discharge of debts. Trustees are appointed or elected to collect the debtor's property, and to administer the debtor's estate.

I. Duties of the Debtor and Dismissal of the Petition

A. Generally, with a voluntary petition or within forty-five days after commencement of bankruptcy proceedings, the debtor is required to **file** the following (under oath and signed as being complete and accurate):

1. list of all creditors with addresses and amounts owed,
2. schedule of assets and liabilities,
3. schedule showing current income and expenses,
4. statement of financial affairs,
5. statement of intention to retain or surrender any property (which secures a consumer debt), and to specify property claimed exempt from bankruptcy proceedings,
6. certificate from an approved credit-counseling agency,
7. a statement of the amount of monthly income itemized to show how the amount is calculated,
8. a copy of debtor's federal income tax return for most recent year prior to filing,
9. proof of payments received from employers during last six months,
   a. Note: (6-9 from 2005 Bankruptcy Act)

   and
10. **To cooperate fully and to respond truthfully during examinations by the trustee or creditors, appear at all hearings, and to surrender to trustee all property, books, and records subject to the bankruptcy proceedings. Failure by the debtor is grounds for denial of discharge of debts.**

B. Even prior to the Bankruptcy Reform Act of 2005, a bankruptcy court could dismiss a Chapter 7 petition if the use of Chapter 7 would constitute a "substantial abuse" of that Chapter. Courts looked at a "totality of the circumstances" test, which included a debtor's ability to pay his or her debts out of future "disposable income," or, as one court put it, whether the debtor is honest and in such a financial predicament to warrant a discharge in exchange for liquidation of assets. The Bankruptcy Reform Act of 2005 established a system of "means testing" of the debtor's income to determine whether the debtor's petition is "presumed" to be a "substantial abuse."

1. When abuse is Presumed -- If the debtor's family income in the state in which the petition is filed is greater than the median family income in that state, the trustee or any party of interest (such as a creditor) can file a motion to dismiss the Chapter 7 petition. Median incomes vary from state to state and such are calculated and reported by the U.S. Bureau of the Census. The debtor's current monthly income is calculated by using the last six-month's average income less "allowed expenses" as basic needs of the debtor (there is a detailed listing). The monthly income is then

multiplied by twelve. If the resulting income exceeds that state's median income by $6,000 or more, abuse is presumed and a petition to dismiss can be filed. A debtor can rebut the presumption of abuse by a showing under oath "special circumstances that justifies expenses or adjustments of current monthly income for which there is not reasonable alternative." (An example might be anticipated medical costs not covered by insurance.)

2. When Abuse is not Presumed -- If the debtor's income as calculated is below the state median or the debtor has successfully rebutted the means - test assumption, abuse is not presumed. This does not preclude, however, the court from still finding under the "totality of the circumstances" test grounds to dismiss.

3. There are a number of grounds for dismissal of a petition besides substantial abuse:

   a. failure of the debtor to provide required documents and schedules,

   b. debtor has been convicted of a violent crime or a drug-trafficking offense (here, victim files motion to dismiss),

   c. debtor fails to pay post-petition domestic -- support obligations (such as child and spousal support).

II. Duties of the Trustee

A. In a Chapter 7 bankruptcy proceeding, after an order for relief is entered, the U.S. Trustee (a government-appointed official) appoints an interim trustee (who usually becomes the permanent trustee of the debtor's estate unless the creditors, at their meeting, elect a different trustee).

B. Basic trustee duties include:

1. Collect and reduce to money debtor's property preserving the interests of the parties.

2. Accountable for all property received and to make a final report accounting for the administration of the debtor's estate.

3. Investigate the financial affairs of the debtor, examine and object to claims of creditors, oppose debtor's discharge where appropriate, and operate business with proper reporting as required by the court.

4. To furnish information and reports concerning the debtor's estate to interested parties.

5. Review all materials filed by the debtor and issue (not later than ten days after first creditors' meeting) a statement whether the case is presumed an abuse under the means test and then file an appropriate motion.

6. Provide notice information to domestic -- support creditors.

C. Trustee is the representative of the debtor's estate (acts more like an executor -- no longer takes title).

III. Automatic Stay -- One of the most important rules in bankruptcy is that the filing of any petition places an automatic stay (with certain exceptions) on the creditor's right to continue to collect from the debtor or to satisfy the debt from the debtor's property outside of the bankruptcy proceedings.

A. **The moment any petition is filed (voluntary or involuntary), --** creditors have an **automatic stay** placed on them, which **prevents any further action toward collecting the debt outside of the bankruptcy proceedings**.

1. This means a creditor cannot enforce a judgment or a lien, secured creditors cannot proceed to repossess under Article 9 of the UCC, nor can any creditor commence any action to enforce the debt - except

2. some of the following actions or proceedings are not stayed:

   a. Criminal prosecution of the debtor,

   b. Collection of child support and other domestic support obligations and proceedings related to divorce, domestic violence, and child custody and visitation,

   c. Tax audits,

   d. Investigations by a securities regulatory agency,

   e. Withholding from a debtor's wages for repayment of a retirement account loan.

3. For secured creditors, a consumer-debtor, within thirty days after filing or before first creditors' meeting, must file with the clerk a statement of intention with respect to the secured collateral (redeem the collateral, continue use, making payments, etc.) and the trustee is required to enforce this intent within forty-five days of the meeting of the creditors.

B. **Stays can be vacated (canceled) by petition, --** such as a secured creditor claiming lack of **"adequate protection"** (value of collateral depreciating) because of the stay. If so, petitioned court must hold a hearing within 30 days. Court could grant the petition by turning over the property to the creditor, requiring cash payment(s), or providing additional or replacement collateral. If a hearing is not held, the stay is terminated automatically after 60 days of a request for relief from the stay.

Example:
Carl is a secured party on a $10,000 debt Susan owes with Susan's fishing boat put up as collateral for the debt. Susan is in default to Carl and two weeks later petitions herself into bankruptcy. Carl cannot proceed to repossess Susan's boat to satisfy the debt because Susan's petition into bankruptcy put a ("hold") stay on any such proceedings. Carl could petition the court for adequate protection noting that Susan's continuing use of the boat is depreciating its value and Carl's security interest. The court could require the trustee or Susan to make periodic payments, a single cash payment, or even vacate the stay, allowing Carl to proceed to repossess and sell the boat.

C. **If a creditor knowingly violates the automatic stay, --** this not only constitutes a crime, but the creditor will be liable **for any actual damages, costs, attorney fees**, and even **possibly punitive damages**.

Debtor's Estate and Exemptions

The debtor's estate, from which creditors will be paid, consists of all property the debtor owns and has rights in at the time of the filing of the petition, and certain property acquired within 180 days after the petition is filed. Individual debtors can claim certain property as exempt from the bankruptcy proceedings. Although the majority of states restrict the lists of exempt property to those permitted by the state, for those states who do not, there is a federal exemption list from which to choose.

I. **Debtor's Estate Includes:**

   A. All **tangible and intangible property** (all legal and equitable interests) of the debtor held at the **commencement of the bankruptcy proceedings**. This includes all exempt property.

   B. The following **after-acquired property** which debtor acquires **within 180 days after the petition is filed**.

      1. Property by **inheritance or gift,**

      2. Property by **divorce, separation, or property settlement,**

      3. **Beneficiary proceeds from a life insurance policy.**

   C. Any **property appreciation, income**, etc. **from existing property but excludes withholdings for employee benefit plan contributions**.

   D. Property **reacquired by trustee's avoidable powers such as preferences, fraudulent transfers, transfer by mistake, under duress**, etc.

II. **Exemptions --** Only **individuals**, not partnerships or corporations, **can claim** exemptions.

   A. **Two lists of exemptions -- state and federal. Congress** has authorized **states to limit exemptions to those of the state** and a majority of states have done so. **However, if the homestead is acquired within three and a half years preceding the date of filing, the maximum** state **homestead equity exempted is $136,875 and the debtor must have domiciled in the state for two years**.

   B. For the **other states**, the debtor **can chose either the state or the federal exemptions below:**

      1. The debtor's interest in a homestead used as a residence up to a value of **$20,200**;

      2. The debtor's interest in a motor vehicle up to **$3,225**;

      3. The debtor's interest up to **$525 per item** in household furnishings (includes one computer, one television, one videocassette recorder, and educational materials and equipment, but excludes items such as works of art, antiques over $500 in value, and electronic entertainment equipment with a fair market value of over $500), appliances, wearing apparel, animals, crops, or musical instruments which are owned primarily for personal uses, subject to a total of **$10,775** for all such;

      4. The debtor's interest in any kind of property ("wildcard" exemption) up to a limit of **$1,025**;

      5. Any unused portion of the $20,200 homestead exemption, subject to a limit of **$10,125**;

      6. The debtor's interest in implements, tools, or professional books used in his or her trade, not to exceed **$2,025** in value;

7. Any unmatured life insurance policies owned by the debtor (except for credit life policies) plus interests in accrued dividends and interest up to **$10,775**;
8. Professionally prescribed health aids;
9. The **debtor's right** to receive various government benefits, such as unemployment compensation, social security, veteran's benefits, etc.
10. The debtor's right to receive various private benefits, such as alimony, child support, pension payments, disability benefits, etc.
11. The **right** to receive damages for bodily injury up to **$20,200**; and
12. The debtor's interest in jewelry up to a total of **$1,350**, which is owned primarily for personal purposes.

Creditors' Meetings, Trustees' Powers, and Debtor's Avoidance

The first creditors' meeting is called by the U.S. Trustee. It is important because the debtor can, under oath, be examined at this meeting as to his or her financial affairs. A permanent trustee can be elected. This usually sets the beginning of the time period for creditors to file claims. The trustee has priority to a debtor's collateral over an unperfected secured party, and nonfiled mortgage and deed interests. The trustee also has avoidance power. It is important for you to know the law concerning the right to set aside fraudulent transfers and transfers called preferences. Debtors can avoid judicial liens and nonpossessory, nonpurchase money security interests in certain types of property.

I. **Creditors' Meetings**

   A. The **first creditors' meeting** is called by the **U.S. Trustee** on behalf of the Court (not less than ten days nor more than forty days from the order for relief). The judge does not attend.

   B. **Creditors** may **elect a permanent trustee by majority vote if at least 20% of total unsecured claims filed are in attendance. If not**, the trustee is **appointed** (usually the interim trustee).

   C. **Debtor** is **usually required to appear and may under oath be examined about his or her assets and any matter relevant to a discharge. Failure to answer truthfully is grounds for denial of discharge**.

II. **Trustees' Powers**

   A. **"Equivalent" Rights -- Generally**, the trustee has "**equivalent**" rights of the following parties:

      1. **Lien creditors** -- means trustees have **priority** to the debtor's property over an **unperfected secured party**.

      2. **Bona fide purchaser of real estate from the debtor** -- which means for example that the trustee has priority over all unfiled interests such as mortgages, deeds, etc.

   B. **Avoidance powers --** Power to set aside transfers of the debtor's property. Four voidable transfers are:

      1. Trustee can set aside transfers due to **duress, mistake, undue influence, failure of consideration, debtor's incapacity**, etc.

Example:
Debtor at time of transfer was a minor. Debtor now in bankruptcy still has right to disaffirm the transfer due to his or her minority. The trustee can set aside this transfer.

      2. Trustee can set aside **all fraudulent transfers** (includes both fraud in fact and fraud in law transfers which are made within **two years** of the **filing of the petition**).

Example:
Debtor, three days before the filing for bankruptcy, transfers a boat (nonexempt property) to his daughter retaining possession and use, and converts nonexempt property into cash, buying a $100,000 life insurance annuity contract. The debtor already has substantial amounts of life insurance. Both the transfer of the boat and the purchase of the $100,000 policy can be set aside and become property subject to the bankruptcy proceedings.

3. Trustee can set aside any transfer of property of the estate made by the debtor **after** the **debtor became subject to the bankruptcy proceeding**, except those made with permission of the trustee or the court.
4. Trustee can set aside any transfer made, which results in a **legal preference** -- a voluntary or involuntary transfer that **favors one creditor over others**.

ELEMENTS FOR ALL DEBTORS

VERY IMPORTANT

A transfer of **debtor's property to a creditor,**

For an **antecedent or preexisting debt,**

Made within **ninety (90) days of the filing of the petition,**

Made while the **debtor was insolvent (any transfer made within 90 days of the petition being filed, insolvency of the debtor is presumed).**

The **creditor receives more than** he or she **would receive in a Chapter 7 liquidation proceeding.**

ELEMENTS FOR ALL INSIDERS

IMPORTANT

(An insider is an individual or business, which has a close relationship with the debtor. For example, a relative, a partner, a corporation (board of directors of which the debtor is a member or as an officer of the corporation).

All elements above, except the transfers, include those made within **one year** from date **of the filing of the petition,**

but

the presumption of insolvency extends only to the **90-day window** from the date of filing of the petition. Therefore, for the trustee to set aside a transfer made during the one-year period outside of the 90-day window, the trustee must **prove in fact that the debtor was insolvent at the time of transfer.**

C. **EXCEPTIONS**

1. **To A Transfer During The 90-Day Period Being A Preference**

a. A **contemporaneous exchange** between the debtor and a creditor **for new value**.

Example:
Debtor retailer purchased new inventory and paid two days later in cash.

b. or

Example:
Debtor purchases new inventory to be delivered on May 1 with the seller-creditor taking a **purchase money security interest** in the new inventory to be delivered. If the secured seller-creditor perfects its security interest within **twenty (20) days after the debtor takes possession**, the security interest is not a preference.

c. The **payment of a debt incurred in the ordinary course of business or financial affairs** of the debtor.

Example:
Debtor pays upon receipt its utility bills.

d. A **consumer debtor's payment** of **up to $5,475** is not a preference.

e. Payments for **paternity, alimony, maintenance, and child support** are not preferences.

III. **Debtor's Avoidance**

A. Debtors can avoid **judicial liens** on exempt property.

B. Debtors can avoid nonpossessory, nonpurchase money security interests on household goods, wearing apparel, appliances, books, animals, crops, musical instruments, personal jewelry, implements, and tools of trade, professional books, or professionally proscribed health aids.

C. For implements, professional books, tools of trade, farm animals, and crops, avoidance is only on amounts which do not exceed $5,475.

Claims, Leases, and Distribution of Estate

All legal obligations, including disputed and unliquidated claims, can be filed as claims, and except for a few as listed are automatically allowed. For unexpired leases of the debtor, the trustee can assume, assign, sublease, or reject the lease. This is very important, starting with the top priority being perfected security interests in a debtor's collateral, on down the line to employee back wages, employee benefits, to prepaid consumer debts, to tax claims, etc. You should be familiar with the list, and the limitation within each class.

I. **Filing Proof of Claim --** Any creditor, equity security holder, co-debtor, surety or guarantor, the debtor on behalf of a creditor, or trustee may file proof of any legal claim or interest.

   A. Time for filing -- determined by Rules of Bankruptcy Procedure. (Must be filed within 90 days from first meeting of creditors. Same for Chapter 12 and Chapter 13 bankruptcies). Taxing and governmental units have 180 days.

   B. All legal obligations of the debtor are claims; thus, there is no need to prove a claim. This includes disputed and unliquidated claims for which the court may estimate value.

II. **Allowance of Claims --** Any claim filed is deemed allowed unless a party in interest objects. Generally, the following claims will be disallowed, at least to amount held unenforceable:

   A. Claims unenforceable due to fraud, usury, illegal (unconscionable), failure of consideration, etc.,

   B. Claim for unmatured interest,

   C. Claim subject to offset,

   D. Claims for taxes which exceed value of the property taxed,

   E. Claims of insiders (relatives or those in close association with debtor) or debtor's attorney which exceed reasonable value of services,

   F. Claims from breach of a lease of real property by a landlord, which exceed the greater of rent due without acceleration for one year, or 15% of the remaining lease terms (not to exceed three years) after the earlier of date of filing petition, or possession or surrender of the premises,

   G. Claims for termination of employment contracts, which exceed one year of compensation (plus unpaid compensation earned) from the date of the filing of the petition or termination of services, whichever is earlier.

III. **Leases --** For **unexpired leases of the debtor**, the trustee can:

   A. Assume and perform the lease.

   B. Assume and assign or sublease.

   C. Reject the lease (if not assumed within 60 days, lease is rejected.)

IV. **Distribution of Estate**

   A. **Perfected Secured Parties --** Perfected secured parties have **priority** to the **collateral or proceeds** therefrom **over general creditors and the trustee. Unperfected secured parties are treated in bankruptcy as general creditors.**

      1. If the security agreement so provides, the secured party has priority also from the collateral to cover costs of default plus reasonable attorney fees.

2. If there is insufficient collateral or value to cover the perfected secured creditor debt entitlement, the creditor can file a claim as a general creditor. Any amount which exceeds the secured creditor's entitlement is available for general creditor distribution.

Example:
West Bank is a perfected secured party on a loan balance of $10,000 with a security interest in $14,000 of the debtor's equipment. The debtor is in default. West Bank has repossessed the equipment and stored it for $500 pending its sale. West Bank also has $1,000 in attorney fees due to debtor's default. If the equipment is sold for $11,000 by either the debtor or trustee, assuming West Bank's security agreement also covers default costs and attorney fees, West Bank would receive the entire $11,000 and would have filed a claim as a general creditor for $500.

B. **General Creditor Priorities** -- The **balance of the debtor's estate** is distributed in the **following group order:** (When there are insufficient proceeds to cover any particular group, the funds are prorated among the members of that group and subsequent groups receive nothing).

1. **First** -- claims for domestic support obligations, such as child support and alimony.
2. **Second** -- all **costs and expenses of the bankruptcy proceedings**. This includes trustee, attorney, and accountant fees.
3. **Third** -- if an **involuntary petition has been filed but the trustee has not yet been appointed** (such as when the debtor challenges the involuntary petition), **any expenses incurred by the debtor in the ordinary course of business from date of filing to the appointment of the trustee or order of relief** (called "gap creditors").

Example:
Three creditors whose aggregate unsecured, non-contingent claims are $50,000 sign an involuntary petition putting Elizabeth, sole owner of a clothing store, into bankruptcy. Elizabeth immediately challenges the petition. A hearing is held two weeks later when the court rules in favor of the creditors, an order of relief is issued and a trustee is appointed. During the two-week period, Elizabeth has continued to do business and has incurred debts to ABC Wholesale Clothes and XYZ Janitorial Services. When distribution of Elizabeth's estate is to take place, ABC and XYZ will be third in line of general creditors to get paid.

4. **Fourth -- employee claims for back wages, salaries, or commissions** (including vacation, severance, sick leave, and other benefits) but **limited to those earned within 90 days of the filing of the petition or cessation of business** (whichever is first) to a **maximum amount of $10,950**.
   a. **IMPORTANT** -- Any amount of back wages, etc., owed, **regardless of when owed or amount owed above the $10,950 during the 90 day period above, is still a claim but for priority purposes goes to the last category -- general creditors**.

Example:
Clara is employed as the manager of a clothing store. She is paid $5,000 per month. The clothing-store owner suffers financial reverses and, based on promises, Clara manages the store for four months without pay. The owner now goes into a Chapter 7 bankruptcy. Clara will file a claim for her entire $20,000 owed in back salary, with $10,950 (earned during the last 90 days) as a priority. The remaining $9,050 will be treated as a last general creditor priority. If Clara had worked one month without pay, quit, and the owner continued to manage the store for three months, before she shut down the business and filed for bankruptcy, Clara would get no employee priority (earned outside the 90-day window) and her entire claim would be treated last with the general creditors.

5. **Fifth -- any claim for contributions to an employee benefit plan arising from services performed within 180 days before the filing of the petition or cessation of business** (whichever comes first) **up to $10,950 per employee (less the aggregate amount** paid to employees under the fourth priority above). Any amount above is treated as a general creditor claim.
6. **Sixth --** claims of **farm producers and fishermen** against **debtors who own or operate grain storage facilities or a fish storage or processing facility** up to the **amount of $5,400 per creditor**. Any **amount above** is treated as a **general creditor claim**.
7. **Seventh -- consumer creditors** who **deposit or prepay for the purchase, lease, or rental of goods or services for personal, family, or household use up to an amount of $2,425 per creditor. Any amount above $2,425** is treated **as a general creditor claim.**

Example:
John contracts with a yard fertilizer and maintenance company to mow his home yard weekly and fertilize it eight times during the coming year. The price is $3,000 less 10% if paid in advance. John pays $2,700 to the company. Before any services are performed, the company goes into Chapter 7 bankruptcy. John has a priority claim of $2,425 if there are funds remaining for this category and a general creditor priority claim of $275.

8. **Eighth --** Claims of **governmental units for various taxes**. These are subject to **time limits** that **vary on the type of tax**.
9. **Ninth --** claims for **death or personal injury resulting from operation of a vehicle or vessel because debtor was intoxicated from use of alcohol, drugs, or other substances**.
10. **Tenth --** All **general unsecured creditors**.
11. If any **amount is left, it goes to the debtor.**

C. **SUMMARY - Priority Distribution**

1. Perfected Secured Claims,
2. Unsecured Claims,
    a. Domestic support obligations,

b. Administrative expenses,
c. Gap creditors -- involuntary petition,
d. Back wages and salaries,
e. Employee benefit plans,
f. Grain producers and fishermen,
g. Prepayments by consumers,
h. Taxes,
i. Death or injury claims from operation of a vehicle or vessel due to intoxication,
j. General creditors,

3. Debtor.

Discharge, Reaffirmations, and Summary Questions

Although most debts of the debtor are discharged, there are a number of conditions under which discharge may be denied, and there are those debts which are not discharged under any circumstances (most important ones for the exam are listed). A reaffirmation is an agreement between a debtor and creditor made prior to the issuance of a bankruptcy decree. It states that a debt shall not be discharged in bankruptcy. It must be filed with the court and, if the debtor is not represented by an attorney, court approval is required. The debtor can, under certain circumstances, rescind the reaffirmation. The following section also provides two summary questions to assist in the review of Chapter 7 information.

I. **Generally** - after the estate has been distributed, the **court will grant the debtor a discharge decree** (at a hearing), which **releases the debtor from further liability of his or her debts**. This decree is revocable for one year.

II. **Conditions under which Discharge May Be Denied**

   A. A **partnership** or **corporation cannot get a discharge decree** under Chapter 7 (can under other Chapters), **only individuals can**.

   B. A debtor will be **denied a discharge if he or she received a discharge within eight (8) years before the filing** of the current petition.

   C. **Any of the following acts by the debtor is a ground for denial of the discharge decree:**

      1. any intentional concealment, distribution, or transfer of assets or records to the detriment of creditors or the trustee (without justification),

      2. any fraudulent claims, statements, oaths, or receipt or transfer of property,

      3. any refusal to obey lawful orders, failure to file required or requested tax documents, failure to testify after grant of immunity, or explain loss or deficiency of assets,

      4. failure of debtor to complete the required consumer education course.

   D. **Consumer Debts** (Can be rebutted by debtor):

      1. any consumer debt incurred within 90 days of filing of petition (order of relief) of more than $525 to a single creditor for luxury goods or services,

      2. any cash advance more than $825 by the debtor using a credit card or other open-ended consumer credit if incurred within 70 days of the filing of the petition (order of relief).

III. **Debts Not Discharged (by Statute) under Any Circumstances --** (the most important ones):

   A. **Unpaid taxes** (2 years) - includes charges incurred to pay U.S. taxes,

   B. **Debts incurred through fraud, larceny, or embezzlement,**

   C. **Debts of creditors who had no knowledge of bankruptcy proceedings** (those not listed in debtor's schedules),

   D. **Unpaid claims for alimony, maintenance, and support,**

E. **Claims** based on **debtor's willful or malicious torts,**

F. **Fines and penalties** payable to a governmental unit,

G. **Student loan debts or benefits (exception if debtor can demonstrate undue hardship),**

H. **Claims arising from a judgment or consent decree awarded against a debtor where liability was incurred as a result of the debtor's operation of a motor vehicle while legally intoxicated**.

IV. **Tax claims discharged --** if trustee requests a tax audit (determination of unpaid taxes) and the taxing authority does not notify the trustee within 60 days that the audit has been commenced, or if the audit is not completed within 180 days, both the trustee and debtor are discharged from tax liability.

V. **Reaffirmations -- agreements** between a **debtor and creditor** that a **debt will not be discharged in bankruptcy**.

A. To be **enforceable:**

1. The agreement must be **entered into prior to the granting of the discharge decree in bankruptcy**.

2. The **agreement must be signed and filed with the court**.

3. If **debtor is represented by an attorney, no hearing or court approval is required if the attorney files an affidavit or declaration that the debtor has been fully advised of the legal consequences of the agreement and such is not a hardship on the debtor or his or her family. If not represented by an attorney, a hearing and approval is required.**

4. The **agreement must include a statement for debtor's right to rescind the agreement at any time prior to the discharge decree being granted or within sixty (60) days of the filing of the agreement, whichever is later. This statement must be** clearly **and** conspicuously stated.

B. **2005 Act** added the following:

1. If debtor's monthly income less debtor's monthly expenses is less than scheduled payments on reaffirmed debt a rebuttable due hardship is presumed. To rebut, debtor can file a written explanation and debtor's attorney must certify that in his or her opinion the debtor is unable to make the payments.

2. The debtor must receive several disclosures before signing a reaffirmation. These disclosures include notice that debtor is not required to affirm any debt, liens on secured property (such as real estate mortgages and liens on cars) will remain in effect even if debt is not reaffirmed, state the amount of debt affirmed with rates of interest and when payments begin, plus the right to rescind. These disclosures must be signed by the debtor, certified by the debtor's attorney, and filed with court with the reaffirmation agreement.

VI. **Summary Questions**

A. **Question 1: MAY 1995 EXAM (Modified for Existing Law)**

1. Dart Inc., a closely held corporation, was petitioned involuntarily into bankruptcy under the liquidation provisions of Chapter 7 of the Federal Bankruptcy Code. Dart contested the petition.

2. Dart has not been paying its business debts as they became due, has defaulted on its mortgage loan payments, and owes back taxes to the IRS. The total cash value of Dart's bankruptcy estate after the sale of all assets and payment of administration expenses is $100,000.

3. Dart has the following creditors:

    a. Fracon Bank is owed $75,000 principal and accrued interest on a mortgage loan secured by Dart's real property. The property was valued at and sold, in bankruptcy, for $70,000.

    b. The IRS has a $12,000 recorded judgment for unpaid corporate income tax.

    c. JOG Office Supplies has an unsecured claim of $1,000 that was timely filed.

    d. Nanstar Electric Co. has an unsecured claim of $1,200 that was not timely filed.

    e. Decoy Publications has a claim of $16,000, of which $2,000 is secured by Dart's inventory that was valued and sold, in bankruptcy, for $2,000. The claim was timely filed.

4. **Question 1-1**

Question: Which of the following creditors must join in the filing of the involuntary petition?

I. JOG Office Supplies

II. Nanstar Electric Co.

III. Decoy Publications

A. I, II and III.

B. II and III.

C. I and II.

D. III only.

Answer:
D. III only.

5. **Question 1-2**

Question: Which of the following statements would correctly describe the result of Dart's opposing the petition?

A. Dart will win because the petition should have been filed under Chapter 11.

B. Dart will win because there are not more than 12 creditors.

C. Dart will lose because it is not paying its debts as they become due.

D. Dart will lose because of its debt to the IRS.

Answer:
C. Dart will lose because it is not paying its debts as they become due.

6. Question 1-3

Question: Which of the following events will follow the filing of the Chapter 7 involuntary petition?

	A trustee will be appointed	A stay against creditor collection proceedings will go into effect
A.	Yes	Yes
B.	Yes	No
C.	No	Yes
D.	No	No

Answer:
A. Yes Yes

7. Question 1-4

Question: Assuming that the bankruptcy estate was distributed, what dollar amount would Nanstar Electric Co. receive?

1. $0
2. $800
3. $1,000
4. $1,800

Answer:
1. $0

8. Question 1-5

Question: What total dollar amount would Fracon Bank receive on its secured and unsecured claims?

1. $70,000
2. $72,000
3. $74,000
4. $75,000

Answer:
3. $74,000

9. **Question 1-6**

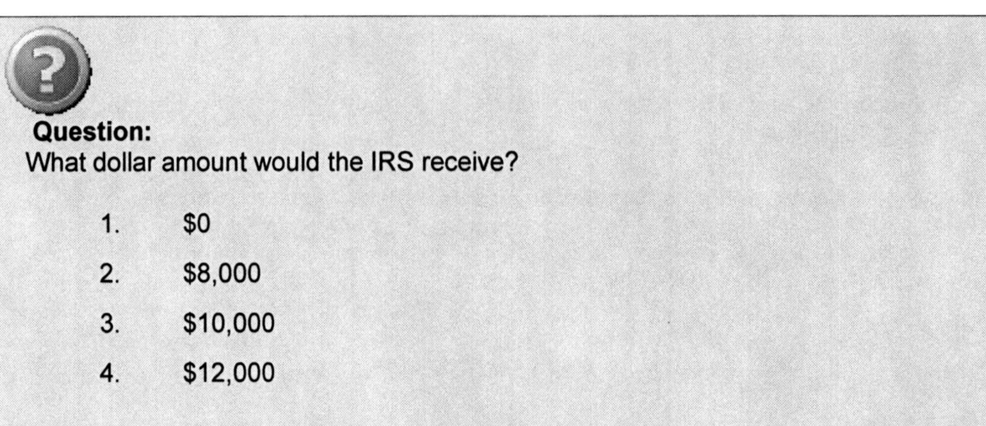

Question:
What dollar amount would the IRS receive?

1. $0
2. $8,000
3. $10,000
4. $12,000

Answer:
4. $12,000

B. Question 2: NOVEMBER 1995 EXAM

1. On June 1, 1995, Rusk Corp. was petitioned involuntarily into bankruptcy. At the time of the filing, Rusk had the following creditors:

- **a.** Safe Bank, for the balance due on the secured note and mortgage on Rusk's warehouse
- **b.** Employee salary claims
- **c.** 1994 federal income taxes due
- **d.** Accountant's fee outstanding
- **e.** Utility bills outstanding

2. Prior to the bankruptcy filing, but while insolvent, Rusk engaged in the following transactions:

- **a.** On February 1, 1995, Rusk repaid all corporate directors' loans made to the corporation.
- **b.** On May 1, 1995, Rusk purchased raw materials for use in its manufacturing business and paid cash to the supplier.

3. For each of the following select from this list:

A. I only.

B. II only.

C. Both I and II.

D. Neither I and II.

C. Question 2-1.

Question:
I. Safe Bank's claims will be the first paid of the listed claims because Safe is a secured creditor.

II. Safe Bank will receive the entire amount of the balance of the mortgage due as a secured creditor regardless of the amount received from the sale of the warehouse.

Answer:
A. I only

D. Question 2-2.

Question:
I. The employee salary claims will be paid in full after the payment of any secured party.

II. The employee salary claims up to $10,950 per claimant will be paid before payment any general creditor's claims.

Answer:
B. II only

E. Question 2-3.

Question:
I. The claim for 1994 federal income taxes due will be paid as a secured creditor claim.

II. The claim for 1994 federal income taxes due will be paid prior to the general creditor claims.

Answer:
B. II only

F. Question 2-4.

Question:
I. The February 1 repayments of the directors' loans were preferential transfers even though the payments were made more than 90 days before the filing of the petition.

II. The February 1 repayments of the directors' loans were preferential transfers because the payments were made to insiders.

Answer:
C. Both I and II

G. Question 2-5.

Question:
I. The May 1 purchase and payment was not a preferential transfer because it was a transaction in the ordinary course of business.

II. The May 1 purchase and payment was a preferential transfer because it occurred within 90 days of the filing of the petition.

Answer:
A. I only

Chapter 11, 12, and 13 Bankruptcies

Although used primarily by businesses, individuals can also be involuntarily petitioned into, or may voluntarily petition themselves into, a Chapter 11 bankruptcy. This permits the debtor (usually) to stay in possession of all assets and by a plan, reorganize its debt structure. If the plan is approved and followed, most debts are discharged. Businesses with debts of less than $2.9 million can use a "Fast Track" Chapter 11 proceeding. Chapters 12 and 13 permit the debtor to adjust debts. By making disposable income available during (usually) a three-year period, they also permit the debtor to discharge most debts. Chapter 12 applies only to family farmers with total debts of less than $3,544,525. Chapter 13 is available only to individuals (not partnerships or corporations) with regular income, whose unsecured debt is less than $336,900 and secured debt is less than $1,010,650.

I. **Chapter 11 Bankruptcy - Reorganizations**

A. **Introduction**

1. Can be by **voluntary or involuntary petition (court can dismiss for cause)**.
2. Can be **filed by any person who can file a Chapter 7 bankruptcy petition except stock and commodities brokers**.
    a. Includes individuals (with some limitations) as well as businesses.
    b. Includes **railroads that are excluded under Chapter 7**.

B. **Basic Differences and Important Similarities**

1. **Automatic Stay --** basically same as Chapter 7 and more important here because for reorganization business must be continued (exception if debtor refiled within two years).
2. **Trustee --** Generally, **not appointed or elected** as in Chapter 7. Usually, the **debtor-in-possession (DIP) acts and has same powers (avoidance, etc.) as a Chapter 7 trustee. Court could appoint a receiver.**
3. **Creditor committees --** U.S. trustee will appoint **a committee of unsecured creditors** and either the **court or trustee may appoint other creditors' committees** to represent **special interests** of creditors, such as **secured creditors** or, in a **debtor corporation, shareholders**.

C. **Reorganization plans**

1. Only **debtor files** within **first 120 days (180 days for small business debtor) after filing of petition (can be extended but not beyond 18 months from date of order of relief)**.
2. If **debtor** does **not file, get an extension, or get creditor approval, any party can file up to 20 months (for small business debtor)**.
3. Plan must **divide claims into common interest creditors** (employees, secured creditors, bondholders, etc.) and **indicate how the claims within each class will be paid, how and to what extent, and payment of tax claims over a five-year period**.

D. **Approval of plan --** (confirmation)

1. The reorganization plan will be **approved** if:

> **Note:**
> If the plan is **not approved** or **does not work as planned**, the proceeding could **be converted to a Chapter 7 liquidation proceeding**.

a. **Each class of creditors** has a vote of **at least 1/2 of the number of creditors** in that class with **at least 2/3 of the amount of claims voted approval**, and

b. the court rules that the plan is **fair and equitable to all classes. (In the best interests of the creditors.)** For example, equity holders by the plan would not recover under the plan unless secured and unsecured creditors recovered in full, and unsecured creditors would not recover unless secured creditors recovered in full. In addition, the debtor must certify all post-petition domestic support obligations have been paid.

2. **If only one class of claims has been approved, the court can still approve the entire plan** (called **"cram-down provision"**) if the court finds the **plan is fair** (does not unfairly discriminate) and **equitable; however, even if all creditor classes have been approved, a former spouse or child can block the plan if payments to them are not in cash**.

E. **Discharge**

1. **After confirmation of the plan, except for individual debtors, all debts not provided for in the plan are discharged, except for those which are not discharged in a Chapter 7 liquidation proceeding. For individual debtors, debts are not discharged until the plan is completed.**

2. All debts **satisfied by the plan are automatically discharged**.

II. **Fast Track -- Chapter 11**

A. Applies **only to businesses with debts of less than $2.9 million**.

B. Permits **creditors' committees to be avoided**.

C. **Shortens filing period** (debtor to 100 days - others to 160 days).

III. **Chapters 12 and 13**

A. **Criteria to petition**

1. Only **voluntary petitions** are permitted. Upon filing, an automatic stay takes effect for a consumer debt but not a business debt or domestic support obligation.

2. **Adjustment of Debts of a Family Farmer -- Chapter 12**

a. Applies only to a **family farmer** -- a farmer whose gross income is at least 50% farm dependent and whose debts are at least 50% farm related.

b. The <u>total debt</u>, secured and unsecured, <u>cannot exceed $3,544,525</u>.

c. A **partnership** or **closely held corporation** is eligible if <u>at least 50% of the organization is owned by a family farmer.</u>

3. **Adjustment of Debts of a Family Fisherman -- Chapter 12**

a. Applies only **where fisherman's gross income is at least 50% dependent on commercial fishing and whose debts are at least 80% related to commercial fishing**.

b. The **total debt**, secured and unsecured, **cannot exceed $1,642,500**.

c. A **partnership** or **closely held corporation** can also qualify.

4. **Adjustment of Debts of an Individual with Regular Income - Chapter 13**

a. Applies only to **individuals (not partnerships or corporations)** who have a **regular source of income** with **fixed unsecured debts of less than $336,900 and secured debts of less than $1,010,650.** (Note, regular income is liberally construed and includes individuals on welfare, those with investment income, farmers who at least yearly sell crops or livestock, etc.)

Example:
John works full time for Z-Corp. His salary is $60,000 per year. Over a period of time, he has acquired a mortgage on his home for $225,000, and credit-card debt and open account debt at a variety of stores for $39,000. Z-Corp. merges with ABC and John's position is eliminated. John gets a half-time job but does not earn enough to pay his debts. His creditors are pressing for payment. John is eligible to file for a Chapter 13 bankruptcy because he is an individual whose unsecured debt of $39,000 is less than $336,900, and his secured debt ($225,000 mortgage) is less than $1,010,650.

b. The U.S. Trustee will always appoint a trustee in an Adjustment of Debt bankruptcy -- to receive future earnings and to distribute disposable income of the debtor.

B. **Filing of Plans**

1. **Both Chapters** require the filing of a **plan -- Chapter 13 called a repayment plan**.
2. Only **debtors can file the plan**.
3. The **content** of the plans are **basically the same** for both chapters (over-simplified).
    a. **Secured creditors** retain liens and are entitled to either the collateral and/or payments under the plan. Chapter 12 -- secured debt is reduced to the value of the property.
    b. **Unsecured creditors** -- receive from disposable income (income in excess of necessities required by the debtor and family) of the debtor payments over a three-year period (can be a longer period - by court approval up to five years - and if the debtor's family income is greater than the state median family income under the means test, the proposed plan must be for five years.

C. **Confirmation of Plans**

1. **Hearing** is held (at least 20 days but not more than 45 days after meeting of creditors).
2. **Court confirms** if secured parties are provided for, unsecured creditors receive any disposal income, and domestic support obligations have been paid. (Note, in determining disposal income, debtor can deduct from gross income up to 15% for charitable contributions.)

D. **Discharge**

1. **Pending discharge**, debtor continues in business, farming, fishing, and possession of assets (both exempt and nonexempt).
2. **Upon completion of payments** (after three or five-year period), **court grants debtor a discharge** (with a few exceptions such as alimony and support, judgments based on DWI claims, and educational loans).
3. A discharge can be revoked within one year if the discharge was procured by fraud.

Government Regulation of Business

Federal Securities Acts

Defining a `Security`

The first step in mastering securities regulation is logically to understand what a "security" is. The definition, it turns out, is rather broad.

I. Definition

A. The statutory definition ('33 Act) contains a laundry list, plus catch-all terms, broadly defining a **security** to mean:

> "Any note, stock, treasury stock, bond, debenture, evidence of indebtedness, certificate of interest or participation in a profit-sharing agreement, collateral-trust certificate, preorganization certificate of subscription, transferable share, **investment contract**, voting-trust certificate, certificate of deposit for a security, fractional undivided interest in oil, gas, or other mineral rights, any put, call, straddle, option, or privilege on any security, certificate of deposit, or group of index of securities (including any interest therein or based on the value thereof), or any put, call, straddle, option, or privilege entered into on a national securities exchange relating to foreign currency, or, in general, any interest or instrumentality common known as a 'security,' or any certificate of interest or participation in, temporary or interim certificate for, receipt for, guarantee of, or warrant or right to subscribe to or purchase, any of the foregoing."

B. The 1934 Act's definition is quite similar.

1. A share of corporate stock is the prototypical security. It is always a security and any other investment interest that seems to share most of its features, especially an investment of money to be managed by others with an expectation of profit, is probably a security.

II. The most important of the catch-all categories is the investment contract

A. Elements of an investment contract:

1. Investment of money,
2. in a common enterprise,
3. with an expectation of profit,
4. to be earned primarily by the actions of others.

Example:
Promoters seeking to develop an orange grove could have incorporated and sold stock in the corporation to raise funds. Instead, they sold the actual trees to investors. If an investor put in 1/20th of the money, then he was deemed owner of 1/20th of the trees. All oranges were tended, harvested, and sold by the promoters. The owner of 1/20th of the trees would receive 1/20th of the profits. Although the promoters insisted that they were selling trees, the court held that they were actually selling "securities" in the form of an investment contract. The investors invested money in a common enterprise (if the weather was good all could profit; if there was a serious freeze, all investors would lose money). They did so hoping to make money primarily by the planting, cultivating, harvesting, and marketing efforts of the promoters.

III. Key distinctions to remember

A. Passive investors need legal protection more than investors who are actively involved in the enterprise and their investments are more likely to be deemed securities.

Example:
General partners invest money in a common enterprise (the partnership business) with an expectation of profit. However, because they are general partners, they can protect themselves by being actively involved in the enterprise. General partnership interests usually are not securities.

Example:
Limited partners invest money in a common enterprise (the partnership business) with an expectation of profit. Additionally, because they must sit on the sidelines in order to protect their limited liability and may not take an active role in directing the enterprise, they, unlike general partners, hope to profit by the efforts of others (the general partners). Limited partnership interests usually are securities.

B. A transaction involving an investment purpose is more likely to create a security than a transaction involving a purpose of consumption.

Example:
A loans $50,000 to B so that B can start a business. B signs a note promising to pay the money back with interest. This is more likely to be a security than if B had borrowed the money (and signed the note) in order to buy a luxury boat that he wanted to cruise around in during his spare time.

The Registration Process

The registration process can be expensive and time-consuming, but it has as its goal ensuring that investors have the opportunity to receive the information needed to make wise investment decisions regarding newly offered shares.

I. Requirements and Basic Procedure

A. The 1933 Act's requirements cover

1. Initial public offerings, wherein companies sell to the general investing public for the first time.
2. Seasoned offerings, wherein public companies print and sell new securities to the public.
3. Secondary offerings, wherein persons controlling or closely affiliated with public companies sell their securities under circumstances where it is appropriate to treat the transaction as if it were being made by the company itself.

B. Basic procedure

1. Issuer files registration statement with SEC.
2. Issuer waits 20 days for SEC approval, during which time preliminary "red herring" prospectus is disseminated, and oral offers and limited types of written offers can be made.
3. Registration statement is deemed "effective" and sales can begin.

II. The Distribution Process for Securities is Similar to that for Products

A. **Product --** Manufacturer-Wholesaler-Retailer-Customer.

B. **Security --** Issuer-Underwriter-Broker-Investor.

III. Basic Legal Framework

A. The process breaks down into three periods

1. The pre-filing period, before the registration statement is filed with the SEC.
2. The waiting period, after the issuing company has filed but before the SEC has given permission for selling to begin (the effective date).
3. The post-effective period.

B. **During the pre-filing period --** a company can neither offer to sell securities nor sell them.

C. **During the waiting period --** a company may make oral offers and certain types of written offers but cannot sell the securities.

D. **Elaboration --** During the waiting period, oral offers are permitted along with certain specified types of written offers, most importantly:

1. the preliminary or "red herring" prospectus, and
2. the "tombstone" ad, a black-bordered advertisement usually placed in the Wall Street Journal that would contain only:
    a. the name of the issuer,
    b. the full title of the security and the amount being offered,

c. a brief description of the company's business,

d. the price range of the security,

e. the name of the managing underwriter,

f. the contemplated date of the issuance,

g. a few other minor items.

3. Both the red herring prospectus and the tombstone ad will contain cautionary words that they constitute neither offers to sell nor solicitations of offers to buy and that no binding contract can be entered into until after the registration statement becomes effective.

E. **During the post-effective period --** an issuer may both offer and sell the securities.

IV. **Contents of Registration Statements include, among other items**

A. Financial Statements audited by independent CPA,

B. Names of issuer, directors, officers, underwriters, etc.,

C. Risks,

D. Description of Issuer's business,

E. Description of Security and Intended Use for Proceeds.

V. **Disclosure to Investors --** Much of the registration statement's contents go into the Prospectus, a part of the Registration Statement that must be delivered to buyers.

A. The Preliminary ("Red Herring") Prospectus is used during the waiting period, but cannot be used thereafter; it contains most of the information that the final prospectus will contain, except for information such as the final price to be charged and fees to underwriters that cannot be determined until the effective date.

B. The Final Prospectus is used after the effective date.

C. The Final Prospectus must be delivered to investors before, or along with, the purchased securities (or written confirmation of purchase).

D. The final prospectus may be supplemented by written advertising material called "free writing" that is not permissible during the waiting period.

VI. **SEC Review**

A. **Theoretically --** the SEC reviews the registration statement during a 20-day waiting period and the registration statement becomes effective on 20th day after filing.

B. **Fact --** The SEC usually does not review the registration statements of seasoned issuers and often allows them to "accelerate" their registration statements and sell before the theoretical 20-day waiting period has expired. When the SEC does review registration statements, such as for all companies going public for the first time, it usually takes much longer than 20 days, typically 60-80 days. Nonetheless, the AICPA tests the theoretical legal framework rather than the actual practice.

C. **Key Point --** The SEC does not review the merits of the securities being offered nor make any guarantees to investors as to the quality of the securities. Issuers can sell the worst securities imaginable so long as they fully disclose how bad they are. Nor does the SEC guarantee the thoroughness and accuracy of the registration materials. When it allows a registration statement to become effective, the SEC is simply indicating that it has not found anything wrong with the disclosures contained therein. Nothing prevents the SEC from finding problems later and acting on them.

VII. Shelf Registration -- Before shelf registration, a company that had two or more offerings in a relatively short time frame would have to go through the entire registration process for each offering, which was very duplicative and wasteful. The SEC realized that this was somewhat wasteful and began allowing the largest 2,000 or so companies to file a single registration statement that would cover the securities they expected to sell during the next two years. Then, whenever an advantageous "market window" presented itself, these firms could pull the securities "off the shelf" and begin selling them within just a day or two.

VIII. Securities Offering Reform Program (SORP)

A. In December 2005, through the Securities Offering Reform Program (SORP), the SEC expanded the "shelf registration" concept to what might be considered "company registration." The largest firms, which are widely followed in the marketplace, are allowed to file a registration statement covering 3-year periods. They can then largely ignore the traditional rules covering permissible activities in pre-filing and waiting periods. The notion is that these firms are so widely followed in the market every day that a registration statement really does not add much in the way of meaningful information. Therefore, they can talk about their companies and even their companies' stock, largely without restriction.

B. Two particular concepts should be noted.

1. First, the SORP rules divide issuers into several categories, the largest of which are called Well-Known Seasoned Issuers (WKSIs - pronounced "wicksees"). These are firms that have been reporting regularly to SEC for at least a year, (b) eligible to use Form S-3 or F-3, and (c) have either (i) $700 million of worldwide public common equity float, or (ii) have issued $1 billion of registered debt in previous 3 years. These firms make up only 30% of listed firms but they control 95% of listed firms' assets. It is only these firms that are allowed to take full advantage of the new SORP rules, although more limited benefits flow to many smaller issuers.

2. Second, it is important to know the concept of a "free writing prospectus" (FWP). Traditionally, after the effective date, firms were allowed to supplement the final prospectus with additional literature called "free writing." WKSIs are now allowed to use additional material (FWPs) at any time with few restrictions other than the material usually has to be filed with the SEC. Some of the other categories of issuers are allowed to use FWPs on a more restricted basis (typically only *after* filing a registration statement).

Exempt from Registration Process

Because registration is expensive and time-consuming, companies seeking to raise capital would generally prefer to avoid it. They may if they sell exempt securities or sell nonexempt securities through exempt transactions. Let's start with exempt securities.

I. Bank and Government Securities

- **A. Rationale --** Bank and government securities are heavily regulated by other federal and state laws.
- **B. Limitation --** Public utilities are not exempt.

II. Short-Term Notes -- Commercial notes (not notes for investment purposes) are exempt if carrying maturity of less than 9 months.

III. Charitable Organizations' Securities -- Nonprofit educational, religious, benevolent, fraternal, or charitable organizations.

IV. Others

- **A.** Regulated Savings & Loans.
- **B.** Federally Regulated Common Carriers.
- **C.** Receivers or Trustees in Bankruptcy (with court approval).
- **D.** Insurance and Annuity Policies (but not regular securities issued by insurance companies)
  - **1.** Limitation: Regular securities issued by insurance companies are not exempt.

Example:
Prudential Insurance Co. sells annuities. These carry many of the same characteristics of securities but are exempt from registration. Prudential Insurance Co. decides to have a public offering of its own securities to raise capital. This transaction is not exempt from registration on grounds that the offeror is an insurance company.

- **E.** Domestic Governmental Organizations.

Registration Exempt Offerings

The time and expense inherent in registration make exempt transactions attractive. This is one of the areas in securities law that receives the most attention on the CPA Exam. It is especially important to master the Regulation D exemption rules.

I. **Three major types --** Congress has authorized **three major types** of transaction exemptions wherein the securities need not be registered with the SEC even though they are not exempt securities.

   A. **"Small offering" exemptions --** (authorized by Sec. 3(b) of the 1933 Act).

      1. **Rationale --** These offerings need not be regulated because of the relatively small threat to the public posed by small offering.

Example:
Regulation A, and Rules 504 and 505 of Regulation D.

   B. **Private placement exemptions --** (authorized by Sec. 4(2) of the 1933 Act).

      1. **Rationale --** These offerings need not be regulated because of the sophisticated nature of offerees who can protect themselves.

      2. **Key Concept --** Accredited Investors (AIs)who can look out for themselves and therefore do not need the protection of the 1933 Act's disclosure provisions, include: millionaires, persons who make $200,000/yr (or $300,000/yr with spouse), institutional investors, insiders of the issuer, and charitable, educational, or religious organizations worth at least $5 million.

Example:
Rule 506 of Regulation D.

   C. **Intrastate offering exemptions --** (authorized by Sec. 3(a)(11) of the 1933 Act).

      1. **Rationale --** These offerings need not be federally regulated because they happen primarily inside a single state's borders and can be adequately regulated by that state.

Example:
Rule 147 under Sec. 3(a)(11) of the 1933 Act.

II. **Characteristics of Key Transaction Exemptions**

   A. **Rule 504 of Regulation D**

      1. Rule 504 can be used mostly by small companies, not by 1934 Act reporting companies or investment companies.

2. **Limitation on Amount** -- Rule 504 can be used to raise only $1 million in any 12-month period.
3. **Manner of Offering** -- General solicitation and advertising are not allowed unless either (a) the securities are registered under a state law requiring public filing and delivery of a substantive disclosure document to investors before sale, or (b) the securities are issued under a state law exemption that permits general solicitation, as long as sales are made only to accredited investors.
4. **Purchaser Requirements** -- There are no such requirements; Rule 504 securities may be sold to anyone.
5. **Information Requirements** -- There are none.
6. **Filing Requirements** -- The issuer need only file a Form D with the SEC within 15 days of the first sale of securities under the exemption. Even failure to comply with this requirement will not disqualify the offering from the exemption, but the SEC may prevent the issuer from using Reg D again in the future.
7. **Resale Restrictions** -- Resale is restricted unless the conditions mentioned for the manner of offering are met.

B. **Rule 505 of Regulation D**

1. Can't be used by investment companies or companies that have recently been in trouble with the SEC ("bad boys").
2. Can be used to raise only $5 million in any 12-month period.
3. **Manner of Offering** -- Cannot use general solicitation or advertising.
4. **Purchaser Requirements** -- Can sell to an unlimited amount of accredited investors but no more than 35 unaccredited investors.
5. **Information Requirements** -- Same as Rule 506.
6. **Filing Requirements** -- Form D within 15 days.
7. To prevent easy circumvention of the rule's restrictions, the shares' resale is restricted for a year and the issuer must take steps to ensure that buyers know that they are restricted, such as by printing a legend on the securities.

C. **Rule 506 of Regulation D**

1. **Nature of Issuer** -- No restrictions.
2. **Limit on Amount** -- None.
3. **Manner of Offering** -- Cannot use general advertising or solicitation.
4. **Purchaser Requirements** -- Can sell to an unlimited number of accredited investors but no more than 35 unaccredited investors. Furthermore, all of the unaccredited investors must either be "sophisticated" in their own right or act through "purchaser representatives" who have the skill to evaluate the investments for them.
5. **Information Requirements** -- No particular information must be disclosed if sales are exclusively to accredited investors, but if some sales are made to unaccredited investors, there are certain minimal disclosure requirements. The more funds are raised, the higher the disclosure requirements.
6. **Filing Requirements** -- Form D within 15 days.
7. **Resale Restrictions** -- To prevent easy circumvention of the rule's restrictions, the shares' resale is restricted for a year and the issuer must take steps to ensure that buyers know that they are restricted, such as by printing a legend on the securities.

D. Regulation A

1. **Nature of Issuer --** Cannot be used by '34 Act reporting companies, investment companies, or "bad boys."
2. **Limit on Amount --** Can raise $5 million in any 12-month period.
3. **Manner of Offering --** Unique "testing the waters" provision allows offeror to make some preliminary offers to determine whether there is sufficient interest in the securities and to cancel the deal completely without violation if there is not.
4. **Offeree and Purchaser Requirements --** None.
5. **Information Requirements --** Simplified disclosure includes current balance sheet and 2 years unaudited financial statements.
6. **Filing Requirements --** Must file simplified Form 1-A, any sales materials used, and Form 2-A report to the SEC of sales and use of proceeds.
7. **Resale Restrictions --** None.

E. Rule 147 Intrastate Offering

1. **Nature of Issuer --** Issuer must be organized and doing business in the state in which it plans to do the offering. To be safe, should meet "80%" test, including having at least 80% of its assets in-state, making 80% of its revenue in-state, and using 80% of the proceeds of the offering in-state.
2. **Limit on Amount --** No limit.
3. **Manner of Offering --** No limitation, except that must stay intrastate.
4. **Offeree and Purchaser Requirements --** All offerees and purchasers must be in-state residents; offer to even one out-of-state resident can disqualify the exemption.
5. **Information Requirements --** None.
6. **Filing Requirements --** None.
7. **Resale Restrictions --** For 9 months can resell only to other residents of the state.

III. The Exemptions in Table Form

A. The Exemptions in Table Form - Reg. D

Type of Offering	Nature of Issuer	Limit on Amount	Manner of Offering	Offeree and Purchaser Requirements	Info. Req.	Filing Req.	Resale Restrictions
Rule 504	No.'34 Act reporting co's or inv. co's	$1m/12mo.	No general solicitation or advertising. (*)	No requirements	None	Form D w/in 15 days of first date	Restricted resale. (*)
Rule 505	No "bad boys" or inv. co's	$5m/12mo.	No general advertising or solicitation	35 non-AIs unlimited AIs	None if all AIs. If sell to non-AIs, disclosure requirement varies with whether issuer is reporting co. and amount of offering.	Form D	Restricted; take reasonable care to prevent resale
Rule 506	No limitation	No limit	No general advertising or solicitation	35 non-AIs unlimited AIs, but all non-AIs must be "sophisticated" or act thru	Same as 505	Form D	Same as 505

				"purchaser reps"			

(*) Under Rule 504, the limitations on general solicitation and resale are lifted if either (a) the securities are registered under a state law requiring public filing and delivery of a substantive disclosure document to investors before sale, or (b) the securities are issued under a state law exemption that permits general solicitation and advertising, so long as sales are made only to Ais.

B. The Exemptions in Table Form - Non-Reg. D

Type of Offering	Nature of Issuer	Limit on Amount	Manner of Offering	Offeree and Purchaser Requirements	Info. Req.	Filing Req.	Resale Restrictions
Reg. A	No'34 Act reporting co's, inv. co's or "bad boys"	$5m/12mo.	"Testing the waters" permitted before filing Form 1-A	No requirements	Simplified disclosure; financials (current BS and 2 yrs) need not be audited	File Form 1-A, any sales materials, and Form 2-A report to SEC of sales and use of proceeds	None
Rule 147	Issuer must be organized and doing bus. in state (80% test) and use 80% of proceeds in state	No limit	No limit, but must stay intrastate	All offerees must be residents of state	None	None	Limited to other residents for 9 mo.

IV. Key Point -- Reg A, Reg D, and Rule 147 are issuer exemptions. Additionally, Section 4(1) exempts everyone except issuers, brokers, and underwriters so that "Joe Blow" investors can resell their shares at any time without registering (unless they are "restricted resale" shares).

Note:
Misconception: Many people do not realize that these exemptions are simply exemptions from registration, not from federal antifraud rules. Therefore, if in the course of an exempt offering an issuing company makes any misrepresentations, it can be sued by the SEC or by investors.

Blue Sky Laws

Since 1996, blue sky laws, which are state securities regulation provisions, are a little less important than they previously were. It is still useful to learn the role they still play and the way in which recent legislation reduced their role.

I. Much state regulation, except for anti-fraud rules, was preempted by Congress in 1996

- **A.** The National Securities Markets Improvement Act (NSMI) preempts state regulation of "covered" securities, including:
    - **1.** Those listed on any national exchange.
    - **2.** Those issued by registered investment companies.
    - **3.** Those sold to "qualified purchasers."
    - **4.** Those sold pursuant to federal exemptions authorized by Sec. 4(2) [e.g., Rule 506].
- **B.** The NSMI did not preempt state regulation of securities issued under Sec. 3(b), so issuers selling pursuant to Regulation A and Rules 504 and 505 must still follow individual blue-sky laws.

II. In particular, the NSMI ends state "merit regulation."

III. The NSMI allows states to continue to:

- **A.** enforce antifraud statutes; and
- **B.** require "notice" filing.

IV. The Securities Litigation Uniform Standards Act of 1998 -- provides that any class action securities fraud suits must be brought in federal, not state, court.

Purposes of the 1934 Act

The average company files a registration statement under the 1933 Act only once every nine years or so. If 1933 Act registration statements were the only source of public information about companies, investors would be in trouble. The 1934 Act is aimed in large part at ensuring that the more important companies deliver a stream of steady information to the investing public via annual reports, quarterly reports, etc.

I. Regular Disclosure -- Provide regular disclosure by major companies even when they are not raising capital by filing registration statements.

II. Punish fraud -- in communications regarding the purchase and sale of securities of corporations of any size.

- **A.** Corporate Disclosure Cases
- **B.** Insider Trading Cases

III. Created SEC -- This Act created the Securities Exchange Commission to enforce all federal securities laws. Among other things, the SEC:

- **A.** Enforces the 1933 Act's registration and anti-fraud provisions.
- **B.** Enforces the 1934 Act's continuous disclosure and anti-fraud provisions.
- **C.** Registers and regulates broker-dealers.
- **D.** Registers and regulates investment-advisers.
- **E.** Enforces rules regarding proxy solicitations and tender offers.
- **F.** Enforces criminal provisions of the federal securities laws by investigating fraud and referring cases to the Department of Justice for prosecution.

Disclosure Requirements

***Purposes** of Disclosure Requirements: 1. Provide regular disclosures by major companies, even when they are not raising capital, by filing registration statements. 2. Punish fraud in communications regarding the purchase and sale of securities of corporations of any size.*

I. Who are reporting companies who must file documents regularly with SEC?

A. All companies whose shares are traded on national exchanges.

B. All companies with more than <u>$10 million</u> in assets and more than <u>500 shareholders</u> in a single class.

- **1.** This $10 million figure was changed from $5 million in 1996.

C. A company that made a registered public offering during the year.

D. NASDAQ "Bulletin Board" companies.

II. What documents must they file?

A. An initial registration form (Form 10) disclosing such information as:

- **1.** Names of officers and directors.
- **2.** Nature of business.
- **3.** Financial structure of firm.
- **4.** Bonus and profit-sharing provisions for officers and directors.

B. Continuous disclosure forms:

- **1.** 10-Ks -- annual reports (containing certified F/S).
- **2.** 10-Qs -- quarterly reports (F/S need not be certified).
- **3.** 8-Ks -- interim reports covering important developments to be filed within 4 business days of when the development occurs.

III. Other 1934 Act Filing Requirements

A. Concentrations of Shares (Sec. 13(d))

- **1.** Any one individual (or group working in concert) who acquires 5% of a class of equity securities of a 1934 Act reporting company must within 10 days file a Schedule 13D, disclosing:
  - **a.** The purpose of the purchase.
    - **i.** The key question is whether they are merely investing in the company or have acquired this block of shares as a prelude to takeover.
  - **b.** Amount and source of funds.
  - **c.** Name and background of acquirer.
- **2.** Purpose of Requirement: to alert shareholders to potential changes in control of their corporations.

B. Tender Offers

1. If an acquirer makes a tender offer to shareholders of a target corporation for control of the target, the 1934 Act imposes substantial filing requirements on both parties.
2. Acquirer filings must disclose much the same information required by Schedule 13D and should include a discussion of plans for change if the acquisition succeeds.
3. Target filings must include the target management's position regarding whether target shareholders should tender their shares or resist the takeover.
4. Purpose of Requirement: So that shareholders of target corporation can make an informed judgment as to whether they should tender or retain their shares.

C. Proxy Solicitations (Sec. 14)

1. Virtually all reporting companies must solicit proxies from shareholders in order to achieve the necessary quorum to hold their state law mandated annual meetings to elect directors and special meetings to approve transactions that shareholders are entitled to vote on, including mergers.
2. The 1934 Act mandates that such solicitations must be accompanied by proxy statements containing SEC-mandated disclosures including:
    a. All material facts about matters to be voted on.
    b. Extensive background on nominees if it is a Board of Directors' election.
    c. Extensive information on the advantages and disadvantages of a transaction if it is a special election for matters such as mergers or sale of major assets.
3. All issuer proxy statements must include:
    a. <u>Proper</u> **shareholder proposals**, which are proposals for corporate action suggested by the shareholders themselves to be voted on at the annual or special meeting of shareholders.
        i. Can be omitted on various grounds, including:
            1. Matters of personal grievance,
            2. Matters of "ordinary business" within the discretion of management,
            3. Matters "not significantly related" to the issuer's business, and
            4. The fact that they call for violation of state or federal law.
    b. Two years' audited F/S.

D. Insider Trading

1. Sec. 16(a) of the '34 Act provides that three classes of persons must disclose their transactions in their own company's stock.
    a. Officers
    b. Directors
    c. Holders of at least 10% of the company's registered equity securities
        i. **Rationale --** These three categories of persons have significant control over their company and could abuse it by engaging in insider trading; disclosure of their trades to the world should minimize any abuses.
        ii. In addition to filing with the SEC an initial report regarding their holdings when they attain the status of officer, director, or 10% holder, these

persons must report any significant transactions in their company's shares within 2 days of the transaction.

2. If a reporting company's officers, directors, or 10% holders do not comply with the Sec. 16(a) reporting requirements, the company itself must disclose these violations in its proxy statements and Form 10-Ks.
3. Sec. 16(b) of the '34 Act provides that any officer, director, or 10% holder must disgorge any profits derived from "shortswing" transactions in their company's stock.
    a. **A "short-swing" transaction** occurs almost any time the insider buys within six months of selling or sells within six months of buying.

Example:
If a director of A Corp. buys 100 A shares on July 1 for $60 and sells 100 A shares on December 10 for $70, a "short-swing" profit of $1,000 has been gained and must be disgorged.

IV. Any intentionally misleading statement in any of these 1934 Act documents is actionable.

Liability Provisions: 1933 Act

The 1933 Act contains three explicit liability provisions--Sec. 11, Sec. 12(a)(1), and Sec. 12(a)(2). For exam purposes, Sec. 11 is the key. It is based upon common law fraud provisions, but dramatically relaxes some of the requirements of a common law fraud claim in a pro-plaintiff way.

Because the 1933 Act focuses on the initial sale of securities, accountants' liability arises primarily due to inaccurate audited financial statements contained in the registration statement that must be filed with the SEC (unless an exemption applies). The Securities Exchange Commission (SEC) can bring civil actions alleging 1933 Act violations, and injured investors can also bring lawsuits for civil damages.

I. There are three primary causes of action for violation of 1933 Act provisions.

- **A.** Sec. 11 remedies misleading statements and omissions contained in the registration statement as of its effective date.
- **B.** Sec. 12(a)(1) remedies violations of Sec. 5.
  - **1.** Offering a security before filing a registration statement.
  - **2.** Selling a security before the registration statement becomes effective.
  - **3.** Selling a security without providing a prospectus.
  - **4.** Providing a prospectus that does not comply with Sec. 10 requirements.
- **C.** Sec. 12(a)(2) remedies misstatements or omissions in the initial sale of securities that occur outside the registration statement.
  - **1.** Until 1996, 12(a)(1) and 12(a)(2) were known as 12(1) and 12(2), respectively.

II. Sec. 11 is Main Focus for Accountants.

- **A.** Accountants are deemed "experts" with special responsibility.
- **B.** Only "sellers" of securities are liable under Secs. 12(a)(1) and 12(a)(2), so unless accountants "solicit" sales, they should not be liable under those sections.

Example:
Only "sellers" of securities are liable: ABC Accounting Firm certifies financial statements included in a registration statement. The financial statements are materially inaccurate. Additionally, the issuer sent out prospectuses that did not conform to Sec. 10 requirements. ABC may well be liable under Sec. 11 as an expert, but it will not be liable under Sec. 12(a)(1) if all it did was certify the financial statements.

Example:
Only "sellers" of securities are liable: ABC Accounting Firm was asked by its tax clients for investment advice. ABC advised the clients to invest in a company that was owned in large part by partners of ABC. The clients lost a large amount of money and sued ABC under Sec. 12(a)(2). The clients were able to win because ABC's partners had gone beyond their role as accountants and actually solicited investments by the clients.

III. Elements that Plaintiffs Must Prove to Win a Sec. 11 Claim.

A. A false statement or omission of fact appeared in a registration statement.

1. The accounting firm is liable only for that part of the registration statement (financial statements) that it prepared.

Example:
ABC Accounting Firm certifies the financial statements for a registration statement filed by XYZ Computer Co. The financial statements are accurate but some of the textual portion of the registration statement describing XYZ's business history is inaccurate. ABC is not liable for these inaccuracies.

Example:
ABC Accounting Firm certifies the financial statements for a registration statement filed by XYZ Computer Co. The financial statements are accurate as of the effective date of the registration statement, but soon thereafter, the company suffers severe business reverses. The financial statements no longer accurately reflect XYZ's status. ABC cannot be liable under Sec. 11 for these problems.

B. The misstatement or omission was material.

Example:
ABC Accounting Firm certifies the financial statements for a registration statement filed by XYZ Computer Co. The financial statements indicate that XYZ's earnings in the previous year were $3.2 million, when really they were only $3.18 million. The $20,000 error is probably immaterial to any investor's decision and ABC is not liable for the inaccuracy.

C. Plaintiff bought securities that were issued under the defective registration statement.

1. Need not be first purchaser, but must be able to "trace" shares to registration statement.

Example:
ABC Accounting Firm certifies the financial statements for a registration statement filed by XYZ Computer Co., a company going public for the first time. The financial statements are materially inaccurate and Joe, who bought his shares from Sam, sues ABC under Sec. 11. Joe can maintain the action despite not being the first purchaser. Because XYZ has just gone public for the first time, these shares were necessarily issued under the defective registration statement.

Example:
ABC Accounting Firm certifies the financial statements for a registration statement filed by XYZ Computer Co., a company that went public a few years ago and is now making this seasoned offering. The financial statements are materially inaccurate. Joe read about the offering in the paper, called his broker, and said that he wanted to buy $10,000 worth of XYZ shares. Unless Joe can prove that the shares he bought were issued under the defective registration statement and were not previously issued shares, he cannot recover under Sec. 11.

D. Plaintiff suffered damages.

IV. Defenses for Accountant Under Sec. 11.

A. Due Diligence.

1. Elements of Due Diligence

a. Reasonable investigation.

b. Reasonable basis.

c. Good faith belief.

B. Special burden on accountants who are "experts." Other individual defendants are allowed to rely upon "expertised portions" of registration statement.

C. The issuing company itself has no due diligence defense; it is strictly liable for errors in the registration statement.

Note:
A Sec. 11 plaintiff need not prove that the accountant defendant (or any other defendant) acted in bad faith - with what the law calls scienter. Indeed, a Sec. 11 plaintiff need not even prove that the accountant defendant (or any other) acted negligently. Negligence is the standard under Sec. 11, but the burden of proof is upon the defendant accountant to prove that he or she did not act negligently.

Example:
ABC Accounting Firm certifies the financial statements for a registration statement filed by XYZ Computer Co. Notwithstanding the fact that ABC ensured that GAAP and GAAS were complied with and that ABC believed in good faith that the financial statements were accurate, it turns out that they contained materially misleading errors. Injured investors sue ABC, XYZ, and XYZ's officers and directors. ABC and all of XYZ's officers and directors who believed the financial statements were accurate have due diligence defenses and will not be liable. However, XYZ itself has no due diligence defense nor do any of its officers and directors who knew, or should have known, that ABC was making errors.

D. Lack of Reliance by P.

Example:
ABC Accounting Firm certifies the financial statements for a registration statement filed by XYZ Computer Co. The financial statements were materially erroneous, a fact that was later discovered and reported in the newspaper. Joe bought XYZ shares after having read the newspaper articles. Joe could not recover against ABC under Sec. 11 because he did not rely on the false statements.

E. Alternative Causation.

Example:
ABC Accounting Firm certifies the financial statements for a registration statement filed by XYZ Computer Co. The financial statements were materially erroneous. The price of XYZ stock dropped 15% following the announcement of the errors. However, the entire stock market declined an average of 15% during this same time frame, and computer stocks declined, on average, even more. ABC has a very good chance of convincing a jury that the decline in XYZ shares was not caused by the errors it made in certifying the financial statements.

F. Statute of Limitations: P must sue:

1. Within one year from when s/he discovered (or should have discovered) the false statements or omissions; and
   a. Inquiry notice: If P is put on notice that there is a problem, most courts start the 1-year period running; they do not wait until P knows the full dimensions of the problem.
2. Within 3 years after the security was bona fide offered to the public (usually the effective date).

Example:
On May 1, 1997, XYZ Computer Company's registration statement became effective. ABC Accounting Firm had certified the financial statements contained therein. In June of 1997, rumors began to circulate that XYZ had been claiming revenue from sales that were not final. Several financial publications published articles regarding these rumors. In August of 1998, investors filed a Sec. 11 lawsuit against ABC and XYZ seeking to prove that the financial statements contained in the registration statement had been materially misleading. Because the plaintiffs had been put on notice of the potential errors in June 1997, yet they waited 14 months to file the lawsuit, they are probably barred by the statute of limitations. They filed within the 3-year of the offering deadline but missed the 1-year of notice deadline.

V. Damages Under Sec. 11.

A. Defendants, including accountants, are jointly and severally liable under Sec. 11, except for:

1. Outside directors (who are only severally liable), and

2. Underwriters (whose liability is capped at the amount of securities they underwrote).

Example:
ABC Accounting Firm certifies the financial statements for a registration statement filed by XYZ Computer Co. The financial statements were materially erroneous. Investors sued for $1,000,000. Defendants included ABC, XYZ, Sam (XYZ's CEO), Ed (an outside director on XYZ's board), and Big Chief Co., an underwriter that handled $100,000 of the offering. A jury found Ed to be 5% at fault because he had ignored some red flags indicating that the financial statements were inaccurate. All other defendants were also held to be potentially liable. Ed's maximum liability is $50,000 because he is an outside director. Big Chief's maximum liability is $100,000 because that is the amount of the offering that it underwrote. All of the other defendants, including the accounting firm, could be held liable for the full $1,000,000 if their co-defendants are insolvent.

B. Calculation of Sec. 11 Damages.

1. First, calculate the "amount paid," which is the <u>lesser</u> of
   a. the amount actually paid by P, or
   b. the price at which the security was offered to the public.

Example:
LMN Corp. files a registration statement and sells its stock to the public at $18/share. On the second day of public trading, P buys on the secondary market at $20/share. The "amount paid" is $18/share.

2. Apply the proper formula.
3. When P sells the shares prior to filing suit,
4. **Damages = "Amount paid" - sale price.**

Example:
P bought LMN shares at $10/share, the public offering price. After disclosure of errors in the financial statements contained in the registration statement, LMN shares dropped to $6/share. P sold at that price and soon thereafter filed a Sec. 11 lawsuit against Longhorn and its auditor. At the time the lawsuit was filed, LMN shares were trading at $4/share. P won the suit. Damages would be $4/share.

5. When P still owns the shares at the time of judgment,
6. **Damages = "Amount paid" - value at "time of suit."**

Example:
P bought LMN shares at $10/share, the public offering price. After disclosure of errors in the financial statements contained in the registration statement, LMN shares dropped to $6/share. LMN shares were trading at $7/share on the day that P filed a Sec. 11 suit against LMN and its auditor. The shares were trading at $4/share on the day a jury rendered a verdict in favor of P against Ds. Damages would be $3/share.

7. When P sells the shares during the litigation at a price higher than the price "at time of suit," price.
8. **Damages = "Amount paid" - sale.**

Example:
P bought LMN shares at $10/share, the public offering price. After disclosure of errors in the financial statements contained in the registration statement, the price of LMN shares dropped to $5/share on the day that P filed a Sec. 11 suit against LMN and its auditor. During the course of suit, the market rallied and P sold the shares at $9/share. LMN shares were trading at $4/share on the day a jury rendered a verdict in favor of P. P's damages would be $1/share.

9. When P sells during litigation at a price lower than the price "at time of suit,"
10. **Damages = "Amount paid" - value at time of suit.**

Example:
P bought LMN shares at $10/share, the public offering price. After disclosure of errors in the financial statements contained in the registration statement, P filed a Sec. 11 suit against LMN and its auditor. On the day suit was filed, LMN shares were trading at $7/share. During the lawsuit, P sold the shares for $2/share. A jury later returned a verdict for P. P's damages would be $3/share.

11. **Key Point:** Punitive damages are not allowed under Sec. 11 or any other federal securities law provision.

VI. Charts Summarizing 1933 Act Civil Liability

A. Elements of Recovery

Cause of Action?	Wrongful Act?	Scienter?	Reliance ?	Causation ?	Damage ?	Potential Ds
Sec.11	Misleading statement or omission in RS	No; nor must P prove negligence	No, but must be able to "trace" shares to defective RS	No	Yes	Issuer and its insiders, underwriters, auditors, and other experts. Privity not necessary.
Sec.12(a)(1)	Illegal offer or sale (usually sale w/o registration where no exemption applies)	No; virtual strict liability	Same as Sec.11	No	Yes	All "sellers" -- those who transfer title or who "solicit" the transaction. Privity not necessary.
Sec.12(a)(2)	Misleading statement	No; nor must P prove negligence	Same as Sec.11	No	Yes	Same as Sec.12(a)(1)

B. Defenses

Cause of Action	Statute of Limitations	Due Diligence	No Reliance by P	Alternate Causation
Sec.11	1 yr. from date misstatement was or should have been discovered and 3 yrs. from first bona fide offer to public.	Yes; all Ds except issuer	Yes, if P knew of error or 12-mo. earnings statement sent	Yes
Sec.12(a)(1)	1 yr. from date of violation and 3 yrs. from first bona fide offer to public	No, but Rule 508 protects unintentional and incidental violation of Reg.D.	No	No
Sec.12(a)(2)	1 yr. from date misstatement was or should have been discovered and 3 yrs. from sale to P	Yes	Yes, if P knew of error	Yes

Civil Liability Provisions

The most important federal securities law provision in the world is probably Section 10(b) of the 1934 Act and its implementing rule, Rule 10b-5. It has been estimated that in 1993 alone, the Big Six firms in the U.S. paid $373.4 million just in 10b-5 cases. That's a lot of money.

I. **Sec. 10(b) and Rule 10b-5 --** of the '34 Act apply to all securities, no matter how big or small the company is, whether it is registered or unregistered with the SEC, and whether an initial offering or secondary trading is involved. The Sarbanes-Oxley Act of 2002 made some important changes to the 1934 Act.

A. **Key Points**

1. If there is a false statement in a registration statement, such as erroneous financial statements certified by an accounting firm, plaintiffs can sue under both Sec. 11 of the '33 Act and Sec. 10(b) of the '34 Act. However, whereas the standard of liability under Sec. 11 is mere negligence (and the burden of proof is on the defendant), the standard of liability under Sec. 10(b) is scienter (bad intent) and the burden of proof is upon the plaintiff.
2. The SEC can bring civil charges alleging violations of Sec. 10(b) and injured investors can also bring civil suits for damages.

II. **What Plaintiffs Must Prove to Win a 10b-5 Claim.**

A. **False statement or omission of material fact.**

B. **Scienter by Defendant**

1. "Recklessness" is sufficiently similar to bad intent to satisfy the requirement.

Example:
Recklessness - ABC Accounting Firm certified the financial statements of XYZ Computer Co. that were included in XYZ's 10-K filing with the SEC. ABC did not comply with GAAP. Indeed, it cut corners in several respects and ignored several "red flags." Nonetheless, ABC thought the financial statements might be accurate and truly hoped that they were. ABC's actions are sufficiently reckless that, if the financial statements turn out to be inaccurate, they will probably be liable under Sec. 10(b).

2. Unlike under Sec. 11, mere negligence will not suffice.

C. **Reliance by Plaintiff**

1. Omission case: Plaintiff need not prove reliance.
   a. In an omission case, plaintiff is not claiming that any affirmative lies were told, only that material facts were omitted.

Example:
Omission Case - ABC Accounting Firm certified the financial statements of XYZ Computer Co. that were included in XYZ's 10-K filing with the SEC. ABC did comply with GAAP. However, XYZ had some unusual financial considerations not covered by GAAP that, when omitted, rendered the financial statements materially misleading. Plaintiff investors suing under Sec. 10(b) and Rule 10b-5 would not have to prove reliance for it is very difficult to prove that you relied on something that was hidden from you.

2. Active Misrepresentation Case: Plaintiff must prove reliance.

   a. May satisfy by proof of "fraud on the market," i.e., by P showing that although s/he did not read the particular false statement (i.e., a faulty financial statement contained in a 10-K), market professionals did and their reaction established a market price upon which P relied when in purchasing the securities.

Example:
Active Misrepresentation Case - ABC Accounting Firm certified the financial statements of XYZ Computer Co. that were included in XYZ's 10-K filing with the SEC. The financial statements reported earnings of $10,000,000. This was surprisingly good news and the stock market reacted by boosting XYZ's share price by $10/share. It turned out that the financial statements were inaccurate having overstated XYZ's earnings by 50%. Plaintiff investors under Sec. 10(b) need not show that they read the 10-K in order to sue. Rather, they relied upon the accuracy of the market price as established by the professional analysts and institutional investors who did read the 10-K and whose activities largely establish the market price. The investors were indirectly misled.

D. Causation

1. Transaction Causation - To establish transaction causation, plaintiff must show that the false statements or omissions caused him to enter into the transaction (overlaps reliance element).

Example:
Sam bought ABC shares from his girlfriend who had just become a stockbroker and was assigned the task of pushing ABC shares. It turns out that ABC's financial statements as contained in its most recent 10-K were inaccurate. Because Sam had not read those financial statements and did not really care what they said -- he was buying to help out his girlfriend -- he cannot establish transaction causation. Whatever misstatements were in the financials statements are not what caused him to buy the shares.

2. Loss Causation - To establish loss causation, plaintiff must show that the false statements or omissions are what actually caused his financial loss; alternative causation may doom P's claim.

Example:
Seeking a tax shelter, Paul wished to invest in an oil and gas limited partnership in the early 1980s. He invested in ABC LP. Unfortunately for Paul, the entire oil and gas industry crashed just after he invested and he lost lots of money. He sued ABC proving that ABC had not disclosed that its promoters were not entirely honest and not very experienced in the oil and gas business. Paul may be able to show transaction causation ("I would not have bought ABC shares had I known the truth.") but he cannot show loss causation. Even if he had not invested in ABC, he would have invested in another oil and gas limited partnership and would have lost money there due to the industry-wide crash.

3. The fraud occurred in connection with a purchase or sale of securities.
    a. P must have bought or sold shares in order to have "standing" to sue.

Example:
Connection with a purchase or sale of securities - A has held ABC shares since 1980. He proves that defendant officers and directors of ABC have manipulated its shares for their own personal goals causing its value to drop. Shares A bought in 1980 at $30/share are now worth only $20/share. Nonetheless, A cannot successfully sue under Sec. 10(b) because he cannot prove that he bought or sold shares in connection with the false statements. He merely held the same shares.

    b. SEC can always sue.
4. Plaintiff suffered damages.

III. Sec. 10(b) Defenses

A. Statute of Limitations -- plaintiff must sue:

1. Within 2 years of when the fraud was or should have been discovered, and
2. Within 5 years of the fraud.

Example:
Statute of Limitations - On May 1, 2002, XYZ Computer Company's registration statement became effective. ABC Accounting Firm had certified the financial statements contained therein. In June of 2003, rumors began to circulate that XYZ had been claiming revenue from sales that were not final. Several financial publications published articles regarding these rumors. In August of 2005, investors filed a Sec. 10(b) lawsuit against ABC and XYZ, seeking to prove that the financial statements contained in the registration statement had been materially misleading. Because the plaintiffs had been put on notice of the potential errors in June 2003, yet they waited 26 months to file the lawsuit, they are probably barred by the statute of limitations. They filed within the 5-year violation deadline but missed the 2-year notice deadline.

B. Fraudulent or reckless conduct by plaintiff

Example:
Plaintiff is an officer of XYZ Computer Corp. and buys some of its shares. The shares plummet in price when it is learned that XYZ's most recent 10-K contained inaccurate financial statements. Plaintiff sues XYZ's accounting firm, ABC, under Sec. 10(b). ABC may avoid liability if it can prove that plaintiff, as an officer of XYZ, was in a position to see red flags that should have alerted him as to XYZ's troubles.

C. Bespeaks Caution Doctrine -- If in a forward-looking statement, such as a prediction of earnings for the upcoming year, a company clearly identifies specific risk factors that might occur to prevent the prediction from coming true, that cautionary language which "bespeaks caution" will likely prevent recovery in any securities fraud suit based on a failure of the company to realize its predicted earnings. This defense was developed by the courts, but has been codified in the PSLRA of 1995.

D. Secondary Liability

1. **Note**, that in a recent and very important decision, the Supreme Court held that there is no such thing as "aiding and abetting" liability under Sec. 10(b).
2. This recent decision should limit such liability for accountants who formerly have often been held liable just for "standing around" the clients who happened to be crooks; henceforth, accountants will probably be liable only for their own false statements or omissions, although this is unsettled.
3. In 1995, Congress restored the SEC's authority to bring "aiding and abetting" claims, but private damage plaintiffs still cannot use this theory.

E. Damages -- (assuming P is a buyer)

1. If P still owns shares: Amount paid minus market value at time of suit.
2. If P has sold shares: Amount paid minus sale price.
3. Punitive Damages are not allowed in any federal securities law case, including Sec. 10(b).

IV. Chart summarizing Sec. 10(b) Elements

Cause of Action or Omission	Sec.10(b)
Misstatement	Yes
Materiality	Yes
Scienter	Yes (recklessness will suffice)
Causation	Yes, transaction (lie made me trade) and loss (lie caused stock price decline) both needed
Reliance	Omission: No Active misrep: Yes, but can satisfy by "fraud on the market"
Privity	No
Damages	Yes

Criminal Liability

The SEC has the authority to refer to the Department of Justice for criminal prosecution ANY intentional violation of ANY provision of the 1933 or 1934 Acts.

I. 1933 Securities Act

A. Accountants are liable for any "willful" violation of any provision of the 1933 Act.

B. Penalties: Up to $10,000 fine and/or 5 years in jail.

II. 1934 Securities Exchange Act

A. Accountants are liable for any "willful" violation of any provision of the 1934 Act.

B. Penalties: Up to $2,500,000 fine and/or 20 years in jail (up to $25 million fine if defendant is a firm).

C. These criminal penalties are cumulative; they may be imposed on top of the civil liability discussed elsewhere.

D. The SEC cannot bring criminal charges itself; rather, it refers these cases to the Department of Justice, which actually files and prosecutes the cases, often based on evidence provided by the SEC.

Private Securities Litigation Reform Act

At the instigation of lobbyists for the accounting profession and high tech firms, Congress overrode President Clinton's veto to pass the PSLRA of 1995. The PSLRA was aimed primarily at making it more difficult for plaintiff's attorneys to drive class action 10b-5 litigation against accounting firms and others. However, among a sea of anti-plaintiff provisions, the PSLRA also contains a provision that burdens accountants with a whistle-blowing duty.

I. PSLRA of 1995

A. In 1995, in response to lobbying by accountants, Congress passed the PSLRA which, in general, made it harder to bring securities fraud class action lawsuits by:

1. Putting in procedural hurdles for plaintiffs seeking to bring class actions, and

2. Raising the bar regarding some procedural and substantive matters regarding the causes of action.

3. The most important procedural hurdle was a requirement that discovery be stayed in actions after defendants filed motions to dismiss. Plaintiffs' class action attorneys evaded this bar on discovery by filing parallel securities fraud actions in state court. This ploy was ended when Congress passed the Securities Litigation Uniform Standards Act of 1998, which requires all class action securities fraud suits to be brought in federal, not state, court.

B. Interestingly, the most important part of this generally pro-accountant law is a provision that imposes upon accountants an arguable duty to "blow the whistle" on their clients to the SEC when illegal activity is discovered.

II. New Rules for Auditors

A. Each audit required by the 1934 Act shall include:

1. Procedures designed to provide reasonable assurance of detecting illegal acts that would have a direct and material effect on the determination of financial statement amounts.

2. Procedures designed to identify material related-party transactions.

3. An evaluation of whether there is substantial doubt about the issuer's ability to continue as a going concern.

B. If, during the audit, the accountant becomes aware of information indicating that an illegal act (whether or not material) has occurred, then the accountant shall:

1. Determine whether it is likely that an illegal act has occurred.

2. If so, determine the possible effect on the issuer (in terms of fines, penalties, damages, etc.).

3. As soon as practicable, inform the appropriate level of management of the issue and assure that its audit committee or board of directors is adequately informed.

C. If, after the audit committee or board of directors is informed, the accountant concludes that:

1. The illegal act has a material effect on the financial statements.

2. The senior management has not taken timely and appropriate remedial action regarding the illegal act.

3. The failure to take such action is reasonably expected to warrant departure from a standard report of the auditor or, when made, warrant resignation from the audit engagement.

D. The accountant shall directly report its conclusions to the board. When the board receives such a report of an illegal act, it shall inform the SEC within 1 business day and provide a copy of the notice to the accountant. If the accountant fails to receive a copy of this notice, within one business day, s/he shall:

   1. Resign from the engagement, or

   2. Furnish to the SEC a copy of its report not later than one business day.

E. If an auditor resigns, it shall, within one business day following the issuer's failure to inform the SEC, furnish the SEC with a copy of the illegal act report.

F. "No independent accountant shall be liable in a private action for any finding, conclusion, or statement expressed in a report made to (the issuer or the SEC)."

G. If an auditor willfully violates these requirements, the SEC may impose a civil penalty under Sec. 21C

Public Company Accounting Oversight Board (PCAOB)

The Enron era scandals prompted Congress to create the PCAOB to oversee auditing of public companies selling securities in the U.S. This ended the self-regulation era of public auditing and ushered in significant and long-lasting changes for the public accounting profession. Accountants in almost every area will be impacted by the PCAOB, so its powers and priorities should be a significant focus on the CPA exam.

I. **Purpose --** Sarbanes-Oxley created the PCAOB to have power over auditors similar to that exercised by the NASD over broker-dealers.

   A. The SEC will oversee the PCAOB.

      1. The PCAOB's members (5, 3 of whom may not be accountants) will be selected by the SEC.

II. **Scope --** PCAOB will not regulate firms that service only private companies

   A. Register public accounting firms.

      1. Establish auditing, quality control, ethics, independence, and other standards relating to the preparation of audit reports, or adopt such standards as proposed by existing professional groups or new advisory committees.
      2. Conduct inspections of registered public accounting firms.
      3. Conduct investigations and disciplinary proceedings concerning registered public accounting firms and associated persons.
      4. Enforce compliance with SOX, the PCAOB's rules, professional standards, and the securities laws relating to the preparation of audit reports by registered public accounting firms and associated persons.
      5. Perform such other services as the PCAOB or the SEC determines are necessary or appropriate to promote high professional standards, protect investors, or further the public interest.

III. **Registration**

   A. In order to prepare, issue, or participate in the preparation or issuance of any audit report with respect to any public company, a public accounting firm must register with the PCAOB.

   B. **Information to be disclosed will include**

      1. names of all audit clients in the past year;
      2. annual fees for audit and nonaudit services received from each client;
      3. a statement of firm quality control policies;
      4. a list of all accountants associated with the firm who participated in the audits;
      5. information relating to criminal, civil, or administrative proceedings pending against the firm or any associated person in connection with any audit report;
      6. copies of any disclosure filed by a client with the SEC in the last calendar year disclosing a disagreement between the auditors and the firm; and
      7. any other information that the PCAOB or the SEC believe should be disclosed.

C. Each firm will also have to submit an annual report and pay a registration fee each year.

IV. New Standards

A. The PCAOB has broad power to consult experts to establish auditing, quality control, ethics, and independence standards.

B. The auditing standards must include at least these three rules

1. Auditors must retain for at least 7 years audit work papers and other information in sufficient detail to support the conclusions reached in the audit report.
2. An accounting firm must provide a concurring or second partner to review and approve each audit.
3. The firm must describe in each audit report the scope of the auditor's testing of the internal control structure and procedures of the issuer and present the findings of such testing, an evaluation of the internal control structure, a description of material weaknesses in such internal controls, and any material noncompliance found.

V. Inspections

A. The PCAOB must conduct a "program of inspections" to assess registrant's compliance with the Act, SEC and PCAOB rules, and professional standards.

1. Annual inspections for firms doing more than 100 audits per year.
2. Inspections every 3 years for firms doing fewer than 100 audits.

B. Firms can seek SEC review of PCAOB inspection reports if they disagree.

VI. Investigations and Discipline

A. The PCAOB is authorized to investigate any act, practice, or omission by a registrant to any associated person that may violate any provision of the Act, the PCAOB's rules, securities rules, or professional standards.

B. The PCAOB can require testimony and production of audit work papers or other documents.

C. The PCAOB must notify the SEC and coordinate with its enforcement division.

D. PCAOB may refer any investigation to the SEC, other federal regulators, or, at the SEC's direction, federal prosecutors.

E. In any disciplinary proceeding, the PCAOB must bring specific charges, give notification, allow for an opportunity to defend, and keep a record of the proceedings (which will generally be nonpublic).

F. Board sanctions may include

1. temporary suspension or permanent revocation of registration of a firm (only for intentional or knowing conduct, or repeated negligent conduct);
2. temporary or permanent suspension or bar of a person from working with a registered public accounting firm (only for intentional or knowing conduct, or repeated negligent conduct);
3. temporary or permanent limitation on the activities, functions, or operations of a firm or person (only for intentional or knowing conduct, or repeated negligent conduct);
4. a civil penalty for each violation up to $100,000 for an individual and $2 million for an entity or, in the case of intentional or knowing conduct, or repeated negligent conduct, up to $750,000 for an individual and $15 million for an entity;
5. censure;

6. required professional education or training; or

7. any other appropriate action.

G. The PCAOB may sanction a firm or its supervisors if they failed to reasonably supervise an "associated person" who violated rules or standards.

VII. Foreign Firms -- Foreign accounting firms are presumptively subject to the Act, but the SEC may create exemptions.

VIII. SEC Oversight

A. The SEC must approve all PCAOB rules.

B. The SEC has broad power to oversee the board, limit its activities, and remove its members.

C. Creation of the PCAOB does not limit in any way the SEC's authority to enforce the securities laws, set standards for auditors, or take legal action.

D. A violation of the Act, any SEC rule based on the Act, or any PCAOB rule is deemed equivalent to a violation of the 1934 Securities Exchange Act.

Auditor Independence

While the most important audit independence rules derive from Rule 101 of the AICPA's Code of Professional Conduct, the SEC and PCAOB have the authority, of course, to supplement or override AICPA rules where public company audits are concerned. Therefore, it is helpful to know the new post-Enron rules embodied in SOX.

I. An independent auditor cannot perform the following services for an audit client:

- **A.** bookkeeping or other services related to the accounting records of financial statements;
- **B.** financial information systems design and implementations;
- **C.** appraisal or valuation services, fairness opinions, or contributions-in-kind reports;
- **D.** actuarial services;
- **E.** internal audit outsourcing services;
- **F.** management functions or human resources;
- **G.** broker or dealer, investment adviser, or investment banking services;
- **H.** legal services and expert services unrelated to the audit; and
- **I.** any other service that the PCAOB determines is impermissible.

II. Non-Audit Client Services -- Firms may provide these services to non-audit clients and to private companies.

III. Non-Audit Services -- Other non-audit services may be performed by public audit clients **if** preapproved by the audit committee and disclosed in client's periodic reports.

- **A.** There are **no** requirements for issuers to rotate audit **firms**
- **B.** but audit firms must rotate both the lead audit partner and the reviewing audit partner at least every 5 years.

IV. Auditor Report

- **A.** Audit firms are now selected and compensated by the audit committee rather than management
- **B.** Each firm must timely report to the client's audit committee:
    - **1.** all critical accounting policies and practices to be used;
    - **2.** all alternative treatments of financial information within GAAP that have been discussed with management officials, ramifications of the use of such alternative disclosures, and the treatment preferred by the accounting firm; and
    - **3.** other material written communications between the accounting firm and the issuer's management, such as any management letter or schedule of unadjusted differences.

V. Cooling-Off Periods

- **A.** An audit firm may not perform an audit for a client if its CEO, controller, CFO, CAO, or any person serving in an equivalent capacity was employed by the firm and participated in the audit during a one-year period preceding the date of the initiation of the audit.
- **B.** If the individual worked for the audit firm but did not participate in the client's audit: no problem.

Other Government Regulation

Title VII Civil Rights Acts

It seems inconceivable now, but until 1964 most companies could legally say: "We won't hire you because we don't hire African-Americans...or women...or Jews...etc." Fortunately, Congress banned many types of discrimination in both public accommodations (restaurants, hotels, airlines, etc.) and in private employment in 1964.

I. Forbids discrimination in employment based on:

A. Race

Example: Three employees, one black and two white, were caught stealing from the employer. The employer fired only the two white employees. There was no apparent basis for the distinction other than race. This is impermissible discrimination under Title VII, which protects all races from racially-based discrimination.

B. Color

Example: A light-skinned person of African-American descent fired all the dark-skinned persons of African-American descent in the department. This could easily constitute discrimination prohibited by Title VII.

C. Religion

Example: Title VII protects both religious beliefs and religious practices. An employer's responsibility is to "reasonably accommodate" the employee's need, although the courts have not construed this responsibility in too onerous a fashion.

1. A Lutheran church had an opening for a pastor. Plaintiff, a Jewish rabbi, applied for the job. Here is an exception to the protection accorded by Title VII. Naturally, an accounting firm could not refuse to hire someone because they were Jewish, but the Lutheran church could in this instance.

D. Sex

Example:
Plaintiff, a male, wished to be a flight attendant but defendant airline had a "women only" policy. This was held to be a Title VII violation. The law protects men as well as women from gender discrimination.

E. National Origin

Example:
Plaintiff was fired because he was from London and had a British accent that annoyed his boss. This was prohibited discrimination under Title VII.

Chart of Protected and Unprotected Discriminations		
	Protected Against	**Not Protected Against**
Discrimination against African-American	x	
Discrimination against Asian-Americans	x	
Discrimination against Polish-Americans	x	
Discrimination against American Indians	x	
Discrimination against Hispanics	x	
Discrimination against whites	x	
Discrimination against white employee because of interracial marriage	x	
Discrimination against the elderly		x [but see ADEA]
Discrimination against women	x	
Discrimination against men	x	
Discrimination against Jews	x	
Discrimination on basis of pregnancy and childbirth	x	
Discrimination on basis of sexual preference		x
Discrimination in form of quid-pro-quo sexual harassment	x	
Discrimination in form of hostile environment	x	
Discrimination against the disabled		x [but see ADA]

II. Title VII applies to:

A. *Employers*

1. Having 15 or more employees for at least 20 weeks; **and**
   - **a.** (In 1997, the Supreme Court held that in counting employees, courts must include those who work part-time or are on leave.)
2. Whose business affects interstate commerce.
   - **a.** (Virtually every business affects interstate commerce in some way, so this is not an especially burdensome requirement for plaintiffs.)

B. *Employment Agencies*

C. *Labor Unions*

D. *Federal, State, and Local Government Employees*

1. **Fact** -- Charitable organizations are not generally exempt, nor are religious employers (though they may hire on the basis of religious belief and practice).

III. **Title VII covers virtually all employment practices, including:**

A. *Hiring*

B. *Promotion* (Including promotion to partnership in an accounting firm.)

C. *Transfers*

D. *Firings*

E. *Compensation*

F. *Job Assignments*

IV. **Title VII is enforced by:**

A. *Equal Employment Opportunity Commission (EEOC)*, and/or

1. If EEOC cannot resolve a Title VII case initiated by employee complaint, it issues a "right to sue" letter to the complaining party.

B. *Civil Actions* by individual plaintiffs.

1. Suits must be against the employer, not the offending individual supervisor.

V. **Title VII does not preempt similar state laws** -- Virtually every state has laws comparable to Title VII, and some provide even greater levels of protection in terms of the practices they prohibit, the classes of persons they protect, and the size of the employers they regulate.

VI. **Types of Discrimination**

A. **Intentional** -- (Disparate Treatment)

1. An employer assigned Hispanic customers to Hispanic employees and white customers to white employees. This was held to be intentional discrimination.

2. In a "mixed motive" case, P wins if illegal criterion was a "motivating factor" in decision, even if other factors were present.

Example: Employer fired plaintiff partly because he was male and partly because he was somewhat slow in carrying out his duties. If the plaintiff would not have been fired solely on the basis of his performance, then he has a plausible Title VII claim.

B. **Discriminatory Impact** -- (Disparate Impact)

1. Disparate Impact cases arise primarily in situations where facially neutral job criteria such as height, weight, strength, or education standards have a discriminatory impact on protected groups; such discrimination is often proved by statistical evidence.

Example:
Employer requires a high school diploma of employees seeking to be custodians. This requirement eliminates 10% of all white applicants from the applicant pool, but knocks out 40% of all African-American applicants in the area. Because it is unlikely that one needs a high school diploma to be a custodian, this requirement is probably discriminatory.

VII. Defenses for Employer

A. Bona Fide Occupational Qualification -- (BFOQ)

1. If a requirement that has a discriminatory impact is a bona fide occupational qualification pertaining directly to the needs of the job, then it is not a Title VII violation.

Example:
Plaintiff was a Sikh whose religion prohibited him from shaving. He worked as a machinist for defendant. Unfortunately, his beard prevented the achievement of an airtight seal on the respirator that federal safety regulations required all machinists to wear. Defendant offered him a number of similar positions for which he was qualified that would not require him to wear a respirator, although all were slightly lower paying. The safety regulations provided defendant employer with a legitimate BFOQ defense.

B. Bona Fide Seniority or Merit System

1. No affirmative action plan can override such systems.

Example:
A city fire department was all white for many years. Only recently did it begin to hire African-Americans. Then budget cutbacks necessitated layoffs, which were done on a seniority basis. Naturally, most of those laid off were African-Americans because they had not had the opportunity to gain much seniority. Nonetheless, the layoffs are not a violation of Title VII if they are based on a valid seniority system.

Note:
Misconception:
Although many people seem to believe that it is improper to ever fire members of protected classes, it is always permissible to fire employees on the basis of merit criteria.

C. Professional-Developed Ability Test

1. **Purpose --** To prove that standards or requirements serve a legitimate business purpose.

VIII. Sexual Harassment -- Although Congress probably did not have sexual harassment in mind when it passed Title VII, the courts have come to recognize two forms of sexual harassment that are prohibited under the Act.

A. Quid Pro Quo ("This for That") has these elements:

1. Boss (or someone for whom boss is responsible) makes unwelcome request for sexual favors; and
2. Compliance is reasonably seen as term or condition of employment.

Example:
Plaintiff worked for a fast food company. He received good evaluations and consistent promotions until he refused to sleep with his new supervisor. She began giving him poor evaluations and soon fired him. He had a valid Title VII claim.

B. Hostile Environment Harassment has these elements:

1. The employer creates or tolerates an intimidating, hostile, or offensive working environment.

Example:
Plaintiff was one of the first females to be employed at a shipyard. She was often subjected to comments by coworkers about her body and coworkers displayed "pin-ups" of naked women. Plaintiff complained to her supervisor who laughed at her and put up his own pin-ups. Plaintiff had a legitimate hostile environment sexual harassment claim.

C. A series of important Supreme Court decisions in 1998 established that:

1. same-sex sexual harassment is prohibited by Title VII,
2. employers may be liable for sexual harassment by their employees and supervisors even though that harassment does not aid the employer in any way, and
3. if victims of sexual harassment suffer an adverse job result (firing, demotion, etc.), the employer is strictly liable,
4. if a sexual harassment victim does not suffer an adverse job result, employers can avoid liability by establishing, communicating, and enforcing a zero-tolerance policy.
5. employees who do not take advantage of their employer's internal procedures for handling complaints will probably be barred from pursuing court litigation.

ADEA

When Congress passed Title VII in 1964, it did not prohibit discrimination on the basis of age. Many years later, Congress remedied this omission by passing the ADEA to protect persons 40 years and older. Remember, there is no protection for discrimination against the young.

I. **Purpose: --** To supplement Title VII, which did not address age discrimination, by eliminating discrimination against older workers.

II. **Protects: --** Individuals 40 years and older.

  A. Main Effect: Prohibit mandatory retirement.

    1. Exemption for executives 65 or older.

    2. Former exemption: Tenured professors.

  B. Also protects from discrimination in all other areas of employment practice.

  C. There is no cause of action for "reverse age discrimination" against the young.

III. **Applies to:**

  A. Businesses employing at least 20 people,

  B. State and Local Governments,

  C. Unions (with at least 25 members),

  D. Employment Agencies.

IV. **Procedures, Remedies, and Defenses are generally same as under Title VII.**

ADA

Title VII did not protect the disabled from discrimination in employment or public accommodations, either. Again, many years after 1964, Congress remedied this omission. The most controversial part of this act during its passage, and the most difficult part in its application since passage, is that relating to disabilities arising from mental illness.

I. **Purpose: --** Ensure our economy takes advantage of the skills and abilities that disabled persons have to offer.

II. **Applies to:**

  A. Employers with 15 or more employees.

  B. All state and local governments.

  C. Most private businesses that provide accommodations, goods, or services to the public.

  D. Public services and transportation.

III. **Enforced by: --** EEOC and private suits, like Title VII.

IV. **Forbids discrimination against "any qualified individual with a disability," defined as:**

  A. a physical or mental impairment that substantially limits one or more "major life activities" of such individual;

  B. a record of any such impairment; or

  C. being regarded as having such an impairment.

  D. Note: In 2008, Congress made several important changes to the ADA, including:

    1. Providing a non-exhaustive list of major life activities, including: "caring for oneself, performing manual tasks, seeing, hearing, eating, sleeping, walking, standing, lifting, bending, speaking, breathing, learning, reading, concentrating, thinking, communicating, and working."

    2. Providing that the determination whether an impairment substantially limits a major life activity must be made "without regarding to the ameliorative effects of mitigating measures" such as medication, artificial aids, assistive technology, and reasonable accommodations. There is an exception for eyeglasses and contact lenses. If they can improve a person's vision sufficiently, the person is no longer considered "disabled," even if s/he is unable to see without them. However, a person who can walk with prosthetic legs or can function at work when taking antidepressant medication, is still "disabled" if s/he cannot walk without the prosthetics or cannot work without the medication.

V. Protected Disabilities Chart

	Protected	Not Protected
Muscular dystrophy	X	
HIV infected	X	
Mental retardation	X	
Alcoholism	X	
Emotional illness	X	
Homosexuality		X
Bisexuality		X
Transvestitism		X
Transsexualism		X
Pedophilia		X
Exhibitionism		X
Voyeurism		X
Sexual behavior disorders		X
Compulsive gambling		X
Kleptomania		X
Pyromania		X
Psychiatric substance disorders resulting from current illegal use of drugs or abuse of alcohol		X

VI. Employers must:

A. Not discriminate in hiring or other employment practices.

Example:
Employee informed employer that he had been diagnosed with brain cancer and would have to undergo chemotherapy. The employer promptly fired the employee without determining whether or not the employee would be able to continue to perform his responsibilities. This was held as an ADA violation.

Example:
Employee informed his supervisor that he had tested HIV-positive. The supervisor told the employee's coworkers and had them vote on whether or not they wished to continue to work with him. He lost by an 18-14 vote and was fired. This was an ADA violation.

B. Establish nondiscriminatory hiring standards by:

1. Identifying the "essential functions" of the job,

2. Ensuring that any employment standards that might exclude a disabled person is "job related and of business necessity,"

3. Determining if a "reasonable accommodation" would permit the disabled person to meet the standard.

C. Make reasonable accommodations by, among other things:

1. Making facilities accessible,

2. Providing adaptive hardware,

3. Hiring readers or interpreters,

4. Providing part-time or modified work schedules.

Federal Social Security Act

The Social Security system was established back in the 1930s as one of the earliest parts of our social welfare system. It has always been controversial, but there seems little likelihood that it will be eliminated any time soon. The system's focus is upon retirement income, but it has a broader scope than just that. Nearly one in every seven Americans receives social security benefits, so the importance of the system cannot be gainsaid.

I. Purpose: -- To provide **partial** replacement of earnings when a worker retires.

II. Mechanism: -- Monthly benefits are paid to retired insured worker from age 62 onward.

III. Insured Worker -- A **"fully insured" worker** is entitled to some benefits, although the amount payable changes often.

- **A.** To be "fully insured," one must accrue a minimum of 40 quarters (10 years) of contributions.
- **B.** A "fully insured" worker is eligible for these benefits:
  - **1.** Survivor benefits for widow or widower and dependents.
  - **2.** Disability benefits for worker and family.
  - **3.** Old age retirement benefits to worker and dependents.
    - **a.** Benefits can be reduced by:
      - **i.** Early retirement before age 65:
        - **1.** Retire at 62 = 80% of benefits
        - **2.** Retire at 63 = 87% of benefits
        - **3.** Retire at 64 = 93% of benefits
      - **ii.** For most of Social Security's existence, workers were entitled to full benefits at age 65. However, for reasons of fiscal solvency, the "full benefits" threshold has been changed and is sliding later and later. For example, someone born in 1937 or before was entitled to full benefits at age 65. Someone born in 1938 is entitled to full benefits at age 65 and two months. Someone born between 1943 and 1954 is, or will be, entitled to full benefits at age 66. Someone born after 1960 will be entitled to full benefits at age 67.
    - **b.** Lump-sum death benefits.
- **C.** A "currently insured" worker is eligible for:
  - **1.** Limited survivor benefits (usually limited to dependent minors or those caring for dependent minors).
  - **2.** Benefits for disabled workers and dependents.
  - **3.** Lump-sum death benefits.

IV. Medicare

- **A.** Covers portion of costs of hospitalization and medical benefits of insured workers and spouses 65 and older.
- **B.** Can cover younger disabled workers in some cases.

V. Disability Benefits

A. Covers worker who suffers a severe physical or mental impairment preventing that person from working for a year or more or expected to result in the victim's death.

B. The disability need not be work related, but must be total.

C. After 24 months of disability, Medicare is made available.

1. Unlike Medicare, Medicaid payments are separate from the Social Security system.

FICA

Often, when small businesses struggle financially, they begin to cut corners by not making timely FICA contributions. This is often a fatal error. Every employer, and every employer's CPA, should know the basics of the FICA rules.

I. Imposes Social Security tax on:

A. Employers,

B. Employees, and

C. The self-employed (under the Self-Employment Contributions Tax Act).

II. Application -- The tax applies only to that part of compensation that is deemed "wages."

Example:
Compensation deemed "wages": salary, commissions, bonuses, fees, tips, fringe benefits, etc. (generally: active income).

Example:
Compensation not deemed "wages": reimbursed employee expenses, interest on bonds owned, dividends on stock owned, investment income (generally: passive income).

III. Features of FICA

A. Rates generally the same for employer and employee.

B. Rates change often [Currently 7.65%, which breaks down to 6.2% for Social Security and 1.45% for Medicare].

C. Social Security taxes are paid on only a base amount of income that is adjusted annually for inflation [$104,000 in 2008 and adjusted annually for inflation]; income levels for taxes for the Medicare component are not similarly capped.

1. **Maximum Amount --** After tax is deducted from maximum amount of taxable income (for Social Security purposes only), no more will be deducted until the next calendar year.
2. **Refund --** An employee who works for more than two employers may have a total higher than the base amount deducted by employer; employee is entitled to a refund.

IV. FICA is also used to fund Medicare (not Medicaid)

V. Employers' Responsibilities:

A. Pay own share.

B. Withhold employee's equal share and remit it in a timely fashion.

C. Pay employee's share if fail to withhold ("double tax").

D. Furnish employee with written statement of wages paid and contributions withheld.

E. Supply Taxpayer Identification Numbers when filing returns.

VI. Employers' Rights:

A. Collect employee's share from employee (though employer may voluntarily pay employee's share and deduct that amount as additional compensation, making it taxable to employee).

B. Deduct as a business expense the contributions made on its own behalf to FICA.

Payroll Tax Liability

I. Introduction

A. Certain corporate taxes are treated as "trust fund" taxes and must be remitted to tax authorities.

B. Failure to remit may lead to penalty of 100% of the tax not paid being imposed on "any responsible officer and director" who willfully fails to pay the tax.

C. The key section is 6672 of Title 26 (Internal Revenue Code).

II. Who is a "Responsible Person?"

A. The statute imposes liability on "any person required to collect, truthfully account for, and pay over any tax" who willfully fails to do so.

B. Many courts look at seven factors, none of which is alone determinative:

1. Is the person an officer or director?
2. Does the person own part of the company?
3. Is the person active in management of day-to-day affairs?
4. Does the person have the ability to hire and fire?
5. Does the person have discretion to decide which, when, and in what order debts or taxes will be paid?
6. Does the person exercise control over daily bank accounts and disbursement records?
7. Does the person have check-signing authority?

C. Some courts say the key question is whether the person had the actual authority or ability, given his or her role within the corporation, to pay the taxes owed.

D. Accountants have been held not to be responsible persons where:

1. They were bookkeepers who were neither officers nor managed day-to-day affairs of company.
2. They performed part-time accounting duties with check-writing authority, but were not officers and wrote checks only as directed by sole stockholder.
3. They performed financial services and had signatory power for checks, but signed such checks only at the request of an officer.
4. Their authority ran solely to preventing double payment of invoices by the corporate employer.
5. They served for several weeks as controller of their normal employer's subsidiary and had the authority to sign checks but would have needed cosigner for checks over $2,000 and were told they would be fired if they wrote a check to IRS without superiors' authorization.

E. Accountants have been held to be responsible persons where:

1. They cosigned corporate employer's checks as representative of third party and exercised third party's authority to choose which creditors corporation should pay.

F. More than one person may be a "responsible party."

III. What is "Willful Failure?"

A. Conduct that is accidental or inadvertent is not willful.

B. However, willful need **not** include an intent to defraud the government.

C. Willfulness means the awareness of the obligation and a conscious and voluntary payment of someone else with funds that should have been used to pay the tax owed.

Self-Employment Contributions Act

Self-employed persons do not escape the coverage of FICA, but special adjustments must be made to accommodate the persons' dual role as employers and employees.

I. Self-employed persons must pay social security tax on their own self-employed taxable earnings

A. Self-employed Income: Net business profits, director's fees.

B. Not "Income": Gifts.

II. Features of Self-employed Tax:

A. Base rate = that of FICA rate for employer and employee combined [Currently 15.3%].

B. Base rate reduced by any "wages" earned during the year, because of the FICA paid on the wages.

C. Self-employed can deduct <u>50%</u> of FICA from taxes.

FUTA

Another key part of our country's social safety net is unemployment compensation...a temporary bridge of support for those who have involuntarily lost their jobs. As with many areas of the law, this one is mandated by the federal government, but substantial responsibility to administer the system is placed upon the states.

I. Purpose: -- Provide unemployment compensation benefits to workers who lose jobs and can't find new ones.

II. Mechanism:

A. Federal unemployment tax must be paid by employer who employs persons covered by the act.

1. Deductible by Employer, not employee.

B. State unemployment tax must also be paid.

1. State tax is credited against employer's federal tax up to a maximum of 90% of the federal tax.

2. State tax may go up or down depending on claims against employer.

3. Additional credit against federal tax is created by good claims record.

Example:
ABC Co. has an excellent record and under its state's system is entitled to pay unemployment tax of only 4% as contrasted to the general state rate of 5%. ABC is entitled to take a credit of 5% against the federal unemployment tax rate of 6.2%.

C. Only the first $7,000 paid to each covered employee is taxable under FUTA, although many states require that the state tax be paid on a higher amount than that.

D. The maximum federal rate is currently 6.2% with a maximum state tax offset credit of 5.4%, so many employers pay a federal tax of only 0.8% after receiving credit for state unemployment tax.

E. Though federally-mandated, the system is administered primarily by the states.

F. Employer must file if s/he pays $1,500 or more in wages during any calendar quarter, or has at least one full or part-time employee during at least 20 weeks during the year.

III. Coverage is mandatory for qualifying employees -- Employees usually must have worked for a minimum specified period and earned a minimum amount of wages to be eligible for benefits.

IV. Eligibility for Unemployment Benefits usually requires:

A. That employee was terminated involuntarily.

	Eligible	Not Eligible
Fired because of business reverses.	x	
Quit because of boredom with job.		x
Fired because of refusal to accept transfer to new department.		x
Fired for embezzling from client.		x
Laid off because of temporary decline in boss's contracts.	x	
Seasonal worker paid on yearly basis (e.g., baseball player).		x
Quit due to sexual harassment by co-employees.	x	
Fired because of carelessness on the job.	x	
Fired for repeatedly and vehemently arguing with boss.		x
Quit because firing was imminent and didn't want bad mark on record.		x

Example:
Employer and employee got into a screaming match. The employee stalked toward the door, stopped then stomped and turned around. The employer told him: "Keep on walking." This was held to be a termination, so the employee was entitled to recover unemployment compensation. If the employer had kept quiet, it probably would have been a "voluntary quit" and the employee would not have been entitled to unemployment compensation.

B. Employee is currently available for and looking for work, **and**

	Eligible	Not Eligible
Refused suitable job offer.		x
Has not looked for new job.		x
Enrolled full time in school.		x
Is taking a few night school classes.	x	

C. Employee is not receiving disqualifying income.

	Eligible	Not Eligible
Receiving disability benefits.		x
Receiving pension income.		x
Receiving holiday, vacation, and back pay from earlier job.		x

D. In some states, such income does not disqualify from benefits, but simply requires dollar-for-dollar reduction in benefits.

FLSA

The most difficult thing about the FLSA is its multi-dimensional aspect. We often hear about overtime, minimum wage, and child labor rules. All these are aspects of the FLSA, and all employers and employers' CPAs should be familiar with their basic rules. Additionally, the FLSA has an equal pay provision that supplements Title VII's rules against general discrimination in employment.

I. Introduction

A. Applies to all businesses that affect interstate commerce.

B. Four major sections:

1. Minimum Wage.
2. Overtime Standard.
3. Child Labor Restrictions.
4. Equal Pay Provision.

II. Four Major Sections

A. Minimum Wage Rules

1. "Covered Employees" must be paid the minimum wage (currently $5.85/hr, and higher in may states).
2. The minimum wage is determined on the basis of each work week, so year-end bonuses and the like are not factored in.

Example:
ABC Co. pays Tom $4.00/hour during the year and on December 31 writes him a check for his share of a profit-sharing plan. The profit-sharing bonus, when added to what Tom has been paid during the year, makes his total compensation more than he would have received had he been paid the minimum wage all year. Nonetheless, this is a violation of the rules.

Example:
Due to a stalemate in the legislature, the State of California did not pay wages until 15 days after they were due because there was no budget and no state funds appropriated for payment of salaries. Highway workers sued, arguing that because they were paid zero, they did not receive the minimum wage...in violation of the FLSA. The court agreed, holding that FLSA wages are "unpaid" unless they are paid on the employees' regular payday.

3. Potential Problem: **Interns**, who must be paid minimum wage, if:

    a. Their work gives the company an "immediate advantage," or

    b. They displace a regular worker.

4. Independent contractors are not covered.

B. **Overtime Standard**

1. Employees working more than 40 hours per week must be paid 1-1/2 times their hourly wage for extra hours.

    a. Public employers, such as states and counties, are allowed under limited circumstances to compensate employees who work overtime with extra time off instead of overtime pay.

2. There is no "offset" for weeks in which employees work less than 40 hours.

Example:
Sam, an eligible employee, works 45 hours one week and 35 the next. Although this averages out to an even 40 hours/week, there is no offset for the short week. Therefore, Sam is entitled to receive 5 hours worth of overtime for the first week.

3. An employer may utilize an hourly, weekly, or monthly pay base for a covered employee provided the minimum hourly rate of pay and overtime pay standards are met.

4. When an employee is "on call" in circumstances that s/he cannot spend his/her time in the way s/he would choose to do, this is viewed as "working time" rather than "waiting time" and must be counted for determining overtime compensation.

Example:
Plaintiff was a physician's assistant at a State Correctional Facility. She worked 40 hours per week and, in addition, was required to provide emergency medical services to inmates in several area facilities after regular working hours. She was compensated time-and-a-half for the time she actually spent at the facilities, but not for the "on-call" periods when she had to stay at home in order to be able to respond within 20 minutes to any call for services. The court found that plaintiff was unable to use the "on call" time as her own and therefore should be compensated for it at time-and-a-half.

5. Employees Not Covered by Either - Minimum Wage or Overtime:

    a. **Key Point:** Minimum wage coverage is broader than overtime coverage.

	Not Covered by Either	Covered by Min.Wage but Not by Overtime
Professionals, like CPAs	x	
Executives	x	
Administrative Employees	x	
Outside Salespersons	x	
Taxi Drivers		x
Railroad Employees		x
Commercial Fishing Workers	x	
Child Actors	x	
Some Agricultural Workers	x	
Air Carrier Employees		x
Sailors on American Vessels		x

C. FLSA also has **"Child Labor" Provisions**

1. Excluding those under 18 years of age from certain occupations designated as "hazardous," including mining, logging, and excavation work.
2. Sixteen is the basic minimum age for employment for any nonhazardous work.
3. Fourteen and fifteen year olds are limited to certain occupations, such as sales and clerical work; they cannot work in manufacturing, or mining, or other occupations that would interfere with their schooling or their health.
4. Children under fourteen cannot work except for their parents or pursuant to court-approved contracts for entertainment (child actors) or athletic contracts.

D. **Equal Pay**

1. Prohibits an employer from discriminating between employees on the basis of sex by paying unequal wages for the same work.
2. Allows pay variance based on:
   a. Seniority.
   b. Merit.
   c. Quality or Quantity of Work.
3. Unlike the rest of the FLSA, the equal pay provisions:
   a. Cover executive, administrative, and professional employees.
   b. Cover state and local government employees.

III. **Enforcement**

A. The FLSA is **enforced by** Department of Labor's Wage and Hour Division and private lawsuits.

ERISA

In the late 1960s, many companies went under and their employees, who believed that they had company-sponsored pension plans to fall back on, learned that their employers had robbed the pensions plans and there was little or nothing left for the employees. Congress responded to this gap in employee protection by passing ERISA.

I. Purpose:

A. Protect employee rights in existing pension plans.

B. Offer tax incentives to employers and employees to fund employee benefit plans by providing that if the plans meet IRS requirements:

1. employers get a current tax deduction for contributions,

2. - **and** - employees are able to defer taxation of benefits until they actually receive them.

II. Characteristics:

A. ERISA broadly preempts state laws regulating pensions.

B. ERISA applies to two types of plans:

1. Employee pension benefit plans,

2. Employee welfare benefit plans.

C. ERISA prohibits plans that discriminate against lower-level employees.

D. ERISA set up the Pension Benefit Guaranty Corp. (PBGC) to administer plan termination insurance for defined benefit pension plans; employers are required to purchase pension termination insurance.

III. ERISA does not require -- employers to set up pension plans.

A. If employers do set up pension plans for employees, they **must meet these standards:**

B. Employee contributions must "vest" (that is, the employee acquires the right to the contribution) immediately.

C. Employees' rights to their employers' contributions generally fully vest after 5 years of employment.

D. ERISA also provides for partial vesting.

Example:
Partial vesting - A plan may provide that partial vesting of employers' contributions begins at 20% in the third year and escalates at 20% per year until full vesting occurs in the seventh year. So, if after five years in such a plan Sam left having matched his employer's contribution of $10,000 with $10,000 of his own, Sam would be entitled to his own $10,000 (of course) and to $6,000 of his employer's contribution.

E. Standards on investment of funds must be followed to avoid mismanagement.

  1. Every plan must provide written procedures specifying means of funding the plan.

  2. Every plan must designate a fiduciary with authority to manage and control the plan's operation and management.

Example:
Fiduciaries must invest funds in accordance with "prudent person" standard, must not engage in "self-dealing," etc.

F. Certain disclosures must be made to employees and to the government.

IV. Coverage -- ERISA does not apply to

A. Federal, state, and local government pension plans,

B. Church plans.

V. ERISA is enforced by

A. Depts. of Labor and Treasury,

B. Private lawsuits.

VI. Types of Pension Plans

A. Defined-Benefit Plans ensure eligible employees and their beneficiaries a specified monthly income for life; in other words, they start with the benefits to be provided and then attempt to calculate what will be needed in the way of contributions to provide those benefits.

  1. Such plans are insured by Pension Benefit Guaranty Corp. (PBGC).

  2. Some plans are "integrated" with Social Security benefits.

Example:
Integration of SS Taxes - Employer can offset benefits with the employee's anticipated benefits from Social Security, since employer is already contributing to the employee's retirement income by paying Social Security Taxes.

B. Defined-Contribution Plans specify annual fixed-share contributions to be made by an employer into a retirement account; in other words, they focus on the contributions to be made and then hope that wise investing will provide generous benefits.

  1. Employer contributions may be tied to employee contributions or may be separately calculated.

2. These funds are invested on behalf of the employee who receives proceeds upon retirement

3. Unlike in a defined-benefit plan where the investment decisions are made exclusively by the plan's fiduciary's in a defined-contribution plan, the employee typically has discretion to allocate the investment among a number of mutual funds.

4. There is no PBGC insurance for defined-contribution plans.

C. Under a 401(k) plan, an employee can reduce his/her reportable income by making pretax contributions to the plan (but cannot withdraw contributions prior to termination of employment absent exceptions such as death, disability, or perhaps hardship).

Pension and Retirement Plan Liability

ERISA not only encourages employers to form retirement and benefit plans, it also establishes standards for those plans and imposes potential liabilities upon those who operate and administer those plans. CPAs may be among those targeted for liability.

I. Introduction

A. The Employee Retirement Income Security Act of 1974 (ERISA) imposes a fiduciary duty upon retirement plan "fiduciaries."

B. The purpose is to protect plans by establishing standards of responsibility and conduct upon plan fiduciaries.

II. Who is a Fiduciary?

A. "Fiduciaries" include:

1. Anyone named in a benefit plan as a "fiduciary," and
2. Anyone who:
    - **a.** exercises any discretionary management or control over management of the plan;
    - **b.** renders investment advice for a fee; or
    - **c.** has discretionary authority or responsibility in administration of the plan.
3. Accountants who merely audit plans will not be fiduciaries.
4. Accountants might become fiduciaries if:
    - **a.** A management accountant who has responsibility to calculate plan benefits also has authority to authorize or disallow benefit payments when a dispute exists about the meaning of plan provisions.
    - **b.** A management accountant who provides advice about interpretation of the plan and knows that the trustee is almost certain to follow the advice.
    - **c.** An accounting firm that offers benefit consulting services to a client on a regular basis.
    - **d.** An accountant with authority to make withdrawals from a bank account holding ERISA plan assets exercises discretionary control over the funds.

III. Duties of Fiduciaries

A. Act with reasonable care; and

B. Discharge duties solely in the interests of plan's participants.

IV. Participating in a Fiduciary Breach

A. It appears that accountants can also be liable, even if they are not fiduciaries themselves, if they participate in a fiduciary's breach of duty.

B. Accountants, actuaries, attorneys, benefits consultants, and other non-fiduciaries may yet be liable under ERISA Section 502(1)(3), which does not limit the world of ERISA defendants to fiduciaries, if they:

1. Participate in a fiduciary's breach of fiduciary duty in violation of Section 404 of ERISA; or
2. Participate in an illicit transaction with a "party in interest" in violation of Section 406(a) of ERISA.
   a. "Parties in interest" include entities such as accountants, lawyers, banks, and brokers who provide services to a plan.
   b. Prohibited transactions include those in which a plan fiduciary causes the plan to loan money to a party in interest, pay excessive compensation for accounting or other services, or transfers assets to a party in interest.
3. Section 402(a)(3) authorizes a civil penalty of 20% of the recovery amount.

C. Accountants and others may also be liable for assisting such breaches or for other errors under common law malpractice causes of action that most courts hold are not preempted by ERISA.

1. Thus, a plan administrator was allowed to pursue against an accountant a malpractice action alleging faulty auditing with respect to loans approved by the plan's investment advisory committee.

COBRA

Few political issues have been more controversial in recent years than health care. One of the major holes in our social safety net seems to be in the area of health insurance coverage. COBRA is Congress's attempt to plug a few of the holes in that net.

As amended by the Health Insurance Portability and Accountability Act of 1996.

I. **COBRA Amended ERISA --** to provide health insurance in some circumstances after a job loss.

II. **For an employee, there are two "qualifying events" that give rise to COBRA coverage**

   A. Termination (including quits, firings, and layoffs) causing loss of health insurance.

      1. Unless it is for "gross misconduct" (in which case the employee is not protected).

   B. Reduction of hours causing loss of health insurance.

III. **Upon the occurrence of a qualifying event, an employee may retain his previous group health insurance coverage**

   A. If s/he pays for it.

   B. Coverage:

      1. Ex-employee,

      2. Spouse,

      3. Dependent children.

   C. Length of Extra Coverage

      1. Usually 18 months after the qualifying event.

      2. **Exception:** The period is 29 months if insured was "disabled" at the time of the qualifying event.

         a. The extra 11 months applies to any beneficiary, not just the employee, who has a disability any time within the first 60 days of continuation coverage.

         b. There are a few circumstances where COBRA coverage can last up to 36 months. For example, if an insured spouse becomes entitled to Medicare, but his or her spouse is not yet so qualified, the latter may gain COBRA benefits for 36 months. Similarly, if divorce, legal separation, or death of the employee are the "qualifying events" for a spouse, he or she may enjoy 36 months of coverage. Finally, when a dependent child loses dependent status, as when a child graduates from college, he or she may purchase group health benefits under COBRA for up to 36 months.

         c. Also, if an employee moves from one group plan to another, the new plan cannot impose a preexisting conditions exclusion that exceeds 12 months for conditions for which medical advice, diagnosis, or treatment was received or recommended within the previous 6 months. So, assume that X was covered by an employer group plan at Company A for two years. X then went to work for Company B and elected to join its group health care plan. Because the new plan cannot impose a preexisting exclusion that exceeds 12 months and because X had two years of coverage at Company A that Company B must credit, Company B's health plan cannot apply the preexisting condition limitation. However, under the rules, if there were a gap between X's leaving Company A's plan and joining Company B's plan that exceeded 63 days, then Company B would not have to credit X's coverage at Company A and could apply its preexisting condition exclusion.

d. Important, COBRA applies only to companies with 20 or more employees.

FMLA

The FMLA moves the U.S. toward the European practice of mandating family - friendly employment practices, at least in a modest way. It has been controversial with employers, but it seems likely that it will be expanded rather than repealed in coming years. Therefore, employers and their CPAs had best be at least passingly familiar with its provisions.

I. Purpose: -- Balance employee's workplace demands with needs of family.

- **A.** The first real federal requirement that an employer provide government-mandated benefits.

II. An eligible employee is entitled to: -- 12 weeks of unpaid leave without losing his job.

III. Leave Is Provided for:

- **A.** Birth of a child.
- **B.** A serious health condition that makes the employee unable to perform his job.
- **C.** Caring for a spouse, child, or parent who has a serious health condition.

IV. To be eligible, an employee must have worked for employer

- **A.** for at least 12 months;
- **B.** - **and** - at least 1,250 hours during the previous 12 months.

V. Employee must request -- such leave; employers need not volunteer it.

VI. FMLA Covers:

- **A.** Employers with over 50 employees in a 75 mile radius, and
- **B.** State and local government agencies.

Workers' Compensation Act

Workers' compensation was originally called "workmen's compensation." That label had to change with the tremendous influx of women into the workforce. One of the older aspects of the social safety net in the U.S., workers' compensation, involves a trade-off. In exchange for forfeiting the right to sue their employer if they are injured on the job due to the employer's negligence, employees receive the nearly-automatic right to obtain workers' compensation benefits when injured within the scope of employment even when the employer is blameless.

I. **Purpose:** Provide nearly-automatic compensation for employees who suffer work-related injuries or diseases.

   A. Many people think of workers' compensation as remedying only on-the-job injuries, but it also provides compensation for work-related diseases, such as asbestosis.

   B. Independent contractors usually are not covered by workers' compensation.

II. **Mechanism:**

   A. Employers carry workers' comp insurance, which provides established levels of benefits that are given automatically to workers for job-related injuries or diseases.

   B. Employer's liability is strict: Employee need not prove negligence or other fault by the employer.

      1. The employer's common law defense's to lawsuit are eliminated.

         a. Assumption of risk.

Example:
Assumption of risk - Sam is a roofer and is injured on the job. Sam knows, of course, that it is dangerous up on those roofs and that workers occasionally fall off roofs and are seriously injured. At common law, Sam's employer could often have successfully raised the defense that Sam "assumed the risk" by taking a dangerous job like roofing. Under workers' compensation systems, this is no defense. Sam is entitled to recover his workers' comp benefits.

      2. Negligence of fellow employee.

Example:
Negligence of fellow employee - Sam works on an assembly line and is seriously injured when Roy, who works right beside him on the line, carelessly drops a piece of heavy equipment on Sam's leg. At common law, Sam's employer could often have successfully raised the defense that the real fault lay with Sam's co-worker. Under workers' compensation systems, this is no defense. Sam is entitled to recover workers' comp benefits.

3. Employee's contributory negligence.

Example:
Employee's contributory negligence - Sam works on an assembly line and one day his mind wanders slightly and he allows his clothes to become caught in some moving parts. He is injured. At common law, Sam's employer could often have raised the defense that the real fault lay with Sam because his own carelessness caused his injury. Under workers' compensation systems, this is no defense. Sam is entitled to recover workers' comp benefits.

C. **Chart: Effect of Elimination of Employer Common Law Defenses**

	Covered	Not Covered
Injured due to own negligence on the job	x	
Injured due to failure to follow boss's safety rules	x	
Injured because of intoxication on the job		x
Injured self intentionally to "get a chance to catch up on Oprah"		x
Injured by negligence of fellow employee	x	
Injured while working on machine known to be defective	x	

D. In exchange for having to pay benefits automatically, employer is given immunity from civil damage suit by employee.

1. If coverage exists, employee cannot decline benefits and claim right to sue.

Example:
Sam is seriously injured while on the job. He thinks that he can prove both that his boss was negligent and that his injuries are so serious that a jury would award him many times what the workers' compensation scheme allows as recovery. Sam rejects proffered workers' compensation benefits and sues his boss for negligence. Sam will not recover if the boss was in compliance with the workers' compensation system requirements.

2. Exceptions to immunity: Boss guilty of intentional tort or gross negligence.

Example:
Ed's supervisor, Sandy, loses her temper over an incident of incompetence by Ed and hits him with a hammer. Ed's recovery is not limited to workers' compensation because Sandy's tort is an intentional one.

3. Mandatory versus elective coverage:

   a. Most states require all employers to carry workers' comp plans.

   b. In some states it is elective, but those who elect not to carry benefits can be sued by injured employees.

III. **Workers are Covered --** if they are injured on the job or in the course of employment, i.e., within the scope of authority to advance the employer's purposes (which is broadly construed in this context).

	Covered	Not Covered
Scope of Authority		
Injured while doing assigned task	x	
Injured while commuting to work in the morning		x
Injured while making a delivery for boss on way home	x	
Traveling sales rep injured while driving from motel to first call	x	
Injured while doing something the boss requires although it's not employee's ordinary job	x	

IV. **Procedure: --** The employee reports the injury or disease to the employer and then files a claim with the state workers' compensation board or the insurance carrier administering the plan.

V. **Actions Against Third Parties**

A. Availability of workers' comp benefits bars injured employees' suits against employer and co-employees, but not against third-parties.

Example:
X is injured on the job in part because his boss told him to operate a complicated machine without giving X adequate training, in part because X's co-employees were careless, and in part because the machine was defectively designed and manufactured. X's employer is in compliance with the state's workers' compensation statute.

Injured Employee's Remedy	WC Benefits	Civil Damages
Against Employer	x	
Against Co-Employee	x	
Against Manufacturer		x

Example:
Actions against third parties - A is an employee of X Co. B is an independent contractor for Y Co. Both drive trucks and are involved in a collision that is A's fault. A was speeding. Additional evidence shows that X Co's faulty maintenance of the brakes on A's truck also contributed to the accident. Both X Co. and Y Co. are in compliance with workers' compensation statutes.

	Yes	No
A can recover workers' comp benefits from X Co.	x	
A can sue X Co. for its negligence		x
B can recover workers' comp benefits from Y Co.		x
B can sue X Co. for its negligence	x	
B can sue A for A's negligence	x	

1. Any recovery against third-party achieved by employee that compensates injuries for which s/he has already received workers' comp is subject to claim by employer or employer's insurance carrier.
    a. If employee had chosen not to sue manufacturer, the employer or its insurance carrier could have obtained and pursued that right of action.

VI. **Benefits:** -- Employees who file timely claims are usually entitled to these benefits:
    A. Medical care expenses.
    B. Disability protection (payment of partial wages).
    C. Death benefits (to be paid to widows/widowers and minor children).
    D. Retraining expenses (where necessary).
    E. Scheduled payments for various losses (finger, arm, leg, etc.).

OSHA

Ideally, the responsibility for providing workers' compensation benefits encourages employers to provide a safe work place for employers. Nonetheless, there are both federal and state regulations that add even more incentives for job safety. The most important federal act is OSHA, which was passed in response to evidence that, among other things, during each year in the late 1960s approximately 14,500 persons were killed while working on the job.

I. OSHA Applies To Most Employers Except:

A. Federal government.

B. State government.

C. Certain industries subject to other safety regulations.

Example:
Federal Mine Safety and Health Act regulation of mining.

II. Purpose: -- To promote safety standards and job safety.

A. Employer need not guarantee a 100% safe work place.

B. Employer must:

1. Provide a workplace free from "recognized hazards" likely to cause death or serious physical harm (injury or disease).

a. A workplace should be free of toxic substances, asbestos dust and the like; the work environment should be adequately lit, ventilated, and heated; and tools and equipment should be in proper working order.

2. Comply with OSHA standards for safety and health.

Note:
OSHA supplements, but does not replace, state safety rules.

C. Fact: Over 10,000 workers die on the job each year in America and 100,000 are permanently disabled.

III. Mechanism: -- OSHA has broad powers to:

A. Develop standards.

B. Require employers to keep records of job-related injuries and report them to OSHA.

C. Investigate complaints and inspect workplaces.

1. If employer resists search, OSHA usually must obtain a search warrant from a court.

2. Need not show probable cause, but only a "reasonable basis."

3. A reasonable basis can be provided by:

a. A higher-than-usual accident rate.

b. Employee complaints.

c. Proof of a fair, random surprise search system needed to keep employers on their toes because OSHA lacks funds and employees to do continuous and thorough searches.

4. Warrantless searches are authorized:

a. In cases of extreme emergency.

b. Where employer consents (most cases).

c. Inspector is merely observing what is open to public view, for there can be no expectation of privacy in such a place.

D. Determine whether violations have occurred.

E. Assess remedies by:

1. Ordering correction of unsafe conditions.

2. Imposing civil fines (per violation).

3. Referring case to the Department of Justice for criminal prosecution, if willful violation caused death of one or more employees.

IV. Employee Rights

A. If a violation threatens physical harm or imminent danger, employee may:

1. File a request for an inspection.

2. Refuse in good faith to work if there is no time to wait for inspection.

B. Employees may not be punished by employers for exercising these rights.

C. Employees themselves may be fired for failing to comply with OSHA rules.

Union and Employee Relations

Although unions are not as powerful an influence in the American economy as they once were, it is wise to be familiar with the essential rules governing union and employee relations

I. Introduction

A. Much strife accompanied early attempts of workers to organize in unions when bargaining with their employers, causing Congress to pass several important laws, including:

1. **The Norris-LaGuardia Act --** it prohibited court injunctions against many union organizing activities, particularly peaceful strikes.
2. **The National Labor Relations Act of 1935 --** (NLRA or the "Wagner Act"), which is the most important law today. Its primary purpose is to protect employees':
   a. right to form, join, or assist unions;
   b. right to bargain collectively through their chosen union; and
   c. right to engage in concerted activities (such as strikes) for the purpose of collective bargaining or other mutual protection.
3. **The Labor-Management Relations Act of 1947 --** ("Taft-Hartley Act"), which tilted federal labor policy toward a more neutral (less pro-labor) perspective by prohibiting union coercion of employees and secondary boycotts.
4. **The Labor-Management Reporting and Disclosure Act of 1959 --** ("Landrum-Griffin Act"), which responded to corruption in unions by protecting workers from unfair treatment by their unions and requiring certain union reforms such as financial disclosure by union leaders.

B. The National Labor Relations Board (NLRB) enforces the NLRA.

II. NLRA Coverage

A. The NLRA applies to all employers involved in or affecting interstate commerce, a concept that is broadly construed.

B. Several categories of workers are exempt from NLRA coverage:

1. Independent contractors.
2. Government employees.
3. Managerial and supervisory employees.
4. Airline and railway employees who are covered by other statutes.

III. The Right to Organize

A. Once 30% of eligible employees in an appropriate job category sign authorization cards, an employee group may petition for an election to certify a union as their bargaining representative.

1. Management may voluntarily recognize the union as the workers' representative, but if it does not do so an election must be held.

B. The NLRB monitors the election to ensure fairness.

C. Employers who resist the election must avoid committing "unfair labor practices," because that would result in automatic certification of the union via an NLRB "bargaining order."

D. Employer "unfair labor practices" include:

1. Interfering with union organizing efforts
   - **a.** employers should not bribe workers to vote against a union;
   - **b.** employers should not threaten workers who wish to vote for a union.
2. Dominating or interfering with the union
3. Discriminating against a union member, or
4. Refusing to bargain collectively.

E. Unions also must refrain from "unfair labor practices," such as:

1. Coercing employees, or
2. Requiring employers to agree not to do business with nonunion companies that the union is trying to unionize ("hot cargo clause"),
3. Refusing to bargain collectively,
4. Engaging in an illegal strike or secondary boycott.

F. Lock-outs: Employers may bar workers from coming to work, sometimes in anticipation of a threatened strike. The legality of such a lock-out depends upon an employer's intent, and is illegal if the employer locks out employees in order to:

1. Destroy the union,
2. Punish workers for organizing, or
3. Avoid its good faith bargaining responsibilities.

G. Federal law prohibits "closed shops" (an employer's agreement to hire only members of a union, effectively giving unions a veto power over hires).

H. Federal law does allow states to enact "right-to-work laws" (and about half have done so) that prohibit two types of agreements that are otherwise legal:

1. "union shops" (agreements requiring newly hired employees to join the union within a specified period after beginning employment), and
2. "agency shops" (agreements allowing employees not to join the union but to pay fees to cover union services).

I. Employers may take bankruptcy in order to discharge their contractual obligations, including those under a collective bargaining agreement. The employer is required to provide a plan that treats all its creditors, including workers, "fairly and equitably" and unions are to be kept informed so that they may evaluate the proposed plan.

IV. Collective Bargaining

A. Negotiations between management and a union are called collective bargaining.

B. Once a union is certified, management cannot bargain with anyone else purporting to represent the employees regarding "mandatory subjects of bargaining," including:

1. wages,
2. hours, and

3. other conditions of employments, such as discharge, seniority rights, retirement and pension plans, insurance plans, and grievances.

C. The NLRA imposes a duty on both sides to bargain in good faith.

1. Withholding information important to fair bargaining is probably acting in bad faith.

2. Presenting "take it or leave it" ultimatums is probably acting in bad faith.

3. The requirement of bargaining in good faith does not include an obligation to actually reach an agreement.

D. Unions may strike to support their rights.

1. To be legal, strikes must be supported by a majority of members.

2. Once a union has agreed to a collective bargaining agreement, it must give the employer 60 days notice before it strikes seeking modification or rescission.

3. So-called "wildcat" strikes by a disgruntled minority of workers are illegal.

4. Secondary strikes (secondary boycotts) against third-parties to coerce them to oppose management are illegal.

5. Workers on strike at a multi-employer work site, like a construction site, must picket just the relevant part of the site and not the entire work place, because that puts pressure on third-parties.

6. Workers, generally, have no right to picket on the employer's private property.

E. Characteristics of a collective bargaining agreement:

1. Union usually agrees not to strike and the company agrees not to lock;

2. Employer agrees to submit disagreements and grievances that arise during the term of the agreement to binding arbitration;

3. Matters such as pay scales, seniority, overtime pay, insurance, vacation holidays, etc. are addressed.

V. Replacement Workers

A. During a strike, management may hire "replacement workers."

B. Following settlement of an authorized "unfair labor practice strike" protesting unfair management practices, management must reinstate the strikers.

C. Following settlement of a typical strike over wages and related matters ("economic strikes"), management need not lay off the "replacement workers," but cannot discriminate against the strikers if it rehires more workers.

Antitrust Law

The main goal of antitrust law is to promote economic competition.

I. Overview

A. The main goal of antitrust law is to promote economic competition.

B. Among the most important antitrust statutes are:

1. **The Sherman Act (1890)**
   - **a.** Section 1 prohibits "contracts, combinations, and conspiracies in restraint of trade." It requires at least two actors.
   - **b.** Section 2 prohibits "monopolization, attempts to monopolize, and conspiracies to monopolize." It looks at the conduct of a single economic actor.
2. **The Clayton Act (1914)**
   - **a.** Section 2 prohibits price discrimination.
   - **b.** Section 3 prohibits some tying and exclusive dealing arrangements.
   - **c.** Section 7 forbids anticompetitive mergers.
   - **d.** Section 8 prohibits interlocking directorates among large corporations that compete with one another.
3. **Federal Trade Commission Act (1914)**
   - **a.** Created the Federal Trade Commission (FTC) to enforce antitrust laws.
   - **b.** Section 5 prohibits "unfair methods of competition."
4. **Robinson-Patman Act (1936)**
   - **a.** Section 2 amends the Clayton act to make the law against price discrimination more effective.

C. Antitrust laws cover business activity, including that of foreign companies, that either directly involves or substantially affects interstate commerce.

D. Remedies

1. The Department of Justice's Antitrust Division can bring criminal or civil lawsuits against violators.
2. The FTC can enforce the Clayton, Robinson-Patman, and FTC Acts.
3. Private parties can file civil lawsuits claiming a violation of the Sherman, Clayton, or Robinson-Patman Acts and seek treble damages (three times the actual damages).

E. Exceptions

1. Labor union collective bargaining activity is generally exempt from the antitrust laws.
2. Public utilities and common carriers are generally exempt as well because they are subject to separate regulation.
3. Activity that did not affect interstate commerce would also be exempt, but that term is so broadly construed that this exception virtually never applies.

II. Monopolization

A. Section 2 of the Sherman Act forbids monopolization, defining a monopoly as "a firm having such an overwhelming degree of market power that it is able to control prices or exclude competition."

B. Elements of a Section 2 violation include:

   1. Overwhelming market power; and

   2. Intent to monopolize.

C. **Market power --** is the ability to raise prices without losing most customers.

   1. Market share is the key component in measuring market power, and less than 50% is usually insufficient to monopolize, and a 75% share is often sufficient.

   2. Other structural factors besides market share include:

      a. Relative size of other firms in the market.

      b. Size and power of customers.

      c. Entry barriers that prevent competitors from entering the market, such as high costs of capital for potential competitors.

      d. Dynamics of the market - does it change rapidly?

   3. Markets are defined in terms of:

      a. Product market, including cross-elasticity of demand (could consumers switch to buttons if zippers were priced too high), and cross-elasticity of supply (could button makers respond quickly to such an increase in demand).

      b. Geographic market-consumers might drive quite a ways to avoid buying an overpriced car, but not so far to avoid an overpriced loaf of bread.

D. Intent to Monopolize

   1. Because monopolist must willfully acquire or maintain a monopoly, there can be legal monopolies, such as those that exist because a firm owns a patent or trade secret. One famous case noted that a business that acquires a monopoly position "merely by virtue of its superior skill, foresight, and industry" has not violated Section 2.

   2. Typically, intent to monopolize is inferred from:

      a. predatory (below cost) pricing with intent to drive out competitors; or

      b. nonprice predation via such means as:

         i. tying up customers with long-term contracts that are not justified by cost savings;

         ii. taking away key employees from a small competitor;

         iii. falsely disparaging the products of competitors;

         iv. forcing smaller firms into unjustified lawsuits and administrative expenses; and

         v. sabotage.

   3. Attempts to monopolize are also illegal if they present a dangerous probability of success.

> **Note:**
> Some practices that do not alone violate the antitrust laws may do so in the presence of overwhelming market power.

III. Mergers

A. Section 7 of the Clayton Act prevents one company from acquiring another if the acquisition is likely to diminish competition in a substantial way in the relevant market.

1. **Horizontal mergers --** between competitors are especially likely to diminish competition and will likely draw regulatory attention if the combined market shares of the companies exceeds 30%, although that number is scarcely hard and fast and is affected by numerous other factors, including the number of competitors in the market.

2. **Vertical mergers --** between companies in a distribution chain (e.g., a steel manufacturer acquires a key ore supplier or a manufacturer of products made of steel) are less likely to diminish competition and are unlikely to be successfully challenged unless the vertically combined market is already highly concentrated and both companies have a large market share.

3. **Conglomerate mergers --** that have neither horizontal nor vertical characteristics (e.g., a steel manufacturer buys a chain of ice cream stores) are very unlikely to face serious antitrust challenge.

IV. Horizontal Restraints of Trade -- Section 1 of the Sherman Act bans "contacts, combinations, or conspiracies in restraint of trade."

A. **Collusion --** is the key to such violations, and may be evidenced by communications between the parties, opportunity to conspire, uniformity of action, etc.

Example:
When 69,000 members of the National Society of Professional Engineers voted for an ethical rule that prohibited competitive bidding by all members, the Supreme Court found illegal collusion among the members.

B. **Rule of Reason --** Collusion violates Section 1 only if it "unreasonably" restricts competition. Defendants may raise a "rule of reason" defense focusing on the purpose and effect of the conduct.

1. Purpose: if the predominant purpose of the conduct is to restrain competition, it will probably be viewed as illegal even if the effect on competition is rather slight; but if the primary purpose of the conduct is not to restrain competition, then a violation will be found only if competition is diminished in a substantial way.

2. Effect: The most important factor affecting competition is the collective market power of the group. If the group could have achieved the claimed legitimate goal with a less restrictive alternative, a court is more likely to find a Section 1 violation.

C. **Per Se Illegality --** Certain types of activities are automatically (per se) illegal and cannot be saved by a "rule of reason" defense.

1. Price Fixing: when competitors agree to charge a specific price, or establish a floor price, or agree not to submit competitive bids, or to rotate bids among a group, etc.

2. Market Division: when competitors agree to divide markets by territory, customer allocation, or product line.

3. Boycotts: Company A can choose not to deal with Company C, usually. But if competitors Company A and Company B agree to boycott Company C for anticompetitive reasons (for example, they are worried that Company C is thinking about a vertical acquisition, which would allow it to compete with them), a per se violation occurs.

V. Vertical Restraints of Trade

A. Resale Price Maintenance (RPM) -- (vertical price fixing) occurs when a seller and a buyer agree on the price at which the seller will resell to its own customers. Usually, a manufacturer tells its dealers or distributors the minimum price at which they may resell its product. This practice inhibits intrabrand competition, preventing dealer A from underpricing dealer B. Section 1 of the Sherman Act forbids RPM.

B. Until recently, RPM was per se illegal, but the Supreme Court recently held that it should now be judged by a rule of reason analysis.

VI. Vertical Nonprice Restrictions

A. Vertical Nonprice Restrictions (VNRs) also violates Section 1 of the Sherman Act by restricting intrabrand competition.

Example:
Territorial Restrictions: Manufacturer guarantees its dealers that they will have the exclusive right to market its products in their geographic territory.

Example:
Customer Restrictions: Dealers agree to resell only to particular customers.

B. VNRs are analyzed via a rule of reason.

VII. Tying Arrangements

A. Tying occurs when Co. A agrees to sell a desirable computer (the tying product) to Co. B only if B will also purchase a software package (the tied product) that Co. A sells that is not nearly as popular.

Example:
In the early days of business machines, IBM was found guilty when it required customers who leased its tabulating machines to also use its tabulating cards.

B. Tying may violate both Section 1 of the Sherman Act and Section 3 of the Clayton Act, although the latter is usually redundant.

C. Tying can occur only if the defendant has substantial market power in the market for the tying product. (again, 30% market share is an extremely rough guide).

D. Courts also usually require that the tying arrangement generate a substantial amount of business in the tied market.

VIII. Exclusive Dealing

A. Section 1 of the Sherman Act may ban illicit use of "requirements contracts" and "output contracts."

B. Assume that a customer makes a "requirements contract" with a supplier, promising that it will purchase a particular product only from the supplier. Widespread use of such agreements could make it hard for new competitors to enter the market, because all potential customers would be locked up.

C. Assume that a seller agrees in an "output contract" to sell only to a particular buyer and not to the buyer's competitors. This arrangement is not as worrisome as a requirements contract, but could prevent the buyer's competitors from obtaining products they need to compete.

D. Exclusive dealing is unlikely to be illegal unless a dominant share (roughly 30% or more) of the market is locked away from competitors.

IX. Price Discrimination

A. The Robinson-Patman Act's prohibition on price discrimination is violated if:

1. seller charged different prices to two or more different customers,
2. the transaction involved tangible commodities (not land or services),
3. the transactions were sales rather than leases, or consignments,
4. the goods were essentially the same,
5. likelihood of a substantial injury to competition resulted.

B. Defenses

1. Cost justification: it is okay to charge more to Customer A than Customer B if the former is located farther away, necessitating higher shipping costs;
2. Meeting competition: if defendant charges $100 to Customer A and then learns that a competitor is charging $90, defendant can lower his price to Customer B to meet the competition.
3. Changing conditions: if defendant charges $100 to Customer A and then defendant's suppliers cut their prices, defendant could pass the savings on to Customer B.

Uniform Commercial Code

Negotiable Instruments and Letters of Credit

Introduction and Creation

There are four types of instruments recognized by the UCC: the draft, the check, the note, and the certificate of deposit. Within each type, there are instruments which serve particular functions. It is important to know not only the four types, but within each, the major functional types. There are six factors essential to an instrument being negotiable. These are the requirements of a writing, which is signed by the maker or drawer, with an unconditional promise or order, to pay a sum certain, in money, either on demand or at a definite time, to either bearer or the order of a person. Each of these have special rules with which you should be knowledgeable.

I. Primary Functions -- Negotiable instruments serve two primary functions:

A. a substitute for money -- such as a check, and/or

B. a credit device or loan -- such as a note

II. Governing Law -- Negotiable instruments are governed primarily by Article 3 of the **Uniform Commercial Code** adopted by all fifty states. Article 3 has recently been revised and the revision has been adopted by almost all of the states.

A. Nonnegotiable instruments are governed by **contract law.**

III. Types -- There are basically four types of negotiable instruments:

	Order to pay
Drafts - UCC 3-104(c)	Three party instruments consisting of a **drawer**, who
Checks - UCC 3-104(f)	orders a **drawee**, to pay a **payee.**
	Promises to pay
Notes - UCC 3-104(e)	Two party instruments consisting of a **maker**, who promises
Certificates of Deposit - UCC 3-104(j)	to pay a **payee.**

IV. Classifications -- Within each "type", instruments can be classified depending on certain features or functions. Some of the most common are:

A. Drafts

1. **Sight Draft --** A draft payable immediately upon issue by the drawer and presentment (sight) to the drawee.
2. **Time Draft --** A draft payable by the drawee at a specific time.
3. **Trade Acceptance --** A draft drawn by a seller - drawer on the buyer-drawee for the buyer-drawee's agreement (acceptance) to pay the amount of the purchase price of the sale plus interest upon presentment to the drawee - acceptor. If the draft is drawn on the buyer's bank, it is referred to as a **banker's acceptance.**

Draft

ABC Furniture Mart
/S/ Sally Davenport Pres.

Draft No. 6666 Date: May 1, 19XX

At *** 90 Days From Date ***

Pay to the order of *** Utopia Sofa***
the sum of ***Six Thousand and no/100 *** Dollars $6,000.00

Value received and charge to the account of
To ABC Furniture Mart
Austin, Texas

Utopia Sofa
/S/ Sally Couch
Authorized Signature

Example:
Grayson's Digital Computer World, a retail store, agrees to purchase from Samstone, a new laptop computer company, 500 model Z laptop computers. Grayson's payment policy is to pay ninety (90) days after receipt of the merchandise giving the store a time period to sell the majority of the purchased inventory. Samstone, being a new company with cash flow problems, signs as drawer a ninety (90) day trade acceptance naming itself as payee and Grayson as drawee and requests Grayson to sign (accept) the instrument sending the trade acceptance back to Samstone. If Grayson signs (accepts), Grayson has agreed to be primarily liable for payment at the end of the ninety day period. In the meantime, Samstone can take the signed trade acceptance and sell it with a discount to its bank giving Samstone instant cash.

Note:
Misconception: There is a belief that a drawee bank is required to certify a check if the drawer has presently sufficient funds to cover the check in the bank. This is in error. Certification is a voluntary act by the drawee bank and the bank's refusal to certify a check is not an act of dishonor.

Note:
A **money order** which is payable on demand and drawn on a bank is a check.

B. **Checks --** A draft drawn on a bank (includes savings bank, savings and loan associations, credit unions, and trust companies) payable on demand.

1. **Example - CHECK**

ABC Furniture Mart May 1 19 XX 70-681/7-19

PAY TO THE ORDER OF Utopia Sofa Corporation $ 6,000.00

ONLY Six Thousand and no/100 Dollars

BANK OF WEST AUSTIN
Austin, TX

ABC Furniture Mart

FOR Invoice 06666 BY: /S/ Sally Davenport
Pres.

071908814

2. **Cashier's Check --** A draft in which the drawer and drawee are the same bank or branches of the same bank - UCC 3-104(g)

3. **Teller's Check (the old bank draft) --** A draft drawn by one bank on another bank (or payable at or through another bank) - UCC 3-104(h)
4. **Traveler's Check --** A draft payable on demand drawn on a bank or through a bank that requires as condition of payment a countersignature by a person whose specimen signature appears on the instrument - UCC 3-104(i)
5. **Certified Check --** A check drawn by a drawer on which the drawee bank accepts (by its signature) a primary and absolute obligation to pay the check upon presentment.

C. **Notes --** A written promise by a maker to pay money to another party or to bearer.

1. **Promissory Note --** A note payable on demand or a definite time to a specific payee (or order) or to bearer.

$ 6,000 . 2 May 19 XX

Ninety (90) days after date the undersigned promise to pay to

the order of Utopia Sofa Corporation

Six Thousand and no/100 --
Dollars

at ten percent interest per annum

Value received ABC Furniture Mart

NO. 62636 by Sally Davenport President

2. **Function Notes --** The note is classified depending on its purpose or function.
   a. **Mortgage note --** A promissory note secured by a mortgage on realty.
   b. **Collateral note --** A promissory note secured by personal property.
   c. **Installment note --** A promissory note which calls for periodic payments of principal and interest.

D. **Certificate of Deposits (CDs) --** A note made by a bank, which acknowledges it has a deposit of funds payable to the holder (usually payee) - UCC 3-104(2)(c)

1. Most CDs are time-interest instruments but can be demand CDs.
2. Small CDs - amounts up to $100,000.
3. Jumbo CDs - amounts of $100,000 or more.

BANK OF WEST AUSTIN 22-1 13992
NEGOTIABLE CERTIFICATE OF DEPOSIT 960

AUSTIN, TX. February 15 19 XX
THIS CERTIFIES to the deposit in this Bank the sum of $ 6000.00
----------------Five thousand and no/100--------------DOLLARS

which is payable to bearer on the 15th day of August ,19 XX against presentation and surrender of this certificate, and bears interest at the rate of 5 1/2% per annum, to be computed (on the basis of 360 days and actual days elapsed) to, and payable at maturity. No payment may be made prior to, and no interest runs after, that date.

BANK OF WEST AUSTIN

By John Vault, Pres.
SIGNATURE

a.

E. **Nonnegotiable Instruments --** The following are not negotiable instruments under Article 3 of the UCC:

1. Letters of Credit
2. Warehouse Receipts
3. Bills of Lading
4. Stocks and Bonds
5. Contracts

V. Other Definitions

A. **Accommodation Party --** A "person" who signs an instrument in any capacity for the purpose of lending his/her name as credit to another party on the instrument - UCC 3-419.

Example:
Daughter is the named payee on a check, but Money Mart will not cash the check unless mother co-endorses the check. Mother is an accommodation indorser.

B. **Negotiation --** the transfer of possession of a negotiable instrument to a party who becomes a holder - UCC 3-201.

C. **Indorsement --** A signature, other than that of maker, drawee, or acceptor, usually for the purpose of negotiation of the instrument -- UCC 3-204(a).

D. **Indorser --** The party who endorses the instrument - UCC 3-204(b).

E. **Presentment --** the demand by a holder that the drawee pay (or where required accept) a draft or check, or that the maker pay a note or a certificate of deposit - UCC 3-501(a).

F. **Issue --** the first delivery of an instrument by the maker or drawer to another giving holders rights on the instrument - UCC 3-105.

G. Allonge -- Endorsements written on a separate piece of paper affixed to the instrument - UCC 3-204(a)

VI. Creation

A. Importance -- If the instrument is negotiable, its transfer can be to a holder in due course who takes the instrument free of most defenses, which can be claimed by a party who is responsible to pay the instrument. Negotiable instruments are treated as liquid assets.

Note:
Misconception: A nonnegotiable instrument is totally unenforceable. This is incorrect. A nonnegotiable instrument is a simple contract and is totally enforceable unless the person or persons responsible to pay have a legal defense against having to do so.

B. Requirements -- to be a Negotiable Instrument - UCC 3-104:

1. **Written --** The instrument must be in **writing**. It can be written on anything providing the matter has a degree of permanence and is readily transferable.

Example:
A promissory note written on a blackboard in chalk is not a negotiable instrument - has neither permanence or transferability.

Example:
A promissory note written in ink on the back of test paper is negotiable because it meets both tests.

2. **Signed --** The instrument must be **signed** by the **maker or drawer**.
   a. **Signature to Authenticate --** Any symbol, mark, or signature executed or adopted by a party with the intent to authenticate a writing is a signature. UCC 1-201(39)
   b. **Other Legal Signatures --** A person's initials, rubber stamp, nickname, and even a person's X (usually must be accompanied by a signed witness) is a signature.

Example:
A typewritten name is not a signature but handwritten initials (G.A.J) for Gaylord A. Jentz would be.

   c. The signature can appear any place on the instrument.
   d. **Contract Liability Established --** Signature of maker or drawer establish a contract liability to pay the instrument.

Note:
Misconception: A drawer or maker's signature must appear in the lower right hand corner. This is totally in error -- signature could even be in the body of the instrument.

3. **Unconditioned Promise or Order --** The instrument must contain an **unconditional promise or order to pay**. [UCC 3-106]
   a. **Definite Promise --** A note or CD must contain a definite promise to pay, not a mere acknowledgment of a debt.

Example:
"I/We promise to pay ..." is a definite obligation to pay.

b. A draft or check must contain language which orders the drawee to pay.

Example:
The word "Pay" on a check is an order to the drawee meeting this criteria.

c. **Conditional Instrument --** Instruments expressly conditioned on the happening of an event or subject to a holder having to read another instrument or document to see whether or on what terms payment will be made renders the instrument conditional and nonnegotiable.

i. **Examples**

1. Permitted Unconditional Clauses

1. Purpose of payment stated (on check "May rent").

2. Consideration received ("payment is for 10 bales of cotton received").

3. Reason for instrument or mere "reference" to another writing ("note is in accordance with security agreement #222 of even date").

4. Account to be debited ("charge to petty cash").

2. Prohibited Conditioned Clauses

1. Payment is expressly conditioned ("upon my daughter getting married").

2. Payment is subject to another instrument or document ("payment of this note is subject to a security agreement of even date").

4. **Sum Certain in Money --** The stated amount of the instrument must be a sum certain (fixed) payable in money. [UCC 3-104]

a. General rule is that the **sum is certain** if a holder can calculate the amount owed at time payment is due or any time thereafter.

i. Thus the instrument can be payable:

1. with a stated interest rate or by stated installments.

2. at different rates of interest before and after maturity.

3. at a stated discount for early payment.

ii. Also, a sum is certain even if:

1. tied to a variable interest rate (such as tied to a consumer price index).

2. payment includes costs of collection and/or attorney fees upon default.

b. **Money --** is any medium of exchange recognized by a government as its currency (not goods or services).

Example:
A check payable in Mexican pesos is negotiable because the peso is recognized by the Mexican government as its medium of currency.

Note:
Misconception: A note payable in U.S. gold is a payment in money. This is not correct, because gold in and of itself is not a currency recognized by the United States government as a medium of exchange.

5. **Payable on Demand or at a Definite Time --** The instrument must be payable on **demand** or **at a definite time**. [UCC 3-108]

   a. **Types of Instruments**

      i. **Demand instruments --** Those that are payable immediately upon issue, such as "payable at sight" or "payable upon presentation", or those which no time period is specified (such as a check).

      ii. **Time instruments --** Those payable at a specific time after issue which include:

         1. A time instrument, which allows the maker or drawer to pay before a specific date. ("On or before Oct. 1, 20XX, I promise ...").

         2. An acceleration clause (for any reason), which permits a holder to demand full payment upon the happening of an event.

         3. Extension clauses to extend for a specific definite time by the maker, drawer, or the happening of a specified event.

6. **Payable To Order Or Bearer --** The instrument must be payable to **order** or **bearer**. [UCC 3-109]

   a. **Order** instruments are payable to the order of:

      i. An identified person (pay to order of G.A.Jentz).

      ii. An agent, trust, estate, office, or organization (pay to Travis County Tax Assessor).

      iii. Specific Rules:

         1. The "person" must be identified with certainty (so a person can tell who must indorse instrument).

         2. Can be payable to the order of persons jointly or alternatively.

         3. Not a requirement for a check to be negotiable (neither is term bearer).

   b. **Bearer** instruments are payable to:

      i. Bearer.

      ii. An identified person or bearer (Payable to John Smith or bearer).

      iii. Cash or some nonidentified person.

C. **Important Summary - Memorize --** Six elements for a negotiable instrument must be:

   1. in <u>writing</u>,

   2. <u>signed</u> by maker or drawer,

   3. <u>unconditioned</u> promise or order,

   4. <u>sum certain</u> in <u>money</u>,

5. payable on demand or at a definite time,

6. payable to order or bearer (except a check).

VII. Factors not Affecting Negotiability

A. **Contradictory Terms --** Typewritten words prevail over printed and handwritten over both typewritten and printed. Written word amounts prevail over numerical amounts unless written amount is ambiguous. [UCC 3-114]

Example:
A check is written for the amount five hundred twenty-five dollars and the numerical amount is $505. This contradiction does not affect the negotiability of the instrument and the sum certain is the written amount of $525.

B. **Omission of Date --** Unless necessary to determine a definite time for payment for a time instrument. Thus, no date on a check (a demand instrument) does not affect the check's negotiability. [UCC 3-113]

C. **Postdating or Antedating --** Neither affect negotiability. [UCC 3-113]

D. **Collateral --** Additional promises to maintain, give additional, or the notation that collateral has been given as security do not affect the negotiability of the instrument.

Transfer of Instruments and Holders in Due Course

To be either a contractual obligation (nonnegotiable instrument) or a substitute for money (negotiable instrument) the instrument must be transferred. Negotiable instruments are usually transferred by negotiation allowing the holder to qualify as a holder in due course. Negotiation of a bearer instrument is by mere delivery, but negotiation of an order instrument is by delivery and indorsement. There are four types of endorsement. You should know all four and the legal effect of each. A holder in due course can have better rights to the collection on an instrument than a contractual assignee. There are three elements which must be met for a holder to become a holder in due course: holder must take for value, take the instrument in good faith, and take the instrument without knowledge of defense or claim, previous dishonor, or that the instrument is overdue. Each has special rules.

I. **Nonnegotiable Instruments --** Transfer of a nonnegotiable instrument, or a negotiable instrument without a required proper indorsement, is by assignment (See: Contract Law).

II. **Negotiable Instruments --** Transfer of a negotiable instrument is by negotiation allowing the holder (if criteria is met) to become a holder in due course. [UCC 3-201]

   A. **Bearer Instruments --** Are negotiated by mere delivery to a holder.

   B. **Order Instruments --** Are negotiated only by a delivery plus an indorsement.

III. **Indorsements**

   A. There are four types of indorsements; Blank, Special, Qualified, Restrictive.

   B. **Blank** and **Special** indorsements indicate how a holder will continue to negotiate the instrument to another holder. **Qualified** and **Restrictive** indorsements limit, usually to some extent, the liability of the indorser to subsequent holders.

      1. **Blank Indorsements --** Specify no particular holder to receive payment.

Example:
A check payable "to the order of Erin Marie" is negotiated by Erin Marie to Able Red by Erin's signature on the back of the check and delivery of the check to Able Red. [UCC 3-205(b)]

         a. **Legal effect of a blank indorsement**

            i. Converts an order instrument into a bearer instrument and Able Red can negotiate the check to Robin Orange by delivery only above.

            ii. Transfer warranties (to be discussed later) are extended to Able Red and any subsequent holders such as Robin Orange above. [UCC 3-416]

            iii. Blank indorser has a (signature) secondary liability to pay to all subsequent holders (Able Red and Robin Orange in example). [UCC 3-415]

      2. **Special Indorsements --** Specifies a person to whom payment or to whose order payment is to be made. Requires the signature indorsement of person specified plus delivery to further negotiate the instrument.

Example:
A check is payable "to bearer" or "to order of Erin Marie." Erin Marie will negotiate the instrument to Able Red by delivery plus she will indorse the instrument "Pay to Able Red" signed "Erin Marie." [UCC 3-205(a)]

a. **Legal effect of a special indorsement**

i. Converts a bearer instrument into, or continues an order instrument as, an order instrument for further negotiation. To further negotiate the instrument, Able Red can indorse in blank, converting the instrument to a bearer instrument, or Able Red can indorse the instrument to a specific person such as Robin Orange by special indorsement.

ii. Transfer warranties are extended to Able Red and any subsequent holder such as Robin Orange. [UCC 3-416]

iii. Special indorser has a (signature) secondary liability to pay to all subsequent holders (Able Red and Robin Orange in illustration). [UCC 3 - 415]

3. **Qualified Indorsements**

a. **Without Recourse --** Usually, indorsement includes words "without recourse" or similar words.

Example:
A check is payable to Able Red. Able Red indorses the check "without recourse /s/ Able Red" and transfers the check to Robin Orange. This is a blank qualified indorsement.

b. **Legal Effect of a qualified indorsement**

i. Disclaims contract signature (secondary party) liability. [UCC 3-415 (b)]

ii. Transfer warranties are extended to Robin Orange and all subsequent holders. [UCC 3-415]

4. **Restrictive Indorsements**

a. **Four types --** [UCC 3-206]

i. **Conditional --** Payment is conditional upon the happening of an event.

Example:
Indorsement states "Pay to Able Red upon her delivery of a laptop computer as per our contract of January 15. /s/ Erin Marie."

ii. **Prohibitive --** Purports to prohibit further transfer of the instrument.

> **Note:**
> **Misconception:** A restrictive indorsement, which states that further negotiation is prohibited, does in fact stop further transfer by negotiation preventing subsequent holders from becoming holders in due course. This statement is incorrect -- the UCC specifically provides that such an indorsement does not prevent further transfer or negotiation of the instrument.

Example:
Indorsement states "Pay to Able Red only. /s/ Erin Marie."

iii. **For Deposit or Collection --** Makes the indorsee (usually depositary) bank a collection agent of the indorser. [UCC 3-206(c)]

Example:
A check is made payable to Erin Marie drawn on Green Bank. Erin Marie indorses the check "For Deposit /s/ Erin Marie" and deposits the check with her bank (West Bank). West Bank is now the collecting agent for Erin Marie and must so act (not binding on an intermediary bank or the drawee bank - Green Bank).

iv. **Trust Indorsement --** Indorsement is made to benefit a third person.

Example:
A check is payable to Erin Marie. Erin indorses the check either "Pay to Able Red as agent of Robin Orange" or "Pay to Able Red in trust for Robin Orange."

b. **Legal Effect**

i. Restrictive indorsement <u>does not prohibit further negotiation</u> of the instrument and subsequent holders can become holders in due course. [UCC 3-206 (e)]

ii. <u>Except</u> for the <u>conditional restrictive indorsement</u>, the indorser's liability to subsequent holders is limited to the restriction being met. If a conditional indorsement or restriction is met, the indorser can be held secondary (contract) liable. [UCC 3-206(b)(f)]

C. Other Indorsement Issues

1. **Misspelled Name --** A payee or indorsee whose name is misspelled can indorse with the misspelled name, the correct name, or both. [UCC 3-204(d)]

2. **Multiple Payees**

   a. If payable to two or more <u>jointly</u> - all must indorse.

   b. If payable to two or more <u>in the alternative</u> - anyone of the parties can indorse.

IV. Holder in Due Course (HDC)

A. HDC Status

1. **Importance --** An HDC can have better rights than an assignee in seeking payment.

Example:
Erin Marie has contracted for $500 to purchase ten chairs from Able Red. Erin Marie makes out a check payable to Able Red for $500. Able Red negotiates the check to Robin Orange. Able Red never delivers the chairs. If Robin Orange is a HDC, Robin Orange can recover $500 from Erin Marie. If Robin Orange is an assignee, any defense (such as breach of contract) Erin Marie has against paying the check to Able Red is also a defense against having to pay Robin Orange (contract law - assignment).

2. **Time of Determination --** HDC status is usually determined at time HDC receives the instrument.
3. **Elements --** The following criteria must be met to become an HDC [UCC 3-302]:
    a. must be a **holder,**
    b. must take the instrument **for value,**
    c. **in good faith**, and
    d. **without notice** that the instrument is:
        i. **overdue,**
        ii. **been previously dishonored**, or
        iii. **of any claim or defense** on the part of any person.

B. **Elements Examined**

1. **Holder --** A "person" who possesses a negotiable instrument "if the instrument is payable to bearer or in the case of an instrument payable to an identified person, if the identified person has possession." [UCC 1-201(20)]
    a. Simply - Anyone who takes possession of a negotiable instrument through issue or negotiation.
2. **Value --** A holder takes for value if:
    a. The holder gives consideration (see contract law), but the holder is only a HDC to the extent that the agreed-upon consideration **has been performed**. If what has been performed is **all** that the parties have intended to be done, the holder is a HDC for the **face value** stated on the instrument. [UCC 3-303]

Example:
A check is drawn payable to Erin Marie for $500. Erin Marie negotiates the check by blank indorsement to Robin Orange with Robin Orange paying $300 and promising to pay Erin Marie $200 next week when she gets her pay check. Robin Orange is presently only a HDC for the amount paid (performed) $300.

Example:
Erin Marie negotiates the above check by blank indorsement to Robin Orange with Robin Orange paying $450 for the $500 check. Robin Orange has no further obligation to pay. Robin Orange has fully performed the consideration promised and is a HDC for $500.

Example:
Erin Marie presently has $1000 in her checking account. She has received a $500 check drawn by Robin Orange on West Bank and immediately deposits the check in her bank - East Bank. The same day, Erin Marie drafts checks amounting to $1,200 and all of these checks are paid by East Bank. Three days later, Robin Orange's check is received back by East Bank with the notation that it was dishonored by West Bank because of insufficient funds in Robin Orange's account. East Bank is a HDC of the $500 check because East Bank paid value (its own funds in the amount $200) but only a HDC against Robin Orange to the amount it has paid. This is referred to as the FIFO rule.

b. **Antecedent Debt** -- If the holder takes the instrument in **payment** of, or as **security for, an antecedent debt.**

Example:
A check is issued to Erin Marie for $500. Erin Marie owes Robin Orange $500 for legal services Robin Orange had previously provided Erin Marie. Erin Marie gives the check to Robin Orange to satisfy her debt. Robin Orange has taken the check for value.

c. **Negotiable Instrument**

   i. If the holder gives a **negotiable instrument** in payment for it.

Example:
A check is issued to Erin Marie for $500. Erin Marie negotiates the check to Robin Orange with Robin Orange paying Erin Marie $200 in cash and giving Erin Marie a negotiable promissory note for $300. Robin Orange is a HDC having given value ($200 cash plus the $300 negotiable note). Had this been a nonnegotiable promissory note, Robin Orange would have been a HDC for only $200 - the consideration paid.

3. Good Faith

Definition:

Good Faith: "Honesty in fact and the observance of reasonable commercial standards of dealing." [UCC 3-103(a)(4)]

a. **Assumed --** Generally assumed unless taken under very usual circumstances.

Example:
A holder who took a $1,000 negotiable certificate of deposit in an alley at 2:00 am paying $250 for it, most probably did not take in good faith.

4. Without Notice

a. **Overdue**

i. A **time instrument** is overdue if taken one minute after its due date. [UCC 3-304]

ii. A **demand instrument** is overdue if taken after the instrument has been outstanding for an unreasonable period of time after its date, or the instrument is taken on the day after the day a demand for payment has been duly made. [UCC 3-304(a)]

iii. A **check** is overdue if taken more than ninety (90) days after its date. [UCC 3-304(a)(2)]

Example:
A check drawn by Erin Marie is dated May 1 but not issued to Robin Orange until May 30 because Robin Orange is out of town. Robin Orange misplaces the check but finds it on August 3 and she indorses the check to her landlord for her August rent. Unknown to the landlord, Erin Marie and Robin Orange had a dispute over services rendered for the check and Erin Marie stopped payment because of the personal dispute. If the landlord is a HDC, the landlord can collect fully from Erin Marie on the check. If not, assuming Erin Marie's defense is a legal defense, the landlord's claim is subject to Erin Marie's defense. Here, the landlord is not a HDC. Although the landlord took the check within ninety days of issue, it was not taken within ninety days of its May 1 date. The landlord is not a HDC.

iv. If an instrument is **payable in installments,** any nonpayment of an installment or lack of full payment of the installment principal (not interest) is notice the instrument is overdue. Note effect of this rule when an installment note provides that any payment will be applied first to interest and the balance to principal.

b. **Previously Been Dishonored --** Requires actual knowledge. [UCC 3-302(a)(2)]

Example:
A check has been stamped on its face "Insufficient Funds" by the drawee bank. No subsequent holder can be a HDC.

c. **Claim or Defense --** Requires actual knowledge. [UCC 3-302(a)(b)]

i. **Irregular --** Holder has notice if the instrument is so incomplete, bears such visible evidence of forgery or alteration, or is otherwise so irregular or incomplete as to call into question its authenticity. [UCC 3-302(a)(1)]

Example:
An instrument's amount in which the sum of $25 is crossed out and in a different colored ink is raised from $25 to $2,500 would be a visible alteration and a holder taking this instrument would not be a HDC. But an instrument originally payable as $7.00 (seven), and clearly in the same ink is added a zero and a 'ty' ($70.00 and seventy) would not be a visible alteration and subsequent holders could qualify as HDCs.

ii. **Prior Notice --** Holder has notice if holder has knowledge that the obligation of any party is voidable or that all parties have been discharged.

Example:
A note is payable to the order of Erin Marie, a minor. Erin Marie indorses the note in blank to her father, Harry Marie. Harry Marie cannot be a HDC because Harry Marie knows his daughter is a minor and that she can disaffirm her liability as an indorser and transferor of the note.

C. **Holder through an HDC: Shelter Rule (Provision) --** Any holder who cannot qualify as an HDC but took the instrument through an HDC, has the same rights as if an HDC.

1. **Use law of assignment**

Example:
A and B are special indorsers and C is the holder of a note. A is qualified as a HDC, but B is not because B did not take the note for value, and C is not a HDC because C took the note with notice the note is overdue. Although C is not a HDC and did not take the note from a HDC (B), C has the rights of a HDC. Using the law of assignment, A as a HDC transferred these rights to B, the assignee, and B, as an assignor, transferred these rights to C.

2. **Shelter Provision Limitation** -- A holder, however, cannot improve his or her position under the Shelter Provision by a negotiation of an instrument to a HDC and the subsequent reacquirement of it.

Example:
Erin Marie acquires a note by fraud and negotiates the note to Robin Orange who qualifies as a HDC. Later Erin Marie repurchases the note from Robin Orange. Here, the Shelter Provision would not apply and Erin Marie does not have the rights of a HDC.

Defenses and Liabilities of Parties

Parties who have liability on an instrument may have a legal reason (defense) to attempt to avoid responsibility for payment. These defenses are divided into personal and real defenses. Real defenses are absolute and completely dissolve liability of the party. Personal defenses can only be asserted against holders, not against a holder in due course or a holder with rights of a holder in due course. Knowledge of six major real defenses is essential. Parties on an instrument can have signature or transfer (sometimes presentment) warranty liability, or both. For signature liability, you should know who has, and to what extent liability flows to agent's signatures, primary party liability signatures, and those with secondary liability. Transfer warranty law primarily applies to indorser type transfers. This includes general indorsers (blank and special), qualified indorsers, and nonindorsers. Those who obtain payment or acceptance of a draft or check also make certain warranties to the payor or acceptor. You should know in detail not only the laws on signatures, but what warranties are made on transfer or presentment.

I. Two Types

A. Personal,

B. Real or Universal

II. Legal Effect [UCC 3-305]

A. Personal defenses can be asserted against ordinary holders but not against a HDC or a holder with rights of a HDC under the Shelter Provision

B. Real or universal defenses can be asserted against all holders, including HDCs and holders with rights of a HDC.

III. Real or Universal Defenses

A. Forgery -- Only those whose authorized signatures appear on an instrument can be held liable.

Example:
Erin Marie's blank check is stolen by Eric Crook and Eric Crook forges Erin Marie's name as drawer of the check. Erin Marie would not be liable on the check even to a HDC of the check.

B. Fraud in Execution -- A person is deceived into signing a negotiable instrument believing that what is being signed is some other document. This does not apply if the person signing should have known the nature of the document they are signing.

Example:
Robert Gonzalas is a single male from Mexico who does not read English. Eric Crook, a deceitful neighbor, delivers a small package to Gonzalas asking him to sign a "receipt," which, in fact, is a $10,000 negotiable promissory note. Gonzalas signs what he believes is a receipt. This is fraud-in-execution. This would not apply to you, as an accountant, because you obviously can read English and have the intelligence to understand what you are signing.

C. **Minority** -- However, this is a universal or real defense only to the extent that state law recognizes minority as a defense to a simple contract (voidable right). (See Contracts)

Example:
Erin Marie is a minor who purchases by check an $800 CD player. Since this is not an item of necessity, Erin Marie can disaffirm (avoid) the purchase and her obligation to pay the check claiming her minority as a real defense.

D. **Discharge Decree In Bankruptcy** -- The petition into bankruptcy is not a real defense, but the discharge decree issued by the Bankruptcy Court discharging the obligation to pay the instrument is.

E. **Void Events** -- Any event that renders an obligation or instrument void is a real or universal defense.

   1. **Illegality** -- Any law which renders an instrument void because it was executed in connection with illegal conduct. If the law merely makes the instrument voidable, it is a personal defense.

Example:
In state X, it is illegal to gamble but the payment of a gambling debt is merely unenforceable (voidable). In this state, a check written to pay off a gambling debt would be unenforceable by the payee-winner, but the drawer would be fully liable to a HDC of the check.

   2. **Mental Incapacity** -- Any instrument drawn, or made, or indorsed by a person who has been adjudicated (declared) by a court as mentally incompetent is a void instrument and it cannot be enforced by a HDC. If the person has not as yet been adjudicated mentally incompetent, but is mentally incompetent, it is a personal defense.

   3. **Duress** -- Any person who signs an instrument under "extreme" duress (threat or force which would result in death or serious injury, for example) has a real defense because the instrument is void.

F. **Material Alteration** -- Changing the contract terms or obligations in any way between any two parties - such as adding clauses, changing dates, or amounts, or interest, deleting clauses, completing an instrument in an unauthorized manner - is a material alteration.

1. Material alterations can be:

   a. **Complete Defense --** Against both an ordinary holder and a HDC.

   b. **Partial Defense --** Where the original tenor of the instrument is altered cleverly (changing $7. 00 to $700.00), the altered amount is a real defense ($693), but a HDC can enforce the instrument for its original tenor ($7).

   c. **No Defense --** If an original instrument is incomplete but later completed in an unauthorized manner, this alteration is no longer a defense against a HDC and the HDC can enforce the instrument as completed.

Example:
Erin Marie has contracted with Eric Crook to repair her damaged car. Erin Marie is leaving town and drafts a check payable to Eric Crook leaving the amount blank. It is agreed that Eric should fill in the amount upon completion of the repairs but the amount would not exceed the $1,000 estimate. Instead, Eric fills in the amount $3,000 and negotiates the check to Emily Elizabeth, a HDC. Emily Elizabeth can fully hold Erin Marie on the check for $3,000.

IV. **Personal Defenses: --** Any legal defense that is not real or universal is a personal defense and cannot be used against a holder with rights of a HDC.

A. **Types**

1. **Breach of Contract --** Includes breach of warranty.

2. **Failure of Consideration**

Example:
Erin Marie issues a $1,000 note to Megan Orange as a gift. There is no consideration for the note and thus the note is unenforceable, but this is only a personal defense.

3. **Fraud in Inducement --** Ordinary fraud.

Example:
Erin Marie contracts to buy Eric Crook's "race horse" for $10,000. Erin Marie gives Eric Crook a check for this amount not knowing that the horse has a condition, which will not allow the horse to race. Eric Crook knew of the condition. Crook has negotiated the check to Megan Orange who is not a HDC. If Erin Marie refuses to pay the check (has stopped payment), Megan Orange cannot enforce payment. If Megan Orange had been a HDC, Erin Marie would be liable to Orange on the check for $10,000.

4. **Unauthorized completion --** Of an incomplete instrument

5. **Nondelivery of Instrument**

Example:
Erin Marie issued a bearer note to Megan Orange. Eric Crook stole the note and negotiated it to Emily Elizabeth. If Emily Elizabeth is not a HDC, Erin Marie need not pay the note. If Emily Elizabeth is a HDC, Erin Marie must pay.

6. **Voidable Transactions**
   a. Illegal obligation.
   b. Ordinary duress.
   c. Incapacity, other than minority.
7. **Prior Payment**

Example:
A note signed by Erin Marie reads "Payable on or before May 1." On April 20, Megan Orange, the holder of the note, secures Erin Marie's payment but Erin Marie does note take possession of the note. On April 28, Megan Orange transfers the note to Eric Edward. On May 1, Eric Edward presents the note to Erin Marie for payment. If Eric Edward is not a HDC, Erin Marie does not have to pay, but if Eric Edward is a HDC, Erin Marie is liable.

V. **Liability of Parties**

A. **Two Types**

1. **Signature** Liability.
2. **Warranty** Liability.

B. **Signature Liability**

1. **General Rule --** No person can be held contractually liable on their signature unless their signature appears thereon. [UCC 3-401]
2. **Agent's Signature**
   a. **Authorized Agent - Principal --** Liable if:
      i. Principal's name only is signed by agent, or
      ii. Principal is named and agent signed indicating agency. [UCC 3-402(a)]

Example: ABC Inc.

/s/ I.M. Kind, Pres.

   b. **Authorized Agent - Agent --** Liable if:
      i. Only signature of agent appears (to parties who do not know of agency).
      ii. Principal is not named but agency status is disclosed (unless parties know agent is not intended to be liable).

Example: I.M. Kind, Agent

iii. Principal is named but nothing indicates agency relationship (unless parties know of agency and agent not intended to be liable. [UCC 3-402(b)]

Example: ABC Inc., I.M. Kind.

c. **Unauthorized Agent --** Only the agent is liable unless principal's negligence substantially contributes to the making of the unauthorized signature or principal ratifies signature. [UCC 3-403, 3-406]

3. **Primary Party Liability**

a. **Primary Parties** are:

i. **Makers of CDs and notes.**

ii. **Acceptors of drafts or checks** [UCC 3-409]

1. Only drawees can become acceptors.

2. Acceptance only required when instrument requires it (trade acceptance), or time period is fixed by date of acceptance.

3. Certification by a drawee of a check, although not required, is an acceptance. Drawer of a cashier's or teller's check is treated the same as a maker of a note or drawee (acceptor) of a certified check. [UCC 3-411]

b. **Absolute Liability --** Unless the primary party has an appropriate defense, the primary party has an absolute contractual duty to pay the instrument at the tenor stated on the instrument at the time of signing. [UCC 3-412, 3-413]

4. **Secondary Party Liability**

a. **Secondary parties** are:

i. **Drawers of an ordinary check or draft.**

ii. **Indorsers** (unqualified).

b. **Liability** is conditioned on:

i. **Presentment**

Definition:
Proper Presentment: To properly present an instrument, the holder must present the instrument to the right person for the correct reason in the right manner timely. [UCC3-501]

Example:
A time note must be presented to the maker for payment on due date. A check must be presented to the drawee bank for payment either at the drawee bank or by deposit in the depositary bank within thirty days after date to hold drawer liable and within thirty days after indorsement to hold an indorser liable. [UCC 3-414(f), 3-415(e)]

ii. Dishonor

Definition:
Dishonor: Generally, any refusal to pay or, where required accept, is a dishonor except where holder refuses to show identification, or show evidence of authority to receive payment, exhibit the instrument, or sign a receipt (anywhere on the instrument) that the holder has received payment. [UCC 3-501, 3-502]

iii. Notice of Dishonor is received:

Definition:
Notice of Dishonor: Must be given within 30 days of dishonor or within 30 days after notice of dishonor is received. For banks, notice of dishonor must be given by midnight of the next banking day or the bank can be held accountable for the instrument. Deferred posting allows checks received after a stated time (i.e., 2:00pm) to be presented for the midnight rule the next succeeding banking day (i.e., received at 3:00pm on Friday, which would not post presentment until Monday, giving bank until midnight on Tuesday to dishonor). [UCC 3-503]

1. Notice can be given by any reasonable means and, once received, is effective notice for all subsequent holders. [UCC 3-503(b)]
2. To give notice by protest (used usually when there is dishonor of an instrument drawn in one country but payable in another) is by a certificate made by a U.S. consul, notary public, or person authorized to administer an oath in the country of dishonor. [UCC 3-505(b)]

iv. Presentment and Notice can be Excused -- Generally, if such cannot be made with reasonable diligence, the drawer or indorser waives such, or by the instrument terms (such as adding word "payment guaranteed"), excuses such. In addition, presentment is waived if drawer instructed drawee not to pay or accept instrument, maker or acceptor is deceased, or drawer disclaimed contract liability (such as signing "without recourse"). [UCC 3-304]

v. Failure to Present Properly or Give Timely Notice of Dishonor

1. **Indorser's secondary** (contract signature liability) is <u>completely discharged</u>. [UCC 3-415(e)]
2. Drawer's secondary (contract signature) liability is excused from liability <u>only to extent the drawer is deprived of funds</u> due to such failure. [UCC 3-414(f)]

Example:
Green has $150,000 in her checking account. On May 1, Green issues to Smith a check for $110,000 for the purchase of an expensive lake lot. Smith negotiates the check to a land development company on May 20. On June 15, the land development attempts to cash the check only to learn that Green's drawee bank was closed on June 12 due to financial reasons. The FDIC Insurance only covers $100,000. The land development company wants to hold Green for the full $110,000 but, due to improper presentment (more than 30 days from date), Green's liability is excused to extent he/she was deprived of funds (here, $10,000 because, had there been proper presentment, the check would have been fully honored).

5. **Unauthorized Signature Liability**

   a. **Unauthorized signatures** include those that are forged and those made by persons knowing that they are not entitled to payment.

   b. A **forged signature**, for liability purposes, is treated as the signature of the forger.

   c. **Imposter** -- A person who procures an instrument impersonating that he/she is someone else by mail, telephone, in person, etc., and indorses the instrument in the name personated, (although fraudulent) the indorsement is effective. The drawer or maker cannot treat the indorsement as unauthorized and is liable to any person who, in good faith, pays the instrument or takes it for value or collection. [UCC 3-404(a)]

Example:
Eric Crook calls Erin Marie and tells her he is Jerry Lewis and is soliciting funds in his (Jerry Lewis's) own name for a charity. Erin Marie makes out a check payable to "Jerry Lewis" and sends it to the address Crook gives her over the phone. It is Crook's address. Crook indorses the check "Jerry Lewis," transfers the check to a co-conspirator, Jeff Slug, and Slug cashes the check at Erin Marie's bank. Erin Marie cannot claim that her bank paid a "forged" instrument and recover the funds from her bank.

   d. **Fictitious Payees** -- Important for exam. Generally involves a dishonest employee who either drafts checks for the employer's signature or has authority to draft and sign checks for the employer, made out to persons not entitled to payment. Indorsements by these payees (although fraudulent) are effective in favor of any person who in good faith pays the instrument or takes it for value or collection. [UCC 3-404 (b)]

Example:
Sly Green is a bookkeeper for Able Cook's restaurant. Green drafts all checks for Cook's signature, distributes the signed checks, and reconciles Cook's bank statement. Unknown to Cook, Green is a compulsive gambler and owes money to a number of bookmakers. Green drafts checks payable to the bookmakers telling Cook these are suppliers of food products for the restaurant. Cook signs the checks. The bookmakers indorse the checks in their own names and cash the checks. All are paid by Cook's bank. An audit reveals the fraudulent payments. Cook claims the indorsements are unauthorized and wants reimbursement from his bank. Unfortunately for Cook, the fictitious payee rule is applied, the indorsements are effective and Cook suffers the loss (can still sue Green and bookmakers, however).

6. **Accommodation Signature Liability**

   a. Since the **accommodation party** signs an instrument to lend his/her name to guaranty the liability of the **accommodated party**, the signature liability rules of the accommodation party are the same as those applied to the accommodated party. Thus, an accommodation party who signs to accommodate a maker has primary liability, to accommodate a drawer secondary liability, and to accommodate an indorser secondary liability. [UCC 3-410]

b. **Accommodation Party --** Basically, the accommodation party is treated as a surety or guarantor (See: Debtor-Creditor Relationships). Thus, a holder does not have to demand payment from the accommodated party before holding the accommodation party liable.

c. **Incapacity Defenses --** Defenses, such as incapacity of the accommodated party, cannot be asserted by the accommodation party.

d. **Accommodated Party Pays --** If the accommodated party pays, the accommodated party cannot recover from the accommodation party but if the accommodation party pays, the accommodation party is entitled to reimbursement from the accommodated party.

C. Warranty Liability

1. Transfer Warranty Liability

a. **General and Qualified Indorsers --** who receive consideration make to all subsequent holders the following transfer warranties: [UCC 3-416]

> **Note: Misconception:** Nonindorsers have no liability on an instrument. This is true for contract signature liability but even nonindorsers who receive consideration make to the immediate transferee transfer warranties and are liable if one is breached.

i. transferor is entitled to enforce the instrument (has good title),

ii. all signatures are authorized and genuine,

iii. instrument has not been altered,

iv. instrument is not subject to a claim or defense by any party, which can be asserted against the transferor, and

v. the transferor has no knowledge of any insolvency proceeding commenced with respect to the maker, acceptor, or drawer.

b. **Cannot be Disclaimed --** These warranties cannot be disclaimed as to checks, but can be to other types of instruments.

c. **Claim for breach --** of warranty must be made within 30 days of breach and the time claimant knows of warrantor's identity.

d. **Nonindorsers --** who receive consideration make the same transfer warranties but these only flow to the transferor's immediate transferee.

Example:
A check is made payable to Erin Marie. Erin Marie, as a gift, indorses (blank indorsement) the check to Megan Orange. Megan Orange for consideration transfers the check without indorsement to Eric Edward. Eric Edward for consideration transfers the check (by special indorsement) to you as a holder. Erin Marie cannot be held for any transfer warranty liability because she receives no consideration. Megan Orange has no transfer warranty liability to you because as a nonindorser you are not her immediate transferee. Eric Edward does pass all five transfer warranties to you but you have to show a breach.

2. Presentment Warranties

a. Anyone who obtains payment or acceptance of a draft or check warrants to the party who pays or accepts:[UCC 3-417]

i. The person obtaining payment or acceptance is authorized to do so and is entitled to enforce the instrument.

ii. The instrument has not been altered (does not apply to a HDC).

iii. The person obtaining payment or acceptance has no knowledge that the signature of the drawer is unauthorized (does not apply to a HDC).

b. **Cannot be Disclaimed --** These warranties cannot be disclaimed as to a check and claim for breach must be made within 30 days of knowledge of breach and identity of the warrantor is known by the claimant.

Discharge

There are five acts which either discharge the instrument or liability of the parties on it. You should have a general knowledge of each.

I. Types of Discharge

A. Payment or Tender of Payment

1. All parties are discharged when the party liable to pay (maker, acceptor, drawee) pays holder the full amount. [UCC 3-602] Payment by any other party (such as an indorser) only discharges that party and any subsequent parties.
2. Tender of payment, which is refused, discharges all parties who would have rights against the party making the tender (but only to extent of the tendered amount). [UCC 3-603]

B. Cancellation or Renunciation

1. Any intentional and voluntary act, such as surrender of the instrument, destruction, mutilation, or cancellation of the instrument (such as writing on the instrument "paid"), is a discharge of all parties from liability. [UCC 3-604]
2. The striking out of a party's signature discharges that party from liability, as does an agreement not to sue a party in a signed writing.

C. Reacquisition

1. A person who reacquires an instrument previously held discharges all intervening holders, but can be held liable by subsequent holders. [UCC 3-207]

D. Certification of a Check

1. Certification (requested by a holder or drawer) by the drawee discharges the drawer and any prior indorsers from liability. [UCC 3-414(c), 3-415(d)]

E. Impairment of Recourse or Collateral

1. Any impairment of a party's right of recourse, such as the right to seek reimbursement from a prior indorser, or the drawer, or maker, is a discharge of that party to the extent the right of recourse is impaired. [UCC 3-605]

Example:
A holder releases an indorser against whom a subsequent indorser has a right of recourse, or a holder agrees to extend the time of payment of the maker or drawer, which impairs the right of an indorser to recover immediately from other indorsers, resulting in a loss.

2. A holder who impairs the value of collateral (such as releases it, fails to maintain, or preserve it) without the consent of those who would benefit from the collateral in the event of nonpayment, discharges these parties liability to the extent they suffer a loss.

Letters of Credit

Letters of credit are sometimes used in certain real estate sales transactions and, frequently, to finance international business transactions to ensure performance under the contract. Basically, sellers want to avoid delivering goods for which the seller might not be paid, and buyers want assurance sellers will not be paid until there is evidence that the goods have been shipped.

I. Basic Definitions (UCC 5-102)

Definitions:
Applicant: the person at whose request or on whose account a letter of credit is issued.

Beneficiary: the person under the letter of credit terms who is entitled to have the letter honored upon presentation.

Issuer: a bank or person that issues a letter of credit.

Nominated Person: a person whom the issuer designates or authorizes to pay, negotiate, or give value under a letter of credit.

Presentation: delivery of a document to an issuer or nominated person to honor or give value under a letter of credit.

Record: information that is inscribed on a tangible, electronic, or other medium that is retrievable in perceivable form.

II. The Letter of Credit Process -- The following steps should help you to understand the letter of credit process in an international setting;

A. Buyer and seller make a sales contract, included in the terms is a letter of credit to be used to finance the sale.

B. Buyer makes an application to its bank for issuance of a letter of credit.

C. The buyer's bank (the issuer) forwards the letter of credit to a correspondent bank in the seller's country.

D. The correspondent bank sends the letter of credit to the seller (beneficiary).

E. The seller, upon receipt, prepares the goods for shipment and prepares the documents required under the letter of credit delivering the documents to the correspondent bank.

F. The correspondent bank, if it deems the documents are in order, sends the documents to the issuer (buyer's bank) and pays the seller according to the terms of the letter of credit.

G. The issuing bank, if the documents are in order, charges the buyer's account, forwards the documents to the buyer (or a custom broker), and reimburses the correspondent bank.

H. The buyer (or custom broker) takes the documents to the carrier and picks up or has the goods delivered to the buyer.

III. Some Basic Laws

A. General Rules

1. A letter of credit can be issued in any form that is a record and is authenticated by a signature, or in accordance with the agreement of the parties, or standard practice of financial institutions. (UCC5-104)
2. Consideration is not required for the issuance of a letter of credit. (UCC5- 108)
3. A letter of credit can be revocable, if so provided in the letter. (UCC5- 106) In an international sales of goods where shipment is overseas, the letter is irrevocable, unless otherwise agreed. (UCC2-325)
4. Letters of credit, unless stated to the contrary, expire one year after its stated date of issuance or date of issue. If the duration is stated to be "perpetual," the letter expires five years after its stated date or date of issue. (UCC5-106)
5. There is a one year statute of limitations. (UCC5-115)

B. Duties, Rights, and Obligations

1. An issuer must honor a presentation, which by standard practice appears on its face to strictly comply with the terms of the letter. An issuer has seven business days to either honor or give notice of a defect in presentation. (UCC5-108) This does not apply to fraud or forgery.
2. For wrongful dishonor, the issuer is liable for the amount that is the subject of dishonor, or damages for its breach, or, sometimes, specific performance plus incidental (but not consequential) damages, and reasonable attorney fees and other expenses of litigations. (UCC5-111)
3. If presentation is honored, the beneficiary warrants to the issuer there is no fraud or forgery, and to the applicant that there is no violation of any agreement between the parties intended to be augmented by the letter of credit. Note, that these are additional to other warranties if documents or instruments are also part of the transaction. (UCC5-110)
4. Generally, a letter of credit may not be transferred, unless so stated in the letter of credit, or by operation of the law. (UCC5-112, 5-113) Proceeds, however, from a letter of credit are generally assignable. (UCC5-114)
5. A letter of credit is independent of the underlying contract between the seller and buyer. Thus, other laws such as the Sale of Goods (UCC Article 2 or International CISG - Convention on International Sales of Goods) or Secured Transactions law (Article 9 UCC9-306, 9-312)) may apply.

Sales

Introduction and Contract Formation

Sometimes contracts involve both goods and services, or goods and realty. The question is which law applies, i.e., the sale of goods or the contract for services or realty. It is important to know which law is applicable. You should also be able to distinguish a gift and bailment from a sale of goods and from each other. In addition, there are specific rules that apply only when one or both parties are merchants. Thus, the definition of a merchant, plus other definitions, are listed to assist you. Since you are already aware of basic contract formation laws that apply to contracts, you should note here the specific laws which apply only to the Sale of Goods under the UCC.

I. Governing Law

A. **Uniform Commercial Code --** Article 2 is primary source.

1. Adoption: All states except Louisiana have adopted.
2. UCC stresses the express terms parties agree upon and supplies terms, rights, and liabilities in absence of agreement.

B. **Law not covered specifically by UCC --** common law applies (See: Contracts).

II. Coverage

A. Only **applies to sales of goods,** not real estate or service contracts

1. When contract involves **both service and sale of goods** - use predominant test.

Example:
You contract with an artist to paint a portrait of you for a Christmas present. Is this a contract for a good - the finished portrait - or a contract for a service - the painting of the portrait? Obviously, the predominant feature of the contract is the artist painting (service) your portrait.

Example:
You order food to be cooked at a restaurant. Are you purchasing the cooking (preparation) of the food or the food itself? Here, the food itself is the predominant feature and a sale of goods. [See UCC 2-314(1)]

2. **Both Realty and Sale of Goods --** When a contract involves both realty and sale of goods, use UCC 2-107 and common law on fixtures (real property).

Example:
Sale of minerals, oil, gas, or structures on earth to be moved are goods if they are to be severed by the seller; if by the buyer, real estate law governs.

Example:
Sales of growing crops or timber - sale of goods regardless who severs.

Example:
"Things" attached but not deemed fixtures, which can be severed without material harm to realty, are goods.

B. **Specific rules** apply when a seller, buyer, or both are **merchants**.

III. Important Definitions

Definitions:
Sale of Goods: is the passage of title of goods from a seller to a buyer for a price.

Merchant: is a person who deals in goods of the kind being sold, or a person who by occupation holds himself or herself out as having knowledge or skill peculiar to the purchases or goods involved in the transaction.

Examples: (Deals in goods of kind being sold)

a manufacturer of washing machines

a retail seller of washing machines

a farmer who regularly sells crops

a university who five times a year sells used and obsolete equipment

Examples: (Holds self out as having knowledge or skill by occupation)

a restaurant owner who purchases a large oven for the restaurant

a computer division of the IRS who buys a new computer

a university purchasing department who purchases chemistry laboratory equipment

Goods: all movable and tangible personal property other than money, investments, or securities and things in action.

Termination: a right a party has pursuant to the contract to end the contract for reasons other than contract breach.

Example:
Seller puts into contract that price of goods is to be determined six months from present date at time of the shipment. Buyer puts in a termination clause allowing buyer to end the contract without liability if the price at the time of shipment exceeds the present price list by more than 3%.

Cancellation: is when a party puts an end to the contract because of the other party's breach, but can pursue remedies.

Example:
Seller breaches contract by failure to deliver by contracted date of performance. Buyer can cancel (any further performance requirements of buyer) and still pursue remedies (hold seller liable for breach).

Cure: is the right of a seller who prior to performance tenders nonconforming goods which are rejected by buyer, to notify buyer of intent to and does tender timely a corrected shipment.

A. **Shipment and Delivery Terms**
   1. **FOB** - Free on board
   2. **C&F** - Cost and freight
   3. **CIF** - Cost, insurance, freight
   4. **FAS** - Free alongside "vessel"
   5. **Delivery Ex-ship** - From the carrying "vessel"

IV. **Distinguish Sales of Goods From ...**
   A. **Gift --** Transfer of personal property but not for a price
   B. **Bailment --** Transfer of personal property but not title

Example:
A buyer takes home a lawn mower priced at $400 to "try it out." This is called a sale on approval. Until the buyer "approves" the purchase offer, title remains with the seller and this is a bailment.

V. **Contract Formation - General Rule**
   A. Use basic contract law applied to all kinds of contracts except where Uniform Commercial Code sections have specific rules for the sale of goods.

Example:
The contract laws on capacity apply to all kinds of contracts and there is no UCC section, which deals with capacity.

VI. Specific UCC Laws

A. Offer and Acceptance

1. Definiteness of Offer and Acceptance Terms

a. If parties intend to make a contract, a contract for sale of goods is formed as long as the object and quantity of goods are agreed upon. [UCC 2-204(3)]

b. **Terms of Agreement --** The UCC stresses that the terms of the agreement control rights, obligations, and liabilities. The UCC supplies the terms in absence of agreement. For an

   i. **Open Price Term --** a reasonable or market price at the time of delivery will apply, or if price is to be fixed by either party, good faith is required in doing so. [UCC 2-305]

   ii. **Open Payment Term --** payment is due at time and place buyer is to receive the goods. [UCC 2-310]

   iii. **Open Place of Delivery Term --** delivery is at seller's business or, if none, at seller's residence. [UCC 2-308]

   iv. **Open Time for Contracted Performance --** in absence of agreement it is a reasonable time. [UCC 2-309]

Note:
Misconception: A contract cannot be formed if the price for the sale of goods is not stated in the contract or the price is to be determined in amount at the time of shipment. This statement is in error because the UCC specifically allows prices to be determined at time of shipment (sometimes referred to as an "escalation clause") and the price can be what is a reasonable or a market price at time of contract, shipment, delivery, or payment.

B. Firm Offer

1. If the following criteria is met the offer is irrevocable, without payment of consideration (distinguished from an option which requires consideration), for the time of assurance stated in the offer (if no time is stated, a reasonable time) not to exceed three months.

   a. offer made by a merchant (can be either seller or buyer), and

   b. offeror gives assurance offer will not be withdrawn, and

   c. offer is in a signed writing. [UCC 2-205]

Note:
Misconception: Buyer Green is from New Orleans and Seller Smith is from Dallas. Smith offers to sell Green a watch for $100. Green accepts Smith's offer. The contract is silent as to place of delivery. Delivery is at buyer's place in New Orleans. No, in absence of agreement it's Smith's residence in Dallas. Green is required to "pick up" the watch or be in breach of contract.

Example:
Green, a retail seller of TVs, offers in a letter to purchase from Vision Inc. (a manufacturer of TVs) 500 Model X TVs at the current Vision Inc. price list. In the letter, Green states that time is of the essence and that the offer is only good and will not be withdrawn for thirty days from date. One week later, Green decides to withdraw the offer and mails a revocation of the offer. Even if Vision receives the letter of revocation, Vision can, during the thirty day period, accept Green's offer and bind Green to a contract. Green's offer as a merchant, in a letter as a signed writing, gave Vision assurance the offer would not be withdrawn for thirty days. Thus, Green made a firm offer, which was irrevocable without payment of consideration for the thirty day period and cannot legally revoke the offer.

C. **Unilateral Offer by Buyer for Shipment of Goods --** can be accepted by the seller in any one of three methods. [UCC 2-206(1)(b)]

1. By seller's delivery of conforming goods to the carrier - common law acceptance of a unilateral offer.
2. By seller's prompt promise to ship.
    a. Use bilateral contract acceptance law.
    b. Any reasonable medium is an authorized means of acceptance and effective upon seller's delivery of the acceptance to the authorized means. [UCC 2-206(1)(a)]
3. By seller's delivery of nonconforming goods to the carrier without notice to the buyer that the nonconforming shipment is sent only as an accommodation.
    a. Here, there is an acceptance and automatic breach.
    b. If buyer is notified that shipment is sent only as an accommodation, buyer cannot treat the nonconforming shipment as an acceptance.

D. **Conflicting Terms --** Called **Battle of the Forms**

1. **Common Law --** mirror image rule applies. An attempted acceptance with terms that modify or add to those of the offer is treated as a counteroffer.
2. **UCC 2-207 --** modifies the common law as follows:
    a. If the offeree makes a definite expression of acceptance, a contract is formed "even though it states terms additional to or different from those offered," unless the offeree conditions his or her acceptance upon the offeror's "assent to the additional or different terms."

Example:
A seller offers to sell to the buyer 5,000 lbs. of a "specific type" of chicken at 50 cents per pound. The buyer responds "I accept your offer for 5,000 lbs. as certified by public scale weight certificate the specific type of chicken at 50 cents per pound." Since this is a sale of goods (chicken), and because the buyer gave a definite expression of acceptance ("I accept" without conditional assent to the modification), a contract is formed even though the buyer's acceptance with additional terms (public weight certificate) modified the terms of the seller's offer.

   b. **The Terms of the Contract --** (seller's offer or buyer's acceptance) is determined as follows:
      i. If one party, or both parties, are nonmerchants, it is on the offeror's terms.
      ii. If both are merchants, additional (but not conflicting) terms are on the offeree's terms, unless:
         1. the offeror states in his or her offer that acceptance must be on the offeror's terms, or
         2. the additional terms materially alters the contract, or
         3. the offeror specifically, with notice, objects (within a reasonable amount of time) to the additional terms.

Example:
In the sale of 5,000 lbs. of chicken, above, with the offeree's additional terms of a public scale weight certificate, since both parties are obviously merchants, the contract is formed on the offeree's (buyer's) terms unless seller objects with notice to the buyer within a reasonable time. If the seller does object, the contract is formed on the seller's terms (delivery without a required public scale weight certificate).

E. **Modification of Terms of Contract**

1. **Common Law --** An agreement to modify the existing terms of a contract is totally unenforceable unless the modification is supported by consideration.
2. **UCC 2-209 --** "An agreement modifying a contract for the sale of goods needs no consideration to be binding." The modification may have to be in writing if either the original contract or the modification places the contract under the Statute of Frauds.

Example:
ABC Gas Inc. has a requirement contract to furnish Green Industries with all the gas it needs to run its plants for ten years at 50 cents per cubic foot of gas. Exploration and transportation costs triple in the next three years and ABC is starting to lose money on the contract. The present market price is 80 cents per cubic foot. ABC and Green, in writing, agree to raise the price of the gas supplied to Green to 60 cents per cubic foot for the rest of the term of the contract. Even though no consideration is given by ABC for the increase in price, the 60 cents price is now binding on both parties.

F. **Unconscionable Contract or Clause --** [UCC 2-302] Follows common law rule that any contract or clause which "hurts the conscience of society" is illegal and, either the clause only, or the contract is unenforceable.

G. **Statute of Frauds --** Contracts for the sale of goods priced at $500 or more must be in writing to be enforceable [UCC 2-201] except

1. **Between-Merchants --** If one sends the other a written confirmation and the one receiving the confirmation, with knowledge of its contents, does not object in writing within ten (10) days of receipt of the confirmation, the oral contract is enforceable by either party.

Example:
ABC is an auto parts store. ABC, by phone, orders from Auto Warehouse $10,000 worth of parts. Auto Warehouse immediately sends ABC a FAX covering the contract made on the telephone. ABC receives the FAX and reads it. Twelve days later, ABC learns it can buy all of the parts it ordered from another parts warehouse company for $9,500. ABC calls Auto Warehouse and tells Auto Warehouse not to ship the parts because it is claiming the Statute of Frauds as a defense. ABC and Auto Warehouse have an enforceable contract, even though it is an oral contract, for the sale of goods priced at $500 or more because both parties are merchants and Auto Warehouse sent by FAX a written confirmation of the oral contract, which ABC read. Since ABC did not object to the contents of the written confirmation within ten days of receipt, the oral contract is fully enforceable by Auto Warehouse.

2. **Special Ordered Contracted Goods --** Goods, which a seller could not resell in his or her ordinary course of business, are removed from the Statute of Frauds <u>only</u> if the seller has made a substantial beginning of manufacture or commitment for procurement to make the goods.
3. **Admission Under Oath --** If a party admits under oath (disposition, interrogatory, in pleadings, or on the "stand") the existence of the oral contract, that person cannot claim the Statute of Frauds as a defense.
4. **Buyer's Performance --** By either making a payment or taking possession of the goods, Buyer removes the Statute of Frauds as a defense, at least to the amount of goods covered by the payment or the goods possessed.

Example:
Green, owner of ABC Television, orally offers to sell Red a TV for $600. Later, Red calls Green and accepts Greens offer. Later yet, Red changes his mind and does not wish to buy the TV. Because Red has not signed a written contract for the sale of goods priced at $500 or more, and Red has neither taken possession of or made a payment for the TV, Red can claim the Statute of Frauds and Green cannot enforce the oral contract against Red.

5. **Memorandum --** Written evidence of the oral contract removes the Statute of Frauds as a defense for the party who signs the memorandum.
    a. Can be in any written form such as a check, a letter, a FAX, etc.
    b. Must meet the following criteria:
        i. writing indicates a <u>sale was made</u>,
        ii. must be <u>signed by the party</u> sought to be held to the oral contract,
        iii. must specify the <u>quantity</u> of the subject matter of the sale.

Example:

Green orally offers to sell Sarah his car for $800. Sarah orally accepts and immediately writes a letter to Green stating the car, price, and delivery terms of the agreement. Sarah has signed the letter. In this situation, Sarah can no longer claim the Statute Frauds as a defense but, because Green has not signed any writing concerning the sale, Green could refuse to sell his car to Sarah claiming the Statute of Frauds as a defense.

General Rules

Before any interest (title or risk of loss) can pass from a seller to a buyer, the goods must be in existence and identified to the contract. Once in existence and so identified, title and risk pass at the time the parties expressly agree. If the goods are in existence and identified to the contract, and the contract is silent as to when title and risk of loss pass, the passage of title and risk of loss is dependent upon the delivery terms stated in the contract. These delivery terms are important and a matrix is provided in the text to help students learn and remember the law in this area. This section also deals with passage of title and risk of loss when there is a sale on approval or sale or return, and who has superior title to goods where title passage was voidable or void, where goods entrusted to a seller by the owner are sold by the seller, and rights of a seller's creditor to set aside title upon a sale of goods to a buyer.

I. General Rules

A. As between the seller and buyer, the UCC stresses passage of risk of loss more than passage of title, and such is usually reflected in the CPA exam.

Note:
Misconception: In the sale of goods, title and risk of loss always pass at the same time. This is in error because first the parties can expressly determine the exact moment when title and risk of loss pass and second, even in absence of agreement the law, in two situations pass both at different times.

B. With two exceptions, in absence of agreement, title and risk of loss pass to the buyer at the same time.

C. Passage of Title is found in UCC 2-401 and passage of risk of loss in UCC 2-509.

D. Before any interest in goods (title or risk of loss) can pass from a seller to a buyer, the goods must be in existence and identified to the contract. [UCC 2-105(2)]

1. The key in most CPA exams is whether identification has taken place because, in most cases, whether goods are in existence, is obvious.
2. Rule of Thumb for Identification is, unless the contract calls for "all" of a mass of goods, there must be a separation from the mass, such as a marking, actual separation, or some other method indicating clearly the goods, which are being sold to the buyer. Exception: fungible goods.
    a. **Fungible Goods --** Goods, which are so mixed that a person cannot distinguish one unit from another and where the ownership of the mass is intended to be tenants in common.

Example:
Green has 1000 cases of peas in the warehouse and Beyer has contracted to purchase 100 cases. Since the goods are not fungible [Green and Beyer do not intend to own the entire 1000 cases as tenants in common], the 100 cases must be identified (marked or separated from the mass) before title or risk of loss can pass.

Example:
Green and Smith have deposited wheat in a silo. Green's deposit is 5000 bushels and Smith's deposit is 10,000 bushels. Smith sells 2000 bushels to Beyer. The wheat is fungible (mixture of like kind goods with intent to become tenant in common owners) and identified by amount without a separation. Thus, title and risk of loss to 2000 bushels passed to buyer upon the making of the contract (ownership is Green with 5000 bushels, Smith 8000 bushels, and Beyer 2000 bushels). Any loss will be so prorated based on ownership.

3. If the goods are either not in existence or identified, only a contract for sale can take place. If both, a sale may take place immediately.

E. Once goods are in existence and identified, title and risk of loss can pass at the time the parties **expressly agree**.

II. Absence of Agreement

A. **General Rule** -- In absence of agreement, the time title and risk of loss to identified goods passes from the seller to the buyer is dependent upon the delivery terms of the contract.

B. There are **three types of delivery terms:**

1. Delivery by seller's shipment.
2. Delivery by seller to buyer's destination.
3. Delivery by seller without a physical movement of the goods. (Buyer is to pick-up the goods from seller, carrier, or warehouse.)

III. Delivery Terms

A. Delivery Shipment Terms and Law

1. **F.O.B.** -- (free on board) seller's city, business, or warehouse, or "shippoint." Title and risk of loss pass upon delivery (possession) of conforming goods to the carrier. [UCC 2-319(1)(a), 2-509(1)(a)]

Example:
Seller contracts to sell to Buyer 100 personal laptop computers at a given price, FOB seller's warehouse via ABC Truck Lines. Until ABC Truck Lines picks up the 100 laptop computers, risk is on the seller. Once ABC Truck Lines has possession of the 100 laptop computers, the risk of loss is on the buyer.

2. **F.A.S** -- (free alongside vessel) Title and risk of loss pass upon seller's delivery of conforming goods alongside the vessel in the manner usual in that port, or on a dock designated and provided by the buyer. [UCC 2-319(2)]

3. **C.I.F. --** (cost, insurance, freight) - Title and risk of loss pass from seller to buyer when the seller delivers (possession) identified conforming goods to the carrier, obtains a negotiable bill(s) of lading covering transportation to named destination, procures an insurance policy, and forwards to buyer all documents. [UCC 2-320(2)(a)]

4. **C&F --** (cost and freight) Same rule as in C.I.F., except procurement of an insurance policy.

5. **Ship --** If contract merely calls for the seller to ship and there are no other delivery terms, title and risk of loss pass from seller to buyer when the seller delivers (possession) identified conforming goods to the carrier. [UCC 2-509(1)(a)]

B. Delivery to Buyer's Destination Terms and Law

1. **F.O.B buyer's city, business or warehouse, or residence --** Title and risk of loss pass upon the seller's <u>tender</u> of conforming goods at place of contract destination. [UCC 2-319(a)(b), 2-509(1)(b)]

   a. **Tender is the key --** A proper tender is the seller's holding out to the buyer the goods in a reasonable manner, for a reasonable time, to allow the buyer to take possession of the goods. [UCC 2-503(1)]

Example:
Seller contracts to deliver 1000 cases of beans to the buyer F.O.B. buyer's warehouse. The beans are shipped by ABC Truck Lines. The truck arrives at buyer's warehouse at 1:00pm on Monday. Buyer cannot unload the truck until Tuesday morning and asks the carrier to leave the truck at the buyer's warehouse dock until it is unloaded in two hours on Tuesday morning. Carrier agrees. During the night, through no fault of the buyer, the beans are destroyed by fire. The risk of loss has passed to the buyer and the buyer must pay the seller for the beans. This is a destination delivery contract and the seller's tender by the carrier began at 1:00pm on Monday. This was a holding out to the buyer in a reasonable manner and, certainly, if the truck could be unloaded in two hours, the load was held out (the entire afternoon) for a reasonable time to enable buyer to take possession. Risk passed to the buyer Monday afternoon.

2. **Delivery "Ex-ship" --** Title and risk of loss does not pass until the ship arrives at a port of destination <u>and</u> not until the goods leave the ship's "tackle" or are otherwise properly unloaded. This is the converse of a delivery F.A.S. [UCC 2-322]

3. **Deliver --** If contract merely calls for the seller to deliver at the buyer's destination and there are no other delivery terms, title and risk of loss pass from the seller to the buyer upon tender of conforming goods at buyer's destination. [UCC 2-509(1)(b)]

C. Delivery by Seller Without Physical Movement -- Buyer picks up goods.

1. If the goods are <u>not represented by a document of title</u>,

   a. <u>title</u> passes at the moment the contract is made.

   b. if <u>seller is a merchant, risk of loss</u> does not pass until buyer gets possession.

   c. if <u>seller is a nonmerchant, risk of loss</u> passes upon seller's tender of the goods to the buyer.

2. **Delivery Without Physical Movement Represented by a Document of Title**

   a. **Types of Documents of Title --** include bills of lading, warehouse receipts, dock receipts, air bills, and any other document, which in the regular course of business, is treated as evidence that the person in possession is entitled to receive, hold, or dispose of both the document and the goods it represents. [UCC 1-201(15)] Documents can be Negotiable (consigned to order of ABC Inc.) or Nonnegotiable (delivery to ABC Inc.).

   b. **If the document is Negotiable**

      i. **Title and Risk of Loss --** pass to the buyer upon the buyer's receipt of the document. [UCC 2-401(3)(a), 2-509(2)(a)]

Example:
Able Corp. sells 500 boxes of copy paper to Green company. The 500 boxes were shipped to the Fox Warehouse Co. earlier and Fox issued to Able a negotiable warehouse receipt representing the 500 boxes. Able indorses and delivers the warehouse receipt to Green at 4:00pm on Friday. During the weekend, the warehouse burns down and the 500 boxes are completely destroyed. Green suffers the loss because risk of loss passed to Green upon Green's receipt of the negotiable document of title.

   c. **If the Document is Nonnegotiable**

      i. **Title passes to buyer** upon buyer's receipt of the document. [UCC 2-401(3)(a)]

      ii. **Risk of loss passes to buyer** after receipt of the document and buyer has had a reasonable time to present the document, to receive the goods, or to give directions to the bailee. [UCC 2-503(4)(b), 2-509(2)(c)]

Example:
Able Corp. sells 500 boxes of copier paper to Green Company. The 500 boxes were shipped to the Fox Warehouse Co. earlier and Fox issued a nonnegotiable warehouse receipt representing the 500 boxes. The warehouse is only open Monday - Friday 7:30 - 4:30pm. On Friday at 4:00pm, Able delivers the warehouse receipt to Green. During the weekend, the Fox warehouse burns down and the 500 boxes are completely destroyed. Able suffers the loss because, although Green had title, risk of loss would not pass until Green has had a reasonable time to present the document to Fox, or to give directions to the bailee Fox. Most courts would hold 30 minutes not to be a reasonable time period and the risk of loss over the weekend was still with Able.

   d. If the goods are held by a bailee, and no document is transferred to the buyer, risk of loss passes to the buyer when the bailee acknowledges the buyer's right to the possession of the goods.

3. Passage of Title & Risk of Loss in Absence of Agreement

Delivery Situations	Delivery Terms	LAW
Delivery by shipment	Ship, FOB origin or seller's -- FAS, CIF, C&F	Title and risk of loss pass to buyer upon carrier's possession of conforming goods
Delivery to destination	Deliver, FOB buyer's -- Delivery ex-ship	Title and risk of loss pass to buyer upon tender of conforming goods to the buyer
Delivery by seller without physical movement of the goods	Delivery without a document of title	Title passes to buyer upon formation of the contract. Risk of loss passes to buyer -- a. If seller is a merchant, upon buyer's receipt of the goods. b. If seller is a nonmerchant, upon seller's tender of the goods.
	Delivery with a document of title -- Nonnegotiable document	Title passes upon buyer's receipt of the document. Risk of loss passes to buyer after buyer receives the document and a reasonable time has lapsed.
	Delivery with a document of title -- Negotiable document	Title and risk of loss pass upon buyers receipt of the document

D. Nonconforming Goods

1. If goods are so nonconforming due to seller's breach that buyer has a right to reject the goods, risk of loss does not pass to the buyer until the defects are cured or buyer accepts goods despite their nonconformity. [UCC 2-510 (1)]
2. In addition, if the goods have been held accepted and acceptance is revoked, risk of loss goes back to seller to extent buyer's insurance did not cover the loss. [UCC 2-510(2)]
3. If the breach is due to fault of the buyer and risk has not passed, risk shifts immediately to the buyer for a commercially reasonable period after seller learns of the breach, but only to extent not covered by seller's insurance. [UCC 2-510 (3)]

IV. Special Issues

A. Sale on Approval -- Until the buyer approves seller's offer, transfer to the buyer of goods creates a bailment. Title and Risk of Loss remain with seller until buyer accepts. Cost of proper return (rejection of offer) falls on the seller. [UCC 2-327(1)] Buyer can accept by:

1. Due notification ("I accept.")
2. Failure to reject within the time of trial period (keeps goods beyond trial period).
3. Does any act inconsistent with seller's ownership. (Buyer takes home lawn mower to try it out for two weeks. During the two weeks buyer mows fifteen yards for fees.)

B. Sale or Return -- An actual sale with title, risk of loss, and possession with the buyer subject to the condition that buyer can restore title and risk upon the seller by a proper return of the goods. Cost of return is on the buyer. Failure to timely return finalizes the sale. [UCC 2-327(2)] The UCC treats a consignment as a sale or return.

C. Title Problems -- Deals with sales of an imperfect title to an innocent third party (BFP - a bona fide purchaser for value) - who has best title - original owner or BFP.

1. **Void Title --** A void title cannot be passed to anyone. Thus, the original owner has the best title. [UCC 2-403(1)]

Example:
Thomas, a thief, steals your bicycle and sells it to Smith. Smith has no knowledge that Thomas is not the owner or that the bike has been stolen. You discover Smith has the bike. You are entitled to return of your bicycle from Smith because Thomas had a void title (no title) to pass to Smith. Smith , however, can legally recover from Thomas if Smith can find Thomas.

2. **Voidable Title --** A title, that even though passed to a buyer, can be recovered. There is one exception; if the buyer in turn passes title to a BFP. [UCC 2-403(1)]

Example:
Mary is a minor who contracts to sell her bicycle to an adult, Jim, for $250. Mary transfers the bicycle and title to Jim. Since Mary is a minor, Jim receives a voidable title and Mary can disaffirm the sale and recover her bicycle. If Jim, before Mary had disaffirmed the sale, had sold the bicycle to Judy (a bona fide purchaser for value), Mary can still disaffirm the contract with Jim but cannot recover the bicycle from Judy. Judy's title is absolute and cuts off Mary's voidable title.

V. Entrusting of Goods

A. Entrusting of goods to a **merchant** (person who deals in goods of that kind) by a buyer gives the merchant the power to transfer all rights (including title) to a buyer in the ordinary course of business. [UCC 2-403(2)(3)]

Example:
Harry took his TV set to ABC TV Inc. for repairs. ABC sells both used and new TVs. The set is repaired but, by mistake, is sold to a customer of ABC without knowledge of Harry's ownership rights. Since ABC is a merchant (in the business of selling used TVs), ABC passed good title to Harry's set to the customer and Harry cannot recover the set from the customer. ABC has committed a tort of conversion, however, and is liable to Harry in a civil suit.

B. Entrusting of goods to a **nonmerchant** - delivery is a mere bailment, and unless the original owner has given some indicia of ownership to the bailee to lead a buyer from the bailee to believe the bailee is either the owner or has authority to sell, there can be no passage of title (treat as a void title).

VI. Rights of Seller's Creditors

A. **General Rule --** Upon sale and passage of title to a buyer, seller's creditors lose any rights in the goods. [UCC 2-402]

B. **Seller's Retention of Goods**

1. If after sale and passage of title, seller retains possession (and frequently, use) of the goods the following rules apply:

    a. If the sale was done to defraud creditors **(fraud-in-fact)**, a seller's creditor can set aside the sale (void the sale) and the goods become subject to the rights of that creditor. [UCC 2-402(2)]

    b. If the creditor cannot prove fraud-in-fact but the possession is in the hands of a **nonmerchant seller**, the creditor can claim such retention is **presumed fraud-in-law**, which requires the seller and/or buyer to prove the sale was not done to defraud creditors. (If seller/buyer cannot so prove, creditors can set-aside sale.) [UCC 2-402(2)]

    c. If possession is in the hands of a **merchant seller, there is no presumed fraud-in-law** and creditor can only set aside sale if creditor can prove fraud-in-fact.

Products Liability

Product liability can stem from warranties or commission of a tort. There are five types of warranties: express warranties, implied warranty of merchantability, implied warranty of fitness for a particular purpose, implied warranty of title, and implied warranty arising from course of dealing or trade usage. You should know the rules for creation of each, what each covers, and how each can be disclaimed by a seller. The two primary torts are negligence and strict liability. Be sure to know the elements which must be proved for either to be a viable action.

Products Liability consists of Warranty and Tort Liability

I. **Historical Rule - Caveat Emptor --** Let the buyer beware.

   A. Even under "Caveat Emptor," a seller could be liable for fraud of title, negligence, or breach of an express warranty.

II. **Warranties --** There are five types of warranties possible if there is a sale or contract to sell goods.

   A. **Express Warranties --** [UCC 2-313]

      1. **Affirmations of fact or promises --** This suit is 100% wool, or this pump will not overheat even with continuous use.

      2. **Sales by description --** Contract with buyer for a camel's hair coat, seller must deliver a camel's hair coat.

      3. **Sales by Sample or Model --** Bulk or finished product must conform exactly to sample or model.

      4. All above must be part of the bargain or sale. [UCC 2-313(1)]

         a. **General Rules**

            i. Can be oral or written.

            ii. Can be in brochures, advertisements, etc. of seller.

            iii. No need to use words like warranty or guaranty to create an express warranty.

            iv. Statements of value or opinion (seller huffing and puffing) are not express warranties.

   B. **Implied Warranty of Title --** [UCC 2-312]

      1. **Seller warrants**

         a. Seller has a good title and its transfer is rightful.

         b. There are (unknown by buyer) no outstanding liens, encumbrances, or security interests against the goods.

         c. If seller is a merchant, that the goods shall be delivered free from third party infringement (patent/copyright, etc.) claims.

   C. **Implied Warranty of Merchantability --** [UCC 2-314]

      1. To create, need two criteria:

         a. the seller must be a merchant, and

b. the goods are warranted to be fit for ordinary use, of proper kind-quality-quantity, properly packaged and labeled, and conform to affirmations of fact made on the container or label.

2. This warranty applies to food and drink to be consumed on or off the premises of the seller.

Example:
Able purchases a ham from ABC Meat Market. Unknown to Able or ABC Meat Market, the ham is tainted and Able is seriously ill after eating it. Able can recover from ABC Meat Market because it is a merchant seller and the ham was not fit for human consumption (ordinary use) and not of the proper quality, which ham is supposed to be.

D. **Implied Warranty of Fitness for a Particular Purpose --** [UCC 2-315]

1. To create, need two criteria:

a. the seller must expressly or by implication know the purpose or buyer's use of the goods, and

b. the buyer must rely on the seller's selection or recommendation in making the purchase.

Example:
Beyer tells Sallor he needs a water pump that will pump 100 gallons a minute of muddy water out of a mine shaft. Sallor tells Beyer the company has the ideal pump, its Z model. Beyer purchases the pump and, although the pump is not defective and runs to its full capacity, it can only pump 75 gallons per minute. Beyer can hold Sallor liable for breach of the implied warranty for a particular purpose because Beyer made Sallor aware of his needs and Beyer purchased in reliance of Sallor's recommendation that Z model would fulfill Beyer's needs.

E. **Implied Warranty Arising from Course of Dealing or Trade Usage --** [UCC 2-314(3)]

1. The warranty applies when both parties have a knowledge of a well-recognized usage of trade or, by numerous past performances, infer a course of action intended to be performed.

Example:
In Wisconsin, where salt is used on icy roads, it is the custom for all new automobiles to be undercoated by a dealer to prevent rust. Cart Auto Sales, a Wisconsin seller-dealer, fails to undercoat a new car sold to Beyer, causing Beyer's car (underneath) exterior to rust. Cart Auto is in breach of the implied warranty arising from course of dealing and trade usage.

III. Warranty Disclaimers

A. Disclaimer of Express Warranties

1. Disclaimer of oral express warranties must be specific, unambiguous, and clearly and conspicuously called to the attention of the buyer. Cannot be inconsistent with written express warranties. [UCC 2-316 (1)]

B. Disclaimer of Implied Warranties

1. **Disclaimer by Custom or Usage --** In certain industries, it is a long established custom that sales do not carry implied warranties. For example, in a few states sales of used goods carry no implied warranties.
2. **Disclaimer by Words**
3. **Specific Disclaimers**
   a. To specifically disclaim the Implied Warranty of Merchantability:
      i. must mention word merchantability
      ii. and, although it
      iii. can be oral or in writing, if in writing, must be conspicuous. [UCC 2-316(2)]
   b. To specifically disclaim the Implied Warranty of Fitness for a Particular Purpose:
      i. must be in writing and
      ii. conspicuous

Example:
" THERE ARE NO WARRANTIES, WHICH EXTEND BEYOND THE DESCRIPTION ON THE FACE HEREOF." [UCC 2-316(2)]

Example:
Green Inc. contracts to sell Able Industries a piece of equipment. In the contract, in bold type is the following clause:

"THERE ARE NO IMPLIED WARRANTIES OF FITNESS FOR A PARTICULAR PURPOSE OR MERCHANTABILITY, WHICH ACCOMPANY THIS SALE."

This clause disclaims both implied warranties because it is in writing, conspicuous, and mentions the word merchantability.

4. **General Disclaimer Words --** both the implied warranty of merchantability and implied warranty of fitness for a particular purpose can be disclaimed by words such as:
   a. " sold as is"
   b. " sold with all faults"

c. other language, which is called to the buyer's attention and makes plain there is no implied warranty. [UCC 2-316(3)(a)]

C. **Disclaimer by Examination --** [UCC 2-315(3)(a)]

1. If the buyer actually examines the goods prior to the sale, the buyer is bound for all defects found (patent or obvious, and latent or hidden), and all defects buyer should have found (patent).

2. If seller offers buyer the opportunity to examine the goods and the buyer refuses to do so, the buyer is bound by all defects he/she should have found (patent defects) if buyer had examined the goods.

D. **Disclaimer of Title --** [UCC 2-312(2)]

1. Can only be accomplished by specific language or buyer's knowledge of title problems.

Note:
Misconception: The terms of a sale "as is" disclaims all express warranties and the implied warranty of title. This is incorrect. Only the implied warranties of merchantability and fitness for a particular purpose are disclaimed in an "as is" sale.

Example:
A sales contract states "Seller conveys only such title as s/he has." This would effectively disclaim the implied warranty of title. A statement that "seller disclaims all warranties" would not be a sufficient disclaimer.

IV. Warranty Defenses

A. **Lack of Privity --** (not being a party to the sales contract): This is usually not a defense either because of case law (for example the purchase of food and drugs) or because of the UCC 2-318, which extends warranties to third party beneficiaries (those expected to use or consume the product).

Example:
You invite a friend to dinner and to afterward watch a sporting contest on TV. You purchase a frozen turkey for the dinner and cook the turkey without negligence or knowledge that the turkey is tainted. Your friend becomes ill from eating the turkey. Under early common law, your friend could not file suit against the store or the turkey processor under contract law (breach of warranty) because your friend was not a party to the purchase contract. Today, your friend can file an action against either or both because privity is no longer a defense due to case law or the UCC third beneficiary section. If you became ill you can also recover because you obviously are in privity to the store (breach of implied warranty of merchantability) and privity is not a defense for the processor.

B. **Statute of Limitations --** Unless agreed to a lesser period of at least one year, the plaintiff must file suit within four years of tender of delivery. [UCC 2-725(2)] Failure to file timely is a bar to recovery.

C. **Notice of Breach --** Failure to notify seller of the breach of warranty bars the plaintiff from pursuing any remedy for such breach if the buyer has accepted the goods. [UCC 2-607(3)(a)]

Performance, Nonperformance, and Perfect Tender Rule

A seller's tender is complete performance if the seller holds conforming goods at buyer's disposition for a reasonable time and place so that with notice buyer can take delivery. A seller's shipment is performance upon the seller's delivery of conforming goods to a carrier making a proper carrier contract, giving buyer notice of shipment, and, if appropriate, delivery of documents necessary for the buyer to obtain delivery. Any tender which fails to conform to the contract, whether it be in quality or quantity, gives the buyer some important options. You should know these.

I. General Rules

A. Seller's Obligation -- Seller is obligated to ship or tender delivery of conforming goods. [UCC 2-301]

1. If a delivery term - Seller is obligated to put and hold conforming goods at buyer's disposition at a reasonable time and place and give notice so buyer can take delivery. Buyer must furnish facilities reasonably suited for receipt of goods. [UCC 2-503(1)]
2. If a shipment term - Seller must: [UCC 2-504]
    - **a.** Deliver conforming goods to the carrier.
    - **b.** Make a proper carrier contract.
        - **i.** Failure of seller to perform this is a material breach only if the buyer can prove that a material delay or buyer loss has been suffered.
    - **c.** Deliver or tender to buyer any documents of title (such as a negotiable bill of lading) necessary for buyer to take delivery.
    - **d.** Notify buyer of shipment - (Generally, sending invoice documents is notice.)
        - **i.** Failure of seller to perform this is a material breach only if the buyer can prove that a material delay or buyer loss has been suffered.

B. Anticipatory Breach -- This occurs when either the seller or the buyer **repudiates** the **contract prior** to the required contract date of performance. Key is whether there is repudiation. [UCC 2-610]

1. Upon anticipatory breach, the non-breaching party can:
    - **a.** for a commercially reasonable period await performance, or
    - **b.** treat the breach as final and resort to remedies, and
    - **c.** suspend their own performance without liability for breach.
2. Unless non-breaching party has "canceled" (notice of breach and intent to pursue remedies), or materially changed their position based on the breach, or given notice that the anticipatory breach is considered "final," the breaching party can retract (by any method or notice) his or her repudiation, which restores the parties back to their original obligation. [UCC 2-611]

Example:
Seller and buyer have a contract with seller to deliver 200 Garth Brooks's CDs on or before May 1. On April 15, seller sends a FAX to the buyer telling the buyer that the seller cannot deliver by May 1, but would do so on May 15. Seller requests buyer to agree by return FAX to the May 15 delivery date. If buyer sends the FAX agreeing to the May 15 delivery date, there is no breach and the contract has been modified (without consideration). If buyer does not consent to the May 15 delivery date, buyer can treat the repudiation (cannot delivery by May 1) as a material breach and pursue remedies. If buyer does not consent to the May 15 date and merely states that buyer expects seller to deliver on time or be held in breach if not delivered by May 1, seller can (with notice) retract its repudiation. This restores the parties back to the May 1st delivery date.

II. **Perfect Tender Rule --** Any tender by a seller, which fails to conform to the contract in any manner (quantity or quality), allows the buyer to:

A. **reject the entire shipment**, or

B. **accept the entire shipment**, or

C. **accept any commercial unit and reject the rest**.

Example:
Seller's contract calls for delivery of 100 cases of carrots. Seller tenders to the buyer 200 cases of carrots, a nonconforming goods tender. The buyer could reject the entire 200 cases, accept the 200 cases paying for the additional 100 cases, or accept 100 cases and reject the other 100 cases.

III. **Nonperformance --** A seller who tenders nonconforming goods, or uses a different carrier than as contracted, may still have the ability to cure or make use of the substitute carrier without such constituting a material breach. Sometimes there is a casualty, partially or completely, to identified goods, or the seller's performance becomes objectively impossible to perform. Each has ramifications as to the rights of the buyer and the liability of the seller.

A. **Nonperforming Actions By a Seller Without A Material Breach**

1. **Cure --** [UCC 2-508)]

a. If a seller tenders delivery of nonconforming goods prior to the contract date, and buyer rejects the goods, the seller can with notice (before you treat the tender as a breach) indicate the intent to cure. The seller is not in breach if the seller tenders conforming goods within the contract time period.

Example:

Contract terms call for seller to delivery on or before June 1 one hundred model Z wash machines. On May 16, seller tenders one hundred model A wash machines and buyer rejects the shipment. Buyer sends seller a FAX stating seller made an error and the nonconforming shipment is rejected. The seller immediately sends buyer a FAX apologizing for the error and tells the buyer a corrected shipment will be made in two days. Seller has now shown an intent to cure and if the wash machines are delivered before June 1 seller is not liable for breach of contract.

b. If seller tenders nonconforming goods to the buyer but this is a tender which a reasonable buyer would be expected to accept (does not require a money allowance, but frequently this is the case), and yet buyer rejects, seller with notice of intent to cure can tender thereafter conforming goods to the buyer within a reasonable period of time (even if after contracted date of delivery) without being in breach.

Example:

Contract terms call for seller's delivery of 100 model Z tape recorders at $800 per unit on or before June 1. On May 25th, seller discovers that, due to a computer error, seller does not have 100 model Z tape recorders in stock but does have model A tape recorders, which sell for $950 per unit. On May 29, sellers tenders 100 model A tape recorders but only invoices buyer at $825 per unit price. Because of budget limitations, buyer rejects the model A tape recorders. If the seller notifies buyer that a corrected shipment will be made and such is tendered within a reasonable time (even after June 1), seller has made a cure of the contract delivery, is not in breach, and buyer must accept and pay for the goods.

2. **Substituted Performance --** [UCC 2-614(1)]

   a. If, without fault of the seller, the agreed facilities or type of contract carrier is not available or delivery impractical but a commercially reasonable substitute carrier is available, seller must use substitute carrier and buyer must accept delivery and pay. (Usually, any additional costs incurred by buyer must be borne by the seller.)

Example:

Contract terms call for shipment via ABC Truck Lines. ABC Truck employees are on strike and no other drivers will cross the picket line. If XYZ Railroad is available and a reasonable substitute, seller must ship by this rail carrier and such shipment is not a breach of contract.

B. **Either Party's Failure to Perform --** There are basically a duty and a right, which apply to a seller's and buyer's failure to perform or act under the UCC, which are treated as exceptions to the perfect tender rule; the right of assurance and the duty of cooperation.

1. **Right of assurance --** if a party has "reasonable grounds" to believe that the other party will not perform as contracted, he or she may in **writing** demand that the other party give adequate assurance of due performance. [UCC 2-609] If the party does not provide reasonable assurance as demanded within **thirty days**, this failure is a repudiation of the contract and can be treated as an anticipatory breach.
   a. Once a party is entitled to and does demand reasonable assurance, that party can suspend performance without liability until he or she receives the assurance requested.
   b. What are reasonable grounds for insecurity depends on the facts. Between-merchants commercial standards may be used.
   c. What actions of assurance that can be requested, also depends on the facts, and, again between-merchants commercial standards can be used.

Example:
Smith Inc. has contracted to buy a specific piece of equipment from ABC. Smith believes that if it runs this piece of equipment at a certain speed it will increase Smith's productivity by 5%. Smith learns from another buyer (Green) who has previously purchased a similar piece of equipment from ABC, that, although Green seldom ran the equipment at that speed, whenever Green did the equipment broke down. ABC's literature had indicated the equipment could be run at a variety of speeds including the speed Smith anticipated running the equipment.

Question: Is Green's experience sufficient (reasonable) grounds for Smith to believe that ABC's equipment will not perform as contracted?

Answer: Most probably, yes.

Question: What can Smith do before the equipment is delivered?

Answer: In writing, ask for reasonable assurances that the equipment will perform as contracted and for protection if it does not.

Question: What are reasonable requests for assurance?

Answer: Smith could ask for express warranties, money-back guaranty, or, perhaps, even replacement equipment if such is available. The point is, as long as reasonable, ABC must satisfy reasonably Smith's insecurity.

Example:
Smith has two contracts with ABC. One is to sell ABC 100 washing machines with delivery on May 1 with ABC's payment to be made on or before June 1. The second, is to sell ABC 100 dryers with delivery on July 1 with ABC's payment to be made on or before August 1. The washers are timely delivered and accepted by ABC. On July 15, Smith still has not been paid despite two phone calls requesting payment. Smith has reasonable grounds to ask for some assurance for payment of the dryers to be delivered on July 1. Smith, in writing, can demand reasonable assurance (perhaps the washing machine payment plus some other dryer payment, such as cash on delivery). Pending ABC's assurance, Smith can suspend the delivery of the dryers without liability and, if assurance is not forthcoming within thirty days, treat the dryer contract (washer contract already breached) as breached.

2. **Duty of Cooperation --** On occasion, the performance of one party is dependent on the cooperation of the other party. If such cooperation is not forthcoming, the other party has the right to:
   a. suspend his or her performance without liability, and
   b. hold the party in breach and pursue remedies, or
   c. proceed in fulfilling the contract in a reasonable manner. [UCC 2-311]

Example:
Great Falls School District School Board has decided to put computers in all classrooms in four of its ten high schools. Great Falls contracts with ABC Computer Inc. for the sale of these computers with delivery to be made by August 1 at the four schools to be designated by the School Board later. It will take ABC four days from date of shipment to deliver the computers. The contract has the School Board's address on it. Because of various PTA oppositions, as of July 26 the School Board has not designated the four schools for ABC delivery.

Question: What are ABC's options due to the School Board's failure to cooperate?

Answer: ABC could suspend making any shipment and, at ABC's option, hold the School Board in breach pursuing remedies, or ABC could deliver all computers to the School Board address and then, if not paid, sue for the purchase price.

C. **Excused Nonperformance**

1. **Casualty to Identified Goods --** [UCC 2-613]
   a. **Only applied if**
      i. at the <u>time of contract formation</u>, the goods <u>were identified</u> to the contract, and

ii. risk of loss has not passed to the buyer, and

iii. casualty to the goods is not the fault of either party.

1. If loss is total, seller has no liability to buyer.

2. If loss is partial, buyer can demand inspection of remaining goods and has choice of voiding the entire contract without liability, or accepting the remaining goods with due price allowance. In either case, seller has no further liability.

3. Rules also apply to a "no arrive, no sale" shipment. [UCC 2-324(b)]

Example:
Seller owns a 15 acre grapefruit orchard. Seller contracts to sell all the present grapefruit growing in the orchard to a Co-Op buyer at an agreed price, FOB Co-Op's warehouse. Two weeks before the harvest of the grapefruit, a frost destroys half of the grapefruit crop. This is a classic casualty to identified goods case. The grapefruit were identified to the contract (all the present grapefruit growing) at time of contract formation, risk of loss had not passed (destination delivery with risk passing upon tender of delivery at Co-Op warehouse), and casualty (frost) not a fault of the parties. The Co-Op can examine the remaining grapefruit paying half the contract price, or reject the remaining grapefruit without further liability of either party.

2. **Impossibility Due to Presupposed Conditions --** [UCC 2-615]

   a. If a condition arises (through no fault of either party), which renders performance impracticable (objective impossibility), the seller must notify the buyer of the delay or nondelivery. If the impossibility affects only a part of the seller's capacity to perform, the seller has a legal duty to allocate (prorate) whatever production is remaining among contract and regular customers.

Example:
Seller is a grower of cranberries and has contracted to sell 2000 crates of cranberries to the buyer. Some of the seller's cranberry bogs have a disease and the seller sprays the bogs with a legal chemical. Later, the FDA (Food and Drug Administration) discovers through animal tests that eating food sprayed with this chemical could cause cancer and the FDA bans all sales of goods, which has been sprayed with the chemical. Because of the ban, seller does not have enough cranberries from unsprayed bogs to fill all contract orders and those of their regular customers. In this situation, the seller must notify buyer of the impossibility and offer to ship on an allocated basis crates of the remaining cranberries. Buyer can reject or accept the allocation, paying a price based on the allocation. In either case, seller cannot be held liable for breach.

Buyer's Performance and Buyer's Rights

A buyer has a duty to accept conforming goods. It is important to know what action by the buyer constitutes acceptance, and under what conditions a buyer can revoke an acceptance. In addition for any goods accepted, the buyer is required to pay for those goods. The buyer has two basic rights, the right of inspection unless agreed to the contrary, and the right to reject any nonconforming tender. You should know the basic rules governing inspections, and the law on what constitutes a proper rejection.

I. Acceptance -- takes place when buyer [UCC 2-606]:

A. after opportunity to inspect the goods either signifies goods are conforming or will accept even if nonconforming. Payment for the goods in and of itself is not acceptance.

B. fails to reject after inspection or after a reasonable opportunity to do so.

C. does an act inconsistent with seller's ownership (such as knowingly using nonconforming goods).

D. Once buyer accepts, buyer loses right to reject (and certain remedies), and buyer must pay at the contract rate, however, acceptance of nonconforming goods with proper notice to the seller does not preclude all remedies.

II. Revocation of Acceptance

A. Under the following conditions, a buyer can revoke his or her previous acceptance [UCC 2-608]:

1. Buyer was given **reasonable assurance** seller would cure a nonconforming shipment, and cure has not taken place.

Example:
Buyer orders 100 barrels of Brand 52 cleaning solvent. Seller delivers Brand 50 cleaning solvent, a weaker but usable solvent. Seller tells buyer to use what it can of the Brand 50 solvent, and an immediate corrected Brand 52 shipment (cure) will be made. Buyer's use of the Brand 50 cleaning solvent is technically an acceptance. If, however, seller does not deliver immediately the corrected Brand 52 solvent, buyer can revoke it's acceptance and hold seller liable for breach (same as if the original nonconforming shipment had been rejected).

2. Seller has assured buyer that **goods are conforming**, and it is later discovered the goods are nonconforming:

Example:
Buyer orders 20 cardboard boxes of red pens. Each cardboard box has 100 small boxes with a dozen pens in each. The cardboard boxes arrive with the words "Green Pens" on each cardboard box. Buyer, without opening the cardboard boxes, calls the seller and tells the seller of the "Green Pen" notation. Seller assures buyer that the labeling is a mistake and inside the cardboard boxes are red pens. Buyer stores the cardboard boxes and pays the seller for the pens. Six months later, when buyer opens the cardboard boxes, buyer discovers that in fact there are only green pens inside, not the red pens seller had assured buyer. In this case buyer can revoke the acceptance.

3. Where buyer's discovery of the **nonconformity was difficult to detect**.

Example:
Buyer purchases a back-up generator. Buyer has no facility to test the generator and stores it. Six months later, the present generator malfunctions and when the back-up generator is placed into service buyer discovers it is defective. Buyer can revoke its earlier acceptance of the generator.

B. **Revocation Timing:** Revocation must take place within a reasonable time of discovery or time buyer should have discovered the defect, and revocation is not effective until the seller has notice of it.

III. Buyer's Tender of Payment -- [UCC 2-511]

A. Any customary means of payment (check, credit card etc.) is sufficient.

B. Note, however, a check is a conditional tender subject to the check being honored.

C. In absence of agreement a seller has a right to demand cash, but seller must give the buyer a reasonable time to procure the cash.

IV. Buyer's Rights - Inspection

A. Unless agreed to the contrary (i.e., a C.O.D. shipment), a buyer has a right before payment to inspect the goods at any reasonable time, place, or manner. [UCC2-513]

B. Costs of inspection is on buyer if goods are conforming, or seller if nonconforming.

V. Rejection of Nonconforming Goods -- [UCC 2-601]

A. To reject and pursue remedies, the purchaser must do so properly:

1. Rejection must be within a reasonable time after tender of or delivery. [UCC 2-602]
2. Rejection is not effective until known by seller. [UCC 2-602]

3. Specific reasons for rejection should be given. If not given, buyer cannot pursue remedies if seller could have cured, or if seller made a request in writing for a written statement of reasons. [UCC 2-605]
4. If buyer has possession of the nonconforming goods, the buyer must act as a bailee (use reasonable care over the goods) [UCC 2-602], and if buyer is a merchant, the buyer must follow any seller's reasonable instructions at seller's cost (buyer's reimbursement) concerning the disposition of the nonconforming goods. [UCC 2-603]
5. If goods are perishable or threaten to rapidly decline in value, buyer must make a reasonable effort to sell, and is entitled to reimbursement for all costs in caring for and selling the goods, plus a 10% sales commission, out of the proceeds of the sale. [UCC 2-603]
6. If seller does not give buyer instructions (and the goods are not perishable or rapidly declining in value), the buyer can store the goods for seller's account (storage charge), reship back at seller's expense, or sell the goods deducting costs and sales commission from the proceeds. [UCC 2-604].

Remedies

A seller has eight basic remedies for a buyer's material breach, but these remedies or combinations depend generally on who has possession of the goods; i.e., the seller, carrier in transit, or buyer. This is a good way to learn and remember each. Be sure to know the law on seller's stoppage in transit. A buyer has nine basic remedies for a seller's material breach, but choice of these remedies can be subdivided into three situations listed in the text. The parties can by contract limit the types of remedies available, those excluded, and within statutory limits the time period for filing actions (called Statute of Limitations). The latter is important to know.

I. **If seller still has possession --** (includes goods reclaimed from carrier through stoppage in transit), seller's remedies are:

A. **Withhold Delivery**: (without liability) and can pursue one of the remedies below, or, if buyer is insolvent, can demand full payment in cash. [UCC 2-702, 2-703(a)]

B. **Identify Goods to the Contract:** Then proceed with remedies listed below.

1. This permits a seller in the process of manufacture (when buyer repudiates the contract) to proceed to complete the manufacture and resell the finished product rather than the unfinished goods as scrap. [UCC 2-704]

C. **Cancel and/or Rescind Contract**: Seller must notify buyer of cancellation promptly and either proceed with remedies below, or, if rescission, seller is entitled to be indemnified to return to original position before contract was made. [UCC 2-703(f)]

Note:
Important: Any profit goes to seller, but if there is a deficiency (proceeds of sale do not cover breach and sales costs plus contract price) seller is entitled to a deficiency judgment against the buyer. [UCC 2-706]

D. **Resell Goods:**

1. Sale must be conducted in a reasonable commercially manner (public or private sale).
2. Seller must always give buyer notice of private sale, and, except for perishable or rapidly declining value goods, must give buyer notice of a public sale.
3. Sale must be conducted at a reasonable time and place, and in a public sale seller may buy.

E. **Sue for Breach of Contract**: Used mostly if breach takes place before delivery or buyer improperly rejects goods. **Measure of damages is difference between market price at time of place of tender and the unpaid contract price plus incidental (costs of breach) damages. [UCC 2-708]**

II. **If Goods are in Transit --** neither seller nor buyer has possession. [UCC 2-705]

A. If **buyer is insolvent** (not paying debts when due, or in ordinary course of business, or insolvent under Bankruptcy Act), seller (upon buyer's repudiation) can stop any quantity shipped.

B. If **buyer's repudiation** is other than insolvency, seller can only stop if quantity shipped is a carload, truckload, planeload, or larger shipment.

Example: Contract calls for seller's delivery of five cases of peas to buyer's place of business. The five cases are loaded on ABC Truck carrier's truck. The truck is also hauling five other seller's products. Buyer repudiates the contract claiming that seller's peas are of poor quality. Seller cannot stop the goods in transit because buyer's repudiation is not due to insolvency and the shipment (five cases) is not a truckload.

C. Seller can **stop shipment** until buyer gets possession, there is a negotiation to buyer of a negotiable document of title, or an acknowledgment to buyer:

   1. by a bailee that the bailee holds the goods for the buyer, or

   2. by a carrier that goods are held for shipment or held as a warehouseman.

III. Buyer Has Possession

A. If buyer received the goods on credit while insolvent, seller may reclaim the goods within ten (10) days of receipt by buyer. Important: Reclamation here precludes any other remedies, however. [UCC 2-702]

B. Seller can sue for the purchase price. [UCC 2-709]

IV. Remedies

A. Where seller tenders nonconforming goods and buyer properly rejects the goods, or seller refuses to deliver conforming goods.

B. Where the buyer accepts nonconforming goods.

C. Where seller refuses to deliver identified nonconforming goods and buyer wants the goods (specific performance, replevin, and buyer makes a payment to an insolvent seller).

V. Details of Remedies

A. This division is a good way to study and remember in some detail each remedy. In addition, the UCC permits liquidated damage (not penalty) clauses.

   1. If **seller tenders nonconforming** goods (buyer rejects) or seller refuses to deliver conforming goods, buyer's remedies are as follow:

      a. **Cancel and with notice rescind** the contract restoring parties back in the position they would have been before entering the contract. [UCC 2-711]

      b. **Cover -** Permits buyer to make in good faith (and without unreasonable delay) a reasonable substitute purchase (such as on open market) and buyer can recover the difference between the cost of cover and the contract price plus incidental damages (costs of breach) and consequential damages (foreseeable loss) less expenses saved in consequence of seller's breach. [UCC 2-712]

      c. **Sue for Breach of Contract -** Buyer's lawsuit to recover as damages the difference between the market price at time buyer learned of the breach and at place of tender, or if goods are rejected or acceptance revoked at place of arrival, and contract price plus incidental and consequential damages. [UCC 2-713]

      d. **Specific Performance -** may be decreed where the goods are unique, or in other proper circumstances such as where the remedy to cover is not available. Rarely, will specific performance be granted where damages are appropriate as a remedy.[UCC 2-716]

Example:
Seller agrees to sell to buyer an original painting by Picasso. Later, seller refuses to deliver the painting even though buyer has tendered fully the contract price. Buyer can in a court in equity file an action for specific performance (painting is unique -- one of a kind) requiring the seller to transfer the painting to buyer.

e. **Replevin -** If seller refuses to tender delivery of identified goods to the buyer, and the buyer cannot cover, the buyer can file a suit in equity requiring the seller to deliver the goods to the buyer. [UCC 2-716(3)]

f. **Buyer's Payment -** If the buyer makes a payment and seller is or becomes insolvent within ten (10) days of receipt of the payment, if the goods are identified the buyer can tender the balance owed and is entitled to the goods. [UCC 2-502]

2. If **buyer accepts nonconforming goods,** the buyer can **with notice** pursue the following remedies: (Notice is important because failure to give notice bars buyer from any remedies.) [UCC 2-607(3)(a)]

   a. **Sue for ordinary damages** incurred in the ordinary course of business and in a proper case receive incidental and consequential damages. [UCC 2-714(1)]

   b. **Sue for breach of warranty -** buyer can recover the difference between the value of the goods accepted and the value the goods would have had, had they been as warranted (unless special circumstances show proximate damages of a different amount) plus, if appropriate, incidental and consequential damages. [UCC 2-714(2)]

Example:
An accounting firm purchases a computer warranted to be a $40,000 value for $30,000. Upon delivery, due to a defect, the computer (although usable) is worth only $20,000. Unless special circumstances would show proximate damages of a different amount, the buyer should recover $20,000, the difference between the value as warranted, $40,000, and the value of the computer as delivered, $20,000.

   c. **Deduction of damages from purchase price** (called the "sell-help" remedy) - Buyer can deduct all or any part of the damages from the price still due and payable to the seller. [UCC 2-717]

   d. Buyer should note clearly to seller that the amount tendered is in "Full Accord and Satisfaction" or "Payment in Full," and seller's acceptance of the deducted amount is full satisfaction of the debt.

Example:
Buyer has contracted for ten new file cabinets priced at $300 each. The new file cabinets are tendered but two, although fully usable, are scratched. The buyer, with notice, can accept all ten file cabinets and tender to the seller a check for $2,900 ($50 per scratched cabinet deduction to cover refinishing costs) and a letter indicating clearly on the check and the letter that the check is intended as final payment and is in full accord and satisfaction of the contract price. If seller cashes the check, the buyer has fully paid and has no further liability.

3. **Liquidated Damages -** The parties by agreement in the contract can predetermine the amount of damages in case of a future breach. The amount must be reasonable in anticipation of what the actual loss would be, there will be difficulties in the proof of loss, and other adequate remedies will probably not be available. If the court holds the amount to be a penalty, the liquidated damage provision is void. If valid, the parties are limited to the liquidated damages stated. [UCC 2-718]

Example:
Seller agrees to deliver certain inventory to the buyer knowing that failure to deliver timely could result in buyer having to shut-down or limit production at its factory. Seller and buyer agree, that for every day seller delays in making delivery, it will cost the buyer a loss of somewhere between $4,000 and $8,000. The contract contains a liquidated damage clause of $5,000 per day for each day's late delivery. This is a liquidated damage clause and is valid because it appears to be a reasonable amount in expectation of buyer's loss, the proof of loss would be difficult to ascertain, and no other adequate remedy could be available.

VI. Limitations

A. **Contract Limitation -** Parties can agree to limit (or even add) remedies otherwise available under the UCC. For example, by agreement a buyer's remedies can be limited to a seller's repair or replacement of defective goods. [UCC 2-719(1)]

B. **Installment Contract -** Unless a breach of one or more installments substantially impairs the value of the whole contract, or the contract so provides, breach of an installment by a seller is not a breach of the whole contract, and a buyer's remedies is limited to that installment. [UCC 2-612]

C. **Statute of Limitations -** Time period from date of cause of action party must file or be barred from recovery. [UCC 2-725]

1. Must be filed within four years from cause of action.
2. Parties can lessen by agreement time period to not less than one year, but cannot extend period.
3. For breach of warranty, the cause of action begins at time of tender of delivery, not when breach is discovered by buyer.

Documents of Title

Definitions, Forms, Negotiation and Transfer, Limitations-rights

A document of title is much like an instrument, but it represents title to goods and the right of a holder to take possession of the goods. The most common documents are bills of lading and warehouse receipts.

I. Definitions and Forms

Definition:
Document of Title (Article 7 - UCC): Includes bills of lading, dock warrants, warehouse receipts, air bills, and any other document, which in the regular course of business evidences that the person in possession has title to and is entitled to receive the goods. [UCC 1-201(15)]

A. Two most common documents in the business world are the bill of lading and warehouse receipt.

Definitions:
Bill of Lading: a document evidencing the receipt of goods by a carrier for shipment. [UCC 1-201(6)]

Warehouse Receipt: a receipt issued by a person engaged in the business of storing goods. [UCC 1-201(45)]

Issuer: a person who is a bailee and issues (delivers) the document to the bailor or a third person. [UCC 7-102(1)(g)] Does not apply to unaccepted delivery order.

Delivery Order: an order by the bailor or a third person for the bailee to deliver goods. [UCC 7-102(1)(d)]

Consignor: a person who delivers goods to a carrier named in a bill of lading. [UCC 7-102(1)(c)]

Consignee: a person named in a bill of lading to whom or whose order the goods are to be delivered. [UCC 7-102(1)(b)]

B. Negotiable Document:

1. A document is negotiable if:

   a. by its terms the goods are to be delivered to the bearer or order of the consignee or person to whom delivery is to be made.

Example:
A negotiable bill of lading is referred to as an order bill of lading. A nonnegotiable bill of lading is referred to as a straight bill of lading.

2. it is an international document, and it runs to a named person or assigns. [UCC 7-104(1)]

II. Duty of Care

A. **Carrier** -- has absolute or strict liability with some exceptions.

B. **Warehouse Company** -- has high degree of care (See: Sales Law for Passage of Title and Risk of Loss).

III. Liens

A. Both warehouse company and carrier have a right to place possessory liens on goods for any storage or carrier charges and costs not paid by the bailor.

1. Enforcement is by private or public sale, but such must be commercially reasonable with proper notice. [UCC 7-209, 7-210, 7-307, 7-308]

IV. Forms

A. **Warehouse receipts** - need location of goods, date of issue and number, whether order or bearer, rates, description, any liens, signature of warehouseman, and a statement if warehouseman is owner.

B. **Bill of lading** - must be in writing and adequately describe goods shipped.

1. **Through bill** - more than one carrier. [UCC 7-302]

2. **Destination bill** - one to be issued at destination -- place of delivery. [UCC 7-305]

V. Transfer and Negotiation

A. **A nonnegotiable document** -- goods are transferred by assignment. Use basic assignment law discussed in contracts and negotiable instruments; assignee acquires only title and rights of the transferor-assignor and is subject to all defenses and claims against the assignor. [UCC 7-504]

Example:
Green, by fraud, has purchased from Fraser 1440 cases of Green Valley Peas. Green deposits the cases into lots (144 cases of peas per lot) with the Able Warehouse Company. Able issues to Green ten (10) nonnegotiable warehouse receipts. Green sells one of the warehouse receipts to Beyer. Before Beyer can pick up the lot, Fraser, by court order, has repossessed the cases of peas held by Able. Beyer received a voidable title to the goods through the nonnegotiable warehouse receipt. Thus, Beyer has no title or rights to goods repossessed by Fraser.

B. **A negotiable document** - through due negotiation, the holder can acquire better rights than the transferor-assignor. [UCC 7-501, 7-502]

1. Negotiation depends on whether the document is bearer (delivery only) or whether it is an order document (delivery plus an indorsement).

2. Negotiation becomes duly negotiated to a holder if the holder takes the document in good faith, without notice of defense or claim of a person to the document or goods, for value, and in the ordinary course of business. (Note: except for the latter, same as a holder in due course of a negotiable instrument.)

C. **Duly Negotiable:** A duly negotiated holder acquires title to the goods and a right to have delivery or possession of these goods according to the terms of the document contract.

1. Shelter Principle is applicable (see: Negotiable Instruments). [UCC 7-504(1)] (Even though holder cannot qualify as a holder through due negotiation, the holder can have the rights of a holder through due negotiation if the holder took through a holder with due negotiation.)

2. Indorsers warrant to the holder that the negotiable document is genuine, that the indorser has no knowledge of claims or facts that would impair the goods or documents value, and that the transfer is rightful. [UCC 7-502] There is no guaranty of bailee's performance, however.

VI. Limitation of Rights

A. **Forgery of the document or any indorsement defeats rights of any holder to either the document or the goods**. (Treat like a Real Defense under Negotiable Instruments.)

Example:
Able, via ABC Truck Lines, ships 100 model Z personal computers to Beyer. Able sends a negotiable bill of lading to Beyer. Before the bill of lading reaches Beyer, it is stolen by Theef. Theef forges Beyer's name as an indorsement on the bill of lading and transfers the bill to you. Able, upon learning that Beyer had not yet received the bill of lading, orders ABC to stop delivery. Able can legally do so because the forged indorsement is a real defense to delivery of the goods, and the forged indorsement defeated any rights you had to the goods.

B. **Documents for stolen goods do not pass title**. [UCC 7-503(1)]

C. **Buyers of fungible goods in the ordinary course of business have priority over document holders**. [UCC 7-205]

Secured Transactions

Importance, Application, Terminology, and Security

The creditor in secured transactions wants two things in the event of the debtor's default. First, the creditor wants to be able to satisfy the debt out of specific property the debtor has rights in, and second this creditor, who is now a secured party, wants to have priority rights to that collateral over third parties such as other creditors, trustees in bankruptcy, and purchasers. Note this law only applies to interests in personal property (includes fixtures, accounts, and chattel paper) and not security interests in realty, (real estate mortgages, mechanics' liens etc.), or possessory service liens (artisans' liens etc.), nor judgments and judgment liens. Six basic terms and definitions must be known in order to explain how a security interest is created, and how generally the secured party obtains priority by perfection. You should also be familiar with the definitions of the various types of collateral subject to an Article 9 security interest. Three elements are necessary to create a security interest. Note that although there is usually a security agreement, a security interest can be created by possession, and if there is a security agreement, it needs only to be signed or authenticated by the debtor.

I. Importance and Application

A. Creditor, at time of giving credit, wants **two things to take place** in contemplation that debtor may go into future default.

1. Creditor can resort to specific collateral debtor owns, or has rights in, for satisfaction of the debt, and,
2. in the event of default, to have priority to that collateral:
   - **a.** Creditor satisfies the first contemplation, becoming a secured party, by creation of a security interest in the debtor's collateral.
   - **b.** Secured party usually satisfies the second by a perfection of the security interest.

B. Applies to any **security interest** in **personal property or fixtures by contract** (includes goods, documents, instruments, general intangibles, chattel paper, and accounts), **an agricultural lien, to any sale of accounts, chattel paper, and payment intangibles, to promissory notes, and to commercial consignments of $1,000** or more. [UCC 9-109]

1. Transactions excluded from secured transactions law (other laws apply):
   - **a.** Landlord liens.
   - **b.** Mechanics liens.
   - **c.** Artisan liens.
   - **d.** Assignment of wages.
   - **e.** Tort claims.
   - **f.** Insurance (except proceeds from policies covering covered collateral).
   - **g.** Judgments.
   - **h.** Leases.
   - **i.** Real estate mortgages.

II. Basic Terminology

A. **Definitions** - (Most Important for Creation and Perfection by Filing)

Definitions:
Secured Party: the creditor who has a security interest in the debtor's collateral. Can be a seller, or lender, or a buyer of accounts or chattels. [UCC 9-102(a)(72)]

Debtor: the "person" who owes payment or other performance of the secured obligation. [UCC 9-102(a)(28)]

Security Interest: the interest in the collateral (personal property, fixtures etc.), which secures payment or performance of an obligation. [UCC 1- 201(37)]

Security Agreement: an agreement that creates or provides for a security interest. [UCC 9-102(a)(73)]

Collateral: is the subject of the security interest. [UCC 9-102(a)(12)]

Financing Statement: referred to as a UCC-1 form, is the instrument usually filed to give public notice to third parties of the secured party's security interest. [UCC 9-102(a)(39)]

B.

SUMMARY

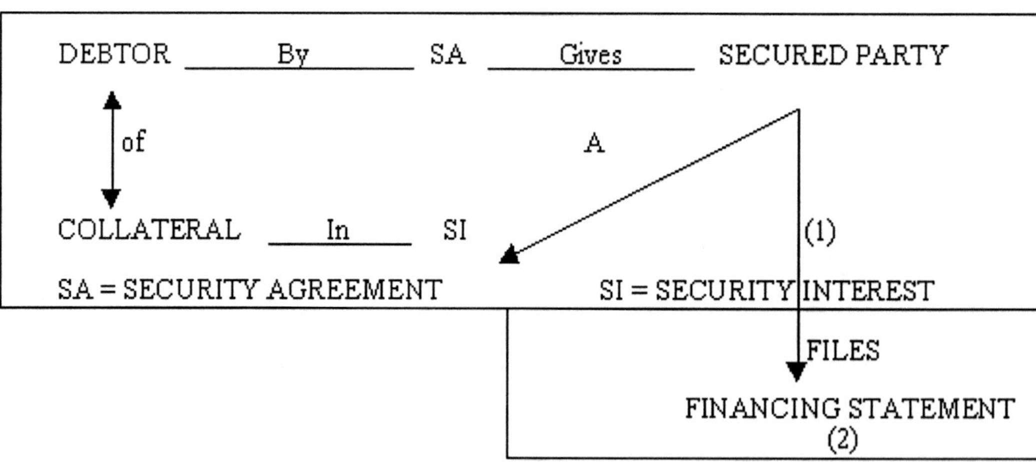

(1) Creates the security interest
(2) Gives notice and priority over other 3rd parties to the debtor's collateral.

C. Collateral Definitions And Classifications:

1. Tangible Goods:

Definitions:
Consumer Goods: used or bought primarily for personal, family, or household purposes. [UCC 9-102(a)(23)]

Equipment: used or bought primarily for use in a business, and not part of inventory or farm products. [UCC 9-102(a)(33)]

Farm Products: such as crops (including aquatic goods) and livestock, or supplies produced in a farming operation such as ginned cotton, milk, eggs, maple syrup etc. [UCC 9-102(a)(34)]

Inventory: held by a person for sale under a contract of service or lease, or raw materials held for production and work in progress. [UCC 9-102(a)(48)]

Fixtures: personal property, which become so attached or so related to realty that an interest in them arises under real estate law. [9-102(a)(41)]

Accessions: personal property that is so attached, installed, or fixed, to other personal property (goods) that it becomes a part of the goods (other personal property) i.e., installing a compact disk-tape recorder radio in an automobile. [UCC 9-102(a)(1)]

2. **Intangibles:**

Definition:
Chattel paper: a writing or writings (records), which evidences both a security interest in goods and/or software used in goods and a monetary obligation to pay - such as a security agreement, or a security agreement and a promissory note.

Instruments: a negotiable instrument (check, note, CD, or draft) or other writing, which evidences a right to the payment of money and is not a security agreement or lease, but a type which can ordinarily be transferred (by endorsement, if necessary) by delivery. [UCC 9-102(a)(47)]

Accounts: any right to receive payment for:

any property (real or personal) sold, leased, licensed, assigned, or otherwise disposed of - includes intellectual licensed property,

services rendered or to be rendered - such as contract rights (e.g., as a right to payment under a construction contract at various stages of construction),

incurring surety obligations,

policies of insurance,

use of a credit card,

winnings of a government sponsored or authorized lottery or other game of chance,

health-care - insurance receivables (defined as an interest or claim under a policy of insurance to payment for health-care goods or services provided). [See 9-102(a)(2), (a)(46)]

Note:
If the record or records consist(s) of information stored in an electronic medium, the collateral is called "electronic chattel paper." If the information is inscribed on a tangible medium, it is called "tangible chattel paper." [9-102(a)(11), (a)(31), (a)(78)]

Deposit accounts: any demand, time savings, passbook, or similar account maintained with a bank. [UCC 9-102(a)(29)]

Agricultural liens: a nonpossessory statutorily lien on a debtor's farm products. [UCC 9-102(a)(5)]

Commercial tort claims: a claim arising out of a tort in which the claimant is an organization, or arose in the course of a claimant's business or profession, and does not include damages for death or personal injury. [UCC 9-102(a)(13)]

General Intangibles: means any personal property other than goods, accounts, chattel paper, deposit accounts, commercial tort claims, investment property, letter of credit-rights, documents, instruments, and money (i.e., oil royalties, copyrights, patents, etc.). [UCC 9-102(a)(42)]

Note:
Misconception: To create a security interest for the secured party, there must be a written security agreement and the agreement must be signed by both the debtor and secured party.
Both are incorrect. A security interest can be created by the secured party taking possession of the collateral under an oral agreement, and if the security agreement is in writing or authenticated, only the debtor's signature is required to create the security interest.

- **a.** Payment intangibles - a general intangible under which the principal debtor's obligation is to pay money (such as a loan without an instrument or chattel paper). [UCC 9-102(a)(61)]
- **b.** Software is a good, if the software is so embedded in a computer that it is considered a part of the computer, but if it is independent from the computer or a good, it is a general intangible. [UCC 9-102(a)(44), (a)(75)]

III. Creation of Security Interest

Note:
Misconception: The debtor must be the "owner" (have title) of the collateral before the secured party can have a security interest in the collateral.
Although the debtor does have title in most cases, it is not a requirement. Thus, a beneficial interest in a trust, where title to the trust property is held by the trustee, may be the subject of a security interest for a loan made to the beneficiary by a creditor (secured party).

A. Security Interest Attachment [UCC 9-203] - Binds Debtor and Secured Party if:

1. Unless the collateral is in the possession of the secured party, there must be a written or authenticated security agreement describing the collateral subject to the security interest signed or authenticated by the debtor. [Authenticated includes any agreement or signature inscribed on a tangible medium or stored in an electronic or other medium which is retrievable - see UCC 9-102(a)(7)(69). The Revised Article 9 also gives examples of what constitutes a sufficient description of the collateral [UCC 9-108(b)] such as "specified listing, category, quantity, UCC defined collateral, etc." and states that supergeneric descriptions, such as "all the debtor's assets," or "all the debtor's personal property," or words of similar import are not a sufficient description. See UCC 9-108(c)]
2. The secured party must give to the debtor something of value (such as a binding commitment to extend credit, or security, or satisfaction of a preexisting debt, or consideration to support a simple contract). [UCC 1-201(44)]
3. The debtor must have "rights" in the collateral.

Perfection

*Perfection is a means to give third parties notice of the secured party's priority security interest. There are three methods of perfection and you should know all three. Note the most common use of a perfection by attachment and **where** (the jurisdiction) to properly perfect a security interest by filing. For tangible collateral, this is now in the jurisdiction where the debtor is **located**. This is very important for the exam.*

Definition:
Perfection: is a means by which a secured party gains priority to a debtor's collateral over other third parties who also claim to have an interest in the same collateral. Types of third parties who may claim a conflicting interest are unsecured creditors, secured parties (unperfected) including lien holders, perfected secured parties, trustees in bankruptcy, and purchasers of the collateral.

I. Methods of Perfection (Three Methods)

A. Attachments - perfection is automatic upon creation of the security interest (no filing or possession required). Applies only in a few situations. Two most important are:

1. A **purchase money security interest** in **consumer goods**. [UCC 9-309(1)]

   a. **Consumer goods** are goods used or bought **primarily** for **personal**, **family**, or **household purposes**. [UCC 9-102(a)(23)]

   b. Purchase money security interest is created when the interest is taken or retained by the seller of the collateral to secure the price, [UCC 9-103(a)(2)]

Example:
Beyer wants to purchase a large screen TV from Sallor TV Inc. for $1,500. Beyer pays $200 down, and signs a security agreement giving Sallor TV a security interest in the set being purchased until the balance of $1,300 is paid. Sallor has a purchase money security interest.

   c. OR, when the interest is taken by a person who advanced or gave value to the debtor to enable the debtor to acquire rights in or the use of the collateral if, in fact, the value is so used. [UCC 9-107(b)]

Example:
Beyer wants to buy a large screen TV from Sallor TV Inc. Beyer goes to West Bank seeking a loan to buy the set. West Bank loans Beyer the money having Beyer sign a security agreement giving West Bank a security interest in the to be purchased TV set. If Beyer does purchase the set, West Bank has a purchase money security interest in the set. Note, if Beyer purchased a large refrigerator-freezer instead of the TV, West Bank would be an unsecured creditor.

2. A **security interest** created by an **assignment** of a **beneficial interest** in a **decedent's estate**. Note: This does not apply to a beneficial interest in a trust - filing is now required. [UCC 9-302(1)(c)]

3. Some **Other Collateral Subject To Automatic Perfection** are:

   a. A sale of payment intangibles.

   b. A sale of promissory notes.

   c. An assignment of health-care-insurance receivables to the health care provider.

   d. Supporting obligations such as letter-of-credit rights, secondary obligations (guarantees, etc.) that support payments on accounts, chattel paper, instruments, general intangibles, etc. [9-308(d), 9-309]

B. **Possession and Control**

1. Generally, Article 9 requires filing for perfection, but it also allows perfection by either possession or another method of perfection. [UCC 9-310, 9-312(a), 9-313] For example, instruments (whether negotiable or nonnegotiable) can be perfected by filing or possession.

2. **Possession** is usually impracticable - however a pledge, pawn of goods, or transfer of instruments or chattel paper are illustrations.

3. **Special Rules**

   a. **Letter of Credit Rights** - Perfection is by control unless it is a supporting obligation. [UCC 9-308(d), 9-312(b)(2)]

   b. **Electronic Chattel Paper** - Perfection is by filing or control unless it is a supporting obligation. [UCC 9-310(a), 9-313(a), 9-314(a)]

   c. **Deposit Accounts** - used as original collateral can be perfected only by control. [UCC 9-312(b)(3)]

   d. **Money** - can only be perfected by possession. [UCC 9-312(b)(3)]

   e. **Investment Property** (such as securities, security accounts, security entitlements, etc.) may be perfected by filing [UCC 9-312(a)] or control. [UCC9-314] For priority purposes, perfection by control prevails over perfection by filing. [UCC 9-328(1)]

C. **Filing --** Either a UCC-1 form or the security agreement.

1. **Filing Location for Perfection** - For all classifications of collateral, except those listed below or where perfection is <u>limited</u> to possession, or control, or specified in a statute, perfection is in the state where the <u>debtor is located</u>. [UCC 9-301]

   a. The **location of the debtor is determined** as follows: [UCC 9-307]

      i. For **individual debtors**, it is his or her principal residence.

      ii. For a **chartered or entity created by a filing,** it is the state of charter or filing. (For example, a Delaware chartered corporation who received a secured loan from a Texas bank, the Texas bank to perfect by filing is in Delaware.)

      iii. For **all other entities**, it is the location of the business or, if more than one, the state where the chief executive office is located.

   b. **Exceptions:**

i. For **fixtures, timber to be cut**, and collateral to be **extracted** (such as oil, coal, gas, minerals) filing is in the jurisdiction where the collateral is located and the filing must include a description of the realty. [UCC 9-301(3)(4), 9-502(b)]

ii. For **possessory** security interests, perfection (and priority) is in the jurisdiction where the collateral is **located**. [UCC 9-301(2)]

iii. For **certificated securities** - perfection is where the security certificate is located, but for uncertificated securities it is the location of the issuer. [UCC 9-305(a)(1)(2)]

II. Temporary Perfection -- [UCC 9-312(e)(f)(g)]

A. Without filing or possession for 20 days from creation of the security interest by authenticated security agreement:

1. Certificated securities, negotiable documents, and instruments if new value is given.

B. If perfected, remains perfected for 20 days without a filing:

1. For goods in possession of a bailee or a negotiable document where the secured party makes available the goods or documents to the debtor for sale, exchange, loading, shipping, etc.

2. For a certificated security or an instrument where the secured party delivers the security certificate or instrument to the debtor for sale, exchange, collection, presentation, etc.

How Good is Perfection?

Perfection gives the secured party, upon the debtor's default, priority over most third parties who also may claim an interest in the debtor's collateral subject to the secured party's security interest. Divide your study into three groups: (a) perfected secured party versus most other creditors and most buyers not in the ordinary course of business; (b) perfected secured party versus buyers (know particularly priority of a buyer in the ordinary course of business); and (c) priority between two perfected secured parties in the same collateral of the debtor. These latter two are very important. Lastly, perfection permits the secured party to have a floating lien by allowing the perfected security interest to float to after-acquired collateral by the debtor, to future advances made by the secured party, to proceeds from the debtor's collateral, to continue a secured party's priority to collateral after a debtor has moved into a new jurisdiction.

I. General Rule

A. A perfected secured party's interest has priority over the following parties: [UCC 9-317, 9-322]

1. Unsecured Creditors.
2. Unperfected Secured Parties.
3. Subsequent Lien Creditors - such as a judgment creditor who acquires a lien by levy of execution on the collateral.
4. Trustees in Bankruptcy - at least to proceeds from sale by trustee.
5. Most Buyers - who purchase not in the ordinary course of business. (Possible exception - a buyer of consumer goods.)

II. Priority of Perfected Secured Parties Over Buyers

A. Buyers in the ordinary course of business - a buyer in the ordinary course of business takes free of a secured party's security interest, even if it is perfected, and buyer knows of the security interest at time of sale. [UCC 9-320(a)]

1. Exception - If buyer knows that seller has no authority to pass title without secured party's consent.

> **Definition:**
> *A buyer in the ordinary course of business*: is a buyer who buys goods from a merchant (a seller who deals in goods of that kind). [UCC 1-201(9)]

ILLUSTRATION

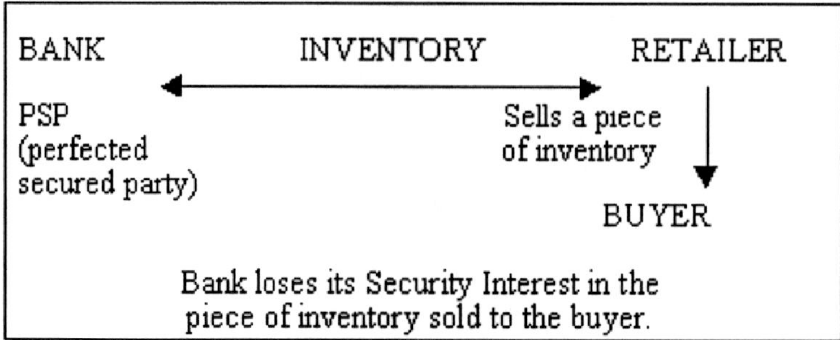

2.

Example:
West Bank has a perfected security interest in a tractor owned by a farmer. After the harvest season, the farmer sells the tractor to a farm implement dealer (one who sells and buys used and new tractors). The farmer goes into default and West Bank claims priority to the tractor purchased by the farm implement dealer. The farm implement dealer claims it is a buyer in the ordinary course of business because it buys and sells used tractors. Here, West Bank has priority because the farm implement dealer is not a buyer in the ordinary course of business. The reason is the farmer (the seller) does not regularly sell tractors, thus, does not deal in goods of that kind.

B. **Buyer not in the ordinary course of business of consumer goods** (the secured party must be perfected by attachment) - a buyer not in the ordinary course of business of consumer goods will prevail over a previously perfected secured party by attachment, if the buyer can prove the following: [UCC 9-320(b)(e)]

1. Buyer must give value to the seller-debtor.
2. Buyer must not know of secured party's security interest.
3. Buyer must buy for personal use (as consumer goods).
4. Buyer must buy before the secured party perfects by filing.
    a. If buyer cannot prove all four, the perfected secured party has priority.

Example:
Beyer purchases a large screen TV for personal use from Ralph's TV store. Beyer cannot pay the full purchase price and, upon making a downpayment, signs a security agreement giving Ralph a security interest in the set purchased. Ralph has a perfected purchase money security interest without a filing (perfection by attachment). Later, while still making payments to Ralph, Beyer sells the set to her next-door-neighbor Sally Hawks. Hawks is a buyer not in the ordinary course of business. Due to some financial reverses, Beyer goes into default to Ralph's TV. If Hawks did not know of Ralph's security interest at the time of sale, and Hawks purchased the TV as a consumer good (for her personal, family, or household use), Ralph cannot repossess the set from Hawks. Had Ralph's TV perfected its security interest (also) by filing before the sale to Hawks, Ralph's TV can repossess the TV from Hawks to satisfy the balance of Beyer's debt.

C. **Buyers of Chattel Paper** - A buyer of chattel paper (such as security agreements held by a retailer) from a debtor-retailer will prevail in priority over a previously perfected secured party (even if perfection is by filing) providing the buyer:

1. gave the debtor new value (not as security for a preexisting debt for example), and,
2. took possession in the ordinary course of the buyer's business (such as an investment or the buyer is in the business of selling and buying chattel paper), and,
3. took without actual knowledge of the secured party's security interest (there is no indication on the chattel paper of an assignment of the secured party's security interest). [UCC 9-330]

D. **Buyers of Negotiable Instruments or Documents or Securities** - Buyers who are holders in due course of instruments, holders to whom a negotiable document has been duly negotiated, or bona fide purchasers of securities have priority over a previously perfected security interest. [UCC 9-330(d), 331(a)]

E. **Buyers of Farm Products** - Buyers of farm products in the ordinary course of business take free of a secured party's perfected security interest under the Food Security Act (not the UCC) unless one of the following events take place:

   1. The buyer has received notice from the secured party of the security interest within one year before the purchase.

   2. The buyer fails to register with the secretary of state's office before the purchase and the secured party has centrally perfected his or her security interest.

   3. The state has an approved (Dept. of Agriculture) EFS (effective financing statement) plan by which the secured party files an EFS form in addition to a UCC filing.

III. Priority Between Two Perfected Security Interests In the Same Collateral

A. **General Rule** - Priority between two perfected secured parties in the same debtor's collateral, including agricultural liens unless a state statute states otherwise, is first in time of perfection is first in priority right. [UCC 9-322(a)(1)]

B. **Exceptions:**

   1. **Livestock** - Generally, a perfected purchase money security interest in livestock (as farm products) has priority over a conflicting security interest in the same livestock providing two events take place before the debtor takes possession of the livestock:

      a. The purchase money security interest perfects, and,

      b. the purchase money security interest secured party sends and the conflicting security interest party receives authenticated notice of the purchase money secured party's security interest. [UCC 9-324(d)]

   2. **Inventory** - A **purchase money security interest** in a debtor's **inventory** will have priority over a previously perfected nonpurchase money security interest providing these two events take place before the debtor takes possession of the collateral.

      a. The purchase money security interest secured party perfects, **and**

      b. the purchase money security interest secured party sends, and the nonpurchase money security interest receives, written notice of the purchase money security interest. [UCC 9-324(b)]

Example:
Ralph's TV Inc. has a cash flow problem and on May 1 secures a loan from West Bank putting up all of Ralph's present inventory and any inventory thereafter acquired. This is a nonpurchase money security interest and West Bank properly perfects its security interest by a filing that same date. On August 1, Ralph learns that it can purchase directly from one of its suppliers, Inter TV, 100 TV sets. Ralph cannot pay cash but does pay 20% of the purchase price down, and signs a security agreement giving Inter TV a security interest in the 100 TV sets Ralph is purchasing. Delivery of the 100 TV sets is to be on or before September 1. Inter TV has a purchase money security interest. On August 2, Inter TV perfects its security interest by a proper filing, and on August 20 sends West Bank a FAX, which is received, notifying West Bank of Inter TV's security interest. If Ralph goes into default to both West Bank and Inter TV, Inter TV would have priority over West Bank's after-acquired collateral interest in the 100 sets purchased by Ralph because Inter TV has a purchase money security interest properly perfected, and West Bank was sent and it received written notice of Inter TV's security interest prior to Ralph's possession of the 100 TV sets.

3. **Collateral Other Than Livestock or Inventory** - For any other types of collateral, a purchase money security interest will have priority over a previously perfected nonpurchase money security interest providing the purchase money security interest secured party perfects before or within twenty (20) days after debtor takes possession of the collateral. No notice is required. [UCC 9-324(a)]

Example:
Cross, a manufacturer, has a cash flow problem and on May 1 secures a loan from West Bank putting up all of its equipment presently owned and equipment it thereafter acquires as collateral. West Bank properly perfects its nonpurchase money security interest that same date. On July 1, Cross purchases a new piece of equipment from Equip Inc. Cross cannot pay cash, but does pay 20% of the purchase price down, and signs a security agreement giving Equip Inc. a purchase money security interest in the new piece of equipment to be delivered on August 1. If Equip Inc. perfects its security interest by the August 1 delivery, or within twenty (20) days thereafter, Cross takes possession (assuming Cross is in default) would have priority over West Bank's prior perfected security interest.

4. **Software** - applies **only** to a **purchase-money security** in **software** if **used in goods subject to a purchase-money security interest**. **Priority** is **determined the same as if the goods are inventory** (if the goods are inventory), or if **not** as if the **goods are other than inventory**. UCC 9-103(c), 9-324(f)]

IV. Perfection and the Floating Lien

A. Floating Lien Concept - The floating lien concept allows the (perfected) secured party to have a security interest in collateral not in existence at time of its creation, apply to payments made on sale or destruction or exchange of the collateral, to apply to future advances of funds, to comingled goods, and even continues when collateral is moved into a different jurisdiction. In short, a perfected secured party could have a single security interest in raw materials to be used in the manufacture of goods, and this interest would continue during the manufacturing process to the finished goods, continue during shipment to another state jurisdiction, and to the proceeds from the sale or exchange of these goods.

B. Floating Lien Types:

1. **After-acquired collateral clauses** [UCC 9-204] - A security agreement can provide for not only a security interest in the present collateral of the debtor, but it can also be applied to any collateral the debtor acquires in the future. (This includes consumer goods when given as additional collateral if debtor acquires rights in them within ten (10) days after the secured party gives value.)

Example:
West Bank has a perfected security interest in the present and after-acquired inventory of a retailer. The retailer purchases for cash some new inventory. West Bank's prior perfection also applies to the new inventory just purchased.

2. **Future Advances** [UCC 9-204] - A perfected security interest in collateral of the debtor can also be applied to future loans made by the perfected secured party using the same collateral as security without a new perfection for the new loans.

Example:
On May 1, West Bank has a perfected security interest (for a loan of $200,000) in $1,000,000 worth of the debtor's collateral. The security agreement includes a future advance clause, which allows for the debtor to borrow up to $400,000 using the same million dollars of collateral. On August 1, the debtor borrows $100,000 from East Bank giving East Bank a security interest in the same collateral (East Bank is treating its loan like a second mortgage). On September 1, the debtor, through the future advance clause, borrows another $200,000 from West Bank. West Bank does not perfect this loan. On October 1, the collateral has rapidly depreciated in value to $400,000 and the debtor goes into default on all three loans. In this case, because of the future advance clause, West Bank is entitled to the full $400,000 even though its last loan was subsequent to East Bank's $100,000 loan.

3. **Proceeds** [UCC 9-315] - not only does a security interest continue in collateral even after sale or exchange, but it also applies to any proceeds (usually payments) payable to the debtor from the sale or destruction (assume insurance policy with debtor as beneficiary) of the collateral. If perfection by filing includes proceeds, perfection also gives the secured party priority to proceeds. If proceeds are not perfected by filing, priority only extends for twenty-one (21) days after the debtors receipt unless the secured party perfects the proceeds by filing within the twenty-one (21) day period.

Example:
West Bank has a filed perfected security interest in all of Ralph's TV present inventory, any after-acquired inventory, and the proceeds from any of these TVs. Able purchases a TV from Ralph signing a security agreement in which she is to make monthly payments. Ralph goes into default to West Bank. Although West Bank cannot repossess the TV sold to Able (Able is a buyer in the ordinary course of business), West Bank is entitled to the monthly payments by Able as proceeds.

4. **Commingled Goods** [UCC 9-336] - If two perfected secured parties have security interests in two different or separate collaterals (piles of raw materials for example), they do not lose their individual perfected interests if the debtor mixes the two piles of raw materials into making a finished product whereby the raw materials have lost their identity. Both secured parties have equal priority but rank according to the cost ratio each raw material contributed to the making of the finished product.
5. **Debtor Moved To A New Jurisdiction** [UCC 9-316] - If collateral is perfected in one jurisdiction (for example, in State A) and the debtor moves into another jurisdiction (State B), the perfected secured party (State A) has priority over a subsequent perfected secured party in the new jurisdiction (State B) for a period of four (4) months (or for the period of time remaining under the original perfection - whichever is earlier) from the date the debtor changes his/her location into the new jurisdiction (State B). Where there is a transfer of the collateral to another debtor who then becomes the debtor and is located in another jurisdiction, the priority period is one year [9-316(a)(3)]. If the perfected secured party in the original jurisdiction perfects in the new jurisdiction within the four months period, its priority continues until the perfection expires.

Example:
West Bank has a perfected security interest in Wisconsin on Able's equipment. (Able is a sole proprietorship located in Wisconsin.) Able has built a new plant in Illinois and on May 1, without West's consent, transfers some of the Wisconsin plant equipment to the Illinois plant and installs the equipment with some newly purchased equipment there. On June 1, Able gets a loan from East Bank in Illinois putting up all the Illinois plant equipment as collateral. Before making the loan, East Bank had checked for prior filings on the equipment in Illinois. If Able goes into default to both West Bank and East Bank on August 1, West Bank has priority over East Bank as to the equipment moved to Illinois because West Bank's perfection in Wisconsin still has priority over the equipment transferred to the Illinois plant until September 1.

Perfection by Filing and Secured Party and Debtor Rights

It is necessary to know the requirements for a perfected filing, such as names and addresses required of both debtor and secured party, and a description of the collateral. You should also know when the filing is actually perfected, for how long the filed perfection is good, and the time period only when perfection can be continued. In addition, secured parties can release, assign, and amend a filed perfection, plus they can file for information on filed interests on a prospective debtor before extending credit. If the secured party is in possession of the collateral, the secured party has the same duties as a bailee of goods, such as the requirement to exercise reasonable care for preserving the value of the collateral. Debtors have the right to have a confirmation or accounting request of the amount of indebtedness and collateral still subject to the security interest, plus debtors are entitled to either the filing of a termination statement or the secured party furnishing one upon the debtor's payment of the balance of the debt. This is important for the exam.

I. Perfection by Filing Laws

A. Filing Requirements: [UCC 9-502]

Note:
Debtor's signature is not required and a uniform national form is provided in UCC 9-521. In addition, addresses of the debtor and secured party should be stated or the filing officer will reject the filing. [UCC 9-516b(4)(5), 9-520(a)]

1. Must state names of both the debtor [for registered organizations, estates, and trusts, the sufficiency of the debtor's name must meet certain criteria-UCC 9-503(a)] and secured party.
2. Must contain a description of the collateral subject to the security interest. (For land related security interests, a legal description of the land is required and notice that the security interest is filed in real property records.) The description can be a supergeneric description such as "all assets" or "all personal property." [UCC 9-504]

B. Time of Perfection:

1. A **financing statement** can be filed before a security agreement is made or a security interest attaches, but debtor authorization is required. [UCC 9-502(d), 9-509] Authentication of a security agreement constitutes the debtor's authorization for the filing of a financing statement. [UCC 9-509(b)]
2. A **security interest** is perfected upon communication (allows electronic filings, if so authorized) of a financing statement (or security agreement) and tender of the filing fee to the filing officer **- OR -** acceptance of the financing statement by the filing officer. [UCC 9-516(a)]
   a. A filing is effective even if filing officer refuses it unless, generally, [UCC 9-516(d)]:
      i. the proper filing fee is not tendered,
      ii. the name of the debtor is not provided (which would prevent indexing),
      iii. the record filing is communicated in an unauthorized (as set by the filing offices) medium,
      iv. where required, there is not a sufficient description of the realty. [UCC 9-516(b)]

b. Generally, a person (such as the debtor) can file a correction statement if it is believed that the original financing statement is inaccurate or wrongfully filed, but this does not affect the effectiveness of the initial financing statement. [UCC 9-518]

3. A **filed financing statement** is effective for five (5) years from date of filing, and can be extended for another five (5) years if a continuation statement is filed (only) during the six-month period prior to the expiration of the five year period. [UCC 9-515]

Note:
For public-finance transactions or manufactured home transactions, the effective period is thirty (30) years. [9-515(b)]

Example:
The five-year period for a perfected (by filing) security interest will expire on December 1. If the secured party wants to extend its perfection for another five years, the secured party must file a continuation statement at anytime from June 1 to December 1 (the six months period before the expiration). Should the secured party file the continuation before the six months window, the continuation would not be effective and its perfection would expire on December 1.

C. **Rights of Secured Parties:**

1. **Release** -- a secured party can release all (used as a termination statement) or part of any collateral described in the filing thereby terminating its security interest in that collateral. Record of the release is by filing a uniform amendment form. [UCC 9-512, 9-521(b)]

2. **Assignment** -- a secured party can assign all or any part of the security interest to a third party assignee, and the assignee can become the secured party of record if the assignment is filed by use of a uniform amendment form. [UCC 9-514, 9-521(a)]

3. **Amendment** -- if debtor and secured party so agree, the filing can be amended (such as, by adding new collateral if authorized by the debtor) by filing a uniform amendment form, which indicates by file number the initial financing statement. [UCC 9-512(a)] The amendment does not extend the time period of perfection, but, if the amendment adds collateral, the perfection date (for priority purposes) for the new collateral only begins at date of the filing of the amendment. [UCC 9-512(b)(c)]

4. **Information Request** -- any person, such as a prospective creditor, can request of the filing officer "information" on previously filed security interests of a specific debtor. For a fee, a certificate or copies of previous filings are furnished. [UCC 9-523(c), 9-525(d)]

II. Secured Party and Debtor

A. **Secured party in possession of collateral** (either for perfection or after debtor's default): [UCC 9-207]

1. Must use reasonable care in the keeping and preserving of the value of the collateral, and the debtor must reimburse the secured party for all reasonable costs in the keeping of the collateral.

2. Cannot use the collateral except as agreed, or to preserve its value.

Example:
The secured party who repossessed a horse, upon debtor's default, could ride the horse to exercise it to preserve the health of the horse, but could not use the horse to plow up land owned by the secured party.

3. Entitled to any increase in value of the collateral (except cash).

Example:
Secured party has possession of ten cows. Two of the cows give birth to calves. The calves can also be held by the secured party as security for the debt.

4. **Must keep the collateral identifiable** (not mix with other person's collateral) unless the collateral is fungible (like wheat to be stored in a grain elevator).

Note:
that **additional duties** are imposed when the secured party has control over deposit accounts, electronic chattel paper, investment property, and letters-of-credit rights if the debt has been paid and the secured party is not committed to make advances. These duties must be performed within ten (10) days of receipt by the secured party of an authenticated demand by the debtor. Failure of the secured party will result in the same remedies as failure to provide a termination statement discussed below. [UCC 9-208, 9-625(b)(e)]

B. **Confirmation Request of Debtor** - the debtor has a right, in a record authenticated by the debtor, to indicate what the debtor believes the unpaid debt amount to be and/or a listing of the collateral subject to the security interest for secured party's approval or correction. [UCC 9-210]

1. **Time Frame for Complying:** Upon receipt, the secured party must comply with the request by authenticating and sending to the debtor an accounting within fourteen (14) days after receipt, or the secured party will be liable for any loss suffered by the debtor plus $500. [UCC 9-210, 9-625(f)]

2. **No Charge:** The debtor is entitled to one request without charge every six months. For any additional requests, the secured party is entitled to a statutory fee up to $25. [UCC 9-210]

C. **Termination** - upon payment (with no commitment to make an advance) by the debtor, if perfection is by filing, the debtor is entitled to have a termination statement filed, which shows to the public an ending of the filed perfected security interest. [UCC 9-513]

1. If the collateral is **consumer goods**, the secured party (not the debtor) must file the termination statement (or a release) within one month of the final payment or within twenty (20) days of receipt of debtor's authenticated demand - whichever is earlier.

2. If the collateral is **other than consumer goods**, the secured party, (only) upon an authenticated demand by the debtor, must send to the debtor a termination statement or file within twenty (20) days. There is no requirement that the secured party file.

3. **Failure** of the secured party to comply with the filing or sending of the termination statement as requested allows the debtor to recover $500, and for any loss suffered. [UCC 9-625(e)(4), (f)]

Debtor's Default

Upon debtor's default, the secured party has certain rights, including obtaining peaceful possession of the debtor's collateral. Once the secured party has possession, under certain circumstances, the secured party can keep the collateral in full satisfaction of the debt, or the secured party can sell the collateral. Know the requirements for keeping the collateral and what is required upon selling it. You should also know how the proceeds of the sale are to be distributed.

I. **General Rule --** Upon debtor's default, the secured party can proceed under the Uniform Commercial Code, or can proceed with any existing judicial remedy (for example, reduce debt to judgment and levy on the debtor's non-exempt property -- property other than the collateral, or garnish etc.) [UCC 9-601].

II. **Uniform Commercial Code**

A. **Duty to Assemble** - if the security agreement so provides, the secured party can require the debtor to assemble the collateral upon debtor's default and place the collateral at a location reasonably convenient to both parties. [UCC 9-609(c)]

B. **Render Collateral Unusable** - upon default, the secured party can, without removal of the collateral, render the collateral unusable (not damage) to the debtor. [UCC 9-609(a)] (Some states prohibit this.)

Example:
A lumber saw mill owner is in default and the secured party has a security interest in the huge machine that saws timber into lumber. The secured party could, under this law, remove the saw blades from the huge machine rendering the machine unusable.

C. **Peaceful Possession** - the self-help remedy. Upon debtor's default, the secured party is entitled to take peaceful possession of the collateral without the use of judicial process. [UCC 9-609(b)]

1. The UCC does not define peaceful possession. General rule is if secured party can take possession without committing any of the acts listed below the collateral has been taken peacefully:

a. trespass onto realty,

b. assault and/or battery, or

c. breaking and entering.

D. **Judicial Process** - if the collateral cannot be taken peacefully or secured party does not wish to try, the secured party can secure possession through a judicial petition and hearing. [UCC 9-609(b)(1), (c)]

E. **Disposal of Possessed Collateral**

1. **Keep Collateral** - in full or partial satisfaction of the debt (always with debtor's consent). [UCC 9-620(a)(1), (c)]

a. **Must Sell When:** Cannot keep, but must sell if the collateral is consumer goods and 60% or more of the debt or price has been paid. [UCC 9-620(e)]

b. In all other situations the secured party can keep collateral if:

i. Secured party sends notice to the debtor and junior security interests, who gave notice of their claim or have filed a statutory security interest. [UCC 9-620(a), 9-621] **and**

ii. the secured party has not received notification or objection from any of the above parties within 20 days after notice was sent.

c. Time Requirement for Sale: If objection is received or secured must sell, the secured party must dispose of the collateral within ninety (90) days after taking possession or the secured party can be held liable for tort of conversion, or, if the collateral is consumer goods, for any loss and an amount not less than the credit service charge plus 10% of the principal amount of the debt, or the time price differential plus 10% of the cash price. [UCC 9-620(f), 9-625(c))]

2. Sell Collateral - secured party can always sell. [UCC 9-610(a)]

a. Reasonable Manner: The UCC only requires that sale, lease, or license be conducted in a commercially reasonable manner. [UCC 9-602(7), 9-603, 9-610(a)] This generally means:

i. sale can be public or private.

ii. secured party must give debtor notice of time and place of disposition, and, except for consumer goods junior lien holders who have given notice of their claims (notice is not required if collateral is perishable, rapidly declining in value, or to be sold on a recognized market), to junior lien holders of record 10 days before notification date (contents of notification are stated-UCC 9-613 for commercial transactions and UCC 9-614 for consumer transactions).

iii. disposition must be at a reasonable time and place.

iv. secured party can disclaim disposal warranties.

v. secured party can "buy" if a public sale, goods are sold on a recognized market or one where there are widely distributed price quotations. [UCC 9-610, 9-611]

b. Distribution of Proceeds:

i. Expenses incurred by secured party in repossession, keeping, and resale.

ii. Balance of debt owed to the secured party.

iii. Junior lien holders who have made written demands.

iv. Debtor (unless the collateral is accounts or chattel paper, then to secured party unless provided for to the contrary to the debtor in the security agreement.) [UCC 9-608(a), 9-615(a)]

c. If the secured party receives noncash proceeds from the disposition, the secured party is required to make a value determination and apply this value in a reasonable commercially manner. [UCC 9-608(a)(3), 9-615(c)] The amount received from a disposition does not in and of itself give grounds that the sale was not conducted in a reasonable manner, however, the price may suggest the need for judicial scrutiny. [UCC 9-627(a), but see Official Comments 10 to UCC 9-610 and Comment 6 to UCC 9-615]

d. Deficiency of Sale Funds: Unless the collateral is accounts, chattel paper, payment intangibles, or promissory notes, if the proceeds are insufficient to cover the expenses and balance of the debt, the secured party is entitled to a deficiency judgment, which enables the secured party to get a writ to levy on other property (nonexempt) of the debtor. If the collateral is accounts, chattel paper, payment intangibles, or promissory notes the secured party is only entitled to a deficiency judgment, if it is so provided for in the security agreement. [UCC 9-615(d)(e)]

e. Failure of the secured party to conduct the disposition in a reasonable manner or give proper notice, the deficiency of the debtor is reduced to the extent such failure affected the price received at the disposition. [UCC 9-627(a)(3)]

f. **Redemption** - If the secured party is not allowed to keep the collateral in possession in full satisfaction of the debt, until there is a sale the debtor or any other secured party has a right of redemption and by doing so can regain possession of the collateral. [UCC 9-623]

g. **Waiver** - only after default, the debtor can waive the compulsory requirement of the secured party to dispose, and the debtor's right of redemption. [UCC 9-624]

III. **The Soldiers and Sailors Civil Relief Act (1940) --** Prohibits a secured party (whose security interest has been previously created) from repossession if the debtor (in default) has, after the security interest was created, enlisted or is called into active duty in the military. This does not apply if the debtor is in the active military service at the time the security interest is created. This prohibition from repossession extends the entire period the debtor is in active service and can extend up to six months thereafter.

Note:
Misconception: Upon a debtor's default, only the secured party with priority has rights to the debtor's collateral. This is incorrect because junior lien holders who have given the secured party written notice of their claims are entitled to notice (except for consumer goods) if the secured party wants to keep the collateral in full satisfaction of the debt and can object forcing a sale. If there is a sale the secured party must turn over to them any proceeds remaining after the expenses of default and balance of debt owed the secured party are satisfied.

Real Property, Including Insurance

Real Property Interests

To develop a clear understanding of real and personal property, the following terms should be fully comprehended. Real property acquisition law is somewhat parallel to that of personal property such as by inheritance, sale, and gift; but adverse possession law, although in reality rare, has appeared in past exams. Interest in and ownership of real property is an area that has extensive coverage and you should first divide your study into two broad groups: freehold estates and nonfreehold estates, divided into possessory and nonpossessory interests.

I. Property Overview

Definition:
Property: Consists of a bundle of rights. These rights extend from rights of ownership, rights of possession, and rights of use to rights in the financing of the property.

A. Property is either:

Definitions:
Real Property: Consists of land, building, plants, trees, and fixtures thereon.

Personal Property: Property that can or is intended to be moved or transferred by men or women, or can move under its own power.

Tangible: Has a physical substance in and of itself, such as a car, or a cow.

Intangible: Represents rights, such as a stock certificate or a patent.

Example:
A live cow is personal property because it can move under its own power. A dead cow is personal property because it is intended to be moved by men or women. A stock certificate is personal property because it can be transferred by either a man or woman.

1. **Fixtures**
   - **a.** All fixtures are initially personal property. Trade fixtures, such as store coolers or glass display cases, remain personal property.
   - **b.** Once attached to the realty, it becomes a part of the realty and a fixture if:
     - **i.** The person who attached intends the property to be a fixture. Intent is frequently based on whether removal would cause substantial damage to the realty; and/or
     - **ii.** The property is so attached to the realty that its adaptation becomes a permanent part of the realty itself.

Note:
Misconception: Statues and fountains placed in your yard are personal property because they can be removed without substantial damage to the realty. This is in error, because the statues and fountains are intended to be a part of the yard (land) and are an adaptation as a permanent part of the land.

Example:
1. A two ton statue placed on land - the person intends it to be a part of the land and its placement is an adaptation as a permanent part of the land.

2. A mobile home with the axles and tires removed sitting on top of a cement foundation.

3. A built-in to the wall refrigerator - cannot be removed without substantial damage to the wall, plus adaptation to become a part of the realty.

II. Real Property Acquisition

A. General - same as an acquisition of personal property in the following:

1. **Gift**.
2. **Will or Inheritance**.
3. **Sale - Contract:**
    a. Contract must generally be in writing with a legal description of the land, the parties identified, price stated, and signed. Broker (real estate agent) contract must also be in writing and signed.
        i. Broker's listing of the property is usually open (available to any agent to "sell" the property) or exclusive (only the broker can "sell" the property).
    b. Most contracts require buyer to pay an amount upon the signing of the contract called earnest money. Upon default of buyer, this money is usually treated as liquidated damages.
    c. Seller agrees in the contract to give the buyer a marketable title. This is a title which does not contain serious defects.
    d. The seller agrees to furnish the buyer either an abstract (a history of the title of the property) or title insurance, a policy which insures the good title and will compensate the buyer for any loss due to title defects.
    e. Modern law gives the buyer an implied warranty of habitability, which requires the seller to disclose to the buyer material property defects.
    f. All monies paid by buyer are usually placed in an escrow account held by a third party as escrow agent, such as a title company.
    g. Contracts are assignable unless expressly prohibited in the contract.
    h. Closing is the final settlement of the contract (payment by buyer and passage of title by the seller).
4. **Adverse Possession** - the obtaining of title without a contract or deed through continuous hostile possession contrary to the true owner rights.
    a. For title to pass, the possession must be:
        i. **actual and open** (must not be secretive or hidden) and possessor must "live" on the premises.

ii. **continuous** for the required statutory period (ten to twenty years).

iii. **exclusive and hostile** - adverse to all, including the owner, and not be on the property with the owner's permission.

Example:
Green operates a 360-acre farm. Green fences in the boundaries of the farm and, by mistake, fences in a strip of land owned by his neighbor. For twenty-five years Green has plowed and grown crops on the land and paid taxes on the land, including this strip. Green has in the past removed hunters and others from his land, including those found on the strip. Green's neighbor is now selling the land and a survey discovers Green's error. The neighbor wants the land back, which he/she claims is included in the deed. In this situation, Green gets to keep the land because of his adverse possession (his ownership was actual, open, continuous, and it was exclusive and hostile for the twenty-five year period).

III. Interests in, and Ownership of, Real Property

A. Freehold Estates: Possessory Interests

1. **Fee Simple Estate:** Person has complete ownership for an unlimited duration to do with the property as he or she legally chooses.

2. **Fee Simple Defeasible Estate:** An estate in which ownership is automatically terminated upon the happening of a particular event, and the property reverts back to the grantor or a third party.

Example:
Green conveys the property to Smith, subject to the condition that should ever alcoholic beverages be sold on the property, the property would revert back to Green.

3. **Life Estate:** Title is held by the grantor or a third party but subject to a holder of a life estate to the possession, use, and ordinary profit (not to waste estate assets) derived from the property for the duration of the life tenant's life or the life of another party. Absolute title passes to the third party or grantor upon the life tenant's death.

   a. Life estate interests are taxable as a gift or inheritance and can be mortgaged. Life estates can be created by law, such as dower or courtesy rights (upon a husband or wife's death).

   b. Life tenant is required to maintain the property and pay the real estate taxes.

Example:
Smith owns a large lake house. Smith conveys the lake house to his two children, but reserves to his elderly mother a life estate in the lake house. Title passes to his two children, but Smith's mother has the right to the exclusive possession and use during her lifetime. If, instead of a lake house, it is an apartment building, Smith's mother could take possession and use of an apartment and could collect rent on the occupancy of the other apartments. She could not, however, demolish the building (waste the property) without the children's consent.

B. Nonfreehold Estates: Possessory Interests

1. **Leasehold Estates - Four types:**

    a. **Tenancy For Years:** a lease for a specified duration (can even be one day or a month). Lease automatically terminates at end of the period and no notice to the tenant is required.

    b. **Tenancy From Period to Period:** a lease which is automatically renewed for the same fixed period until the lease is terminated. Usually, the period is the same as the rent period; for example, a month-to-month tenancy begins with a one month lease with the rent paid for the month, and then the lease continues until terminated on a month-to-month basis. To terminate, tenant or landlord must receive written notice of termination, usually prior to payment of the last month's rent; for example, on a month-to-month tenancy with rent payment due on the first of each month, the tenant or landlord, to terminate the lease on January 31, would have to give written notice sometime prior to the January 1 (at least a month's notice) rent payment.

    c. **Tenancy at Will:** a tenancy that simply continues with permission of the landlord. Until treated as a periodic tenancy, a tenancy at will can be terminated by either party without notice.

Example:
Smith has a one-year lease (tenancy for years), which expires on May 31, when Smith is supposed to move into his/her newly-built home. Because of weather, Smith's home is not yet finished, but expected to be completed in ten days. Because Green does not as yet have a tenant to replace Smith, Green tells Smith to continue to occupy the premises. This is a tenancy at will.

    d. **Tenancy at Sufferance:** a tenancy without consent of the landlord. Since the tenant is technically a trespasser, the landlord can terminate the tenancy by eviction by the landlord. (In some states, landlord can remove tenant and place possessions of tenant "on the curb" after serving of the eviction notice.)

Example:
A tenant under a tenancy for years refuses to leave after the lease's termination despite the landlord's request. This is a tenancy at sufferance.

2. **Types of Nonpossessory Interests**

   a. **Easements** - the right of a person to make limited use of another's realty, usually without taking anything from it, or possession of it. Types of easements are:

      i. **Appurtenant** - one created specially for use in connection with an adjacent piece of realty; for example, Able and Smith own adjoining tracts of land, and Able grants Smith the right to cross A's land to reach a county road.

      ii. **In Gross** - one created specifically for use in connection with a single tract of land; for example, Able gives the Inca Power Company an easement to run power lines on towers across his/her property.

      iii. **Profit** - an easement for a party to go upon another's realty and take part of the land or product of the land; for example, Able contracts with Gravel Inc. to come upon his property and remove 500 tons of sand and gravel.

      iv. **Grant** - conveyance by contract or deed.

      v. **Implication** - created when parties demonstrate, by circumstances which indicate implied consent, that an intent to create an easement exists; for example, Able and Smith have been neighbors for years. Smith always drives his tractor across Able's pasture to reach a field Smith owns without any objection from Able.

      vi. **Necessity** - created by law to allow a party access to a use of another piece of property or part of the realty; for example, if you lease the third floor of an office building you have automatically an easement to use the stairs or elevator to reach the third floor. The same is true if you bought a land-locked piece of realty and the only way to reach a highway is to cross another's realty.

   b. **License** - a revocable right to come upon another's land, usually to enjoy it or perform a function; for example, an electric meter reader has a license to come upon your property to read the meter, or you, as a ticket holder to a sporting event, have a license to enter upon the realty to watch the event.

   c. **Mortgage** - a nonpossessory security right, which upon default of the **mortgagor** (debtor realty owner) allows the **mortgagee** (creditor holding the mortgage) to foreclose (sell or take title) on the property.

      i. A **mortgage** is a security interest in realty the landowner voluntarily grants to a lender to secure payment of a debt. If the mortgage is given to purchase the realty, it is called a purchase money mortgage and this "lien" is usually given priority over other liens and claims.

      ii. Mortgages must be in writing to be enforceable, signed by the mortgagor, containing a legal description of the property, delivered to the mortgagee.

      iii. Mortgages are recorded (like deeds) to give purchasers and others notice of the mortgagee's lien, and that they take the property subject to the mortgagee's interest.

      iv. **Mortgage Theories:**

         1. **Title theory** - mortgagee takes title.

         2. **Lien theory** - mortgagor has title.

         3. **Deed of Trust** theory - title held by a third party such as an abstract company.

v. The latter two are the most common and treated very similarly upon mortgagor's default.

vi. **Mortgagor Rights:**

1. to possess realty and have reasonable use.
2. to lease or sell the realty, unless prohibited by mortgage, without mortgagee's consent.
3. to right of redemption upon default before foreclosure sale.

vii. **Mortgagee Rights:**

1. to freely assign mortgage.
2. to collect mortgage payments.
3. to foreclose upon default; most common foreclosures are by judicial sale or by a power pursuant to the mortgage.

viii. **Sale to a Buyer:**

1. **Subject to the mortgage** - title to the realty passes to the buyer with the buyer making payments to the mortgagor. The mortgagee still has a lien on the realty, and can hold the mortgagor liable on the mortgage note (unless released by mortgagee) if there is a default, but the mortgagee cannot hold the buyer personally liable.
2. **Assumption of mortgage** - the buyer takes title and makes mortgage payments to the mortgagee. The mortgagee still has a lien on the realty, can hold the mortgagor liable on the mortgage note (unless released by mortgagee), and upon default as a creditor beneficiary can hold the buyer personally liable.

ix. **Mortgage Termination:**

1. Performance - mortgagor making final payment.
2. Merger - mortgagee takes title to the realty.
3. Tender - mortgagor's full tender and mortgagee's refusal.

d. **Liens on Realty**

i. **Mechanics or Materialman's Lien -** a nonpossessory filed lien to secure payment for work performed or materials added to the realty not paid for. Lien holder can foreclose on realty same as mortgagee.

ii. **Judgment Lien -** a party in a law suit who receives a judgment may place a lien upon the debtor's real property (unless the property is an exempt homestead) by filing a copy of the judgment with a proper county official.

C. **Future Interests** - (not covered in depth on CPA exam) a future interest is a nonpossessory interest where the right to possession and use is postponed to a possible future time. Two basic types are:

1. **Reversion Interest -** owner of a fee simple interest transfers an interest which, when terminated, reverts back to the owner. For example, Green conveys a fee simple defeasible title to Smith whereby, should Smith ever divorce Green's daughter, title would revert back to Green.
2. **Remainder Interest -** owner of a fee simple transfers a lesser estate, such as a life estate, to his son with title to his grandchildren. The grandchildren have a remainder interest, with full title passing upon the expiration of the life estate interest.

Concurrent Ownership and Deeds

Concurrent ownership questions are frequently asked. Knowledge of the differences between a tenancy in common and joint tenancy with right of survivorship is essential. There are five types of deeds. The more important ones are the warranty deed and quit claim deed. The recording of a deed or mortgage is by a filing. Thus, it is a public notice of a claim to the realty and it is a superior claim to subsequent third party claims. Although really not that important, past exams required you to know the three types of recording statutes.

I. Types and Transfer

Definition:
Tenancy in Common: two or more persons own jointly undivided shares in the property. Can transfer interest without consent to a third party who is now the tenant in common.

Example:
Mary and Jim are close friends and buy a 10-acre tract of land to be held by both as tenants in common. Mary and Jim each own a half interest in the 10 acres.

Definitions:
Joint Tenancy with Right of Survivorship: Upon death, the interest goes to the surviving member. It goes to the heir, if it is a tenancy in common.

Tenancy by the Entirety: A joint tenancy with right of survivorship between a husband and wife. Transfer of an interest can be made only with the consent of the other joint tenant(s), and the recipient then becomes a tenant in common.

Community Property: Two or more persons own jointly undivided interests in the property, but upon death of a co-owner the property goes to the surviving joint owner (not the heirs of the deceased owner).

Example:
Mary and Jim own a 5-acre tract of land as joint tenants with right of survivorship. If Jim dies, Jim's interest passes to Mary, and she becomes the sole owner of the land.

II. Creation and Termination

A. Joint Tenancy

1. To create:

a. One generally must designate the joint tenancy specifically with a "right of survivorship" or the joint tenancy will be treated as a tenancy in common.

b. Joint interests must unite together, i.e., title, interest, and possession, at same time.

c. One cannot have a joint tenancy with right of survivorship with a corporation because of corporation's perpetual existence.

2. **To terminate:** A joint tenancy can be terminated before death by a sale or gift. The recipient then becomes an owner as a tenant in common.

B. Tenancy-By-The-Entirety

1. Simply, a joint tenancy with right of survivorship between a husband and wife.
2. Generally, a joint tenant in a tenancy by the entirety cannot transfer his or her interest without the consent of the other spouse.
3. Divorce terminates.

C. Community Property

1. Only a limited number of states have community property law.
2. Most property acquired (except gift or inheritance) by a spouse during marriage is jointly owned (each a half interest).

III. Deeds – Titles - Types:

Definitions:
Warranty Deed: gives buyer the greatest number of warranties and covenants. A deed must name the grantor and grantee, signed by the grantor, with a legal description of the realty, and delivered to the grantee.

Covenant of Seisin: grantor (person transferring title) warrants he or she has good title and authority to convey to the grantee (person receiving title).

Covenant Against Encumbrances: grantor warrants there are no outstanding liens or other encumbrances except those so stated or are in a public record.

Covenant of Quiet Enjoyment: grantor warrants that the grantee's possession will not be distributed by eviction, or a person with a lien or superior title.

Special Warranty Deed: grantor warrants only that the grantor has not previously done anything to lessen the value of realty, such as mortgage the property.

Quitclaim Deed: grantor does not make any warranties, but conveys to the grantee any interest the grantor may have in the realty.

Example:
Smith wants to build an attached garage onto his/her home. To do so, and meet building code setbacks of property from a property line, Smith wants to buy one foot of her neighbor's property without an expensive survey. The neighbor will sell the one foot strip of land, but will only give Smith a quitclaim deed. This means that the neighbor doesn't warrant that she has title to the land or any interest thereon, but if she does own or have an interest, she is releasing it to Smith.

Definitions:
Grant Deed: (sometimes referred to as a bargain and sale deed) - treated like a quitclaim deed but, by statute, grant deeds usually carry an implied warranty that the grantor owns the property transferred and grantor has not previously encumbered it or conveyed it to a third party.

Sheriff's Deed: a deed of title given a buyer at a sheriff's sale to pay off a judgment, tax lien etc. Does not warrant anything, but extinguishes all owners' rights except the statutory right of redemption (which period begins with the giving of the deed).

IV. Recording is the act of filing a mortgage or deed. -- It gives notice of a superior claim to third parties.

- **A.** If recorded by the grantee, a subsequent buyer of the realty takes title subject to the grantee's superior ownership.
- **B.** If not recorded by the grantee, a subsequent bona fide purchaser (BFP) from the grantor has superior title over the grantee.

Example:
Green sells his/her house for $200,000 to Smith, giving Smith a warranty deed. Smith does not record the deed. Later, Green fraudulently sells the same house to Jones for $180,000. Unless Jones knew of the previous sale to Smith, Jones takes superior title over Smith, being a bona fide purchaser for value. Note, Jones, or an abstract company, could check the records to see who has title to the house, but the search would only show Green as the owner. Jones should immediately record the deed to avoid a similar problem.

- **C. Types of Recording Statutes.**
    1. **A notice statute** - regardless of who files first, a BFP takes superior title, unless the purchaser had notice of previous transfer.
    2. **A race statute** - regardless of knowledge, the first to file is first in superior title.
    3. **A race-notice (notice-race) statute** - a BFP has superior title only if the subsequent purchaser files first and does not know of previous conveyance.

Landlord-Tenant, Assignment and Subleasing

This is a fairly extensive area of law. 1. First, be sure you know what is required to create a leasehold and what is covered in leases. 2. Second, and most important, you should be well aware of the rights and duties of both the tenant and the landlord. Pay particular attention to the implied warranty of habitability of the premises, who has the duties to maintain or repair the premises and the rights of a tenant if the landlord has such a duty and fails to do so, a landlord's rights for a tenant's nonpayment of rent and a landlord's right of entry onto the leased premises, and who is responsible for injuries to third parties who come upon the premises. The difference between an assignment and sublease and corresponding rights of the parties is important. Most leases do not permit either without consent of the landlord.

I. **Relationship** -- is created by an owner's transfer of temporary possession without title to another, usually in return for payment of rent.

> **Definitions:**
> *Lease*: The agreement for transfer.
>
> *Lessor*: The landlord, owner of the property.
>
> *Lessee*: The person (tenant) taking possession of the property.

II. **Creation**

A. Created by contract or agreement. Remember, a tenancy by sufferance is illegal.

B. Most states require leases of more than one year to be in writing. Leases for a lesser period can be made orally.

C. Lease agreements cannot violate environment or discrimination laws.

D. The lease must at least:

1. indicate an intent to create a landlord-tenant relationship,
2. identify the parties,
3. identify the premises.

> **Note:**
> **Misconception**: Because a lease of realty is an interest in real estate, all leases must be in writing under the Statute of Frauds to be enforceable. This is incorrect, because all states permit leases of less than one year in duration to be made orally.

E. Leases often provide additionally for:

1. **Covenants** -- various promises of the parties, such as duties of repair, duty of tenant to pay rent by certain dates, duty of maintenance, duty to not interfere with tenants possession and use, etc.
2. **Conditions** -- events where the consequences provide for termination of the lease and relief of the other party from performing obligations, such as excessive noise, failure to provide heat, etc.

III. **Rights and Duties**

A. Landlord has a duty to transfer, and tenant has a right to retain possession of the property.

1. **English Rule**: Must give tenant actual possession.
2. **American Rule**: Must give tenant the legal right to possess.

Example:
A tenant's lease has terminated, but the tenant remains on the property and refuses to leave. The new tenant cannot take possession. Under the English Rule, the landlord is in breach of the duty to transfer. Under the American Rule the landlord is not in breach.

B. Tenant has a right to have quiet possession, enjoyment, and use of the premises.

1. Duty can be breached by the landlord, by someone acting under landlord's authority, or by someone with a superior title, but generally not by other third parties.
2. Landlord's interference is a breach of the covenant of quiet enjoyment and treated as an eviction. Evictions are:
    a. **Intentional**: Landlord changes locks, padlocks the premises, or otherwise prevents tenant from entering the premises.
    b. **Constructive**: Allowing conditions which make it impossible for the tenant to occupy the premises, such as failure to provide heat in the winter.
    c. **Retaliatory**: A wrongful eviction by the landlord, such as terminating the lease because of the tenant's report to city officials of the unhealthful conditions of the premises.

C. Tenant has right to have the property fit for use, such as human occupancy.

1. Most states give tenants an **implied warranty of habitability** of the premises.

Example:
A tenant who unknowingly leased a house infested with rats, or with a roof which severely leaked during any rain storm, could bring an action against the landlord for breach of the implied warrant of habitability.

D. Tenant has a duty to only make legal use of the premises, and to use the premises consistent with the basic purpose for which the premises were leased. Alterations by tenant consistent with use is permitted, as long as such does not diminish value of the realty.

Example:
A tenant who leases a single family home cannot convert the house into a fast-food restaurant without the landlord's consent.

E. Tenant has a duty not to remove, damage, or alter the premises (such as adding on a room), or waste the realty without the landlord's consent.

Example:
A tenant could not remove walls within a house, but does have a right to paint the existing walls.

F. Landlord has a duty to maintain the premises, but tenant has a duty to make ordinary repairs and emergency repairs to prevent substantial damage (such as replacing a broken water pipe, with reimbursement by the landlord).

   1. **At common law**, landlord has no duty to repair or maintain premises. Tenant took premises "as is." Today, building codes, express lease covenants, the implied warranty of habitability, common areas of office and apartment buildings laws, etc., place a duty on the landlord to maintain the premises in a livable and useful condition.

   2. For failure of landlord to maintain premises, tenant may:

      a. **Withhold rent**: Statutorily called a rent-strike.

      b. **Repair and Deduct**: Statutes permit tenant to repair if landlord has a duty to do so, and then deduct costs of repair from rent.

      c. **Sue for Damage**: Recover damages suffered from the lack of repair.

      d. **Terminate the lease**: Treat as a constructive eviction.

G. Tenant is liable for any negligent or intentional damage to the realty.

   1. A tenant who has altered the premises, either in accordance with his or her use, or with permission of the landlord, may want to remove these alterations, such as built-in cabinets at the end of tenancy. General rules are:

      a. if a residential tenancy, the items cannot be removed at the end of the tenancy.

      b. if a commercial tenancy, the items are known as trade fixtures (personal property) and can be removed.

H. Landlord, in absence of lease contract, has a duty to pay real estate taxes.

I. Tenant has duty to pay rent (and, if provided by agreement, a security deposit).

   1. Failure of tenant to pay rent allows the landlord to:

      a. Make a **late payment charge**.

      b. Exercise a possible **landlord's lien** (lien on tenant's property on the premises).

      c. **Sue for past-due** rent.

      d. **Recover possession by:**

         i. Eviction Proceedings.

         ii. Unlawful Detainer (summary eviction).

         iii. Right of Entry (peaceful possession).

J. Landlord has right of entry, usually limited to:

   1. **Collection of rent**.

   2. **Making required repairs**.

3. **Inspect premises** -- only if provided in lease, or probable cause of violation of lease, law, etc.

4. **Upon eviction**.

5. **Show premises** at end of lease to a new prospective tenant, unless prohibited.

K. Injuries

1. **Landlords** are liable for injuries incurred on any realty the landlord controls (such as hallways or stairway in an apartment building) due to structural damage of the realty or failure to make necessary repairs.

2. **Tenants** are liable for injuries to guests and to those that are incurred on the property the tenant controls.

IV. Assignment

Definition:
Assignment: the tenant's transfer of the balance of his or her entire interest in the leased premises to a third person.

A. Unless prohibited by the lease contract, leases can be assigned without the consent of the landlord. Most leases prohibit assignment without landlord's consent.

B. Assignee assumes all lease duties and rights of the assignor original tenant.

C. Assignee becomes primarily liable to pay rent, but assignor is secondarily liable, unless released by the landlord.

V. Sublease

Definition:
Sublease : a tenant's partial transfer of tenant's interest in the leased property.

A. Unless prohibited by the lease contract, a tenant can sublease to a third party without the landlord's consent.

B. **Important**: A lease provision prohibiting assignment does not prohibit subleasing, and vice versa.

C. Difference from assignment: sublessor is still primarily liable for the rent and obligations and sublessee is only liable to the sublessor for the rent.

Example:
Smith is a student at State University. Smith has a four-year contract lease with landlord Green. If, after two years, Smith drops out of State University, unless prohibited by the lease, Smith can assign the remaining two years of the lease to Jones. If Smith decides not to attend summer school, unless prohibited by the lease, Smith can sublet the apartment to Jones for the three summer month period. In the assignment, Jones becomes primarily liable under the lease and Smith is liable only for any breach or default by Jones. In the sublease, Smith remains primarily liable, and Jones simply makes rental payments to Smith.

Termination and Sale of Realty

A list of methods of termination are given in the text. You should be aware of these as well as events or actions which do not terminate the lease.

I. Methods of Termination

A. **Automatically** - at end of term lease (specified period) without notice to the landlord.

Example:
Smith has a one-year lease ending on December 31. This lease automatically terminates at midnight on December 31.

B. **Notice** - Periodic tenancies and Tenancies at Will (which become periodic tenancies) are terminated only by proper written notice given the other party.

Example:
Smith has a month-to-month tenancy with rent payable on or before the first of each month. If Smith wants to terminate his/her lease on May 31, he/she would be required to give the landlord written notice of termination on or before May 1.

C. **Merger** - whereby the tenant purchases the realty.

D. **Abandonment** - tenant moves off the realty without intent to return.

E. **Destruction of the Realty** - automatically terminates the lease unless provisions in the lease require landlord to rebuild.

F. **Eviction** - unless wrongful, an eviction, actual or constructive, terminates the lease.

G. **Death of Tenant** - only applies if there is a periodic tenancy or tenancy at will.

II. In absence of agreement, leases are not terminated due to:

A. **Assignment** by either landlord or tenant.

B. **Sublease** by the tenant.

C. **Death** of landlord.

D. **Sale** by landlord. Thus, a buyer generally takes possession subject to the lease.

Insurance and Limitation of the CPA Exam

A general knowledge of contract law governing insurance contracts is essential. Pay attention to the fact that the application is an offer, that in life insurance it becomes a part of the insurance contract, and how acceptance takes place. Provisions, rights and duties is the second most important part of the law in this area. Be sure to know the difference between a hostile and a friendly fire, law on insurable interest, the fact that most fire insurance policies cannot be assigned, and, most importantly, the formula and law on coinsurance clauses and the proportionate liability on multiple insurance pro rata clauses. The latter two are frequent questions.

I. Governed by general contract law and a state's statutes and regulations.

A. Application is an offer for fire and property insurance. The application can be made orally or in writing by prospective insured. If in writing, the application is usually attached to and made a part of the policy (for life insurance, it is always made in writing and, by attachment, made a part of the contract). If false statements have been made in the application, the insurer can usually either void the policy, modify it, or limit the recovery under the policy.

B. Acceptance by the insurer can come in various ways.

1. For Fire and Property:
   - **a.** Orally or in writing, even before delivery of the policy.
   - **b.** Insurance is effective upon acceptance of the insurer.
2. By a binder (common in life insurance) which temporarily binds the parties subject to issuance of a policy.
3. By delivery of the policy to the insured or his or her broker.
4. At a time the parties agree the policy is effective.

> **Note:**
> In life insurance, coverage is not effective until a premium is paid.

> **Note:**
> **Important**: For **fire and property** insurance the insurable interest must be present at time of loss.

C. The Statute of Frauds does not apply unless contract (policy) coverage of insurance is for more than one year. State laws, however, may require either the contract and/or policy be in writing.

D. Legal Capacity. Both parties must have legal capacity to enter into a contract, and the subject matter insured must be legal and in existence.

II. Fire Insurance

A. Only covers "**hostile fires**" (fires that occur outside of places where fires usually burn) and not "friendly fires" (smoke damage due to a fire in a fireplace).

B. Only persons with an **insurable interest** (a substantial relationship between the risk and insured to protect the insured from suffering a financial or economic loss) can recover under the policy.

C. Generally, all owners, lien holders, and any party which has an interest in the property (such as a tenant) are eligible to have insurable interests (to the extent of their interest) in the property.

> **Note:**
> **Misconception**: If a seller of a home has a one-year fire insurance policy on the home, and sells the house (with title) to the buyer with six months insurance coverage still remaining on the house, the seller is entitled to recover under the policy for the total loss of the house in the buyer's possession three months after the sale.
> No, seller cannot recover under the policy even though the policy contract period has not ended. The reason is that at the time of loss the seller no longer had an insurable interest in the house.

III. Dual Party Insurable Interest -- In the following situations, both parties have an insurance interest:

A. Bailor and Bailee.

B. Mortgagor and Mortgagee.

Note:
For **life insurance**, the insurable interest must be present at the time of contract formation and, for example, can consist of persons with a close family relationship to the insured. Thus, children can take out a life policy on their mother or father's life, wife on her husband's life, etc. The relationship can also be a business one. Thus, a partnership could take out a life policy on each partner.

C. Landlord and Tenant.

D. Seller and Buyer under a contract to sell.

Example:
Green owns a house and leases the house to Smith. Both have separate fire insurance policies in existence when, due to lightning, a fire completely destroys the house. Both Green and Smith have insurable interests in the house at the time of loss (Green as owner and Smith as tenant), and both can recover under their respective policies.

IV. Proof of Loss -- Insured must report loss to insurer within a stated or reasonable period of time from date of loss. The notice requirement is usually a condition subsequent to insurer's liability to pay.

V. Assignment

A. Policy is usually not assignable by insured without the insurer's consent because:

1. Assignment is prohibited by express terms in the fire insurance contract, and/or
2. Courts treat a fire policy as a personal contract, and/or
3. Assignment could increase risks of insurer.

B. Proceeds for loss, however, are fully assignable.

VI. Subrogation -- Once an insurer pays for the loss, the insurer is subrogated (has the rights of the insured) to any cause of action the insured has against a third party who caused the loss.

Example:
Smith is the sole owner of his home and has a standard fire policy with ABC. Through no fault of Smith, an arsonist burns down Smith's house. ABC is required to pay Smith for the loss under the policy. Upon payment, ABC is subrogated to any rights Smith has against the arsonist (here, the filing of a tort action and recovery for loss against the arsonist).

VII. Coinsurance Clauses -- This is a provision to encourage owners to insure property as close to full market value as possible.

A. Typically, a coinsurance clause provides that if the owner insures up to a specified percent -- **usually 80 percent** of fair market value -- the owner can recover for any loss up to the face amount of the policy.

B. If the owner insures for less than the fixed percentage (80 percent), the owner is responsible for a proportionate share of the loss. **This does not apply if there is a total loss**.

Formula:

Actual Loss x Amount of Insurance / Coinsurance % x FMV* = Amount paid to insured

* FMV = Fair Market Value of Property at Time of Loss

Example:

Facts: Insured has $40,000 policy

Loss is $30,000

FMV is $100,000

$30,000 x $40,000 / $80,000 (80% of $100,000) = $15,000 paid to insured

VIII. Multiple Insurance Pro Rata Clauses -- An insured with multiple insurance policies covering the same risk, and the coverage of these exceed the loss, can collect from each insurer only that proportionate share of each insurer's liability to the total coverage.

Example:

Facts: Loss is $50,000

Insurance Coverage

A Insurance Company ..... $ 60,000 = 60%

B Insurance Company ..... $ 40,000 = 40%

Total = $100,000

A Insurance Company ..... $ 30,000

B Insurance Company ..... $ 20,000

IX. Representations and Warranties

A. Representations are statements made, which induce the parties to enter into a contract for insurance.

B. Warranties are statements, which become part of the insurance contract and are conditions precedent to the insurer's liability.

Note:
Important: Breach of a material warranty statement, which increases insurer's risk, excuses insurer from liability. Thus, many state statutes and/or insurance policies provide that all statements made are warranties.

X. Occupancy Clause for Fire and Homeowner's Policies -- For recovery, an owner usually must occupy the premises at the time of loss. If premises become unoccupied or vacant for a period of time without insurer's consent, coverage is suspended.

XI. Limitation of CPA Examination -- Past exams have limited questions to about eight areas, but the three most important are what constitutes an insurable interest and when, the laws on coinsurance, and multiple insurance pro rata clauses. You will note that definitions are standard for all types of insurance, although when you review the classifications of fire insurance (types) and property insurance, it is important by definition to distinguish between the different types. Most important for you to know are the various types of fire policies (blanket, floater, open, specific and valued) and their differences, particularly between a valued and open policy.

A. The eight areas include the following:

1. Fire and Property (Liability) Insurance -- not life insurance.
2. Formation of Insurance Contract.
3. *Insurable Interest.
4. Warranties and Representations.
5. Assignment.
6. Subrogation.
7. *Coinsurance.
8. *Multiple Insurance Pro Rata Clauses.

B. Definitions

Definitions:
Insurance: A means of shifting and compensating for risk of loss.

Insured: The party who is to be protected by insurance (compensated for loss).

Insurer: The party, who for a premium, contracts to undertake certain risks of loss of the insured.

Beneficiary: The party to be compensated for an insured loss.

Policy: The written insurance contract.

Premium: Consideration paid by the insured to the insurer for the insurance coverage.

C. Fire and Property Insurance

1. **Fire Insurance Policies**

Types of Policy	Coverage
Blanket	Covers a class of property with a maximum overall liability rather than specific property, because the property is expected to shift or vary in nature. A policy covering the inventory of a business is an example.
Floater	Usually supplements a specific policy. It is intended to cover property that may change in either location or quantity. To illustrate, if the painting mentioned under "specific policy" were to be exhibited during the year at numerous locations throughout the state, a floater policy would be desirable.
Open	A policy in which the value of the property insured is not agreed upon. The policy usually provides for a maximum liability of the insurer, but payment for loss is restricted to the fair market value of the property at the time of loss or to the insurer's limit, whichever is less.
Specific	Covers a specific item of property at a specific location with insurer's maximum liability for each item. An example is a particular painting located in a residence, or a piece of machinery located in a factory or business.
Valued	A policy in which, by agreement, a specific value is placed on the subject to be insured to cover the eventuality of its total loss. Value is inclusive and amount paid.

2. **Types of Property Insurance:**
    a. **Homeowners:** Protects homeowners against some or all of the risks of loss to their residences and the residences' contents, and against liability related to such property.
    b. **Marine:** Covers movable property (ships, freight, or cargo) against certain perils or navigation risks during a specific voyage or time period.
    c. **Automobile:** May cover damage to automobiles resulting from specific hazards or occurrences (such as fire, vandalism, theft, or collision); normally, provides protection against liability for personal injuries and property damage resulting from the operation of the vehicle.
    d. **Renters:** Covers renter's personal property located on the premises against loss due to fire, theft, etc.
    e. **Mortgage:** Covers a mortgage loan; the insurer pays the balance of the mortgage to the creditor upon the death or disability of the debtor.
    f. **Casualty:** Protects against losses that may be incurred by the insured as a result of being held liable for personal injuries or property damage sustained by others.

Federal Taxation

Introduction

Introduction to Tax Review

This introduction describes the AICPA contents for the tax portion of the Uniform CPA exam and the organization of these review materials. In addition, this introduction describes some strategic considerations in preparing for the tax portion of the exam and provides some suggestions for taking the exam.

I. **Federal Taxation Content --** The AICPA provides a brief listing of the subject areas that are considered for inclusion in the tax portion of the Uniform CPA exam. This roster somewhat reduces the amount of material that needs to be reviewed for the exam. For example, the AICPA does not include international or state taxes in the listing of subject areas.

A. **AICPA Outline --** The AICPA provides an outline of the tax contents (and their approximate weights) for the REG portion of the exam.

1. **Federal tax procedures and accounting issues (8% - 12%)**
    a. Federal tax procedures
    b. Accounting periods
    c. Accounting methods including cash, accrual, percentage of completion, completed contract, and installment sales
    d. Inventory methods, including uniform capitalization rules
2. **Federal taxation of property transaction (8% - 12%)**
    a. Types of assets
    b. Basis of assets
    c. Depreciation and amortization
    d. Taxable and nontaxable sales and exchanges
    e. Income, deductions, capital gains and losses, including sales and exchanges of business property and depreciation recapture
3. **Federal taxation - individuals (12% - 18%)**
    a. Gross income - inclusions and exclusions
    b. Reporting of items from pass-though entities, including passive activity losses
    c. Adjustments and deductions to arrive at taxable income
    d. Filing status and exemptions
    e. Tax computations, credits, and penalties
    f. Alternative minimum tax
    g. Retirement plans
    h. Estate and gift taxation, including transfers subject to the gift tax, annual exclusions, and items includible and deductible from gross estate

4. **Federal taxation - entities (22% - 28%)**
    a. Similarities and distinctions in tax reporting among such entities as sole proprietorships, general and limited partnerships, Subchapter S corporations, Subchapter C corporations, limited liability companies, and limited liability partnerships.
    b. Subchapter C corporations
        i. Determination of taxable income and loss, and reconciliation of book income to taxable income
        ii. Tax computations, credits, and penalties, including alternative minimum tax
        iii. Net operating losses
        iv. Consolidated returns
        v. Entity/owner transactions, including contributions and distributions
    c. Subchapter S corporations
        i. Eligibility and election
        ii. Determination of ordinary income, separately stated items, and reconciliation of book income to taxable income
        iii. Basis of shareholder's interest
        iv. Entity/owner transactions, including contributions and liquidating and nonliquidating distributions
        v. Built-in gains tax
        vi. Partnerships
            1. Determination of ordinary income, separately stated items, and reconciliation of book income to taxable income
            2. Basis of partner's interest and basis of assets contributed to the partnership
            3. Partnership and partner elections
            4. Partner dealing with own partnership
            5. Treatment of partnership liabilities
            6. Distribution of partnership assets
            7. Ownership changes and liquidation and termination of partnership
        vii. Trusts
            1. Types of trusts
            2. Income and deductions
            3. Determination of beneficiary's share of taxable income
    d. **Ethics and responsibilities in tax practice (2% - 5%)**

II. **Course Structure --** To facilitate preparation for the exam, the review materials are divided into the following sections and lessons:

Introduction		
	1	Introduction to Tax Review
Property Transactions		
	2	Classification of Assets
	3	Nonrecognition Transactions
Income		
	4	Income - Basic Principles
	5	Nonrecognition - Double Tax
	6	Nonrecognition - Subsidies
Deductions		
	7	Individual Deductions - For AGI
	8	Itemized Deductions
	9	Business Deductions
	10	Limitations on Business Deductions
Individual Income Taxation		
	11	Personal and Dependency Exemptions
	12	Filing Status
	13	Additional Taxes
Other Income Tax Issues		
	14	Personal and Business Tax Credits
	15	Taxpayer Responsibilities
Taxation of Corporations		
	16	Formation of a Corporation
	17	Corporate Income Computation
	18	Corporate Alternative Minimum Tax
	19	Penalty Taxes - Corporations
	20	Distributions from a Corporation
	21	Corporate Redemptions and Liquidations
	22	Taxation of Related Corporations
	23	Corporate Reorganizations

Taxation of S Corporations		
	24	S Corporations - Introduction
	25	S Corporation - Income and Basis
Taxation of Partnerships		
	26	Partnerships - Introduction
	27	Formation of a Partnership
	28	Taxation of Partners
	29	Partnership Sales and Liquidations
Estate and Gift Taxation		
	30	Introduction to Transfer Taxes
	31	Federal Gift Tax
	32	Federal Estate Tax
Fiduciaries		
	33	Income Taxation of Fiduciaries

III. Exam Preparation -- The AICPA provides a brief outline of the skills candidates should possess for the exam.

A. AICPA Indicated Tasks: The AICPA indicates that candidates will be asked to perform the following tasks:

1. Analyze information and identify data relevant for tax purposes
2. Identify issues, elections, and alternative tax treatments
3. Research issues and alternative tax treatments
4. Formulate conclusions

B. AICPA Recommended Publications: The AICPA recommends that candidates study the following publications:

1. Internal Revenue Code and Income Tax Regulations
2. Internal Revenue Service Circular 230
3. AICPA Statements on Standards for Tax Services
4. U.S. Master Tax Guide
5. Current federal income tax textbooks

Note:
I am certain that a thorough examination of the Internal Revenue Code and Regulations will prepare a candidate for the exam. Unfortunately, most of us have other things to do over the next 20 years. The AICPA suggestions are not, however, completely without insight. The recommendation to review Circular 230 and the statements of responsibility in tax practice indicate that the AICPA is serious about familiarity with professional responsibilities in tax practice.

C. Advice for preparation

1. Use review materials strategically.

a. Use review material to organize preparation for thorough coverage.

b. The review materials can be used to briefly review familiar topics (refresh the memory) or focus on new material.

c. Detailed preparation is facilitated by combining review materials with materials from tax courses, such as tax textbooks. Example: If a candidate has no exposure to estate and gift taxation, then the review materials would be greatly enhanced by also reviewing an estate and gift textbook.

d. Use review materials to facilitate preparation by studying the brief explanations and clarifying examples.

e. Use review problems and questions as a mechanism for calibrating study efforts.

f. Watch the multi-media portions of the review course, then read all text materials, and finally complete all problems.

2. **Keep the ultimate objective in mind** (to pass the exam), and study topics strategically.

   a. An old adage is that any score over 75 was wasted effort. Coordinate preparation for the entire exam.

   b. Tax topics constitute only 60% of the REG portion of the exam. Integrate the study of taxation with an overall strategy on the REG. This strategy minimizes the risk that a poor score on one topic will cause a failure on this portion of the exam.

Example:
A risky strategy is to ignore a topic because of a relatively strong understanding of topics in the same part of the exam. This strategy is risky because the topical coverage is approximate and it may be difficult to score high enough in one topic to offset a poor score in another topic.

   c. The initial time invested in understanding new topics may have a higher payoff than additional time invested in perfecting comprehension in other topics.

Example:
If individual taxation is relatively clear, but corporate taxation is confusing, a good strategy would be to concentrate on corporate topics. A relatively superficial understanding of corporate topics could result in immediate gains because some of the questions on corporate topics are likely to be relatively easy.

D. Preparation for Tax Questions

1. No essay questions will be given on the tax portion of the exam.

   a. Tax questions are objective and will likely have unambiguous answers. Hence, the questions will probably avoid uncertain interpretations of the law

Example:
The determination of whether an activity qualifies as "hobby" is quite uncertain because this determination is based on numerous factors. Hence, objective questions are unlikely to ask about the determination of hobby status.

b. "Nit picking" questions are likely because details are unambiguous.

Example:
While the determination of hobby status is uncertain, the hobby loss presumption is unambiguous. A profit in three of five consecutive years results in the presumption that an activity is not a hobby. Hence, a question is more likely to be asked about this detail rather than the more ambiguous determination of hobby status.

c. Integrated problems are unlikely because there are too many interactions in even simple tax problems.

Example:
A miscalculation in determining adjusted gross income (AGI) could undermine other calculations based upon AGI. Hence, the "integrated" problems on the tax portion often consist of a series of independent questions.

2. **How much detail should be studied?** There are over 2,000 pages in the Internal Revenue Code, so it is difficult to say. A few suggestions follow:

   a. The scope of the exam is limited to the law in effect as of six months before the beginning of the testing period in which you take the exam. More recent changes should be ignored.

   b. Besides changes in the law, the tax code is replete with transition rules (temporary rules existing until a change in the law becomes permanent). Questions about temporary changes are unlikely, but questions about phase-in rules are possible.

      - Note that in recent years many new tax provisions have been passed that are intended to be in effect for only one or two years. This is particularly true for many provisions in 2009 and 2010 which have been legislated to stimulate the economy. I have included only the changes that I believe are the most important of this nature. However, note that the likelihood that these provisions will be tested is not as high as for other material due to their temporary status.

c. A focus on specific numbers is also unlikely because there are too many specific numbers in the law and many are indexed to change each year. Any figure that is indexed to inflation does not have to be memorized. I have included these figures in the materials so you will be aware of them, but generally include a date after the number to indicate the year for that particular number (e.g., exemption amount is $3,650 (2009)).

Example:
The limit on the election to expense will change each year for the next several years. Past exam questions (disclosed) have asked about this limit, and this indicates that, despite the changes in the law, the limit may be important on future exams.

d. The review materials are limited to the topics most likely to be addressed given past exams (at least those that are public), public notices by the AICPA, and the author's experience in testing tax topics.

IV. Test Taking Tips

A. Often, even an expert cannot eliminate all alternatives on a tax question (remember there are 2,000 pages to the code). Hence, educated guesses are a critical part of an exam strategy. An "educated" guess is made by eliminating all incorrect alternatives and then using general concepts (or principles) to select between the remaining alternatives.

Example:
A question several years ago asked if a taxpayer is entitled to deduct jury pay that the taxpayer had to give to his employer because the employer paid the employee during the time the employee spent on a jury. There is an obscure provision that covers this situation, but who would have studied it (given its obscurity)? An "educated" guess would be a deduction "for" adjusted gross income because the employee must include the jury pay in income, but should not be taxed on it because he was forced to remit it to his employer. An itemized deduction would have not been fair because the limits placed on these deductions might have caused the employee to be taxed on the jury pay.

B. Should you anticipate specific topics (e.g., new provisions)? With the exception of a few disclosed questions, the exams have been closed since 1996. The questions on disclosed exams indicate that exams do not stress new provisions, perhaps because of the ambiguity involved with the application of new law.

C. The AICPA examines the validity of proposed questions by including "trial" questions on the exam. These questions are not scored, but they are interspersed with actual test questions. Hence, an inability to answer some tax questions should not be cause for concern -- these questions could be trial questions.

D. Advice for exam performance

1. Stay cool and don't be hasty.
2. Budget your time.
3. Eliminate alternatives.
4. Use your common sense.
5. Think positively and be confident.

Property Transactions

Classification of Assets

Assets can be classified into one of three mutually exclusive categories: ordinary assets, capital assets, and Section 1231 assets.

I. *Only a "sale or exchange" of a "capital" asset is eligible for capital gains netting.*

Definitions:
A sale or exchange: is any disposition except a casualty, theft, or other involuntary conversion, such as a condemnation. The lapse, cancellation, or expiration of valuable rights to personalty and realty (options) is considered a sale or exchange.

Capital assets: do not include inventory, accounts receivable, depreciable assets in trade, realty in trade, creative works (in the hands of the creator), or certain miscellaneous assets (such as government publications or obligations). Note that through 2010, self-created musical works are treated as capital assets even though these are creative works.

Note:
Misconception: Only losses of sales from investment and business assets are deductible. Hence, while personal assets are capital assets, losses of these assets are not deductible.

A. Short Cut -- Investment assets and personal use assets are capital assets. Common investment assets include stocks, bonds, and real estate.

II. *Each capital gain and loss is classified according to whether the asset is long-term or short-term.*

A. Long-term assets are those held over one year.

B. Definition -- The holding period begins and ends on the date title passes. For stock sales, the holding period ends with the execution date.

C. Holding periods "tack" for transactions in which an asset takes a substituted basis.

Example:
TP's pickup was destroyed in a storm and he replaced it with a similar pickup. If TP elected to defer the gain as an involuntary conversion, then the holding period of the old pickup will tack onto the holding period for the new pickup.

D. There are automatic holding periods for "nonbusiness" bad debts (short-term) and inheritances (long-term).

III. *The combination of the net short-term gain or loss and the net long-term gain or loss determines whether any gain is eligible for a preferential tax rate.*

Note:
Misconception: A capital loss (whether short-term or long-term) must be deductible in order to be netted with gains. Losses on the sale of personal use assets are not deductible despite the fact that these assets are capital assets.

Definitions:
The net short-term gain or loss: is the accumulation of all short-term capital gains and all deductible short-term losses.

The net long-term gain or loss: is the accumulation of all long-term capital gains and all deductible long-term losses.

A. If the combination of net short-term and net long-term gains and losses is negative, then individuals can deduct this "net capital loss" up to $3,000 per year. The deduction is "for" AGI and is limited to taxable income (any excess loss carries forward).

Definition:
A net capital loss: occurs if a net loss results from combining net short-term gains and losses with net long-term gains and losses.

Example: This year TP realized a net short-term gain of $2,000 and a net long-term loss of $3,000. TP can deduct a net capital loss of $1,000 for AGI.

B. If the combination of net short-term and net long-term gains and losses is positive, then this is deemed capital gain net income.

C. "Net capital gain" is the portion of capital gain net income (if any) that is eligible for a reduced tax rate.

Definition:
A net capital gain: is net long-term capital gain in excess of a net short-term capital loss (if any).

Example: This year TP realized a net short-term gain of $5,000 and a net long-term loss of $3,000. TP's capital gain net income of $2,000 is comprised of net short-term gains and, accordingly, is taxed at the regular income tax rates. There is no "net capital gain" in this instance.

D. Corporations can only use a "net capital loss" to offset capital gain net income. Net capital losses are carried over as short-term capital losses, and these losses are carriedback three years and forward five years.

IV. Preferential Tax Rates -- The special tax treatment accorded a "net capital gain" is a lower tax rate.

A. *The tax calculation is made by computing the regular tax on income without the net capital gain plus the preferential tax rate times the net capital gain.*

B. *The preferential tax rate depends on the composition of the net long-term gain.*

1. Net capital gain is taxed at a maximum rate of 15 percent. If the taxpayers regular tax rate is 15 percent or lower, then the maximum tax rate is reduced to 0 percent (this lower rate was 5% before 2008).

2. Net capital gain attributable to straight-line depreciation claimed on real estate is taxed at a maximum rate of 25 percent.

3. Net capital gain from "collectibles" is taxed at a maximum rate of 28 percent.

Definition:
A collectible: is tangible personalty such as coins, art, and antiques purchased for investment purposes. Gold and silver are also classified as collectibles subject to the 28% rate.

Example: In 2009, TP has a 35 percent marginal tax rate on regular taxable income. He realized the following gains:

$9,000 gain on the sale of art held 5 years.

$20,000 gain on the sale of securities held 15 months.

$15,000 gain on the sale of securities held 3 years.

$7,000 gain on the sale of long-term rental realty attributable to depreciation.

The $9,000 gain is taxed at a maximum of 28 percent, while the $15,000 and the $20,000 gains are taxed at maximum 15 percent. The $7,000 gain is taxed at a maximum rate of 25 percent.

C. *Special rules exist for netting losses against various categories of long-term gains.*

1. A net short-term loss is applied against a net long-term gain (the group of long-term gains taxed at the highest rate is offset first).

Example: In 2009, TP has net short-term capital loss of $20,000. He has also realized a net long-term gain of $50,000 comprised of the following net gains and losses:

$10,000 gain on the sale of coins held 3 years.

$25,000 gain on the sale of securities held 3 years.

$15,000 gain on the sale of realty (attributable to depreciation).

TP has a net capital gain of $30,000. The short-term capital loss first offsets the gain on the collectibles, and then offsets $10,000 of the gain attributable to depreciation. Hence, the net capital gain of $30,000 is comprised of $5,000 gain taxed at 25 percent (the realty) and a $25,000 gain taxed at a maximum rate of 15 percent.

A net loss in one of the long-term groups is first applied to the group of long-term gains taxed at the highest rate.

Example:
In 2009 TP has a net long-term gain of $20,000 comprised of the following capital gains and losses:

$5,000 loss on the sale of coins held 3 years.

$15,000 gain on the sale of securities held 3 years.

$10,000 gain on the sale of realty (attributable to depreciation) held 4 years.

The long-term capital loss from the collectibles first offsets part of the long-term gain attributable to depreciation. Hence, the net long-term gain of $20,000 is comprised of $5,000 gain taxed at 25 percent (the realty) and a $15,000 gain taxed at a maximum rate of 15 percent.

D. **Special Situations --** *Some special rules exist for certain capital gains and losses.*

1. For gains and losses incurred by partnerships and "S" corporations, the determination of the maximum tax rate is made at the entity level.
2. Beginning in 2008, special rules apply for preferred stock issued by financial institutions and sold to the federal government as part of the economic stabilization process. Gain from the sale of this specific type of preferred stock is treated as ordinary income.
3. Gains from the sale of "qualifying small business stock" by noncorporate taxpayers are eligible for a 50% exclusion. *Qualifying small business stock* is stock of a small business corporation (less than $50 million in capital) held for five years. The maximum gain eligible for the exclusion is the lower of ten times the taxpayer's basis in the stock or $10 million in aggregate. 50% of the qualifying gain is excluded from income. The remaining gain is taxed at a maximum rate of 28%.
   - For qualifying small business stock acquired after February 17, 2009 and before January 1, 2011, the 50% gain exclusion is increased to 75%.

Example:
ABC corporation, a qualified small business corporation, issued 100 shares of stock to TP for $20,000 in 1994. On September 25 of 2009, TP sold the stock for $300,000 and realized a gain of $280,000. The gain eligible for the exclusion is the lower of $200,000 (ten times TP's basis) or $10 million. Hence, 75% of the qualifying gain of $200,000 is excluded from income, or $150,000. The remaining $50,000 of the excluded gain is taxed at 28%. The $80,000 gain not qualifying as small business gain is taxed at the regular capital gains rate (maximum of 15%).

E. If a nondealer, noncorporate taxpayer subdivides real property into at least two lots for resale, the gain from the sale of the lots will be treated as capital gain as long as the taxpayer had held the property for at least five years and no substantial improvement has been made to the lots by the taxpayer. All gain on the first five lots sold will be capital gain. For all lots sold over five, 5 percent of the selling price will be treated as ordinary income.

Example:
This year ABC Corporation began operations and realized taxable income of $36,000. ABC also recognized the following gains and losses.

Short-term capital gains	$8,500
Short-term capital losses	(4,500)
Long-term capital gains	1,500
Long-term capital losses	(3,500)

Question: What is ABC corporation's taxable income?

Answer: ABC is taxed on $38,000, ordinary income of $36,000 and $2,000 of capital gains.

V. **Section 1231 --** Section 1231 is designed to provide capital gain treatment to a net gain generated from transactions involving involuntary conversions and the disposition of trade assets.

A. *The scope of section 1231 is determined by the nature of the asset and the type of disposition.*

1. Section 1231 applies to the sale or exchange of "section 1231" assets.

Definition:
Section 1231 assets: are assets used in the trade and held for over 12 months (long-term). Section 1231 assets include realty and depreciable property but excludes capital assets, inventory, accounts receivable, copyrights, and government publications.

a. **Short Cut:** "Section 1231" assets include realty and depreciable personalty held in a trade for over 12 months.

2. Section 1231 also applies to all involuntary conversions of business assets.

B. *First stage of netting is recharacterization of part of gain attributed to accumulated depreciation (called recapture of depreciation).*

1. Recapture of depreciation reduces the amount of gain eligible for section 1231 treatment by recharacterizing the gain.

2. "Section 1245 recapture" recharacterizes gain on personalty as ordinary income to the extent of accumulated depreciation.

3. "Section 1250 recapture" is recapture of accumulated accelerated depreciation in excess of straight-line depreciation as ordinary income.

4. "Unrecaptured Section 1250 gain" recharacterizes gain on realty as eligible for a special (25 percent) tax rate to the extent of accumulated straight-line depreciation.

Definitions:
Section 1245 recapture: refers to depreciable personalty (movables).

Section 1250 recapture: applies to depreciable real estate.

a. **Short Cuts:**

- Recapture does not recharacterize losses.
- Gains on the sale of land held long-term in a trade are 1231 gains.
- Gains on the sale of machinery held long-term are ordinary income, unless sold for an amount greater than the original purchase price.
- Gains on the sale of buildings held long-term in a trade are 1231 gains but will be taxed as ordinary to the extent of accelerated depreciation in excess of straight-line with the straight-line depreciation being recaptured at the 25 percent rate.

Example:
TP sells a machine held long-term with an original cost of $10 and accumulated depreciation of $7. If the machine is sold for $5, then TP will have a realized gain of $2 (TP's adjusted basis is $3). TP would characterize this gain as ordinary to the extent of accumulated depreciation. Hence, the entire gain is taxed as ordinary income.

Example:
TP sells a machine held long-term in the trade with an original cost of $10 and accumulated depreciation of $7. If the machine is sold for $14, then TP will have a realized gain of $11. TP would characterize this gain as ordinary to the extent of accumulated depreciation ($7). Hence, $7 of gain will be taxed as ordinary income and the remaining $4 of gain will be Section 1231 gain.

Example:
TP sells a building held long-term in the trade with an original cost of $100 and accumulated depreciation of $45. If the building is sold for $120, then TP will have a realized gain of $65 (TP's adjusted basis is $55). This gain would be taxed as a Section 1231 gain, but $45 of the gain would be taxed at a rate of 25 percent (assuming all depreciation is straight-line depreciation) whereas the remaining $20 of gain would be eligible for a rate of 15 percent or 5 percent (0 percent in 2008).

C. *Subsequent stages of 1231 netting involve separate netting for business casualties, other involuntary conversions, and trade assets.*

1. To the extent section 1231 gains exceed section 1231 losses, the net gain is treated as a long-term capital gain.

2. If section 1231 losses exceed section 1231 gains, the loss is deductible as an ordinary loss (subject to a lookback limit for gains during the previous 5 years). The lookback provision states that the net Section 1231 gains must be offset by net Section 1231 losses from the five preceding tax years that have not previously been recaptured. To the extent of these losses, the net Section 1231 gain is treated as ordinary income.

VI. **Gifts and Inheritances --** Gifts and inheritances are taxed under the Federal Estate and Gift Tax law. To avoid the double taxation of these transfers, their value is excluded from the income of the recipient.

A. Gifts are excluded if the purpose of the transfer was detached generosity (no quid pro quo or consideration was expected in return for the transfer).

B. Income accrued up to time of gift is still taxed to the donor, whereas income accruing after the gift is taxed to recipient (donee).

> **Note:**
> **Misconception:** Whether an item is a gift depends on the intent of the donor, not the intent of the done. For example, S rakes the leaves in T's yard as a gesture of kindness, but T decides to pay her $20 for her work. Even though S did not expect to be paid, S has $20 of income because T's intent was to pay him for the services he rendered.

C. Basis issues for Gifts and Inheritances:

1. **If property is gifted to a taxpayer, the donee's basis is:**

a. *Gain basis* = adjusted basis of the donor.

b. *Loss basis* = lower of

i. FMV at date of gift, or

ii. adjusted basis of the donor.

c. *Depreciable basis* = gain basis.

d. The basis is increased for the portion of any gift tax paid by the donor due to appreciation in the property:

> Adjustment to basis = (Unrealized appreciation)/FMV at date of gift - annual exclusion X Gift Tax paid

> **Study Tip:**
> *The gain and loss basis differs only when the FMV of the property is less than its basis. The law allows a built-in gain to be transferred to another individual, but does NOT allow a transfer of a built-in loss.*

D. Tax Effects of basis for gifts

1. A gain is recognized only if the donee sells property for more than the gain basis.

2. A loss is recognized only if the donee sells property for less than the loss basis.

3. If the property is sold by the donee for an amount in-between the gain and loss basis, no gain or loss is recognized.

Example:
TP receives a used auto from his father as a gift. The father bought the auto for $10,000 several years ago and the auto is worth $15,000 at the time of the gift. TP will take his father's basis ($10,000) in the auto.

If the father had a basis of $20,000 in the auto, in TP's hands the auto would have a gain basis of $20,000 and a loss basis of $15,000. Loss can only be recognized to the extent that the auto is sold for less than $15,000. Gain can only be recognized to the extent that the auto is sold for more than $20,000. If the automobile is sold for an amount between $15,000 and $20,000, no gain or loss is recognized.

E. Holding Period of Gifted Property

1. If the *gain basis* is used to compute realized gain or loss, the holding period of the property for the donee includes the holding period of the donor.
2. If the loss basis is used, the holding period of the donee begins on the date of the gift.

F. Inheritances - Basis and Holding Period

1. The basis of property acquired from a decedent is the fair market value at the date of death, or the FMV on the alternate valuation date (six months after the date of death) if that date is selected by the executor as the valuation date.
2. Holding period is deemed to be long-term.

Nonrecognition Transactions

The tax on realized gain or loss from certain dispositions is postponed (or in one case excluded).

I. **Short Cut --** One should assume that all realized gains and losses are recognized, unless aware of a specific exception. This lesson summarizes the most important situations for which gains and losses are not recognized. Note, that if not recognized, gains and losses can be deferred or excluded. If deferred, they will be recognized at some time in the future. If excluded, they will never be recognized. Generally, losses from the sale of personal use property are not recognized. The only time a loss on personal use property is deductible is if the disposition qualifies as a personal casualty.

II. **Like-Kind Exchanges**

A. **Overview: --** The deferral provision for direct (like-kind) exchanges is a prototype for deferral provisions governing transactions that are not in substance dispositions. In a classic direct exchange, the taxpayer simply exchanges one asset for another, like-kind asset. Losses are never recognized from a like-kind exchange. Recognized gain is the lesser of:

1. realized gain, or
2. boot received.

B. Rules are mandatory, not elective.

C. **Qualifying Property --** *Qualifying property must be exchanged*

1. Only business and investment property qualifies for deferral

Definitions:
Business property: is any property used in a trade or held for investment. In contrast, property held for other reasons is referred to as personal-use or "personal" property.

Realty: is land and any property attached thereto.

Personalty: refers to tangible property that is not realty.

Example:
Example: An apartment building is realty, but a truck is personalty.

2. Exchanges of inventory and receivables do not qualify for deferral.
3. The property received in the exchange must be "like-kind" property.

Definition:
Like-kind property: has the same general character as the property given up.

a. The IRS has devised a complex classification system for determining the character of tangible personalty. In general, all realty is considered like-kind. So, the exchange of land for an office building is like-kind.

b. Personalty is divided into 13 broad asset classes, and assets must be within the same class to be like-kind. Examples of asset classes are office furniture, fixtures, and equipment; computer equipment; automobiles; and light-duty trucks. However, an exchange of real property for personalty is NEVER considered like-kind.

c. Business property can be exchanged for investment property.

Example:
An exchange of a pickup truck for a dump truck may qualify as a like-kind exchange. However, an exchange of an apartment building for a barge cannot be like-kind, because it is an exchange of realty for personalty.

d. Property located outside the United States will not qualify as like-kind when exchanged for property located inside the United States.

e. There are special rules that apply to like-kind exchanges when like-kind property is acquired from related taxpayers.

D. **Holding Period --** Holding period of like-kind property surrendered tacks on to the holding period of like-kind property received.

III. **Like-Kind exchanges and the Receipt of Boot --** *The receipt of "boot" triggers gain recognition.*

Definition:
Boot: is defined as nonqualifying property received by the taxpayer.

A. Cash and nonqualifying (not like-kind) property are considered boot.

B. Note, that mortgage relief is treated as boot received if the taxpayer's mortgage that is assumed is greater than the mortgage that the taxpayer assumes on the new property he is receiving. However, if (as in this problem) the taxpayer assumes a larger mortgage than he gives up, this excess reduces his amount realized, but it does not reduce other boot received.

Example:
TP transfers whiteacre to B in exchange for blackacre. If whiteacre is subject to a mortgage of $100 but blackacre is only subject to a mortgage of $80, then B will have assumed $20 more liabilities than TP. This excess liability will be treated as boot received by TP.

1. Boot does <u>not</u> cause realized losses to be recognized.

2. The basis of like-kind property received can be computed as follows:

FMV of property received
- Postponed gain
+ Postponed loss
Basis of like-kind property
==================

a. Basis of non-like kind property received is the property's FMV, since gain has been recognized to that extent.

Example:
Leker exchanged a van that was used exclusively for business and had an adjusted tax basis of $20,000 for a new van. The new van had a fair market value of $10,000, and Leker also received $3,000 in cash. What was Leker's tax basis in the acquired van?

Leker has a realized loss on this exchange of $7,000 ($13,000 amount realized - $20,000 adjusted basis). He received $3,000 of boot, but boot does not cause realized losses to be recognized. Therefore, the recognized loss is zero and the postponed loss is $7,000. Leker's basis in the acquired can is its FMV ($10,000) plus the postponed loss ($7,000), or $17,000.

IV. Involuntary Conversions

A. **Overview:** -- *The involuntary conversion of property resulting in a realized gain is eligible for deferral*. This deferral provision does NOT apply to losses. The deferral provision governing involuntary conversions applies when a gain is generated because an asset is destroyed, stolen, or condemned. Taxpayers may elect to defer gains if the proceeds from the conversion are reinvested in similar property within a reasonable period of time. Hence, after reinvesting in similar property, the taxpayer has no wherewithal to pay the tax, and in addition, no disposition of substance has occurred.

Study Tip:
Note, that while the deferral rules for like-kind exchanges are MANDATORY, the rules for involuntary conversions are ELECTIVE. Also, gains and losses are deferred under the like-kind exchange rules, while only gains are deferred for involuntary conversions.

1. **Eligible for Deferral**

a. The disposition qualifies as an "involuntary conversion."

Definitions:
An involuntary conversion: is the result of a casualty (an unexpected, unavoidable outside influence like a storm, fire, or shipwreck), a theft, or a condemnation.

A condemnation: is a taking by the government. An imminent threat of condemnation is considered sufficient to trigger an involuntary conversion.

b. Gains from conversion of any kind of property are eligible for deferral (not just business property).

Note:
Misconception: Gains are eligible for deferral because of an involuntary conversion, but losses are recognized (e.g., not postponed).

2. **Defer Gain** -- *If the taxpayer replaces the converted property with similar property, he may elect to defer gain from the transaction.*

a. **Replacement Property**

i. The replacement property must be **similar or related in the service or use** made by the taxpayer.

Definition:
The phrase: similar or related in the service or use: means the end use of the replacement property must be similar to the use of the converted property. The determination of whether replacement property qualifies is similar to the process for determining if property qualifies as like-kind. However, this test is generally narrower than the like-kind test, because the properties must also have similar end uses.

b. **Replacement Time Period**

i. The replacement must be made within two years from END of tax year in which the gain is realized.

1. The replacement period is extended to three years if the conversion was a condemnation of business realty. The replacement period can also be extended with IRS permission, or if the area of the conversion is declared a disaster area.

2. Excess proceeds over replacement cost causes recognition of gains.

Amount realized from conversion

\- <u>Adjusted basis of old property</u>

Realized gain/loss

================================

Amount realized from conversion

\- <u>Cost of replacement property</u>

Recognized gain, limited to realized gain

==============================

c. **Adjusted Basis**

i. The adjusted basis of the new property is its cost reduced by any deferred gain.

Example:
TP's pickup was destroyed in a storm. The pickup has an adjusted basis of $2,000, and TP received $4,500 in insurance proceeds. Thus, TP realized a gain of $2,500 from the conversion of the pickup. If TP only spends $4,300 on a similar pickup within the replacement period, then TP will recognize $200 of gain (the amount of proceeds that were not reinvested). The adjusted basis of the new pickup will be $2,000 ($4,300-$2,300).

ii. **Short Cut:** -- If the taxpayer invests less than the entire proceeds in the replacement property, then the adjusted basis of the replacement property will often be the same as the adjusted basis of the converted property.

B. **Holding Period** -- Holding period carries over for qualified replacement property.

V. Other Loss Disallowances

A. **Overview:** -- There are three common provisions that mandate deferral of losses because of opportunities to manipulate taxes. The first, wash sales, are losses from the sales of securities that often occur near year-end. The second provision governs losses from the sale of business property to related parties. In both cases, there is an attempt to recognize a loss without giving up control of the underlying asset. The third area relates to short sales of assets.

> **Study Tip:**
> Note that the wash sale rules apply only to losses, not to gains.

B. **Wash Sales** -- Losses from the sale of securities are not recognized if similar securities are purchased within 30 days of the sale.

> **Note:**
> **Misconception:** The "repurchase" of a security can occur either before <u>or</u> after sale of the original security -- the 30 day period is a window centered on the sale date. The repurchase period is 61 days, the day of sale plus 30 days before and after this day.

> **Definition:**
> *A wash sale*: results from the purchase of "substantially identical" stock or securities within a 30-day window around the sale date.

1. The taxpayer takes an adjusted basis in the new securities equal to the cost plus the deferred loss from the wash sale.
2. Holding period of the new stock or securities includes the holding period of the old stock or securities.

> **Example:**
> TP sold 100 shares of XYZ stock on December 22 for $1,200. The stock had an adjusted basis of $2,000, and TP realized a loss of $800. If TP purchased 100 shares of XYZ on January 15 of the next year for $1,400, the loss on the December 22 sale would be deferred as a wash sale. The stock held by TP would have a basis of $2,200 ($1,400 plus $800).

C. **Losses: Related Parties**

1. Losses from sales of business property to related parties are not recognized.

> **Study Tip:**
> In-laws are not considered related parties, although they are eligible to be claimed as a dependent; nor are aunts and uncles related parties.

> **Definition:**
> *A related party*: for purposes of loss deduction, includes family members -- brother, sister, spouse, ancestors, and descendants, and controlled entities (corporations where the taxpayer owns more than 50% of the stock; partnerships where a partner owns more than 50% of the partnership's capital). In addition, beneficiaries of estates and trusts can also be treated as related parties.

2. Deferred losses create a "right of offset" which can be used to reduce a gain upon the ultimate sale of the property to an unrelated taxpayer. However, the right of offset cannot create a loss, nor make a loss greater.
3. **Holding period** -- of original buyer does not include holding period of the seller; begins on date of purchase of property from related party.

Note:
Misconception: The related party rules are not applicable to the sale of personal use property because these losses are not deductible under any circumstances. The only time a loss on personal use property is deductible is if the disposition qualifies as a personal casualty.

Example:
TP sold stock to S, his brother, for $1,000. TP had an adjusted basis in the stock of $2,500, but he cannot deduct the realized loss of $1,500 because S is a related party. S takes a basis in the stock of $1,000. If S eventually sells the stock to an unrelated third party for $1,800, S can offset the $800 gain with $800 of the deferred loss. The remainder of the deferred loss ($700) is not recognized.

D. Short Sale

1. A "short sale" of appreciated stock held by the taxpayer is treated as constructive sale on the date of the short sale.

Definition:
A short sale: (also called "selling short against the box") is a transaction where the taxpayer borrows and sells shares identical to those already owned. This transaction has the effect of eliminating the taxpayer's risk of loss and opportunity for gain potential.

2. The short sale rule causes taxpayers to recognize gains on any short sales even if the sale was not closed through the purchase of additional stock or the delivery of shares previously owned. This rule is referred to as "marking to market," because the gain is measured by the value of the shares at the end of the year.
3. The short sale rule also requires taxpayers to defer losses. Losses are deferred until the short position is actually closed.

VI. Sale of Principal Residence

A. Overview: -- The law provides for an exclusion of gains from a principal residence once every two years.

1. A taxpayer may exclude realized gains up to $250,000 ($500,000 if filing joint) on the sale of a residence if all of the following are true:
   a. **Either** -- the taxpayer or spouse meets the ownership test.
   b. **Both** -- the taxpayer and spouse meet the use test.
   c. During the 2-year period ending on the date of the sale, neither the taxpayer nor spouse excluded gain from the sale of another home (frequency limit). Alternatively, if only one spouse qualifies, that spouse can claim only a $250,000 exclusion.

Example:
TP , a single taxpayer, sold his residence. He had an adjusted basis in the residence of $55,000 and received $415,000 on the sale before commissions. If TP paid sales commissions of $10,000, then he realized a gain of $350,000 on the sale. TP may be eligible to exclude $250,000 of the gain. The remaining gain ($100,000) would be taxed as a capital gain.

d. Any depreciation taken after May 5, 1997 must be recaptured on the sale (e.g., the gain attributed to portion of the home depreciated as an office). As long as the business portion is not a separate building, the gain does not need to be allocated between the business and personal portions of the residence.

e. For sales after 2007, if the sale occurs not later than two years after the death of a spouse, the surviving spouse may exclude $500,000 of gain. Note, that the rules in "a" and "b" must have been met at the date of death of the deceased spouse for this provision to apply.

Example:
TP has owned and occupied his residence for the past seven years. In January of this year, TP married S who moved into TP's residence. Immediately prior to the marriage, S sold her residence and excluded the gain. In June, TP and S sold TP's residence. TP qualifies for the exclusion, but S violates the frequency test. Nonetheless, TP can elect to exclude $250,000 of gain on the sale.

f. For sales after 2008, the exclusion will not apply to the extent that the property was not used as a principal residence during a portion of the five-year testing period. For example, if during the five-year window the property is used as a residence for three years and rented as a vacation home for two years, 40% of the gain (2 years/5 years) cannot be excluded from income.

B. Ownership and Use Tests

1. The residence must be owned and used by the taxpayer as a principal residence for at least two of the preceding five years (ownership and use tests).

   a. The amount of time need not be continuous (e.g., ownership and use must only total 730 days during the previous 5 years).

   b. Short or temporary absences (e.g., vacations) are ignored and use is imputed for taxpayers who are institutionalized (e.g., unable to care for themselves). Additionally, an individual can suspend the running of the five-year test period if serving in the uniformed services, Foreign Service, Peace Corps, or intelligence community.

   c. For married taxpayers, either spouse can meet the ownership test, but both must meet the use test. If only one spouse meets the use test, then that spouse can only claim a $250,000 exclusion.

Example:
TP has owned and occupied his residence for the past five years. In January of this year, TP married S who moved into TP's residence. In June, TP sold his residence. TP qualifies for the ownership and use test, but S violates the use test. Hence, TP can elect to exclude a maximum of $250,000 of gain on the sale.

C. Other Unforeseen Circumstances

1. If a residence is sold prematurely due to changes in employment or health (or other unforeseen circumstances such as a natural disaster, multiple births, or change in wedding plans), then the maximum amount of the exclusion is prorated based upon the number of qualifying months (ownership or use) divided by 2 years (or equivalent in months or days). The qualifying months is the lesser of the number of ownership/use months or the number of months since the last sale.

Example:
TP has owned and occupied his residence for the past 18 months. TP was transferred across the country and subsequently sold his residence for a gain of $200,000. TP does not qualify for the exclusion because he has not owned and occupied his residence for two years. Nonetheless, because of the change in employment TP can elect to exclude up to 75% (18/24) of the maximum ($250,000) from the sale. In this situation, TP can exclude $187,500 of the gain ($12,500 will be a taxable gain).

VII. Installment Sales

A. Overview -- The deferral of gains through installment sale is the traditional example of a deferral provision motivated by equitable considerations. The installment sale deferral automatically defers gains (not losses) when payment is made in later periods. Although taxpayers can elect to recognize gains currently, the installment sale treatment prorates the gain recognition according to the proportion of cash received in each year. *A sale where one payment is deferred into a future year is eligible for installment treatment.*

- Taxpayers who are dealers cannot use installment method for sales of inventory.
- Even if the installments method is elected all depreciation recapture must be recognized in year one (the year of sale).

B. Recognition of Deferred Gain -- *Recognition of deferred gain is triggered by receipt of cash.*

- A "gross profit percentage" is multiplied by the cash received to determine the gain recognized.

Definition:
Gross profit percentage: The gross profit percentage is ratio of gain to be recognized to contract price (the total cash to be received).

Example:
TP sells his car (AB=$3) for $12 to be paid in the future. TP expects to receive $2 next year, $4 in the second year, and $6 in the third year (plus interest). Because TP has a realized gain of $9 and a contract price of $12, TP will have a gross profit percentage of 75%. Hence, he will be taxed on a gain of $1.5 next year, $3 in the second year, and $4.5 in the third year. In addition, the interest payments will be taxed as interest income.

C. Installment Obligation

- *A disposition of the installment obligation will trigger recognition of the deferred gain.* The entire gain will be recognized immediately if the installment note is sold or otherwise encumbered.
- The installment obligation (note receivable) must have market interest rate or a portion of the gain will be treated as imputed interest.

Income

Income - Basic Principles

Tax accounting consists of specialized rules for realizing and accounting for income. The accounting rules also apply to expenses, but these rules are described in detail in the section covering deductions. Like financial accounting, the rules used to determine taxable income are premised upon ascertaining net income. Unlike conservative financial accounting rules, the tax rules treat ambiguous circumstances ***liberally****, by assuming income is recognized. Thus, the tax rules are normally structured to recognize a larger, rather than smaller, tax liability.*

I. **Tax Accounting** -- Tax accounting consists of specialized rules for realizing and accounting for income. The accounting rules also apply to expenses, but these rules are described in detail in the section covering deductions. Like financial accounting, the rules used to determine taxable income are premised upon ascertaining net income. Unlike conservative financial accounting rules, the tax rules treat ambiguous circumstances **liberally**, by assuming income is recognized. Thus, the tax rules are normally structured to recognize a larger, rather than smaller, tax liability.

II. **Realization**

> **Definition:**
> *Realization*: is the event that triggers the taxation of income. Like realization for financial accounting, realization is difficult to define precisely.

A. *Realized income is presumed to be taxable.*

1. Realization generally occurs when a transaction results in the receipt of property or a right capable of valuation.
2. Income cannot be realized or recognized if the property received by the taxpayer is not susceptible of valuation. For example, a taxpayer may not be able to value a promise to pay for property based upon future events.

B. *Return of capital is not income.*

1. Receipts are not recognized as income to the extent the receipts represent the cost of goods or the cost of property sold.

> **Definition:**
> *Return of capital*: is the cost of goods or the cost of property sold.

> **Example:**
> SH purchases $10,000 of Motorola stock, and later sells the stock for $13,000. SH is allowed to recover her cost/capital of $10,000 before realizing income. Therefore, her realized income is $3,000 ($13,000 - cost basis of $10,000).

C. *Congress has enacted specific exceptions for untaxed (unrecognized) income.*

1. Nonrecognition provisions may exclude income from taxation or merely defer taxation of the income until a later period.
2. Each type of unrecognized income may be subject to specific, unique limits.

Definition:
Gross income: is the amount of realized income after eliminating deferred and excluded income.

D. *Corollary: Expenses are presumed nondeductible.*

1. Nondeductible expenses do not influence taxable income.
2. Congress only authorized deductions for a list of specific expenses.
3. Similar to nonrecognition provisions, each type of deduction may be subject to specific, unique limits.

III. Accounting Methods and Periods

A. Year-Ends -- Regular corporations do not have restrictions on the year-end that they can choose. However, partnerships and S corporations have significant limitations. These limitations are discussed in the partnership and S corporations sections of the course.

B. Accrual Method -- *The accrual method for taxes is very similar to financial accounting, but exceptions to accrual are usually income increasing*

- For tax purposes, unearned income is recognized in the year received, rather than the year earned.
- Taxpayers may elect to defer recognition of service income into the next year if the service is to be provided within the following year.
- Taxpayers may elect to defer recognition of advance payments for goods if the method of accounting for sales is the same for tax and financial reporting purposes.
- To the extent that accrued expenses are deductible, the deduction can be claimed in the period in which the liability becomes certain (all events).

C. Cash Method -- *The cash method of accounting recognizes income (and expenses) in the year in which payment is received (or paid).*

Note:
Misconception: A cash basis taxpayer does not need reduce property to cash to trigger income recognition.

- This rule only addresses the timing of income (and expense), not whether income has been realized.
- Under the cash basis, a taxpayer has no accounts receivable because no accounting entry is made for sales on account (no property has been received).
- Prepaid expenses are prorated for cash basis taxpayers if recognition of the total expense in the current year would distort taxable income.

D. Cash versus Accrual Accounting -- In general, the following entities cannot use the cash method of accounting:

Note:
Misconception: A cash basis taxpayer cannot write off accounts receivable but can write off a loan. No entry is made for sales on account, but a loan requires an entry (debit loan receivable and credit cash).

1. Regular C corporations.
2. Partnerships that have regular C corporations as partners.
3. Tax shelters. Note that the exceptions listed below do NOT apply to tax shelters.

Definition:
Tax shelter: A tax shelter is an entity other than a C corporation for which ownership interests have been offered for sale in an offering required to be registered with Federal or State security agencies.

- Notwithstanding the above, the following entities can use the cash method:

a. Any corporation or partnership whose annual gross receipts do not exceed $5 million. The test is satisfied for a prior year if the average annual gross receipts for the previous three-year period do not exceed $5 million. Once the test is failed, the entity must use the accrual method for all future tax years.

b. Certain farming businesses.

c. Qualified personal service corporations.

> **Definition:**
> *Qualified personal service corporation*: A qualified personal service corporation exists if 1) substantially all of the activities of the business consist of services in health, law, engineering, architecture, accounting, actuarial science, performing arts, or consulting, and 2) at least 95% of its stock is owned by the employees performing the services.

E. Special Inventory Rules

1. In general, business with inventories must use the accrual method to report purchases (cost of goods sold) and sales. This method is known as the hybrid method of accounting if other accounts are kept using the cash basis.

2. Taxpayers whose annual gross receipts do not exceed $1 million can use the cash method for purchase and sales accounts also. The test is satisfied for a prior year if the average annual gross receipts for the previous three-year period do not exceed $1 million. Once the test is failed, the entity must use the accrual method for all future tax years.

3. Taxpayers whose annual gross receipts exceed $1,000,000 but are less than $10 million can use the cash method for purchase and sales accounts if their primary business is delivering services (not manufacturing, wholesale, or retail).

4. Manufacturers and certain retailers and wholesalers are required to use the **uniform capitalization method** to capitalize all the direct and indirect costs allocable to property they produce and for property bought for resale. These costs are then allocated to ending inventory and property sold during the year. Property is produced if the taxpayer constructs, builds, installs, manufactures, develops or improves property. Exceptions to the uniform capitalization method include: small personal property dealers; long-term contracts; costs incurred in certain farming businesses and in raising and harvesting crops and timber; certain creative expenses and personal property; intangible drilling and development costs; natural gas acquired for resale; and research and experimental expenditures. Small personal property dealers are defined to be those with $10 million or less in gross receipts during the preceding three years.

5. Virtually all indirect production costs must be capitalized for tax purposes. Marketing, selling, advertising and distribution expenses are not required to be capitalized under the uniform capitalization rules. Storage costs are required to be capitalized to the extent that they can be traced to an off-site storage or warehouse facility. Those storage costs attributed to an on-site facility are not required to be capitalized.

6. Costs can be allocated between ending inventory and cost of goods sold using FIFO, LIFO, weighted average, or specific identification. However, LIFO can be used only if it is also used for financial reporting. During a period of rising prices, LIFO produces a higher cost of goods sold and lower taxable income.

7. Taxpayers can value inventory at the lower of cost or market unless they are using LIFO (in which case cost must be used). Market is defined as replacement cost or reproduction cost.

F. Changes in Accounting Methods

1. Once a taxpayer has selected a particular method of accounting it cannot be changed without the consent of the IRS.
2. In general, any adjustment to income required due to a voluntary change in accounting method is spread over four years beginning with the year of change. A voluntary change includes changing from an incorrect to a correct method. If the adjustment is less than $25,000 the taxpayer can include all income in the year of change.
3. If the change in accounting method is initiated due to an IRS examination, any positive adjustment to income is included in the earliest tax year under examination.

IV. Prepaid Items and Long-Term Contracts

A. Prepaid interest, rents, and royalties -- are usually taxed when received. Lease deposits are not income when received if they can be returned to the lessee at the end of the lease term. They are taxed when the lessor receives an unrestricted to them.

B. The taxpayer can elect to include prepaid service income in gross income when received. However, under the deferral method the taxpayer only has to include the payments in gross income in the year of receipt if they are also included in the taxpayer's financial statements. The remaining payments are taxed in the following year (even if not yet earned). The deferral rule also applies to payments received by hotels and other venues where significant services are provided to the lessee.

C. Revenue from the advanced payment of goods can be deferred until earned as long as the same reporting method is used for financial accounting.

D. Prepaid dues and subscriptions are reported over the membership or subscription period.

E. Long-term contracts -- are contracts related to the construction of property for which the completion of the property is generally not completed in the year that construction began. Income from long-term contracts is reported under the percentage of completion method. Under the percentage method, the percentage of the contract completed during the tax year is multiplied by the total gross profit from the contract to compute the income inclusion.

- Under the completed contract method no income is recognized until the construction process is completed. This method is permitted for home construction contracts and for contracts completed by contractors whose average annual gross receipts for the three preceding year do not exceed $10 million.

F. Leasehold Improvements -- The fair value of leasehold improvements is income to the landlord if the improvements are made in lieu of rent.

V. Interest Income -- Interest is included in income when received (cash basis) or accrued (accrual basis). Special imputed interest rules apply to obligations purchased at a discount or premium.

A. Bond Premiums -- Premiums occur when the stated rate for the bond is more than the market rate *Individuals on the cash basis may amortize bond premiums (deduction).*

1. For taxable bonds, taxpayers may elect (one time election for all bonds held) to amortize premium (constant-yield method) and claim the amortization as a deduction.

2. For tax exempt bonds, taxpayers must amortize premium, but no deduction is available.

3. Interest is accrued on bonds purchased between interest dates, and the portion earned prior to the purchase is treated as a return of capital.

B. **Bond Discounts --** Discounts occur when the stated rate for the bond is less than the market rate. *Individuals on the cash basis may amortize bond discounts (as interest income).*

1. Original issue discounts must be amortized using the effective interest rate method.

> **Definition:**
> *Original issue discount*: is a loan made that requires a payment at maturity exceeding the amount of the original loan. This additional payment is a discount and constitutes interest.

2. Cash basis taxpayers can elect to defer the original issue discount on US savings bonds (series EE bonds -- not series H) until maturity.

3. Individuals can elect to amortize discounts on bonds purchased in the secondary market (straight-line method is allowed).

C. *Short-term discounts are taxed at maturity as ordinary income for cash basis taxpayers. It is reported as earned for accrual basis taxpayers.*

1. A short-term obligation has a maturity of one year or less.

2. This rule also applies to original issue discounts for short-term government bonds.

3. In order to defer recognition of the discount, the interest cannot be withdrawn or made available without penalty.

D. **Series EE Bonds --** Interest on Series EE bonds is not paid annually but when the bond matures. The interest is not included in income until maturity unless the taxpayer elects to include the annual increases in the value of the bond as income each year. If the election is made it applies to all future years also. *Interest on series EE savings bonds can be excluded at maturity or when redeemed if the taxpayer uses the proceeds to pay higher education expenses in the year of redemption.*

1. The exclusion is available if the owner of the bond is at least 24 years old (the bond must not be held in a child's name).

2. The interest is excluded in proportion to the educational expenses (tuition and fees) of the taxpayer, spouse, or dependent that are not reimbursed by scholarships.

3. The exclusion is phased-out for 2009 when modified AGI exceeds $69,950 ($104,900) for single (filing joint) status. The phase-out is proportionate over a range of $15,000 ($30,000 for married-joint).

VI. **Interest-Free and Below-Market Loans**

A. If the interest charged for a loan is less than the current market rate (which is based on the Applicable Federal Rates published monthly by the IRS) then special rules may apply. In general, it is assumed that the borrower pays the current market rate of interest to the lender. The borrower will have interest expense and the lender interest income for this hypothetical payment.

- The lender is then assumed to make a payment to the borrower equal to the hypothetical payment (since the payment was not actually made). The tax consequences to the borrower for this deemed payment is:

1. Compensation income if the borrower is an employee.

2. Dividend income if the borrower is a shareholder.
3. A gift in most other circumstances

Example:
Beth works for Publishing, Inc. and receives a $100,000 non-interest bearing loan from Publishing. Assume that the current market rate of interest is 10%. Beth is assumed to pay interest of $10,000 ($100,000 x 10%) to Publishing. The deductibility of this interest is governed by the specific rules related to interest deductions. Publishing recognizes $10,000 of interest income. Since Beth is an employee, she is also deemed to receive $10,000 of compensation income (subject to payroll taxes).

B. Several types of loans are exempt from the below-market rules:

1. In general loans are excluded if the loan amount does not exceed $10,000 and the borrower does not use the proceeds to purchase investment assets.
2. If the amount of the loan does not exceed $100,000 and there is not a tax-avoidance motive, the deemed interest paid by the borrower is limited to the borrower's investment income on the loan proceeds. The investment income is deemed to be zero if $1,000 or less.
3. Loans made to continuing qualified care facilities.

VII. Dividends on Stock -- Generally, distributions of cash or property to shareholders is taxed as dividend income if the distribution is made from the corporation's retained earnings (called "earnings and profits" for tax purposes).

A. Definition -- Any distribution of cash or property from a corporation to its shareholders is a "dividend" to the extent of earnings and profits.

B. *The* <u>*value*</u> *of the property received in a dividend is the amount included in income to the extent the dividend is paid from earnings and profits.*

1. A liquidating dividend or a dividend not out of earnings and profits is treated as a return of capital until the basis of the stock is recovered; amounts in excess of basis are taxed as gains from a sale of the stock.
2. Earnings and profits are the tax version of retained earnings.
3. Dividends are taxed to cash basis taxpayers in the period in which the property is made available (typically when received).

C. Dividend income is taxed at 5% if the taxpayer is in the 10% or 15% bracket (this rate drops to 0% after 2007). For higher tax brackets, dividend income is taxed at 15%. To qualify for this lower rate, the dividend must be received from a domestic corporation or a foreign corporation whose stock is tradable on an established U.S. securities market. If the stock was held for 60 days or less during the 121-day period beginning 60 days before the ex-dividend date, then the dividend does not qualify for this lower rate.

Note:
Stock dividends and splits are not taxable events.

D. Stock dividends are not taxable as long as the dividend is proportionate (same percentage for all shareholders). A stock dividend or split requires the taxpayer to adjust the basis of the stock's new number of shares.

Example:
TP owns 40 shares in XYZ Corporation purchased at a cost of $10 per share ($400 total). TP received an additional 10 shares as a stock dividend. He has realized no income and his shares now have a basis of $8 each ($400 divided by 50 shares).

E. An option to receive cash in lieu of stock (whether or not exercised) triggers recognition of dividend income.

F. Distributions from mutual funds are usually characterized as either ordinary dividends or capital gains. All ordinary dividends are treated as dividend income and the mutual fund will indicate if any of these are qualified dividends taxed at 15% or lower rates. All capital gain distributions are treated as long-term capital gains.

VIII. Judicial Concepts -- The courts have constructed several special rules to address income recognition in unusual circumstances.

A. Constructive Receipt -- *Constructive receipt requires a cash basis taxpayer to include the value of property in income in the period in which the right to (or control of) the property is acquired.* The income is not constructively received if substantial restrictions exist on the taxpayer's use of the funds. For example, if the taxpayer would have to forfeit future bonuses to receive the funds then a substantial restriction exists.

Example:
TP received a check on December 28 for services this year. He must recognize the income because he has control over the property (the check).

B. Tax Benefit Rule -- *The tax benefit rule requires a taxpayer to include an expense reimbursement in income if the expense was deducted in a prior period and the deduction reduced the taxpayer's taxable income.*

Example:
TP deducted a $200 business expense last year, but because of limitations the deduction only reduced his taxable income by $120. This year a client reimbursed $150 of the original expense. TP must include $120 of the reimbursement in his income this year.

C. Claim of Right Doctrine -- *The claim of right rule requires the taxpayer to include property in income in the period in which an apparent claim to the property materializes.*

1. A later repayment of the property (because the claim was not valid) generates a deduction, but does not influence the earlier recognition of the income.

Example:
Last year TP was paid a $100 bonus, but this year TP's employer discovered an error and required TP to repay $90 of the bonus. TP should include the $100 bonus in his income last year and claim a $90 deduction for the repayment this year.

IX. Income from Community Property

A. Community property law divides income into separate property and community property.

1. Separate property consists of assets owned before marriage or acquired by gift or inheritance while married.
2. Community property is property acquired during a marriage unless by gift or inheritance.

B. Allocation of Income

1. Income from separate property may be separate property (Idaho, Louisiana, and Texas) or community property (Alaska, Arizona, California, Nevada, New Mexico, Washington, and Wisconsin) depending on the state. If community property each spouse is taxed on 50% of the income. If separate property the income is reported by the spouse who owns the property.
2. Personal service income is usually community property.

X. Stock Options

A. Key dates for stock options are:

1. Grant date - date the option is granted to employee.
2. Exercise date - date that the option is exercised and the stock is purchased.
3. Sale date - date that the stock is sold.

B. Non-Qualified Stock Options

1. No income is recognized when the option is granted.
2. On the exercise date, the employee recognized ordinary income equal to:
   a. (FMV of Stock - Exercise Price) x # of shares exercised.
   b. The employer receives a salary deduction for this same amount.
   c. The employee has a basis in the stock equal to its FMV on the exercise date. When the stock is later sold, this basis is used in computing the gain/loss from the sale.

C. Incentive Stock Options -- No income *is recognized (except for AMT) when the option is* granted or exercised. *The consequences when the stock itself is later sold vary:*

1. The gain on sale is LTCG if acquired stock is:
   a. held more than one year, and
   b. not sold until after two years from the date the option was granted.
   c. The employer does not receive a deduction.

Study Tip:
For an ISO, the exercise price cannot be less than the FMV of the stock on the grant date.

2. If these requirements are not met, the option is treated like a **non-qualified stock option:**

   a. the gain on the stock sale is ordinary income and the employer receives a deduction equal to the stock's FMV on the exercise date over the exercise price.

   b. the difference in the FMV on the sale date and the FMV on the exercise date is capital gain or loss.

Note:
Note, that even the tax effects are like those for a NQSO; the timing of the income recognition still takes effect on the date the stock is sold, not the exercise date.

SUMMARY OF TAX EFFECTS OF STOCK OPTIONS

	INCENTIVE STOCK OPTION	NON-QUALIFIED STOCK OPTION
GRANT DATE	NONE	NONE
EXERCISE DATE	NONE (EXCEPT AMT)	ORDINARY INCOME
SALE DATE	ORDINARY INCOME/CAPITAL GAIN (AMT ADJ. REVERSES)	CAPITAL GAIN

3. Corporation receives deduction for ordinary income portion only.

Nonrecognition - Double Tax

There are many provisions that allow taxpayers to exclude income under special circumstances. This section describes exclusion provisions that are designed to avoid taxing income twice.

I. Life Insurance Proceeds

A. Life insurance proceeds are generally subject to estate tax at the time of the decedent's death. Hence, subjecting the beneficiary to income taxation upon receipt of the proceeds would constitute a double tax on the proceeds.

B. *Proceeds of life insurance received due to the death of the insured are excluded from income.*

1. The exchange/sale of a life insurance policy for the cash surrender value is treated like a sale and the proceeds in excess of the cost are income. One exception to this rule is the surrender of a policy by a terminally ill taxpayer.
2. One exception to this rule is the surrender of a policy by a terminally ill taxpayer. Accelerated death benefits from a life insurance policy can be excluded from income if the insured taxpayer is terminally or chronically ill. Terminally ill means that a physician has certified that death is likely to occur in 24 months or less. Chronically ill means that the individual cannot perform some common daily activities (e.g., eating, bathing, etc.)

C. *A life insurance policy purchased (from the insured or the owner of the policy) for consideration is treated like an asset and the proceeds in excess of the cost are income.*

Example:
TP owned a life insurance policy on his spouse, but was short of cash. He sold the policy for $100 to B, an unrelated individual. Upon the death of TP's spouse, B received $500 from the life insurance company. B will be taxed on $400 of income ($100 is return of capital). If TP had not sold the policy, then TP would have received $500 tax free.

II. Gifts and Inheritances

Gifts and Inheritances -- Gifts and inheritances are taxed under the Federal Estate and Gift Tax law. To avoid the double taxation of these transfers, their value is excluded from the income of the recipient.

Note:
Misconception: Whether an item is a gift depends on the intent of the donor, not the intent of the done. For example, S rakes the leaves in T's yard as a gesture of kindness, but T decides to pay her $20 for her work. Even though S did not expect to be paid, S has $20 of income because T's intent was to pay him for the services he rendered.

A. Gifts are excluded if the purpose of the transfer was detached generosity (no quid pro quo or consideration was expected in return for the transfer).

B. Income accrued up to time of gift is still taxed to the donor, whereas income accruing after the gift is taxed to recipient (donee).

C. Basis issues for Gifts and Inheritances:

1. **If property is gifted to a taxpayer, the donee's basis is:**
   - a. *Gain basis* = adjusted basis of the donor.
   - b. *Loss basis* = lower of
     - i. FMV at date of gift, or

ii. adjusted basis of the donor.

c. *Depreciable basis* = gain basis.

d. The basis is increased for the portion of any gift tax paid by the donor due to appreciation in the property:

Adjustment to basis =	(Unrealized appreciation) / FMV at date of gift - annual exclusion	X Gift Tax paid

Study Tip:
The gain and loss basis differs only when the FMV of the property is less than its basis. The law allows a built-in gain to be transferred to another individual, but does NOT allow a transfer of a built-in loss.

D. Tax Effects of basis for gifts

1. A gain is recognized only if the donee sells property for more than the gain basis.

2. A loss is recognized only if the donee sells property for less than the loss basis.

3. If the property is sold by the donee for an amount in-between the gain and loss basis, no gain or loss is recognized.

Example:
TP receives a used auto from his father as a gift. The father bought the auto for $10,000 several years ago and the auto is worth $15,000 at the time of the gift. TP will take his father's basis ($10,000) in the auto.

If the father had a basis of $20,000 in the auto, in TP's hands the auto would have a gain basis of $20,000 and a loss basis of $15,000. Loss can only be recognized to the extent that the auto is sold for less than $15,000. Gain can only be recognized to the extent that the auto is sold for more than $20,000. If the automobile is sold for an amount between $15,000 and $20,000, no gain or loss is recognized.

E. Holding Period of Gifted Property

1. If the *gain basis* is used to compute realized gain or loss, the holding period of the property for the donee includes the holding period of the donor.

2. If the loss basis is used, the holding period of the donee begins on the date of the gift.

F. Inheritances - Basis and Holding Period

1. The basis of property acquired from a decedent is the fair market value at the date of death, or the FMV on the alternate valuation date (six months after the date of death) if that date is selected by the executor as the valuation date.

2. Holding period is deemed to be long-term.

III. Alimony -- Alimony is taxed to the recipient and the payor is granted a deduction ("for AGI"). In this way, the income is only taxed once to the ultimate recipient. Payments to a former spouse that do not qualify as alimony are treated as a division of property: nontaxable to the recipient and nondeductible by the payor.

A. Alimony -- alimony is taxable to the one receiving the payments and deductible by the one making the payments. To qualify as alimony, the payments must be:

Study Tip:
It is permissible for alimony to terminate before the spouse's death, it just cannot extend beyond death.

1. Required by decree or written agreement and not characterized as something other than alimony
2. Made in cash
3. Paid to or on behalf of former spouse
4. Terminate upon death of recipient, and
5. Payor and payee cannot be members of the same household.

B. **Child Support** -- child support is not taxable to the one receiving the payments and is not deductible by the one making the payments.

C. **Property transfers** -- other than cash to a former spouse under a divorce decree are not a taxable event. The transferor's basis in the property transfers to the transferee.

D. If the required amount of child support and alimony are not received, payments are first assumed to be child support.

E. Special front loading rules require recapture of deductions and income if alimony payments decline more than $15,000 over the first 3 years after the divorce.

Nonrecognition - Subsidies

The government provides for the deferral or exclusion of income in order to provide indirect subsidies to certain activities.

I. Damages

A. **Personal Injuries --** *Amounts received to compensate for* **physical injury or illness** *are not subject to income taxation.* Note that worker's compensation is also excluded from income since it is paid due to physical injuries incurred while working.

> **Definition:**
> *Compensation for physical injuries*: includes any payment that compensates for damages due to a physical injury or illness. As long as the action generating a payment is due to a physical injury or illness, then all damage payments received, except for punitive damages, are excludable from income. This is the case even if the injured party is being reimbursed for lost wages.

B. Damages received for emotional distress, employment or age discrimination, or injury to reputation must be included in gross income.

C. **Punitive damages --** in general, must be included in gross income.

> **Note:**
> If a taxpayer receives a judgment or settlement as a result of a discrimination suit, the damages received are typically included in gross income. Attorney's fees and other costs incurred as part of the suit are deductible for AGI, limited to the amount of the proceeds that are included in income

> **Example:**
> TP was in an accident caused by Smith. TP received $1,000 to compensate him for medical expenses, $5,000 for emotional distress due to injury, and $2 million for punitive damages. TP is taxed on $2 million but not on the compensation for expenses or emotional distress (it was due to a physical injury).

II. Insurance Benefits Received

A. **Benefits from Taxpayer Purchased Policies --** *Health and disability insurance proceeds are excluded if the taxpayer paid the premiums.*

1. Benefits under a policy purchased by the taxpayer are excluded even if payments are a substitute for lost wages.

B. **Benefits from Employer Purchased Policies --** *Health and disability insurance proceeds may also be excluded if the taxpayer's employer paid the premiums.*

1. Medical expense reimbursements are excluded as long as the expenses reimbursed are for qualified medical expenses, or

2. If payment is received for loss of (or the use of) a body part or permanent disfigurement.

   - These exclusions apply for the employee and the employee's spouse and dependents.

C. Benefits received from long-term care policies are excluded from income up to $280 per day in 2009, but excess amounts over this limit are not included if the funds were used for actual long-term care services.

Example:
TP was disabled last year. TP's employer-provided health insurance paid his medical expenses of $50,000, and paid TP $40,000 for the wages TP lost while he was disabled. TP may exclude the $50,000, but TP is taxed on the disability proceeds of $40,000 because the employer paid the insurance premiums.

III. Fringe Benefits

A. **Life insurance premiums --** *paid by an employer are excluded on group-term life insurance.*

1. The limit on this exclusion is the amount of premiums necessary for a group-term policy of $50,000 face value.
2. For amounts over $50,000, the insurance benefits are taxable based on the rates in an IRS table. The rates are based on the age of the taxpayer.

Example:
UT, Inc. provides life insurance for its employees equal to their annual compensation. T's annual compensation is $80,000 and the includible income per $1,000 of coverage is $1.20 per month (T is 42 years old).

T can exclude payments for the first $50,000 of coverage from income. She is taxed on the excess coverage of $30,000 ($80,000 - $50,000). She has 30 excess increments ($30,000/1,000) each of which is taxed at $1.20 per month, so her income inclusion is $432 (30 x $1.20 x 12).

B. **Employer Purchased Health and Long-Term Care Plans**

1. **Health insurance premiums --** *paid by an employer are excluded.*
   a. Corollary: Self-employed individuals can deduct 100% of health insurance premiums paid for coverage of self, spouse, and dependents. However, the deduction cannot exceed the taxpayer's net earnings from self-employment.
2. Employer paid premiums for **long-term care policies** are also excluded from income.

C. **Accountable Plans**

1. If employee business expenses are reimbursed under an accountable plan, then the reimbursement is not taxable (for FICA or income tax) and the employee gets no deduction for the expense. Technically, the tax law requires the reimbursement to be included as income and the employee's deduction is FOR AGI. Since this always nets to zero, the IRS allows the income and deduction to not be reported.
2. If the expenses are reimbursed, but not under an accountable plan, the reimbursement must be included in income (for FICA and income tax) and the deduction is a 2% miscellaneous itemized deduction.
3. If the expenses are not reimbursed by the employer, the employee's deduction is a 2% miscellaneous itemized deduction.
4. For a plan to be accountable:

a. must substantiate all expenses to be reimbursed, and

b. excess reimbursements must be returned to the employer.

D. **Personal Expenses Paid by Employer** -- *If an employer pays the expenses of an employee, the payment is income to the employee because it is compensatory in nature.*

Example:
In lieu of additional salary, an employer makes a $200 car payment for an employee. The $200 payment is income to the employee.

E. **Food and Lodging** -- *The value of food and lodging provided by employer to employees is excluded from the income of the employee if the food and lodging is provided for the employer's convenience.*

1. Convenience of employer, means the food and lodging must be provided for a non-compensatory reason. For example, a hospital may provide free meals in the hospital's cafeteria for doctors so they will be on call in case an emergency occurs. The employer must require the employee to accept lodging as a condition of employment to be excluded from income.

2. Convenience of the employer, has also been interpreted as meaning that employer-provided meals must be provided in kind on the employer's premises.

Example:
EE employs TP as a manager of a motel. EE provides lodging worth $2,000 to TP in order to keep TP on call in case of complaints. TP may exclude the value of the lodging if EE requires that TP accept the lodging as a condition of employment.

F. **Working condition** -- *fringe benefits are excluded from the employee's income.*

1. A working condition benefit is a benefit provided by the employer that would be deductible (as an employee business expense) if the employee had instead paid the expense.

Example:
T is an attorney and his law firm reimburses him for his dues to the American Bar Association and his subscription to the *National Law Review*. These reimbursements are excluded from income as working condition fringe benefits

G. **De Minimus Fringes** -- *are excluded because these benefits are small in value and infrequent.* Examples include occasional use of the copy or fax machine, typing services, and free coffee provided in the office.

H. **No Additional Cost Fringes** -- *are excluded benefits when provided to employee, their spouses, or dependents.*

Note:
Exclusion applies only to services provide by employers, not to products given to or sold at a discount to employees. If an employee is allowed to take groceries home that have met their expiration date, the value of the groceries would not be excluded since they are a product and not a service.

1. These benefits are those provided by employers at no substantial additional cost, such as plane tickets provided to airline employees when there are empty seats.
2. For businesses with more than one line of business (e.g., operate a hotel and a rental car service) the exclusion only applies for services provided in the business line that the employee works in.

I. **Employee discounts --** *(except on realty and marketable securities) are excluded if the discount is not excessive.*

1. The discount is limited to 20% of the value of services.
2. The limit on the discount for purchases of merchandise is the average gross profit percentage for the employer.

Example:
T is employed at an office supply store and is allowed to buy a computer that cost the store $900 (offered for sale at $1,300) for $1,000. Since T is paying at least the store's cost, the discount does not exceed the gross profit and is excluded from income.

If the store also provides shipping services for customers, and T is allowed to ship items at a 50% discount, the portion of the discount that exceeds 20% of the value of the services is included in T's income.

J. **Nominal Gifts --** *The value of nominal gifts to employees are excluded up to $25 per employee.*

Example:
TP is employed by a grocery store that provides all employees with a complimentary turkey for Thanksgiving. If the value of the turkey is less than $25, then the gift is excluded by TP.

K. **Safety and Length of Service Achievement Awards --** *are excluded from income subject to a limit of $400 if not a qualified plan, and $1,600 if part of a qualified plan.* The award will be taxed if it is made in cash.

L. **Transportation and Parking --** *Employer reimbursements for mass transit transportation ($120 per month) and parking ($230 per month) are excludable up to the limits shown in 2009. However, beginning March 2009 the mass transit exclusion is increased to $230 per month to match the parking exclusion.*

M. Beginning in 2009, reimbursement for commuting with a bicycle can be excluded up to $20 per month. Qualified expenses include the purchase, repair, and storage of the bike if it is regularly used for commuting to work.

Example:
TP is employed by a firm that provides all employees with monthly parking passes. If the value of the parking is less than $230 per month (2009), then this benefit is excluded by TP.

N. **Other special** -- *"qualified" benefits provided by employer may be excluded, including:*

1. Employees can exclude (up to $5,000; $2,500 if married filing separately) from gross income the value of **child and dependent care services** provided by the employer, if the services are provided so that the employee can work.
2. Employees can exclude (up to $5,250) from gross income the value of assistance provided by the employer **for** *undergraduate and graduate* **tuition, fees, books, and supplies**.
3. Employees can exclude from gross income up to $12,150 (in 2009) of **expenses incurred to adopt a child**, if these expenses are reimbursed by the employer. The exclusion is phased-out at AGI levels between $182,180 and $222,180. (Amounts are indexed to inflation so they do not need to be memorized.)
4. If the adoption expenses are actually paid by the taxpayer, the taxpayer receives a non-refundable credit for qualified adoption expenses up to the same $12,150 limit per child.
5. Employer reimbursement of moving expenses, but only if the moving expenses would have been deductible by the employee if she had paid for them.
6. Use of athletic facilities provided at a location owned or leased by the employer. This benefit applies to the employee, employee's spouse and dependents, and retirees.
7. Employer provided retirement advice.
8. Qualified tuition reduction by nonprofit educational institutions. Applies to the employee and employee's spouse and dependents. Applies only for undergraduate education, except graduate students who receive tuition waivers for serving as a graduate assistant can exclude the tuition reduction.
9. Benefits paid to the family of a deceased employee are included in income.

IV. **Government Payments** -- Certain transfers from state and local government and governmental entities are not taxed in order to help subsidize governmental activities.

A. **Municipal Interest** -- *Interest on state or local governmental obligations is excluded.*

1. The exclusion does not extend to some special types of municipal bonds, such as "arbitrage" bonds.
2. The exclusion does not mean that interest on municipal bonds cannot be used in other tax calculations, such as in the computation of the alternative minimum tax or the exclusion of social security benefits.
3. For bonds issued after February 17, 2009 or in 2010, certain issues can elect for the bonds to be treated as Build America Bonds. These are municipal bonds but the election means that the interest on the bonds will be included in income, but the holder will receive a tax credit equal to 35% of the interest.

Note:
If the state or local bond is sold at a gain, such gain is taxable. Losses are also deductible. The character of the gain/loss is capital since bonds are an investment asset.

B. Social Security Benefits -- generally, SSB are not included in income. However, if the taxpayer's provisional income (PI) exceeds a specified amount, up to 85% of the benefits may be included in income.

1. **PI = AGI + tax-exempt interest + 50% (SSB)**
2. The following base amounts (BA) must be used:

	BA1	BA2
Married taxpayers filing jointly	$32,000	$44,000
Married taxpayers that file separately	$ 0	$ 0
All other taxpayers	$25,000	$34,000

3. **If PI exceeds BA1 but not BA2**, then the taxable amount of SSB is the lesser of:
   a. 50% x SSB
   b. 50% x [PI - BA1].
4. **If PI exceeds BA2**, then the taxable amount of SSB is the lesser of:
   a. .85 x SSB, or
   b. .85 x [PI - BA2), plus the lesser of
      i. amount included based on first formula, or
      ii. $4,500 (unless married filing joint, then $6,000).

Study Tip:
If PI is less than $25,000, then none of the SSB are included in income.

C. Unemployment compensation -- is taxable. However, in 2009 up to $2,400 of unemployment compensation can be excluded from income.

Study Tip:
This is taxable because it is a replacement for wages.

D. Foster child payments -- are excluded from income if they are for reimbursement for expenses incurred to care for the foster child.

V. Prizes and Awards

A. The fair market value of these items must be included in income.

B. Prizes or awards can be excluded if they are for civic, artistic, educational, scientific, or literary achievement and the recipient is:

1. selected without action on his/her part,
2. not required to perform services,
3. the amount is paid directly to a tax-exempt or governmental organization.

VI. Scholarships

A. Amounts received as scholarships can be excluded from income to the extent that the funds are used for tuition, fees, books, supplies, and equipment required for courses.

B. Amounts received for room and board are treated as earned income.

Note:
If the payments from the university are in return for services rendered, the amounts are taxable as wages, even if the services are a condition for receiving the degree, or required of all candidates for the degree.

VII. Retirement Savings -- Contributions made by an employer (and sometimes the contributions by an employee) to a "qualified" retirement plan are not subject to tax until the contributions are withdrawn from the plan.

A. **Qualified Pension Plans** -- *Contributions of salary to "qualified" pension plans are deferred until distributions are made from the pension.*

1. For a plan to be "qualified," it must meet nondiscriminatory, funding, vesting, and certain participation/coverage requirements.
2. Early withdrawals (before age 59 1/2) trigger a penalty in addition to the taxation of the withdrawal.

B. **Individual Retirement Accounts (IRAs) --** The income earned on contributions made to an individual retirement account is not subject to tax in the current year. The taxation of these contributions varies according to the type of the account -- traditional, Roth, or educational.

C. **Traditional IRAs --** *provide a deduction for eligible contributions.*

1. **Contributions --** The limit on any IRA contribution (deductible or nondeductible) is $5,000 in 2008 and 2009, or compensation (an additional $1,000 catchup contribution is allowed for taxpayers over the age of 50). Hence, for a married couple, the limit on IRA contributions is $10,000, or combined compensation. Excess contributions are subject to a 6% excise tax each year until withdrawn.
2. **IRA Deductions --** If the taxpayer is not a participant in a qualified pension plan, the IRA contributions can be deducted "for" AGI. IRA contributions can also be deducted by taxpayers who are active participants in qualified plans, but this deduction is phased out proportionately over a $10,000 range ($20,000 if married filing joint) if the taxpayer's AGI exceeds the AGI limit below.

Taxable years beginning in	Joint Returns Phase-out range
2009	$89,000 - $109,000

Taxable years beginning in	Single Taxpayers Phase-out range
2009	$55,000 - $65,000

Example:
TP is a single taxpayer who has AGI of $57,000. This year (2009), TP is covered by a qualified pension plan, and he made a $5,000 contribution to an IRA. Because of the phase out, TP loses 20% of the IRA deduction [(57,000 - 55,000)/10,000]. Hence, TP deducts $3,200 of the IRA contribution. The remaining $800 is a nondeductible contribution.

3. Note, that the phase out of the IRA deduction is always rounded up to the nearest $10 and the minimum deduction is $200 if the entire deduction is not phased-out.
4. A married taxpayer who is not an active participant can deduct contributions even if the taxpayer's spouse is an active participant. However, this deduction is phased-out proportionately over a $10,000 range if the joint AGI exceeds $166,000 in 2009.
5. Taxpayers who cannot deduct IRA contributions can nonetheless defer the income earned by nondeductible IRA contributions to traditional IRAs.

D. **Roth IRA --** *contributions are not deductible.*

1. "The limit on contributions to a Roth IRA are the same as those to a traditional IRA (compensation or $5,000, or $6,000 for those 50 or older ($10,000 if married joint) for 2009) without consideration to the rule about participation in a qualified pension. The limit on Roth contributions is coordinated with other IRAs so that combined contributions to all IRAs cannot exceed these limits.

2. Covered contributions to a Roth IRA are phased-out proportionately if the taxpayer's AGI for 2009 exceeds $166,000 for married-joint (a $10,000 range) or $105,000 for single taxpayers (a $15,000 range).

E. **Conversion of a Traditional IRA to a Roth IRA --** Taxpayers can convert a traditional IRA to a Roth IRA in years that their AGI is $100,000 or less. The taxpayer must recognize gain at the time of the conversion to the extent that the conversion amount exceeds the tax basis in the IRA.

F. **Roth 401(k) Plans --** Beginning in 2007, taxpayers may create a Roth 401(k). Similar to Roth IRAs, after-tax dollars are contributed to these plans, but all distributions from these plans are tax-exempt. There are no income limitations on contributions to a Roth 401(k).

G. **Coverdell Savings Account --** *Contributions to a Coverdell Education Savings Account (former Education IRA) are not deductible, but income may not be subject to tax.*

1. A Coverdell Savings Account must be established exclusively to pay higher education costs (tuition, fees, books, and room and board reduced by tax-free scholarships and similar payments, including elementary and secondary school expenses) for a beneficiary who is under age 18 (unless a special needs student).

2. Contributions to a Coverdell Savings Account are limited to $2,000 per beneficiary, per year. The contribution is phased-out proportionately if the taxpayer's AGI exceeds $190,000 for married-joint (a $30,000 range) or $95,000 for single taxpayers (a $15,000 range).

3. Corporations or tax-exempt entities may make contributions to Coverdell Savings Accounts regardless of the income of the entity.

VIII. Retirement Distribution

A. **Withdrawals from a "traditional" IRA --** *are taxed as income in the year of withdrawal.*

1. If the taxpayer has made nondeductible contributions to the IRA, then withdrawals are prorated between the total nondeductible contributions and the remaining balance in the account (because the taxpayer has basis for the nondeductible contributions). The portion of withdrawals constituting nondeductible contributions are not subject to tax.

2. Withdrawals from a traditional IRA may be subject to a penalty tax of 10%. This tax is not imposed if the taxpayer is disabled or age 59 1/2. Withdrawals are also exempt from the penalty when due to death or disability or:

   a. Made in the form of certain periodic payments.

   b. Used to pay medical expenses in excess of 7-1/2% of AGI.

   c. Used to purchase health insurance of an individual who is unemployed for at least 12 weeks.

   d. For first-time home buyer expenses.

   e. Distributed for the qualified higher education expenses.

   f. Amounts are levied by the IRS.

   g. Made by individuals called or ordered to active military duty.

3. Withdrawals from a traditional IRA must begin when the taxpayer reaches age 70 1/2.

4. In 2008 and 2009, up to $100,000 of distributions from an IRA will be tax-free if contributed to a charitable organization by an individual age 70 1/2 or over.

B. **Withdrawals from a "Roth" or "Coverdell Savings Account"** -- *may be tax exempt.*

1. Withdrawals of contributions from a Roth IRA are not taxed as income. Withdrawals are assumed to be from contributions first, rather than prorated between contributions and accrued income.
2. Withdrawals of income accumulated in a Roth IRA are not taxed as income if the distribution occurred five years or more from the date of the initial contribution, and it is made on or after an individual attains age 59 1/2. Withdrawals of income are also not taxed if due to the death or disability of the taxpayer, or if for first-time homebuyer expenses, or certain education expenses.
3. Withdrawals of contributions of income from a Coverdell Savings Account are not subject to tax if used to pay higher education expenses, or rolled into a Coverdell Savings account for a member of the beneficiary's family.
4. Taxpayers may waive the exclusion for withdrawals from a Coverdell Savings Account if they prefer to claim the Hope/Lifetime credits for the educational expenditures.
5. If a withdrawal (or a portion of a withdrawal) from a Coverdell Savings Account is not used for education expenses, then the withdrawal is prorated between total contributions and accumulated income. The portion of the withdrawal constituting income is subject to tax plus the 10% penalty tax.

C. **Special Retirement Plans** -- Self-employed taxpayers may make deductible contributions to special retirement plans.

1. "Keogh" plans have the same limits as pension plans, except the maximum percentage limit is based upon self-employment earnings. For 2009, contributions are limited to the lesser of $46,000 or 100% of earned income. Earned income equals net earnings from self-employment less 50% of the self-employment tax less the allowable Keogh contribution.
2. A 401(k) plan allows voluntary employee contributions to reduce taxable salary up to a maximum of $16,500, plus $5,500 catchup for those 50 and over for 2009.

IX. Health Savings Accounts

A. Qualified taxpayers can contribute funds to a Health Savings Account and receive a deduction for AGI in the year the contributions are made. In 2009, annual contributions are limited to $3,000 for singles, and $5,950 for families. Distributions must be used exclusively for qualified medical expenses (health insurance premiums are not qualified).

B. To qualify, a taxpayer must only be covered under a high-deductible health plan and may not be entitled to benefits under Medicare. In 2009, a high-deductible health plan must have a deductible of at least $1,150 ($2,300 for family coverage) and annual out-of-pocket expenses cannot exceed $5,800 ($11,600 for family coverage).

X. Forgiveness of Debt

A. Generally, the forgiveness of debt results in income to the borrower unless the forgiveness is a gift, or the forgiveness is related to a bankruptcy proceeding.

B. If the taxpayer is bankrupt or insolvent, the debt forgiveness is not taxable. However, the taxpayer must reduce tax attributes such as NOLs, credit carryovers, and the basis of property. The taxpayer can elect to reduce the basis of property first rather than other tax attributes.

C. A taxpayer that is insolvent, but not bankrupt, can exclude forgiveness of debt only to the extent of the insolvency.

Example:
UNA, Inc. has assets of $500,000 and debts of $750,000. Therefore, their insolvency is $250,000. If creditors forgive $400,000 of debt, the first $250,000 will be excluded from income. The remaining $150,000 will be included in income. UNA will reduce other tax attributes for the $250,000 of excluded income.

D. For cancellation of debt on real property used in a trade or business, no income is recognized even if the taxpayer is not bankrupt or insolvent. However, the taxpayer must reduce the basis of the property by the amount of forgiven debt.

E. For discharges of indebtedness in 2007 - 2012 on a taxpayer's principal residence in connection with a debt restructure or foreclosure, up to $2 million of debt relief may be excluded from income. This debt is limited to indebtedness to acquire, construct, or substantially improve a principal residence. Thus, home equity loans, whose proceeds are not used for these purposes, are not included in this exclusion.

XI. Annuities

A. Annuity Definition

1. Annuities require an insurance company to make certain payments to a taxpayer for a specified period of time. Annuities are often used as part of a retirement plan.
2. The amount paid for an annuity is the taxpayer's basis in the asset.
    a. If the annuity is purchased from an insurance company, the taxpayer's basis equals the amount paid.
    b. If the annuity is funded through a retirement plan, the taxpayer only receives tax basis for the contributions to the retirement plan if made from after-tax income.
    c. The taxpayer receives NO BASIS for employer contributions and contributions made by the employee which were tax deductible (e.g., contributions to 401(k) plans).

B. Tax Consequences

1. Each payment from the annuity is part income and part return of basis.
2. The expected return from the annuity is the annual payment times the expected remaining life of the taxpayer (determined by tables provided by the IRS).

$$\text{Excluded portion} = \frac{\text{Cost of Annuity}}{\text{Expected Return}} \times \text{Payment}$$

3. Exclusion ratio stays during the expected life of the taxpayer. If the taxpayer lives longer than expected, additional payments are fully taxable.
4. If annuitant dies before the total basis is recovered, unrecovered cost is a deduction on taxpayer's final return. It is a miscellaneous deduction (not subject to the 2% rule).

Example:
T's basis in his retirement annuity is $100,000. He retires in 2008 at the age of 62 and is to receive payments of $1,000 per month for life. His expected life under the IRS tables is 260 months. Thus, his expected return is $260,000 ($1,000 x 260 months).

T's exclusion ratio is 38.46% ($100,000/$260,000). If he receives payments of $12,000 in 2008, he can exclude $4,615 ($12,000 x 38.46%) and has taxable income of $7,385.

T's basis at the end of 2008 is $95,385 ($100,000 - $4,615). If he dies on January 1, 2009, he can deduct the unrecovered basis of $95,385 on his final tax return as a miscellaneous itemized deduction. If he lives longer than 260 months, then for month 261 and all future months, the entire $1,000 monthly payment is included in income.

XII. Section 529 Plans

- **A.** These plans are used to save for college expenses through a vehicle that allows the earnings to be excluded from gross income.
- **B.** Contributions are not deductible, and a beneficiary must be specified for the plan. States typically allow lifetime contributions to the plan of as much as $250,000.
- **C.** Earnings in the plan are tax deferred.
- **D.** Distributions from the plans are excluded from income to the extent the distribution is used to pay for tuition, fees, book, etc., and reasonable room and board costs. Distributions not used for a qualified purpose are subject to income taxation and a 10% penalty. For 2009 and 2010, computer technology and equipment and internet access and related services qualify as higher education expenses.

XIII. Income in respect of a decedent (IRD)

- **A.** IRD is income which the decedent had earned before his death, but had not yet recognized as income because of his method of accounting.
- **B.** IRD must be included in the gross income of the person that receives it, and it has the same character as it would have had if the decedent had recognized it.
- **C.** Some common examples of IRD are accrued income, accrued interest on U.S. savings bonds and on savings accounts, and dividends for which the record date was before the date of death.

Deductions

Individual Deductions - For AGI

Because the tax laws only allow the deduction of certain specific expenses, it is necessary to identify qualifying expenditures. Each deduction is classified as either "for" AGI or "from" AGI. This lesson focuses on deductions for AGI.

I. **Types of deductions --** Because the tax laws only allow the deduction of certain specific expenses, it is necessary to identify qualifying expenditures. Each deduction is classified as either "for" AGI or "from" AGI. This lesson focuses on deductions for AGI.

> **Definition:**
> *AGI*: refers to "adjusted gross income" and AGI is calculated by subtracting deductions "for" AGI from gross income.

II. **Deductions for AGI**

A. Deductions "for" AGI primarily consist of business related expenses. These deductions are subject to few(er) limits than itemized deductions.

B. **Business expenses** *associated with a "trade" are deductible for AGI.*

> **Definition:**
> *A trade*: is an activity with a continuous level of profit seeking, such as a self-employed taxpayer who depends on the activity for his livelihood.

1. Deductions "for" AGI are often claimed on separate forms where the deductions serve to directly offset the income generated by the activity.

> **Example:**
> "Trade" expenses offset trade income directly on Schedule C, whereas rental expenses offset rental revenues on Schedule E.

2. Expenses associated with rental and royalty activities are deducted "for" AGI whether or not the activity is considered a "trade."

C. **Non-business Deductions:** - *There are several major categories of non-business deductions, which are deducted "for" AGI.*

1. Alimony payments (discussed in Lesson 5: Nonrecognition - Double Tax).
2. One-half of self-employment taxes paid by self-employed taxpayers.
3. 100% of the medical insurance premiums (not exceeding self-employment income) paid by a self-employed taxpayer (including spouse and dependents) for taxpayers (and spouse) who are not eligible to participate in an employer subsidized health plan.
    - The same applies for premiums paid for long-term care insurance by self-employed individuals who are not eligible to participate in an employer subsidized long-term care plan.
4. Moving expenses.

5. IRA (Keogh) contributions and other contributions to self-employed retirement plans(discussed in Lesson 6: Nonrecognition - Subsidies).
6. Interest on student loans.
7. Qualified higher education expenses.
8. Contributions to Health Savings Accounts (discussed in Lesson 6: Nonrecognition - Subsidies).
9. Attorney's fees and court costs for discrimination suits.
10. Educator expenses.
11. Penalty for early withdrawal of savings.
12. Domestic Production Activities Deduction (discussed under Lesson 17: Corporate Income Computation).
13. Other deductions "for" AGI include forfeited interest on premature withdrawals, repayment of jury pay, and expenses associated with reforestation, clean fuels, and performing artists.

III. Moving expenses -- To be deductible, moving expenses must be *associated with a job change or a first job.*

A. The new job location must add 50 miles to the old commute to justify deduction.

B. The taxpayer must be active in a new job for a substantial period after the move.

> **Definition:**
> *A Substantial Period of Employment*: is 39 weeks during the next 12 months for an employee. A self-employed taxpayer must meet this requirement, as well as an additional requirement of 78 weeks during next 24 months.

C. Qualifying expenses for the move are limited to reasonable amounts paid to move possessions and transportation costs (not meals) for taxpayer and others residing with the taxpayer. If a personal automobile is used, transportation costs are computed at 19 cents per mile in the first six months of 2008 and 27 cents during the last six months.

Example:
TP was transferred from New York to Florida by his employer. TP incurred the following expenses:

lodging and travel while moving	$1,000
pre-move house hunting	$1,200
costs of moving personal effects	$1,800

What is the deductible moving expense if TP is employed full-time? Assuming TP meets the employment test after the move, then $2,800 can be deducted "for AGI."

IV. Student Loan Interest -- Interest paid on student loans is deductible.

> **Definitions:**
> *A Student Loan*: is one whose proceeds are used to pay "qualifying" educational expenses of the taxpayer, his spouse, or dependents (at the time of the expenditure).
>
> *Qualifying Educational Expenses*: include tuition, fees, and room and board reduced by educational exclusions (scholarships, education IRAs, education savings bonds, etc.).

A. The deduction is limited to $2,500 of interest that is not otherwise deductible.

B. The deduction is phased out in 2008 proportionately for married taxpayers with AGI in excess of $110,000 over a range of $30,000 ($55,000 for unmarried over a range of $15,000).

V. Qualified higher education expenses *are deductible.*

> **Definition:**
> *Qualified Higher Educational Expenses*: are the same as under the "Hope" credit - tuition and academic fees required for enrollment or attendance at post-secondary educational institution for the taxpayer, spouse, and/or dependents.

A. The deduction is limited to $4,000 of otherwise nondeductible expenses reduced by other tax-free benefits (such as scholarships or Coverdell Education Savings Account distributions). The deduction cannot be claimed for a student if the Hope or Lifetime credit has been claimed with respect to that same student.

B. The deduction is permitted for taxpayers with a modified AGI that does not exceed $65,000 ($130,000 for joint returns). If AGI exceeds these amounts, a deduction of $2,000 is permitted if AGI does not exceed $80,000 ($160,000 for joint returns). If AGI exceeds these higher limits, then no deduction is allowed.

VI. Educator Expenses -- An individual who is a teacher in grades kindergarten through grade 12 can deduct, as a deduction for AGI, up to $250 for expenses related to books, equipment, and supplies that are used in the classroom. Any excess over $250 is a 2% miscellaneous itemized deduction.

Itemized Deductions

There are six major categories of itemized deductions. Besides the Requirement that total itemized deductions exceed the standard deduction, many of these individual deductions are subject to unique limitations.

I. Itemized Deductions ("from AGI") -- Itemized deductions consist primarily of non-trade business expenses (employee and investment expenses) and a few personal expenses that can be deducted. These deductions are subject to individual limits, and in the aggregate must exceed the standard deduction before any benefit will be realized.

A. Personal Itemized Deductions -- *Six types of personal expenses may be itemized.*

1. Medical expenses.
2. Interest.
3. Taxes.
4. Charitable contributions.
5. Casualty losses.
6. Miscellaneous deductions.

II. The Standard Deduction -- The standard deduction *may be claimed in lieu of itemized deductions.*

A. Standard deduction amounts vary according to filing status (2009).

single	$ 5,700
head of household	$ 8,350
married-joint	$ 11,400
married-separate	$ 5,700

B. An additional amount is added to the standard deduction if either the taxpayer or their spouse is (1) over age 65 or (2) blind. In 2009 the amount of the addition is $1,400 for unmarried and $1,100 for married taxpayers.

C. Taxpayers choose to itemize if aggregate itemized deductions (after application of limits specific to each individual type of deduction) exceeds the standard deduction.

D. For 2008 and 2009, the standard deduction is also increased by the real property tax deduction, which is the lesser of:

1. the amount that qualifies as state and local real property taxes per the itemized deduction rules, or
2. $500, or $1,000 for a joint return.

E. For 2009, the standard deduction is increased by the sales and excise taxes paid on the first $49,500 of the purchase price for new vehicles. See the discussion below under "Taxes" for more details.

F. Spouses filing separately must file consistently (if one elects to itemize, both must itemize).

III. Medical Expenses

A. Uninsured medical expenses are eligible for deduction if the total expense exceeds a limit based upon AGI.

> **Study Tip:**
> Note, that medical expenses is the only deduction allowed for payments made on behalf of someone other than the taxpayer (i.e., dependents).

> **Definition:**
> *A Medical Expense*: is any expenditure for the care, prevention, cure, or treatment of disease or bodily function. Deductible for taxpayer, spouse, and dependent (gross income and joint return tests do not apply for this purpose).

B. Must exceed 7.5% of AGI to be deductible.

C. Deductible items include dental, medical, and hospital care; prescription drugs; equipment such as wheelchairs, crutches, eyeglasses, hearing aids, contacts; transportation for medical care; medical insurance premiums; qualified long-term care expenses and insurance; alcohol and drug rehabilitation; weight-reduction programs if as part of medical treatment.

D. Non-deductible items include funeral, burial, and cremation expenses; nonprescription drugs (except insulin); bottled water; toiletries; cosmetics; health spas; stop-smoking clinics; unnecessary cosmetic surgery.

E. Nursing home expenses qualify if the primary reason for being there is for medical reasons.

F. Capital expenditures may qualify if 1) incurred based on the advice of a physician, 2) the facility is primarily used by the patient alone, and 3) the expense is reasonable. Cost is fully deductible in year incurred. An expense can only be taken to the extent that it exceeds the increase in the value of the property.

G. Qualifying automobile expenses are actual expenses or 24 cents (2009) per mile.

H. Lodging is deductible up to $50 per night; also applies for someone required to travel with patient. No deduction is allowed for meals, unless part of treatment program.

I. Medical expenses are not deducted until paid, and not until the year in which treatment is received, unless prepayment is required by provider.

> Qualified Medical Expenses
>
> \- Reimbursements from Insurance
>
> \- <u>7.5% of AGI</u>
>
> = Deductible Medical Expense

> **Note:**
> Taxpayers can **elect to deduct state and local sales taxes** instead of state and local income taxes. If this election is made, the amount of sales taxes can be determined by using actual receipts or by using a table provided by the IRS. The table includes state sales taxes only so an adjustment is required to add local sales taxes. Taxpayers may also add to the table amount sales taxes on major purchases such as cars, motorcycles, motor homes, SUVs, trucks, boats, and airplanes.

IV. Taxes -- Property taxes and income taxes imposed by state, local, or foreign governments can be deducted as an itemized deduction. For cash basis taxpayers, the taxes are deductible in the year paid or withheld.

A. *Personal income taxes imposed by state, local, or foreign governments are deductible.*

B. Federal taxes, death, excise, and sales taxes are, in general, not deductible.

C. For purchases of **new** vehicles on or after February 17, 2009, the sales and excise taxes paid on the first $49,500 of purchase price is deductible. This deduction is phased out between modified AGI of $125,000 - $135,000 ($250,000 - $260,000) for single (married) taxpayers. This provision applies to passenger automobiles, light trucks, motorcycles, and motor homes.

D. **Property taxes** *imposed on personal-use property owned by taxpayer are deductible as an itemized deduction.*

1. Property taxes on property used for business purposes can be deducted as a business expense.
2. Property taxes do not include special assessments unless these assessments are for repair or maintenance of the property, or imposed for interest payments.
3. Personal property taxes based on the value of the property (ad valorem) are deductible.
4. Special assessments are not deductible.
5. Fees, licenses (dog, automobile, hunting and fishing, etc.) are not deductible.

E. *Taxes are deducted in year withheld or paid, even if payment relates to a different tax year.*

V. **Interest**

A. **Home Mortgage Interest --** Interest paid on debt secured by a personal residence can be deducted as an itemized deduction.

1. *Interest paid on debt relating to the taxpayer's principal place of abode and second home is eligible for deduction.*
   a. Interest on a maximum of $1 million of acquisition indebtedness can be deducted if the debt was used to purchase, construct, or improve the residence.
   b. Interest on the lower of 1) $100,000 or 2) the equity in the home (FMV - other mortgages) can be deducted regardless of how the proceeds of the debt were used.
2. *"Points" can be deducted if paid by taxpayer in the year of purchase or improvement of the residence.*

> **Definition:**
> *Points*: are compensation paid to a lender solely for the use or forbearance of money. Fees paid for services do not qualify as points.

   a. Points paid for refinancing are considered repaid interest that must be amortized over life of loan.
   b. Premiums for qualified mortgage insurance related to acquisition indebtedness on a qualified residence are treated as qualified mortgage interest. This deduction phases out if AGI exceeds $100,000. 10% of the deduction is lost for each $1,000 of AGI, or portion thereof, that exceeds $100,000.

B. **Investment Interest expense --** is limited to net investment income (investment income less investment expenses).

1. Investment income includes interest, dividends, rents, royalties, and annuities if not derived from a trade/business, a passive activity, or a real estate activity for which there is active participation.
2. Net capital gain attributable to the sale of investment property or to qualified dividend income is not included unless the taxpayer elects to do so. If the taxpayer elects to include this as investment income, this gain must be taxed at ordinary income rates, rather the preferential capital gain rates.

3. Investment expenses are expenses related to the production of investment income. Note, that investment expenses are included in computing net investment income only to the extent that they are deductible after application of the 2% phase-out rule for itemized deductions. 2% expenses, other than investment expenses, are applied against the phase-out first.
4. Disallowed investment interest is carried over to future years.

C. **Personal Interest --** *which includes credit card interest, car loan interest, and interest on income tax underpayments, is not deductible.*

D. **Other interest rules**

1. Prepaid interest must be allocated to the years to which the payments relate. Interest is deducted when paid on the cash basis. Accrual basis taxpayers deduct interest ratably over the life of the loan. Mortgage prepayment penalties are deductible as interest.
2. Not deductible if related to the production of tax-exempt income.

VI. **Charitable Contributions --** An itemized deduction is allowed for contributions of cash or property to qualified charities.

A. *Charitable contributions must be made to qualified donees (recipients).*

1. Public ("A") charities are government subdivisions, hospitals, churches, schools, and similar institutions operated for religious, scientific, educational, or charitable purposes.
2. Private ("B") charities include fraternal orders, cemetery companies, and private foundations operated for religious, scientific, educational, or charitable purposes.
3. Political organizations do not qualify as charities.

B. *Contributions can include cash or property, but not services.*

1. All contributions must be reduced by any value or benefit received by the taxpayer.
2. For LTCG and Section 1231 property:
   a. FMV is deductible.
   b. This deduction is limited to 30% of AGI.
   c. The 30% of AGI limitation for capital gain property can be removed if the taxpayer elects to deduct the FMV reduced by the appreciation in the property.
   d. The deduction is limited to the adjusted basis of tangible personal property if the charitable organization does not use the property in a manner that is related to its tax-exempt purpose.
   e. For contributions of tangible personal property exceeding $5,000, if the donee organization sells the property within three years of contribution, the taxpayer must recapture (in the year of sell) the deduction to the extent it exceeded the basis of the property. This recapture can be avoided if the donee organization certifies that the property had been used for an exempt purpose and that this use was substantial.
3. **All other property**, the deduction is the **lesser** of:
   a. the adjusted basis of the property, or
   b. the FMV of the property.
4. Unreimbursed costs (including $0.14/mile) can be deducted.

5. For contributions of clothing and household goods, the value of these contributions can be deducted only if the items are in good used condition or better. Deductions may be disallowed for contributions of clothing or household items with minimal value, such as used socks or undergarments. This rule does not apply if the value of a single item exceeds $500 and a qualified appraisal is attached.

6. In 2008 and 2009, up to $100,000 of distributions from an IRA will be tax-free if contributed to a charitable organization by an individual age 70 or over. This contribution will also not be subject to the 50% or 30% limitation discussed above.

C. *Written records of the contribution are required.*

1. No deduction is allowed for a single contribution of $250 or more unless the donor has written acknowledgment of the amount and purpose of the contribution from the donee organization. A canceled check is not sufficient.

2. Contributions of cash are not deductible unless the donor has a canceled check, credit card statement, or written statement from the charity.

3. For property valued at more than $500, a description of the property must be provided.

4. A qualified appraisal is required for donations of property worth more than $5,000.

5. For property valued at more than $500,000, the qualified appraisal must be attached to the tax return.

6. The requirements for property valued at more than $5,000 and $500,000 do not apply to cash, intellectual property, inventory, publicly-traded securities, and qualified vehicles.

D. Rule for Contributions of Autos, etc. -- If an auto, boat, or airplane with a claimed value of more than $500 is donated, and the donee sells the vehicle without significant use of the vehicle, the deduction is limited to the gross sales proceeds from the sale of the vehicle. The donee organization must provide substantiation of this amount for the donor to attach to the return.

E. Deduction Limitations -- *Limitations of the aggregate contribution deduction are based on AGI.*

1. Deduction is limited to 50% of AGI for aggregate contributions of cash combined with contributions of property.

2. Deduction for contributions of capital gain property to "A" charities is limited to 30% of AGI (ignoring cash contributions).

3. Deduction for contributions of capital gain property to "B" charities is limited to 20% of AGI (ignoring cash contributions).

4. Contributions in excess of the limits carryforward 5 years.

VII. Casualty Losses -- Casualty losses involving personal assets are eligible for deduction if the total unreimbursed loss exceeds a limit based upon AGI. Casualty losses of business assets are deducted as business losses.

> **Note:**
> **Misconception:** Any type of property can generate a casualty loss. However, a casualty of business property qualifies as a business loss. Hence, only casualty losses of personal assets are deducted as itemized deductions.

A. *A casualty loss is calculated by subtracting the adjusted basis of the damaged property from any insurance proceeds.*

> **Definition:**
> *Casualty*: is a sudden, unexpected event damaging or destroying an asset. A casualty includes the theft of an asset.

B. Amount of Casualty Loss -- *For purposes of calculating the casualty loss, the adjusted basis of the damaged property is limited to lesser of the adjusted basis or the decline in the value of the asset due to the casualty.*

1. This limit does not apply to the complete destruction of a business asset.
2. The loss is deducted in the year that the casualty occurs or the theft is discovered.

C. *For personal casualty losses, the deduction is computed as follows:*

	Lower of decline in FMV or AB of property
-	Insurance Reimbursements
-	$100 per casualty (this increases to $500 in 2009)
-	10% x AGI
	________________________________
	Casualty loss deduction
	==============================

D. If a gain results from the casualty (insurance reimbursement exceeds property's adjusted basis), then all casualty gains and losses are netted. A net casualty gain is treated as a capital gain.

E. Appraisal fees (to determine fair market value) are 2% miscellaneous itemized deductions.

VIII. Miscellaneous Itemized Deductions -- Certain business-oriented expenses are not associated with "trade" activities but are, nonetheless, deductible as itemized deductions. These deductions are referred to as "miscellaneous" itemized deductions. Some of these expenses are subject to a 2% of AGI floor, while others are merely added with other itemized deductions.

A. *Operation of the 2% of AGI floor limitation.*

1. The floor limit is applied by subtracting 2% of AGI from the aggregate amount of the deductions subject to the floor.
2. Any excess deductions over the floor are included with other itemized deductions.

Example:
TP has AGI of $100,000 and miscellaneous itemized deductions subject to the 2% floor of $3,500. TP can include $1,500 of these deductions with his other itemized deductions.

B. *There are five major types of miscellaneous deductions subject to the 2% floor.*

1. Employee expenses not reimbursed under an accountable plan. If reimbursed under an accountable plan, then these expenses are deducted for AGI.
2. Investment expenses (not royalty or rental expenses).
3. Tax return preparation expenses.
4. Home office expenses of an employee.
5. Hobby expenses.

C. Other miscellaneous itemized deductions subject to the floor include appraisal fees to determine casualty loss and legal fees to procure alimony.

D. *There are several types of deductions NOT subject to the 2% floor.*

1. Bond premium amortization on bonds purchased before October 23, 1986.
2. Repayments previously included in income under the claim of right doctrine.
3. Remaining basis of terminated annuity.
4. Gambling losses to extent of winnings.
5. Other miscellaneous deductions not subject to the floor include work expenses of handicapped taxpayers, estate taxes related to income in respect of a decedent, short sale expenses, and expense relating to cooperative housing corporations.

IX. Overall Limitation on Itemized Deductions.

A. Taxpayers whose AGI exceeds a threshold ($166,800 in 2009) must reduce the total amount claimed for itemized deductions.

B. *The reduction* was 3% of the amount of AGI in excess of the threshold *before 2007.* For 2007, this reduction is reduced to 2%, and the reduction is 1% in 2008 and 2009.

C. *Itemized deductions NOT subject to the phase-out are medical expenses, investment interest expenses, casualty and theft losses, and gambling losses.*

D. The reduction is the lower of:

1. 1% x (AGI - $166,800), or
2. 80% x (taxes + home mortgage interest + charitable contributions + 2% miscellaneous deductions).

Example:
H and W are calendar-year married taxpayers filing a joint return for 2009. The couple has AGI of $800,000 and $25,000 of itemized deductions consisting of $15,000 taxes, $6,000 of contributions, and $4,000 of mortgage interest. The couple's total itemized deduction of $25,000 is reduced by $6,332 to $18,668. The $6,332 reduction amount is the smaller of (a) or (b) computed as follows:

(a) 1% of excess AGI: $6,332 [1% of $633,200 (i.e., $800,000 AGI less $166,800 applicable amount)].

(b) 80% of otherwise allowable itemized deductions: $20,000 (i.e., 80% of $25,000).

Business Deductions

While there are several different levels of business activity (trade, investment, and employee), all business expenses are subject to similar requirements and prohibitions.

I. **Requirements and Prohibited Deductions --** The law generally allows the deduction of business expenses, but prohibits the deduction of certain other types of expenditures.

A. *The expenditure must be directly connected with a bona fide profit motive.*

1. The expenditure must be "ordinary and necessary."

> **Definition:**
> *Ordinary and Necessary*: are usually interpreted to mean the nature of the expenditure is customary and appropriate under the circumstances.

2. The expenditure must be "reasonable" in amount.

> **Definition:**
> *Reasonable*: is usually interpreted to mean that an expenditure cannot be extravagant in amount.

a. **Short Cut --** Reasonableness is generally a concern when the expenditure is associated with enjoyable activity, such as travel, entertainment, or compensation paid to a related taxpayer, such as a child or spouse.

B. **Disallowed Deductions --** *There are four prohibited deductions.*

1. No personal expenses are deductible unless specifically allowed, including personal legal expenses.
2. Expenditures benefiting more than one period must be capitalized rather than expensed.
3. No expenses can be deducted if the expenditure is against public policy (e.g., illegal). Payments in violation of public policy are not necessary and not deductible. Examples include bribes, fines, penalties, and expenses of operating an illegal drug business. However, cost of goods sold can be deducted for an illegal drug business. Note that the ordinary, necessary, and reasonable expenses of operating other illegal businesses are permitted (as long as the expense itself is not against public policy).
4. No expenses can be deducted if the expense is used to generate tax-exempt income.
5. Lobbying expenses at the state and federal level; deductions are permitted at the city and county government level.
6. Executive compensation for the CEO and the four other most highly compensated officers that exceeds $1 million per person is not deductible unless the income is based on a performance based compensation plan.
7. Specific disallowed deductions from previous exams include life insurance premiums, funeral expenses, and disability insurance premiums.

C. Accounting Methods

1. Expenses are deemed paid under the cash basis when charged to a credit card.
2. Recall from Lesson 4 *Income: Basic Principles* that the accrual method must be used to expense inventory sold unless average gross receipts are less than $1,000,000.
3. For prepaid expenses under the cash method, an immediate deduction can be taken when paid as long as the benefits from the expenditure do not extend beyond the earlier of:
   - 12 months after benefits first begin, or
   - The end of the year after the year in which the payment was made.
   - If the 12 month rule is not meet then the expenses are amortized over the benefit period.
4. Notwithstanding the above, prepaid interest must always be amortized over the life of the loan.
5. Under the accrual method of accounting, there are times when it is not clear when economic performance has occurred. Therefore, the following rules have been established:
   - If there is an obligation to **perform** services or goods in the future (i.e., repairs) the deduction does not occur until the goods or services are provided.
   - If there is an obligation to **pay** for future goods or services, the deduction does not occur until the recipient has received the goods or services.
   - The taxpayer can only deduct refunds, rebates, awards, prizes, provision of warranty work or service contracts, taxes, and insurance premiums when actually paid.
   - If the expenditure is a recurring item, and economic performance occurs within 8 and one-half months after the close of the tax year (or when the return is filed if earlier), then the expenditure can generally be deducted in the year incurred.
   - Vacation pay and bonuses are deducted only if paid within two and one-half months after the close of the tax year.

II. Education Expenses

A. Education expenses are <u>not deductible</u> if:

1. To <u>meet minimum standards</u> of current job, or
2. To <u>qualify taxpayer for a new trade or business</u>.

B. Education expenses are <u>deductible</u> if:

1. To <u>maintain or improve existing skills</u> required in current job, or
2. To <u>meet requirements of employer</u> or imposed by law to retain employment status.

C. Note, that even if these rules are not met, a general deduction for higher education expenses up to $4,000 is allowed as a deduction for AGI. See Lesson 7 - Deductions for AGI for more details. Therefore, the rules listed above apply for expenses not deductible under the $4,000 provision.

Study Tip:
No deduction is allowed for CPA Review Courses. Sorry!!

Example:
Law school tuition cannot be deducted because it is required to qualify for a new profession (even if the taxpayer never intends to practice as a lawyer).

III. **Losses --** Losses on the disposition of business assets can generally be deducted, but the deduction of losses from the disposition of personal (non-business) assets is prohibited.

A. *Deductible losses are generated with the disposition of business assets.*

1. A disposition occurs with a sale, exchange, or worthlessness of an asset.
2. The disposition of personal assets will not generate deductible losses unless the disposition qualifies as a personal casualty.

Definition:
A Business Asset: is an asset used in a trade, held for investment, or used by an employee in an employment capacity. A personal asset is an asset used for a motive other than profit seeking (e.g., a personal reason).

3. An asset that is used partially for business purposes and partially for personal purposes is generally treated as two distinct assets based upon the proportion of time the asset is used for each purpose.

B. *Requirements for deducting the cost of worthless assets.*

1. In general, the asset must be totally worthless (no residual value).
2. The asset must be a business asset.
3. A worthless asset is treated as being sold for nothing on last day of the year.

C. **Bad debts** *are deductible if the loan is made in a trade activity.*

1. Loans can only be deducted using a direct write off method.
2. Business loans can be deducted to the extent that the loan is partially worthless.

Note:
Misconception: A cash basis taxpayer can deduct losses from worthless loans, but not losses generated by the failure of customers to pay for sales on account. A cash basis taxpayer never establishes a basis for an account receivable (sale on account), whereas a basis for a direct loan is created with the transfer of cash.

D. **"Non-business" bad debts** *are also deductible.*

Definition:
A Non-business Bad Debt: is any bona fide loan that is not made in a trade capacity, but has a bona fide profit motive.

1. Whether a loan is bona fide or a disguised gift, depends on facts such as whether interest is charged and collateral is required.
2. Non-business bad debts are deductible as short-term capital losses in the year of complete worthlessness (no partial worthlessness is allowed).

E. **Limitations** *on deduction of losses.*

1. Losses on the disposition of trade assets are subject to the netting rules under 1231, and losses on investment assets are subject to the netting rules for capital assets. In general, these netting procedures allow deductible losses to offset gains without limit.
2. If capital losses exceed capital gains, then this "net capital loss" is subject to $3,000 deduction limit.

3. Special rules apply if Section 1244 qualifying small corporation stock is sold at a loss or becomes worthless (losses are deductible up to $100,000 as ordinary losses, but gains are still taxed as capital gains).

F. Net Operating Losses

1. NOLs must be carried back to the two preceding tax years (beginning with the second prior year) unless an election is made in the year of the NOL to forego the carryback. The carryover period is 20 years.
2. NOLs are only allowed for business losses and casualty losses. Any nonbusiness losses or expenses must be added back to the taxable loss to determine the NOL.
3. The net operating loss of a corporation is, in general, equal to its taxable loss for the tax year. A corporation is allowed to include the dividends received deduction in computing its net operating loss.
4. For an individual, the following cannot create an NOL:
   a. Personal exemptions.
   b. Standard deduction or itemized deductions (except for casualty loss), and other non-business deductions in excess of non-business income.
   c. Excess of non-business capital losses over non-business capital gains (limited to $3,000)
   d. An NOL deduction from another year.
5. In the year to which the NOL is being applied, the NOL is a deduction for AGI for an individual and a regular business deduction for a corporation. For an individual, any deductions that were based on AGI for the carryback year must be recomputed except for the charitable contribution deduction.

IV. Depreciation -- Depreciation deductions are allowed for assets used to produce income, but the deductions must be calculated using cost recovery rules.

A. Amortization Rules -- *There are special rules for amortizing resources and intangibles.*

1. Natural resources are subject to straight-line depletion.
2. **Intangible assets** that are acquired, not created, can be amortized on a straight-line basis over a 15-year period beginning with the month in which they are acquired.

B. Examples include goodwill, going concern value, information bases, know-how, government licenses and permits, franchises, trademarks, etc.

C. Other assets (covenants not to compete, computer software, film, sound recordings, video tapes, patents, copyrights) qualify if acquired in connection with the acquisition of a trade or business.

D. Organization and Start-Up Expenses

1. Expenses incurred in connection with the **organization of a corporation.**
2. $5,000 of these expenses may be deducted, but the $5,000 is reduced by the amount of expenditures incurred that exceed $50,000. Expenses not deducted must be capitalized and amortized over 180 months (unless an election is made to not do so), beginning with the month that the corporation begins its business operations. Election must be filed with first corporate tax return. Same rules apply **for start-up costs**. Start-up costs are expenditures that would be deductible except that the corporation has not yet started its trade or business operation.

3. Typical organizational expenses are legal services incident to organization, accounting services, organizational meetings of directors and shareholders, and fees paid to incorporate. They must be incurred before the end of the taxable year that business begins (but they do not have to be paid, even if on the cash basis).

4. Costs of issuing and selling stock (syndication expenses) must also be capitalized, but cannot be amortized.

E. **Cost Recovery Rules -- Cost recovery** *is computed under a uniform method using the class life period (MACRS).*

1. Double-declining-balance is used for personalty and straight-line is used for realty.
    a. **Definition:** Realty is land and other assets affixed thereto (buildings). "Personalty" is any tangible assets that can be moved (not fixed to land).

2. Recovery for personalty is computed as though assets are purchased at mid year (mid-year convention), while recovery for realty uses a mid-month convention. In the year of purchase, these conventions are already incorporated into the percentages provided in the MACRS tables so no adjustment is necessary to these numbers.

3. While there are numerous class lives for personalty, some of the more common are five-year (automobiles, trucks, computers and peripheral equipment, copiers) and seven-year (furniture and fixtures, most machinery).
    - In 2008 and 2009, qualified leasehold property and qualified restaurant property are recovered over 15 years. In 2009, restaurants can include buildings as 15-year property as long as more than 50% of the building's square footage is for the preparation and consumption of prepared meals. Additionally, certain improvements made to retail space in 2009 (only) are recovered over 15 years.
    - Many types of farm machinery or equipment placed in service during 2009 (only) can be depreciated over 5 years. Grain bins, fences, and other land improvements are not included for farms.
    - Beginning in 2009, race horses are depreciated as 3-year MACRS property. Previously, many race horses were 7-year property.

4. A disposition of the asset follows the appropriate convention. For example, personalty that is sold anytime during 2009 is eligible for 50% of the depreciation that would have been permitted if the asset had not been sold. If reality is sold on March 3, 2009, the taxpayer is allowed 2.5 months depreciation (one-half month for March) for 2009.

5. Bonus depreciation is allowed for property purchased and placed in service in 2008 and 2009. Note, that bonus depreciation will be used unless the taxpayer elects to not do so. 50% bonus is allowed for new tangible property with a recovery period of less than or equal to 20 years, computer software, and certain leasehold improvements. A taxpayer can elect to not use bonus depreciation for a class of property (in which case the election applies to the whole class). The bonus depreciation is allowed for both regular and AMT purposes. No AMT depreciation adjustment is required for any property that uses bonus depreciation. An election can be made to treat AMT and research credits as refundable in lieu of bonus depreciation.

6. A mid-quarter convention is used for all new personalty if more than 40% of personalty acquired during the year is purchased in last quarter of the year.

Example:
On August 1 of this year TP purchased and placed into service an office building costing $264,000 including $30,000 for the land.

Question: What is TP's MACRS deduction for the office building?

Answer: $234,000 is depreciated straight-line over 39 years, but TP is only entitled to 4.5 months (note that a half month is allowed for August using the mid-month convention) this year. Hence, the cost recovery is $2,250 this year.

F. **Section 179 Election --** *There is a Section 179 election to expense a limited amount of tangible personalty if used in a trade activity. Note, that Section 179 expensing is taken into account before bonus depreciation is computed. Off-the-shelf computer software also qualifies under Section 179.*

1. The maximum amount expensed in any year is limited to the lesser of business income or $250,000 for 2009.
2. The Section 179 expense cannot exceed the income from the business, reduced for all expenses except Section 179. Any election to expense in excess of the business income limit is carried forward (indefinitely) and used in a year when income is sufficient.
3. The Section 179 election is phased out (dollar for dollar) if qualified assets purchased exceed $800,000 for 2009.
4. A carryforward is not allowed if the Section 179 deduction is reduced due to the excess purchase provision.
5. The taxpayer can revoke the Section 179 election in later years as long as the return is still eligible to be amended.

Example:
TP purchased $841,000 (2009) of tangible assets for use in his trade. The Section 179 limit of $250,000 is reduced by $41,000 ($841,000 - $800,000) to $209,000. There is no carryforward of the $41,000.

Example:
TP, a self-employed taxpayer, had business income of $15,000 in 2009 prior to deductions associated with cost recovery. This year TP purchased equipment for $25,000.

Question: What is TP's deduction under the election to expense the cost of the machinery?

Answer: TP can elect to expense $25,000, but the deduction is limited to the business income of $15,000. The remaining $10,000 can be carried forward indefinitely and expensed in future years when there is sufficient business income.

Example:
TP, a self-employed taxpayer, purchased equipment in 2009 for $1,200,000.

Question: What portion of the cost may TP elect to treat as an expense rather than as a capital expenditure?

Answer: Since $1,200,000 exceeds the $800,000 trigger by $400,000, the overall limit of $250,000 is reduced to zero.

G. *The taxpayer can elect several alternatives to MACRS.*

1. Straight-line can be used for personalty over the class life of the asset.
2. The AMT system can be used which is one-and-one-half declining balance.
3. The alternative depreciation system (ADS) provides for straight-line over an extended life. ADS must be used for computing earnings and profits, and for listed property used 50% or more for personal purposes.
4. The units of production method can be elected if appropriate for the type of asset.

H. Luxury Auto Limits -- *Autos are subject to an annual ceiling on recovery.*

1. Special rules limit the amount of depreciation that can be claimed on a passenger automobile (GVW of 6,000 pounds or less). However, these limits are adjusted annually for inflation, so the exact dollar limits do not need to be memorized for the exam. For 2009, first year depreciation is limited to $2,960 ($3,160 for trucks and vans). $10,960 ($11,160 for trucks and vans) is the limit including 50% bonus depreciation as discussed above. The additional $8,000 of depreciation is allowed in 2008 and 2009 only.
2. Trucks, vans, and SUVs (and any other vehicle) that weigh more than 6,000 pounds are exempt from the luxury automobile rule. However, for these heavier vehicles, the Sec. 179 election is limited to $25,000 (assuming 100% business use). Regular MACRS rules apply for the remaining basis, including bonus depreciation.
3. Note, that the limits mentioned above assume 100% business/investment use. For mixed-use autos, the limit is multiplied by the percentage of business/investment use.

Example:
A taxpayer can claim first year cost recovery of $2,960 (2009) for an auto costing $30,000. However, if the taxpayer uses the auto 30 percent of the time for personal purposes, then the taxpayer can only claim recovery of $2,072 ($2,960 * 70%). Including bonus depreciation, the limit is $7,672 ($10,960 * 70%).

I. Listed property *must pass business use test.*

Definition:
Listed Property: includes assets, such as computers, cell phones, and vehicles, that can be used for both business and personal purposes.

1. To use cost recovery the business use of listed assets must exceed 50% of total use.
2. For purposes of this test business use is limited to use in the trade or for the convenience of the employer. That is, investment use is not considered for meeting the 50% test.
3. Failure to meet the business use test means cost recovery is limited to straight-line (ADS). However, both the business and investment use of the asset may be depreciated. ADS depreciation must be used for the entire depreciable life of the asset, even if the 50% test is met in future years. Additionally, if the 50% test is failed in the current year but accelerated depreciation had been taken in previous years, the excess depreciation from prior years must be recaptured.

Example:
In Year 1 and Year 2 a computer is used 60% for business use. In Year 3 the business use percentage is 45% and investment use is 12%. For Year 3, ADS straight-line depreciation must be used because the 50% test is failed, but 57% of the asset's basis can be depreciated. Excess depreciation over straight-line from Years 1 and 2 must be recaptured in Year 3. Additionally, the asset must be depreciated using ADS for the remainder of its depreciable life.

Limitations on Business Deductions

Certain business expenditures can be associated with personal enjoyment or tax avoidance. While Congress does not want to prohibit legitimate business deductions, it does not want to subsidize personal activities or sanction tax avoidance. Hence, the deductibility of certain expenditures are subject to restrictions.

I. Hobby Losses

A. Hobby expenses may be deducted if the hobby generates revenue.

> **Definition:**
> *A Hobby*: is an activity that is not primarily profit oriented because it is primarily undertaken for personal enjoyment.

1. The expenses from this activity are deductible, but only to the extent the activity generates revenues. In other words, no hobby loss (expenses in excess of revenue) is deductible.

B. *To avoid the hobby designation, the taxpayer must produce evidence that there is a real profit motive in conducting the activity.*

> **Example:**
> TP is a wealthy doctor who also owns a ranch in Colorado. TP only visits the ranch during the summer when he uses the ranch to conduct recreational activities. If the ranch is not operated at a profit, then expense deductions are limited to the revenue produced by the ranch.

C. *The deductions associated with a hobby are limited to the gross profit generated by the activity.*

1. Expenses can only be deducted as "2% miscellaneous" itemized deductions. Expenses not allowed due to insufficient income, do not carryover to future tax years.

2. The limitation is imposed by deducting expenses in the following order:

a. interest and taxes (fully deductible as itemized deductions),

b. cash expenses, and

c. depreciation.

Example:
TP paints landscapes in the mountains during his summer vacations. This year, TP incurred $400 in airfares and lodging, but only sold $50 in paintings.

Question: How much can TP deduct?

Answer: TP can deduct hobby expenses up to the amount of hobby income. In this case, TP can deduct $50 as a miscellaneous itemized deduction subject to the 2% of AGI limit.

D. *The burden of proving a lack of profit motive can be shifted to the IRS.*

1. When the activity generates a profit in three out of five consecutive years, the IRS must prove the taxpayer has no profit motive in conducting the activity.
2. If there are losses in at least three of the previous five years, the taxpayer has the burden to prove that the activity is a business.

II. Travel Expenses -- Deductions for cost of travel are limited to trips with a business purpose.

A. *The cost of transportation is deductible when the primary purpose is business.*

1. Commuting between the taxpayer's residence and the place of business is never deductible. However, travel from one job or work area to a second job or work area is deductible. Also, travel from home to a "temporary work location" is deductible if the assignment is short-term in nature.
2. The amount and purpose of the transportation must be substantiated.
3. Transportation costs include direct costs (airfare, tolls, gas, depreciation of a vehicle, insurance, etc.), or a mileage rate of 55 cents (2009) can be claimed for auto use. If the mileage rate is used, the only costs added to this amount are for parking and tolls.

B. *Meals and lodging expenses can be claimed when the taxpayer is "away from home" overnight.*

Definitions:
Away From Home: overnight means the trip is of sufficient duration to require the taxpayer to rest.

Home: is defined as the taxpayer's principal place of business. If the taxpayer is assigned to a new location for an indefinite period of time or for more than a year, the "tax home" shifts to the new location. Thus, there would be no travel expenses to this location. Rather, this would now be commuting to the new business home.

1. The cost of meals is reduced by 50%. This reduction does not apply just when traveling, but also when entertaining. If an employer reimburses the meal then the deduction for the meal is 100%.
2. For business travel that is mixed with personal travel, the travel to the location is deductible only if greater than 50% of the total days are business days. If the 50% test is met, all of the transportation costs to the location are deductible. If not met, then none of the transportation costs are deductible. If Friday and Monday are both business days, then the weekend can be counted as business days also.

C. *Other travel related limits include the following:*

1. Travel cannot be a form of business education (e.g., a French teacher travels to France).
2. The cost of a companion is deductible if the companion is an employee of taxpayer or serves some legitimate business purpose.
3. No deduction is allowed for travel to "investment" seminars.
4. For foreign travel, if the travel is primarily business the costs of transportation are fully deductible if the travel outside the United States does not exceed one week or if more than 75% of the days on the trip were business days. If more than 50% of the days were business but one of these tests is not met, then the travel costs are pro-rated based on business days as a percentage of total days. If the trip was not primarily for business then none of the transportation costs are deductible. Business expenses in the foreign country are deductible.
5. Significant restrictions are placed on deductions for conventions and seminars held on cruise ships or in foreign countries.

III. Entertainment -- Deductions for the cost of entertainment are closely regulated and limited to 50% percent of expenditures.

A. *Business must be conducted in association with the entertainment or be directly related to the operations of the business.*

1. Entertainment must involve a person with a business relation (e.g., customer, client, employee, partner, etc.).
2. A substantial discussion must occur.
3. The discussion must either occur before, during, or after the entertainment on the same business day.
4. No deductions for facilities or club dues.
5. Dues to clubs organized for pleasure or recreation are not deductible. Dues for public service clubs (e.g., Kiwanis), professional organizations, and trade associations are deductible.
6. The deduction for tickets to an entertainment activity is limited to the face value of the ticket (before the 50% disallowance).
7. Business gifts are limited to $25 per donee, per year.

B. *Contemporaneous written records are required.*

1. The record must establish the cost, time, activity, relationship, and business purpose of the entertainment.
2. "Accountable" reimbursement plans and per diem expenditures are exceptions to the record requirements.

C. *The cost of deductible meals and entertainment is reduced by 50% (to represent the personal enjoyment of the taxpayer).*

1. No reduction is made when the entertainment is provided to employees as compensation, or if provided as a means of advertising or marketing.

Example:
TP provided a Florida vacation to his highest volume salesperson this year. TP can deduct the entire cost of the vacation because it is compensation to the employee.

IV. Business use of the Home -- Deductions associated with a home office or the rental of a personal residence are subject to special limits.

A. Home office expenses -- *can be deducted for portion of residence used as an office.*

1. Business use of the office must be exclusive and regular.
2. The office must be a principal place of business.
3. If the office is not a principal place of business, then it can still qualify if it is used as the ordinary place for meeting clients or for the administration of the business (there is no other fixed location used for substantial administration).
4. If the taxpayer is an employee, then the office must be used for the convenience of the employer.
5. Expenses must be allocated between the portion of the dwelling used as residence and the office.
6. Office deductions are limited to income after non-office expenses. Office deductions are applied toward income in the same order as the hobby loss limit (mortgage interest and real estate taxes, cash expenses, depreciation), but excess deductions carryforward and can be used in future years when business income is sufficient.

Example:
TP, a self-employed taxpayer, uses one fourth of her apartment exclusively and regularly as her office. She conducts business only at this location. This year she received fees of $5,000 and paid rent, utilities, etc., on her apartment of $8,000.

Question: What amount may she deduct in conjunction with the home office?

Answer: TP may deduct one-fourth of her rent ($2,000) "for AGI." This will be reported on Schedule C with her other business income and expenses.

B. Vacation home expenses -- *occur when a personal residence is rented.*

1. If rented for less than 15 days a year, it is treated as a **personal residence**. Rent income is excluded and mortgage interest and property taxes are deductible on Schedule A.
2. If rented for 15 days or more, and if it is not used for personal purposes for more than the greater of 1) 14 days or 2) 10% of the total days rented, it is treated as **rental property**. All rent is taxable, net of all regular rental expenses, pro-rated for the percentage of rental days only. A rental loss is allowable.
3. If rented for 15 days or more, and if it is used for personal purposes for more than the greater of 1) 14 days or 2) 10% of the total days rented, it is treated as **personal/rental property**. All regular expenses are pro-rated as above for rental days, but a rental loss is not allowed. Expenses must be deducted in the same order as for a "hobby."

Example:
TP owns a duplex. He rents one side of the duplex and lives in the other side. The rental was occupied all year and TP received $7,200 in rent. This year TP paid real estate taxes of $6,400, fire insurance of $600, and TP paid $800 to have the rental painted.

Question: If depreciation on the entire duplex is $5,000, how much will the rental increase TP's adjusted gross income?

Answer: TP's AGI will increase by $400. The $7,200 of revenue will be offset by $3,200 in taxes, $300 in insurance, $800 of maintenance, and $2,500 of depreciation (deducted in that order).

V. Passive Activity Losses -- Deduction of expenses is limited to the revenue produced by the business activity if the taxpayer does not participate in the management of the activity.

A. *The expenses and revenues from "passive" activities are combined (netted) and the expenses in excess of revenue (the passive loss) is suspended.*

Definition:
A Passive Activity: is a profit-seeking activity in which the taxpayer does not materially participate in the management of the activity.

1. Material participation means being involved in the operation of the activity in a continuous, substantial way. Two specific ways to meet this requirement is to work more than 500 hours in the activity, or more than 100 hours if no other individual works more than 100 hours.
2. All limited partners and most rental activities are considered passive without regard to the taxpayer's participation. Exceptions to this rule are allowed for car rentals, hotels, golf courses, and other activities where the average rental time is seven days or less, or 30 days or less if significant personal services are provided by the owner in connection with the rental.
3. Real estate professionals are excepted from the limit. A real estate professional must perform more than 50% of his/her personal services in trades or businesses involving real property, and must perform more than 750 hours of services in real property trades or businesses in which he/she materially participates.

B. Rental Real Estate -- *An exception to the limitation of passive losses exists for taxpayers who "actively" manage rental reality.*

Definition:
Active Management: occurs for taxpayers who own at least 10% of the property and significantly participate in decision making. This is a much easier benchmark to meet that material participation.

1. An active manager can deduct a maximum loss of $25,000 per year.
2. The exception is phased-out for taxpayers with AGI over $100,000 at the rate of 50% ($1 of deduction for each $2 of AGI over $100,000).

Example:
TP has AGI of $130,000 and is an active manager in rental realty. If the rental activity generates a loss of $20,000 TP is limited to a deduction of $5,000 ($20-[($130-100)x 50%]).

C. Suspended losses become deductible in later years if income is generated or the activity is sold.

VI. Investment Interest -- The deduction of interest paid on loans whose proceeds are used for investment activities is an itemized deduction limited to the ordinary income produced by investments. (Recall that interest paid on loans whose proceeds are used in a trade are deducted "for" AGI with no limitation.)

A. *Deduction of investment interest is limited to net investment income.*

Definition:
Net Investment Income: is interest, dividends (qualified dividends taxed at 15% are excluded), ordinary income from recapture, short-term capital gains (not long-term capital gains) less deductible investment expenses (excluding interest). Long-term capital gains and dividend income can be included as net investment income if these items are taxed as ordinary income.

1. More details are provided in Lesson 8 (*Itemized Deductions*).

Example:
TP has AGI of $100,000 and $1,200 of investment expenses and $800 of investment interest expense. If TP has investment income of $500, then TP can deduct $500 of investment interest expense. The investment expenses do not exceed the 2% of AGI floor so net investment income is $500.

Individual Income Taxation

Personal and Dependency Exemptions

Exemptions provide a flat deduction of $3,500 (2008) that reduces AGI in determining taxable income.

I. **Personal Exemptions --** Most taxpayers can claim an exemption in computing taxable income on their own return.

   A. *No personal exemption can be claimed for a taxpayer (or spouse) who is claimed as a dependent by another taxpayer.*

      1. Personal exemptions include the taxpayer and spouse if married filing jointly.

   B. A personal exemption can be claimed on the taxpayer's final return even if the taxpayer or spouse dies during the tax year.

II. **Dependency Exemptions --** The tests for a dependency exemption are applied on the last day of the year, or the last day the dependent was alive (if the dependent died during the year). One must meet all tests to claim an individual as a dependent.

> **Definition:**
> *Dependency Exemptions*: are flat deductions allowed for individuals (other than the taxpayer) who satisfy several specific tests.

   A. One can qualify as a dependent as either a qualifying child or a qualifying relative.

   B. **A Qualifying Child --** can be claimed as a dependent if the following tests are met:

      1. **Relationship test --** natural child, stepchild, adopted child, foster child, sibling, step-sibling, or a descendant of any of these. Note, that this definition includes brothers, sisters, nieces and nephews.

      2. **Residence test --** The dependent must have the same principal place of abode as the taxpayer for more than one half of the tax year. Note, that one could live with several individuals who potentially qualify to claim the individual as a dependent (mother, aunt, grandfather) at the same time.

      3. **Age test --** Must be less than 19 at the end of the tax year, or less than 24 if a full-time student for at least five months of the tax year. Beginning in 2009, the qualifying child must also be younger than the taxpayer claiming the QC as a dependent. There is no age limitation if the individual is permanently and totally disabled.

      4. **Joint return test --** A dependent cannot file married-joint.

         a. A dependent can file joint to obtain a refund (the dependent is not required to file according to gross income level). Otherwise, a married-joint taxpayer will not qualify as dependent despite passing all of the other tests.

      5. **Citizenship/residency test --** A dependent must be a citizen, resident of U.S., or resident of Canada or Mexico.

      6. **Not self-supporting test --** To be claimed as a dependent, the individual must not have provided more than 50% of his/her own support.

      7. **Other requirements --** In addition to the above, a qualifying child must be younger than the taxpayer who is claiming the child as a dependent and cannot be married. Also, if a parent qualified to claim the child as a dependent but declines, no other individual can claim the individual unless that individual's AGI is higher than that of any parent.

C. Tie-Breaker Rules -- If more than one individual qualifies to claim the potential dependent, the following rules apply:

1. If one individual is a parent, the parent claims the exemption.
2. If both individuals are parents and they do not file a joint return, the parent with whom the child resided the longest during the tax year claims the exemption.
3. If same as "b" and the child lives with both parents at the same time, the parent with the highest AGI claims the exemption.
4. If none of the individuals are parents, the taxpayer with the highest AGI claims the exemption. However, note that beginning in 2009, if a parent is eligible to claim the qualifying child, then no one else may do so unless another eligible individual has a higher AGI for the tax year than any parent eligible to claim the child.

D. The Qualifying Relative rule -- defines "relative" very broadly, including all common relatives except for cousins. The term also includes any person who lives in the taxpayer's home for the entire tax year. A qualifying child cannot also be a qualifying relative. In addition to the relationship test, the following tests must be met to claim a qualifying relative as a dependent:

1. **Support test --** The taxpayer must provide more than 50% of the dependent's total support. The multiple support agreement provision continues to apply.

Definition:
Support: is defined as all necessary living expenses including food, clothes, and other necessities. Support does not include services provided by the taxpayer, but does include the fair market value of housing and food provided by the taxpayer.

   a. The support test traces the source of the funds used to pay for necessities.
   b. Scholarships do not count as support.

Note:
Misconception: A child under age 19 can receive significant amounts of income and not violate the support test. The income would not violate the support test if it was not used to pay for necessities (e.g., the income was placed in savings).

Example:
A child of the taxpayer (under age 19) earned $5,000 this year and received a scholarship that paid tuition of $8,000. If the child uses the funds from wages for necessities, the child will still satisfy the support test if the taxpayer provides at least $5,001 of necessities (5,001/10,000 > 1/2).

2. **Gross income test**
   a. The dependent's gross income must be less than the exemption amount for the year ($3,650 for 2009). Gross income is defined as only income that is taxable.
   b. There are two exceptions to this test. These apply for a child/stepchild (adopted and foster also)
      i. that is less than 19 at the end of the tax year, or
      ii. that is less than 24 at the end of the tax year and is a full-time student for at least five months during the tax year.
3. **Joint return test --** same as above.
4. **Citizenship/residency test --** same as above.

Note:
A dependent cannot claim others as a dependent. Additionally, the dependent's social security number must be listed on the return for the exemption to be claimed.

E. Additional Requirements

III. Other Dependency Rules -- There are situations in which individuals may be supported but not meet all tests for a dependency exemption. In two circumstances, multiple support agreements and divorced parents, the law provides for a dependency exemption despite the technical violation of one or more of the tests.

A. Multiple support agreements -- *allow a group of taxpayers who (together) support an individual more than 50%.*

1. Except for the support test, each individual in the group would otherwise be eligible to claim the individual as a dependent.
2. Each individual in the group provides over 10% but less than half of the support.
3. A written agreement allocates the dependency exemption to a member of the group. All members providing more than half of the support must sign.

Example:
TP lives alone and has no income. She is supported by the following people:

	Support	Percent
A (an unrelated friend)	$2,400	40%
B (TP's sister)	2,400	40%
C (TP's son)	720	12%
D (TP's son-in-law)	480	8%

B. Divorced Parents -- *An exception applies for children who are supported by parents who are divorced or legally separated for the last six months of the year.*

1. The parent with custody (over half the year) is entitled to dependency exemption in the absence of any written agreement.
2. The custodial parent can waive the exemption to other parent (in writing).

IV. Phase Out of Exemptions -- Exemptions are subject to a phase-out for wealthy taxpayers. The phase-out is triggered by a high AGI and the amount of the phase out is determined through a stepwise increment.

A. *The AGI trigger for the phase-out varies by filing status.*

Filing Status	AGI - Beginning of Phaseout (2009)	AGI Above Which Exemption Fully Phased Out
Code section 1(a) Married Jointly	$250,200	$372,700
Code section 1(c) Single	$166,800	$289,300

B. *Two percent of total exemptions are lost for each $2,500 increment (or portion) above the trigger AGI.*

C. For 2008 and 2009, the phase-out is only one-third of the amount it would otherwise be.

1. Each $2,500 increment is called a "step." Each step is rounded upward and multiplied by two percent. This percent is then multiplied by the total amount of exemptions claimed, and the product is added to taxable income.

Example:
A single taxpayer has AGI that is $48,500 over the trigger. This is 19.4 steps ($48,500/$2,500). The total steps are rounded up to 20 and each step results in a loss of 2% of the exemptions. In other words, the taxpayer will lose 40% of his exemptions. If the taxpayer claimed a personal exemption of $3,650 (2009), the phase out will be $3,650 x 40% x 33.33%, or $487.

2. **Short Cut --** All exemptions are phased out when AGI is $122,501 over the trigger ($122,501 divided by $2,500 results in 50 steps). Since each step results in a 2% reduction, 100% of the exemptions are lost.

Example:
TP is a single taxpayer who claims two personal (dependency) exemptions. If TP's AGI exceeds the phase-out trigger by $25,300, what portion of the exemptions is subject to a phase-out?

TP's AGI is $25,300 over the trigger, and this translates into 11 steps ($25,300/$2,500). Hence, TP would lose 22 percent of the exemptions (times 1/3 in 2009).

<u>Formula for Tax Calculations</u>

Adjusted Gross Income

less

Itemized Deductions or **Standard Deduction**

and

Personal and Dependent Exemptions

equals

Taxable Income

times

Tax Rates

(determined by Filing Status)

equals

Gross Tax

less

Tax Credits

plus

Additional Taxes

equals

Net Tax

Filing Status

Filing status determines the tax rate to be applied to taxable income. In addition, each filing status has a unique standard deduction. The determination of filing status occurs at year-end (or the death of the taxpayer or spouse). As an aside, it is important to note that most taxpayers are required to calculate their tax using a "tax table" instead of the tax rate schedule.

Study Tip:
An abandoned spouse is a married taxpayer who is allowed to file as though they are unmarried. *An* **"abandoned" spouse** *may file as a head of household.* The following requirements must be met:
The taxpayer's spouse does not live in the home for the last 6 months of calendar year.

The taxpayer must provide more than half the cost of maintaining a home for self and a dependent child.

Definition: *Child* means a descendant of the taxpayer (e.g., son, daughter, or grandchild), or a stepchild, adopted child, or foster child.

Note:
Misconception: A taxpayer whose spouse dies in the current tax year is usually eligible to file married-joint in the current year regardless of **surviving** spouse status. The surviving spouse exception applies to the following two tax years during which the taxpayer will file married-joint (despite the absence of a spouse).

I. **Married Filing Joint --** Married taxpayers are treated to wider tax brackets if they choose to file married-joint. This election generally means that any tax liability is joint and several. *Joint status may be elected by a married couple*

   A. Marital status is determined on the last day of the year, or the last day the taxpayer is alive.

   B. A spouse can avoid joint liability when income is omitted from a joint return if the spouse qualifies as an "innocent" spouse (the spouse has no reason to know of an omission from income and the error can be attributed to the other spouse).

II. **Married Filing Separate --** *Others, who are married, must file as married-separate.*

   A. Married filing separately requires that the spouses divide income and expenses (according to ownership).

III. **Surviving Spouse --** Taxpayers, who are not married, may nonetheless qualify for a more advantageous tax rate schedule if they are a surviving spouse.

   A. *A "surviving" spouse may file married-joint for two years after the taxpayer's spouse has died.* To qualify as a surviving spouse, the taxpayer must provide more than half of the cost of maintaining the household (rent, mortgage interest, taxes, home insurance, repairs, food, utilities, etc.) for a *dependent child* (step, adopted, also).

IV. **Head of Household --** Head of Household status *represents a de facto family for certain single taxpayers.*

   A. The taxpayer must provide more than half of the cost of maintaining the household for a **qualifying child or a qualifying relative** (a non-relative living in the home for the entire tax year does not qualify). This home must be the qualifying child's or qualifying relative's principal residence for more than half of the tax year.

   B. Two exceptions to these rules:

      1. If the **qualifying child** is an unmarried child (step, adopted, and grandchild also), the child need not qualify as a dependent.

      2. If the **qualifying relative** is a parent, the parent need not live with the taxpayer, but the taxpayer must provide more than 50% of the cost of maintaining the parent's home.

V. **Single**

   A. Everyone who is unmarried and does not qualify for surviving spouse or head of household must file single -- the default filing status.

   B. **Short Cut --** A taxpayer who resides with a dependent child is most likely to be eligible for some "special" tax treatment, such as abandoned or surviving spouse status.

VI. **Standard Deduction - Overview --** The standard deduction is an automatic deduction that reduces the taxable income of most taxpayers.

A. *Taxpayers can elect to deduct standard deduction in lieu of itemized deductions, and the amount varies by filing status.*

Filing Status	2009 Standard Deduction
MARRIED INDIVIDUALS FILING JOINT RETURNS AND SURVIVING SPOUSES (section 1(a))	$11,400
HEADS OF HOUSEHOLDS (section 1(b))	$8,350
UNMARRIED INDIVIDUALS (OTHER THAN SURVIVING SPOUSES AND HEADS OF HOUSEHOLDS) (section 1(c))	$5,700
MARRIED INDIVIDUALS FILING SEPARATE RETURNS (section 1(d))	$5,700

1. **Short Cut --** To determine most amounts (limits, cutoffs, etc.,) for a taxpayer filing married-separately, divide the amount for married-joint in half.

B. *Special adjustments are made to the standard deduction in two instances.*

1. Taxpayer (or spouse if filing-joint) is blind at year end or reaches age 65.
   - **a.** In this instance, the standard deduction determined above is increased by $1,100 if the taxpayer who is blind or at least age is 65 is married or is a surviving spouse. Otherwise, the amount of the additional standard deduction is $1,400. Note, that if a taxpayer is 65 and blind, she would receive two additional standard deductions.
   - **b.** For 2008 and 2009, the standard deduction is also increased by the real property tax deduction, which is the lesser of:
     - **i.** the amount that qualifies as state and local real property taxes per the itemized deduction rules, or
     - **ii.** $500, or $1,000 for a joint return.
   - **c.** These additions do not apply to dependents.
   - **d.** For 2009, the standard deduction is increased by the sales and excise taxes paid on the first $49,500 of the purchase price for new vehicles. See the discussion under "Taxes" in the *Itemized Deductions* lesson for more details.

Study Tip:
For most tax items that vary based on filing status, married taxpayers receive higher amounts than single taxpayers. However, this is not the case for the additional standard deduction.

VII. Special Rules for Dependents on Another Return -- *A taxpayer claimed as a dependent by another is entitled to a "mini" standard deduction and no personal exemption.*

A. The "mini" standard deduction is $950 (2009).

1. A dependent can "earn" a regular standard deduction by earning income. The amount of the standard deduction is the greater of the mini standard deduction or earned income plus $300 (2009) (limited to the regular standard deduction).

Example:
TP is claimed as a dependent on her parent's return. This year TP received interest of $1,200 and wages of $2,200. TP is eligible for a standard deduction of $2,500, $2,200 + $300 (2009).

Definition:
Earned Income: is income generated by personal services (wages, self-employment income, etc.,) as opposed to income generated by property (interest, dividends, etc.,).

VIII. Kiddie Tax -- The so-called kiddie tax is designed to discourage taxpayers from giving income-generating property to children in order to have the income taxed at the child's low tax rates.

A. The kiddie tax includes all children who are under 18 and children between 19 and 23 who are full-time students. However, children between 18 and 23 are included only if their earned income does not exceed 50% of their total support for the year.

1. Taxable income for the child is divided into net unearned income and other income.
2. Net unearned income is taxed at the parent's tax rate, while other income is taxed at child's tax rate.

B. *Net unearned income is computed by reducing unearned income.*

1. Taxpayers who don't itemize subtract $1,900 from unearned income (2009).
2. Taxpayers who itemize subtract $950 plus itemized deductions allocated to unearned income (2009).

Examples:	**One**	**Two**	**Three**
Unearned Income	$1,950	$500	$3,000
Earned Income	250	800	5,500
	2,200	1,300	8,500
Standard Deduction	(950)	(1,100)	(5,700)
Personal Exemption	0	0	0
Taxable Income	$1,250	$ 200	$2,800
	=====	=====	=====
Taxed at Parent's Rate	$ 50	$ 0	$1,100
(Unearned Income > $1,900)			
Taxed at Child's Rate	$1,200	$ 200	$1,700

Additional Taxes

There are two additional taxes that "piggyback" onto the federal income tax: the self employment tax (SE) and the alternative minimum tax (AMT). The SE tax is levied on self employment income because this income is not subject to the social security (OASDI) tax. The AMT is imposed if the income tax computed under regular rules is insufficient compared to the taxpayer's level of economic income.

I. **Self-Employment Tax** -- The SE tax and the social security tax (OASDI) operate in tandem. Each tax consists of two parts, a retirement rate and a health insurance rate. The retirement rate is capped by a maximum amount of wages and income subject to the tax. If the tax is imposed on wages exceeding the maximum (for example, the taxpayer changed jobs), then the excess tax can be claimed as a refund.

A. *The SE tax consists of two parts imposed at twice the OASDI tax rate.*

1. The first part of the SE rate is 12.4% on the first $106,800 (2009) of SE income (the ceiling).
2. If wages are earned in addition to SE income, then the ceiling is reduced by the wages subject to OASDI.
3. The second part of the SE rate is 2.9% on all SE income (no ceiling).

Example:
TP earned $20,900 in wages and $100,000 in self-employment income. While all $120,900 is subject to the 2.9% tax, only $85,900 (2009) of the SE income is subject to the 12.4% tax ($20,900 has already been subjected to FICA).

B. *The SE tax is imposed on income from self-employment.*

1. Self-employment income is gross income from self-employment less deductions associated with the activity. SE income includes director's fees.
2. Self-employment income must exceed $400 for application of the SE tax.
3. The last step in calculating the tax is to multiply self employment income by 92.35%.
4. **Reminder:** One-half of the SE tax is deductible "for" AGI.

Study Tip:
The deductible business expenses incurred by self-employed taxpayers are deductible for "AGI".

Example:
TP is a self-employed cash-basis taxpayer who recorded the following this year:

Receipts	$45,000
Dividends (investments)	300
Cost of sales	22,000
Other operating expenses	4,500
State business taxes	950
Federal self-employment tax	1,400

Question: What is TP's net earnings from self-employment?

Answer: $17,550 is SE earnings (the dividends are not earned and the self-employment tax is not deductible in calculating net earnings).

Example:
TP is a cash-basis self-employed repairman with gross receipts of $20,000 this year. TP paid the following this year:

Repair parts	$2,500
Listing in Yellow Pages	2,000
Estimated federal income taxes	1,000
Business long-distance phone calls	400
Charitable contributions	200

Question: What is TP's net self-employment income?

Answer: $15,100 ($20,000 - $2,500 - $2,000 - $400). Note that the charitable contributions are deducted on Schedule A.

Example:
TP, a retired corporate executive, earned consulting fees of $9,000 and director's fees of $4,000 this year.

Question: What is TP's gross income from self-employment this year?

Answer: $13,000

C. Nanny Tax -- Taxpayers, who employ domestic workers, must withhold and pay FICA if cash wages exceeds $1,700 (2009).

II. Alternative Minimum Tax

A. The alternative minimum tax is a separate tax system that calculates a broader tax base by modifying taxable income for both individuals and corporations. These modifications generally serve to increase taxable income by adding items of income not recognized by the regular tax and disallowing deductions that do not necessarily represent economic outlays. The AMT only applies to taxpayers whose net regular liability is less than the "tentative" tax calculated under the broad AMT rules. This outline covers the individual AMT.

Formula for computing the AMT is as follows:

	Regular taxable income
+/-	Adjustments
+	Preferences
	AMT Income
-	Exemption
	AMT Base
x	Rate
	Tentative Minimum Tax before Foreign Tax Credit
-	Certain credit (see discussion below)
	Tentative Minimum Tax
-	Regular Tax Liability
	AMT (if positive)
	================

B. Adjustments -- AMT adjustments are specific adjustments that can either increase or decrease taxable income when computing alternative minimum taxable income. These adjustments often represent income or deductions used to defer the taxation of economic income. Hence, many (but not all) of these adjustments are merely timing differences that will reverse in future periods.

1. The AMT adjustment applies only to MACRS 3-, 5-, 7-, and 10-year property that is depreciated using the 200 percent declining balance method. For AMT, the 150% declining-balance method is used over the MACRS life.
   - Note that no AMT adjustments are required for assets purchased in 2008 that use bonus depreciation. For more information on bonus depreciation see Lesson 9 Business Deductions.
2. Percentage of completion contract income over completed contract income.
3. For itemized deductions:
   a. The phase-out of itemized deductions is subtracted from taxable income (i.e., phase-out does not apply for AMT).
   b. Medical deduction is allowed only to extent it exceeds 10% of AGI.
   c. No deduction is allowed for taxes (so must be added back to taxable income).

Study Tip:
Problems focusing on the accelerated portion of cost recovery will likely give the total amounts for the regular tax and the AMT. You will use this information to compute the AMT adjustment for depreciation.

Note:
Misconception: There is no difference between AMT cost recovery and regular cost recovery for real property. Different methods are required only for personalty.

d. 2% miscellaneous deductions are not allowed.

4. Personal exemptions and the standard deduction (if used) are added back.

5. The compensation element on the exercise date for an incentive stock option.

C. **Preferences --** Preferences always increase AMT income. The most common preference items for individuals are:

1. Tax-exempt interest on private activity bonds has been a preference items for many years, but a few recent exceptions have been enacted. For bonds issued after July 30, 2008, the interest on tax exempt housing bonds is not treated as a preference item if the bonds are for low-income housing developments, are mortgage bonds, or are mortgage bonds for veterans.

   - For any private activity bonds issued in 2009 and 2010, the interest earned from these bonds will NOT be include in AMT income.

2. Percentage depletion in excess of cost basis on certain mineral properties.

3. Gain on the sale of qualified small business stock.

D. *AMT exemption* -- Taxpayers are entitled to an AMT exemption of *$70,950 if married filing joint ($46,700 for others)* in 2009.

1. The exemption is subject to a phase-out triggered by AMTI over $150,000 (married, $112,500 for others).

2. The phase-out rate is 25% of the amount of AMTI over the trigger.

3. For children subject to the kiddie tax, the AMT exemption cannot exceed the sum of the child's earned income plus $6,700 (in 2009).

Example:
With a married taxpayer with AMTI of $346,000, the phase-out is triggered because AMTI exceeds the $150,000 trigger. This taxpayer is $196,000 over the trigger which means that $49,000 of the exemption will be lost ($196,000 x 25%).

4. *The* **AMT tax rate** *is 26% up to $175,000 and 28% over $175,000.*

E. **Tax Credits**

1. The foreign tax credit is allowed for the AMT, as are the adoption credit, child tax credit, residential energy efficient property credit, and the saver's credit. The right to offset the AMT with these credits is a permanent provision, in contrast with the next rule below.

2. For 2009, other nonrefundable personal credits may also offset the AMT, as well as the regular tax. This means that all personal credits, in addition to refundable credits such as the adoption credit, child tax credit, and saver's credit, may be used to reduce AMT. Examples include the child and dependent care credit, credit for higher education expenses, and energy credits.

   a. For 2010, these nonrefundable credits will not reduce the AMT unless Congress takes action to extend this provision to 2010.

   b. Recent legislation has included the alternative motor vehicle credit as a reduction to the AMT beginning in 2009.

3. The preferential rates on capital gains are available for a net capital gain when calculating the AMT tentative tax.

4. Taxpayers pay the greater of the AMT tentative tax or regular tax (before credits).

5. The amount of AMT paid, that is due to timing differences between regular taxable income and AMTI, creates an *AMT credit* that can be used to offset regular tax liability (but not below the tentative minimum tax for a given year) in future years. The AMT credit can be carried forward indefinitely.

F. Refundable Credit -- The AMT credit may be used to generate a limited refund, even if the AMT liability for the year does not exceed the regular tax liability.

- The AMT refundable credit is the greater of:

a. The amount of the AMT refundable credit for the preceding tax year, or

b. 50% of the long-term unused minimum tax credit.

- The long-term unused minimum tax credit for a tax year is the regular AMT credit carryforward reduced by any minimum tax credit for the three immediately preceding tax years.
- Note, that the regular minimum tax credit is still nonrefundable.

Other Income Tax Issues

Personal and Business Tax Credits

Tax credits offset a tax liability on a one-for-one basis. Credits can be triggered by many different types of actions.

<u>Tax Credit Categories</u>

Personal Credits:

Child Tax Credit

Saver's (IRA) Credit

Education Tax Credits

Dependent Care

Adoption Expense Credit

Elderly Credit

Alternative Motor Vehicle Credit

Alternative Fuel Vehicle Refueling Property Credit

Qualified Plug-In Electric Drive Motor Vehicles Credit

Personal Energy Tax Credit

Residential Energy Efficient Property Credit

Foreign Tax Credit

General Business Credits:

Research and Development

Rehabilitation

Miscellaneous

Refundable Credits:

Earned Income

Child Credit

Health Coverage Tax Credit

First-time Homebuyers

I. **Order of Credits --** Credits are applied against the tax liability in a predetermined order.

A. *The order of applying credits against tax is determined by the nature of the credit:*

1. Personal credits (except for the foreign tax credit) are limited to gross tax, and there is no carryover of any excess.
2. The general business credit is limited to a percentage of gross tax after personal credits, and any excess carries over (back 1 year and forward 20 years).

Study Tip:
Credits reduce "regular" tax regardless of the tentative tax imposed under the alternative minimum tax.

3. Refundable credits (earned income and withholding; child credit) are applied last because these credits have no limit based upon tax (any excess, or a portion of the excess, is refunded to the taxpayer).

B. **AMT** -- See Lesson *Additional Taxes* for discussion of credits for the AMT.

II. **Personal Credits** -- Personal credits are allowed for a number of activities deemed socially desirable.

A. **Child Credit** -- *A $1,000 Child Credit is allowed for each* **qualifying child (as defined under the dependency rules)** *under the age of 17.*

1. Qualifying children include a dependent son, daughter, stepchild, or grandchild whose name and social security number is included on the return.

2. The credit is phased out for married taxpayers with AGI in excess of $110,000 ($75,000 for unmarried). The credit is reduced $50 for each $1,000 (or portion) over the trigger AGI amount.

Example:
TP is married (filing joint) with two dependent children under the age of 17. This year TP has AGI of $123,500. TP will be able to claim a credit of $1,300 because TP's gross credit of $2,000 is reduced by $700 (14 x $50).

3. The child tax credit is refundable to the extent of 15% of the taxpayer's earned income in excess of $3,000 (for 2009 and 2010). Combat pay is treated as earned income for purposes of computing this refundable credit, even though combat pay is not taxable.

III. **Education Credits**

A. *A* **"Hope" Credit** *is allowed up to a maximum of $2,500 (2009) per year for each eligible student.* This credit has been renamed as the American Opportunity Tax Credit for 2009 and 2010 but is referred to as the Hope Credit in this discussion.

1. The credit is computed as 100% of the first $2,000 and 25% of the next $2,000 of qualified educational expenses.

2. Qualified educational expenses are nondeductible tuition and academic fees (reduced by tax-free benefits, such as scholarships) incurred during a student's first four years of post-secondary education. The expenses must relate to an academic period beginning in the current tax year, or the first three months of the next tax year. Course materials are also included.

3. A qualifying student includes the taxpayer, spouse, or any dependent of the taxpayer enrolled at least half time in an institution of higher education. To be eligible, the student must be enrolled in a degree program.

4. The credit is phased out ratably for married taxpayers with AGI in excess of $80,000 ($160,000 in the case of a joint return) (2009). The credit is phased out over a $20,000 range ($10,000 for unmarried) and, thus, is completely gone when AGI reaches $90,000 ($180,000 unmarried joint return) (2009).

5. The credit can be claimed against the AMT and 40% of the credit is refundable.

B. *A* **"Lifetime Learning Credit"** *is allowed up to a maximum of $2,000 per taxpayer per year.*

1. The credit is computed as 20% of $10,000 of qualified educational expenses incurred for the taxpayer, spouse, or dependent.

2. Qualified educational expenses are nondeductible tuition and academic fees (reduced by tax-free benefits, such as scholarships) incurred by a taxpayer. The expenses must be for post-secondary education, but need not relate to a degree program. Student does not need to be at least half-time for expenses to qualify.

3. Like the Hope credit, the lifetime learning credit is phased out ratably for married taxpayers with AGI in excess of $50,000 ($100,000 in the case of a joint return) and is phased out over a $10,000 range ($20,000 for married joint).

4. The Hope credit, the lifetime learning credit, and distributions from educational IRAs are mutually exclusive in that an educational expenditure can never simultaneously qualify for more than one benefit (e.g., no double or triple "dipping").

Example:
TP spent $3,000 in tuition for his first year in post-secondary education. He was reimbursed $500 through a tax-exempt scholarship, and he recorded AGI of $20,000. TP can use the unreimbursed tuition of $2,500 to claim a $2,125 Hope credit (100% of $2,000 and 25% of $500).

a. **Shortcut** -- The two credits differ in the percentage applied to calculating the credit (100% and 25% for the Hope versus 20% for the lifetime), the total expenses eligible for the credit ($4,000 per year for the Hope versus $5,000 total for the lifetime), and the type of expenses covered by the credit (first four years of post-secondary education in a degree program for the Hope versus any post-secondary education for the lifetime). The Hope applies per student ($2,500 per student), whereas the Lifetime Learning Credit applies per tax return (maximum $2,000 credit per year).

C. *A **"Saver's Credit"** is allowed for voluntary contributions to IRA and qualified retirement accounts.*

1. The credit is a maximum of $1,000 (in addition to any exclusion or deduction that would otherwise apply) and is based upon IRA contributions (Roth or traditional).

2. The taxpayer must be 18 or older, not a full-time student, or claimed as a dependent on another return, and cannot receive a distribution from the account.

3. No credit is allowed for taxpayers with AGI in excess of $55,500 ($41,625 for head of household and $27,750 for single taxpayers).

4. Taxpayers with AGI below $33,000 ($24,750 for head of household and $16,500 for single taxpayers) receive a credit of 50% of IRA contributions. If AGI is over $33,000 but not over $36,000, the credit percentage is 20%. If AGI is over $36,000 but not over $55,500, the credit percentage is 10%. If AGI is over $55,500 no credit is allowed. Head of household is 75% of these amounts, and individuals are 50% of these amounts.

Example:
TP is married (filing joint) and has AGI of $23,500. If TP contributes $2,000 to an IRA, TP will be able to claim a credit of $1,000 (2009) because TP's AGI is below $30,000. This credit is in addition to a $2,000 IRA deduction.

Example:
TP is single and has AGI of $12,000. If TP contributes $3,000 to a Roth IRA, TP will be able to claim a credit of $1,000 (2009) because TP's AGI is below $15,000

IV. Dependent Care Credit -- The dependent care credit is designed to provide a tax credit for a portion of the expenses incurred for care-giving while the taxpayer is employed.

A. *To be eligible for the credit, a person needing care must live with the taxpayer for more than half the year.*

1. A qualifying child or dependent under the age of 13 automatically qualifies (the child can violate the gross income test and still qualify for care).

2. Other dependents or a spouse will also qualify if they are incapable of self-care (physical or mental disability). This individual must live in the same household as the taxpayer for more than half of the tax year.

B. *Expenditures for household services and care are required for the credit.*

1. Care can be given within the home, but the care-giver cannot be a dependent relative or child of the taxpayer.

2. The taxpayer must be employed and earn at least as much as the amount of the expenses. If married, then the taxpayer must file joint (unless abandoned) and the spouse must also be employed.

3. Income is imputed to a spouse incapable of self-care or a full-time student.

4. Other rules include:

- Expenses for a child below kindergarten qualify; expenses for before or after school care of a child in kindergarten or higher grade may qualify.
- Full amount paid for day camp or similar programs, even if the program specializes in a particular activity.
- Summer school and tutoring programs are education and do not qualify.
- Sick child centers may qualify for either the credit or a medical expense, but not as both.
- For boarding school, amounts paid for food, lodging, clothing, and education must be separated from amounts paid for other goods or services.
- Additional cost of providing room and board for a caregiver may qualify if expenses are in addition to normal household expenses.
- Cost of overnight expense does NOT qualify.

C. *The credit is calculated by multiplying the qualifying expenditures by the appropriate credit percentage.*

1. The credit percentage begins at 35% if AGI is less than $15,000, and is reduced by 1% for each $2,000 increment (or part) in AGI above $15,000. The minimum dependent care credit is 20%.

a. Short Cut -- Taxpayers with AGI over $43,000 will receive the minimum dependent care credit of 20%.

2. The maximum amount of expense eligible for the credit is $3,000 ($6,000 if more than one individual qualifies for care) or earned income (of the lesser-earning spouse if married).

Example: TP is a single parent with a 10-year-old child at home. This year TP earned $8,000 and paid $2,000 for the care of the child while TP worked. TP qualifies for a dependent care credit of $750 ($2,000*35%).

Example: TP is a self-employed taxpayer who pays $3,000 for the after-school care of her dependent 9-year-old child. TP has an AGI of $86,000.

Question: What amount of the expenses is eligible for the child care credit?

Answer: For one dependent, the maximum eligible amount is $3,000 or earned income. The credit percentage in this case would be 20%.

V. Adoption Credit -- Many credits are designed to provide tax relief for individuals with special needs.

A. *The adoption credit is allowed for adoption expenses.*

1. Reasonable expenses up to $12,150 (2009) associated with an adoption qualify for the credit.
2. A $12,150 (2009) adoption credit is available for children with special needs regardless of actual expenses.
3. The credit is phased out for taxpayers with AGI in excess of $182,180, and is completely phased out for taxpayers with modified adjusted gross income of $222,180.
4. The credit is limited to regular tax, but any excess credit carries forward for five years.

VI. The Elderly Credit -- *The Elderly Credit is 15% of difference between an initial (flat) amount and income.*

A. The taxpayer or spouse must be age 65 or totally disabled.

B. The flat amount is $5,000 if one spouse is eligible, or $7,500 for two.

C. Income is certain retirement pay plus one-half of AGI over $7,500 ($10,000 if joint).

Example: TP, age 50, is totally and permanently disabled. This year he received social security benefits of $2,000 and had AGI of $2,500.

Question: Is TP eligible for the elderly credit?

Answer: Yes, taxpayers over age 65, and those who are totally and permanently disabled, are eligible. TP's AGI is low enough to trigger the credit.

VII. Motor Vehicle Credits

A. Alternative Motor Vehicle Credit

1. An income tax credit is available for "alternative motor vehicles." The alternative motor vehicles, to which this credit applies, are "qualified fuel cell motor vehicles," "advanced lean-burn technology motor vehicles," "qualified hybrid motor vehicles," and "qualified alternative fuel motor vehicles." The credit is computed differently for each type of vehicle.
2. As part of the alternative motor vehicle credit, for purchases after February 17, 2009 and before 2012, a plug-in conversion credit is added that is 10% of the cost of the vehicle (up to a maximum cost of $40,000). This credit is for plug-in electric drive motor vehicles.
3. The alternative motor vehicle credit is also allowed against the AMT.

B. Credit for New Qualified Plug-in Electric Drive Motor Vehicles.

1. A credit (credit #1) is also allowed for purchases of **new** qualified plug-in electric drive motor vehicles. For 2009, the credit is $2,500 plus an amount based on the capacity of the battery. The credit is limited to $7,500 for most passenger cars and trucks, but can go as high as $15,000 for large commercial vehicles. After 2009 the credit is limited to $5,000 for most passenger cars and trucks, but can go as high as $7,500 for large commercial vehicles. This credit phases out based on the number of vehicles sold during the year.
2. After February 17, 2009 a credit (credit #2) is allowed for purchases of **new** qualified plug-in electric drive vehicles that are low-speed vehicles or that have two or three wheels. The credit is 10% of the cost and is limited to $2,500. This credit is not allowed if credit #1 has already been claimed. That is, credit #1 and credit #2 cannot both be claimed for the same vehicle.

VIII. Personal (Nonbusiness) Energy Tax Credit -- For 2009, this credit is 30% of the amount spent for energy efficiency improvements to one's personal residence including windows, each advanced main air circulating fan, qualifying furnaces or boilers, energy efficient heat pumps, water heaters, and central air conditioners. The total credit for 2009 and 2010 cannot exceed $1,500 and it can also offset the AMT.

IX. Residential Energy Efficient Property Credit

A. Individual taxpayers can take a credit for 30% of the cost for residential energy efficient property (REEP), including qualified solar electric property, qualified solar water heating property, qualified fuel cell property (limited to $500 for each .5 kilowatt of capacity), qualified small wind energy property, and qualified geothermal heat pump property.

B. Note, that for 2009, the $2,000 maximum credit no longer applies for qualified solar electric property, qualified solar water heating, geothermal heat pump, and small wind energy property.

C. The REEP credit is also allowed against the AMT.

X. Foreign Tax Credit -- The US taxes income from all sources, including income from foreign countries. The purpose of this credit is to prevent double taxation of foreign income that is subject to income tax in the foreign jurisdiction. Note that the scope of the CPA exam specifically excludes questions about the application of state, local, or foreign taxes.

A. *The credit is limited to the foreign tax paid, or the proportion of U.S. tax allocable to U.S. income.*

1. The proportion of U.S. tax allocable to U.S. income is determined by multiplying U.S. tax times the ratio of foreign taxable income to total taxable income.

Example:
TP records 20% of his income from abroad. TP can claim a foreign tax credit in the amount of the lesser of his foreign tax paid or 20% of the US tax on global income.

2. Excess foreign tax credits carry over -- back 2 years and forward 5 years.

B. *In lieu of a credit, a taxpayer can elect to mitigate foreign taxes in two other ways.*

1. Taxpayers can claim the foreign tax as an itemized deduction.
2. Taxpayers can elect to exclude income earned (in excess of housing costs) while a bona fide resident in a foreign country. The exclusion is a maximum of $85,700 if the taxpayer is physically present in the foreign country for 330 days in any 12 consecutive months.

Example:
TP earned $83,000 from working 340 days in France. TP can exclude $79,830 (340/365 x $85,700) because he was in residence more than 330 days.

XI. Earned Income Credit -- The earned income credit is a complex method of mitigating employment taxes for low income taxpayers. This is a refundable credit.

A. *The credit is generated by earning income.*

1. The credit percentage increases if the taxpayer maintains a home with qualifying children (descendents under age 19, or students under age 24, or permanently disabled).
2. The credit is phased out based on earned income or AGI (if greater) exceeding a threshold that also depends upon the number of qualifying children.
3. The credit is disallowed if disqualified income, such as interest, dividends, tax exempt interest and other investment income exceeds $3,100 (2009).

B. *Taxpayers between the ages of 25 through 64 without qualifying children are also eligible if they are not claimed as a dependent on another's return.*

C. Combat pay is included as earned income for purposes of this credit.

XII. First-time Homebuyers Credit

A. For purchases after April 8, 2008, the amount of the credit is the lesser of $7,500 or 10% of the home's purchase price. For purchases after 2008 and before December 1, 2009 the maximum credit is increased to $8,000. Additionally, for purchases in 2009 the taxpayer can elect to treat the purchase as if made on December 31, 2008 so the taxpayer can benefit from the credit in 2008.

B. The credit is phased out between modified AGI of $75,000 and $95,000 ($150,000 and $170,000 if joint return).

C. For purchases after April 8, 2008 and before 2009, the credit is unusual in that it must be recaptured over 15 years on a straight-line basis beginning in the 2nd tax year after the year in which the home is purchased. If sold during the 15 year period, the unrecaptured credit must be added to the tax liability. No recapture is required if the taxpayer dies. Since no interest is charged over the 15 years, the credit is essentially an interest free loan.

D. For purchases after 2008 and before December 1, 2009, the recapture rule does not apply. Thus, for these purchases the credit is actual financial support to encourage home purchases. A recapture rule does apply, requiring the repayment of the entire credit, if the home is sold or ceases to be used as a principal residence during the 36 months beginning with the purchase of the home.

E. To qualify as a first-time homebuyer, the taxpayer cannot have had an interest in a principal residence for the three years before the purchase date.

F. The credit also offsets the AMT.

XIII. **Health Coverage Tax Credit --** Refundable tax credit for unemployed workers who have lost their jobs due to shifting of production to foreign countries (and certain other eligible taxpayers) based on the amount a taxpayer pays for qualified health insurance. The credit had been 65% of the insurance costs but increased to 80% as of May 1, 2009.

- Additionally, for workers terminated between September 1, 2008 and December 31, 2009, the government will provide a subsidy of 65% of COBRA health coverage continuation payments for up to nine months. Taxpayers with modified AGI greater than $125,000 ($250,000 for families) will not benefit from this provision. Note that the 65% is actually paid by the employer and then reimbursed by the government.

XIV. **Marking Work Pay Credit --** This credit allows a credit equal to the lower of 6.2% of earned income or $400 ($800 for a joint return). The credit is refundable but is phased out at higher income levels. The credit applies for 2009 and 2010 only and is implemented by reducing withholding from an employee's pay.

XV. **General Business Credits --** The **General Business Credit** consists of a combination of credits designed to subsidize certain activities. While each credit is calculated independently, the combination of credits is subject to an overall limit.

A. *The overall credit is limited to "net regular" tax.*

1. **Definition:** The net regular tax liability is the regular tax less personal credits.
2. The limit is net regular liability less 25% of net regular liability over $25,000.

B. *The upshot of the credit is that the business credit cannot offset all of the regular tax if the liability exceeds $25,000.*

1. Unused credits are carried back one year and then forward 20 years.
2. Credits cannot reduce the regular liability below the "tentative" tax required to be paid under the alternative minimum tax.

Example:
TP has a net regular tax liability of $125,000 this year. TP has a general business tax credit of $70,000 and no other credits.

Question: What amount of general business tax credit is TP eligible to claim?

Answer: The maximum credit TP could claim would be $100,000 [$125 - ($125-25)x.25]. Since he has a credit of only $70,000, he can claim the entire credit.

Question: What if TP also had a tentative minimum tax liability of $105,000?

Answer: If his tentative tax was $105,000, he could only reduce his regular tax liability to the tentative tax by claiming a maximum credit of $20,000.

XVI. The Rehabilitation Credit -- is typical of the credits available under the general business credit. There are a number of other credits that are available for specific activities. Each credit has unique requirements and limits, but the rehabilitation credit is a good example.

- **A.** *The rehabilitation credit percentage depends upon the type of expenditure.*
  1. Expenditures to rehabilitate property placed in service before 1936 are eligible for a 10% credit.
  2. Expenditures to rehabilitate certified historic structure are eligible for a 20% credit.
- **B.** *Qualifying expenditures are often used to adjust basis, and may be subject to recapture.*
  1. The adjusted basis of the property is reduced by the amount of credit.
  2. Rehabilitation credit is recaptured if the building is held less than five years (the recapture rate is 20% per year).

XVII. Miscellaneous Credits -- *There are many types of business credits designed to subsidize specific activities.*

- **A.** The cost of operating employee child care facilities generates a 25% credit for employers up to $150,000 per year.
- **B.** Incremental research expenditures are eligible for a 20% credit. The research must be conducted within the U.S. and does not apply to research for commercial production, surveys, or social science research.
  - Taxpayers may elect to use an alternative simplified research credit. This is equal to 12% (14% in 2009) of the excess of qualified research expenses over 50% of the average research expenses for the last three years.
- **C.** Energy credits are granted for certain solar and geothermal property at a rate of 10%-30% of qualified expenditures. Credits are also allowed for facilities using marine and hydrokinetic renewable energy or wind to produce electricity, as well as biomass, landfill gas, trash, and hydropower.

D. Contractors may claim a credit for each new efficient home, which is used as a residence after sale. The credit is either $1,000 of $2,000 depending on the reduction in energy usage (30% or 50%).

E. Welfare to work credits are calculated on the amount of wages paid per eligible employee during the first two years of employment. The maximum credit is $2,400 per employee.

F. Other credits include credits for disabled access, low-income housing, enhanced oil recovery, orphan drugs, employer provided child care, and alcohol fuel.

Taxpayer Responsibilities

Taxpayers have two important responsibilities: file accurate tax returns and remit an appropriate amount of taxes during the tax year. Controversies about whether a taxpayer has met their responsibilities are restricted to those during a recent time period by the statute of limitations.

I. **Filing Requirements --** All taxpayers who have income in excess of a predetermined limit must file an income tax return.

A. *An individual, whose "gross income" exceeds the individual's automatic deductions, must generally file a tax return.*

1. Automatic deductions include the personal exemption, the standard deduction, and the increment to the standard deduction for taxpayers who are over age 65.
2. Taxpayers must also file a return if net self-employment income exceeds $400 during the tax year.

> **Note:**
> **Misconception:** The filing requirement includes the standard deduction and the increment for age 65, but does not include the increment to the standard deduction for blind taxpayers.

II. **Filing Deadlines --** *The due date for individual returns is the 15th day of 4th month (April 15, generally).*

A. If the due date falls on a weekend or holiday, then the return is due the next business day.

B. An automatic six-month filing extension (generally October 15) is granted to individuals upon application and payment of any estimated tax.

C. Corporations are entitled to an automatic six-month extension, as trusts. Partnerships can receive a five-month extension for filing. In all cases, the estimated tax due must be paid with the application for the extension.

> **Note:**
> **Misconception:** The due date for corporate returns is the 15th day of the 3rd month following the close of the tax year. Like individuals, partnerships and trusts must file returns on the 15th day of the 4th month.

III. **Penalties are imposed on taxpayers under four circumstances. --** First, a penalty is imposed if the taxpayer fails to file a required tax return. Second, a penalty is imposed if the taxpayer fails to make adequate tax payments during the year (underpayment). Third, a penalty if imposed if the taxpayer fails to pay the tax reflected on the tax return (delinquency). Finally, a penalty is imposed if the taxpayer files an inaccurate tax return.

A. **Nonfiling Penalty --** *A nonfiling penalty is imposed on taxpayers (who must file a return) if the return is not filed by the due date.*

1. The penalty for late filing is 5% per month of the tax due with the return.
2. The maximum penalty is 25% of the tax due, and the minimum penalty is the lesser of $100 ($135 beginning in 2009) or the amount of the tax due.
3. If the failure to file is fraudulent (intentional), the penalty is increased to 15% per month up to a maximum of 75% of the tax due with the return.

> **Note:**
> **Misconception:** No penalty is imposed if no tax is due with the return, or the taxpayer is eligible for a refund.

B. **Underpayment Penalty --** *An underpayment penalty is imposed for failure to remit taxes during the year.*

> **Definition:**
> *A Tax Underpayment*: is the difference between the tax due and the amount of tax paid on or before the filing of the return plus credits.

C. Required Tax Payments for Individuals

1. Taxes are remitted during the year through withholding or, if withholding is insufficient, through estimated tax payments. Taxpayers must make estimated payments (on the 15th of April, June, September, and January) if the amount of tax owed is at least $1,000 after subtracting withholding and credits.
2. No penalty is imposed if the tax due with the return is less than $1,000.
3. No penalty is imposed if the tax payments during the year were at least 90% of current year taxes or 100% of last year's taxes. If the taxpayer's AGI exceeds $150,000, then tax payments during the year must be at least 110% of last year's taxes.
4. For 2009 only the 100% of last year's taxes requirement is reduced to 90% for individuals (and estates and trusts) with AGI less than $500,000 for the preceding tax year if at least 50% of the gross income is derived from a small trade or business.

D. Required Corporate Tax Payments

1. Estimated tax payments are due (if annual tax payments are at least $500) on 4/15, 6/15, 9/15, and 12/15 for a calendar year corporation.
2. There is no estimated tax underpayment penalty if the payments are at least equal to the lower of:
   a. 100% of current year's tax, or
   b. 100% of the preceding year's tax.
   c. The penalty can also be avoided if the annualization exception is met. For this exception the actual income for each quarter is computed, and then each estimated tax payment is based on that income computation.
3. A corporation with $1 million or more of taxable income in any of its three preceding tax years can use the preceding year's tax exception only for its first installment. The other installments must be based on the current year's tax to avoid penalty.

Example:
TP remitted $8,000 in withholding this year, but his total income tax is $10,000. Hence, $2,000 is due with TP's return. TP will be subject to an underpayment penalty unless his total income tax paid in the preceding year was at least $8,000 (if his AGI was less than $150,000).

E. Interest *and* Delinquency *Penalties are imposed if the taxes shown on the return are not paid on the filing date.*

1. Interest on late payments starts on the due date for filing and is calculated using Federal short-term interest rate.
2. Any tax due must be paid at the time of filing, or else a penalty of 0.5% of the underpayment is imposed per month (up to 25% in total).

Example:
TP paid a tax of $1,000 twenty-five days after filing his return. In addition to interest on the underpayment, TP owes $5 ($1,000 *.005) as a delinquency penalty.

3. If both the delinquency penalty and the non-filing penalty are imposed, the maximum penalty is limited to 25% of the tax due.
4. Neither the nonfiling nor the delinquency penalties are imposed if the taxpayer has a reasonable cause for failing to file or failing to pay.

Definition:
Reasonable Cause: is a cause outside the control of the taxpayer and not due to neglect, such as irregularities in mail delivery, death or serious illness, unavoidable absence, or disaster. A taxpayer, generally, has the burden of proving that a failure was due to reasonable cause.

Example:
The taxpayer failed to file a timely return and pay taxes because his records were destroyed in a fire. This excuses both penalties, but not the interest on the underpayment.

F. **Accuracy Penalties --** *Additional penalties may be imposed if the taxpayer underpays the actual tax because of an "inaccurate" position taken on a tax return.*

Definition:
An Inaccurate Position: occurs when a taxpayer disregards the tax rules without reasonable cause.

1. A penalty of 20% of the tax due to the inaccuracy is imposed if the inaccurate position is due to negligence. The penalty is waived if the taxpayer had a reasonable basis for the position taken.

Definition:
Negligence: is an intentional disregard of rules and regulations without intent to defraud.

2. A penalty of 20% of the tax due to the inaccuracy is imposed if the taxpayer "substantially" understates the tax. This penalty is waived if there was substantial authority for the position taken, or if the position was adequately disclosed on the tax return. The substantial authority standard is less stringent than the "more likely than not" standard, but more stringent than the "reasonable basis" standard.

Definition:
Substantial Understatement: For individuals, a "substantial" understatement results when the additional tax due exceeds the *greater* of $5,000 or 10% of the total tax on the return. For corporations, a "substantial" understatement results when the understatement exceeds the lesser of 10% of the tax required to be shown on the return (or $10,000 if that is greater) or $10 million.

3. A penalty is imposed if there is a "substantial" or "gross" overstatement of the value or basis of any property. The penalty is 20 percent of the tax understatement for a substantial misvaluation and 40 percent for a gross misvaluation.

> **Definition:**
> *A Substantial Misvaluation*: occurs if the property is stated at 150 percent or more of the correct amount. A "gross" misvaluation occurs if the property is stated at 400 percent or more of the correct amount.

4. The penalty for fraud is 75% of underpayment and an addition of 50% of the interest due on the underpayment.

> **Definition:**
> *Fraud*: is a deliberate action by the taxpayer to conceal, misrepresent, or deceive tax authorities about a tax deficiency.

IV. The statute of limitations encourages controversies to be settled in a timely way -- The statute bars tax disputes after a period of time has elapsed from filing the return.

A. *The primary statute of limitations expires after three years from filing of the return.*

1. The statute begins to run from the due date or filing date, whichever is later.

B. *There are several exceptions to the three-year rule.*

1. The statute is extended to 6 years if 25% or more of the gross income is understated on the original tax return.
2. The statute never expires if the taxpayer commits fraud or fails to file a tax return.

C. The Statute of Limitation for filing a claim for refund (on form 1040X) is the later of:

1. Two years from the payment of tax, or
2. Three years from the date the return was filed (or April 15 if filed before the original due date).

V. Penalties may also be imposed on tax preparers. -- Note: You may want to review Section VI below before continuing to reference definitions of key terms used in this section.

- For tax returns or claims filed in 2008 or later, these penalties apply to all tax return preparers, including preparers for estate, gift, employment, excise, and exempt organization returns.

A. A tax return preparer, who prepares a return or refund claim, which includes an "unreasonable position," must pay a penalty of the greater of $1,000 or 50% of the income derived by the preparer for preparing the return. A position is unreasonable if there is not **substantial authority** for it.

1. There is an exception to this rule if the position was disclosed and there is a reasonable basis for it. However, this exception applies to reportable transactions and tax shelters only if the position has a "**more likely than not**" chance of being sustained.
2. The reasonable cause and good faith exceptions apply.

B. If the understated tax liability is due to an unreasonable position and the preparer *willfully attempts* to understate the tax liability or recklessly or intentionally disregards rules or regulations, the penalty is the greater of $5,000 or 50% of the income earned by the tax preparer for preparing the return or claim.

Definition:
Unreasonable Position: A position is unreasonable if it does not have substantial authority.

C. Additional penalties may be imposed on preparers for:

1. Not signing returns done for compensation.
2. Not providing a copy of the return for the taxpayer.
3. Not keeping a list of returns filed.
4. Endorsing or negotiating a refund check.
5. Disclosing information from a tax return, unless for quality or peer review, or under an administrative order by a regulatory agency.
6. A preparer can be fined $100 if he does not exercise due diligence in determining if a taxpayer is eligible for the earned income credit.

D. Beginning January 1, 2009 tax preparers are subject to new penalties related to "knowingly or recklessly" disclosing tax return information. If a tax preparer uses or discloses tax return information without the client's explicit, written consent, each violation could result in a fine of up to $1,000 or one year imprisonment, or both.

VI. Summary of Terminology for Penalties

A. Not frivolous = not patently improper

B. Reasonable basis = at least one authority that has not been overruled (Treas. Reg. Sec. 1.6662-3(b))

C. Substantial authority = more than a reasonable basis

D. Realistic possibility = 1 in 3 chance of success (Treas. Reg. Sec. 1.6694-2(b))

E. More likely that not = more than 50% chance of succeeding

Taxation of Corporations

Formation of a Corporation

The contribution of property and services in the formation of a corporation can be a taxable event to the contributing shareholders.

The recognition of gain or loss on a contribution of property in exchange for stock is determined by the ownership levels of the contributing shareholders.

I. Deferral -- *Deferral of gain and loss is required for members of the control club.*

> **Definition:**
> *The Control Club*: is the group of individuals, who participate in a transfer of property to a corporation, and are in control of the corporation immediately after the transfer.

A. To be eligible for membership in the control club, property must be contributed (services rendered to the corporation is not property).

B. The property must be transferred solely in exchange for stock.

> **Definition:**
> *Stock*: is any equity interest except that "nonqualified" preferred stock (NPS) is treated as boot. NPS is preferred stock that is expected to be redeemed within 20 years.

1. Immediately after the transfer, the transferor(s) are in control, and control is defined as owning at least 80 percent of the voting and nonvoting stock.
2. The receipt of "boot" triggers gain but not loss.

> **Definition:**
> *Boot*: is property received other than stock. Liabilities transferred with property are boot to the extent the liabilities exceed the adjusted basis of the property.

C. If boot is received, the gain recognized to the shareholder is the lower of:

1. realized gain, or
2. the fair market value of the boot received

D. If stock is received in exchange for services,

1. the transferor has wage income equal to the fair market value of the stock received (and basis in the stock equal to that amount),
2. the corporation has a salary expense deduction (unless the services rendered were an organizational expense).

E. Reminder: The corporation does not realize any gain or loss on issuing stock.

II. Basis Issues -- *The adjusted basis for qualifying property is a carryover basis.*

A. The corporation takes an adjusted basis in the property from the transferor plus any gain recognized by the transferor.

B. The corporation's basis in the property received is:

	Shareholder's basis in the property
+	Gain recognized by the shareholder

C. The shareholder's stock takes the adjusted basis of the transferred property plus any gain recognized less any boot received.

D. The shareholder's basis in the stock received from the corporation is:

	Basis of all property transferred to the corporation
+	Gain recognized by shareholder
-	Boot received by shareholder
-	Liabilities assumed by corporations

1. **Short Cut --** A carryover basis is the fair value of the property less the gain deferred (or plus any loss deferred). This short cut works only if the value of the property is known.

E. Debt Assumption -- A contribution of encumbered property requires that the transferor reduce the basis of the stock by the amount of debt assumed by the corporation.

F. Basis Adjustment for Loss Property

Study Tip:
It may be helpful to think about the accounting entries that the contributing shareholder and the corporation would make on the transfer of encumbered property.

1. If the total basis of the property transferred by a shareholder is greater than the fair market value of the property, a basis adjustment is required to prevent the shareholders and the corporation from both benefiting from this unrealized loss. The downward basis adjustment is allocated proportionately among all assets contributed by the shareholder that had a built-in loss.
2. Note, that if the shareholder and corporation elect, the shareholder's stock basis can be reduced rather than the corporation's assets.

Example:
As part of a corporate formation, TP contributes property with an adjusted basis of $100 and a FMV of $75. The corporation's basis in this property will be reduced to $75, and TP's stock basis will be $100. Alternatively, TP and the corporation could elect to leave the property's basis at $100 and reduce TP's stock basis to $75.

Example:
TP contributes a building worth $200,000 to a corporation in exchange for 100 percent of the corporate stock. TP has an adjusted basis of $100,000 in the building, but the property is subject to a $25,000 mortgage. The corporation takes an adjusted basis of $100,000 in the building, but TP takes an adjusted basis of $75,000 in his stock.

III. Debt Assumptions -- Gain may be recognized in two circumstances if the corporation assumes the shareholders' debt.

A. If the total liabilities assumed by the corporation exceed the total adjusted basis of property transferred by the shareholder, then gain must be recognized as follows:

Gain Recognized = Liabilities Assumed - Basis of Property Transferred

B. If the debt was not incurred by the shareholder for valid business reasons, then the corporate assumption will cause ALL of the debt relief to be treated as BOOT. This will cause gain to be recognized, but only to the extent of the realized gain.

IV. Holding Period

A. The shareholder's holding period for the stock may or may not include the amount of time he/she held the property just given to the corporation.

1. Capital asset or Section 1231 asset transferred to corporation - property holding period is tacked on to stock holding period.
2. All other property - holding period of property does not tack on. Holding period for stock begins on day after the transfer.

B. The corporation's holding period in the property received always includes the period that the transferor held the property before the exchange.

V. Special Issues for Certain Shareholders -- The capitalization of a corporation determines whether special tax provisions apply when initial shareholders sell their stock, and whether loans to a corporation can be reclassified as equity.

A. *Two special provisions govern gains or losses from the sale or worthlessness of certain small business corporation stock.*

1. Section 1244 allows shareholders to claim an ordinary loss deduction (up to $50,000, or $100,000 filing joint) on the sale of worthless "small business" stock. To qualify under this provision, the corporation must issue stock for less than $1 million and conduct an active business.
2. There is an exclusion of 50% of gain on sale of "qualified" small business stock. Qualified stock must be held for five years after the initial issuance from an active corporation with assets less than $50 million.

VI. Debt vs. Equity -- *Corporate debt can be reclassified as equity, but this is a question of fact.*

A. Debt characteristics are important (instrument, collateral, interest, etc.).

B. The corporation is not thinly capitalized (debt equity ratio too high).

Corporate Income Computation

The corporate income tax is imposed on business operations that qualify as corporations.

I. **Definition of a Corporation --** It is necessary to identify which businesses qualify as corporations in order to impose the corporate tax. For tax purposes, it is not essential that a business be formally incorporated to be taxed as a corporation, but under the tax regulations, owners have some control over the tax status of unincorporated entities.

A. *The* **"check-the-box"** *regulations permit unincorporated entities to elect to be taxed as a corporation or treated as a partnership for tax purposes.*

1. Some associations are automatically taxed as corporations and are not eligible to make an election. These "per se" corporations include business entities formed under statutes that refer to the entities as incorporated.

   a. **Short cut:** The check-the-box election is applicable to entities such as limited liability companies (LLCs), limited liability partnerships (LLPs), and partnerships. "Incorporated" entities are taxed as per se corporations.

2. Unless qualified as a "per se" corporation, single-owner firms are not eligible for corporate status under the check-the-box election.

3. For multiple-owner firms, the default classification is partnership treatment.

4. An election under the check-the-box regulations is effective for the tax year if made within the first 75 days of the year.

5. An election can be changed after 5 years or with IRS permission.

6. Subchapter S electing corporations are not subject to the corporate tax, but must pass income through to shareholders regardless of dividend distributions (more on these entities in the section on Subchapter S Corporations).

II. **Corporate Tax Formula --** The corporate tax calculation is very similar to the formula used to calculate individual taxes. Taxable income is calculated by subtracting business and special deductions from realized income.

> **Definition:**
> *C Corporation*: A corporation subject to the corporate income tax is often referred to as a "C" corporation because the rules governing the corporate tax are contained in Subchapter C of the Internal Revenue Code.

A. *The corporate formula is analogous to the individual formula.*

1. Expenses are generally deductible as business deductions (subject to the limits placed on business deductions, such as reasonable, ordinary, etc.).

2. There are four categories of special deductions subject to special limitations (analogous to itemized deductions).

3. Deductible capital losses are offset against recognized capital gains, but there is no deduction for a net capital loss. Rather, a net capital loss is carried over (back 3 years/forward 5 years) to offset against capital gains in other years.

B. *Special Rules:*

1. Corporations can choose a fiscal year unless the corporation makes an "S" election or qualifies as a "personal service" corporation.

> **Definition:**
> *A Personal Service Corporation*: is a corporation whose principal activity is the performance of personal services performed by employees who own substantially all of the stock; for example, a medical corporation whose owners are also the doctors providing the medical services.

2. Accrual accounting is required except for small corporations (gross receipts less than $5 million), certain personal service corporations, and "S" corporations. Recurring expenses, however, must be paid within one-and-one-half months of the fiscal year end and expenses to certain related taxpayers (e.g., cash basis shareholders) can only be deducted when paid.
3. Multiple tax brackets are not available for members of a "controlled group" (see Lesson 22 Taxation of Related Corporations) or for personal service corporations (a flat 35% tax rate).
4. Passive loss limits do not apply to corporations (except personal service corporations and certain "close" corporations).
5. The due date for a corporate return is the 15th day of the 3rd month following the end of the tax year, but there is a six-month extension to file granted upon request. Estimated corporate tax payments are required if the tax liability exceeds $500.

The Corporate Income Tax Formula

Realized Income

less

Nonrecognition of Income:

Deferrals and Exclusions

Cost of goods sold

equals

"Gross Income"

less

Deductions

equals

Taxable Income before Special Deductions

less

Special Deductions

equals

Taxable Income

times

Tax Rates

equals

Gross Tax

less

Credits and Payments

plus

Other Taxes

equals

Net Tax

Example:
ABC, a calendar-year accrual-basis corporation, received $10,000 of life insurance proceeds due to the death of its controller. ABC was the owner and beneficiary of this policy.

Question: What amount of taxable income do the proceeds generate?

Answer: None. Life insurance proceeds are excluded.

Example:
ABC, a calendar-year accrual-basis corporation, paid $3,000 of insurance premiums on the life of its manager (ABC is the beneficiary of this $100,000 policy) and $4,000 of group term insurance premiums for the corporation's four employees (the employees' spouses are the beneficiaries of these $10,000 policies).

Question: What amount should ABC deduct for insurance premiums this year?

Answer: $4,000. The "key man" premiums are not deductible.

C. **Book Income versus Taxable Income --** *Schedule M-1 is a reconciliation of book income to taxable income.* Corporations with total assets of $10 million or more are required to file schedule M-3, which provides much more detail than Schedule M-1.

Study Tip:
In the past the exam has focused on this reconciliation beyond its importance in practice or theory.

1. Nondeductible expenses are added to book income (federal tax expense, net capital loss, expenses in excess of limits, etc.).
2. Income that is taxable but not included in book income is added to book income (for example, prepaid income included in taxable income).
3. Nontaxable income that is included in book income is subtracted from book income (municipal interest, life insurance proceeds, etc.).
4. Deductions not expensed in book income are subtracted from book income (dividends received deduction, election to expense, etc.).

Example:
Book income of $100 includes federal tax expense of $22 and municipal interest of $13. The two adjustments to taxable income are identical to reversing entries - add expense of $22 and subtract income of $13 to book income. Hence, taxable income is $109.

Example:
This year ABC Corporation, an accrual-basis calendar-year corporation, reported book income of $380,000. Included in that amount was $50,000 of municipal bond interest, $170,000 for federal income tax expense, and $2,000 of interest expense on debt incurred to carry the municipal bonds.

Question: What amount should ABC report as taxable income on Schedule M-1 of Form 1120?

Answer: $502,000, as calculated by reducing book income by $50,000 and increasing it by $172,000.

Example:
This year ABC corporation, a calendar-year accrual-basis corporation, had net book income of $100,000. Included in the computation were the following:

provision for federal income tax	$26,000
net capital loss	11,000
keyman insurance premiums	4,000

Question: What is ABC's taxable income?

Answer: $141,000 -- computed by adding these adjustments to book income.

Example:
This year ABC corporation reported book income of $140,000. Included in that amount was $50,000 for meals and entertainment expense, and $40,000 for federal income tax expense.

Question: What amount should be reported as ABC's taxable income in the form M-1 reconciliation?

Answer: $205,000 -- computed by adding back one-half of meals and all of federal taxes to book income.

III. **Special Corporate Deductions --** Corporate special deductions are not ordinarily allowed as expenses of doing business. They are deducted in a specific order because each one is limited to the amount of income after reducing taxable income by the prior deduction.

Corporate Tax Formula - Special Deductions

Gross Income

Less: Deductions (except charitable, Div. Rec'd, NOL carryback, STCL carryback)

Taxable income for charitable limitation

Less: Charitable contributions (<= 10% of above)

Taxable income for Div. Rec'd deduction (however, note that NOL carryforwards are not allowed for computing the DRD limit, additionally, the U.S. production activities deduction is not allowed for the DRD limit)

Less: Dividends received deduction

Taxable income before carrybacks

Less: NOL carryback and STCL carryback

TAXABLE INCOME

IV. Expenses incurred in connection with the organization of a corporation.

A. $5,000 of these expenses may be deducted, but the $5,000 is reduced by the amount of expenditures incurred that exceed $50,000. Expenses not deducted must be capitalized, and amortized over 180 months, beginning with the month that the corporation begins its business operations, unless an election is filed not to do so. Same rules apply **for start-up costs**. Start-up costs are expenditures that would be deductible except that the corporation has not yet started its trade or business operation.

B. Typical organizational expenses are legal services incident to organization, accounting services, organizational meetings of directors and shareholders, and fees paid to incorporate. They must be incurred before the end of the taxable year that business begins (but they do not have to be paid, even if on the cash basis).

C. Costs of issuing and selling stock (syndication expenses) must also be capitalized, but cannot be amortized.

V. Charitable Contributions -- *can be deducted after the amortization of organizational expenditures.*

A. **Charitable contribution** rules are the same as for individuals, with the following exceptions:

1. A contribution of inventory or depreciable or real property used in its trade or business, by corporations only, to charities that use the property in a manner related to the exempt purpose and solely for the care of the ill, needy, or infants, or where the property is used for research purposes under specified conditions, are subject to special rules.
2. The deduction is the lower of:

AB of property + 50% x (FMV - AB),

or

2 x AB

B. This rule also applies for contributions of books and food inventory by corporations to a public elementary or secondary school that uses the books in an appropriate manner.

C. This deduction also applies to computer equipment donated to schools or libraries and to contributions of newly manufactured scientific equipment to a college or university (if for research).

D. The corporation can elect to deduct accrued contributions if the contributions are actually paid in first 2-and-one-half months following the year-end.

E. The limit on the deduction is 10 percent of taxable income (before special deductions for charity, dividends received, and carryovers).

F. Any excess charitable contribution (above the 10 percent limit) carries forward for 5 years (there is no carryback).

VI. Dividends-Received-Deduction -- *The dividends-received deduction (DRD) is a percent (%) of domestic dividends.*

A. To be eligible, the stock must be of a domestic corporation held over a 45-day window (90 days for preferred stock). This prevents dividend stripping.

Note:
Misconception: The dividends-received deduction is not limited by taxable income if the full dividends-received deduction creates or adds to a net operating loss. For example, suppose ABC corporation received $100 in dividends from a domestic corporation (ABC owned less than 20% of the stock). If ABC has taxable income (before the DRD) of $10, then the DRD is $70 because it exceeds taxable income and thereby creates a net operating loss (an NOL of $60).

B. The DRD percentage depends on the level of stock owned by the corporation.

1. **Short cut** -- If the corporation owns less than 20% of the stock of another corporation, then the dividends-received deduction (DRD) is 70% of the dividends received. If the corporation owns 80% or more, then the DRD is 100% of the dividends received. All ownership levels between these two extremes are entitled to an 80% DRD.

C. The DRD is limited by taxable income (before the DRD), unless the DRD creates or adds to a net operating loss.

Example:
ABC corporation received $100 in dividends from a domestic corporation (ABC owned less than 20% of the stock). If ABC has taxable income (before the DRD) of $200, then the DRD is $70. If ABC has taxable income (before the DRD) of $90, then ABC is only entitled to a DRD of $63 (70% of $90).

1. **Short Cut** -- To determine if taxable income limits the DRD, compare the amount of eligible dividends to taxable income before the DRD. If income exceeds the dividends, then taxable income will not limit the DRD.

D. Additional limits are imposed on the DRD if debt is used to finance the investment in stock (DRD is limited to the proportion of dividends that are not financed by debt).

VII. Net Operating Loss -- *A net operating loss (NOL) is negative taxable income carried from other tax years.*

A. The carryover period is back 2 years and forward 20 years.

B. Any carryover from a previous or prior year is not included in calculating the current year NOL (specific for each year).

C. The current year carryover ignores carryovers created in other years. Multiple carryovers to one year are used in a FIFO order.

D. For NOLS occurring after 2007, electing small businesses can carryback the NOL for 3, 4, or 5 years per the taxpayer's election. The carryforward period is not affected by the election.

- An eligible small business is one whose average annual gross receipts for the three-year period ending with the tax year in which the NOL occurred is $15 million or less. This rule applies to corporations, partnerships, and sole proprietorships.

VIII. Domestic Production Deduction -- Corporations engaged in production activities within the United States qualify for a deduction equal to 6% times the lower of qualified production activity income or taxable income. Beginning in 2009, the DPD is reduced for the production of oil, gas, and related products.

A. Qualified production activity income is equal to:

1. Gross receipts from domestic production less:
2. Cost of Goods Sold, direct expenses allocated to this income, a pro-rate share of indirect expenses allocated to this income.

B. This deduction may not exceed 50% of the wages allocable to domestic production income.

Example:

Hanover Company produces computer chips and has the following information:

Gross receipts from qualified production activities	$1,000,000	
Related cost of goods sold	400,000	
Direct costs related to receipts (not including wages)		200,000
Indirect costs related to receipts	100,000	
W-2 wages related to receipts		100,000

40% of the indirect costs relate to the qualified production activities. Hanover Company's taxable income is $350,000.

Hanover's qualified production income is:

Gross receipts from qualified production activities:	$1,000,000	
Related cost of goods sold	- 400,000	
Direct costs related to receipts (not including wages)		- 200,000
Indirect costs related to receipts	- 40,000	
W-2 wages related to receipts		- 100,000
	$ 260,000	
	=======	

Hanover's qualified production activities deduction is:

6% x the lower of 1) QPAI of $260,0000, of

2) Taxable income of $350,000

6% x $260,000 = $15,600.

Note that the QPAD cannot exceed 50% of the W-2 wages related to the qualified production income, which is $50,000 ($100,000 x 50%).

IX. Temporary Income Rule for reacquisitions of corporate debt

A. To help troubled companies avoid bankruptcy, special income rules apply for companies who buy back their own debt at a price lower than its issue price.

B. This rule applies for 2009 and 2010 only.

C. For debt discharge income realized in 2009, if elected the gross income is included ratably over five years beginning with the 5th tax year following the year of recognition. If the discharge is in 2010, the same rule applies except beginning with the 4th tax year following the year of recognition.

Example:
In 2009 Corporation BOA reacquires bonds it had issued with an issue price of $1,100,000 for $600,000. The $500,000 of debt discharge income would be included in 2009. However, if the election is made, the income is recognized from 2014 - 2018 at the rate of $100,000 ($500,000/5 year) each year.

Corporate Alternative Minimum Tax

The corporate alternative minimum tax (AMT) is designed to impose a tax on those corporations with a combination of relatively low regular tax and high economic income.

The corporate AMT formula is very similar to the individual formula in that taxable income is modified by adding "tax preferences" and adding or subtracting "adjustments" to income. The tax is called an alternative tax because it is imposed in lieu of the regular tax when the AMT's "tentative" tax exceeds the regular tax.

I. Small Corporation Exemption -- *The AMT does not apply to small corporations, but other firms need to calculate the AMT to determine if it applies in any given year.*

A. The corporate AMT doesn't apply to small corporations meeting a gross receipts test. The tentative minimum tax (TMT) is zero if the corporation's average annual gross receipts for all three-tax-year periods ending before the tax year doesn't exceed $7,500,000. For 2009, the three-year testing period is 2006-2008. If a corporation fails this test for any year, then it will be subject to the AMT for ALL future years.

B. The above gross receipts test is applied by substituting $5,000,000 for $7,500,000 for the first three-year-tax period (or portion thereof) of the corporation that's taken into account under the test. For new corporations, the TMT is always zero for its first year of operations. A corporation formed in 2009 would be subject to the following tests:

2009 - exempt from AMT for first year

2010 - testing period is 2009

2011 - testing period is 2009-10

2012 - testing period is 2009-11

II. Adjustments and Preferences -- *Adjust Taxable Income (before NOL carryovers) for "tax preferences" and "adjustments" similar to individual formula.*

A. Preferences

Definition:
Tax Preferences: increase taxable income when computing alternative minimum taxable income (AMTI). They often represent economic income excluded from regular taxable income or excessive deductions.

1. *Tax-exempt interest* on private activity bonds (net of related expenses). Interest from general obligation bonds is not added back. For bonds issued after July 30, 2008, the interest on tax exempt housing bonds is not treated as a preference item if the bonds are for low-income housing developments, are mortgage bonds, or are mortgage bonds for veterans. For any private activity bonds issued in 2009 and 2010, the interest earned from these bonds will NOT be included in AMT income.

2. *Realty (and leased personalty)* - excess of accelerated over straight-line depreciation for pre-1987 acquired property.
3. Excess of *percentage depletion* deduction over property's adjusted basis.

B. Adjustments

> **Definition:**
> *AMT Adjustments*: are specific adjustments that can either increase or decrease taxable income when computing alternative minimum taxable income. These adjustments often represent income or deductions used to defer the taxation of economic income.

> **Note:**
> **Misconception:** There is no difference between AMT cost recovery and regular cost recovery for real property. Different methods are required only for personalty.

1. The AMT adjustment applies only to MACRS 3-, 5-, 7-, and 10-year property that is depreciated using the 200 percent declining balance method. For AMT, the 150% DBM is used over the MACRS life. Note, that no AMT adjustments are required for assets purchased in 2008 and 2009 that use bonus depreciation. For more information on bonus depreciation see Lesson 9 Business Deductions.
2. Differences in gain/loss between regular tax and AMT caused by *different bases in assets* (due to different depreciation methods).
3. Difference in *percentage of completion method income over completed contract method income.*

III. Adjusted Current Earnings (ACE) -- The adjustment for ACE is a recognition that the list of preferences and adjustments contained in the AMT formula was not all-inclusive. Congress addressed this problem by using the adjustments for calculating E&P as a basis for providing a better yardstick for comparing AMTI with economic income.

A. *A positive ACE represents high pretax economic earnings.*

1. To calculate ACE, modify AMTI by adding economic income and adjusting for timing differences analogous to E&P adjustments. For example, AMTI is increased by municipal interest and reduced by the nondeductible expenses associated with producing the municipal interest.
   - However, note that for any tax exempt bonds issued in 2009 and 2010, the interest earned from these bonds will NOT be included in ACE.
2. If ACE exceeds AMTI (before the ACE adjustment), then 75 percent of this difference is used as an adjustment for calculating AMTI.
3. Because of timing differences, ACE can also be a negative adjustment, but it is limited to cumulative amount of prior positive adjustments.
4. The dividends-received deduction is allowed for ACE if the corporation is entitled to a deduction of 80% or more.
   a. **Short Cut:** The dividends-received deduction must always be added back to taxable income in computing E&P. However, for ACE, the dividends-received deduction can be ignored if it is based on ownership of 20 percent or more (the DRD percent is 80% or 100%).
5. There is no deduction for federal income tax.
6. There is no adjustment for excess charitable contributions, net capital losses, penalties, or disallowed T&E.

IV. Other Items in Corporate AMT Formula -- *Special characteristics of the corporate AMT formula include the AMT NOL deduction and the corporate AMT exemption.*

A. The AMT NOL deduction is allowed for the carryover of net operating losses under the AMT in prior years, and is limited to 90 percent of AMTI (before NOL).

B. The AMT exemption for corporations is $40,000, and it is phased out for AMTI over $150,000 (25% of the amount of AMTI over this trigger).

Example:
ABC corporation has AMTI of $250,000. ABC will be entitled to claim an exemption of $15,000 ($40,000 less 25% of $100,000).

1. **Short Cut --** An exemption for the corporate AMT is completely phased out when AMTI equals $310,000. This is $160,000 over the phase-out trigger of $150,000, and this means that the entire $40,000 exemption is phased out (25% of $160,000).

C. Corporations pay the greater of the AMT tentative tax or regular tax, but the regular tax is not reduced by the foreign tax credit.

D. Several credits can reduce the AMT liability, including the low-income housing credit, alcohol fuels credit, work opportunity tax credit, rehabilitation credit, energy credit, and the credit for electricity produced from certain renewable resources.

V. AMT credit limitation -- The AMT credit is limited to the amount of AMT generated from timing differences, and this credit is available in a year in which the tentative tax is less than regular tax.

- **Short Cut --** The AMT credit is only available when a corporation has paid the AMT in prior years because of timing differences (such as the use of accelerated depreciation or installment sales). Hence, no AMT credit is available unless both conditions are present (prior AMT payments and timing differences).

VI. Formula for Corporate AMT:

Formula for Corporate AMT
Taxable Income
plus
Tax Preferences
plus or minus
AMT Adjustments
and
ACE Adjustment
equals
Alternative Minimum Taxable Income (AMTI)
minus
Minimum Tax Exemption
equals
Tax Base
times
Tax Rate (20%)
equals
Tentative Tax
less
Regular Tax
equals
Alternative Minimum Tax (AMT)

Penalty Taxes - Corporations

Both penalty taxes operate to force corporations to distribute dividend income to shareholders. The rate of the penalty tax, 15 percent, is the current top tax rate on dividend income. Hence, the taxes are designed so that corporations would prefer to pay dividends (and subject their shareholders to double taxation on corporate dividends) rather than pay the penalty tax. The two penalty taxes are mutually exclusive -- only one will apply in any year.

I. **Accumulated Earnings Tax --** Corporations are sometimes used to avoid high individual tax rates. For example, the first $25,000 of corporate taxable income is taxed at only 15 percent. This use of the corporate form to reduce tax rates only works if the income remains in the corporation. If the income is distributed as dividends, then it is subject to the individual tax and no tax savings is realized. The accumulated earnings tax is designed to mitigate this use of the corporate form. Unnecessarily high levels of accumulated taxable income trigger this penalty tax, and it operates by imposing a penalty tax on any undistributed income. Hence, the accumulated earnings tax can be avoided either by documenting business reasons for accumulating income, or by distributing income as dividends.

   A. *An accumulated earnings tax of 15% is imposed on undistributed accumulated taxable income.*

      1. Accumulated taxable income is computed by adjusting taxable income to reflect retained economic income.
      2. Dividend distributions reduce accumulated taxable income because income is not "accumulated" if dividends are paid out to shareholders.
      3. For purposes of the accumulated earnings tax, dividends include "consent dividends" and dividends paid within two-and-one-half months of year-end.

> **Definition:**
> *A Consent Dividend*: is not actually paid to shareholders. Instead, shareholders consent to be taxed as though a dividend (identified in the consent) was paid. The purpose of a consent dividend is to allow a shareholder to avoid a penalty tax by distributing dividends after the year-end.

      4. Finally, an accumulated earnings credit is subtracted from any accumulation to represent the "reasonable" accumulation of earnings for business purposes.

The Accumulated Earnings Tax Formula

Taxable Income

plus or minus

Adjustments:

- corporate income tax

- excess charitable contributions

- net capital loss

- net capital gain (after tax)

+ dividends received deductions

less

Dividends paid or deemed paid

less

Accumulated earnings credit

equals

"Accumulated Taxable Income"

B. **Adjustments:** *There are six modifications made to taxable income to reflect economic accumulations of income.*

1. Taxable income is reduced by (1) accrued income taxes, (2) excess charitable contributions, (3) net capital loss, (4) net capital gain after tax.

Definition:
Excess: charitable contributions is the amount of contributions to charity in excess of the corporate deduction limit (10 percent of taxable income).

a. **Short cut:** The adjustments for net capital loss and net capital gain are mutually exclusive in that only one can occur in any given year. That is, either the corporation will have capital losses in excess of gains (a net capital loss) or vice versa (a net capital gain).

2. Taxable income is increased by adding back (5) the dividends-received deduction and (6) any net operating loss or capital loss carryovers.

C. **Accumulated Earnings Credit:** *The accumulated earnings credit is the greater of two numbers related to earnings and profits.*

1. One number is the amount of the current earnings and profits needed for the "reasonable needs" of the business.

Definition:
The Reasonable Needs: of a business is a question of fact, but it has been found to include amounts necessary to finance business expansion (actual or planned), to provide working capital, or to retire liabilities. Reasonable needs, however, does not include amounts retained for unrealistic needs or for loans to shareholders.

2. A flat $250,000 ($150,000 for service corporations) less the accumulated earnings and profits at the close of proceeding year.

    a. **Short cut:** Earnings and profits are critical for determining the maximum amount of the accumulated earnings credit. However, a rule of thumb is that the credit will not be less than $250,000.

II. **Personal Holding Company Tax --** Corporations are sometimes used to hold investments because corporations are entitled to deduct a portion of dividends received. Hence, taxable income will be less if dividends are received by a corporation rather than an individual. The personal holding company tax is designed to mitigate this use of the corporate form. This penalty tax is triggered by relatively high levels of investment income in a corporation and it operates by imposing a penalty tax on any undistributed income. Hence, the personal holding company tax can be avoided either by keeping investment income levels relatively low, or by distributing income as dividends.

The Personal Holding Company Tax Formula
Taxable Income
plus or minus
Adjustments:
- corporate income tax
- excess charitable contributions
- net capital gain (after tax)
+ dividends received deduction
+ net operating loss carryover (not previous year)
equals
Adjusted Taxable Income
less
Dividends paid or deemed paid
equals
"Undistributed PHC Income"

A. *A PHC tax of 15% is only imposed on corporations qualifying as a "personal holding company" (PHC).*

    1. Banks, insurance, and finance companies are exempt from the tax because their business purpose is to manage investments.

    2. The tax base for the PHC tax is taxable income adjusted to reflect retained economic income.

3. Like the accumulated earnings tax, the PHC tax can be avoided by paying dividends.

B. **Income and Ownership Tests:** *A corporation is a personal holding company if it "passes" two tests: the income test and the ownership test.*

1. The "income" test is met if passive income constitutes 60% of adjusted ordinary gross income (AOGI).

Note:
Misconception: A corporation that "passes" the tests as a personal holding company may be subject to the PHC tax only if it also has undistributed PHC income.

Definitions:
Passive Income: includes dividends, interest, and sometimes, rents, royalties, and personal service contracts. Income from rents, royalties, and personal service contracts is defined as passive under special circumstances.

Adjusted Ordinary Gross Income: (AOGI) is gross income excluding capital and 1231 gains and reduced by expenses associated with the production of rent and royalty income.

2. The "ownership" test is met if more than 50% of the value of the stock is owned directly or indirectly by five or fewer individuals any time during the last half of the year.

Definition:
Indirect Ownership: is determined by stock "attribution" rules. These rules define ownership to include the stock held by an entity (the portion relating to a corporation, partnership, trust, or estate) or by family members (collaterals, spouse, ancestors, and lineal descendants).

a. **Short Cut:** A corporation with 10 or more equal and unrelated shareholders would not be a PHC because it will not pass the ownership test.

C. **Adjustments:** *PHC income is taxable income modified by five adjustments.* The adjustments to taxable income are designed so that the tax base (undistributed PHC income) reflects retained economic income.

1. Taxable income is reduced by (1) accrued income tax, (2) excess charitable contributions, and (3) net capital gain (after tax).

2. Taxable income is increased by adding back (4) the dividends-received deduction and (5) the carryover for net operating losses from year prior to the previous year.

a. **Short cut:** The adjustments for the PHC are similar to those used for the accumulated earnings tax except that there is no adjustment for net capital losses and the adjustment for net operating loss carryovers does not include an NOL from the previous year.

D. **PHC Tax:** *The PHC tax is imposed on undistributed PHC income.*

1. To reduce PHC income, dividends must be pro rata (the dividends cannot be paid disproportionately).

2. For purposes of the PHC tax, dividends include dividends paid during the year, "consent" dividends, and dividends paid within 2-and-one-half months of year-end.

3. A "deficiency" dividend can also be paid to avoid the PHC tax.

Definition:
A Deficiency Dividend: is a dividend expressly declared to avoid the tax and is paid within 90 days of tax imposition (the finding of a deficiency due to the PHC tax).

Distributions from a Corporation

The calculation of earnings and profits is critical to determining whether a corporate distribution is a dividend (taxable to a shareholder) or a return of capital (tax free up to the shareholder's basis). A distribution qualifies as a dividend if earnings and profits are positive. Hence, earnings and profits is the tax analog to retained earnings.

I. **Earnings and Profits --** To properly classify distributions from a corporation, one must know the corporation's "earnings and profits." To determine earnings and profits, taxable income must be adjusted to represent economic income. Hence, many of the adjustments will be very similar to the reconciling items used to adjust taxable income with book (accounting) income, except the direction of the change will be reversed.

A. *Additions to taxable income are made for exempt income or deductions that do not represent an economic outlay.*

1. Municipal interest and life insurance proceeds are added to taxable income because they are economic inflows excluded from taxable income.

2. The dividends-received deduction does not represent an economic outlay, so it is added back to taxable income in computing E&P.

3. Deductions claimed for carryovers from previous years (carryforwards) are added back to taxable income.

B. *Some expenditures are not deductible, but represent economic outlays. These expenditures reduce taxable income in computing E&P.*

1. The amount of federal income tax (net of credits) reduces taxable income in computing E&P because it represents an economic outlay.

2. Net capital loss and the excess amount of charitable contributions also reduce E&P. Other examples are penalties, life insurance premiums for a "key" man, and the disallowed portion of entertainment expenses.

C. *Some modifications to taxable income are timing differences and can be positive or negative.*

1. The deferred portion of a gain from a current installment sale (but not other deferrals) is also added to taxable income because it represents an economic inflow. When the gain is recognized in later years, it reduces taxable income because it has already been included in E&P in the year of the sale.

2. The amount of depreciation deducted in excess of straight-line is viewed as a form of deferral and it is added back to taxable income (like the installment gain, this is a timing adjustment that will reverse in later years).

D. *Distributions generally reduce E&P.*

1. Cash distributions reduce E&P.

2. Distributions of property reduce E&P by the greater of the value of the property or the adjusted basis and this amount is then reduced by any liabilities that are assumed by the shareholder.

3. A distribution of appreciated property will first increase E&P by the amount of the gain recognized on the distribution.

4. Distributions cannot create a deficit in E&P - only losses can create a deficit.

> **Note:**
> **Misconception:**
> Distributions cannot create a deficit in E&P, but E&P can have a negative balance due to net operating losses (negative taxable income).

Example:
If Corporation Mouse distributes property with a FMV of $1,000 and a basis of $1,200 to shareholder Cat and Cat assumes a liability attached to the property of $300, E&P is reduced by $900 ($1,200 - $300).

II. Dividend Treatment -- The taxation of distributions as dividend income to shareholders depends upon the earnings and profits (E&P) accumulated in the corporation prior to distribution. Distributions are:

A. Taxable as dividend income to extent of the shareholder's pro-rata share of E&P.

B. Excess is tax-free to extent of shareholder's basis in stock (and reduces the basis).

C. Remaining distribution amount is taxed as a capital gain.

D. *Both current and accumulated E&P are used to determine whether a distribution is a dividend. There are four possible scenarios.*

Definitions:
Current E&P: is that generated during the year (up to the year-end.)

Accumulated E&P: is the amount on the 1st day of year (ignoring current E&P).

Study Tip:
Questions about distributions from E&P will typically use year-end distributions or describe income as "earned ratably" throughout the year. This language simplifies the calculation of the E&P balance on the date of the distribution (necessary to determine whether the distribution is from current or accumulated E&P).

1. **Scenario #1:** If both current and accumulated E&P are negative, then distributions are a return of capital (tax-free up to adjusted basis -- and then capital gain).
2. **Scenario #2:** If both current and accumulated E&P are positive, then the distribution is taxed as a dividend. Distributions are first taken from current E&P by allocating E&P up to the distribution date. Once current E&P is depleted, then distributions reduce accumulated E&P.
3. **Scenario #3:** If current E&P is positive but accumulated E&P is negative, then a distribution is a dividend only to extent of current E&P.
4. **Scenario #4:** If accumulated E&P is positive but current E&P is negative, then a distribution is a dividend to the extent of net E&P (accumulated E&P less an allocated portion of the deficit in current E&P) on the date of the distribution.

E&P STATUS AT TIME OF DISTRIBUTION	*Accumulated E&P is* **negative**	*Accumulated E&P is* **positive**
Current E&P is **negative**	Scenario 1: Distributions are a return of capital	Scenario 4: Dividend income to extent of accumulated E&P after netting against deficit in current E&P
Current E&P is **positive**	Scenario 3: Dividend income to extent of current E&P	Scenario 2: Dividend income to extent of current E&P, then accumulated E&P

III. Property Distribution -- *Distributions of property (in kind distributions).*

A. The value of the property distributed (net of any debt assumed by the shareholder) is the amount eligible for dividend treatment.

B. The distribution of appreciated property causes the corporation to recognize gains (not losses) like a sale of the property.

C. Amount distributed = FMV - liabilities on property

D. Basis of the property to the shareholder is the fair market value.

E. Constructive dividends are also treated as distributions.

Definition:
A Constructive Dividend: is a payment to a shareholder that, although not formally declared as a dividend, is regarded as a dividend. Property distributions to shareholders will often be treated as a constructive dividend.

Example:
TP is the sole shareholder of Green Incorporated. This year, Green paid TP a salary of $200,000 when a reasonable amount of compensation for TP's services would have been $50,000. The excess salary ($150,000) is unreasonable compensation and is not deductible by Green. Instead, this amount is construed as a dividend payment to TP.

Corporate Redemptions and Liquidations

A corporation may engage in two types of transactions that can be viewed as a purchase of the stock held by a shareholder. A corporation may redeem stock by purchasing it from a shareholder. On the other hand, a corporation may dissolve and thereby cause the stock held by shareholders to be liquidated. Unfortunately, these transactions are not always treated as simple sales of stock because these transactions can also be structured to avoid taxes.

I. **Redemptions** -- A redemption of stock occurs when a corporation repurchases stock from a shareholder. The redemption is generally treated by the shareholder as a sale of the stock that will trigger recognition of gain or loss. However, a redemption of stock can also be structured to have the identical effect of a dividend distribution. Hence, the tax rules are constructed to assure that redemptions, that have the effect of a dividend, are taxed as dividends rather than sales of stock.

- There are two advantages of redemption treatment. First, the shareholder is able to offset stock basis against the redemption proceeds. Second, any resulting gain is treated as capital gain, which is often advantageous as compared to dividend income.

Example:
TP owns 100 shares that constitute 100 percent of Blue Inc. This year, in lieu of a $100 dividend, Blue redeems 1 share of stock for $100. This redemption is essentially a disguised dividend because TP remains the sole shareholder of Blue after the redemption.

II. **Three Methods to Qualify** -- *In order for a redemption to be taxed as a sale, it must qualify under one of three circumstances:*

A. **First** -- a redemption will be treated as a sale, if the distribution is "not essentially equivalent to a dividend" (**NEED**).

Definition:
Not Essentially Equivalent to a Dividend: This phrase has been interpreted to mean that there is a "meaningful" reduction in the shareholder's rights, including voting rights and rights to earnings.

1. **Short Cut** -- NEED is a question of fact that is very ambiguous.

B. **Second** -- a "substantially disproportionate" redemption will also qualify as a sale if the shareholder passes two tests: the **"control"** test and the **"reduced interest"** test.

Definitions:
The Control Test: means that the shareholder must own less than 50% of the voting shares after the redemption.

The Reduced Interest Test: means that the shareholder must own less than 80% of the shares that were owned prior to the redemption.

Example:
A owns 40 shares of XYZ corporation (one-third of the outstanding stock), and the remaining 80 shares are owned by B. If XYZ redeems 10 of A's shares and 10 of B's shares, the redemption would not be substantially disproportionate for A. Although A owns less than 50% of XYZ shares after the redemption (30/100), his interest has only declined from 33% (40/120) to 30% (30/100). Thus, the redemption would not meet the reduced interest test because A's interest did not decline to 80% of the previous ownership level.

C. **Third --** a **"complete termination"** of the shareholder's interest in the corporation qualifies as a sale.

Definition:
A Complete Termination: means that the shareholder must surrender the stock owned directly and indirectly (through stock attribution).

1. For complete terminations, family attribution can be waived with the execution of an agreement by the taxpayer to notify the IRS of any subsequent acquisitions of stock for the next 10 years.

III. **Attribution --** *For purposes of the redemption tests, the shareholder's interest includes stock owned direct and indirectly. Indirect or constructive ownership is determined through stock "attribution" rules.*

Definitions:
Stock attribution: means that a shareholder is deemed to own stock held by other related taxpayers. There are two forms of attribution: attribution from an entity and attribution from family.

Entity Attribution: means that stock owned by corporation, partnership, trust, or estate is deemed to be owned by a taxpayer who is an owner or beneficiary of the entity. Additionally, stock owned by the owner or beneficiary may be deemed to be owned by the entity.

A. A corporation is only subject to entity attribution if the corporation is controlled by the taxpayer (50% or more of the value of the stock). In this case, the taxpayer is deemed to own a proportionate interest of the stock held by the corporation.

B. Stock owned by a partner is deemed to be owned in full by the partnership. Stock owned by a greater than 50% shareholder is deemed to be owned in full by the corporation.

Example:
1. A taxpayer owns a 10% interest in a partnership. If the partnership owns 100 shares of a corporation, then the partner is deemed to own 10 shares of the stock (10% of the stock held by a partnership).

2. TP owns 10% in Corporation A. If Corporation A owns 100 share of Corporation R, TP is not attributed any stock of Corporation R. However, if TP owns 60% of Corporation A, then TP would be deemed to own 60 shares (100 X 60%) of Corporation R.

Note:
Misconception: The scope of attribution rules is not uniform across various tax topics. For example, the attribution rules applying to redemptions is narrower than the attribution rules applying to the personal holding companies. The latter rules include siblings (brothers and sisters) who are not included for the redemption rules.

Definition:
Family Attribution: means that stock is owned by family members. It is defined to include spouse, children, grandchildren, and parents.

Example:
XYZ corporation is owned equally by TP and his three children. Under the family attribution rules, TP is deemed to own all of the stock of the corporation while each child is only deemed to own TP's shares (no attribution between siblings).

IV. Consequences to Corporation

A. If the corporation distributes appreciated property as part of the redemption, the appreciation is recognized by the corporation. However, the loss in distributed assets that have decline in value is not recognized. If the property has been depreciated, the corporation may have to recognize Section 1245 or Section 1250 recapture.

B. The corporation must reduce its earnings and profits for redemptions. The reduction is the lower of 1) the redeemed stock's proportionate share of E&P, or 2) the amount of the redemption.

- If the redemption is actually treated as a dividend, E&P is reduced by the greater of the FMV or adjusted basis of the property distributed, reduced by any liabilities attached to the property.

V. Partial Liquidations

A. *A partial liquidation is treated as a sale by noncorporate shareholders, so it is a fourth method to qualify for redemption treatment.* There are two tests for partial liquidations, one objective and one subjective.

Definition:
A Partial Liquidation: is a contraction of the corporate business. Hence, the determination for sale treatment is made by looking for a contraction at the corporate level.

B. The objective test requires that the corporation must completely terminate a "qualifying" business and must continue to operate at least one qualifying business.

> **Definition:**
> *A Qualifying Business*: is a trade conducted for five years prior to the determination.

C. To meet the subjective test, the distribution must qualify as not essentially equivalent to a dividend in that it results from a genuine contraction of the corporate business, and not just from the sale of excess inventory.

> **Note:**
> **Misconception:** "Not necessarily equivalent to a dividend" for purposes of a partial liquidation is different from the definition of NEED for redemptions. The former focuses on the source of the distribution at the corporate level, while the latter examines the effect of the distribution at the shareholder level. However, both definitions are similar in that they are very subjective tests.

VI. Redemption Used to Pay Death Taxes

A. *A redemption used to pay death taxes may also be treated as a sale under two conditions.*

B. The death of a shareholder in a valuable closely-held corporation may result in significant death taxes. However, if the corporate stock is the primary asset of the estate, then a redemption may be necessary in order to pay the estate tax. If the stock held by the estate is treated as a sale, no additional tax is usually due because adjusted basis of stock is increased to FMV on date of death.

1. The stock held by the decedent must be a large portion of the estate (35% of adjusted gross estate).
2. The redemption is limited to the amount of federal and state death taxes and funeral and administrative expenses.

VII. Stock Distributions

A. Stock distributions are not taxable to the shareholder if there is no option to receive property in lieu of stock and there is no change in proportionate interests of the shareholders.

B. A stock "bailout" is treated as a dividend to the shareholder to the extent of earnings and profits at the time of the sale or redemption.

> **Definition:**
> *A Stock Bailout*: is a distribution of nonvoting stock followed by sale (or redemption) of the stock by the corporation.

VIII. Complete Liquidations -- A distribution in complete liquidation occurs with the dissolution of a corporation and the distribution of remaining assets. A complete liquidation is similar to a redemption in that the shareholders receive assets in exchange for canceling the shares of stock.

A. *Shareholders recognize gain or loss on the liquidating distribution.*

1. The gain or loss is determined by subtracting the adjusted basis of the stock from the value of the distribution.
2. Any gain or loss recognized by the shareholder will generally be a capital gain or loss (depending on whether the stock is a capital asset).
3. If the distributed property is subject to a liability, then the shareholder reduces the fair market value of the property by the amount of liabilities.
4. The adjusted basis of the property received in the distribution is its fair market value on the date of distribution.

Example:
TP received realty worth $100 in liquidation of XYZ corporation. TP had a basis of $25 in the XYZ stock and the realty was subject to a mortgage of $40. TP will recognize a gain of $35 because the net value received was $60 reduced by an adjusted basis of $25. TP will have an adjusted basis in the realty of $100.

B. *A corporation will recognize gain or loss when it makes a liquidating distribution.*

1. The computation of the gain or loss is computed by subtracting the adjusted basis from the fair market value of the property distributed on the date of distribution.
2. The nature of the gain or loss depends on the nature of the asset distributed (ordinary, capital, or Section 1231).
3. If the distributed property is subject to a liability, then the fair market value of the property cannot be less than the amount of liabilities.

Example:
As part of a corporation liquidation, Corporation T distributes land with a FMV of $50,000, adjusted basis of $20,000, and debt attached to the property of $65,000. Corporation T recognizes gain of $45,000 ($65,000 - $20,000).

4. Expenses incurred in the liquidation are deducted on the last corporate return.

Example:
ABC corporation liquidated by distributing inventory worth $200 to its shareholders. If the inventory had an adjusted basis of $70, ABC would recognize ordinary income of $130 on the liquidation.

5. If the corporation realizes a loss on the distribution of property in complete liquidation to a shareholder owning more than 50% in value of the corporation's stock), then the loss is not recognized if:
   a. The distribution of each asset is not pro rata, or
   b. The property distributed is disqualified property (i.e., property acquired by the liquidating corporation in a tax-free incorporation or as a contribution to capital during a five-year period ending on the date of the distribution).
6. Built-in losses will be disallowed on distributions of some disqualified property to any shareholder, if the principal purpose was to recognize loss by the corporation in connection with the liquidation.
   a. Such a purpose is presumed, if the transfer occurs within two years of the adoption of the plan of liquidation, unless a business purpose can be established.
   b. Any decline in value for the property after its contribution to the corporation results in a deductible loss to the liquidating corporation. Only the built-in loss at the time of contribution is disallowed.

Study Tip:
Under the related-party rule, all losses are disallowed. Under the non related-party rule, only built-in losses are disallowed.

C. *No gain or loss is recognized on the liquidation of a subsidiary by the parent under two conditions.* When a controlled subsidiary is liquidated, no real disposition of the assets has occurred. The assets have merely been transferred from one corporate pocket to another. The key to deferring gain and loss is the establishment of control and the timing of the liquidation.

1. First, the parent must own 80% of the voting stock and other stock of the subsidiary.
2. Second, the subsidiary must distribute its assets within the tax year (or within three years of the close of the tax year of the first distribution).
3. The parent corporation takes a carryover basis in the distributed assets and inherits the subsidiary's tax attributes.

Taxation of Related Corporations

There is a tax incentive to create multiple corporations to avoid the limits placed on individual corporations. Congress created limits on related corporations to mitigate these incentives and create a mechanism for identifying and taxing related economic entities.

Overview: Corporations can be directly related through inter-corporate ownership or indirectly related through common shareholders.

I. **Affiliated Groups --** An "affiliated group" exists when one corporation owns at least 80 percent of the voting power of another corporation and holds shares representing at least 80 percent of its value. This test must be met on every day of the year.

Example:
P corporation owns 80 percent of S corporation and 20 percent of X corporation. S owns 70 percent of X but all other shares are held by unrelated individuals. P and S form an affiliated group. Because in aggregate P and S also own more than 80 percent of the stock of X, this corporation is also included in the affiliated PSX group.

II. **Eligible affiliated corporations can elect to file a consolidated return.**

Note: Misconception: Ownership of a corporation is determined by examining the amount of voting stock, as well as other classes of stock. To qualify as a parent, a corporation must own 80 percent or more of each class.
Once a parent and subsidiary exist, then related corporations can be included in the affiliated group if the total ownership (including all corporations within the group) rises to 80 percent or more.

A. Consolidating permits the corporations to eliminate intercompany profits and losses, allows the profitable corporation to offset its income against losses of another corporation, and permits net capital losses of one corporation to offset capital gains of another.

B. Gains and losses on intercompany sales are deferred until disposition outside the group. These gains and losses will be recognized at the time of the eventual disposition outside the consolidated firm but the nature of the gain or loss is determined by the use of the property at the time of the intercompany sale.

C. Foreign corporations, exempt corporations, S corporations, and insurance companies are not eligible to consolidate.

D. The election to consolidate must be unanimous and it is binding on future returns (irrevocable) and creates a joint and several tax liability.

E. The members of the group must conform their tax year to the parent's tax year.

F. Intercompany dividends are eliminated from consolidated taxable income.

G. The parent adjusts the basis of the stock of a consolidated subsidiary for allocable portion of income, losses, and dividends.

III. **Controlled Groups --** Controlled groups are parent-subsidiary corporations, brother-sister groups, and certain insurance companies.

A. A controlled group of corporations is entitled to one $250,000 accumulated earnings tax credit and is limited to taxable income in each of the first two brackets, as though the group was one corporation. A controlled group also receives only one Sec 179 expense deduction and one AMT exemption.

Example:
Rather than form a corporation that expects to generate $100,000 of taxable income, a taxpayer might try to form four corporations with $25,000 of taxable income each. This tactic would allow each corporation to be taxed at 15% instead of the higher tax rates imposed on taxable income over $25,000. However, the four corporations would form a controlled group and would only be eligible for one set of tax brackets that could be allocated among the group.

B. The following tests are applied on the last day of the year.

C. **Parent-Subsidiary** -- The focus here is on *corporate ownership*. A parent-subsidiary controlled group exists if

1. stock possessing *at least 80% of the* voting power *of all classes of stock entitled to* vote, OR *at least 80% of the total* value *of shares of all classes of stock* of each of the corporations, except the common parent, is owned by one or more of the other corporations, and

2. the common parent owns stock possessing at least 80% of the total combined voting power of all classes of stock entitled to vote, OR at least 80% of the total value of shares of all classes of stock *of at least one of the other corporations.*

D. **Brother-Sister** -- The focus here is on individual ownership. A brother-sister controlled group exists if

1. Two or more corporations are owned by five or fewer persons (individuals, estates, or trusts),
   a. who have a common ownership of *more than 50%* of the total combined voting powers of all classes of stock entitled to vote, or *more than 50%* of the total value of shares of all classes of stock of each corporation.
   b. who possess stock *representing at least 80% of the total combined voting power of all classes of stock entitled to vote,* or *at least 80% of the total value of shares of all classes of each corporation*, and
   c. the 80% test does not apply for determining brother-sister corporations in some circumstances. These circumstances include determining corporate tax brackets, the accumulated earnings credit, and the minimum tax exemption.

Example: A, B, and C corporations are owned by X and Z (unrelated individuals) as follows:

	Corporations		
Individuals	A	B	C
X	40%	30%	60%
Z	10%	65%	30%

A cannot be a member of a controlled group because it fails the control test (X and Z only own 50%). B and C both meet the total control test (80% or more by five or fewer individuals) and this group also passes the common ownership test (60%). Thus, BC is a controlled group!

2. **Shortcut** -- Set up potential controlled groups in a table like that in the above example. The control test is made by adding down each column. The common ownership test is conducted by adding the smallest percentage in each row as follows:

	Corporations		
Individuals	B	C	common
X	30%	60%	30%
Y	65%	30%	30%
tests	95%	90%	60%

Corporate Reorganizations

Acquisitions typically result in the recognition of gains and losses by the shareholders of the acquired firm. However, "reorganizations" are specific forms of acquisitions that qualify shareholders for non-recognition treatment. Rather than the imposition of tax, reorganizations result in deferral of gains and losses for the shareholders of the acquired firm until the future sale of the stock.

I. **Acquisitions and Reorganizations --** Mergers, stock acquisitions, and asset acquisitions can all qualify for reorganization status if the shareholders of the acquired corporation receive sufficient equity from the acquiring corporations.

A. A Reorganization

Definition:
A type 'A' reorganization: is a merger or consolidation under state law (called a statutory merger). Note, that Target is exchanging its assets for Acquired's stock. Once Target dissolves, the shareholders of Target own Acquiring stock.

1. In a merger, the acquired corporation (target) dissolves into another corporation (the acquiring corporation).
2. In a consolidation, both the acquired and the acquiring corporations dissolve into a new (surviving) corporation.
3. A merger only qualifies as a reorganization if a majority (> 50%) of the equity (stock) of the target is exchanged for equity (qualified stock) in the acquiring firm. This is called the "continuity of interest" requirement.
4. The shareholders of the acquired firm can only defer gains and losses to the extent they receive equity of the acquiring corporation. Note, that both voting and/or non-voting stock can be used in Type A reorganization.
5. Forms of payment, that do not qualify as equity, are considered "boot."

Definition:
Boot: is defined as property that does not qualify for nonrecognition. Boot triggers the recognition of gain, but not the recognition of losses.

Example:
T corporation merges into B corporation. All T shareholders receive B stock in exchange for their T shares. T shareholders will defer gains and losses on the disposition of their T shares because this transaction qualifies as a reorganization. If B corporation transferred consideration other than voting stock in the acquiring firm, these payments would be considered boot. These payments would not disqualify the merger unless more than 50% of the consideration received by a majority of T shareholders consisted of received boot instead of equity (violation of continuity of interest requirement).

B. B Reorganization

Definition:
A type 'B' reorganization: is an acquisition of the stock of the target solely in exchange for voting stock of the acquiring firm. Acquiring exchanges its own stock for stock in Target. Target remains in existence, but it is now owned at least 80% by Acquiring. The former Target shareholders now own stock in Acquiring.

1. The acquiring firm must exchange its own voting stock (or that of its parent company) for the stock of the target. Note, that the use of non-voting stock will disqualify the transaction from being a tax-free B reorganization.
2. The acquiring firm must own at least 80% of the stock of the target firm (voting and all other classes of stock) after the most recent acquisition of stock. Note, that 80% does not need to be acquired during this acquisition; rather, total ownership must be 80% after the transaction.
3. Any consideration other than voting shares in the acquiring corporation, will violate the requirements of the reorganization.

Example:
B corporation offers B stock to the shareholders of T corporation. If 90 percent of the T shareholders exchanged their T shares for B shares, then these shareholders would defer any gains or losses on the disposition of their T shares.

C. C Reorganization

Definition:
A type 'C' reorganization: is an acquisition of "substantially all" of the assets of the target solely in exchange for voting stock of the acquiring firm. Note, that Target is exchanging its assets for Acquired's stock. Once Target dissolves, the shareholders of Target own Acquiring stock.

1. The target firm then distributes the stock and other assets to its shareholders.
2. "Substantially all" of the assets, is defined by the IRS as 90% of net asset value and 70% of gross asset value.
3. The stock that Acquiring transfers to Target can be voting stock only. Also, other consideration provided (i.e., boot) cannot exceed 20% of the total consideration provided by Acquiring.
   - If liabilities attached to Acquiring's assets are assumed by Target, this liability relief is not considered as boot (and therefore not subject to the 20% test) unless other boot is also given. If other boot is also given, then the total amount of boot and liability relief cannot exceed 20% of the consideration.

Example:
B corporation transfers B common stock to T corporation in exchange for all of T's assets. T then distributes the B stock to its shareholders. The shareholders of T would defer gains and losses on the cancellation of their T shares. The shareholders would have an adjusted basis in the B shares equal to their adjusted basis in the old T shares.

D. D Reorganization

Definition:
A type 'D' reorganization: is (typically) a divisive reorganization (not acquisitive) in that a corporation (the parent) divides by transferring assets to a subsidiary in exchange for subsidiary shares.

1. The parent then distributes the subsidiary shares to its shareholders (spin-off) or redeems P stock with the S stock (split-off). Alternatively, the parent could be liquidated into two new corporations (a split-up).
2. In all events, the parent corporation must receive and distribute control of the subsidiary in the exchange (80% of the vote and other classes of stock).

Example:
P corporation creates a subsidiary, S corporation, and contributes an office building to S in exchange for all of the S shares. If P then distributes the S shares to its shareholders, this transaction would qualify as a spin-off. The shareholders of P would defer any gains and losses on the distribution and would allocate the adjusted basis of their P stock between their P shares and the S shares.

E. *Other Reorganizations exist to defer gains and losses on specialized transactions.*

1. "E" and "F" reorganizations are recapitalizations and nominal changes (such as changes in the name of the corporation or the state of incorporation).
2. "G" reorganizations are related to bankruptcy recapitalizations.

II. Deferral of Gains/Losses and Basis Issues -- Generally, a reorganization does not require income recognition at the corporate level (by either the target or the acquiring corporation).

A. *In a reorganization, the* **acquiring corporation** *does not recognize gain or loss on the transfer of its stock for the acquired corporation.*

1. An exception to this rule occurs if the acquiring corporation distributes appreciated property (in addition to stock). The appreciated property will trigger gain recognition to the acquiring corporation just as if the acquiring firm sold the assets.

B. *In a reorganization, the* **acquired corporation** *does not generally recognize gain or loss.*

1. A distribution of appreciated property to shareholders in connection with the acquisition will trigger gain recognition by the acquired corporation.

2. **Short Cut --** Whenever a corporation distributes appreciated property (property with a value in excess of adjusted basis), the corporation will recognize the gain. This applies regardless of whether the distribution is related to a reorganization, a redemption, or a liquidation.

C. No gain or loss is recognized to the **shareholders** of the corporations involved in a tax-free reorganization if they receive only stock in exchange for property of the acquiring organization.

1. If shareholders receive other property in addition to stock, it is treated as boot and gain is recognized equal to the lower of:

a. boot received, or

b. realized gain

2. The basis to the shareholder in the stock received is:

	Basis in stock surrendered
+	Gain recognized
-	Boot received

III. **Tax Attributes: --** *The tax attributes of the target firm (such as net operating loss carryovers) survive in reorganizations.*

Definition:
Tax attributes: are defined as tax characteristics of the firm. The code lists 24 different characteristics but the most common attributes are the adjusted basis of assets, the earnings and profits of the corporation, carryovers (including net operating loss, capital loss, and excess charitable contributions), accounting methods (including depreciation methods), and tax credit carryovers.

A. If the target firm disappears (in a merger or asset acquisition), then the acquiring corporation is entitled to the target's tax attributes.

Example:
B acquires the assets of T in a merger, that qualifies as a reorganization. The adjusted basis of T's assets does not change even though the assets are now owned by B. In addition, the depreciation methods used on the T assets will continue to be used by B.

B. If the target survives as a subsidiary (e.g., after a stock acquisition), then the tax attributes stay with the target corporation. The acquiring firm can avail itself of a limited amount of the target's attributes through a consolidation with the target. The use of tax attributes by a surviving corporation or a parent is strictly limited through the application of complex provisions designed to limit tax incentives for corporate acquisitions.

C. **Specific Limitations**

1. Earnings & Profit of the target firm carries over to Aquiring. However, if Target has a deficit in E&P, that deficit can be used to offset only future earnings of the combined companies (not past E&P of Acquiring).

2. An NOL of Target is limited as follows for Acquiring's first tax return after the reorganization:

(Income of Acquiring x # of days in year after transfer) / 365 days

3. Additionally, if there is a significant change in the ownership of Target (generally > 50%) the amount of Target's NOL that can be used in all future years is strictly limited to:

FMV of Target's stock before the change x the long-term tax-exempt rate

IV. Other Types of Acquisitions -- The corporate tax consequences of a taxable acquisition (not a reorganization) depend upon the form of the acquisition.

A. Subsidiaries -- *If the acquiring firm purchases the stock of the target and operates the target as a subsidiary, then neither firm recognizes any gain or loss.*

1. The tax attributes of the target survive, albeit trapped in the target firm.
2. The acquiring firm uses the purchase price of the target's shares as the adjusted basis of the subsidiary.
3. The adjusted basis of the target's assets does not change.

B. Section 338 Elections -- *Under certain conditions in a taxable stock purchase, the acquiring firm can elect to step up the basis of the target's asset to FMV.*

1. This election, referred to as a "338" election, requires the recognition of any gain generated by the difference between the adjusted basis of the target's assets and the fair market value of the stock.
2. The benefit of the election (step up in the basis of the acquired assets) is generally less than the tax cost triggered by gain recognition. Hence, the election is rarely invoked.

C. Taxable Mergers -- *If the acquiring firm merges the target or acquires the assets of the target, then the target corporation recognizes gains and losses on the transfer of its assets.*

1. The adjusted basis of the target's assets is their fair market value. Any excess purchase price is allocated to goodwill and amortized over 15 years.

Taxation of S Corporations

S Corporations - Introduction

Shareholders in corporations meeting the eligibility requirements can elect to have the corporate tax waived under Subchapter S.

I. **Legal Status --** The S election can only be made by a corporation and the corporation retains its legal corporate status after the election.

   A. *S corporations retain corporate status and their corporate characteristics*

      1. Shareholders are not liable for corporate debt.
      2. Shares can be freely transferred.
      3. Shareholders can be employees (separation of ownership and management).

   B. **Tax Characteristics --** *Unlike C corporations, S corporations act as conduits for taxable income.*

      1. Like partners, S shareholders are taxed on portion of income or loss, regardless of distributions.
      2. There is no imposition of the corporate AMT, PHC, or accumulated earnings taxes. Individual (not corporate) tax preferences are allocated to shareholders.
      3. The adjusted basis of shareholders' stock is generally adjusted at year end.
      4. Shareholders recognize gains when the value of distributions (cash or property) exceeds the adjusted basis in the stock.
      5. Partners in a partnership are not eligible to benefit from many fringe benefit exclusions because partners who work for the partnership are not considered to be employees. This same rule applies to S corporation shareholders who own 2% or more of the S corporation.
      6. A 2% or greater S corporation shareholder can deduct premiums paid on health insurance policies issued in his/her own name as a deduction for AGI as long as the shareholder has earned income from the S corporation that exceeds the total of all premiums paid.

   C. **Default Rules for S Corps are the C Corp Rules --** *Despite conceptual similarity to partnerships, corporate rules serve as default rules for S corporations.*

      1. There is no special provision for contributions of property to an S corporation. Hence, the "control club" rule prevails for nonrecognition.
      2. S corporations can elect to amortize organizational expenses.
      3. Distributions of property take an outside basis of FMV (rather than inside basis).
      4. Distributions of built-in gain or loss property do not have any special implications for the contributing shareholder.
      5. Distribution of appreciated property causes recognition of gain at the corporate level (passed through to shareholders).
      6. There is no earnings and profits calculation because all earning are taxed to shareholder, but a special calculation is necessary to distinguish Subchapter S earnings (called accumulated adjustments) from earnings and profits accumulated previously under chapter C status.

II. Eligibility Rules -- To qualify for an S election, a corporation must have the requisite ownership structure and be an eligible entity.

A. Eligibility Entity -- *The corporation must be an eligible entity.*

1. Foreign corporations are not eligible.
2. Certain members of affiliated groups, parents of subsidiaries, financial institutions, and DISCs are not eligible (certain banks are eligible).
3. S corporations may own an 80 percent or more equity interest in a C corporation.
4. S corporations may own a "qualified" subchapter S subsidiary.

Definition:
A 'qualified' subchapter S subsidiary: is a corporation that meets all requirements for subchapter S status and is owned 100 percent by a parent S corporation.

B. Shareholder Requirements -- *Shareholders must be eligible.*

1. Nonresident aliens, C corporations, partnerships are not eligible.
   a. **Shortcut --** An S corporation can be a parent corporation, but it cannot be a subsidiary of any corporation except another subchapter S corporation.
2. Estates (bankruptcy or testamentary) can be shareholders.
3. Trusts can be shareholders, if grantor or testamentary (2-year limit after transfer).
4. Special stock voting trusts and qualified S trusts can be shareholders (all beneficiaries are qualified and electing shareholders).
5. Small business electing trusts and exempt entities are allowed as shareholders.

C. Shareholder Limit -- *An eligible corporation can have no more than 100 shareholders.*

1. All members of a family and their estates are treated as a single shareholder.
2. Each beneficiary of a shareholding trust is counted as a separate shareholder.
3. Co-owners of stock each count as one shareholder.

D. Stock Requirements -- *Only one class of stock is outstanding.*

1. Shares that vary solely in voting rights are not considered two classes of stock.
2. Convertible debt does not violate the requirement unless and until it is converted into a second class of stock.
3. Unissued treasury stock does not violate the requirement.
4. A "safe harbor" exists for shareholder debt to prevent these securities from being interpreted as a second class of equity. The debt must be evidenced by a written promise that is not contingent or convertible. Short-term unwritten loans are sanctioned in amounts under $10,000.

III. Election Requirements -- The shareholders of the corporation must make a qualifying election to obtain or revoke S status.

Note:
Misconception: In its initial year, a corporation must make the S election on or before 15th day of 3rd month after commencing business.

A. *Unanimous consent of shareholders is required for election.*

1. The election is valid for current year, if it is made on or before 15th day of 3rd month (form 2553).
2. An election that is ineligible for the current year is still valid for the next year (if the circumstance causing ineligibility is corrected).

3. All current shareholders (and past shareholders for the current year, up to date of election) must consent to election.

4. Both spouses must consent, if the stock is jointly owned.

B. **Termination Requirements --** *Termination of the election can occur through three circumstances.*

1. A voluntary termination occurs through a majority vote (a majority of all shareholders) specifying a prospective year or made before the 15th day of the 3rd month for the current year.

    - Also note, that if there is a greater than 50% change in the ownership of the S corporation, the new owners must affirm that they wish to continue to S election.

> **Note:**
> **Misconception:** All shareholders (voting and nonvoting) are entitled to a vote in a voluntary termination of an S election.

2. An involuntary termination occurs through a violation of an eligibility requirement and this termination is effective on the date of the violation.

    a. **Reminder --** The IRS can waive an inadvertent termination.

> **Note:**
> An involuntary termination caused by a violation of an eligibility requirement will generally create a short S year and a short C year.

> **Definition:**
> *A 'short year'*: is a tax year consisting of less than 12 months.

3. An involuntary termination can occur due to a violation of the limit on passive investment income for 3 consecutive years (see discussion of S corporate taxes below). This termination is effective on the first day of the 4th consecutive year. This provision only applies if the S corporation has earnings and profits (from previous C corporation years) on its balance sheet.

> **Note:**
> Once terminated, S status cannot be elected without IRS permission for 5 years.

S Corporations - Income and Basis

Shareholders in an S corporation must report their shares of income, and under some circumstances an S corporation may also be subject to income tax.

I. Operating Rules

A. Required Year-End -- Rather than pay the corporate tax, S corporations report income to shareholders on a year-end consistent with that of the shareholders.

B. *A calendar year-end is generally the default for S corporations.*

1. S corporations can elect a fiscal year-end (with IRS permission) if there is a business purpose to the election. The most common business purpose is to elect a "natural" business year.

> **Definition:**
> *A 'natural' business year*: is one in which 25% or more of the gross receipts occur in the last two months of the year (three consecutive years).

2. S corporations may elect a year-end under Section 444 with no more than 3 months of deferral (a deposit with the IRS is required to compensate the government for the deferral benefits to the shareholders if the benefits exceed $500).

II. Reporting Operations -- *S corporations calculate taxable income (reported on form 1120S) in a manner similar to partnerships (e.g., no "personal" deductions).*

A. S corporations may use the cash basis of accounting unless the corporation is a "tax shelter."

B. An "S" corporation reports taxable income (ordinary income) and separately stated items for each shareholder on Schedule K-1 whether or not any dividends were declared.

> **Definition:**
> *Separately stated items*: are any tax items (deductions, income, preferences, etc.,) that might affect owners differently. These items retain their character to the owners and must, therefore, be reported separately for each owner.

C. S corporations are not entitled to most special corporate deductions, such as the dividends-received deduction.

D. S corporations do not pay alternative minimum tax, personal holding company tax, or accumulated earnings tax.

E. S corporations make most of the tax elections (not shareholders), including the election to amortize organization and start-up costs.

III. Flow-Through to Shareholders -- Each shareholder reports income consistent with the period in which the corporate stock was held.

A. *Each shareholder reports income and separately stated items according to pro rata share of stock ownership.*

1. If relative interests change during the year, each shareholder calculates the share of income on a daily basis.

2. To calculate the daily share of income prior to (or after) the change in shares, divide annual income (and separately stated items) by the number of days in the year. Next, multiply this amount by (1) number of days prior to (after) the change and (2) the percentage ownership interest.

Example:
As of January 1 of this year, TP1 owned all of the 100 shares of ABC, a calendar year S corporation. On February 10th (the 41st day of this year), TP1 sold 25 shares to TP2. This year (365 days), ABC reported $73,000 in non-separately stated income and made no distributions to shareholders. What amount of non-separately stated income should TP1 report from ABC?

TP1 should report income of $56,750 calculated using the daily income ($200 per day) for the 40 days TP1 owned 100% and 75% of the daily income for the 325 days after the sale. Note, that the new purchaser is deemed to own the shares on the day of the sale.

3. If a shareholder's interest is completely terminated (death or sale), then the share can be calculated by closing the books as of the termination date (an "interim" close). However, all shareholders, including the departing shareholder, must agree to this treatment.

Example:
As of January 1 of this year, TP1 owned half of the 100 shares of ABC, a calendar year S corporation. On February 10th TP1 sold all of his shares to TP2. This year (365 days) ABC reported $73,000 in ordinary income, that accrued ratably through out the year, and a capital loss of $3,650, that occurred on June 30. What amount of nonseparately stated income should TP1 report from ABC?

Unless the shareholders elect an interim close, TP1 should report ordinary income of $4,000 ($200 per day for the 40 days TP1 owned 50%) and a capital loss of $200 ($10 per day for the 40 days TP1 owned 50%). If all the shareholders elect an interim close, then TP1 still reports the $4,000 of ordinary (it accrued ratably). TP1 cannot, however, report any of the loss because it occurred after he sold his stock.

IV. Adjusted Stock Basis -- *Each shareholder has an adjusted basis in his S stock that must be modified by contributions, income, distributions, and expenses.*

A. First, contributions to capital increase the shareholder's adjusted basis.

B. Second, the shareholder's share of income (including exempt income) increases the shareholder's adjusted basis.

C. Third, distributions to the shareholder decrease the shareholder's adjusted basis.

D. Fourth, the shareholder's share of loss (including nondeductible expenses) decreases the shareholder's adjusted basis. For 2008 and 2009, the shareholder's basis is reduced by the adjusted basis of property given as a charitable contribution (rather than FMV).

Calculation of S Shareholder's Basis

Initial Basis

Plus:

Additional Contributions

Shareholder's share of:

Corporate Income

Exempt Income

Less

Distributions from AAA:

cash

inventory and receivables

other property

Shareholder's share of:

Nondeductible Expenses

Corporate Loss

V. Loss Limitations -- *Loss deductions are limited in four ways.*

A. First, the adjusted basis of the stock limits loss deductions because a shareholder's basis cannot be reduced below zero.

B. Second, the adjusted basis of loans to the corporation by the shareholder can be used for loss deductions once the adjusted basis of the stock is exhausted. However, later increases in basis are used to restore the basis of the debt before basis of the stock.

- Debt basis is created when the shareholder loans his/her own funds to the S corporation.

C. Third, shareholders may only deduct losses to the extent they are "at risk" for investments in the corporation.

D. Fourth, passive loss limits may also limit loss deductions depending upon the nature of the corporate business and the shareholders participation in management activities.

E. Unused losses (due to inadequate basis) are carried forward indefinitely (until the adjusted basis of the stock increases or the S election is revoked).

F. If an S corporation contributes appreciated property to a charitable organization, the corporation can deduct the fair market value of the property. However, S corporation shareholders can reduce their basis by only the contributed property's basis.

Example:
This year S corporation, an S electing corporation, reported the following:

Gross income	$210,000
Business expenses	283,000
Charitable contributions	14,600

S has two shareholders: PW owns 10% of the stock and M owns 90%. What amount should PW report this year from S?

S operated at a $73,000 loss, so PW should report $7,300 of loss and $1,460 of charitable contributions. Suppose that PW sold his stock 60 days after the beginning of the year? If PW sold his stock, then (absent a terminating election) the operating loss would be prorated on a daily basis. Hence, S incurred a daily loss of $200 ($73,000/365) and PW's share would be $1,200 ($200x60x10%). Likewise, the charitable contribution would be $240 ($40x60x10%).

Example:
ABC, a calendar year S corporation, had an ordinary loss of $36,500 this year. TP owned 50% of ABC for the first 40 days of the year before selling the stock to an unrelated party. TP's basis in the stock was $10,000 and TP was a full-time employee of the corporation. What is TP's share of the loss this year?

$2,000 -- calculated by multiplying TP's share (50%) of the daily loss ($100) times the number of days TP held the stock (40).

VI. Distributions -- Distributions may trigger corporate gain, but normally represent a return of capital to shareholders.

A. Corporate Gain -- *The corporation generates gains by distributing appreciated property.*

1. The gain is passed through to shareholders like other income.

Example:
S Corporation distributes land to its sole shareholder. If the land has a value of $100 and an adjusted basis of $80 on the date of distribution, then S Corporation will recognize $20 of income on the distribution. No tax will be imposed on S Corporation. Instead, the gain will be passed through to the shareholder.

B. Shareholder Income if Corporation has no E&P -- *A distribution creates a gain to the shareholder if the distribution exceeds the shareholder's adjusted basis in the stock.*

1. The amount of a distribution is the amount of cash plus the <u>value</u> of any property distributed.

2. Distributions in excess of adjusted basis are taxed as gains from the sale of stock.

3. **Short Cut --** Distributions in excess of adjusted basis will most likely be taxed as capital gains because stock will most likely be a capital asset in the hands of the shareholder (an asset held for investment).

C. **Shareholder Income if S Corporation has E&P --** *Shareholders of S corporations with accumulated earnings and profits (E&P) from previous status as a C corporation are subject to a complex distribution system.*

1. **Short Cut --** An S corporation, that has always been an S electing corporation, will not need to use an accumulated adjustments account unless and until the S election is terminated. In addition, an S corporation, that was previously a C corporation, will not need to use an accumulated adjustments account unless the corporation had earnings and profits from this prior period.

2. Accumulated undistributed income generated during S status is recorded at the corporate level in the "Accumulated Adjustments Account" (AAA).

3. AAA is adjusted in the same way as stock basis except (1) no adjustment is made for tax exempt income (and related expenses) and (2) AAA can be negative (only losses can reduce AAA below zero; distributions cannot create a deficit in AAA).

4. OAA is the "Other Adjustments Account" that tracks tax exempt income earned by the corporation.

5. Distributions follow this order: first tax-free from AAA (previously taxed to shareholders) and then from E&P (dividend income). All other distributions (including from other adjustments account or OAA) are a return of capital (tax-free up to the remaining stock basis, then capital gain).

    - An S corporation can make a "bypass election", which allows the distribution to first come from E&P and then AAA.

6. Distributions from AAA reduce the balance of AAA (but distributions never reduce AAA below zero - only losses can accomplish this feat).

7. Distributions from AAA and OAA reduce the adjusted basis of the shareholder's stock.

Example:
At the end of this year, ABC corporation (an electing S corporation) has AAA of $100 and E&P of $50. If ABC makes a distribution of $180 to its sole shareholder, the shareholder will report the first $100 as a return of capital, the next $50 as dividend income, and the final $30 as a return of capital. If SH had a basis in his ABC stock immediately before the distribution of $80, he would report a gain of $50 ($100 + $30 - $80).

VII. **Built-In Gains Tax --** *An S corporation can be subject to tax if the corporation sells property that contained a "built-in" gain at the time of the S election.*

Definition:
Built-in gain property: for purposes of a tax on an S corporation, is appreciated property (value in excess of adjusted basis) as of the beginning of the first year of the S status.

A. **Short Cut --** A built-in gains tax is not imposed on a corporation that has always been an S electing corporation.

B. The tax is imposed at the highest corporate rate and is limited to the net amount of built-in gain at the time of election.

C. The tax can only be imposed for a period of 10 years after the S election is made. For S corporation tax years beginning in 2009 and 2010, the built-in gains tax is not imposed if the 7th tax year in the 10-year period preceded the 2009 and 2010 tax years. Thus, if the S election was made in 2002 then the built-in gains tax will not apply for 2009 and beyond. If the S election was made in 2003 then the built-in gains tax will not apply for 2010 and beyond.

D. In the year of sell, if property is also sold that had built-in losses at the date of the S election, these built-in losses can offset the built-in gains.

E. The total built-in gain subject to this tax in any given year is also limited to the S corporation's taxable income for that year.

Example:
ABC Corporation made an S election this year and, at the time of the election, it held property with a value of $100 and the basis of $80. ABC will be taxed on this $20 built-in gain (at the highest corporate rate) if the property is sold any time during the next 10 years.

VIII. **Passive Investment Income Tax --** *An S corporation can be subject to the top corporate tax rate if the corporation reports excessive passive investment income and the corporation has E&P from prior status as a C corporation.*

Definition:
Passive income: for purposes of this test includes interest, dividends (except dividends from a subsidiary to the extent the subsidiary is conducting an active trade or business), royalties, and rents (unless substantial extra services are provided).

A. Excessive passive income is passive income over 25% of gross receipts.

B. The IRS may waive this tax if the corporation establishes that it made distributions within a reasonable time of discovering that E&P existed from a prior year.

Example:
ABC Corporation made an S election this year and, at the time of the election, it had E&P. This year ABC will be subject to a tax on excessive passive income if it receives interest of $100 and no other revenue.

C. **Short Cut --** A corporation that has never been a regular "C" corporation or does not have E&P from a prior period as a "C" corporation cannot be subject to the corporate tax on excessive net passive income.

Taxation of Partnerships

Partnerships - Introduction

A business operated as a partnership is not recognized as taxable entities under the income tax laws. Instead, the partners divide the income and expenses of the business and report their share on individual returns. The income is taxed to the owners regardless of distributions. Distributions are, in turn, treated as a return of capital.

I. **Introduction --** A business operated as a partnership is not recognized as a taxable entity under the income tax laws. Instead, the partners divide the income and expenses of the business and report their share on individual returns. The income is taxed to the owners regardless of distributions. Distributions are, in turn, treated as a return of capital. The distinction between partnerships and corporations is important because no tax is imposed on partnerships.

II. **Partnership**

> **Definition:**
> *A partnership*: is an association of two or more taxpayers to operate a business that is not taxed as a corporation.

A. An entity may be exempt from partnership rules if organized for investment purposes.

B. A partnership must be an "association" of two or more taxpayers with the objective of making a profit. The existence of a partnership is a question of fact, but co-ownership and/or joint use of property does not necessarily constitute a partnership. There must be an active conduct of a business with the intent to share profits.

C. Certain publicly traded partnerships (i.e., master limited partnerships) are taxed as corporations.

III. **Check-the-Box --** *Under the "check-the-box" regulations, unincorporated entities may elect to be taxed as an association (corporation) or a partnership.*

A. Some associations are automatically taxed as corporations and are not eligible to make an election. These "per se" corporations include business entities formed under statutes that refer to the entities as incorporated.

B. The default entity is a partnership when the business has more than two owners. This default rule typically applies to partnerships and limited liability companies. If an entity does not prefer the default rule, it can elect to be taxed as a corporation.

C. If an entity has only one owner, then the default classification is that the entity is "disregarded" for federal income tax purposes. These entities can also elect to be taxed as a corporation.

D. An election under the check-the-box regulations is effective if filed within the first 75 days of the tax year.

IV. **General/Limited Partners --** *There are two types of partners: general and limited.*

Definitions:
General partners: can participate in management and have joint and several liability for the partnership's debts. All partnerships must have at least one general partner.

Limited partners: are only liable up to their investment, but they cannot participate in management without losing their limited status.

A. A partnership loss will be a passive loss to a limited partner.

B. A partnership loss may be a passive loss to a general partner depending upon whether the partner meets the material participation test. See Limitations on Business Deductions lesson for more detail.

Study Tip:
Without specific information (e.g., number of hours of activity for the partner), partnerships engaging in rental activities are most likely passive. See Limitations on Business Deductions lesson for more detail.

C. Note, that owners of limited liability companies are known as "members" and they also have limited liability.

D. Limited liability partnerships also usually file as partnerships for federal tax purposes, unless the partners elect differently.

V. Partnership Operations - Distributive Share -- Partnerships report a share of items of income and expense to each partner.

A. *Partnerships are NOT subject to tax, but report taxable income on Form 1065.*

1. Partnerships report taxable income (ordinary income) and separately stated items to each partner on Schedule K-1.

Definition:
Separately stated items: are any tax items (deductions, income, preferences, etc.,) which might affect partners differently -- these items retain their character to the owners.

a. Some common examples of separate items are dividends, capital gains and losses, tax-exempt interest, passive losses, charitable contributions, investment income, section 179 expenses. Section 1245 recapture is never separately stated.

b. Qualified dividends (taxed at a maximum rate of 15%) also flow-through to the partner as a separately stated item.

2. Partnerships may use the cash basis of accounting unless the partnership is a "tax shelter" or at least one partner is a C corporation. Exceptions allow the cash method for farming and where the partnership (or corporate partner) is a small business (average annual gross receipts of $5 million or less for the three prior years ending with the current tax year).

3. Partnerships may elect to amortize organization and start-up costs. $5,000 of organizational expenses may be deducted, but the $5,000 is reduced by the amount of expenditures incurred that exceed $50,000. Expenses not deducted must be capitalized and amortized over 180 months, beginning with the month that the corporation begins its business operations. An election can be made to not deduct or amortize the expenses. The same rule applies for start-up costs. "Syndication" expenditures (cost of selling partnership interests) are capitalized and cannot be amortized.

4. Special simplified reporting (and IRS audit) rules exist for electing "large" partnerships (non-service partnership with over 100 partners).

5. General partners' distributive shares are subject to the self-employment tax, whereas limited partner' share usually are not. However, guaranteed payments for both general and limited partners are subject to the self-employment tax.

6. For partnership returns due after 2008, the extension period has been shortened from 6 months to 5 months. Therefore, for calendar year partnerships the extended due date will now be September 15.

VI. **Partner Interests** -- *Each partner owns a "capital" interest and a "profits" interest.*

A. The capital-sharing ratio represents each partner's share of partnership capital

B. Profit and loss (P&L) sharing ratios are each partner's share of profits and losses, respectively.

VII. **Basis** -- *Each partner has an adjusted basis in his partnership interest that is constantly changing (lots more on this later).*

A. A partner's share of income (or loss) and contributions (withdrawals) increases (decreases) the adjusted basis.

B. Schedule K-1 provides a reconciliation of the capital account to help partners calculate their adjusted basis.

VIII. **Permitted Tax Years** -- *Partners report income in the year that the partnership tax year ends.*

A. Since the partnership and the partners may not have the same year-ends, the partners only report income once the partnership closes it books at the partnership year-end.

Example:
ABC is a partnership with a June 30 fiscal year end. Partner A, however, has a calendar year end. This year ABC earned $24,000 for the fiscal year and also earned an additional $9,000 from July through December. If A is an equal partner in ABC, he should report $8,000 of income this year (one-third of $24,000). A's share of the income from July through December will not be taxed until ABC closes its books next year.

B. Required Tax Year: The required tax year for the partnership is determined as follows:

1. Partnerships use the same year-end as its <u>majority</u> interest partner(s) (more than 50% capital and P&L).

2. If the partnership has no single year for the majority, then the partnership uses same year-end as <u>all</u> of its principal partners (5% P&L interest or more).

3. If neither the majority interest nor principal partner test is met, the required tax year is determined by using the least aggregate deferral method. This method is computationally intensive, but determines the year-end which will provide the least amount of deferral for the entire partnership group.

C. If a partnership does not want to use the required tax year, the partners can elect a fiscal year end (with IRS permission) if there is a business purpose; a natural business year can also be used.

> **Definition:**
> *A natural business year*: is one in which 25% or more of the gross receipts occur in the last two months of the year (3 consecutive years).

D. A second exception to the required tax year is that under Section 444 partnerships may elect a year-end with no more than 3 months of deferral, but a deposit with the IRS is required to compensate the government for the deferral benefits to the partners (only if the deferral benefit exceeds $500).

E. Partnerships are due on or before the 15th day of the fourth month following the year-end. Partnerships can extend their returns for five months from the due date. This would be September 15 for calendar-year partnerships.

Formation of a Partnership

The formation of a partnership does not trigger income, but requires that both the partners and the partnership calculate adjusted basis.

I. **Overview --** The formation of a partnership does not trigger income, but requires that both the partners and the partnership calculate adjusted basis.

   A. Contributions to a partnership are not taxable events, but require partners to calculate a substituted basis for their partnership interest.

   B. **Deferred Gain or Loss:** *Partners and partnerships recognize no gain or loss on contributions in exchange for a partnership interest.*

      1. The "control club" used for corporate contributions is not relevant for partnerships since partnerships are taxed as conduits.

         a. **Reminder:** The "control club"is the 80 percent control requirement necessary to provide shareholders with deferral for contributions to a corporation.

      2. No distinction is made between an initial contribution and later additional contributions.

      3. No deferral is available for contributions to a partnership in exchange for property -- deferral is only available for exchanges of property for a partnership interest.

   C. **Exceptions** *exist for nonrecognition:*

      1. Services contributed for a partnership interest create income in the amount of the value of the partnership interest (which also becomes the adjusted basis of the partnership interest).

      2. There is no deferral for contributions that are essentially disguised sales or attempts to diversify stock holdings.

Example:
There is no deferral of gain on appreciated stock contributed to an investment partnership.

Example:
TP contributes property ($100 FMV and basis of $20) to partnership PS in exchange for a 5 percent interest. Five days later TP withdraws cash of $100. This is a disguised sale and TP will recognize gain of $80 on the "contribution" of the property.

II. **Basis Issues --** Each partner calculates his personal adjusted basis (outside basis) in the partnership, and the partnership calculates the adjusted basis of the assets (inside basis) held by the partnership.

A. Partnership: *A partnership takes a carryover basis (the adjusted basis of the property in the hands of the partners) for contributed property.*

> **Definition:**
> *Inside basis*: of property refers to the aggregate basis of assets in the hands of the partnership.

1. Since the adjusted basis of contributed property carries over from the partners to the partnership, the holding periods and depreciation methods also continue unabated.

B. Partner: *Each partner takes a substituted basis in the partnership interest from the assets contributed to the partnership.*

> **Definition:**
> *Outside basis*: refers to the adjusted basis of each partners' interest in the partnership.

III. Holding Period

A. Holding periods tack for contributions of capital assets and Section 1231 assets. For other assets, the holding period starts when the contribution is received by the partnership.

B. The adjusted basis for contributions of services is the value included in the income of the partner.

C. The adjusted basis for partnership interests purchased from existing partners or interests received as gifts or inheritances are determined like other assets (cost or carryover basis, respectively).

Taxation of Partners

The taxable income or loss of a partnership passes through to the partners according to the partnership agreement. Each partner maintains a unique adjusted basis in his individual partnership interest.

I. **Allocations of Income -- Distributive Share:** Items of income and expense are allocated from the partnership to partners. Partners include these items (known as their distributive share) on the return that includes the year-end of the partnership. Partners modify their adjusted basis in the partnership for these allocations.

A. **Allocations --** *Partners receive a share of income or a (potentially different) share of loss, according to the partnership agreement.*

1. Any "special" allocation must pass a judgmental "substantial economic effect" test that ensures that partners with special allocations bear the economic burden or receive the economic benefit of the special allocation.
2. If no special allocation is provided in the partnership agreement, then separately stated items are distributed in the same proportions as income and loss.

B. **Precontribution (built-in) Gains and Losses --** *are allocated back to the original contributing partners when the property is sold.*

> **Definition:**
> *Built-in gain (or loss) property*: refers to property that has appreciated (declined) in value at the time of its contribution to the partnership (the value of gain property is greater than its adjusted basis, whereas the value of loss property is less than its adjusted basis).

> **Note:**
> **Misconception:** There is **no time limit** on the allocation of the **amount** of built-in gains and losses from sales of property. A time limit (five years) applies to the **characterization** of these gains and losses as ordinary or capital. Another time limit (seven years) applies to the **distribution** of built-in gain property (to partners).

1. The built-in gain or loss is allocated to the contributing partner up to the gain or loss realized on the sale.
2. *The character of the built-in gains and losses is generally determined by the use of the property by the partnership, with two exceptions.*
    a. Sales of contributed ordinary income or loss property (e.g., inventory and accounts receivable) generate ordinary income or loss to the contributing partner. The characterization of income or loss as ordinary from a sale of inventory is limited to five years (five years after the property was contributed to the partnership). There is no time limit for the ordinary income characterization for accounts receivables.
        - Note that **all** gain or loss on the sale is treated as ordinary if the above rule is met. It is not limited to the built-in gain or loss at the time of contribution.

Example:
Partner A is an art dealer and a partner in ABC Partners, a consulting firm. A contributes a painting (he held as inventory) to ABC to decorate the ABC office (a Section 1231 asset). The painting has a FMV of $10,000 and an adjusted basis of $6,000. If ABC sells the painting within five years of the contribution, any gain or loss will be allocated to A (up to the built-in gain or loss) and will be characterized as ordinary income. Thus, if the painting is sold four year later for $11,000, the $5,000 gain ($11,000 - $6,000) is characterized as ordinary income. If ABC sells the painting after five years, then the $5,000 gain is Section 1231 gain. Note, that in both cases, since the built in gain was only $4,000 ($10,000 - $6,000), the first $4,000 of gain is allocated to Partner A. The remaining $1,000 of gain is allocated to A and the other partners based on their profit-sharing ratios.

b. Sales of contributed capital assets with built-in capital losses generate capital losses to contributing partner (again only for five years after the contribution). However, for built-in capital losses, the amount of loss that can be recharacterized as capital is limited to the built-in loss at the time the asset was contributed.

Example:
Partner R contributes a capital asset to RST Partnership, which will be used by the partnership as inventory. The asset has a FMV of $10,000 and adjusted basis of $15,000. The built-in loss is $5,000 and, when this asset is sold, the first $5,000 of recognized loss will be allocated to R. If RST sells the asset three years later for $8,000, the recognized loss is $7,000. The first $5,000 of loss is allocated to R and the other $2,000 of loss is allocated to R and the other partners based on their loss sharing ratios. The $5,000 loss allocated to R is a capital loss (since this was sold within five year), but the remaining $2,000 loss will be characterized based on how the partnership used the asset (inventory = ordinary loss). Note, that only the built-in loss is recharacterized as a capital loss.

C. Family Partnerships -- *Allocations of partnership income related to a partnership interest given to a family member are subject to special limits.*

1. If capital is a material income producing factor, the income allocated to a donated interest cannot exceed the capital percentage.
2. Partnership income must be adjusted by the value of any services provided by donor family members.

Example:
Dad is a half partner in a partnership where capital is a material income producing factor. Dad gives a 20 percent interest to his son. This year, the partnership earns $100 of income and Dad provides services worth $10. The son is allocated partnership income of $18.

II. Basis of Partnership Interest -- Partners continually adjust their outside basis for partnership transactions, including the deduction their share of partnership losses.

A. Increases -- *A partner's basis is increased by contributions of property, income, and increases in liabilities.*

1. A partner's proportionate share of income includes gains and exempt income.
2. A partner's proportionate share includes increases in liabilities (treated like a contribution).

B. Decreases -- *A partner's basis is decreased by distributions, expenses, and deemed distributions.*

1. A partner's proportionate share of expenses, including deductions, losses, and nondeductible expenses (not capital expenditures).
2. A partner's proportionate share of decreases in liabilities (deemed distributions).

Definition:
A 'Deemed' distribution: occurs with any decrease in the partnership liabilities.

3. **Reminder --** A partner's basis in the partnership cannot be reduced below zero.

Example:
Partner R, a 25% partner, contributes property to the partnership with an adjusted basis of $20, FMV of $50, and a liability of $30 which the partnership assumes. R's basis is first increased by $20 for the basis of the property, then decreased by $30 for the debt assumption. However, since the partnership debt increased by $30, and R is responsible for 25% of the debt, or $7.50, his basis is increased by $7.50. The net effect on basis is a decrease of $2.50 (basis of $20 less $22.50 of debt shifted to other partners).

If R's basis before this contribution was $0, he would recognize $2.50 of gain to avoid negative basis. If R's basis before the contribution was $10, his ending basis would be $7.50 ($10 - $2.50).

C. Debt Allocations -- In the example above, we assumed that Partner R was responsible for 25% of the debt since he was a 25% partner. This is usually a reasonable assumption for the CPA Exam. However, the debt allocation rules are actually much more complex than this.

1. Recourse Debt: For recourse debt, each partner's share of debt is measured by his/her economic risk of loss assuming a "constructive liquidation scenario" occurred. While this material is likely too complex for the exam, you should be aware that limited partners are not allocated any share of recourse debt.
2. Nonrecourse Debt: This is debt for which the lender's only recourse, in the event of default, is to take back the property. As above, the allocation of nonrecourse debt is likely too complex for the exam. However, you should be aware that nonrecourse debt is often allocated based on the partners' profit sharing ratios. Also, contrasted with recourse debt, both **general and limited** partners are allocated nonrecourse debt.

D. Loss Limitations -- *A partner's loss deductions are limited by the amount of adjusted basis.*

1. Partners may only deduct losses to the extent they are "at risk" for debt (nonrecourse debt is not "at risk").
2. Passive loss limits may limit loss deductions.
3. Unused losses are carried forward indefinitely.

E. Calculation of Outside Basis

Initial Basis

Plus:

Additional Contributions

Partner's share of:

Debt Increases

Partnership Income

Exempt Income

Less:

Distributions:

Cash Distributions

Debt Decreases

Asset Distributions

Partner's share of:

Nondeductible Expenses

Partnership Loss

III. Transactions between Partners and Partnerships -- Despite the status of partnerships as conduit entities, arms length contracts between a partner and partnership are recognized for tax purposes.

A. Guaranteed Payments -- *Guaranteed payments are those made to partners without regard to partnership income.*

1. Partners are not employees of the partnership, but might receive guaranteed payments for services or capital investment.
2. Guaranteed payments are ordinary income to the recipients at the partnership year-end.
3. Guaranteed payments (for deduction purposes) reduce partnership income and thereby reduce each partner's distributive share of such income.

B. Special Rules -- *Partners may contract with the partnership at arm's length with "normal" consequences, but tax avoidance is restricted.*

1. No deduction for a payment to a partner can be claimed by an accrual partnership until the cash basis partner includes the payment in income.

2. Losses on sales to partnerships in which the taxpayer is a controlling partner (more than 50% interest) are deferred as related party losses.
3. Sales of capital gain property by a controlling partner (majority interest) to a partnership will be deemed noncapital if the asset is not capital in the hands of the partnership.
4. The above two rules also apply for sales between commonly controlled partnerships (brother-sister partnerships).

Partnership Sales and Liquidations

Distributions do not create gain or loss unless a partner receives cash (or cash equivalents) in excess of his adjusted basis. Distributions require re-calculation of adjusted basis.

I. **Gain/Loss Deferral --** *Partnerships generally do not recognize gains or losses on distributions.*

   A. Partners can recognize gains on nonliquidating or liquidating distributions of cash. Cash distributed in excess of outside basis causes gain recognition.

   B. Nonliquidating distributions of property NEVER trigger loss recognition, but losses may be recognized on a liquidating distribution.

II. **Nonliquidating (or Current) Distributions**

> **Definition:**
> *A nonliquidating distribution*: is a distribution to a continuing partner, including a draw by the partner.

   A. Arm's length sales to partners are not distributions.

   B. **Basis Effects --** *For partners, nonliquidating distributions are a return of capital that reduces outside basis (in a specific order).*

      1. First, the partner's adjusted basis is allocated to cash distributions and cash deemed distributed (reductions in liabilities).

      2. Second, the partner's adjusted basis is allocated to distributions of unrealized receivables and inventory in an amount equal to the partnership's basis in these assets.

      3. Finally, the partner's adjusted basis is allocated to other assets distributed. Any deficiency in the partner's adjusted basis is allocated to properties with unrealized losses and any excess basis is allocated to properties with unrealized gains.

      4. Distributed property retains its inside basis (in the hands of the partner) unless the partner runs out of outside basis, then the inside basis of the property is reduced to the outside basis.

      5. If the distributed property consists of multiple assets, then the allocation of basis can be quite complex. A simple approach is to allocate the outside basis by the amount of the inside basis.

> **Example:**
> Two parcels of inventory (parcel A and parcel B) are distributed to a partner in a nonliquidating proportionate distribution at a time when the partner has an outside basis of $12. Parcel A has an inside basis of $6 and Parcel B has an inside basis of $18. Each parcel is worth $20. In this situation, one-fourth [($6/($6+$18)*$12] or $3 of the outside basis is allocated to parcel A. The remaining three-fourths of the outside basis ($9) is allocated to parcel B [$18/($6+$18)*$12].

III. Liquidating Distributions -- A liquidating distribution may result in gain or loss, and it requires the partner to transfer his outside basis to assets received from the partnership.

A. A liquidating distribution occurs when the entire partnership is liquidated or the interest of one partner is redeemed.

1. The distribution can be a series of transfers.
2. The partnership, generally, does not recognize any gains or losses.

B. Basis Effect -- *Liquidating distributions are treated as a return of capital and the partner's outside basis is substituted for the inside basis of distributed property.*

1. Like nonliquidating distributions, distributions of cash (and deemed distributions) trigger gain to the extent cash exceeds outside basis.
2. Distributed property retains its inside basis, but this amount is adjusted (up or down) depending upon the outside basis of the partner. The calculation of this adjustment is complex and unlikely to be tested.
3. Inventory and receivables must be distributed pro rata (a nonpro rata distribution will be "disproportionate").

C. Loss Recognition -- *Unlike nonliquidating distributions, partners can recognize losses on liquidating distributions, but only if two conditions are met:*

1. First, the distribution must consist only of cash, inventory, and unrealized receivables.
2. Second, the outside basis of the partner's interest exceeds the sum of cash plus the inside basis of the receivables and inventory.

IV. Special Issues -- *Complications are created by built-in gains, deemed distributions, and disproportionate distributions.*

A. Deemed distributions (reductions in liabilities) are treated as cash distributions.

B. Distributions of marketable securities (up to the value of the securities less the partner's share of appreciation inherent in the securities) are treated as deemed distributions.

C. Distributions of built-in gain property to "other" partners (not the partner who originally contributed the property) within 7 years of the original contribution causes gain recognition.

D. "Disproportionate" distributions of "hot assets" can also trigger income recognition.

> **Definition:**
> *Hot assets*: generate ordinary income or loss because the partner has not yet been taxed on accrued, but unrealized, income.

- Hot assets are inventory and unrealized receivable. For distributions, inventory has to be substantially appreciated (FMV > 120% x adjusted basis) for it to be classified as a "hot asset."

1. Unrealized receivables generally are receivables of cash basis taxpayers. Potential section 1245 and section 1250 recapture are also included as an unrealized receivable.
2. Inventory is defined as any asset other than cash, capital assets, or Section 1231 assets.

> **Definition:**
> *Disproportionate distributions*: occur when ordinary income assets (inventory and receivables) are distributed to partners without regard to their proportionate ownership interests. Therefore, if a 12% partner receives 12% of the hot assets, then no special rules need to be applied to those discussed above for distributions.

V. Sales of Partnership Interests -- A sale of a partnership interest results in a gain or loss calculated in the manner used for other assets. The portion of any gain or loss due to "hot" assets is not eligible for capital gain treatment.

A. Gain/Loss -- *Sale of a partnership interest results in recognition of a capital gain or loss.*

1. The outside basis is used to calculate the gain or loss.
2. The amount realized includes assets received and liabilities assumed.
3. The partnership determines the partner's share of income or loss on the date of the sale.

B. Exceptions to Capital Gain/Loss Rule

1. Unrealized receivables and inventory are hot assets. To the extent that the selling partner would be allocated ordinary income if the partnership had sold its hot assets, the partner's gain on the sale of the partnership interest will be treated as ordinary income.
2. In addition to hot assets, if the partnership owns collectibles or has Section 1250 assets, these items may also impact the gain from the sale of a partnership asset. The selling partner's gain will be taxed at 28% to the extent it is due to collectibles, and any unrecaptured Section 1250 gain will be taxed at 25%.
   - Collectibles include coins, stamps, antiques, artwork, etc

VI. Terminations -- The termination of a partnership requires the closing of the partnership books.

A. *Termination requires a closing of the partnership.*

1. Termination requires a closing of the partnership tax-year.
2. Termination results is a deemed distribution of assets to the partners.

B. *A partnership terminates for tax purposes if either of two events occur.*

1. No part of the business continues to be carried on by any partner in the partnership form.

> **Note:**
> **Misconception:**
> Generally, partnerships are contracts between the partners that are terminated with the death or withdrawal of any partner. However, the death or withdrawal of a partner doesn't necessarily terminate partnerships for tax purposes. The partnership only determines the share for the decedent partner.

> **Example:**
> In a two-person partnership, one partner sells his interest to the other partner. This is sale terminates the partnership for tax purposes because it will no longer have two owners (it is now a proprietorship).

2. There is a sale or exchange of at least a 50% interest in both capital and profits within a consecutive 12-month period.

C. Mergers and Divisions -- *Partnerships can merge or divide with the original partnership continuing as the reporting entity.*

1. In a merger of partnerships, one partnership continues if its old partners also control the new entity (over 50% interest).
2. In a division of a partnership, one of the new partnerships is a continuation of the old partnership if the partners (in the new partnership) had a controlling interest in the old partnership.

VII. Integrated Review Problem -- A, B, and C formed ABC partnership with the following contributions:

	Asset	AB	FMW	Interest
A	Cash	$40,000	$40,000	50%
B	Land	12,000	21,000	20%
C	Inventory	24,000	24,000	30%

A. The land was a capital asset to B and subject to a mortgage of $5,000, assumed by the partnership. Assume that this year the partnership breaks even, but decides to make distributions to each partner.

1. What is B's initial basis? $8,000 (12,000-5,000+(20%x5,000)).
2. What is C's initial basis? $25,500 (24,000 +(30%x5,000)).
3. A nonliquidating cash distribution may reduce the recipient partner's basis below zero. False.
4. A nonliquidating distribution of unappreciated inventory reduces the recipient partner's basis in the partnership. True.
5. In a liquidating distribution of property other than money, where the partnership's basis of the distributed property exceeds the basis of the partner's interest, the partner's basis in the distributed property is limited to his predistribution basis in the partnership interest. True.
6. Gain is recognized by the partner who receives a nonliquidating distribution of property, where the adjusted basis of the property exceeds his basis in the partnership interest before the distribution. False.
7. In a nonliquidating distribution of inventory, where the partnership has no unrealized receivables or appreciated inventory, the basis of inventory that is distributed to a partner cannot exceed the inventory's adjusted basis to the partnership. True.
8. The partnership's nonliquidating distribution of encumbered property to a partner who assumes the mortgage does not affect the other partners' bases in their partnership interests. False.

Estate and Gift Taxation

Introduction to Transfer Taxes

The gratuitous transfer of property during a taxpayer's life or upon the death of the taxpayer is subject to a federal transfer tax. This tax is called a gift tax when it is imposed on lifetime transfers. The tax is called an estate tax when it is imposed on transfers triggered by the death of the taxpayer. The donor is primarily liable for the gift tax, while the decedent's estate is primarily liable for the estate tax.

I. Key Definitions

Definitions:
A Trust: is a legal entity created by transfer of property from a **grantor**. The purpose of the trust is to hold and administer property for **beneficiaries** according to the terms of the trust instrument. The trust exists for the period determined by the trust instrument and state law.

An Estate: is a legal entity that comes into existence automatically at the death of a taxpayer (the **decedent**). The **executor** of the estate collects the assets of the decedent, pays the decedent's debts, and distributes the remaining assets to the beneficiaries according to the decedent's will or according to the state law governing inheritances. The estate exists for the period required by the executor to perform his duties.

A Donor: is a person who makes a gift to a **donee**.

A Terminable Interest: is one that ends upon the occurrence of a contingency.

A Remainderman: is a person who receives property after a present interest is terminated.

A Contingent Interest: is one that is created upon the occurrence of a contingency.

II. Gifts and Inheritances

A. A transfer during the life of the donor (an *inter vivos* transfer) triggers a gift tax.

B. A transfer at death (a *testamentary* transfer) triggers the estate tax.

C. The donor or decedent can only transfer their ownership interests and not the interests owned by others. In community property states (Texas and California, among others), property acquired during a marriage is owned one-half by each spouse.

  1. The recipient of a gift is called a **donee**, and the recipient of an inheritance is called an **heir**.

D. The donee or heir is secondarily liable for the transfer tax.

E. The decedent's will directs transfers after the death of the decedent.

F. **Reminder --** Gifts and inheritances are not income to recipients. Under the income tax, most donees assume a carryover basis for a gift and the holding period "tacks" from the donor. For inheritances, the heir takes a step-up basis (the fair market value which was included in the estate) and the holding period is always long-term.

III. The generation skipping tax (GST)

> **Definition:**
> *The Generation Skipping Tax*: is a supplemental tax, that prevents the avoidance of the transfer taxes by skipping one generation of recipients.

A. GST is triggered by the transfer of property to someone who is more than one generation younger than donor or decedent (e.g., a grandparent transfers property to a grandchild, rather than a child).

B. The GST is not applicable to a transfer of property to someone who is more than one generation younger than donor or decedent, if the persons in the intervening generation are deceased (e.g., a transfer to a grandchild is not subject to the tax if the grandchild's parents are dead).

C. The GST is not widely applicable because most transfers qualify for an annual gift tax exclusion and each donor/decedent is entitled to a large aggregate exemption ($3.5 million in 2009).

> **Example:**
> Determine whether the transfer is subject to the generation-skipping transfer tax (A), the gift tax (B), or both taxes (C).
>
> TP's daughter, D, has one child, GD. This year TP made an outright gift of $5,000,000 to GD.
>
> C - the GST is an addition to the gift tax because a generation (D) was skipped.

IV. Integration of Gift and Estate Tax -- The federal gift tax and estate tax are coordinated in order to assure that all transfers are only subjected to one of the two transfer taxes. The transfer taxes are integrated so that taxable gifts affect the tax base for the estate tax.

A. The two transfer taxes were unified after 1976 and hence, special transition rules apply to transfers prior to 1976.

B. **Deductions** *for both the estate and gift taxes.*

1. There is an unlimited marital deduction for transfers to a spouse.
2. There is an unlimited charitable contribution deduction for transfers to charity.

C. **Unified Credit --** *A unified credit provides that the first $3.5 million in 2009 of transfers from an estate will not trigger a tax liability. The credit allowed for the first $3,500,000 of transfers is $1,455,800 (which completely offsets the estate tax). The unified credit for transfers by gift is limited to $1,000,000.*

1. The unified credit applies to taxable transfers by gift or bequest to allow a minimum cumulative amount of tax-free transfers. The $1,000,000 exemption for gifts is not in addition to the $3.5 million for estates. For example, in 2009 the maximum unified credit is $3.5 million for transfers during life and at death, but only $1.0 million of the credit may be used for gifts.
2. Because the unified credit applies to taxable transfers, it is not used to offset transfers eligible for a marital deduction (transfers to a spouse) or charitable deduction (transfers to a charity).

Federal Gift Tax

The federal gift tax was created to prevent the lifetime transfers of property that would avoid the federal estate tax imposed on testamentary transfers. The tax is designed to be triggered by large transfers rather than modest gifts or transfers to a spouse.

I. A Gift

Definition:

A Gift: is a transfer of property for less than adequate consideration.

- **A.** Transfers, in a business context, are typically for consideration.
- **B.** Transfers for love and affection or marriage are gratuitous.

II. *The transfer must be complete to be treated as a gift.*

- **A.** The gift must be delivered to the donee.
- **B.** The donor must give up control of the property.
- **C.** The donee must accept the gift; the donee cannot disclaim or refuse the gift or it will be incomplete.

III. Joint Ownership -- *The creation of a joint ownership interest without equal consideration from each co-owner is considered a gift of the excess contribution to the owner making a smaller contribution.* Joint ownership is determined under the law of each state, but typically **"tenants in common"** do not hold property with the right of survivorship. **"Tenancy by the entirety"** and **"joint tenancy with the right of survivorship"** hold property with the right of survivorship. **Right of survivorship** means that when one co-owner dies, the property immediately passes to the other co-owners.

- **A.** The creation of a joint interest without adequate consideration creates a gift regardless of the form of ownership (tenancy in common or joint tenancy).
- **B.** Transfers of cash to joint bank accounts do not constitute a complete gift until the donee withdraws the cash.
- **C.** A purchase of a savings bond held jointly in the name of the donee and the donor is not a complete gift.
- **D.** The creation of a joint interest with a spouse (with the right of survivorship) is not taxed because of the marital deduction.

Example:
TP purchases real estate for $50,000 and this property is owned by TP and his son as tenants in common (one-half interest each). TP made a complete gift of $25,000 to his son. If TP had contributed $40,000 and the son contributed $10,000, then the amount of the gift would be $15,000 ($25,000 - $10,000).

- **E.** The termination of joint ownership may also trigger a tax, if the proceeds are not divided according to each owner's interest.

IV. Exclusions from Gift Tax -- There are several important exceptions to the taxation of gifts, including the annual exclusion.

A. *Certain transfers are not considered gifts.*

1. Payment of another unrelated individual's medical or educational expenses (tuition and fees only) is not considered a gift. However, these payments must be made directly to the medical provider or the educational institution.
2. Political contributions are not gifts.
3. The satisfaction of an obligation is not a gift.

Example:
TP makes a $5,000 child support payment. This is not considered a gift if TP has the obligation to make child support payments.

B. Annual Exclusion -- *An "annual exclusion" of $13,000 (2009) eliminates modest gifts from the application of the gift tax.*

1. The annual exclusion is applied per donee per year.
2. The annual exclusion only applies to a gift of a "present" interest.

Definition:
A Present interest: is the right to income or to enjoy property currently. A gift to a minor is considered a present interest if the minor has a right to the property upon reaching age 21.

V. Gift Splitting -- In community property states, one-half of all property generally belongs to each spouse. Hence, a gift of community property is automatically split between the spouses. To equalize this effect, a gift splitting election is available.

A. *The purpose of a gift splitting election is to equalize treatment of gifts by spouses with the treatment of gifts in a community property state.*

1. The election is available each year.
2. The donor must be married at the time of the transfer.

B. *Under the gift splitting election, a gift is split and treated as being given equally by both spouses.*

1. The value of the gift is divided in two and each spouse is treated as making a gift.
2. Both spouses can use an annual exclusion for gifts of present interests. Note, that both spouses will need to file a gift tax return so that each can elect gift-splitting.

Example:
TP is married to S and this year made a gift of $50,000 to his son. If TP and S elect to gift splitting, the $50,000 gift is treated as two $25,000 gifts to the son, one gift from TP and one from S. Each gift would be eligible for an annual exclusion of $13,000, so each spouse would have made a taxable gift of $12,000.

VI. Deductions -- Two important deductions are available in calculating the amount of taxable gifts.

A. *A* **marital deduction** *is allowed for most gifts to a spouse.*

1. Gifts of "terminable interests," generally do not qualify for the deduction.

Definition:
A Terminable Interest: is an interest in property that terminates upon the death of the recipient. For example, a taxpayer who receives the right to occupy property for the duration of his life has received a terminable interest in that the taxpayer's rights terminate upon his death.

2. The deduction is unlimited in amount.

3. The amount of the deduction is the total gift less any excluded portion (if the annual exclusion applies).

Example: H and W became engaged in April, when H gave W a ring with a value of $50,000. In July H and W were married and H gave W a new car worth $75,000.

Question: What amount of annual exclusion may H claim?

Answer: H can claim $13,000 annual exclusion for the April gift and a $75,000 marital deduction for the new car. The remaining $37,000 for the ring is taxable since H and W were not married at the time of the gift.

Example: TP gives Mrs. TP $60,000.

Question: What is the amount of the taxable gift?

Answer: TP can exclude the first $13,000 under the annual exclusion and then claim a marital deduction for the remaining $47,000. No taxable gift was made.

B. *A* **charitable contribution** *deduction is allowed for gifts to charitable organizations.*

1. A charity is defined similarly to income tax (educational, scientific, religious organizations), but includes foreign charities and excludes cemeteries.

2. There is no limitation on the amount of the deduction.

Example: TP donated $60,000 to his church.

Question: What is the amount of the taxable gift?

Answer: TP can deduct all $60,000 for gift tax purposes because the church qualifies as a charity. No taxable gift was made.

VII. Gift Tax Formula -- The gift tax calculation includes current gifts and past gifts. The purpose of adding gifts from previous periods is to use prior gifts to determine the gift tax rate (since the rates are progressive) on current gifts. To prevent double taxation of these gifts, the gift tax on prior taxable gifts (not the gift tax paid, but the amount of tax computed ignoring payments) is then subtracted from the total gift tax.

Note:
Misconception: The gift tax on previous gifts is computed using the current tax rate schedule and ignores the use of the unified credit. This amount does not represent the amount of gift tax paid.

A. *There are four steps to calculate the gift tax.*

1. First, determine current taxable gifts (gifts reduced by exclusions and deductions).
2. Second, add previous taxable gifts and calculate the total gift tax.
3. Third, reduce the total gift tax by the gift tax computed on taxable gifts from previous periods.
4. Fourth, reduce any remaining gift tax by the unused portion of the unified credit. The unified credit for transfers made by gift is limited to $1,000,000, which will offset $345,800 of gift tax.

Note:
Misconception: The unused portion of the unified credit is used to reduce the total gift tax. The amount of unified credit used must be tracked from each period because the gift tax on previous periods ignores the amount of gift tax actually paid.

B. Filing Requirements -- *The requirement for filing a return is based upon the annual exclusion.*

1. April 15 is the due date for gifts made in the prior year; no fiscal years are allowed.
2. The gift tax return (form 709) is due if gifts exceed the annual exclusion or if a gift is made of a future interest.
3. No gift tax return is required if a gift to charity exceeds the annual exclusion, as long as the entire value of the transfer qualifies for a charitable contribution.

C. The Federal Gift Tax Formula

Current Gifts
Less: 1/2 of split gifts
Plus: 1/2 of split gifts by spouse
Less: ANNUAL EXCLUSION
Less Marital and Charitable Deductions
equals **Current Taxable Gifts**
plus **Prior Taxable Gifts**
equals **Cumulative Taxable Gifts**
times **Tax Rates**
equals **Cumulative Tax**
less **Current Tax on Prior Taxable Gifts**
less **remaining Unified Credit**
equals **Gift Tax Payable**

VIII. Integrated Review Problem -- For each situation, indicate whether the transfer of cash, the income interest, or the remainder interest is a gift of present interest (P), a gift of a future interest (F), or not a completed gift (N).

A. A created a $500,000 trust that provided his mother with an income interest for her life and his sister with the remainder interest at the death of his mother. A expressly retained the power to revoke the income interest and the remainder interest at any time.

1. *The income interest at the trust's creation.*
    a. N - incomplete transfer due to power to revoke.
2. *The remainder interest at the trust's creation.*
    a. N - incomplete transfer due to power to revoke.

B. B created a $100,000 trust to provide her nephew with an income interest until he reaches age 45. When the trust was created, the nephew was age 25 and income distribution was to begin at age 29. The remainder interest, upon the nephew reaching age 45, goes to B's niece.

1. *The income interest.*
    a. F - no transfer to the nephew for 4 years.

C. C made a $10,000 cash gift to his son in May of this year and another gift of $12,000 in cash to his son in August of this year.

1. *The cash transfers.*
    a. P - $13,000 will be excluded. (2009)

D. This year D transferred property worth $20,000 to a trust with the income to be paid to his 22-year old niece. After the niece reaches age 30, the remainder interest is to be distributed to D's brother. The income interest is valued at $9,700 and the remainder interest is valued at $10,300.

1. *The income interest.*
    a. P - complete transfer because the niece is currently receiving the income. This is a gift of a present interest so the annual exclusion applies to it.
2. *The remainder interest.*
    a. F - the brother will not receive the gift for another 8 years. This gift is a future interest so none of it is excluded by the annual exclusion.

E. E made a $40,000 cash gift to his uncle this year. E was married throughout the year and elected with his spouse to gift split.

1. *The cash transfer.*
    a. P - $26,000 will be excluded. (2009)

F. This year F created a $1,000,000 trust, which provides his sister with an income interest for 10 years after which the remainder will pass to F's brother. F retained the power to revoke the remainder interest at any time. The income interest is valued at $600,000.

1. *The income interest.*
    a. P - complete transfer because the sister is currently receiving the income. This is a gift of a present interest so the annual exclusion applies to it.
2. *The remainder interest.*
    a. N - incomplete transfer due to power to revoke. There is no gift tax since it is not a completed gift.

Federal Estate Tax

The estate tax is designed to tax property owned by the decedent at death, and the computation is very similar to the computation used for the gift tax.

I. **Gross Estate --** The gross estate includes property owned by the decedent at death and certain property transfers.

A. *Property owned by the decedent at the date of death is included in the probate estate.*

> **Definition:**
> *The Probate Estate*: includes cash, stocks, and assets such as a residence, clothing, and jewelry. The probate estate is the collection of the decedent's possessions for legal purposes, whereas the gross estate is a measure of the value of these possessions for estate tax purposes.

B. *Property "transferred" by the decedent at death is also included in the gross estate.*

1. Transfer of property occurs without probate through operation of law.

> **Example:**
> Property held in joint ownership with right of survivorship passes to the survivor upon the death of the first owner. The interest held in this property by the decedent would be included in his gross estate.

2. Other forms of property that pass by operation of law include retained life estates, revocable gifts, transfers triggered by death (retirement benefits), and life insurance.

C. **Valuation of Property --** *Property is included in the gross estate at the fair market value.*

1. The valuation date is the date of death, or the executor can elect to have the property valued on an alternative valuation date.

> **Definition:**
> *Fair Market Value*: is a question of fact, but the standard is the amount that a willing buyer and willing seller would agree upon when both are in possession of all relevant information.

2. The alternate valuation date is six months after the date of death or on the date the property is disposed of (if earlier than six months after the date of death).

3. The election to use the alternate valuation date is only available if it causes gross estate and tax payable to decline.

4. An executor can elect to value certain realty used in farming or in connection with a closely held business at a "special use" valuation.

Definition:
Special Use Valuation: allows realty to be valued at a current use that does not result in the best or highest fair market value. This election is available when the business is conducted by the decedent's family, constitutes a substantial portion of the gross estate, and the property passes to a qualifying heir of the decedent.

II. Specific Inclusions in Gross Estate -- Certain property transfers are included in the gross estate because the transfer could be used to avoid the estate tax.

A. Life Insurance -- *proceeds are included in the gross estate under either of two conditions.*

1. The decedent had incidents of ownership (e.g., the right to designate the beneficiary).
2. The decedent's estate or executor is the beneficiary of the insurance policy.

B. Jointly Owned Property -- *is included in the gross estate.*

1. The value of the decedent's interest as a tenant in common is included in the gross estate.
2. For jointly owned property by a husband and wife (right of survivorship or tenancy in the entirety), 50% of the value of the property will be included in the estate of the first spouse to die.
3. For jointly owned property with the right of survivorship (unmarried owners), the amount includable is the portion of the property equal to the proportion of the consideration that the decedent provided to acquire the property.

Example:
TP owns a one-half interest in property worth $100,000. The property was originally acquired for $20,000 and TP provided $5,000 (25%) of the price. If the property is held with the right of survivorship with a person other than TP's spouse, then TP's gross estate will only include $25,000. This is 25% of the value of the property, and this is equal to the portion of the purchase price provided by TP ($5,000/$20,000).

Example:
Bob furnished 80% of the consideration to buy land and his friend Amy furnished the remaining 20%. The land was titled as joint tenants with right of survivorship.

Question: What amount is included in Bob's estate?

Answer: If Bob dies first, 80% of the value of the property (valued as of Bob's death) will be in Bob's gross estate. If Bob and Amy are husband and wife and Bob dies first, his estate will include 50% of the value of the property.

C. Retained Interests -- *Property transferred where the decedent retained an interest or a power.*

1. A retained life estate or the retention of a power to alter, amend, or revoke a transfer are retained interests that cause the property subject to the power to be included in the gross estate.
2. The power to designate possession or enjoyment of property or income (including power created by another that can be exercised in the decedent's favor) will also cause the property to be included in the gross estate.

Definition:
A Life Interest: is an interest in property that is retained for the life of the transferor. For example, a life interest in a residence means that the residence can be occupied for the life of the owner even though the property itself has already been transferred to another individual.

Example:
Donor transferred property in trust with income to self for life and property to go at donor's death to R (remainderman).

Question: What is included in the donor's estate upon his death?

Answer: The trust property will be in the donor's gross estate.

D. **Transfers within 3 Years of Death --** *Certain gifts within 3 years of death are included in the gross estate of the decedent.*
   1. Transfers with retained interests, revocable transfers, and transfers of life insurance are included in the decedent's gross estate if the transfer is made within three years of death.
   2. The property is included at the date of death value.
   3. The gift tax paid on the gift is included in the estate for any gifts made within three years of death (this is the "gross up" provision).

Example:
Two years ago TP transferred a life insurance policy on his life to S (his son), and paid gift tax on the transfer.

Question: When TP died this year, what was included in his estate? Suppose that TP also transferred stock to S?

Answer: The value of the insurance and the gift tax paid on the transfer are included in T's gross estate. If TP had transferred stock, only the gift tax would be in his gross estate because TP did not retain any interest and the transfer was not completed by the death of the decedent.

III. **Marital Deduction --** In order to avoid taxing a married couple's estate twice, a deduction is provided for a transfer or bequest to a surviving spouse.

A. *To qualify for the marital deduction, the spouse must receive property outright and be able to control its ultimate destination.*

1. Property that passes to the surviving spouse as a result of joint tenancy qualifies.
2. Only the net value of property subject to mortgage qualifies.
3. Property rights that are terminable do not qualify.

Definition:
A Terminable Interest: is one that fails due to a contingency or the passage of time. An example of a terminable interest is where the decedent grants the spouse the right to occupy a residence until such time as the spouse remarries.

4. The deduction is unlimited in amount.

B. *Qualified terminable interest property (QTIP) will qualify for the deduction.*

1. An election is made to use the marital deduction for a transfer to a spouse of less than a complete interest in trust.
2. The surviving spouse must receive all of the trust income annually (or more often) for life, but the decedent determines where the property goes at the surviving spouse's death.
3. The property must be included in the surviving spouse's estate at its value when the survivor dies.

C. *No marital deduction is allowed for non-citizen spouses.*

1. An exception to this rule is a transfer to a "qualified domestic trust," which assures estate tax imposition upon non-citizen spouse's death.

Example:
The decedent's will leaves property in trust with income to be paid out annually to surviving spouse for her life. At her death the property goes to the decedent's daughter by a previous marriage.

Question: Is a marital deduction available for this property?

Answer: The marital deduction may be elected on this transfer under the QTIP rules.

IV. Other Deductions -- Deductions are allowed for expenses and losses because the taxable estate represents the net amount transferred to beneficiaries.

A. *Debts of the estate, such as mortgages and accrued taxes, are deductible.*

B. *Final expenses (so to speak) are deductible.*

Example:
Funeral expenses and administration expenses (e.g., attorneys' and accountants' fees) are examples.

C. The executor has option of deducting administration expenses on the estate tax return or the estate's income tax return

D. *Casualty and theft losses are deductible without any floor limitation.*

1. The losses must be incurred during the administration of the estate.
2. The executor has option of deducting casualty and theft losses on the estate tax return or the estate's income tax return.

E. *Charitable contributions are deductible without any limitation.*

1. The same charities as the gift tax (e.g., includes foreign charities, but excludes cemeteries).

V. Estate Tax Computation -- The estate tax calculation uses the taxable estate increased by adjusted taxable gifts (post 1976). Including gifts results in a higher tax rate applied to the estate property. However, these gifts are not double taxed because gift taxes paid reduce the tax imposed on total transfers.

A. *There are four steps to calculating the estate tax.*

1. First, the taxable estate is increased by adjusted taxable gifts.

Definition:
Adjusted Taxable Gifts: are taxable gifts other than gifts already included in the gross estate. Adjusted taxable gifts are included at date of gift values.

Example:
D had a taxable estate of $3,400,000 and had made adjusted taxable gifts of $800,000 that were not included in the estate. D did not pay any tax on the gifts because he used his unified credit to offset the gift tax.

Question: If the unified credit offsets $3,500,000 of taxable transfers (2009), how much of the estate will effectively be subject to the estate tax?

Answer: D's estate will owe tax on $700,000 ($3,400,000 plus $800,000 less $3,500,000).

Note:
Misconception: In contrast to the gift tax calculation, the estate tax calculation uses the amount of gift taxes paid on previous transfers. Because this calculation uses taxes actually paid, the calculation uses the entire unified credit regardless of any amounts previously claimed in computing gifts taxes.

2. Second, apply tax rates to total transfers.
3. Third, reduce the tentative transfer tax by gift taxes paid.
4. Fourth, subtract the unified credit and other credits.
5. *Credits* against the estate tax include the unified transfer tax credit and credit for state and foreign death taxes paid. For 2009, the unified credit for the estate tax is $1,455,800, which will eliminate the tax on a net estate of **$3.5 million**.

B. Other Credits -- *There are several other credits besides the unified credit.*

1. There is a credit for tax on "prior transfers" to adjust for taxes on proximate deaths (deaths within 10 years).

2. A credit is allowed for all or part of the death taxes paid to a foreign country. The requirement for filing a return is based upon whether the gross estate exceeds the exemption equivalent.

C. **Filing Requirement --** *The requirement for filing a return is based upon whether the gross estate exceeds the exemption equivalent.*

1. The estate tax is levied on the estate, but installment payment of estate taxes is available for closely held business interests.
2. The estate tax return (form 706) is due 9 months after date of death.
3. An estate tax return must be filed if the gross estate plus adjusted taxable gifts equals or exceeds the exemption equivalent.

D. *The Federal Estate Tax Formula*

Property Included in Gross Estate

less Expenses, Debts, and Losses

equals **Adjusted Gross Estate**

less Marital and Charitable Deductions

equals **Taxable Estate**

plus **Adjusted Taxable Gifts** (post 1976)

equals **Estate Tax Base**

times **Tax Rates**

equals **Tentative Tax**

less:

Gift Taxes Paid (post 76)

Unified Credit

Foreign Death Tax Credit

Taxes on prior transfers

equals **Estate Tax Payable**

Fiduciaries

Income Taxation of Fiduciaries

Fiduciaries (trusts and estates) can be taxed on the income that accrues during the administration of the fiduciary.

I. **Fiduciaries --** Trusts and estates can be taxed on the income that accrues during the administration of the fiduciary. Fiduciaries are taxed on income retained by the fiduciary and not distributed currently to beneficiaries.

A. **Single taxation:** *Income is taxed only once to either the fiduciary or the beneficiary.*

1. A distribution deduction for fiduciary prevents double tax.
2. Income taxed to beneficiaries retains its character (a conduit approach).

B. **Income Computation:** *Individual income tax rules generally apply to determining the taxable income for fiduciaries.*

1. Fiduciaries get a personal exemption depending on the type of fiduciary: $600 for estates, $300 for simple trusts and for complex trusts that distribute all of their income currently, and $100 for all other complex trusts.

Definitions:
A Simple Trust: (1) must distribute all income currently, (2) make no distributions of corpus currently, and (3) make no current charitable contributions. Any trust that does not qualify as simple must be complex.

A Grantor Trust: is a trust controlled by the grantor through retained powers or the possibility the property in the trust will revert to the grantor.

2. A trust may be simple in some years and complex in others.
3. Fiduciaries get no standard deduction, but can deduct interest, taxes, charitable contributions, and trustee's fees.
4. When income is distributed currently by the fiduciary, then the fiduciary acts as a conduit and the beneficiaries are taxed on the distributed income.
5. The Supreme Court recently ruled in *Knight* that investment advisory fees of nongrantor trusts and estates generally are subject to the 2% of AGI floor as miscellaneous itemized deductions, unless the fees are not "commonly incurred" by individuals.

C. *Fiduciary accounting rules determine what can be disbursed.*

1. Receipts and disbursements of trusts and estates are categorized by the fiduciary instrument or state law as either belonging to income or corpus (principal).

Definition:
Corpus: is the principal or property in a trust or estate. The income earned on the principal is distinguished from the principal.

2. Income and deductions are allocated among beneficiaries according to the trust instrument.

D. **Deduction for Distributions**

1. *Fiduciaries are entitled to deduct distributions* **of income** *to beneficiaries.*
2. Fiduciaries pay income taxes, including an alternative minimum tax (when applicable), if the fiduciary has undistributed taxable income.

II. DNI

A. *Distributions of income create a distribution deduction for the fiduciary.*

1. The distribution deduction cannot exceed the distributable net income.

> **Definition:**
> *Distributable Net Income (DNI)*: is the amount of accounting "income" that's available to be distributed; typically capital gains belong to corpus and are not part of DNI.

2. Property distributions are not generally treated as dispositions of assets, but instead as distributions of DNI.
3. Beneficiaries are taxed on the receipt of distributions (to the extent of DNI).
4. Beneficiaries report income for the beneficiary's tax year in which the estate's or the trust's year-ends.

B. *The calculation of DNI requires adjusting taxable income.*

1. Add back personal exemption, net tax-exempt income, and net capital loss.
2. Subtract net capital gains allocable to corpus (keep net capital gains allocable to income beneficiaries or charity).
3. For estates and complex trusts, there is a two-tier system of allocating income and deductions and a "throwback" rule to discourage tax avoidance by timing trust distributions.

> **Example:**
> This year an estate reports \$50k of capital gains (allocable to corpus), \$100k of interest income, \$25k of administrative expenses (allocable to income), and \$12k of real estate taxes. Taxable income (before the distribution deduction) is \$112,400. DNI is \$63,000 calculated by adding back the personal exemption of \$600 and subtracting out the net capital gains of \$50k.

4. **Shortcut:** To calculate DNI, subtract net capital gains from accounting income.

C. Income Tax Formula for Fiduciaries

Gross Income

less **Deductions:**

interest, taxes, business expenses,

depreciation, and charitable contributions

less **Distribution Deduction**

(maximum is DNI)

less **Personal exemption**

equals **Taxable Income**

times **Tax Rates**

equals **Gross Tax**

less credits

plus additional taxes

equals **Tax Payable**

III. Procedural Rules

A. Trusts must use a calendar year, but estates may choose any year-end. Both must file by the 15th day of the fourth month after the year-end.

B. Trusts must pay estimated income taxes, but estates need only pay estimated income taxes after their first two tax years of operation.

C. Fiduciaries must file an income tax return (form 1041) if gross income exceeds $600, if the fiduciary has taxable income, or if a nonresident alien is a beneficiary.

IV. Income in Respect of a Decedent -- Income in respect of a decedent (IRD) occurs if a decedent was entitled to receive income at the date of death, but the income was not included in the decedent's final tax return. Hence, the income must be taxed as income to the estate (because it has not yet been subjected to any income tax) and also included on the estate tax return (because it is part of the property owned by the decedent at the time of death).

A. *Income and expenses are reported on a decedent's final individual income tax return up to the date of death.*

1. Income actually and constructively received through the date of death is included on the final return. When the decedent was on the cash basis, some income will not be received until after the date of death.

Definition:
Income in Respect of a Decedent: is income earned by the decedent but not included in the decedent's final return.

Example:
D died on July 10. D is a cash basis taxpayer who receives a paycheck at the end of each month. The paycheck covering the period up to July 10 is not received until the end of July. It will be income in respect of a decedent.

2. Deductible expenses paid through the date of death are properly claimed in the decedent's final return.

B. *Income (or expenses) in respect of a decedent are taxed as income to the estate (or beneficiary if distributed).*

Definition:
Expenses in Respect of a Decedent: are deductible expenses paid after the date of death.

C. There is no step up for income in respect of decedent. This income has not yet been subject to income tax.

D. The income is included in both the estate income tax return and the estate tax return.

E. Accrued expenses paid after the date of death attributed to income in respect of a decedent are deducted on both the estate income tax return and the estate tax return.

F. Estates (or beneficiaries) who are taxed on income in respect of a decedent are entitled to deduct the estate tax on this property.

LaVergne, TN USA
12 January 2010
169653LV00001B/1/P

9 780974 654119